racing & football outlook

FOOTBALL GUIDE 2012-2013

Edited by Paul Charlton and Dan Sait

Contributors: Paul Charlton, Steve Cook, Alex Deacon, Andy Dietz, Tom Earl, Sean Gollogly, Derek Guldberg, Dylan Hill, Glenn Jeffreys, Chris Mann, Dan Sait, Danny Hayes, Nigel Speight, Ian Wilkerson

Published in 2012 by Raceform
Compton, Newbury, Berkshire, RG20 6NL

A catalogue record for this book is available from the British Library.

ISBN 978-1-906820-95-4

Printed and bound by the CPI Group (UK) Ltd, Croydon, CR0 4YY

Contents

Stunning campaign a hard act to follow

WOW, what a season. Just when it seemed Spain's Primera Liga was about to claim absolute dominance, the rest of Europe suddenly bit back.

As Barcelona and Real Madrid were threatening to totally eclipse their European rivals, Bayern Munich landed a blow for the Bundesliga by sending Jose Mourinho's Real crashing out of the Champions League semi-final, while the mighty Barcelona found themselves 2-1 up on aggregate in the second leg of their semi-final tie against the sixth-best English side of 2011-12 – a hopelessly out-of-form, managerless, ten-man Chelsea.

The rest, as they say, is history. It may not have been pretty but, against all the odds, caretaker manager Roberto Di Matteo led Chelsea to their first ever Champions League title, with Didier Drogba scoring the deciding penalty – an appropriate finale to a glorious Blues career.

And, after a season in which it seemed some higher power was feverishly wringing every drop of drama from the domestic campaign, it felt almost inevitable that Drogba's final kick would have a major impact elsewhere. Victory for Chelsea denied Spurs, semi-serious title contenders as late as January, a Champions League berth and sealed a season in which extraordinary late drama became the norm.

The pinnacle for that late drama came at Eastlands, where we were treated to easily the most stunning end to a Premier League campaign and arguably one of the most dramatic finales of all time.

Having beaten Man United in their last outing on home turf, a routine home win over QPR was all Man City needed to claim their first title in 44 years. But how Mark Hughes' men put City through the wringer as the R's fought for top-flight survival, somehow clinging on to a shock 2-1 lead as the clock hit the 90-minute mark. However, that epic encore – two goals in injury time – finally brought euphoria to the blue half of Manchester.

While that breathtaking match capped an exceptional season, within 2011-12 lay many darker moments. The sudden and tragic death of Gary Speed stunned the footballing world and when Gary Ablett succumbed to non-Hodgkin's lymphoma just five weeks later we found ourselves robbed of two well-loved and hugely respected men who should have been in their prime.

It was so nearly three following the horror of Fabrice Muamba's collapse during a cup tie at White Hart Lane, and there was sadness and disappointment in equal measure as Stiliyan Petrov was diagnosed with acute leukaemia and, following so much progress in the English game, issues of racism resurfaced.

But, for all the lows, the overriding sensation of 2011-12 was one of entertainment and drama woven among dozens of starkly contrasting narratives. Rangers' collapse will surely lead Scottish football into a period of introspection, and while the Football League's implementation of Financial Fair play may finally begin to bring sanity back to the boardroom, you suspect there will always be a Blackburn Rovers or two floating about.

But let's look forward to the proper football stories – those that play out on the pitch. Wiganesque revivals, promoted sides beating the odds to entertain as they survive, flair proving king and big matches producing big entertainment.

We'll be hoping for plenty more of that next season and, following the *Racing & Football Outlook*'s revamp at the turn of the year, we'll have lots more new stuff for 2012-13. See you every Tuesday!

Gunners can mount a serious challenge

THE big question has been answered – Man City are for real, *writes Figaro*. The next question is whether they can stay there and the answer is "maybe not." You can tell I'm full of confidence!

I just cannot see City as 11-8 favourites for the title. What may surprise you though is that I do not see the main threat coming from their biggest rivals.

Although it was pleasing to see pass master Paul Scholes brought out of mothballs for the second half of the season, it was a sharp indictment of those players who are supposed to be replacing him and clear proof of United's problems in midfield.

With Rio Ferdinand injury prone, Ryan Giggs another year older and Ashley Young having to come to terms with a very poor Euro 2012 showing, there is little reason to expect United to reverse their 2011-12 positions with Man City.

Last term, Man United were stimied by the injury to Nemanja Vidic. You could argue that had he been playing in the 4-4 draw with Everton, the Red Devils wouldn't have surrendered their two-goal lead in that game and would have retained the title.

Every season is full of ifs and buts like that though, and there's no arguing with the fact that the team that does the double over Man United with a 7-1 aggregate score deserves to win the crown.

Just as crucial as the Vidic injury was the prolonged absence of Jack Wilshere at **Arsenal**. Coupled with the loss of Cesc Fabregas, that blew a big hole in the Gunners' midfield creativity, and by the end of the season Arsenal had six players on the long-term injury list.

However, Alex Oxlade-Chamberlain did well enough to catch Roy Hodgson's eye and he might avoid falling just a little short of fulfilling very early promise to the extent that Theo Walcott has.

To be fair, I thought Walcott deserved more game time than he got for England and many felt that now ex-French coach, Laurent Blanc, should have used Olivier Giroud, the striker Arsenal have bought from Montpellier, far more too.

That pair should take the field feeling that they still have something to prove and the latter's performances in France last year suggested he can take some of the burden off Robin van Persie – or fill the void if he leaves the club.

At the time of writing, at the end of June, William Hill had Arsenal in at 6-1 for the title but Paddy Power were offering Arsene Wenger's men at double that. At a third the odds for the place half of the bet, we'll have some of that.

I first mentioned Arsenal as a possibility for the title on the *Soccer Betting Hotline* back in May and there has been so little transfer activity since that nothing has happened to change my mind.

Consider Arsenal's record over the final quarter of the season. They won six of their last seven games against other teams in the top half of the table, a run that included wins at Liverpool and Everton, the 5-2 thrashing of Tottenham where they came back from 2-0 down, plus home wins against Man City and Newcastle.

They thoroughly deserved to snatch third place back from Tottenham and they equally deserve a single digit quote in the title market.

We don't normally stray into European club competitions here but I do think that now Jose Mourinho has seen off Barcelona domestically as well as Pep Guardiola for at least a year, he stands a great chance of bringing the Champions League trophy back to **Real Madrid**.

CHALLENGERS: Arsenal can emerge as Man City's main rivals given better luck

They are a best price of 4-1, second favourites behind Barcelona side that looked as if they were beginning to curl around the edges during the 2011-12 campaign.

Can you see Chelsea becoming the first team to retain the trophy since AC Milan retained the old European Cup without the talismanic Didier Drogba? Me neither, and after the Manchester meltdown last year, neither City nor United, who are correctly out at 14-1 in places, look trustworthy.

Returning to the Premier League, **Swansea**'s survival chances may have disappeared along with Brendan Rogers and I have already suggested backing **Notts County**, **Swindon** and **Bradford** for lower league glory in the *Racing &*

Football Outlook.

I'll hold fire on Scotland and the Championship for the time being, as late transfer activity may clarify the latter, while the positioning of Rangers is crucial for the former. Check out the *Outlook* in August!

Recommendations

Stake 10pts on **Real Madrid** to win the Champions League at 4-1 generally, 5pts each-way on **Arsenal** to win the Premier League at 12-1 (Paddy Power), 20pts on **Swansea** to be relegated at 9-4 (Boylesports), 8pts each-way on **Swindon** to win League 1 at 11-1 (BetVictor), 6pts each-way on **Notts County** to win League 1 at 16-1 generally, 5pts each-way on **Bradford** to win League 2 at 25-1 (BetVictor).

JULY

Tuesday 3-4	Champions League first qualifying round, first leg
Thursday 5	Europa League first qualifying round, first leg
Tuesday 10-11	Champions League first qualifying round, second leg
Thursday 12	Europa League first qualifying round, second leg
Tuesday 17-18	Champions League second qualifying round, first leg
Thursday 19	Europa League second qualifying round, first leg
Friday 20	Champions League third qualifying round draw
	Europa League third qualifying round draw
Tuesday 24-25	Champions League second qualifying round, second leg
Thursday 26	Olympic Football group stage begins
	Europa League second qualifying round, second leg
Saturday 28	Scottish Challenge Cup first round
Tuesday 31	Champions League third qualifying round, first leg

AUGUST

Wednesday 1	Champions League third qualifying round, first leg
Thursday 2	Europa League third qualifying round, first leg
Saturday 4	Olympic Football quarter-finals
	Scottish League Cup first round
	Start of the Scottish Premier League season
Tuesday 7	Olympic Football semi-finals
Tuesday 7-8	Champions League third qualifying round, second leg
Thursday 9	Europa League third qualifying round, second leg
Friday 10	Olympic Football bronze medal match
	Champions League play-off round draw
	Europa League play-off round draw
Saturday 11	Olympic Football final
	FA Cup extra preliminary round
	Start of the Conference Premier season
	Start of Scottish Football League
	Start of the French Ligue 1 season
Sunday 12	FA Community Shield
	Chelsea v Man City
Monday 13 *(w/c)*	League Cup first round
Tuesday 14	Scottish Challenge Cup second round
Wednesday 15	International friendlies
	England v Italy
	Northern Ireland v Finland
	Scotland v Australia
	Serbia v Republic of Ireland
	Wales v Bosnia-Hz
Saturday 18	Start of the Premier League season
	Start of the Football League season
	Start of the Conference North/South season
	Start of the Spanish Primera Liga
Tuesday 21-22	Champions League play-off round, first leg
Thursday 23	Europa League play-off round, first leg
Friday 24	Start of the German Bundesliga season
Saturday 25	FA Cup preliminary round
	Scottish Cup first round
	Start of the Italian Serie A season
Monday 27 *(w/c)*	League Cup second round
Tuesday 28-29	Champions League play-off round, second leg
	Scottish League Cup second round

Thursday 30	Champions League group stage draw
	Europa League play-off round, second leg
Friday 31	Uefa Super Cup
	Chelsea v Atletico Madrid
	Europa League group stage draw

SEPTEMBER

Saturday 1	FA Vase first qualifying round
Monday 3 *(w/c)*	Johnstone's Paint Trophy first round
Friday 7	World Cup 2014 qualifiers
	Kazakhstan v Republic of Ireland
	Moldova v England
	Russia v Northern Ireland
	Wales v Belgium
Saturday 8	World Cup 2014 qualifiers
	Scotland v Serbia
	FA Cup first qualifying round
Sunday 9	Scottish Challenge Cup quarter-final
Tuesday 11	World Cup 2014 qualifiers
	England v Ukraine
	Northern Ireland v Luxembourg
	Scotland v Macedonia
	Serbia v Wales
Saturday 15	FA Trophy preliminary round
	FA Vase second qualifying round
Tuesday 18-19	Champions League group stage, matchday one
Thursday 20	Europa League group stage, matchday one
Saturday 22	FA Cup second qualifying round
Monday 24 *(w/c)*	League Cup third round
Tuesday 25-26	Scottish League Cup third round
Saturday 29	FA Trophy first qualifying round
	Scottish Cup second round

OCTOBER

Tuesday 2-3	Champions League group stage, matchday two
Thursday 4	Europa League group stage, matchday two
Saturday 6	FA Cup third qualifying round
Monday 8 *(w/c)*	Johnstone's Paint Trophy second round
Friday 12	World Cup 2014 qualifiers
	England v San Marino
	Republic of Ireland v Germany
	Wales v Scotland
Saturday 13	FA Vase first round
Sunday 14	Scottish Challenge Cup semi-final
Tuesday 16	World Cup 2014 qualifiers
	Belgium v Scotland
	Croatia v Wales
	Faroe Islands v Republic of Ireland
	Poland v England
	Portugal v Northern Ireland
Saturday 20	FA Cup fourth qualifying round
Tuesday 23-24	Champions League group stage, matchday three
Thursday 25	Europa League group stage, matchday three
Friday 26	Africa Cup of Nations draw
Saturday 27	FA Trophy second qualifying round
Monday 29 *(w/c)*	League Cup fourth round
Tuesday 30-31	Scottish League Cup quarter-final

NOVEMBER

| Saturday 3 | FA Cup first round |
| | Scottish Cup third round |

Tuesday 6-7	Champions League group stage, matchday four
Thursday 8	Europa League group stage, matchday four
Saturday 10	FA Trophy third qualifying round
Monday 12	Fifa Club World Cup draw *(to be confirmed)*
Wednesday 14	World Cup 2014 qualifiers

Northern Ireland v Azerbaijan
International friendlies
Luxembourg v Scotland
Sweden v England

Saturday 17	FA Vase second round
Tuesday 20-21	Champions League group stage, matchday five
Thursday 22	Europa League group stage, matchday five
Saturday 24	FA Trophy first round

DECEMBER

Saturday 1	Fifa Confederations Cup draw
	FA Cup second round
	Scottish Cup fourth round
Monday 3 *(w/c)*	Johnstone's Paint Trophy area quarter-finals
Tuesday 4-5	Champions League group stage, matchday six
Thursday 6	Fifa Club World Cup begins, Japan
	Europa League group stage, matchday six
Saturday 8	FA Vase third round
Monday 10 *(w/c)*	League Cup fifth round
Friday 14	Champions League last 16 draw
	Europa League last 32/last 16 draw
Saturday 15	FA Trophy second round
Sunday 16	Fifa Club World Cup final

JANUARY

Saturday 5	FA Cup third round
Monday 7 *(w/c)*	League Cup semi-final round, first leg
	Johnstone's Paint Trophy area semi-finals
Saturday 12	FA Trophy third round
Saturday 19	Africa Cup of Nations begins, South Africa
	FA Vase fourth round
Monday 21 *(w/c)*	League Cup semi-final round, second leg
Saturday 26	FA Trophy fourth round
	FA Cup fourth round
	Scottish League Cup semi-final

FEBRUARY

Saturday 2	Scottish Cup fifth round
Monday 4 *(w/c)*	Johnstone's Paint Trophy area finals, first leg
Saturday 9	FA Vase fifth round
Sunday 10	Africa Cup of Nations final
Tuesday 12-13	Champions League last 16, first leg
Thursday 14	Europa League last 32, first leg
Saturday 16	FA Cup fifth round
	FA Trophy semi-final, first leg
Monday 18 *(w/c)*	Johnstone's Paint Trophy area finals, second leg
Tuesday 19-20	Champions League last 16, first leg
Thursday 21	Europa League last 32, second leg
Saturday 23	FA Trophy semi-final, second leg
Sunday 24	League Cup final

MARCH

| Saturday 2 | FA Vase sixth round |
| | Scottish Cup quarter-final |

Tuesday 5-6	Champions League last 16, second leg
Wednesday 6	International friendlies
	Wales v Austria
Thursday 7	Europa League last 16, first leg
Saturday 9	FA Cup sixth round
Tuesday 12-13	Champions League last 16, second leg
Thursday 14	Europa League last 16, second leg
Friday 15	Champions League quarter-final/semi-final draw
	Europa League quarter-final/semi-final draw
Sunday 17	Scottish League Cup final
Friday 22	World Cup 2014 qualifiers
	Northern Ireland v Russia
	San Marino v England
	Scotland v Wales
	Sweden v Republic of Ireland
Saturday 23	FA Vase semi-final, first leg
Sunday 24	FA Trophy final
Tuesday 26	World Cup 2014 qualifiers
	Montenegro v England
	Northern Ireland v Israel
	Republic of Ireland v Austria
	Serbia v Scotland
	Wales v Croatia
Saturday 30	FA Vase semi-final, second leg

APRIL

Tuesday 2-3	Champions League quarter-final, first leg
Thursday 4	Europa League quarter-final, first leg
Sunday 7	Johnstone's Paint Trophy final
	Scottish Challenge Cup final
Tuesday 9-10	Champions League quarter-final, second leg
Thursday 11	Europa League quarter-final, second leg
Saturday 13	FA Cup semi-final
	Scottish Cup semi-final
Tuesday 23-24	Champions League semi-final, first leg
Thursday 25	Europa League semi-final, first leg
Tuesday 30	Champions League semi-final, second leg

MAY

Wednesday 1	Champions League semi-final, second leg
Thursday 2	Europa League semi-final, second leg
Saturday 4	FA Vase final
Wednesday 8	Scottish Football League play-off semi-final, first leg
Saturday 11	FA Cup final
	Scottish Football League play-off semi-final, second leg
Wednesday 15	Europa League final, Amsterdam
	Scottish Football League play-off final, first leg
Saturday 18	League 2 play-off final
Sunday 19	League 1 play-off final
	Scottish Football League play-off final, second leg
Saturday 25	Champions League final, Wembley
Sunday 26	Scottish Cup final
Monday 27	Championship play-off final

JUNE

Friday 7	World Cup 2014 qualifiers
	Croatia v Scotland
	Republic of Ireland v Faroe Islands
Saturday 15	Fifa Confederations Cup begins, Brazil
Sunday 30	Fifa Confederations Cup final

Date	Game	Time	Channel	Competition
AUGUST				
Mon 13	Oldham v Sheffield Weds	7.45pm	Sky Sports 1	League Cup
Tue 14	Swindon v Brighton	7.45pm	Sky Sports 1	League Cup
Wed 15	Northern Ireland v Finland	7.45pm	Sky Sports 3	International
	Scotland v Australia	8pm	Sky Sports 1	International
	Wales v Boznia-Hz	7.45pm	tbc	International
Fri 17	Cardiff v Huddersfield	7.45pm	Sky Sports 1	Championship
Sat 18	Leeds v Wolves	12.45pm	Sky Sports 2	Championship
	Newcastle v Tottenham	5.30pm	ESPN	Premier League
Sun 19	Wigan v Chelsea	1.30pm	Sky Sports 1	Premier League
	Man City v Southampton	4pm	Sky Sports 1	Premier League
Mon 20	Everton v Man Utd	8pm	Sky Sports 1	Premier League
Fri 24	Bolton v Nottm Forest	7.45pm	Sky Sports 1	Championship
Sat 25	Swansea v West Ham	12.45pm	Sky Sports	Premier League
	Chelsea v Newcastle	5.30pm	ESPN	Premier League
Sun 26	Stoke City v Arsenal	1.30pm	Sky Sports 1	Premier League
	Liverpool v Man City	4pm	Sky Sports 1	Premier League
Fri 31	Chelsea v Atletico Madrid	TBC	Sky Sports 2	Uefa Super Cup
SEPTEMBER				
Sat 1	West Ham v Fulham	12.45pm	Sky Sports	Premier League
	Man City v QPR	5.30pm	ESPN	Premier League
Sun 2	Liverpool v Arsenal	1.30pm	Sky Sports	Premier League
	Southampton v Man Utd	4pm	Sky Sports	Premier League
Fri 7	Moldova v England	tbc	tbc	World Cup qualifier
	Wales v Belgium	7.45pm	tbc	World Cup qualifier
	Russia v N Ireland	tbc	tbc	World Cup qualifier
	Kazakhstan v Republic of Ireland	tbc	tbc	World Cup qualifier
Sat 8	Scotland v Serbia	3pm	Sky Sports	World Cup qualifier
Sun 9	Coventry v Stevenage	1.15pm	Sky Sports	League 1
	Crawley v Portsmouth	3.30pm	Sky Sports	League 1
Tue 11	England v Ukraine	8pm	ITV	World Cup qualifier
	Northern Ireland v Luxembourg	7.45pm	Sky Sports	World Cup qualifier
	Scotland v Macedonia	8pm	Sky Sports	World Cup qualifier
	Serbia v Wales	tbc	tbc	World Cup qualifier
Fri 14	Charlton v Crystal Palace	7.45pm	Sky Sports	Championship
Sat 15	Norwich v West Ham	12.45pm	Sky Sports	Premier League
	Sunderland v Liverpool	5.30pm	ESPN	Premier League
Sun 16	Reading v Tottenham	4pm	Sky Sports	Premier League
Mon 17	Everton v Newcastle	8pm	Sky Sports	Premier League
Fri 21	Blackburn v Middlesbrough	7.45pm	Sky Sports	Championship
Sat 22	Swansea v Everton	12.45pm	Sky Sports	Premier League
Sun 23	Liverpool v Man Utd	1.30pm	Sky Sports	Premier League
	Man City v Arsenal	4pm	Sky Sports	Premier League
Sat 29	Arsenal v Chelsea	12.45pm	Sky Sports	Premier League
	Man Utd v Tottenham	5.30pm	ESPN	Premier League
Sun 30	Aston Villa v West Brom	4pm	Sky Sports	Premier League
OCTOBER				
Mon 1	QPR v West Ham	8pm	Sky Sports	Premier League
Sat 6	Man City v Sunderland	12.45pm	Sky Sports	Premier League

	West Ham v Arsenal	5.30pm	ESPN	Premier League
Sun 7	Southampton v Fulham	1.30pm	Sky Sports	Premier League
	Newcastle v Man Utd	4pm	Sky Sports	Premier League
Fri 12	England v San Marino	8pm	ITV	World Cup qualifier
	Republic of Ireland v Germany	tbc	tbc	World Cup qualifier
	Wales v Scotland	tbc	tbc	World Cup qualifier
Tue 16	Belgium v Scotland	7.45pm	BBC Scotland	World Cup qualifier
	Croatia v Wales	tbc	tbc	World Cup qualifier
	Faroe Islands v Rep of Ireland	tbc	tbc	World Cup qualifier
	Poland v England	tbc	tbc	World Cup qualifier
	Portugal v Northern Ireland	tbc	tbc	World Cup qualifier
Fri 19	Sheffield Weds v Leeds	7.45pm	Sky Sports	Championship
Sat 20	Tottenham v Chelsea	12.45pm	Sky Sports	Premier League
	Norwich v Arsenal	5.30pm	ESPN	Premier League
Sun 21	Sunderland v Newcastle	1.30pm	Sky Sports	Premier League
	QPR v Everton	4pm	Sky Sports	Premier League
Sat 27	Everton v Liverpool	12.45pm	Sky Sports	Premier League
	Man City v Swansea	5.30pm	ESPN	Premier League
Sun 28	Aston Villa v Norwich	1.30pm	Sky Sports	Premier League
	Chelsea v Man Utd	4pm	Sky Sports	Premier League

NOVEMBER

	Man Utd v Arsenal	12.45pm	Sky Sports	Premier League
Sat 3	Man Utd v Arsenal	12.45pm	Sky Sports	Premier League
	West Ham v Man City	5.30pm	ESPN	Premier League
Sun 4	QPR v Reading	1.30pm	Sky Sports	Premier League
	Liverpool v Newcastle	4pm	Sky Sports	Premier League
Mon 5	West Brom v Southampton	8pm	Sky Sports	Premier League
Sat 10	Aston Villa v Man Utd	5.30pm	Sky Sports	Premier League
Sun 11	Man City v Tottenham	1.30pm	Sky Sports	Premier League
	Chelsea v Liverpool	4pm	Sky Sports	Premier League
Wed 14	Northern Ireland v Azerbaijan	7.45pm	Sky Sports	World Cup qualifier
Sat 17	Arsenal v Tottenham	12.45pm	Sky Sports	Premier League
	Norwich City v Man Utd	5.30pm	ESPN	Premier League
Sun 18	Fulham v Sunderland	4pm	Sky Sports	Premier League
Mon 19	West Ham v Stoke	8pm	Sky Sports	Premier League
Sat 24	Aston Villa v Arsenal	5.30pm	ESPN	Premier League
	Swansea v Liverpool	12.45pm	Sky Sports	Premier League
Sun 25	Sunderland v West Brom	1.30pm	Sky Sports	Premier League
	Chelsea v Man City	4pm	Sky Sports	Premier League
Tue 27	Aston Villa v Reading	8pm	Sky Sports	Premier League
Wed 28	Wigan v Man City	8pm	Sky Sports	Premier League

MARCH 2013

	San Marino v England	tbc	tbc	World Cup qualifier
Fri 22	San Marino v England	tbc	tbc	World Cup qualifier
	Northern Ireland v Russia	tbc	Sky Sports	World Cup qualifier
	Scotland v Wales	tbc	Sky Sports	World Cup qualifier
	Sweden v Republic of Ireland	tbc	tbc	World Cup qualifier
Tue 26	Montenegro v England	tbc	tbc	World Cup qualifier
	Northern Ireland v Israel	tbc	Sky Sports	World Cup qualifier
	Republic of Ireland v Austria	tbc	tbc	World Cup qualifier
	Serbia v Scotland	tbc	BBC Scotland	World Cup qualifier
	Wales v Croatia	tbc	tbc	World Cup qualifier

JUNE 2013

	Croatia v Scotland	tbc	BBC1 Scotland	World Cup qualifier
Fri 7	Croatia v Scotland	tbc	BBC1 Scotland	World Cup qualifier

BBC televised fixtures were unavailable as we went to press

Gap to top two might be too big to bridge

IT was all change last season, with a new name on the Premier League trophy, Chelsea finishing outside the top four, Newcastle in contention for the Champions League places, Everton finishing ahead of Liverpool and the three promoted clubs all staying up, *writes Paul Charlton*.

But at the top, at least, it's worth counting on things staying broadly the same this time with the two Manchester clubs dominating the title betting.

As we go to press, United have been the busier side in the transfer market and Shinji Kagawa, who joined from Borussia Dortmund, looks perfect for them. Nick Powell's progress will be interesting to watch as well, although he looks like one for the future. Neither of the top two will be significantly weaker when they kick off for next season, however.

Of the rest, it is Chelsea who have made the most eye-catching signing, with Eden Hazard a real talent. Roberto Di Matteo is obviously a better fit at Chelsea than Andre Villas-Boas was but the re-building continues and their best work was all done in the cups last season.

Arsenal have been busy in the transfer market too and the question of whether Robin van Persie stays with them or not, unanswered as we went to press, should be less important with the signings of Lukas Podolski and Olivier Giroud.

Podolski brings vast experience with him from Cologne – despite his 101 German caps, he is still only 27 – and scored 18 goals in the Bundesliga last season, while Giroud was the joint top scorer in Ligue 1 last season, scoring 21 goals as Montpellier landed an unlikely title success. He is a good finisher, excellent in the air and can make a goal too, providing nine assists last term. Arsene Wenger will hope to have Jack Wilshere available as well.

But while it's easy to see Arsenal and Chelsea putting up more of a fight this time, last season's 19-point gap to the two Manchester clubs looks too big to bridge. Back a **Man City/Man United dual forecast**.

That brings us nicely onto the golden boot, where you need a player from one of the very top teams. Thierry Henry was the last player to finish as top scorer while playing for a team who finished outside the top three and that was back in 2005-06. Van Persie's future is still up in the air at the time of writing leaving **Sergio Aguero** and Wayne Rooney as joint favourites. As the top scorer in a team that scored 93 goals last season, slight preference is for Aguero, who found the net 23 times in his first Premier League campaign, but further down the list, **Papiss Cisse** is certainly interesting at 25-1. It's hard to see Newcastle having another season like 2011-12 but Cisse

Premier League winner

	b365	Btfrd	Hills	Lads	Pwr	StJms
Man City	5-4	11-8	11-8	11-8	5-4	5-4
Man Utd	9-4	2	**5-2**	9-4	9-4	9-4
Chelsea	9-2	9-2	9-2	9-2	9-2	9-2
Arsenal	10	10	6	10	**12**	10
Tottenham	25	25	**33**	20	25	**33**
Liverpool	28	**33**	20	25	25	**33**
Newcastle	150	150	125	100	**175**	100
Everton	250	250	250	250	**275**	250
Sunderland	**1000**	**1000**	**1000**	**1000**	500	**1000**
Aston Villa	1500	1500	1000	**2000**	1000	1500
Fulham	1000	1000	750	750	1500	**2000**
QPR	1000	**2500**	1000	2000	1500	2000
Stoke	1500	1500	1000	**3000**	1000	1500
West Brom	2500	2500	2500	**3000**	2000	2000
Swansea	2500	2500	2500	**4000**	2500	2000
Norwich	2500	2500	2500	**5000**	2500	3000
West Ham	**5000**	2500	2000	3000	1500	3000
Wigan	2500	**5000**	3000	3000	**5000**	2500
Reading	**5000**	**5000**	3000	**5000**	1500	3000
Southampton	**5000**	2500	1500	3500	**5000**	3000

Win or each-way. See individual bookmakers for terms

CLASS OF THEIR OWN: last year's title race turned into a two-way battle

might be one to do each-way or to back to lay after the way he hit the ground running following his January move from Freiburg.

After finishing ninth in Martin Jol's first season in the dugout, back **Fulham to finish in the top ten** again at 2-1 with Stan James. They've finished in the top half in three of the last four seasons and the year they missed out, they had the distraction of a Europa League campaign that went all the way to the final.

At the bottom, it's unlikely the three promoted teams will all stay up again but the fact that not a single team is odds-on to go down shows how tight the relegation scrap might be. **West Ham** are a bigger price in the relegation betting than either of the teams who went up automatically but their squad looks no better than the side who finished bottom with 33 points two seasons ago. They're worth a bet at 9-4 with Ladbrokes or Coral.

However, the best bet in this market might be for **QPR** to go down at 5-1 with

William Hill. They only survived by a point last season after a great escape style run of results to rival Wigan's (the Latics are 7-4 shots in this market) and only averaged just over 1.1 points a game after Mark Hughes took charge in January (0.85 under Neil Warnock) despite some big names arriving in the transfer window.

By the end of September they will have played Swansea, Norwich and West Ham as well as Man City, Chelsea and Tottenham. If they don't do well against the three fancied to go down, their own relegation odds will tumble. Towards the end of last season there was ample opportunity to trade QPR's relegation price, which remained stubbornly higher than perhaps it should have been for most of the campaign.

Last season's other top-flight newbies, Swansea and Norwich, both finished ten points ahead of the R's but are 9-4 and 7-4 respectively and while both have lost good managers over the summer, both have found solid replacements.

Arsenal

Nickname: The Gunners
Colours: Red and White

Ground: Emirates Stadium **Capacity: 60,361**
Tel: 020-7619-5003 **www.arsenal.com**

A DIFFICULT season started with the sales of Cesc Fabregas, Samir Nasri and Gael Clichy and finished, again, with no trophy but Champions League football.

It didn't help either that Jack Wilshere, who made 49 appearances for Arsenal in 2010-11, didn't kick a ball in anger after injuring an ankle in pre-season.

All of that contributed to a slow start, which saw them lose three of their first five games, including an 8-2 mauling at Old Trafford, but the Gunners turned things around. Robin van Persie was the key man, scoring 30 of Arsenal's 74 league goals, and a 5-2 win over Spurs in February helped them overhaul what was then a ten-point gap to third place as Tottenham's form collapsed in the run-in.

Laurent Koscielny had a great season, Alex Song emerged as a creative force with 11 assists and Alex Oxlade-Chamberlain broke into the England team.

Longest run without loss: 8
Longest run without win: 4
High – low league position 3-15
Clean sheets: 13
Yellow cards: 67 **Red cards:** 4
Players used: 32
Leading Scorer: R van Persie 30 (9,20)

	11-12	Last six seasons at home							
	H A	P	W	D	L	OV	UN	BS	CS
Man City	W L	6	4	2	0	1	5	1	5
Man United	L L	6	3	1	2	5	1	5	1
Arsenal									
Tottenham	W L	6	4	1	1	6	0	4	2
Newcastle	W D	5	3	1	1	3	2	2	2
Chelsea	D W	6	2	2	2	3	3	3	2
Everton	W W	6	4	2	0	3	3	4	2
Liverpool	L W	6	2	3	1	5	3	5	2
Fulham	D L	6	4	2	0	4	2	4	2
West Brom	W W	3	2	0	1	2	1	1	2
Swansea	W L	1	1	0	0	0	1	0	1
Norwich	D W	1	0	1	0	1	0	1	0
Sunderland	W W	5	3	2	0	2	3	2	3
Stoke	W D	4	4	0	0	2	2	2	2
Wigan	L W	6	5	0	1	4	2	2	4
Aston Villa	W W	6	2	2	2	3	3	3	2
QPR	W L	1	1	0	0	0	1	0	1
Reading	- -	2	2	0	0	1	1	1	1
Southampton	- -	0	0	0	0	0	0	0	0
West Ham	- -	5	3	1	1	0	5	0	4

Season	Division	Pos	P	W	D	L	F	A	GD	Pts
2011-12	Prem	3	38	21	7	10	74	49	25	70
2010-11	Prem	4	38	19	11	8	72	43	29	68
2009-10	Prem	3	38	23	6	9	83	41	42	75

Final *Outlook Index* figure: 905

Key Stat: For the third season running, the Gunners conceded more goals than they had in the previous campaign (37, 41, 43, 49)

2011-12 Premier League appearances

	P	G	Y	R
A Arshavin	8 (11)	1	1	0
M Arteta	29	6	5	0
Y Benayoun	10 (9)	4	1	0
N Bendtner	0 (1)	0	2	0
M Chamakh	1 (10)	1	0	0
F Coquelin	6 (4)	0	2	0
A Diaby	0 (4)	0	1	0
J Djourou	14 (4)	0	4	1
E Frimpong	3 (3)	0	2	1
Gervinho	19 (9)	4	0	1
K Gibbs	15 (1)	1	1	0
T Henry	0 (4)	1	0	0
C Jenkinson	5 (4)	0	1	1
L Koscielny	33	2	9	0
H Lansbury	0 (2)	0	1	0
P Mertesacker	21	0	2	0

	P	G	Y	R
I Miquel	1 (3)	0	0	0
S Nasri	1	0	0	0
A O-Chamberlain	6 (10)	2	0	0
Park Chu-Young	0 (1)	0	0	0
A Ramsey	27 (7)	2	3	0
T Rosicky	19 (9)	1	4	0
B Sagna	20 (1)	1	2	0
A Santos	10 (5)	2	2	0
A Song	34	1	10	0
S Squillaci	0 (1)	0	0	0
W Szczesny	38	0	2	0
A Traore	1	0	0	0
T Vermaelen	28 (1)	6	7	0
T Walcott	32 (3)	8	1	0
N Yennaris	0 (1)	0	0	0
R van Persie	37 (1)	30	8	0

Aston Villa

Nickname: The Villans
Colours: Claret and Blue

Ground: Villa Park
Tel: 0121-327-2299

Capacity: 42,785
www.avfc.co.uk

LAST term's seven league victories was Villa's lowest tally since the 1890-91 season, when the Villans played just 22 matches in a 12-team division. Only rock-bottom Wolves won fewer last season.

And only once, in 1969-70, have Villa scored fewer league goals in a season than last term's 37. Only Stoke got fewer.

In fairness to Alex McLeish, who has been replaced by Paul Lambert, he was dealt a difficult hand. An unpopular appointment, taking charge having just overseen the relegation of Villa's city rivals, Birmingham, he lost Stewart Downing and Ashley Young in the summer and saw Darren Bent, whose goals over the second half of 2010-11 had helped the club rally to a top-ten finish, miss the last dozen games through injury.

Their win-rate only stood at 29 per cent when Bent was in the side but without him it dropped to a dismal 11 per cent.

Longest run without loss: 7
Longest run without win: 10
High – low league position 7-16
Clean sheets: 9
Yellow cards: 71 **Red cards:** 2
Players used: 27
Leading Scorer: D Bent 9 (3,8)

| | 11-12 | | Last six seasons at home | | | | | | | |
	H	A	P	W	D	L	OV	UN	BS	CS
Man City	L	L	6	2	2	2	2	4	4	1
Man United	L	L	6	0	3	3	3	3	3	1
Arsenal	L	L	6	0	2	4	4	2	4	1
Tottenham	D	L	6	1	3	2	3	3	6	0
Newcastle	D	L	5	4	1	0	1	4	2	3
Chelsea	L	W	6	2	2	2	2	4	2	3
Everton	D	D	6	2	4	0	2	4	4	2
Liverpool	L	D	6	1	2	3	1	5	1	3
Fulham	W	D	6	3	3	0	2	4	3	3
West Brom	L	D	3	2	0	1	3	0	3	0
Swansea	L	D	1	0	0	1	0	1	0	0
Norwich	W	L	1	1	0	0	1	0	1	0
Sunderland	D	D	5	1	2	2	1	4	2	1
Stoke	D	D	4	1	3	0	1	3	3	1
Wigan	W	D	6	1	3	2	0	6	2	2
Aston Villa										
QPR	D	D	1	0	1	0	1	0	1	0
Reading	-	-	2	2	0	0	2	0	2	0
Southampton	-	-	0	0	0	0	0	0	0	0
West Ham	-	-	5	3	2	0	1	4	1	4

Season	Division	Pos	P	W	D	L	F	A	GD	Pts
2011-12	Prem	16	38	7	17	14	37	53	-16	38
2010-11	Prem	9	38	12	12	14	48	59	-11	48
2009-10	Prem	6	38	17	13	8	52	39	13	64

Final *Outlook Index* figure: 845

Key Stat: Solid Villa played their part in a division-high seven goalless draws last season, five away from home

2011-12 Premier League appearances

	P	G	Y	R
G Agbonlahor	32 (1)	5	6	0
M Albrighton	15 (11)	2	3	0
N Baker	6 (2)	0	0	0
B Bannan	10 (18)	1	2	0
D Bent	21 (1)	9	1	0
S Carruthers	0 (3)	0	1	0
C Clark	13 (2)	1	3	0
J Collins	31 (1)	1	7	0
C Cuellar	17 (1)	0	2	0
N Delfouneso	1 (5)	0	0	0
F Delph	10 (1)	0	3	0
R Dunne	28	1	7	0
G Gardner	5 (9)	0	1	0
S Given	32	0	1	0
B Guzan	6 (1)	0	0	0
C Herd	19	1	2	1

	P	G	Y	R
E Heskey	18 (10)	1	3	0
A Hutton	29 (2)	0	7	1
S Ireland	19 (5)	1	2	0
J Jenas	1 (2)	0	0	0
R Keane	5 (1)	3	0	0
E Lichaj	9 (1)	1	3	0
C N'Zogbia	24 (6)	2	4	0
S Petrov	26 (1)	4	7	0
S Warnock	34 (1)	2	6	0
A Weimann	5 (9)	2	0	0
L Young	2	0	0	0

Chelsea

Nickname: The Blues
Colours: Blue

Ground: Stamford Bridge
Tel: 0871-984-1955

Capacity: 42,449
www.chelseafc.com

ANDRE VILLAS-BOAS went to Chelsea after a superb season at Porto but results were poor and the grand plan – to rejuvenate the first team – stalled.

He left in March with Chelsea fifth in the league and facing an FA Cup replay against Birmingham and an early Champions League exit after losing the first leg of their quarter-final 3-1 to Napoli.

Roberto Di Matteo brought back the old guard and, after a remarkable turnaround against Napoli, the Blues saw off Benfica and Barcelona en route to the final, where they beat Bayern Munich on penalties, a fortnight after beating Liverpool in the FA Cup final.

Di Matteo now faces the same problems but Fernando Torres showed flickers of form, the likes of Juan Mata, Daniel Sturridge and Ramires all impressed, and the signing of Eden Hazard is a major coup for Roman Abramovich.

Longest run without loss: 6
Longest run without win: 4
High – low league position 3-6
Clean sheets: 10
Yellow cards: 75 **Red cards:** 4
Players used: 29 **Leading Scorers:** F Lampard 11 (4,9) D Sturridge 11 (5,10)

	11-12	Last six seasons at home							
	H A	P	W	D	L	OV	UN	BS	CS
Man City	W L	6	5	0	1	4	2	2	4
Man United	D L	6	3	3	0	3	3	4	2
Arsenal	L D	6	3	1	2	3	3	4	2
Tottenham	D D	6	4	2	0	2	4	2	4
Newcastle	L W	5	2	2	1	2	3	2	2
Chelsea									
Everton	W L	6	1	5	0	2	4	5	1
Liverpool	L L	6	2	1	3	1	5	1	3
Fulham	D D	6	3	3	0	3	3	4	2
West Brom	W L	3	3	0	0	2	1	1	2
Swansea	W D	1	1	0	0	1	0	1	0
Norwich	W D	1	1	0	0	1	0	1	0
Sunderland	W W	5	4	0	1	3	2	1	3
Stoke	W D	4	4	0	0	2	2	1	3
Wigan	W D	6	5	1	0	4	2	3	3
Aston Villa	L W	6	2	3	1	4	2	5	1
QPR	W L	1	1	0	0	1	0	1	0
Reading	- -	2	1	1	0	1	1	1	1
Southampton	- -	0	0	0	0	0	0	0	0
West Ham	- -	5	4	1	0	2	3	2	3

Season	Division	Pos	P	W	D	L	F	A	GD	Pts
2011-12	Prem	6	38	18	10	10	65	46	19	64
2010-11	Prem	2	38	21	8	9	69	33	36	71
2009-10	Prem	1	38	27	5	6	103	32	71	86

Final *Outlook Index* figure: 894

Key Stat: Chelsea's W5, D3, L3 Premier League record under Di Matteo did not include a win over any team that finished higher than 14th

2011-12 Premier League appearances

	P	G	Y	R		P	G	Y	R
Alex	3	0	2	0	D Luiz	18 (2)	2	5	0
N Anelka	3 (6)	1	0	0	R Lukaku	1 (7)	0	0	0
Y Benayoun	0 (1)	0	0	0	F Malouda	11 (15)	2	3	0
R Bertrand	6 (1)	0	1	0	J Mata	29 (5)	6	2	0
J Bosingwa	24 (3)	1	5	1	J McEachran	0 (2)	0	0	0
G Cahill	10 (1)	1	2	0	J Mikel	15 (7)	0	4	0
P Cech	34	0	0	0	Ramires	28 (2)	5	4	0
A Cole	31 (1)	0	8	1	Raul Meireles	23 (5)	2	8	0
D Drogba	16 (8)	5	1	1	O Romeu	11 (5)	0	2	0
M Essien	10 (4)	0	3	0	D Sturridge	28 (2)	11	3	0
P Ferreira	3 (3)	0	1	0	J Terry	31	6	8	0
Hilario	2	0	0	0	F Torres	20 (12)	6	4	1
S Hutchinson	1 (1)	0	0	0	R Turnbull	2	0	0	0
B Ivanovic	26 (3)	3	6	0					
S Kalou	7 (5)	1	0	0					
F Lampard	26 (4)	11	5	0					

Everton

Nickname: The Toffees
Colours: Blue and White

Ground: Goodison Park
Tel: 0871-663-1878

Capacity: 40,157
www.evertonfc.com

AS usual, Everton finished stronger than they started. David Moyes' side took 1.24 points a game in 2011 but upped that average to 1.67 points a game in 2012, and beat Man City, Spurs, Chelsea and Newcastle at home.

In contrast to the summer transfer window, which saw Mikel Arteta leave and bit-part players Royston Drenthe and Denis Stracqualursi come in, January saw the arrivals of some influential performers, Landon Donovan and Steven Pienaar returning to the club on loan (Donovan only for just over a month), and Darron Gibson and Nikica Jelavic both signing, the latter finishing as top scorer, with nine goals in 13 league appearances.

They finished seventh, for Everton's eighth top-ten finish in the ten full seasons that Moyes, the Football League's third-longest serving manager, has been in the dugout.

Longest run without loss: 9
Longest run without win: 4
High – low league position 7-17
Clean sheets: 12
Yellow cards: 61 **Red cards:** 1
Players used: 30
Leading Scorer: N Jelavic 9 (4,6)

	11-12		Last six seasons at home							
	H	A	P	W	D	L	OV	UN	BS	CS
Man City	W	L	6	4	1	1	2	4	3	3
Man United	L	D	6	1	2	3	3	3	4	0
Arsenal	L	L	6	1	1	4	3	3	4	1
Tottenham	W	L	6	2	3	1	3	3	3	3
Newcastle	W	L	5	3	1	1	4	1	3	1
Chelsea	W	L	6	3	1	2	2	4	2	3
Everton										
Liverpool	L	L	6	2	0	4	2	4	1	2
Fulham	W	W	6	6	0	0	5	1	3	3
West Brom	W	W	3	2	0	1	1	2	1	2
Swansea	W	W	1	1	0	0	0	1	0	1
Norwich	D	D	1	0	1	0	0	1	1	0
Sunderland	W	D	5	5	0	0	3	2	1	4
Stoke	L	D	4	2	1	1	1	3	2	1
Wigan	W	D	6	4	2	0	5	1	4	2
Aston Villa	D	D	6	0	4	2	4	2	5	0
QPR	L	D	1	0	0	1	0	1	0	0
Reading	-	-	2	1	1	0	0	2	1	1
Southampton	-	-	0	0	0	0	0	0	0	0
West Ham	-	-	5	2	3	0	3	2	4	1

Season	Division	Pos	P	W	D	L	F	A	GD	Pts
2011-12	Prem	7	38	15	11	12	50	40	10	56
2010-11	Prem	7	38	13	15	10	51	45	6	54
2009-10	Prem	8	38	16	13	9	60	49	11	61

Final *Outlook Index* figure: 883

Key Stat: Last season was only the second time that Everton finished ahead of Liverpool since the Toffees won the league in 1987

2011-12 Premier League appearances

	P	G	Y	R
V Anichebe	5 (7)	5	1	0
M Arteta	2 (1)	1	1	0
L Baines	33	4	7	0
R Barkley	2 (4)	0	0	0
J Baxter	0 (1)	0	0	0
J Beckford	1 (1)	0	0	0
D Bilyaletdinov	7 (3)	0	0	0
T Cahill	27 (8)	2	5	0
S Coleman	14 (4)	0	2	0
S Distin	24 (3)	0	4	0
L Donovan	7	0	1	0
R Drenthe	10 (11)	3	5	0
S Duffy	2 (2)	0	0	0
M Fellaini	31 (3)	3	6	0
D Gibson	11	1	3	0
M Gueye	3 (14)	1	1	0

	P	G	Y	R
J Heitinga	29 (1)	1	4	0
T Hibbert	31 (1)	0	1	0
T Howard	38	1	1	0
P Jagielka	29 (1)	2	2	0
N Jelavic	10 (3)	9	1	0
C McAleny	0 (2)	0	0	0
J McFadden	2 (5)	0	0	0
P Neville	24 (3)	0	3	0
L Osman	28 (2)	4	3	0
S Pienaar	14	4	6	0
J Rodwell	11 (3)	2	2	1
L Saha	15 (3)	1	0	0
D Stracqualursi	7 (13)	1	1	0
A Vellios	2 (11)	3	1	0

Fulham

Nickname: The Cottagers
Colours: White and Black

Ground: Craven Cottage   **Capacity: 25,700**
Tel: 0843-208-1222   **www.fulhamfc.com**

FULHAM'S season kicked off last June, with Martin Jol's first match in the dugout a 3-0 victory over Faroese outfit NSI.

Unlike their previous European campaign, when Roy Hodgson took them to the 2009 Europa League final, Fulham bowed out at the group stage, but the upside was that, unlike their last European campaign, their league performance didn't suffer – although Fulham finished a place down on their eighth place in 2010-11, they earned three points more.

Much of the credit must go to Clint Dempsey, who weighed in with 17 league goals, including his first top-flight hat-trick in a remarkable 5-2 win over Newcastle.

He wasn't their only goal threat, however, with Pavel Pogrebnyak getting six goals in 12 league games after joining on loan from Stuttgart on the final day of the January transfer window.

Longest run without loss: 4
Longest run without win: 6
High – low league position 8-17
Clean sheets: 11
Yellow cards: 54 **Red cards:** 0
Players used: 28
Leading Scorer: C Dempsey 17 (7,13)

	11-12		Last six seasons at home						
	H	A	P	W	D	L	OV	UN	BS	CS
Man City	D	L	6	0	3	3	5	1	6	0
Man United	L	L	6	2	1	3	5	1	2	2
Arsenal	W	D	6	3	1	2	4	2	3	1
Tottenham	L	L	6	1	3	2	4	2	5	1
Newcastle	W	L	5	4	0	1	3	2	3	1
Chelsea	D	D	6	0	3	3	2	4	3	1
Everton	L	L	6	3	1	2	2	4	2	3
Liverpool	W	W	6	3	0	3	2	4	2	2
Fulham										
West Brom	D	D	3	2	1	0	1	2	1	2
Swansea	L	L	1	0	0	1	1	0	0	0
Norwich	W	D	1	1	0	0	1	0	1	0
Sunderland	W	D	5	2	2	1	2	3	2	3
Stoke	W	L	4	3	0	1	1	3	1	2
Wigan	W	W	6	4	1	1	2	4	3	2
Aston Villa	D	L	6	2	3	1	2	4	4	1
QPR	W	W	1	1	0	0	1	0	0	1
Reading	-	-	2	1	0	1	1	1	1	0
Southampton	-	-	0	0	0	0	0	0	0	0
West Ham	-	-	5	1	1	3	3	2	3	1

Season	Division	Pos	P	W	D	L	F	A	GD	Pts
2011-12	Prem	9	38	14	10	14	48	51	-3	52
2010-11	Prem	8	38	11	16	11	49	43	6	49
2009-10	Prem	12	38	12	10	16	39	46	-7	46

Final _Outlook Index_ figure: 873

Key Stat: Fulham's away games produced 37 goals, the lowest in the top flight by seven – 14 of their 19 away games finished with under 2.5 goals

2011-12 Premier League appearances

	P	G	Y	R
C Baird	13 (6)	0	6	0
M Briggs	1 (1)	0	0	0
S Davies	3 (3)	0	0	0
M Dembele	33 (3)	2	6	0
C Dempsey	37	17	2	0
M Diarra	8 (3)	1	1	0
D Duff	23 (5)	2	2	0
D Etuhu	9 (13)	0	4	0
K Frei	6 (10)	0	1	0
M Gecov	0 (2)	0	0	0
Z Grygera	5	0	2	0
B Hangeland	38	0	7	0
A Hughes	18 (1)	0	0	0
A Johnson	13 (7)	3	1	0
A Kacaniklic	2 (2)	0	0	0
P Kasami	3 (4)	0	0	0

	P	G	Y	R
S Kelly	21 (3)	0	0	0
D Murphy	33 (3)	2	7	0
P Pogrebnyak	12	6	1	0
J Riise	35 (1)	0	2	0
B Ruiz	17 (10)	2	0	0
O Sa	3 (4)	1	0	0
M Schwarzer	30	0	1	0
P Senderos	21	1	5	0
S Sidwell	12 (2)	1	4	0
D Stockdale	8	0	0	0
M Trotta	0 (1)	0	1	0
B Zamora	15 (1)	5	2	0

Liverpool

Nickname: The Reds
Colours: Red

Ground: Anfield
Tel: 0151-263-2361

Capacity: 45,276
www.liverpoolfc.tv

LIVERPOOL finished 2010-11 with a flourish under Kenny Dalglish – only Man United and Chelsea took more points once he was in the dugout – but they couldn't keep up the pace last season.

While they did finish with a trophy to polish and Europa League football thanks to their League Cup win over Cardiff – and they reached the FA Cup final, too – eighth place wasn't good enough for the board and Brendan Rodgers is in charge for the coming season.

The first part of the campaign was overshadowed by the Luis Suarez affair – the Uruguayan served an eight-game ban for racially abusing Man United's Patrice Evra – but he was comfortably their best player and none of their other expensive signings under Dalglish really excelled, even if Andy Carroll did enough towards the end of the season to earn a place in England's Euro 2012 squad.

Longest run without loss: 8
Longest run without win: 4
High – low league position 5-9
Clean sheets: 12
Yellow cards: 55 **Red cards:** 5
Players used: 26
Leading Scorer: L Suarez 11 (3,9)

	11-12		Last six seasons at home						
	H	A	P	W	D	L	OV	UN	BS	CS
Man City	D	L	6	3	3	0	2	4	3	3
Man United	D	L	6	3	1	2	2	4	3	1
Arsenal	L	W	6	1	3	2	4	2	6	0
Tottenham	D	L	6	3	2	1	3	3	2	3
Newcastle	W	L	5	5	0	0	4	1	1	4
Chelsea	W	W	6	4	1	1	1	5	2	3
Everton	W	W	6	3	3	0	2	4	2	4
Liverpool										
Fulham	L	L	6	3	2	1	1	5	0	5
West Brom	L	W	3	2	0	1	1	2	0	2
Swansea	D	L	1	0	1	0	0	1	0	1
Norwich	D	W	1	0	1	0	0	1	1	0
Sunderland	D	L	5	3	2	0	3	2	2	3
Stoke	D	L	4	2	2	0	1	3	0	4
Wigan	L	D	6	3	2	1	3	3	5	1
Aston Villa	D	W	6	3	2	1	5	1	4	2
QPR	W	L	1	1	0	0	0	1	0	1
Reading	-	-	2	2	0	0	1	1	1	1
Southampton	-	-	0	0	0	0	0	0	0	0
West Ham	-	-	5	4	1	0	4	1	1	4

Season	Division	Pos	P	W	D	L	F	A	GD	Pts
2011-12	Prem	8	38	14	10	14	47	40	7	52
2010-11	Prem	6	38	17	7	14	59	44	15	58
2009-10	Prem	7	38	18	9	11	61	35	26	63

Final *Outlook Index* figure: 865

Key Stat: Their lowest points haul since 1980-81 – a 22-team division, granted, but it was two points for a win and Liverpool won the European Cup too

2011-12 Premier League appearances

	P	G	Y	R
C Adam	27 (1)	2	5	1
D Agger	24 (3)	1	6	0
F Aurelio	1 (1)	0	0	0
C Bellamy	12 (15)	6	6	0
J Carragher	19 (2)	0	1	0
A Carroll	21 (14)	4	5	0
S Coates	4 (3)	1	1	0
Doni	4	0	0	1
S Downing	28 (8)	0	1	0
J Enrique	33 (2)	0	2	0
J Flanagan	5	0	2	0
S Gerrard	12 (6)	5	0	0
J Henderson	31 (6)	2	3	0
G Johnson	22 (1)	1	2	0
B Jones	0 (1)	0	1	0
M Kelly	12	0	1	0

	P	G	Y	R
D Kuyt	22 (12)	2	3	0
Lucas	12	0	5	0
Raul Meireles	0 (2)	0	0	0
J Reina	34	0	0	1
M Rodriguez	10 (2)	4	1	0
J Shelvey	8 (5)	1	2	0
M Skrtel	33 (1)	2	3	1
J Spearing	15 (1)	0	0	1
R Sterling	0 (3)	0	0	0
L Suarez	29 (2)	11	5	0

Man City

Nickname: The Citizens
Colours: Sky Blue and White

Ground: Etihad Stadium   **Capacity: 47,405**
Tel: 0161-444-1894   **www.mcfc.co.uk**

CITY wrapped up their first league title since 1968 and it's worth remembering that they started the season third in the betting at 4-1 after finishing in third place, nine points off Man United, in 2010-11.

A superb start to the season that saw them win 12 of their first 14 games, half by three goals or more, and included the 1-6 win at Old Trafford, was overshadowed by the Carlos Tevez affair, but Tevez was already a bit-part figure at that stage. Nevertheless, Roberto Mancini was able to bring him back to score vital goals late in the campaign.

David Silva weighed in with 15 assists, Vincent Kompany was many pundits' player of the season, Yaya Toure was, once again, a force of nature and Sergio Aguero got 23 goals in his first season in England, including the injury-time strike against QPR that wrapped up the title race on the final day.

Longest run without loss: 14
Longest run without win: 3
High – low league position 1-2
Clean sheets: 17
Yellow cards: 56 **Red cards:** 5
Players used: 24
Leading Scorer: S Aguero 23 (8,16)

	11-12	Last six seasons at home

	H	A	P	W	D	L	OV	UN	BS	CS
Man City										
Man United	W	W	6	2	1	3	0	6	0	3
Arsenal	W	L	6	4	0	2	4	2	2	3
Tottenham	W	W	6	3	0	3	4	2	4	1
Newcastle	W	W	5	4	1	0	4	1	4	1
Chelsea	W	L	6	3	0	3	3	3	3	1
Everton	W	L	6	2	0	4	2	4	2	1
Liverpool	W	D	6	2	3	1	3	3	1	5
Fulham	W	D	6	2	2	2	5	1	5	1
West Brom	W	D	3	3	0	0	3	0	1	2
Swansea	W	L	1	1	0	0	1	0	0	1
Norwich	W	W	1	1	0	0	1	0	1	0
Sunderland	D	L	5	4	1	0	3	2	2	3
Stoke	W	D	4	4	0	0	3	1	0	4
Wigan	W	W	6	4	1	1	2	4	0	5
Aston Villa	W	W	6	5	0	1	3	3	2	3
QPR	W	W	1	1	0	0	1	0	1	0
Reading	-	-	2	1	0	1	1	1	1	0
Southampton	-	-	0	0	0	0	0	0	0	0
West Ham	-	-	5	4	1	0	3	2	3	2

Season	Division	Pos	P	W	D	L	F	A	GD	Pts
2011-12	Prem	1	38	28	5	5	93	29	64	89
2010-11	Prem	3	38	21	8	9	60	33	27	71
2009-10	Prem	5	38	18	13	7	73	45	28	67

Final *Outlook Index* figure: 939

Key Stat: City's goal difference in 2010-11 was a healthy +27. In 2011-12 it was +64, seven shy of the Premier League record

2011-12 Premier League appearances

	P	G	Y	R		P	G	Y	R
S Aguero	31 (3)	23	2	0	M Richards	23 (6)	1	2	0
M Balotelli	14 (9)	13	6	2	S Savic	5 (6)	1	1	0
G Barry	31 (3)	1	9	1	D Silva	33 (3)	6	0	0
G Clichy	28	0	2	1	C Tevez	7 (6)	4	1	0
E Dzeko	16 (14)	14	2	0	K Toure	8 (6)	0	0	0
O Hargreaves	0 (1)	0	0	0	Y Toure	31 (1)	6	8	0
J Hart	38	0	0	0	P Zabaleta	18 (3)	1	5	0
A Johnson	10 (16)	6	1	0	N de Jong	11 (10)	0	5	0
A Kolarov	9 (3)	2	1	0					
V Kompany	31	3	5	1					
J Lescott	30 (1)	2	1	0					
J Milner	17 (9)	3	3	0					
S Nasri	26 (4)	5	2	0					
N Onuoha	1 (1)	0	0	0					
D Pizarro	1 (4)	0	0	0					
A Razak	0 (1)	0	0	0					

Man Utd

Nickname: The Red Devils
Colours: Red and White

Ground: Old Trafford
Tel: 0161-868-8000

Capacity: 75,811
www.manutd.com

NOT for the first time, Betfred paid out early and came unstuck as United appeared to be closing in on a record 20th league title, a battling 0-2 victory at Ewood Park seeing them go five points clear of City with seven games to go.

The momentum had certainly swung in United's favour over the second half of the season, as they put a 1-6 defeat to City in October and a group-stage exit from the Champions League behind them to open up what was, at its peak, an eight-point gap back to the Citizens.

From that high water mark, however, United slipped up. A loss at Wigan and a draw at home to Everton in a game they had led 4-2 in the three games leading up to the Manchester derby meant the pressure was on for the trip to Eastlands and City's 1-0 win meant that, in three weeks, United had gone from champions elect to second on goal difference.

Longest run without loss: 12
Longest run without win: 2
High – low league position 1-2
Clean sheets: 20
Yellow cards: 51 **Red cards:** 1
Players used: 31
Leading Scorer: W Rooney 27 (9,17)

	11-12		Last six seasons at home							
	H	A	P	W	D	L	OV	UN	BS	CS
Man City	L	L	6	4	0	2	5	1	5	1
Man United										
Arsenal	W	W	6	4	1	1	3	3	3	2
Tottenham	W	W	6	6	0	0	3	3	2	4
Newcastle	D	L	5	3	2	0	2	3	2	3
Chelsea	W	D	6	4	1	1	4	2	4	2
Everton	D	W	6	5	1	0	4	2	2	4
Liverpool	W	D	6	5	0	1	5	1	4	2
Fulham	W	W	6	6	0	0	3	2	1	5
West Brom	W	W	3	2	1	0	2	1	1	2
Swansea	W	W	1	1	0	0	0	1	0	1
Norwich	W	W	1	1	0	0	0	1	0	1
Sunderland	W	W	5	4	1	0	1	4	1	4
Stoke	W	D	4	4	0	0	3	1	1	3
Wigan	W	L	6	6	0	0	4	2	1	5
Aston Villa	W	W	6	5	0	1	5	1	3	2
QPR	W	W	1	1	0	0	0	1	0	1
Reading	-	-	2	1	1	0	1	1	1	1
Southampton	-	-	0	0	0	0	0	0	0	0
West Ham	-	-	5	4	0	1	3	2	1	3

Season	Division	Pos	P	W	D	L	F	A	GD	Pts
2011-12	Prem	2	38	28	5	5	89	33	56	89
2010-11	Prem	1	38	23	11	4	78	37	41	80
2009-10	Prem	2	38	27	4	7	86	28	58	85

Final *Outlook Index* figure: 941

Key Stat: Man United have only ever matched or bettered last season's haul of 89 points on four occasions and were 19 points clear of third place

2011-12 Premier League appearances

	P	G	Y	R		P	G	Y	R
B Amos	1	0	0	0	A Lindegaard	8	0	0	0
Anderson	8 (2)	2	2	0	F Macheda	0 (3)	0	0	0
D Berbatov	5 (7)	7	0	0	Nani	24 (5)	8	2	0
M Carrick	27 (3)	2	4	0	M Owen	0 (1)	0	0	0
T Cleverley	5 (5)	0	0	0	J-S Park	10 (7)	2	0	0
J Evans	28 (1)	1	6	1	P Pogba	0 (3)	0	0	0
P Evra	37	0	6	0	Rafael Da Silva	10 (2)	0	2	0
Fabio Da Silva	2 (3)	0	1	0	W Rooney	32 (2)	27	1	0
R Ferdinand	29 (1)	0	4	0	P Scholes	14 (3)	4	3	0
D Fletcher	7 (1)	1	1	0	C Smalling	14 (5)	1	1	0
E Fryers	0 (2)	0	0	0	L Valencia	22 (5)	4	3	0
D Gibson	1	0	0	0	N Vidic	6	0	0	0
R Giggs	14 (11)	2	3	0	D Welbeck	23 (7)	9	3	0
J Hernandez	18 (10)	10	0	0	A Young	19 (6)	6	3	0
P Jones	25 (4)	1	6	0	D de Gea	29	0	0	0
W Keane	0 (1)	0	0	0					

Newcastle

Nickname: The Magpies
Colours: Black and White

Ground: Sports Direct Arena   **Capacity: 52,409**
Tel: 0844-372-1892   **www.nufc.co.uk**

NEWCASTLE had at least three candidates for signing of the season, with Demba Ba, a free transfer from West Ham, superb in the first half of the campaign, Papiss Cisse making an immediate impact after his £9m January move from Freiburg and Yohan Cabaye, a snip at £4.8m Lille, excellent going forward and a very effective ball winner.

It wasn't all about the new arrivals though. Captain Fabricio Coloccini also had an excellent season and Alan Pardew was able to get the best out of the enigmatic Hatem Ben Arfa, who had joined the Magpies from Marseille in 2010 with a reputation for being a troublemaker, and had spent much of his Newcastle career injured. His FA Cup goal against Blackburn was simply stunning.

In the end, they surpassed all expectations to finish fifth, taking points off every other team in the division bar Man City.

Longest run without loss: 11
Longest run without win: 6
High – low league position 3-7
Clean sheets: 15
Yellow cards: 68 **Red cards:** 2
Players used: 26
Leading Scorer: D Ba 16 (5,10)

	11-12		Last six seasons at home							
	H	A	P	W	D	L	OV	UN	BS	CS
Man City	L	L	5	0	1	4	2	3	2	0
Man United	W	D	5	1	2	2	4	1	3	2
Arsenal	D	L	5	0	4	1	2	3	3	2
Tottenham	D	L	5	3	2	0	4	1	5	0
Newcastle										
Chelsea	L	W	5	0	2	3	1	4	1	1
Everton	W	L	5	2	2	1	3	2	4	1
Liverpool	W	L	5	3	0	2	4	1	3	1
Fulham	W	L	5	2	1	2	2	3	2	2
West Brom	L	W	4	1	2	1	4	0	4	0
Swansea	D	W	2	1	1	0	1	1	0	2
Norwich	W	L	1	1	0	0	0	1	0	1
Sunderland	D	W	4	2	2	0	1	3	3	1
Stoke	W	W	3	1	1	1	3	0	2	1
Wigan	W	L	5	3	2	0	3	2	3	2
Aston Villa	W	D	5	4	1	0	3	2	2	3
QPR	W	D	2	1	1	0	2	1	1	1
Reading	-	-	3	3	0	0	3	0	1	2
Southampton	-	-	0	0	0	0	0	0	0	0
West Ham	-	-	4	2	2	0	4	0	3	1

Season	Division	Pos	P	W	D	L	F	A	GD	Pts
2011-12	Prem	5	38	19	8	11	56	51	5	65
2010-11	Prem	12	38	11	13	14	56	57	-1	46
2009-10	Champ	1	46	30	12	4	90	35	55	102

Final *Outlook Index* figure: 888

Key Stat: Newcastle kept clean sheets in nine of their 19 home games – only the two Manchester clubs managed more.

2011-12 Premier League appearances

	P	G	Y	R
Sammy Ameobi	1 (9)	0	0	0
Shola Ameobi	8 (19)	2	3	0
D Ba	32 (2)	16	1	0
J Barton	2	0	2	0
H Ben Arfa	16 (10)	5	2	0
L Best	16 (2)	4	2	0
Y Cabaye	34	4	7	0
P Cisse	13 (1)	13	3	0
F Coloccini	35	0	2	0
S Ferguson	0 (7)	0	1	0
D Gosling	1 (11)	1	2	1
D Guthrie	13 (3)	1	3	0
J Gutierrez	37	2	5	1
T Krul	38	0	4	0
P Lovenkrands	2 (7)	0	0	0
S Marveaux	1 (6)	0	0	0

	P	G	Y	R
G Obertan	18 (5)	1	0	0
J Perch	13 (12)	0	3	0
D Santon	19 (5)	0	1	0
D Simpson	35	0	7	0
A Smith	0 (2)	0	1	0
S Taylor	14	0	1	0
R Taylor	23 (8)	2	5	0
C Tiote	24	0	11	0
H Vuckic	2 (2)	0	0	0
M Williamson	21 (1)	0	4	0

Norwich

Nickname: The Canaries
Colours: Yellow and Green

Ground: Carrow Road
Tel: 01603-760-760

Capacity: 27,224
www.canaries.co.uk

ODDS-ON to go down in the ante-post relegation markets, Norwich ony missed out on a top-ten finish on goal difference.

They did it playing some attractive, positive football which proved more effective against the weaker sides in the division – they won just three games against teams who finished in the top half of the table – and scored more goals than any side outside the top six.

Grant Holt scored 15 times and, despite the fact that only the three relegated sides conceded more goals, John Ruddy did well enough in goal to earn an England call-up, although a broken finger meant he didn't go to Euro 2012.

Losing Paul Lambert, the manager who took the Canaries from League 1 to mid-table in the Premier League in three seasons, was a blow but Norwich have secured a capable replacement in Chris Hughton.

Longest run without loss: 4
Longest run without win: 4
High – low league position 8-13
Clean sheets: 3
Yellow cards: 59 **Red cards:** 3
Players used: 27
Leading Scorer: G Holt 15 (2,12)

	11-12 H A	Last six seasons at home							
		P	W	D	L	OV	UN	BS	CS
Man City	L L	1	0	0	1	1	0	1	0
Man United	L L	1	0	0	1	1	0	1	0
Arsenal	L D	1	0	0	1	1	0	1	0
Tottenham	L W	1	0	0	1	0	1	0	0
Newcastle	W L	1	1	0	0	1	0	1	0
Chelsea	D L	1	0	1	0	0	1	0	1
Everton	D D	1	0	1	0	1	0	1	0
Liverpool	L D	1	0	0	1	1	0	1	0
Fulham	D L	1	0	1	0	0	1	1	0
West Brom	L W	3	0	0	3	2	1	2	0
Swansea	W W	3	2	0	1	2	1	2	1
Norwich									
Sunderland	W L	2	2	0	0	1	1	1	1
Stoke	D L	3	1	1	1	0	3	1	1
Wigan	D D	1	0	1	0	0	1	1	0
Aston Villa	W L	1	1	0	0	0	1	0	1
QPR	W W	5	4	0	1	2	3	1	3
Reading	- -	2	1	0	1	1	1	1	0
Southampton	- -	4	1	1	2	2	2	2	0
West Ham	- -	0	0	0	0	0	0	0	0

Season	Division	Pos	P	W	D	L	F	A	GD	Pts
2011-12	Prem	12	38	12	11	15	52	66	-14	47
2010-11	Champ	2	46	23	15	8	83	58	25	84
2009-10	League 1	1	46	29	8	9	89	47	42	95

Final *Outlook Index* figure: 848

Key Stat: Norwich supporters saw their team win an average of just 4.11 corners a game at Carrow Road, the lowest at home by more than a corner

2011-12 Premier League appearances

	P	G	Y	R
D Ayala	6 (1)	0	2	0
L Barnett	13 (4)	1	2	1
R Bennett	8	0	2	0
E Bennett	22 (10)	1	5	0
A Crofts	13 (11)	0	3	0
A Drury	12	0	2	0
D Fox	23 (5)	0	3	0
G Holt	24 (12)	15	7	1
W Hoolahan	25 (8)	4	4	0
J Howson	11	1	3	0
S Jackson	10 (12)	3	1	0
B Johnson	25 (3)	2	2	0
S Lappin	4	0	0	0
C Martin	3 (1)	0	0	0
R Martin	30 (3)	2	1	0
S Morison	22 (12)	9	1	0

	P	G	Y	R
K Naughton	29 (3)	0	7	0
A Pilkington	23 (7)	8	1	0
D Rudd	1 (1)	0	0	0
J Ruddy	37	0	1	1
A Surman	21 (4)	4	1	0
M Tierney	17	0	2	0
J Vaughan	1 (4)	0	1	0
E Ward	12	0	2	0
Z Whitbread	18	0	4	0
A Wilbraham	2 (9)	1	1	0
R de Laet	6	1	1	0

QPR

Nickname: The R's
Colours: Blue and White

Ground: Loftus Road
Tel: 020-8749-0994

Capacity: 18,439
www.qpr.co.uk

AFTER taking QPR from the brink of relegation from the Championship to the Premier League, Neil Warnock lasted just over half a season back in the top flight.

After a decent start – QPR were in the top ten in November – a run of two points taken from nine games left the club in 17th. Mark Hughes, out of management since leaving Fulham the previous summer, took charge and signed a couple of big names in the January transfer window, Djibril Cisse and Bobby Zamora.

Cisse famously either scored or was sent off in every QPR appearance and finished with six goals from his eight appearances, but Zamora only scored twice for the R's after leaving Fulham.

The end result was finishing exactly where Warnock left them, 17th, and they needed a late rally of five straight home wins that included victories over Liverpool, Arsenal and Tottenham to stay up.

Longest run without loss: 3
Longest run without win: 9
High – low league position 9-18
Clean sheets: 7
Yellow cards: 57 **Red cards:** 9
Players used: 35
Leading Scorer: H Helguson 8 (4,7)

	11-12 H A	Last six seasons at home P	W	D	L	OV	UN	BS	CS
Man City	L L	1	0	0	1	1	0	1	0
Man United	L L	1	0	0	1	0	1	0	0
Arsenal	W L	1	1	0	0	1	0	1	0
Tottenham	W L	1	1	0	0	0	1	0	1
Newcastle	D L	2	0	1	1	0	2	0	1
Chelsea	W L	1	1	0	0	0	1	0	1
Everton	D W	1	0	1	0	0	1	1	0
Liverpool	W L	1	1	0	0	1	0	1	0
Fulham	L L	1	0	0	1	0	1	0	0
West Brom	D L	4	1	1	2	2	2	3	0
Swansea	W D	4	3	1	0	2	2	1	3
Norwich	L L	5	1	2	2	2	3	2	2
Sunderland	L L	2	0	0	2	2	0	2	0
Stoke	W W	3·2	1	0	1	2	1	2	
Wigan	W L	1	1	0	0	1	0	1	0
Aston Villa	D D	1	0	1	0	0	1	1	0
QPR									
Reading	- -	3	2	1	0	2	1	2	1
Southampton	- -	3	1	0	2	2	1	1	0
West Ham	- -	0	0	0	0	0	0	0	0

Season	Division	Pos	P	W	D	L	F	A	GD	Pts
2011-12	Prem	17	38	10	7	21	43	66	-23	37
2010-11	Champ	1	46	24	16	6	71	32	39	88
2009-10	Champ	13	46	14	15	17	58	65	-7	57

Final *Outlook Index* figure: 832

Key Stat: 11 points on the road for the worst away record in the Premier League – QPR conceded two goals or more in 12 of 19 away games

2011-12 Premier League appearances

	P	G	Y	R
P Agyemang	2	0	0	0
B Andrade	0 (1)	0	0	0
J Barton	31	3	8	2
J Bothroyd	12 (9)	2	3	0
Bruno Perone	1	0	0	0
A Buzsaky	10 (8)	2	0	0
D Campbell	2 (9)	1	0	0
R Cerny	5	0	0	0
D Cisse	7 (1)	6	0	2
M Connolly	5 (1)	0	0	0
S Derry	28 (1)	1	4	1
S Diakite	9	1	6	1
K Dyer	1	0	0	0
H Ephraim	0 (2)	0	0	0
A Faurlin	20	1	3	0
A Ferdinand	31	0	2	0
D Gabbidon	15 (2)	0	1	0
F Hall	11 (3)	0	3	0

	P	G	Y	R
M Harriman	0 (1)	0	0	0
H Helguson	13 (3)	8	2	0
C Hill	19 (3)	0	4	1
R Hulse	1 (1)	0	0	0
P Kenny	33	0	0	0
F Macheda	0 (3)	0	1	0
J Mackie	24 (7)	7	2	0
N Onuoha	16	0	2	0
B Orr	2 (4)	0	0	0
J Puncheon	0 (2)	0	0	0
T Smith	4 (13)	2	0	0
A Taarabt	24 (3)	2	3	1
T Taiwo	13 (2)	1	1	0
A Traore	18 (5)	0	2	1
S Wright-Phillips	24 (8)	0	3	0
L Young	23	2	5	0
B Zamora	14	2	2	0

Reading

Nickname: The Royals
Colours: Blue and White

Ground: Madejski Stadium **Capacity: 24,169**
Tel: 0118-968-1100 **www.readingfc.co.uk**

READING lost Shane Long, the scorer of 21 Championship goals as they went to the play-off final in 2010-11, and made a slow start to the season. With 15 games gone, the Royals had a W4, D6, L5 record and in 16th place with nearly a third of the season gone, they looked to be going nowhere.

Results picked up, however, and once Jason Roberts joined in January, they averaged nearly 2.5 points per game and surged to the title, pipping Southampton to the post by a single point.

Kaspars Gorkks also had a big season after joining from QPR at the end of the summer transfer window but perhaps their biggest asset is Brian McDermott, who has shown himself to be top operator in his two seasons in management. There is money at the club now that the takeover by Anton Zingarevich, a rich Russian who studied locally, is complete.

Longest run without loss: 10
Longest run without win: 4
High – low league position 1-15
Clean sheets: 20
Yellow cards: 58 **Red cards:** 1
Players used: 28
Leading Scorer: A Le Fondre 12 (1,9)

	11-12 H A	Last six seasons at home P W D L OV UN BS CS
		P W D L OV UN BS CS
Man City	- -	2 2 0 0 0 2 0 2
Man United	- -	2 0 1 1 0 2 1 0
Arsenal	- -	2 0 0 2 2 0 1 0
Tottenham	- -	2 1 0 1 1 1 1 0
Newcastle	- -	3 2 0 1 2 1 2 1
Chelsea	- -	2 0 0 2 1 1 1 0
Everton	- -	2 1 0 1 0 2 0 1
Liverpool	- -	2 1 0 1 2 0 2 0
Fulham	- -	2 1 0 1 0 2 0 1
West Brom	- -	1 0 1 0 0 1 1 0
Swansea	- -	3 1 1 1 1 2 1 1
Norwich	- -	2 1 1 0 1 1 1 1
Sunderland	- -	1 1 0 0 1 0 1 0
Stoke	- -	0 0 0 0 0 0 0 0
Wigan	- -	2 2 0 0 2 0 2 0
Aston Villa	- -	2 1 0 1 1 1 1 1
QPR	- -	3 1 1 1 0 3 0 2
Reading		
Southampton	D W	2 0 1 1 1 1 2 0
West Ham	W W	3 2 0 1 3 0 0 2

Season	Division	Pos	P	W	D	L	F	A	GD	Pts
2011-12	Champ	1	46	27	8	11	69	41	28	89
2010-11	Champ	5	46	20	17	9	77	51	26	77
2009-10	Champ	9	46	17	12	17	68	63	5	63

Final *Outlook Index* figure: 851

Key Stat: When Jason Roberts' name was on the teamsheet, Reading's win-rate stood at 82 per cent

2011-12 Championship appearances

	P	G	Y	R
B Afobe	1 (2)	0	0	0
M Antonio	2 (4)	0	0	0
S Church	19 (12)	7	0	0
M Connolly	6	0	2	0
S Cummings	32 (2)	0	2	0
T Cywka	1 (3)	0	0	0
A Federici	46	0	0	0
K Gorkss	42	3	6	0
A Griffin	9	0	3	0
B Gunnarsson	1 (4)	0	0	0
I Harte	30 (2)	4	1	0
B Howard	0 (1)	0	3	0
N Hunt	33 (8)	8	6	0
J Karacan	36 (1)	3	5	0
J Kebe	30 (3)	3	2	0
B Khumalo	4	0	0	0

	P	G	Y	R
A Le Fondre	17 (15)	12	2	0
M Leigertwood	41	5	6	0
S Long	1	0	2	0
M Manset	4 (11)	3	2	0
J McAnuff	40	5	5	0
J Mills	13 (2)	0	3	0
H Mullins	6	0	1	0
A Pearce	46	5	6	0
J Roberts	17	6	2	1
H Robson-Kanu	19 (16)	4	3	0
J Tabb	10 (9)	0	1	0

Southampton

Nickname: The Saints
Colours: Red and White

Ground: St Mary's Stadium **Capacity: 32,689**
Tel: 0845-688-9448 **www.saintsfc.co.uk**

BACK in the Championship after winning promotion from League 1 in 2010-11, the Saints thrashed Leeds on the opening day of the season and were never out of the top two. It was a disappointment to miss out on the title, but a return to the top flight is a massive achievement just three years after they started the 2009-10 season ten points adrift at the bottom of League 1 after going into administration.

Rickie Lambert continued to impress in the Championship. He was Southampton's top scorer in their promotion campaign and was awarded the Football League Player of the Year after 27 league goals in 42 Championship appearances, a total which included four hat-tricks.

Dutch defender Jos Hooiveld also made an impact after signing from Celtic and weighed in with some vital goals, including one in each of Southampton's league games against West Ham.

Longest run without loss: 12
Longest run without win: 3
High – low league position 1-2
Clean sheets: 18
Yellow cards: 52 **Red cards:** 4
Players used: 27
Leading Scorer: R Lambert 27 (11,15)

	11-12		Last six seasons at home							
	H	A	P	W	D	L	OV	UN	BS	CS
Man City	-	-	0	0	0	0	0	0	0	0
Man United	-	-	0	0	0	0	0	0	0	0
Arsenal	-	-	0	0	0	0	0	0	0	0
Tottenham	-	-	0	0	0	0	0	0	0	0
Newcastle	-	-	0	0	0	0	0	0	0	0
Chelsea	-	-	0	0	0	0	0	0	0	0
Everton	-	-	0	0	0	0	0	0	0	0
Liverpool	-	-	0	0	0	0	0	0	0	0
Fulham	-	-	0	0	0	0	0	0	0	0
West Brom	-	-	2	1	1	0	1	1	1	1
Swansea	-	-	1	0	1	0	1	0	1	0
Norwich	-	-	4	2	1	1	2	2	2	1
Sunderland	-	-	1	0	0	1	1	0	1	0
Stoke	-	-	2	2	0	0	1	1	1	1
Wigan	-	-	0	0	0	0	0	0	0	0
Aston Villa	-	-	0	0	0	0	0	0	0	0
QPR	-	-	3	0	1	2	2	1	2	1
Reading	L	D	2	0	1	1	1	1	2	0
Southampton										
West Ham	W	D	1	1	0	0	0	1	0	1

Season	Division	Pos	P	W	D	L	F	A	GD	Pts
2011-12	Champ	2	46	26	10	10	85	46	39	88
2010-11	League 1	2	46	28	8	10	86	38	48	92
2009-10	League 1	7	46	23	14	9	85	47	38	73*

Final *Outlook Index* figure: 830

Key Stat: The last two teams to go from League 1 to the Premier League in successive seasons – Man City and Norwich – are still in the top flight

2011-12 Championship appearances

	P	G	Y	R
L Barnard	0 (6)	0	0	0
B Bialkowski	1	0	0	0
D Butterfield	9 (1)	0	0	0
R Chaplow	17 (8)	3	2	1
D Connolly	17 (9)	6	1	0
J Cork	39 (7)	0	5	0
K Davis	45	0	1	0
S De Ridder	5 (27)	3	5	0
G Do Prado	36 (6)	10	3	0
I Falque	1	0	0	0
J Fonte	42	1	6	0
J Forte	0 (1)	0	0	0
D Fox	37 (4)	0	5	1
D Hammond	31 (12)	1	2	1
D Harding	12 (8)	1	3	0
L Holmes	0 (6)	1	0	0

	P	G	Y	R
J Hooiveld	39	7	4	0
A Lallana	41	11	1	0
R Lambert	42	27	2	1
T Lee	4 (3)	1	0	0
A Martin	7 (3)	1	0	0
J Puncheon	4 (4)	0	1	0
B Reeves	0 (2)	0	0	0
F Richardson	33 (1)	0	2	0
M Schneiderlin	29 (13)	2	5	0
D Seaborne	4	0	1	0
B Sharp	11 (4)	9	3	0

Stoke

Nickname: The Potters
Colours: Red and White

Ground: Britannia Stadium   **Capacity: 27,740**
Tel: 01782-367-598   **www.stokecityfc.com**

STOKE finished in their lowest position in the four seasons since they won promotion to the top flight but 14th place was just one position lower than in 2010-11 and 45 points was just two lower than their high of 47 in 2009-10.

All in all, their league campaign was about what was to be expected and looks better when it's remembered that it was combined with a decent Europa League run which saw them go out to Valencia in the knockout rounds.

As usual, they were solid at the Britannia, but while they took points off all the top four at home, that was countered by 11 defeats on the road – they failed to score in over half their away games and only QPR lost more on their travels.

Peter Crouch, an ambitious £10m signing last summer, finished as the club's top scorer, his ten league goals including a stunner against Man City.

Longest run without loss: 4
Longest run without win: 6
High – low league position 7-14
Clean sheets: 9
Yellow cards: 61 **Red cards:** 2
Players used: 23
Leading Scorer: P Crouch 10 (3,9)

	11-12 H A	Last six seasons at home P	W	D	L	OV	UN	BS	CS
Man City	D L	4	1	3	0	0	4	3	1
Man United	D L	4	0	1	3	1	3	2	0
Arsenal	D L	4	2	1	1	3	1	4	0
Tottenham	W D	4	2	0	2	4	0	4	0
Newcastle	L L	3	1	1	1	2	1	2	1
Chelsea	D L	4	0	2	2	1	3	2	1
Everton	D W	4	1	2	1	1	3	2	2
Liverpool	W D	4	2	2	0	0	4	1	3
Fulham	W L	4	2	1	1	1	3	1	2
West Brom	L W	5	3	1	1	2	3	3	2
Swansea	W L	1	1	0	0	0	1	0	1
Norwich	W D	3	3	0	0	2	1	1	2
Sunderland	L L	5	4	0	1	2	3	2	2
Stoke									
Wigan	D L	4	1	2	1	2	2	2	1
Aston Villa	D D	4	2	2	0	2	2	2	2
QPR	L L	3	2	0	1	2	1	2	1
Reading	- -	0	0	0	0	0	0	0	0
Southampton	- -	2	2	0	0	2	0	2	0
West Ham	- -	3	1	1	1	1	2	2	0

Season	Division	Pos	P	W	D	L	F	A	GD	Pts
2011-12	Prem	14	38	11	12	15	36	53	-17	45
2010-11	Prem	13	38	13	7	18	46	48	-2	46
2009-10	Prem	11	38	11	14	13	34	48	-14	47

Final *Outlook Index* figure: 847

Key Stat: Despite having Rory Delap and Ryan Shotton in the team, only two Stoke goals came from throw-ins

2011-12 Premier League appearances

	P	G	Y	R		P	G	Y	R
A Begovic	22 (1)	0	0	0	M Upson	10 (4)	1	1	0
P Crouch	31 (1)	10	2	0	J Walters	38	7	3	0
R Delap	18 (8)	2	4	0	G Whelan	27 (3)	1	4	0
S Diao	2 (4)	0	1	0	D Whitehead	24 (9)	0	5	0
M Etherington	30	3	1	0	A Wilkinson	20 (5)	0	5	0
R Fuller	3 (10)	0	2	1	M Wilson	35	0	8	0
D Higginbotham	1 (1)	0	0	0	J Woodgate	16 (1)	0	3	0
R Huth	31 (3)	3	5	1					
C Jerome	7 (16)	4	0	0					
K Jones	10 (11)	1	0	0					
W Palacios	9 (9)	0	3	0					
J Pennant	18 (9)	0	2	0					
D Pugh	0 (3)	0	0	0					
R Shawcross	36	2	8	0					
R Shotton	14 (9)	1	2	0					
T Sorensen	16	0	1	0					

Sunderland

Nickname: Mackems/The Black Cats
Colours: Red and White

Ground: Stadium of Light
Tel: 0871-911-1200

Capacity: 48,707
www.safc.com

STEVE BRUCE was sacked after just two wins in the first 13 games left Sunderland two points above the relegation places. When Martin O'Neill was appointed three days later, he made an impact almost immediately. They beat Blackburn in his first game in the dugout and won nine of his first 15 games at the helm, a run that included a victory over Man City and an FA Cup win over Arsenal.

When they beat QPR in March, they had climbed from 16th after Bruce's last match in charge to eighth. They failed to win any of their last eight league games but finished comfortably in mid-table.

James McClean was a real find and Nicklas Bendtner a decent loan signing – although he was never far away from a reminder of why Arsenal were happy to loan him out – but the star was Stephane Sessegnon, who earned rave reviews for his pace and skillful runs from midfield.

Longest run without loss: 4
Longest run without win: 8
High – low league position 8-17
Clean sheets: 12
Yellow cards: 61 **Red cards:** 4
Players used: 28
Leading Scorer: N Bendtner 8 (4,8)

	11-12		Last six seasons at home							
	H	A	P	W	D	L	OV	UN	BS	CS
Man City	W	D	5	2	1	2	2	3	2	2
Man United	L	L	5	0	1	4	2	3	1	1
Arsenal	L	L	5	1	2	2	1	4	3	1
Tottenham	D	L	5	2	2	1	2	3	3	2
Newcastle	L	D	4	1	2	1	1	3	3	0
Chelsea	L	L	5	0	0	5	4	1	4	0
Everton	D	L	5	0	3	2	1	4	3	0
Liverpool	W	D	5	2	0	3	0	5	0	2
Fulham	D	L	5	1	3	1	1	4	1	3
West Brom	D	L	4	2	1	1	3	1	2	2
Swansea	W	D	1	1	0	0	0	1	0	1
Norwich	W	L	2	2	0	0	1	1	0	2
Sunderland										
Stoke	W	W	5	3	2	0	2	3	1	4
Wigan	L	W	5	2	1	2	3	2	4	1
Aston Villa	D	D	5	1	2	2	2	3	3	1
QPR	W	W	2	2	0	0	2	0	2	0
Reading	-	-	1	1	0	0	1	0	1	0
Southampton	-	-	1	0	1	0	0	1	1	0
West Ham	-	-	4	2	1	1	2	2	2	1

Season	Division	Pos	P	W	D	L	F	A	GD	Pts
2011-12	Prem	13	38	11	12	15	45	46	-1	45
2010-11	Prem	10	38	12	11	15	45	56	-11	47
2009-10	Prem	13	38	11	11	16	48	56	-8	44

Final *Outlook Index* figure: 850

Key Stat: Stephane Sessegnon either provided the assist or the finishing touch for 16 of Sunderland's 45 league goals last season

2011-12 Premier League appearances

	P	G	Y	R
P Bardsley	29 (2)	1	4	1
N Bendtner	25 (3)	8	2	0
T Bramble	8	1	0	0
W Bridge	3 (5)	0	1	0
W Brown	20	1	2	0
F Campbell	6 (6)	1	3	0
L Cattermole	23	0	10	1
J Colback	29 (6)	1	3	0
J Dong-Won	2 (17)	2	1	0
A Elmohamady	7 (11)	1	0	0
A Ferdinand	3	0	0	0
C Gardner	22 (8)	3	5	1
C Gordon	1	0	0	0
A Gyan	3	0	0	0
M Kilgallon	9 (1)	0	0	0
S Kyrgiakos	2 (1)	0	1	0

	P	G	Y	R
S Larsson	32	7	7	0
J McClean	20 (3)	5	2	0
D Meyler	1 (6)	0	0	0
S Mignolet	29	0	0	0
R Noble	0 (2)	0	0	0
J O'Shea	29	0	5	0
K Richardson	26 (3)	2	5	0
S Sessegnon	36	7	3	1
M Turner	23 (1)	0	3	0
D Vaughan	17 (5)	2	3	0
K Westwood	8 (1)	0	0	0
C Wickham	5 (11)	1	0	0

Swansea

Nickname: The Swans
Colours: White

Ground: Liberty Stadium
Tel: 0844-249-1912

Capacity: 20,520
www.swanseacity.net

SWANSEA'S maiden season in the Premier League was a resounding success. As play-off winners they were 8-13 relegation favourites ante-post but finished 11th, playing some beautiful football and claiming some big scalps along the way.

Their best work was done at the Liberty Stadium, where they had the ninth-best home record in the top flight after finishing with the best home record in the Championship in their promotion season.

Their survival depended on a solid defence – defensively they were as good as Newcastle and, with 51 goals conceded, they were best of the promoted sides by a 15-goal margin. Against that, though, goals were often hard to come by.

New manager Michael Laudrup is a fascinating appointment and won't change Swansea's style much, but it will be hard to match Brendan Rodgers' achievements at the club.

Longest run without loss: 4
Longest run without win: 4
High – low league position 8-15
Clean sheets: 14
Yellow cards: 41 **Red cards:** 2
Players used: 25
Leading Scorer: D Graham 12 (4,11)

	11-12 H A	Last six seasons at home P W D L OV UN BS CS							
Man City	W L	1	1	0	0	0	1	0	1
Man United	L L	1	0	0	1	0	1	0	0
Arsenal	W L	1	1	0	0	1	0	1	0
Tottenham	D L	1	0	1	0	0	1	1	0
Newcastle	L D	2	0	1	1	0	2	1	0
Chelsea	D L	1	0	1	0	0	1	1	0
Everton	L L	1	0	0	1	0	1	0	0
Liverpool	W D	1	1	0	0	0	1	0	1
Fulham	W W	1	1	0	0	0	1	0	1
West Brom	W W	2	1	0	1	1	1	0	1
Swansea									
Norwich	L L	3	2	0	1	3	0	2	1
Sunderland	D L	1	0	1	0	0	1	0	1
Stoke	W L	1	1	0	0	0	1	0	1
Wigan	D W	1	0	1	0	0	1	0	1
Aston Villa	D W	1	0	1	0	0	1	0	1
QPR	D L	4	1	3	0	0	4	1	3
Reading	- -	3	2	1	0	0	3	0	3
Southampton	- -	1	1	0	0	1	0	0	1
West Ham	- -	0	0	0	0	0	0	0	0

Season	Division	Pos	P	W	D	L	F	A	GD	Pts
2011-12	Prem	11	38	12	11	15	44	51	-7	47
2010-11	Champ	3	46	24	8	14	69	42	27	80
2009-10	Champ	7	46	17	18	11	40	37	3	69

Final *Outlook Index* figure: 843

Key Stat: The Swans failed to score in 15 of their Premier League matches, a total matched only by Aston Villa

2011-12 Premier League appearances								
	P	G	Y	R		P	G	Y	R
G Agustien	7 (6)	0	3	0	A Richards	6 (2)	0	4	0
J Allen	31 (5)	4	2	1	W Routledge	17 (11)	1	2	0
F Bessone	0 (1)	0	0	0	G Sigurdsson	17 (1)	7	0	0
L Britton	35 (1)	0	3	0	S Sinclair	35 (3)	8	1	0
S Caulker	26	0	2	0	A Tate	1 (4)	0	0	0
S Dobbie	2 (6)	0	0	0	N Taylor	35 (1)	0	4	0
N Dyer	29 (5)	5	1	1	G Tremmel	1	0	0	0
M Gower	14 (6)	0	2	0	M Vorm	37	0	2	0
D Graham	32 (4)	12	0	0	A Williams	37	1	6	0
L Lita	4 (12)	2	1	0					
J McEachran	1 (3)	0	0	0					
G Monk	14 (2)	0	3	0					
L Moore	3 (17)	2	1	0					
V Moras	0 (1)	0	0	0					
A Orlandi	2 (1)	1	1	0					
A Rangel	32 (2)	0	3	0					

Tottenham

Nickname: Spurs
Colours: White and Navy Blue

Ground: White Hart Lane   **Capacity:** 36,230
Tel: 0844-499-5000   www.tottenhamhotspur.com

TOTTENHAM kicked off the season with a pair of big defeats to Man United and Man City, but after that they never looked back – at least not until Fabio Capello resigned as England manager in February.

At that point, Spurs were third, ten points clear of sixth-placed Arsenal and seven ahead of Chelsea, immediately behind them. They were playing slick football and averaging 2.08 points per game.

But once manager Harry Redknapp was installed as favourite for the England job, results suffered. They scored fewer goals and earnt just 1.36 points a game.

Even though Arsenal overhauled them, they would still be looking at a Champions League campaign if Chelsea hadn't won it, with Luka Modric, Emmanuel Adebayor and Scott Parker all putting in some excellent performances.

Redknapp was sacked in June and is a hard act to follow for Andre Villas-Boas.

Longest run without loss: 11
Longest run without win: 5
High – low league position 3-6
Clean sheets: 14
Yellow cards: 45 **Red cards:** 3
Players used: 29
Leading Scorer: E Adebayor 17 (4,12)

	11-12 H A	Last six seasons at home P	W	D	L	OV	UN	BS	CS
Man City	L L	6	4	1	1	5	1	4	2
Man United	L L	6	0	3	3	3	3	3	2
Arsenal	W L	6	2	3	1	5	1	5	1
Tottenham									
Newcastle	W D	5	3	0	2	3	2	2	3
Chelsea	D D	6	3	3	0	3	3	5	1
Everton	W L	6	2	1	3	2	4	3	1
Liverpool	W D	6	4	0	2	4	2	3	1
Fulham	W W	6	4	2	0	1	5	1	5
West Brom	W W	3	2	1	0	1	2	1	2
Swansea	W D	1	1	0	0	1	0	1	0
Norwich	L W	1	0	0	1	1	0	1	0
Sunderland	W D	5	3	1	1	1	4	2	3
Stoke	D L	4	2	1	1	2	2	3	0
Wigan	W W	6	4	1	1	4	2	3	2
Aston Villa	W D	6	3	2	1	4	2	4	2
QPR	W L	1	1	0	0	1	0	1	0
Reading	- -	2	2	0	0	1	1	1	1
Southampton	- -	0	0	0	0	0	0	0	0
West Ham	- -	5	4	1	0	1	4	0	5

Season	Division	Pos	P	W	D	L	F	A	GD	Pts
2011-12	Prem	4	38	20	9	9	66	41	25	69
2010-11	Prem	5	38	16	14	8	55	46	9	62
2009-10	Prem	4	38	21	7	10	67	41	26	70

Final *Outlook Index* figure: 892

Key Stat: Tottenham finished fourth twice under Harry Redknapp – they had never been better than fifth in the previous 18 seasons

2011-12 Premier League appearances

	P	G	Y	R
M Adebayor	32 (1)	17	3	0
B Assou-Ekotto	34	2	6	0
G Bale	36	9	3	0
S Bassong	1 (4)	0	0	0
V Corluka	1 (2)	0	0	0
P Crouch	1	0	0	0
M Dawson	6 (1)	0	1	0
J Defoe	11 (14)	11	2	0
G Dos Santos	0 (7)	0	0	0
B Friedel	38	0	0	0
W Gallas	15	0	1	0
T Huddlestone	0 (2)	0	0	0
Y Kaboul	33	1	3	1
L King	21	0	0	0
N Kranjcar	9 (3)	1	0	0
C Lancaster	0 (1)	0	0	0

	P	G	Y	R
A Lennon	19 (4)	3	1	0
J Livermore	7 (17)	0	1	0
L Modric	36	4	2	0
R Nelsen	0 (5)	0	0	0
S Parker	28 (1)	0	8	1
R Pavlyuchenko	0 (5)	1	0	0
S Pienaar	0 (2)	0	0	0
D Rose	3 (8)	0	1	1
L Saha	5 (5)	3	0	0
Sandro	17 (6)	0	6	0
A Smith	0 (1)	0	0	0
K Walker	37	2	4	0
R van der Vaart	28 (5)	11	3	0

West Brom

Nickname: The Baggies/Throstles/Albion
Colours: Navy Blue and White

Ground: The Hawthorns
Tel: 0871-271-1100

Capacity: 26,360
www.wba.co.uk

WEST BROM enjoyed an eventful season, finishing tenth with the sixth-best away record in the Premier League and the fifth-worst home record, then lost their manager to the England job.

Steve Clarke, in his first senior managerial role, is an interesting choice after his time as number two to Jose Mourinho at Chelsea and, more recently, Kenny Dalglish at Liverpool, the Baggies' first opponents next season.

There were some excellent wins against the bigger clubs – Chelsea at home, Newcastle and Liverpool away – but most of West Brom's points came from the teams who ended the season below them.

James Morrison put in some big performances all season, Jonas Olsson struck up a solid defensive partnership with Gareth McAuley and captain Chris Brunt impressed again.

Longest run without loss: 4
Longest run without win: 4
High – low league position 10-17
Clean sheets: 10
Yellow cards: 49 **Red cards:** 1
Players used: 25
Leading Scorer: P Odemwingie 10 (5,7)

	11-12 H A	Last six seasons at home P	W	D	L	OV	BS	CS
Man City	D L	3	1	1	1	2	1	1
Man United	L L	3	0	0	3	3	0	2	0
Arsenal	L L	3	0	1	2	3	0	3	0
Tottenham	L L	3	1	1	1	1	2	2	1
Newcastle	L W	4	1	1	2	3	1	4	0
Chelsea	W L	3	1	0	2	2	1	1	1
Everton	L L	3	1	0	2	1	2	1	1
Liverpool	L W	3	1	0	2	1	2	1	0
Fulham	D D	3	2	1	0	1	2	1	2
West Brom									
Swansea	L L	2	0	0	2	1	1	1	0
Norwich	L W	3	1	0	2	1	2	1	1
Sunderland	W D	4	3	0	1	3	1	1	3
Stoke	L W	5	0	1	4	2	3	2	0
Wigan	L D	3	1	1	1	3	0	3	0
Aston Villa	D W	3	1	1	1	2	1	2	1
QPR	W D	4	2	2	0	3	1	3	1
Reading	- -	1	1	0	0	1	0	1	0
Southampton	- -	2	0	2	0	0	2	2	0
West Ham	- -	2	1	1	0	2	0	2	0

Season	Division	Pos	P	W	D	L	F	A	GD	Pts
2011-12	Prem	10	38	13	8	17	45	52	-7	47
2010-11	Prem	11	38	12	11	15	56	71	-15	47
2009-10	Champ	2	46	26	13	7	89	48	41	91

Final *Outlook Index* figure: 853

Key Stat: West Brom lost six of the seven matches that Gareth McAuley missed last season

2011-12 Premier League appearances

	P	G	Y	R		P	G	Y	R
K Andrews	8 (6)	2	2	0	J Olsson	33	2	4	1
C Brunt	25 (4)	2	5	0	S Reid	21 (1)	1	3	0
S Cox	7 (11)	0	2	0	L Ridgewell	13	1	2	0
C Dawson	6 (2)	0	0	0	P Scharner	18 (11)	3	6	0
G Dorrans	16 (15)	3	4	0	N Shorey	22 (3)	0	1	0
M Fortune	12 (5)	2	0	0	G Tamas	7 (1)	0	1	0
B Foster	37	0	0	0	S Tchoyi	6 (12)	1	0	0
M Fulop	1	0	0	0	J Thomas	26 (3)	1	4	0
Z Gera	3	0	0	0	G Thorne	1 (2)	0	0	0
G Jara	1 (3)	0	0	0					
B Jones	17 (1)	0	4	0					
S Long	24 (8)	8	2	0					
G McAuley	32	2	0	0					
J Morrison	23 (7)	5	1	0					
Y Mulumbu	34 (1)	1	5	0					
P Odemwingie	25 (5)	10	2	0					

West Ham

Nickname: The Hammers/Irons
Colours: Claret and Blue

Ground: Boleyn Ground
Tel: 020-8548-2748

Capacity: 35,303
www.whufc.com

THE Hammers were 5-1 title favourites in the ante-post betting and their 86 points and +33 goal difference would have been good enough to secure automatic promotion in four of the previous five seasons.

They had to do it the hard way after a mid-season run of six draws in seven games saw them first lose top spot to Southampton and then miss out on second place after Reading's late surge to the title. Four of the last six play-off winners went straight back down again but while Sam Allardyce hasn't always had the smoothest relationship with Hammers fans, he has plenty of Premier League know-how.

They'll need another big season from Mark Noble and Kevin Nolan in midfield, and for James Tomkins to repeat a good season in defence, which included a couple of vital goals.

Longest run without loss: 11
Longest run without win: 5
High – low league position 1-5
Clean sheets: 17
Yellow cards: 67 **Red cards:** 6
Players used: 33
Leading Scorer: C Cole 14 (5,13)

	11-12	Last six seasons at home							
	H A	P	W	D	L	OV	UN	BS	CS
Man City	- -	5	1	1	3	1	4	2	1
Man United	- -	5	2	0	3	3	2	2	1
Arsenal	- -	5	1	1	3	2	3	1	1
Tottenham	- -	5	1	1	3	2	3	3	1
Newcastle	- -	4	1	1	2	3	1	3	0
Chelsea	- -	5	0	1	4	3	2	3	0
Everton	- -	5	1	1	3	2	3	3	1
Liverpool	- -	5	2	0	3	4	1	3	1
Fulham	- -	5	2	3	0	4	1	5	0
West Brom	- -	2	0	2	0	1	1	1	1
Swansea	- -	0	0	0	0	0	0	0	0
Norwich	- -	0	0	0	0	0	0	0	0
Sunderland	- -	4	3	0	1	2	2	1	2
Stoke	- -	3	2	0	1	2	1	1	1
Wigan	- -	5	3	1	1	3	2	4	0
Aston Villa	- -	5	1	2	2	3	2	4	0
QPR	- -	0	0	0	0	0	0	0	0
Reading	L L	3	0	1	2	1	2	2	0
Southampton	D L	1	0	1	0	0	1	1	0
West Ham									

Season	Division	Pos	P	W	D	L	F	A	GD	Pts
2011-12	Champ	3	46	24	14	8	81	48	33	86
2010-11	Prem	20	38	7	12	19	43	70	-27	33
2009-10	Prem	17	38	8	11	19	47	66	-19	35

Final *Outlook Index* figure: 836

Key Stat: The Hammers failed to win any of their six matches against other sides who finished in the top four

2011-12 Championship appearances

	P	G	Y	R
M Almunia	4	0	0	0
S Baldock	10 (13)	5	1	0
P Barrera	0 (1)	0	0	0
D Bentley	2 (3)	0	0	0
J Carew	7 (12)	2	1	0
C Cole	28 (12)	14	7	0
D Collins	5 (7)	1	1	0
J Collison	26 (5)	4	1	1
G Demel	7	0	0	0
P Diop	14 (2)	1	1	0
J Faubert	28 (6)	1	6	0
A Faye	25 (4)	0	5	0
R Green	42	0	0	1
R Hall	0 (3)	0	0	0
H Ilunga	4	0	0	0
H Lansbury	13 (9)	1	4	0
N Maynard	9 (5)	2	1	0

	P	G	Y	R
G McCartney	36 (2)	1	6	0
R Morrison	0 (1)	0	0	0
M Noble	43 (2)	8	6	0
K Nolan	42	12	10	1
F Nouble	1 (2)	1	0	0
J O'Brien	27 (5)	1	4	1
G O'Neil	9 (7)	2	3	0
S Parker	4	1	0	0
F Piquionne	8 (12)	2	0	1
D Potts	3	0	0	0
W Reid	27 (1)	3	4	0
F Sears	2 (8)	0	0	0
J Stanislas	0 (1)	0	0	0
M Taylor	26 (2)	1	1	1
J Tomkins	42 (2)	4	5	0
R Vaz Te	14 (2)	10	1	0

Wigan

Nickname: The Latics
Colours: Blue and White

Ground: DW Stadium   **Capacity: 25,133**
Tel: 01942-774-000   **www.wiganlatics.co.uk**

IN THE end, Wigan survived fairly comfortably but to say that it had looked unlikely would be a major understatement.

In mid March they were bottom with nine tough games remaining and 2-9 with Ladbrokes was the best price available about the Latics going down.

Wigan had spent most of the season in the bottom three – and much of it in last place – but Roberto Martinez remained optimistic that sticking to his principles and producing good performances would pay dividends. They beat Stoke, Man United, Newcastle and Wolves in their final four home games and Liverpool, Arsenal and Blackburn away to confirm their survival with a game to spare.

Victor Moses had a breakthrough season while Gary Caldwell, who ended the season as the sweeper in a three-man defence, won Wigan's player of the year award.

Longest run without loss: 4
Longest run without win: 9
High – low league position 15-20
Clean sheets: 8
Yellow cards: 68 Red cards: 3
Players used: 23
Leading Scorer: F Di Santo 7 (3,6)

	11-12 H	11-12 A	Last six seasons at home P	W	D	L	OV	UN	BS	CS
Man City	L	L	6	2	2	2	2	4	3	1
Man United	W	L	6	1	0	5	4	2	2	1
Arsenal	L	W	6	1	2	3	4	2	3	1
Tottenham	L	L	6	1	3	2	3	3	3	2
Newcastle	W	L	5	4	0	1	2	3	1	3
Chelsea	D	L	6	1	1	4	3	3	3	0
Everton	D	L	6	1	2	3	1	5	3	1
Liverpool	D	W	6	1	3	2	1	5	2	2
Fulham	L	L	6	0	5	1	0	6	3	2
West Brom	D	W	3	2	1	0	1	2	2	1
Swansea	L	D	1	0	0	1	0	1	0	0
Norwich	D	D	1	0	1	0	0	1	1	0
Sunderland	L	W	5	2	2	1	2	3	3	2
Stoke	W	D	4	1	3	0	1	3	2	2
Wigan										
Aston Villa	D	L	6	0	2	4	4	2	3	2
QPR	W	L	1	1	0	0	0	1	0	1
Reading	-	-	2	1	1	0	0	2	0	2
Southampton	-	-	0	0	0	0	0	0	0	0
West Ham	-	-	5	3	0	2	2	3	1	2

Season	Division	Pos	P	W	D	L	F	A	GD	Pts
2011-12	Prem.	15	38	11	10	17	42	62	-20	43
2010-11	Prem	16	38	9	15	14	40	61	-21	42
2009-10	Prem	16	38	9	9	20	37	79	-42	36

Final *Outlook Index* figure: 866

Key Stat: Backed blindly to a level stake, the Latics were the most profitable team to follow in British league football last season (see page 108)

2011-12 Premier League appearances

	P	G	Y	R
A Al Habsi	38	0	1	0
A Alcaraz	25	2	5	0
J Beausejour	16	0	1	0
E Boyce	26	3	3	0
G Caldwell	36	3	9	1
A Crusat	4 (11)	1	1	0
F Di Santo	24 (8)	7	4	0
M Diame	18 (8)	3	4	0
M Figueroa	37 (1)	0	6	0
S Gohouri	8 (2)	0	3	1
J Gomez	24 (4)	5	4	0
D Jones	13 (3)	0	2	0
S Maloney	8 (5)	3	1	0
J McArthur	18 (13)	3	4	0
J McCarthy	33	0	7	0
C McManaman	0 (2)	0	1	0

	P	G	Y	R
V Moses	36 (2)	6	4	0
Piscu	5	0	2	0
H Rodallega	11 (12)	2	1	0
C Sammon	8 (17)	0	1	1
R Stam	13 (7)	0	3	0
B Watson	14 (7)	3	1	0
P van Aanholt	3	0	0	0

Top scorers 2011-12

		P	W	D	L	F	GFA	PGA	Pts
1	Man City (1)	38	28	5	5	93	2.45	2.3	89
2	Man Utd (2)	38	28	5	5	89	2.34	2.3	89
3	Arsenal (3)	38	21	7	10	74	1.95	1.8	70
4	Tottenham (4)	38	20	9	9	66	1.74	1.8	69
5	Chelsea (6)	38	18	10	10	65	1.71	1.7	64
6	Newcastle (5)	38	19	8	11	56	1.47	1.7	65
7	Norwich (12)	38	12	11	15	52	1.37	1.2	47
8	Everton (7)	38	15	11	12	50	1.32	1.5	56
9	Fulham (9)	38	14	10	14	48	1.26	1.4	52
10	Blackburn (19)	38	8	7	23	48	1.26	0.8	31
11	Liverpool (8)	38	14	10	14	47	1.24	1.4	52
12	Bolton (18)	38	10	6	22	46	1.21	0.9	36
13	West Brom (10)	38	13	8	17	45	1.18	1.2	47
14	Sunderland (13)	38	11	12	15	45	1.18	1.2	45
15	Swansea (11)	38	12	11	15	44	1.16	1.2	47
16	QPR (17)	38	10	7	21	43	1.13	1.0	37
17	Wigan (15)	38	11	10	17	42	1.11	1.1	43
18	Wolves (20)	38	5	10	23	40	1.05	0.7	25
19	Aston Villa (16)	38	7	17	14	37	0.97	1.0	38
20	Stoke (14)	38	11	12	15	36	0.95	1.2	45

Best defence 2011-12

		P	W	D	L	F	GAA	PGA	Pts
1	Man City (1)	38	28	5	5	29	0.76	2.3	89
2	Man Utd (2)	38	28	5	5	33	0.87	2.3	89
3	Everton (7)	38	15	11	12	40	1.05	1.5	56
4	Liverpool (8)	38	14	10	14	40	1.05	1.4	52
5	Tottenham (4)	38	20	9	9	41	1.08	1.8	69
6	Chelsea (6)	38	18	10	10	46	1.21	1.7	64
7	Sunderland (13)	38	11	12	15	46	1.21	1.2	45
8	Arsenal (3)	38	21	7	10	49	1.29	1.8	70
9	Newcastle (5)	38	19	8	11	51	1.34	1.7	65
10	Fulham (9)	38	14	10	14	51	1.34	1.4	52
11	Swansea (11)	38	12	11	15	51	1.34	1.2	47
12	West Brom (10)	38	13	8	17	52	1.37	1.2	47
13	Stoke (14)	38	11	12	15	53	1.39	1.2	45
14	Aston Villa (16)	38	7	17	14	53	1.39	1.0	38
15	Wigan (15)	38	11	10	17	62	1.63	1.1	43
16	Norwich (12)	38	12	11	15	66	1.74	1.2	47
17	QPR (17)	38	10	7	21	66	1.74	1.0	37
18	Bolton (18)	38	10	6	22	77	2.03	0.9	36
19	Blackburn (19)	38	8	7	23	78	2.05	0.8	31
20	Wolves (20)	38	5	10	23	82	2.16	0.7	25

FIRST TO SCORE: Man City scored first in the crucial final-day victory over QPR

Key *Number in brackets refers to final league finishing position. Points do not include any deductions but league positions do. GFA: Goals for average per match, GAA: Goals against average per match, PGA: Average points gained per match, CS: clean sheet, FS: first to score*

Clean sheets 2011-12

		P	CS	%
1	Man Utd (2)	38	20	52.6
2	Man City (1)	38	17	44.7
3	Newcastle (5)	38	15	39.5
4	Swansea (11)	38	14	36.8
5	Tottenham (4)	38	14	36.8
6	Arsenal (3)	38	13	34.2
7	Everton (7)	38	12	31.6
8	Liverpool (8)	38	12	31.6
9	Sunderland (13)	38	12	31.6
10	Fulham (9)	38	11	28.9
11	Chelsea (6)	38	10	26.3
12	West Brom (10)	38	10	26.3
13	Stoke (14)	38	9	23.7
14	Aston Villa (16)	38	9	23.7
15	Wigan (15)	38	8	21.1
16	QPR (17)	38	7	18.4
17	Wolves (20)	38	4	10.5
18	Bolton (18)	38	3	7.9
19	Norwich (12)	38	3	7.9
20	Blackburn (19)	38	3	7.9

First to score 2011-12

		P	FS	%
1	Man Utd (2)	38	30	78.9
2	Man City (1)	38	28	73.7
3	Arsenal (3)	38	23	60.5
4	Chelsea (6)	38	23	60.5
5	Tottenham (4)	38	22	57.9
6	Everton (7)	38	20	52.6
7	Newcastle (5)	38	20	52.6
8	Liverpool (8)	38	17	44.7
9	West Brom (10)	38	17	44.7
10	Sunderland (13)	38	17	44.7
11	Swansea (11)	38	16	42.1
12	Stoke (14)	38	15	39.5
13	Norwich (12)	38	15	39.5
14	Aston Villa (16)	38	15	39.5
15	QPR (17)	38	14	36.8
16	Wigan (15)	38	14	36.8
17	Blackburn (19)	38	14	36.8
18	Fulham (9)	38	13	34.2
19	Bolton (18)	38	10	26.3
20	Wolves (20)	38	10	26.3

Top scorers 2011-12

		Goals
R van Persie	Arsenal	30
W Rooney	Man Utd	27
S Aguero	Man City	23
E Adebayor	Tottenham	17
C Dempsey	Fulham	17
Yakubu	Blackburn	17
D Ba	Newcastle	16
G Holt	Norwich	15
E Dzeko	Man City	14
M Balotelli	Man City	13
P Cisse	Newcastle	13
S Fletcher	Wolves	12
D Graham	Swansea	12
J Defoe	Tottenham	11
F Lampard	Chelsea	11
D Sturridge	Chelsea	11
L Suarez	Liverpool	11
R van der Vaart	Tottenham	11
P Crouch	Stoke	10
J Hernandez	Man Utd	10

Record when keeping a clean sheet 2011-12

		P	W	D	L	F	GFA	PGA	Pts
1	Man Utd (2)	20	20	0	0	50	2.50	3.0	60
2	Blackburn (19)	3	3	0	0	6	2.00	3.0	9
3	Man City (1)	17	16	1	0	39	2.29	2.9	49
4	Everton (7)	12	11	1	0	21	1.75	2.8	34
5	QPR (17)	7	6	1	0	10	1.43	2.7	19
6	Newcastle (5)	15	12	3	0	22	1.47	2.6	39
7	Tottenham (4)	14	11	3	0	26	1.86	2.6	36
8	Arsenal (3)	13	10	3	0	21	1.62	2.5	33
9	Fulham (9)	11	8	3	0	21	1.91	2.5	27
10	West Brom (10)	10	7	3	0	13	1.30	2.4	24
11	Swansea (11)	14	9	5	0	19	1.36	2.3	32
12	Liverpool (8)	12	8	4	0	18	1.50	2.3	28
13	Stoke (14)	9	6	3	0	8	0.89	2.3	21
14	Wigan (15)	8	5	3	0	10	1.25	2.3	18
15	Bolton (18)	3	2	1	0	9	3.00	2.3	7
16	Norwich (12)	3	2	1	0	4	1.33	2.3	7
17	Sunderland (13)	12	7	5	0	14	1.17	2.2	26
18	Chelsea (6)	10	6	4	0	12	1.20	2.2	22
19	Wolves (20)	4	1	3	0	2	0.50	1.5	6
20	Aston Villa (16)	9	2	7	0	3	0.33	1.4	13

Record when first to score 2011-12

		P	W	D	L	F	GFA	PGA	Pts
1	Man Utd (2)	30	27	3	0	80	14	2.8	84
2	Man City (1)	28	25	2	1	82	18	2.8	77
3	Tottenham (4)	22	18	3	1	51	16	2.6	57
4	Newcastle (5)	20	17	1	2	40	15	2.6	52
5	Fulham (9)	13	10	2	1	29	8	2.5	32
6	Arsenal (3)	23	16	3	4	51	23	2.2	51
7	Chelsea (6)	23	16	3	4	54	28	2.2	51
8	Liverpool (8)	17	11	4	2	33	13	2.2	37
9	Swansea (11)	16	10	5	1	33	13	2.2	35
10	Everton (7)	20	12	6	2	38	17	2.1	42
11	Stoke (14)	15	9	5	1	23	12	2.1	32
12	Norwich (12)	15	9	4	2	29	18	2.1	31
13	Bolton (18)	10	6	3	1	23	11	2.1	21
14	West Brom (10)	17	11	1	5	30	19	2.0	34
15	Sunderland (13)	17	10	3	4	32	16	1.9	33
16	QPR (17)	14	8	3	3	23	13	1.9	27
17	Wigan (15)	14	8	3	3	23	15	1.9	27
18	Blackburn (19)	14	7	3	4	28	23	1.7	24
19	Aston Villa (16)	15	5	8	2	22	17	1.5	23
20	Wolves (20)	10	2	1	7	15	18	0.7	7

Top ten over 2.5 goals 2011-12

		P	Over 2.5	Under 2.5
1	Bolton	38	28 (74%)	10 (26%)
2	Wolves	38	27 (71%)	11 (29%)
3	Arsenal	38	25 (66%)	13 (34%)
4	Blackburn	38	24 (63%)	14 (37%)
5	Man City	38	23 (61%)	15 (39%)
	Norwich	38	23 (61%)	15 (39%)
7	Chelsea	38	22 (58%)	16 (42%)
8	Wigan	38	21 (55%)	17 (45%)
	Newcastle	38	21 (55%)	17 (45%)
	West Brom	38	21 (55%)	17 (45%)

Top ten under 2.5 goals 2011-12

		P	Over 2.5	Under 2.5
1	Everton	38	13 (34%)	25 (66%)
2	Swansea	38	15 (39%)	23 (61%)
3	Aston Villa	38	16 (42%)	22 (58%)
	Liverpool	38	16 (42%)	22 (58%)
	Stoke	38	16 (42%)	22 (58%)
6	Fulham	38	18 (47%)	20 (53%)
7	Sunderland	38	19 (50%)	19 (50%)
8	Tottenham	38	20 (53%)	18 (47%)
	Man Utd	38	20 (53%)	18 (47%)
	QPR	38	20 (53%)	18 (47%)

Foxes look far from convincing favourites

LEICESTER are as short as 5-1 to take the 2012-13 Championship title and, at those prices, they remain eminently swervable, *writes Dan Sait*.

As the rich men of the division, Leicester may yet do a QPR and suddenly find the winning formula but it took the R's several seasons to put their wealth to use and they had substantially more financial clout behind them than the Foxes.

Either way, Leicester frustrated those who backed them at 4-1 last term by finishing in ninth place, 23 points behind Reading, so backing them at a best price of 13-2 seems a huge leap of faith.

Behind them, Bolton's player exodus, Wolves' lack of quality, and a slow start for Neil Warnock at Leeds make each of the top four in the market avoidable.

It's **Cardiff**, fifth in the betting, who appeal. There may be scope for fan unrest in the Welsh capital following the re-branding of the club, but solid investment also provides scope for improvement.

The 12-1 shots also start from a solid base, having finished no lower than sixth over the past three seasons, and none of the other contenders are clearly better. Of the sides still in the division, only Birmingham took more points (one) last term and for those concerned about Cardiff's history of choking, simply back to lay – the 12s may not be around very long.

Birmingham looked a great title prospect before losing the excellent Chris Hughton and while his replacement, Lee Clark, has done little wrong during his

fledgling managerial career, wait and see before you bet. If they start well, don't be shy about jumping on the bandwagon.

Blackpool continue to impress under Ian Holloway and look a solid bet for promotion at Paddy Power's 11-2 and progressive new boys **Sheffield Wednesday** look like dark horses for the top six.

Middlesbrough need only to show a little more ruthlessness in their easier games to join those sides in the play-offs and **Watford** could benefit from some quality loan signings now that they are part of the Pozzo empire, and are well priced to sneak into the top six.

It's hard to argue with a market that makes **Barnsley** and **Peterborough** favourites for the drop – with the former looking an absolute banker – but neither Bristol City or Crystal Palace appeal greatly at short prices, as the Robins could make strides under Derek McInnes and Palace are making a habit of beating the drop in recent seasons.

Newly promoted **Huddersfield** could fill the third relegation spot as they tailed off after Lee Clark was harshly sacked midway through the 2011-12 season.

Championship winner						
	b365	Btfrd	Hills	Lads	Pwr	StJms
Leicester	13-2	6	6	6	13-2	11-2
Bolton	8	8	8	7	9	7
Wolves	8	9	8	8	8	8
Leeds	10	12	8	11	12	12
Cardiff	9	12	11	10	12	12
Blackburn	16	12	12	11	16	16
Blackpool	16	14	16	16	13	12
Brighton	16	14	14	14	13	12
Sheff Weds	20	20	20	20	18	16
Birmingham	20	12	10	12	12	18
Nottm Forest	16	16	20	16	20	20
Middlesbrough	22	16	16	16	16	16
Charlton	22	20	20	20	20	20
Ipswich	25	25	20	20	22	20
Hull	33	28	25	28	25	25
Burnley	25	33	25	28	25	25
Huddersfield	33	40	25	33	33	33
Watford	33	50	40	33	35	50
Derby	40	33	50	33	35	40
Millwall	66	50	40	50	50	66
Bristol City	50	66	80	50	60	66
Crystal Palace	66	66	66	80	75	80
Peterborough	150	100	100	100	75	100
Barnsley	200	150	200	66	125	150
Win or each-way. See individual bookmakers for terms						

Barnsley

Nickname: Tykes
Colours: Red and White
Ground: Oakwell (23,287)
Tel: 01226-211-211　　www.barnsleyfc.co.uk

AFTER landing in the Oakwell dugout last summer with the brief of keeping Barnsley up and costs down, Keith Hill did just about all that could be expected of him, ending the season in 21st place.

The Tykes' worrying trajectory suggests this season will be even tougher, as Barnsley started last season brightly but plummeted following the January sale of ten-goal Ricardo Vaz Te. A few interesting signings have arrived at Oakwell but it still looks like 2012-13 will be a struggle.

Longest run without loss: 7/7
High – low league position 12-22
Clean sheets: 8 **Yellow cards:** 62 **Red cards:** 2
Average attendance: 9,897 **Players used:** 37
Leading Scorer: C Davies 11 (3,9)
Key stat: Following Vaz Te's departure to West Ham, Barnsley scored in just three of their final 12 league games of the season

	11-12 H A	Last six seasons at home P	W	D	L	OV	UN	BS	CS
Bolton	- -	0	0	0	0	0	0	0	0
Blackburn	- -	0	0	0	0	0	0	0	0
Wolves	- -	3	2	1	0	0	3	1	2
Birmingham	L D	3	1	1	1	1	2	2	1
Blackpool	L D	4	2	0	2	2	2	2	1
Cardiff	L L	6	1	1	4	2	4	3	1
Middlesbrough	L L	3	2	0	1	2	1	3	1
Hull	W L	4	2	1	1	3	1	3	1
Leicester	D W	5	1	1	3	0	5	1	1
Brighton	D L	1	0	1	0	0	1	0	1
Watford	D L	5	3	2	0	2	3	3	2
Derby	W D	5	2	2	1	2	3	3	2
Burnley	W L	5	3	1	1	2	3	3	2
Leeds	W W	3	3	0	0	3	0	3	0
Ipswich	L L	6	3	1	2	4	2	5	1
Millwall	L D	2	1	0	1	1	1	1	1
Crystal Palace	W L	6	4	2	0	2	4	2	4
Peterborough	W W	2	1	1	0	1	1	1	1
Nottm Forest	D D	4	2	2	0	2	2	4	0
Bristol City	L L	5	2	1	2	4	1	3	2
Barnsley									
Charlton	- -	2	1	1	0	1	1	0	2
Sheffield Weds	- -	4	1	1	2	3	1	2	1
Huddersfield	- -	0	0	0	0	0	0	0	0

Season	Division	Pos	P	W	D	L	F	A	GD	Pts
2011-12	Champ	21	46	13	9	24	49	74	-25	48
2010-11	Champ	17	46	14	14	18	55	66	-11	56
2009-10	Champ	18	46	14	12	20	53	69	-16	54

Birmingham

Nickname: Blues
Colours: Blue
Ground: St Andrew's (29,409)
Tel: 0871-226-1875　　www.bcfc.com

BLUES were in turmoil this time last year. The squad was gutted by 13 big-name departures, Alex McLeish left for Villa and owner Carson Yeung was under arrest.

Then Chris Hughton turned up and worked a minor miracle, stamping his class on an underperforming team, transforming them into an exciting attacking unit and taking them, via a decent European campaign, to the play-offs. However, Hughton's departure leaves new boss Lee Clark with big boots to fill.

Longest run without loss/win: 11/4
High – low league position 3-17
Clean sheets: 14 **Yellow cards:** 63 **Red cards:** 3
Average attendance: 19,127 **Players used:** 25
Leading Scorer: M King 16 (4,14)
Key stat: Birmingham scored more goals away from home than any other Championship side in 2011-12

	11-12 H A	Last six seasons at home P	W	D	L	OV	UN	BS	CS
Bolton	- -	3	2	0	1	2	1	2	1
Blackburn	- -	3	3	0	0	3	0	3	0
Wolves	- -	4	2	2	0	1	3	3	1
Birmingham									
Blackpool	W D	3	2	0	1	1	2	0	2
Cardiff	D L	3	1	2	0	0	3	2	1
Middlesbrough	W L	2	2	0	0	2	0	0	2
Hull	D L	3	1	2	0	1	2	1	2
Leicester	W L	2	1	1	0	0	2	1	1
Brighton	D D	1	0	1	0	0	1	0	1
Watford	W D	2	2	0	0	2	0	1	1
Derby	D L	4	2	2	0	1	3	2	2
Burnley	W W	4	2	1	1	2	2	3	0
Leeds	W W	2	2	0	0	0	2	0	2
Ipswich	W D	3	2	1	0	3	0	3	0
Millwall	W W	1	1	0	0	1	0	0	1
Crystal Palace	W L	3	3	0	0	2	1	2	1
Peterborough	D D	1	0	1	0	0	1	1	0
Nottm Forest	L W	2	1	0	1	1	1	1	1
Bristol City	D W	2	1	1	0	1	1	1	1
Barnsley	D W	3	2	1	0	0	3	1	2
Charlton	- -	1	1	0	0	1	0	1	0
Sheffield Weds	- -	2	2	0	0	1	1	1	1
Huddersfield	- -	0	0	0	0	0	0	0	0

Season	Division	Pos	P	W	D	L	F	A	GD	Pts
2011-12	Champ	4	46	20	16	10	78	51	27	76
2010-11	Prem	18	38	8	15	15	37	58	-21	39
2009-10	Prem	9	38	13	11	14	38	47	-9	50

Blackburn

Nickname: Rovers
Colours: Blue and White
Ground: Ewood Park (31,154)
Tel: 0871-702-1875   www.rovers.co.uk

VERY few positives can be taken from Blackburn's grim relegation in 2011-12, with the fans justifiably enraged by the disastrous performance of owners Venky's.

Revolt in the stands can only harm a team's confidence but it's hard to argue with the fans as they've seen their club dismantled by a group of amateurs.

Steve Kean has taken enough flak to last a lifetime but it seems harsh to judge a rookie boss trying to prove himself in impossible circumstances.

Longest run without loss/win: 3/8
High – low league position 16-20
Clean sheets: 3 Yellow cards: 68 Red cards: 5
Average attendance: 22,551 Players used: 31
Leading Scorer: Yakubu 17 (4,10)
Key stat: Blackburn lost eight of their final nine games as they limped out of the Premier League last season

| | 11-12 | | Last six seasons at home | | | | | | | |
	H	A	P	W	D	L	OV	UN	BS	CS
Bolton	L	L	6	3	1	2	4	2	3	2
Blackburn										
Wolves	L	W	3	2	0	1	3	0	2	1
Birmingham	-	-	3	2	1	0	2	1	3	0
Blackpool	-	-	1	0	1	0	1	0	1	0
Cardiff	-	-	0	0	0	0	0	0	0	0
Middlesbrough	-	-	3	1	2	0	1	2	3	0
Hull	-	-	2	1	1	0	0	2	1	1
Leicester	-	-	0	0	0	0	0	0	0	0
Brighton	-	-	0	0	0	0	0	0	0	0
Watford	-	-	1	1	0	0	1	0	1	0
Derby	-	-	1	1	0	0	1	0	1	0
Burnley	-	-	1	1	0	0	1	0	1	0
Leeds	-	-	0	0	0	0	0	0	0	0
Ipswich	-	-	0	0	0	0	0	0	0	0
Millwall	-	-	0	0	0	0	0	0	0	0
Crystal Palace	-	-	0	0	0	0	0	0	0	0
Peterborough	-	-	0	0	0	0	0	0	0	0
Nottm Forest	-	-	0	0	0	0	0	0	0	0
Bristol City	-	-	0	0	0	0	0	0	0	0
Barnsley	-	-	0	0	0	0	0	0	0	0
Charlton	-	-	1	1	0	0	1	0	1	0
Sheffield Weds	-	-	0	0	0	0	0	0	0	0
Huddersfield	-	-	0	0	0	0	0	0	0	0

Season	Division	Pos	P	W	D	L	F	A	GD	Pts
2011-12	Prem	19	38	8	7	23	48	78	-30	31
2010-11	Prem	15	38	11	10	17	46	59	-13	43
2009-10	Prem	10	38	13	11	14	41	55	-14	50

Blackpool

Nickname: The Seasiders/Tangerines
Colours: Tangerine and White
Ground: Bloomfield Road (16,007)
Tel: 01253-685-000   www.blackpoolfc.co.uk

THE finale to 2011-12 left the Seasiders heartbroken as they undeservedly lost the play-off final. But, when the pain subsides, Blackpool fans will look back with pride.

Ian Holloway had a huge rebuilding job to do last summer, with his squad stripped of almost all of its attacking stars in the wake of their relegation from the top flight.

Just steadying the ship would have been mission accomplished but to do it so quickly while delivering more attractive, attacking football was really impressive.

Longest run without loss/win: 7/3
High – low league position 4-13
Clean sheets: 13 Yellow cards: 55 Red cards: 2
Average attendance: 12,764 Players used: 33
Leading Scorer: K Phillips 16 (3,12)
Key stat: Only promoted pair Southampton and West Ham scored more Championship goals than Blackpool

| | 11-12 | | Last six seasons at home | | | | | | | |
	H	A	P	W	D	L	OV	UN	BS	CS
Bolton	-	-	1	1	0	0	1	0	1	0
Blackburn	-	-	1	0	0	1	1	0	1	0
Wolves	-	-	3	1	2	0	2	1	2	1
Birmingham	D	L	3	1	1	1	2	1	2	1
Blackpool										
Cardiff	D	W	4	0	3	1	0	4	3	0
Middlesbrough	W	D	2	2	0	0	1	1	0	2
Hull	D	W	2	1	1	0	1	1	2	0
Leicester	D	L	3	1	1	1	3	0	3	0
Brighton	W	D	2	1	1	0	1	1	1	1
Watford	D	W	4	1	2	1	1	3	2	1
Derby	L	L	3	1	1	1	1	2	1	1
Burnley	W	L	3	2	0	1	2	1	0	2
Leeds	W	W	1	1	0	0	0	1	0	1
Ipswich	W	D	4	2	1	1	0	4	1	2
Millwall	W	D	2	1	0	1	0	2	0	1
Crystal Palace	W	D	4	1	3	0	3	1	4	0
Peterborough	W	L	2	2	0	0	1	1	1	1
Nottm Forest	L	D	4	1	1	2	2	2	3	0
Bristol City	W	W	5	1	2	2	1	4	2	1
Barnsley	D	W	4	1	2	1	1	3	3	1
Charlton	-	-	2	2	0	0	1	1	1	1
Sheffield Weds	-	-	3	1	0	2	2	1	2	0
Huddersfield	-	-	1	1	0	0	1	0	1	0

Season	Division	Pos	P	W	D	L	F	A	GD	Pts
2011-12	Champ	5	46	20	15	11	79	59	20	75
2010-11	Prem	19	38	10	9	19	55	78	-23	39
2009-10	Champ	6	46	19	13	14	74	58	16	70

Bolton

Nickname: The Trotters
Colours: White and Blue
Ground: Reebok Stadium (28,100)
Tel: 0844-871-2932   www.bwfc.co.uk

RELEGATION will hit Bolton hard. A player exodus followed the Trotters' relegation and while that will help chairman Phil Gartside in his stated aim to halve the wage bill, players leaving for free won't help tackle the club's estimated £100m debt.

With 16 players leaving so far and David Wheater, Fabrice Muamba and Stuart Holden out for lengthy spells, Owen Coyle will have to rely heavily on academy players and loanees – a strong first XI could be let down by a lack of depth.

Longest run without loss/win: 3/6
High – low league position 16-20
Clean sheets: 3 **Yellow cards:** 51 **Red cards:** 5
Average attendance: 23,670 **Players used:** 30
Leading Scorer: I Klasnic 8 (0,7)
Key stat: Bolton didn't lose any of their seven away games to teams in the Premier League's bottom eight last term

	11-12 H A	Last six seasons at home P	W	D	L	OV	UN	BS	CS
Bolton									
Blackburn	W W	6	2	1	3	4	2	4	1
Wolves	D W	3	2	1	0	0	3	1	2
Birmingham	- -	3	2	1	0	3	0	2	1
Blackpool	- -	1	0	1	0	1	0	1	0
Cardiff	- -	0	0	0	0	0	0	0	0
Middlesbrough	- -	3	1	2	0	1	2	1	2
Hull	- -	2	0	2	0	1	1	2	0
Leicester	- -	0	0	0	0	0	0	0	0
Brighton	- -	0	0	0	0	0	0	0	0
Watford	- -	1	1	0	0	0	1	0	1
Derby	- -	1	1	0	0	0	1	0	1
Burnley	- -	1	1	0	0	0	1	0	1
Leeds	- -	0	0	0	0	0	0	0	0
Ipswich	- -	0	0	0	0	0	0	0	0
Millwall	- -	0	0	0	0	0	0	0	0
Crystal Palace	- -	0	0	0	0	0	0	0	0
Peterborough	- -	0	0	0	0	0	0	0	0
Nottm Forest	- -	0	0	0	0	0	0	0	0
Bristol City	- -	0	0	0	0	0	0	0	0
Barnsley	- -	0	0	0	0	0	0	0	0
Charlton	- -	1	0	1	0	0	1	1	0
Sheffield Weds	- -	0	0	0	0	0	0	0	0
Huddersfield	- -	0	0	0	0	0	0	0	0

Season	Division	Pos	P	W	D	L	F	A	GD	Pts
2011-12	Prem	18	38	10	6	22	46	77	-31	36
2010-11	Prem	14	38	12	10	16	52	56	-4	46
2009-10	Prem	14	38	10	9	19	42	67	-25	39

Brighton

Nickname: The Seagulls
Colours: Blue and White
Ground: AmEx Community Stadium (22,500)
Tel: 01273-878-288   www.seagulls.co.uk

BRIGHTON were hoping the momentum of their League 1 winning 2010-11 season might carry them straight to the top flight but, after an extremely promising start, things rather petered out. And, with Brighton winning just three of their final 16 games of 2011-12, there will be fears of second season syndrome striking.

However, the club remains well run, well financed and well supported, and it seems that Gus Poyet will stay put following rumours of an exit early in the summer.

Longest run without loss/win: 12/9
High – low league position 3-16
Clean sheets: 16 **Yellow cards:** 93 **Red cards:** 8
Average attendance: 20,029 **Players used:** 33
Leading Scorer: A Barnes 11 (2,9)
Key stat: There were fewer first-half goals at the Amex Stadium than at any other Championship ground last season

	11-12 H A	Last six seasons at home P	W	D	L	OV	UN	BS	CS
Bolton	- -	0	0	0	0	0	0	0	0
Blackburn	- -	0	0	0	0	0	0	0	0
Wolves	- -	0	0	0	0	0	0	0	0
Birmingham	D D	1	0	1	0	0	1	1	0
Blackpool	D L	2	0	1	1	2	0	1	0
Cardiff	D W	1	0	1	0	1	0	1	0
Middlesbrough	D L	1	0	1	0	0	1	1	0
Hull	D D	1	0	1	0	0	1	0	1
Leicester	W L	2	2	0	0	1	1	1	1
Brighton									
Watford	D L	1	0	1	0	1	0	1	0
Derby	W W	1	1	0	0	0	1	0	1
Burnley	L L	1	0	0	1	0	1	0	0
Leeds	D W	4	0	1	3	2	2	1	0
Ipswich	W L	1	1	0	0	1	0	0	1
Millwall	D D	5	2	1	2	3	2	2	1
Crystal Palace	L D	1	0	0	1	1	0	1	0
Peterborough	W W	3	2	0	1	2	1	2	1
Nottm Forest	W D	3	2	0	1	1	2	1	1
Bristol City	W W	2	1	0	1	0	2	0	1
Barnsley	W D	1	1	0	0	0	1	0	1
Charlton	- -	2	0	1	1	0	2	1	0
Sheffield Weds	- -	1	1	0	0	0	1	0	1
Huddersfield	- -	5	0	3	2	1	4	2	2

Season	Division	Pos	P	W	D	L	F	A	GD	Pts
2011-12	Champ	10	46	17	15	14	52	52	0	66
2010-11	League 1	1	46	28	11	7	85	40	45	95
2009-10	League 1	13	46	15	14	17	56	60	-4	59

Bristol City

Nickname: The Robins
Colours: Red and White
Ground: Ashton Gate (21,804)
Tel: 01179-630-600　　**www.bcfc.co.uk**

JUST six points from their first ten games prompted another managerial change for the Robins, with caretaker-turned-permanent boss Keith Millen the latest to leave.

There will be more changes this summer as Derek McInnes, appointed in October, reshapes a squad that needs trimming and has several players out of contract. The former St Johnstone boss has made a promising start to his managerial career and should be able bring improvement and stability to Ashton Gate.

Longest run without loss/win: 8/10
High – low league position 19-24
Clean sheets: 9 **Yellow cards:** 79 **Red cards:** 6
Average attendance: 13,836 **Players used:** 33
Leading Scorer: N Maynard 8 (3,6)
Key stat: Bristol City's points-per-game average rose from 0.5 to 1.26 after Derek McInnes arrived – that's mid-table form

	11-12 H A	Last six seasons at home P	W	D	L	OV	UN	BS	CS
Bolton	- -	0	0	0	0	0	0	0	0
Blackburn	- -	0	0	0	0	0	0	0	0
Wolves	- -	2	0	2	0	1	1	1	1
Birmingham	L D	2	0	0	2	1	1	1	0
Blackpool	L L	5	2	1	2	2	3	2	3
Cardiff	L L	5	2	1	2	3	2	2	2
Middlesbrough	L D	3	1	0	2	2	1	2	1
Hull	D L	3	2	1	0	2	1	2	1
Leicester	W W	4	2	1	1	1	3	2	1
Brighton	L L	2	1	0	1	0	2	0	1
Watford	L D	5	0	3	2	1	4	2	1
Derby	D L	4	2	2	0	1	3	3	1
Burnley	W D	4	2	1	1	3	1	3	1
Leeds	L L	2	0	0	2	1	1	0	0
Ipswich	L L	5	1	2	2	1	4	1	2
Millwall	W W	3	2	0	1	1	2	0	2
Crystal Palace	D L	5	2	3	0	1	4	3	2
Peterborough	L L	2	0	1	1	1	1	2	0
Nottm Forest	D W	5	0	4	1	2	3	4	1
Bristol City									
Barnsley	W W	5	4	1	0	3	2	3	2
Charlton	- -	2	1	0	1	1	1	1	0
Sheffield Weds	- -	3	1	2	0	1	2	3	0
Huddersfield	- -	1	0	1	0	0	1	1	0

Season	Division	Pos	P	W	D	L	F	A	GD	Pts
2011-12	Champ	20	46	12	13	21	44	68	-24	49
2010-11	Champ	15	46	17	9	20	62	65	-3	60
2009-10	Champ	10	46	15	18	13	56	65	-9	63

Burnley

Nickname: The Clarets
Colours: Claret and Blue
Ground: Turf Moor (21,940)
Tel: 0871-221-1882　　**burnleyfootballclub.com**

BURNLEY never seriously looked like promotion or relegation material and only briefly put together any serious runs of form last season.

The Clarets probably needed to bounce back at the first time of asking if they were to become a yo-yo club or better and after missing out in 2010-11, they look the epitome of a mid-table Championship side.

Given time, manager Eddie Howe, 34, may yet flourish at Turf Moor but fans might need to be very patient.

Longest run without loss/win: 4/7
High – low league position 7-21
Clean sheets: 12 **Yellow cards:** 70 **Red cards:** 2
Average attendance: 14,048 **Players used:** 29
Leading Scorer: C Austin 16 (7,13)
Key stat: Only two Championship sides won fewer home games than Burnley managed at Turf Moor last season

	11-12 H A	Last six seasons at home P	W	D	L	OV	UN	BS	CS
Bolton	- -	1	0	1	0	0	1	1	0
Blackburn	- -	1	0	0	1	0	1	0	0
Wolves	- -	4	1	0	3	2	2	2	1
Birmingham	L L	4	1	1	2	3	1	4	0
Blackpool	W L	3	2	1	0	2	1	2	1
Cardiff	D D	5	1	4	0	2	3	4	1
Middlesbrough	L W	2	1	0	1	1	1	1	0
Hull	W W	5	4	0	1	1	4	0	4
Leicester	L D	4	1	1	2	2	2	2	1
Brighton	W W	1	1	0	0	0	1	0	1
Watford	D L	4	2	2	0	4	0	4	0
Derby	D W	4	2	2	0	2	2	1	3
Burnley									
Leeds	L L	3	1	0	2	3	0	3	0
Ipswich	W L	5	2	1	2	4	1	2	2
Millwall	L W	2	0	0	2	2	0	1	0
Crystal Palace	D L	5	2	3	0	1	4	4	1
Peterborough	D L	1	0	1	0	0	1	1	0
Nottm Forest	W W	3	3	0	0	2	1	1	2
Bristol City	D L	4	1	2	1	1	3	1	2
Barnsley	W L	5	4	0	1	4	1	3	2
Charlton	- -	2	2	0	0	1	1	1	1
Sheffield Weds	- -	3	0	2	1	1	2	3	0
Huddersfield	- -	0	0	0	0	0	0	0	0

Season	Division	Pos	P	W	D	L	F	A	GD	Pts
2011-12	Champ	13	46	17	11	18	61	58	3	62
2010-11	Champ	8	46	18	14	14	65	61	4	68
2009-10	Prem	18	38	8	6	24	42	82	-40	30

Cardiff

Nickname: The Bluebirds
Colours: Red
Ground: Cardiff City Stadium (26,828)
Tel: 0845-365-1115 www.cardiffcityfc.co.uk

CONSIDERING the upheaval Cardiff went through last summer, Malky Mackay did well to guide the club to sixth place.

A League Cup final penalty shootout defeat was hard to take but heartbreak is a familiar feeling to Bluebirds fans after three consecutive play-off failures.

Imminent investment comes with plenty of caveats attached that could undermine Cardiff in the mid-to-long term. But, for bettors, the short-term prospects look promising for the red-shirted Bluebirds.

Longest run without loss/win: 10/5
High – low league position 3-9
Clean sheets: 15 **Yellow cards:** 58 **Red cards:** 0
Average attendance: 22,100 **Players used:** 25
Leading Scorer: P Whittingham 12 (3,12)
Key stat: Tough to beat – Cardiff had the most draws in the Championship last term and the second fewest defeats

	11-12 H A	Last six seasons at home P	W	D	L	OV	UN	BS	CS
Bolton	- -	0	0	0	0	0	0	0	0
Blackburn	- -	0	0	0	0	0	0	0	0
Wolves	- -	3	1	0	2	3	0	2	1
Birmingham	W D	3	2	0	1	1	2	1	2
Blackpool	L D	4	2	1	1	2	2	3	1
Cardiff									
Middlesbrough	L W	3	1	0	2	2	1	1	1
Hull	L L	4	2	0	2	1	3	0	2
Leicester	D L	5	3	1	1	2	3	2	2
Brighton	L D	1	0	0	1	1	0	1	0
Watford	D D	5	3	1	1	4	1	5	0
Derby	W W	5	4	1	0	4	1	4	1
Burnley	D D	5	3	2	0	2	3	3	2
Leeds	D D	3	2	1	0	1	2	2	1
Ipswich	D L	6	1	2	3	4	2	3	1
Millwall	D D	2	1	1	0	1	1	1	1
Crystal Palace	W W	6	2	4	0	1	5	3	3
Peterborough	W L	2	2	0	0	1	1	1	1
Nottm Forest	W W	4	2	1	1	0	4	1	2
Bristol City	W W	5	4	1	0	4	1	3	2
Barnsley	W W	6	4	1	1	4	2	3	2
Charlton	- -	2	1	0	1	0	2	0	1
Sheffield Weds	- -	4	3	0	1	2	2	2	2
Huddersfield	- -	0	0	0	0	0	0	0	0

Season	Division	Pos	P	W	D	L	F	A	GD	Pts
2011-12	Champ	6	46	19	18	9	66	53	13	75
2010-11	Champ	4	46	23	11	12	76	54	22	80
2009-10	Champ	4	46	22	10	14	73	54	19	76

Charlton

Nickname: The Addicks
Colours: Red and White
Ground: The Valley (27,111)
Tel: 020-8333-4000 www.cafc.co.uk

CHRIS POWELL'S overhaul paid off in style last season as the rookie Addicks boss completely rebuilt his defence and revitalised a stale squad to earn a club record 101 points in League 1.

Suddenly, after seven years in the doldrums, the Addicks look a solid, progressive side again and while Powell has played down suggestions of back-to-back promotions, Charlton fans have every right to be aiming for a play-off place rather than merely hoping to survive.

Longest run without loss/win: 12/3
High – low league position 1-2
Clean sheets: 20 **Yellow cards:** 58 **Red cards:** 5
Average attendance: 17,402 **Players used:** 28
Leading Scorer: B Wright-Phillips 22 (9,17)
Key stat: Charlton recorded a stunning 50 points in 23 League 1 away games last term, losing just three times

	11-12 H A	Last six seasons at home P	W	D	L	OV	UN	BS	CS
Bolton	- -	1	1	0	0	0	1	0	1
Blackburn	- -	1	1	0	0	0	1	0	1
Wolves	- -	2	0	0	2	2	0	2	0
Birmingham	- -	1	0	1	0	0	1	0	1
Blackpool	- -	2	1	1	0	2	0	2	0
Cardiff	- -	2	1	1	0	2	0	1	1
Middlesbrough	- -	1	0	0	1	1	0	1	0
Hull	- -	1	0	1	0	0	1	1	0
Leicester	- -	1	1	0	0	0	1	0	1
Brighton	- -	2	0	0	2	2	0	1	0
Watford	- -	3	0	2	1	2	1	2	1
Derby	- -	1	0	1	0	1	0	1	0
Burnley	- -	2	0	1	1	1	1	2	0
Leeds	- -	1	1	0	0	0	1	0	1
Ipswich	- -	2	2	0	0	2	0	2	0
Millwall	- -	1	0	1	0	1	0	1	0
Crystal Palace	- -	2	2	0	0	2	0	2	0
Peterborough	- -	1	1	0	0	0	1	0	1
Nottm Forest	- -	1	0	0	1	0	1	0	0
Bristol City	- -	2	0	1	1	0	2	1	0
Barnsley	- -	2	0	1	1	1	1	2	0
Charlton									
Sheffield Weds	D W	4	2	1	1	2	2	3	1
Huddersfield	W L	3	2	0	1	1	2	1	1

Season	Division	Pos	P	W	D	L	F	A	GD	Pts
2011-12	League 1	1	46	30	11	5	82	36	46	101
2010-11	League 1	13	46	15	14	17	62	66	-4	59
2009-10	League 1	4	46	23	15	8	71	48	23	84

Crystal Palace

Nickname: The Eagles
Colours: Red and Blue
Ground: Selhurst Park (26,225)
Tel: 020-8768-6000   www.cpfc.co.uk

DOUGIE FREEDMAN did a fine job in his first full season as Palace boss, keeping the Eagles a safe distance from the drop zone while landing one of the shocks of the season by beating Man United at Old Trafford in the League Cup quarter-final.

However, slow season ticket sales and hefty debts mean proceeds from the likely sales of star men such as Wilfried Zaha and Nathaniel Clyne are unlikely to be reinvested in the squad and that gives Freedman a mountain to climb.

Longest run without loss/win: 10/9
High – low league position 3-17
Clean sheets: 17 **Yellow cards:** 57 **Red cards:** 2
Average attendance: 15,219 **Players used:** 37
Leading Scorer: D Ambrose 7 (2,7) C Martin 7 (4,6)
Key stat: Selhurst Park saw just 41 goals last season – fewer than any other Championship ground (1.78 goals per game)

	11-12 H	A	Last six seasons at home P	W	D	L	OV	UN	BS	CS
Bolton	-	-	0	0	0	0	0	0	0	0
Blackburn	-	-	0	0	0	0	0	0	0	0
Wolves	-	-	3	0	1	2	1	2	1	0
Birmingham	W	L	3	1	1	1	0	3	0	2
Blackpool	D	L	4	1	2	1	1	3	2	1
Cardiff	L	L	6	1	1	4	3	3	3	2
Middlesbrough	L	D	3	2	0	1	0	3	0	2
Hull	D	W	4	0	4	0	0	4	2	2
Leicester	L	L	5	2	1	2	3	2	3	1
Brighton	D	W	1	0	1	0	0	1	1	0
Watford	W	W	5	3	1	1	3	2	1	3
Derby	D	L	5	3	2	0	1	4	2	3
Burnley	W	D	5	2	3	0	2	3	1	4
Leeds	D	L	3	2	1	0	0	3	1	2
Ipswich	D	W	6	2	1	3	3	3	4	1
Millwall	D	W	2	0	1	1	0	2	0	1
Crystal Palace										
Peterborough	W	L	2	2	0	0	0	2	0	2
Nottm Forest	L	W	4	0	1	3	3	1	2	0
Bristol City	W	D	5	3	1	1		4	1	3
Barnsley	W	L	6	5	1	0		4	2	4
Charlton	-	-	2	1	0	1	0	2	0	1
Sheffield Weds	-	-	4	1	2	1	2	2	3	1
Huddersfield	-	-	0	0	0	0	0	0	0	0

Season	Division	Pos	P	W	D	L	F	A	GD	Pts
2011-12	Champ	17	46	13	17	16	46	51	-5	56
2010-11	Champ	20	46	12	12	22	44	69	-25	48
2009-10	Champ	21	46	14	17	15	50	53	-3	49*

Derby

Nickname: The Rams
Colours: White and Black
Ground: Pride Park (33,502)
Tel: 0871-472-1884   www.dcfc.co.uk

DERBY proved us wrong last season, winning six of their first eight games and never dropping below 16th in the league.

A successful summer recruitment drive was the catalyst, with Craig Bryson, Frank Fielding and Theo Robinson boosting a much-changed starting line-up.

It was badly needed as the club was in danger of going stale and slipping further. However, with the academy also beginning to produce the goods, there is little reason for Rams fans to worry this term.

Longest run without loss/win: 5/7
High – low league position 3-16
Clean sheets: 12 **Yellow cards:** 58 **Red cards:** 1
Average attendance: 26,020 **Players used:** 30
Leading Scorer: S Davies 12 (2,11)
Key stat: Outside of the top six, Derby had the best record against the Championship's top five last term (W4, D3, L3)

	11-12 H	A	Last six seasons at home P	W	D	L	OV	UN	BS	CS
Bolton	-	-	1	0	1	0	0	1	1	0
Blackburn	-	-	1	0	0	1	1	0	1	0
Wolves	-	-	2	0	0	2	1	1	1	0
Birmingham	W	D	4	1	1	2	2	2	3	0
Blackpool	W	W	3	2	0	1	2	2	3	0
Cardiff	L	L	5	2	1	2	3	2	3	1
Middlesbrough	L	L	4	1	1	2	2	2	2	0
Hull	L	W	3	0	1	2	1	2	1	0
Leicester	L	L	4	2	0	2	0	4	0	2
Brighton	L	L	1	0	0	1	0	1	0	0
Watford	L	W	4	3	0	1	2	2	2	2
Derby										
Burnley	L	D	4	1	1	2	2	2	3	1
Leeds	W	W	3	3	0	0	1	2	1	2
Ipswich	D	L	5	1	1	3	3	2	3	1
Millwall	W	D	2	1	1	0	1	1	0	2
Crystal Palace	W	D	5	3	1	1	3	2	3	2
Peterborough	D	L	2	1	1	0	1	1	2	0
Nottm Forest	W	W	4	2	1	1	0	4	1	2
Bristol City	W	D	4	3	0	1	2	2	2	1
Barnsley	D	L	5	1	3	1	2	3	3	2
Charlton	-	-	1	1	0	0	0	1	0	1
Sheffield Weds	-	-	3	3	0	0	2	1	0	3
Huddersfield	-	-	0	0	0	0	0	0	0	0

Season	Division	Pos	P	W	D	L	F	A	GD	Pts
2011-12	Champ	12	46	18	10	18	50	58	-8	64
2010-11	Champ	19	46	13	10	23	58	71	-13	49
2009-10	Champ	14	46	15	11	20	53	63	-10	56

Huddersfield

Nickname: The Terriers
Colours: Blue and White
Ground: Galpharm Stadium (24,554)
Tel: 0870-444-4677   **www.htafc.com**

HUDDERSFIELD held their nerve to win an epic play-off final penalty shootout but they'll need the feel-good factor to play a big role if they're to survive this season.

It won't be easy. The Terriers finished 20 points behind League 1 winners Charlton and their performances tailed off following the extremely harsh sacking of Lee Clark.

The owed nearly half their league goals to 36-goal hotshot Jordan Rhodes, and it's hard to see the Terriers being able to hold on to their in-demand striker.

Longest run without loss/win: 18/3
High – low league position 2-8
Clean sheets: 16 **Yellow cards:** 66 **Red cards:** 2
Average attendance: 14,145 **Players used:** 29
Leading Scorer: J Rhodes 36 (8,19)
Key stat: Huddersfield earned 1.83 points per game under Lee Clark for the first 30 games, but it dropped to 1.63 under Simon Grayson

	11-12		Last six seasons at home						
	H A	P	W	D	L	OV	UN	BS	CS
Bolton	- -	0	0	0	0	0	0	0	0
Blackburn	- -	0	0	0	0	0	0	0	0
Wolves	- -	0	0	0	0	0	0	0	0
Birmingham	- -	0	0	0	0	0	0	0	0
Blackpool	- -	1	0	0	1	0	1	0	0
Cardiff	- -	0	0	0	0	0	0	0	0
Middlesbrough	- -	0	0	0	0	0	0	0	0
Hull	- -	0	0	0	0	0	0	0	0
Leicester	- -	1	0	0	1	1	0	1	0
Brighton	- -	5	3	1	1	5	0	4	0
Watford	- -	0	0	0	0	0	0	0	0
Derby	- -	0	0	0	0	0	0	0	0
Burnley	- -	0	0	0	0	0	0	0	0
Leeds	- -	3	2	1	0	1	2	1	2
Ipswich	- -	0	0	0	0	0	0	0	0
Millwall	- -	4	3	0	1	2	2	2	2
Crystal Palace	- -	0	0	0	0	0	0	0	0
Peterborough	- -	2	1	1	0	0	2	1	1
Nottm Forest	- -	2	0	2	0	0	2	2	0
Bristol City	- -	1	1	0	0	1	0	1	0
Barnsley	- -	0	0	0	0	0	0	0	0
Charlton	W L	3	2	1	0	1	2	2	1
Sheffield Weds	L D	2	1	0	1	0	2	0	1
Huddersfield									

Season	Division	Pos	P	W	D	L	F	A	GD	Pts
2011-12	League 1	4	46	21	18	7	79	47	32	81
2010-11	League 1	3	46	25	12	9	77	48	29	87
2009-10	League 1	6	46	23	11	12	82	56	26	80

Hull

Nickname: The Tigers
Colours: Amber and Black
Ground: The KC Stadium (25,404)
Tel: 01482-504-600   **www.hullcityafc.net**

A PROMISING start to 2011-12 was disrupted when Nigel Pearson was lured away from the KC Stadium in November.

Nicky Barmby initially did well enough as caretaker manager to earn a permanent contract, but a run of one win in 12 games in early spring saw the Tigers miss out on the top six and Barmby was controversially replaced by Steve Bruce in the summer.

Owner Assem Allam says his ambition is the Premier League but the rebuilding project on the pitch is back to square one.

Longest run without loss/win: 11/6
High – low league position 4-10
Clean sheets: 18 **Yellow cards:** 71 **Red cards:** 1
Average attendance: 18,790 **Players used:** 29
Leading Scorer: M Fryatt 16 (7,13)
Key stat: Only Reading had a better defensive record in the Championship last term, but Hull were the fifth-lowest goalscorers in the division

	11-12		Last six seasons at home						
	H A	P	W	D	L	OV	UN	BS	CS
Bolton	- -	2	1	0	1	0	2	0	1
Blackburn	- -	2	0	1	1	1	1	1	1
Wolves	- -	3	2	1	0	1	2	1	2
Birmingham	W D	3	2	0	1	1	2	1	1
Blackpool	L D	2	0	1	1	1	1	1	0
Cardiff	W W	4	2	1	1	3	1	3	0
Middlesbrough	W L	3	2	0	1	3	0	3	0
Hull									
Leicester	W L	4	2	0	2	2	2	2	1
Brighton	D D	1	0	1	0	0	1	0	1
Watford	W D	3	2	1	0	2	1	1	2
Derby	L W	3	1	0	2	1	2	1	1
Burnley	L L	5	2	0	3	2	3	2	2
Leeds	D L	3	0	2	1	2	1	2	1
Ipswich	D W	4	2	1	1	3	1	3	1
Millwall	W L	2	1	0	1	0	2	0	1
Crystal Palace	L D	4	1	2	1	1	3	3	0
Peterborough	W W	1	1	0	0	0	1	0	1
Nottm Forest	W W	2	1	1	0	1	1	1	1
Bristol City	W D	3	2	1	0	1	2	0	3
Barnsley	W L	4	3	0	1	3	1	2	2
Charlton	- -	1	0	0	1	1	0	1	0
Sheffield Weds	- -	2	2	0	0	1	1	1	1
Huddersfield	- -	0	0	0	0	0	0	0	0

Season	Division	Pos	P	W	D	L	F	A	GD	Pts
2011-12	Champ	8	46	19	11	16	47	44	3	68
2010-11	Champ	11	46	16	17	13	52	51	1	65
2009-10	Prem	19	38	6	12	20	34	75	-41	30

Ipswich

Nickname: Town/Tractor Boys
Colours: Blue and White
Ground: Portman Road (30,311)
Tel: 01473-400-500   www.itfc.co.uk

IT'S HARD to get too excited about Ipswich these days, with the Tractor Boys finishing between eighth and 15th in each of the past seven seasons.

Thanks to the continued and significant financial support of owner Marcus Evans, Ipswich have a significant edge over many of their mid-table rivals.

But manager Paul Jewell will be under pressure to make that edge count this season after a disappointing return on Evans' investment in 2011-12.

Longest run without loss/win: 6/7
High – low league position 9-21
Clean sheets: 12 **Yellow cards:** 57 **Red cards:** 5
Average attendance: 18,267 **Players used:** 31
Leading Scorer: M Chopra 14 (5,11)
Key stat: Ipswich showed play-off form from January 31, with a W9, D6, L4 record in their last 19 games

	11-12 H A	Last six seasons at home P	W	D	L	OV	UN	BS	CS
Bolton	- -	0	0	0	0	0	0	0	0
Blackburn	- -	0	0	0	0	0	0	0	0
Wolves	- -	3	1	0	2	1	2	0	1
Birmingham	D L	3	1	1	1	0	3	1	1
Blackpool	D L	4	2	2	0	3	1	4	0
Cardiff	W D	6	4	1	1	3	3	3	3
Middlesbrough	D D	3	0	3	0	1	2	3	0
Hull	L D	4	1	2	1	0	4	1	2
Leicester	L D	5	2	1	2	3	2	2	2
Brighton	W L	1	1	0	0	1	0	1	0
Watford	L L	5	0	2	3	3	2	3	1
Derby	W D	5	4	0	1	1	4	1	3
Burnley	W L	5	1	4	0	0	5	3	2
Leeds	W L	3	3	0	0	2	1	2	1
Ipswich									
Millwall	L L	2	1	0	1	1	1	0	1
Crystal Palace	L D	6	2	1	3	3	3	4	1
Peterborough	W L	2	1	1	0	1	1	1	1
Nottm Forest	L L	4	1	1	2	2	2	3	0
Bristol City	W W	5	4	1	0	3	2	1	4
Barnsley	W W	6	4	1	1	3	3	2	4
Charlton	- -	2	1	1	0	0	2	1	1
Sheffield Weds	- -	4	1	2	1	1	3	2	1
Huddersfield	- -	0	0	0	0	0	0	0	0

Season	Division	Pos	P	W	D	L	F	A	GD	Pts
2011-12	Champ	15	46	17	10	19	69	77	-8	61
2010-11	Champ	13	46	18	8	20	62	68	-6	62
2009-10	Champ	15	46	12	20	14	50	61	-11	56

Leeds

Nickname: United
Colours: White
Ground: Elland Road (37,697)
Tel: 0871-334-1919   www.leedsunited.com

LEEDS set a couple of unwanted club records last term, losing 11 home games in a season and conceding seven goals at Elland Road for the first time.

Simon Grayson was sacked for his part in the former sequence but his replacement, Neil Warnock, oversaw the humiliating 3-7 home defeat to goal-shy Forest.

Warnock is both experienced and a serial promotion winner but he has a big rebuilding project ahead and a tricky environment in which to operate.

Longest run without loss/win: 7/4
High – low league position 5-14
Clean sheets: 10 **Yellow cards:** 75 **Red cards:** 9
Average attendance: 23,283 **Players used:** 34
Leading Scorer: R McCormack 18 (5,15)
Key stat: Leeds' points-per-game average dropped to 0.93 from 1.5 after Neil Warnock was handed the reins

	11-12 H A	Last six seasons at home P	W	D	L	OV	UN	BS	CS
Bolton	- -	0	0	0	0	0	0	0	0
Blackburn	- -	0	0	0	0	0	0	0	0
Wolves	- -	1	0	0	1	0	1	0	0
Birmingham	L L	2	1	0	1	2	0	2	0
Blackpool	L L	1	0	0	1	1	0	2	0
Cardiff	D D	3	0	1	2	1	2	1	0
Middlesbrough	L W	2	0	1	1	0	2	1	0
Hull	W D	3	1	2	0	2	1	2	1
Leicester	L W	4	0	1	3	3	1	4	0
Brighton	L D	4	1	2	1	2	2	3	1
Watford	L D	2	0	1	1	1	1	1	0
Derby	L L	3	0	0	3	1	2	1	0
Burnley	W W	3	3	0	0	1	2	1	2
Leeds									
Ipswich	W L	3	1	2	0	1	2	2	1
Millwall	W W	5	4	0	1	2	3	2	2
Crystal Palace	W D	3	3	0	0	3	0	3	0
Peterborough	W W	2	2	0	0	0	2	0	0
Nottm Forest	L W	3	1	1	1	2	1	3	0
Bristol City	W W	2	2	0	0	2	0	2	0
Barnsley	L L	3	0	2	1	3	0	3	0
Charlton	- -	1	0	1	0	0	1	0	1
Sheffield Weds	- -	1	0	0	1	1	0	1	0
Huddersfield	- -	3	1	1	1	3	0	2	1

Season	Division	Pos	P	W	D	L	F	A	GD	Pts
2011-12	Champ	14	46	17	10	19	65	68	-3	61
2010-11	Champ	7	46	19	15	12	81	70	11	72
2009-10	League 1	2	46	25	11	10	77	44	33	86

Leicester

Nickname: The Foxes
Colours: Blue
Ground: Walkers Stadium (32,312)
Tel: 0844-815-6000   www.lcfc.co.uk

LEICESTER were as short as 4-1 to win last season's Championship but it was no huge surprise that a club awash with cash but lacking clear leadership failed to live up to expectations.

It was even less of a surprise that trigger-happy chairman Vichai Raksriaksorn saw fit to sack Sven-Goran Eriksson after a slow start. Nigel Pearson started his second spell in the Leicester dugout in November, but it's no given that his side will live up to their favourites tag.

Longest run without loss/win: 7/5
High – low league position 8-15
Clean sheets: 14 **Yellow cards:** 65 **Red cards:** 9
Average attendance: 23,037 **Players used:** 30
Leading Scorer: D Nugent 15 (7,14)
Key stat: During 2011-12, Leicester averaged 1.47 points per game under Pearson, just 0.01 better than Eriksson's return of 1.46

	11-12 H	A	Last six seasons at home P	W	D	L	OV	UN	BS	CS
Bolton	-	-	0	0	0	0	0	0	0	0
Blackburn	-	-	0	0	0	0	0	0	0	0
Wolves	-	-	2	0	1	1	1	1	1	1
Birmingham	W	L	2	1	0	1	2	0	2	0
Blackpool	W	D	3	2	0	1	1	2	1	1
Cardiff	W	D	5	3	2	0	2	3	2	3
Middlesbrough	D	D	3	1	2	0	1	2	1	2
Hull	W	L	4	1	1	2	1	3	2	0
Leicester										
Brighton	W	L	2	1	1	0	0	2	0	2
Watford	W	L	4	4	0	0	3	1	3	1
Derby	W	W	4	2	2	0	1	3	1	3
Burnley	D	W	4	1	1	2	1	3	0	2
Leeds	L	W	4	1	2	1	1	3	2	1
Ipswich	D	W	5	3	2	0	2	3	4	1
Millwall	L	L	3	1	0	2	2	1	1	0
Crystal Palace	W	W	5	3	2	0	1	4	2	3
Peterborough	D	L	3	1	2	0	1	2	2	1
Nottm Forest	D	D	3	2	1	0	1	2	0	3
Bristol City	L	L	4	1	1	2	3	1	3	1
Barnsley	L	D	5	4	0	1	2	3	2	3
Charlton	-	-	1	0	1	0	0	1	1	0
Sheffield Weds	-	-	3	1	0	2	3	0	2	1
Huddersfield	-	-	1	1	0	0	1	0	1	0

Season	Division	Pos	P	W	D	L	F	A	GD	Pts
2011-12	Champ	9	46	18	12	16	66	55	11	66
2010-11	Champ	10	46	19	10	17	76	71	5	67
2009-10	Champ	5	46	21	13	12	61	45	16	76

Middlesbrough

Nickname: Boro
Colours: Red and White
Ground: Riverside Stadium (34,998)
Tel: 0844-499-6789   www.mfc.co.uk

THE 2011-12 campaign must go down as a missed opportunity, with Boro having been in second place on New Year's Day but missing out on a play-off berth.

Most frustrating of all will be the fact that they took plenty of points off their promotion rivals but blew the easy games, winning just twice in 12 home games against teams in the bottom half of the table.

But if Tony Mowbray can make his wasteful side a touch more ruthless, Boro could mount another top-six challenge.

Longest run without loss/win: 11/8
High – low league position 2-9
Clean sheets: 15 **Yellow cards:** 78 **Red cards:** 7
Average attendance: 17,558 **Players used:** 29
Leading Scorer: M Emnes 14 (8,13)
Key stat: Only bottom side Doncaster matched Boro's record of just two home wins against the bottom half teams

	11-12 H	A	Last six seasons at home P	W	D	L	OV	UN	BS	CS
Bolton	-	-	3	1	0	2	2	1	2	0
Blackburn	-	-	3	0	1	2	1	2	1	1
Wolves	-	-	0	0	0	0	0	0	0	0
Birmingham	W	L	2	2	0	0	1	1	1	1
Blackpool	D	L	2	0	1	1	2	0	1	0
Cardiff	L	W	3	1	0	2	0	3	0	1
Middlesbrough										
Hull	W	L	3	2	1	0	2	1	2	1
Leicester	D	D	3	0	2	1	1	2	1	1
Brighton	W	D	1	1	0	0	0	1	0	1
Watford	W	L	4	3	0	1	2	2	2	1
Derby	W	W	4	4	0	0	1	3	1	3
Burnley	L	W	2	1	0	1	1	1	1	0
Leeds	L	W	2	0	0	2	1	1	1	0
Ipswich	D	D	3	1	1	1	2	1	2	1
Millwall	D	W	2	0	1	1	0	2	1	0
Crystal Palace	D	W	3	1	2	0	1	2	2	1
Peterborough	D	D	2	1	1	0	0	2	1	1
Nottm Forest	W	L	3	1	2	0	1	2	3	0
Bristol City	D	W	3	0	2	1	1	2	2	1
Barnsley	W	W	3	2	1	0	1	2	2	1
Charlton	-	-	1	1	0	0	0	1	0	1
Sheffield Weds	-	-	1	1	0	0	0	1	0	1
Huddersfield	-	-	0	0	0	0	0	0	0	0

Season	Division	Pos	P	W	D	L	F	A	GD	Pts
2011-12	Champ	7	46	18	16	12	52	51	1	70
2010-11	Champ	12	46	17	11	18	68	68	0	62
2009-10	Champ	11	46	16	14	16	58	50	8	62

Millwall

MILLWALL

Nickname: The Lions
Colours: Blue and White
Ground: The Den (19,734)
Tel: 020-7232-1222   www.millwallfc.co.uk

A FINE run of form to finish 2011-12 left Millwall 17 points clear of relegation but it didn't feel that comfortable for the majority of the season – the Lions bumped along in and around 20th position for most of the second half of the campaign.

The defensive solidity that saw the Lions finish ninth in 2010-11 deserted them, but at least Kenny Jackett's new striking signings, Andy Keogh and Darius Henderson, made successful starts to their Millwall careers.

Longest run without loss/win: 7/10
High – low league position 16-23
Clean sheets: 16 **Yellow cards:** 79 **Red cards:** 2
Average attendance: 11,484 **Players used:** 32
Leading Scorer: D Henderson 15 (5,10)
Key stat: Millwall took just three points from matches in which they went behind last season. Only Barnsley were less resilient

	11-12 H A	Last six seasons at home P	W	D	L	OV	UN	BS	CS
Bolton	- -	0	0	0	0	0	0	0	0
Blackburn	- -	0	0	0	0	0	0	0	0
Wolves	- -	0	0	0	0	0	0	0	0
Birmingham	L L	1	0	0	1	1	0	0	0
Blackpool	D L	2	0	2	0	1	1	1	1
Cardiff	D D	2	0	2	0	1	1	1	1
Middlesbrough	L D	2	0	0	2	2	0	2	0
Hull	W L	2	2	0	0	1	1	0	2
Leicester	W W	3	2	0	1	1	2	1	1
Brighton	D D	5	1	2	2	1	4	2	1
Watford	L L	2	0	0	2	1	1	1	0
Derby	D L	2	1	1	0	0	2	0	2
Burnley	L W	2	0	1	1	0	2	1	0
Leeds	L L	5	3	0	2	3	2	3	0
Ipswich	W W	2	2	0	0	2	0	2	0
Millwall									
Crystal Palace	L D	2	1	0	1	1	1	0	1
Peterborough	D W	2	1	1	0	1	1	1	1
Nottm Forest	W L	4	2	2	0	1	3	1	3
Bristol City	L L	3	1	1	1	1	2	1	2
Barnsley	D W	2	1	1	0	0	2	0	2
Charlton	- -	1	1	0	0	1	0	0	1
Sheffield Weds	- -	0	0	0	0	0	0	0	0
Huddersfield	- -	4	2	1	1	3	1	3	1

Season	Division	Pos	P	W	D	L	F	A	GD	Pts
2011-12	Champ	16	46	15	12	19	55	57	-2	57
2010-11	Champ	9	46	18	13	15	62	48	14	67
2009-10	League 1	3	46	24	13	9	76	44	32	85

Nottm Forest

FOREST

Nickname: Forest
Colours: Red and White
Ground: City Ground (30,576)
Tel: 0115-982-4455   www.nottinghamforest.co.uk

IT COULDN'T have gone much worse for Forest. Quietly fancied for a play-off place last summer, they made a poor start, new manager Steve McClaren resigned citing a lack of ambition from the club, Nigel Doughty resigned as chairman and then, worst of all, Doughty, who was committed to help finance the club in his reduced role as owner, sadly passed away in February.

Doughty's estate should continue fund the club until a buyer is found, but Forest's prospects are tricky to assess at present.

Longest run without loss/win: 4/7
High – low league position 17-23
Clean sheets: 12 **Yellow cards:** 61 **Red cards:** 5
Average attendance: 21,970 **Players used:** 31
Leading Scorer: G McCleary 9 (4,6)
Key stat: Forest's 0.8 points per game average under Steve McClaren only went up to 1.17 under Steve Cotterill

	11-12 H A	Last six seasons at home P	W	D	L	OV	UN	BS	CS
Bolton	- -	0	0	0	0	0	0	0	0
Blackburn	- -	0	0	0	0	0	0	0	0
Wolves	- -	1	0	0	1	0	1	0	0
Birmingham	L W	2	0	1	1	1	1	2	0
Blackpool	D W	4	0	3	1	0	4	1	2
Cardiff	L L	4	1	1	2	1	3	1	1
Middlesbrough	W L	3	3	0	0	0	3	0	3
Hull	L L	2	0	0	2	0	2	0	0
Leicester	D D	3	2	1	0	3	0	3	0
Brighton	D L	3	1	2	0	1	2	2	1
Watford	D W	4	2	1	1	2	2	3	1
Derby	L L	4	2	0	2	4	0	4	0
Burnley	L L	3	1	0	2	1	2	1	1
Leeds	L W	3	0	1	2	2	1	2	0
Ipswich	W W	4	3	1	0	2	2	2	2
Millwall	W L	4	3	1	0	2	2	3	1
Crystal Palace	L W	4	2	0	2	1	3	0	2
Peterborough	L W	2	1	0	1	0	2	0	1
Nottm Forest									
Bristol City	L D	5	3	1	1	1	4	2	2
Barnsley	D D	4	2	2	0	1	3	1	3
Charlton	- -	1	0	1	0	0	1	0	1
Sheffield Weds	- -	2	2	0	0	2	0	2	0
Huddersfield	- -	2	2	0	0	2	0	2	0

Season	Division	Pos	P	W	D	L	F	A	GD	Pts
2011-12	Champ	19	46	14	8	24	48	63	-15	50
2010-11	Champ	6	46	20	15	11	69	50	19	75
2009-10	Champ	3	46	22	13	11	65	40	25	79

Peterborough

Nickname: The Posh
Colours: Blue
Ground: London Road (14,793)
Tel: 01733-563-947   www.theposh.com

THE POSH didn't disappoint on their return to the Championship last season, sticking with the attacking philosophy that made them the highest-scoring side in English football in 2010-11.

But while Darren Ferguson's team survived with some ease and scored 67 league goals along the way, poor defensive displays could catch up with them at some point. Only rock-bottom Doncaster shipped more Championship goals than the 77 Peterborough conceded last term.

Longest run without loss/win: 5/7
High – low league position 10-19
Clean sheets: 4 **Yellow cards:** 55 **Red cards:** 2
Average attendance: 9,111 **Players used:** 27
Leading Scorer: P Taylor 12 (2,11)
Key stat: Peterborough kept just a solitary clean sheet in 24 league and cup away games last season

	11-12 H	A	P	W	D	L	OV	UN	BS	CS
Bolton	-	-	0	0	0	0	0	0	0	0
Blackburn	-	-	0	0	0	0	0	0	0	0
Wolves	-	-	0	0	0	0	0	0	0	0
Birmingham	D	D	1	0	1	0	0	1	1	0
Blackpool	W	L	2	1	0	1	1	1	1	0
Cardiff	W	L	2	1	1	0	2	0	2	0
Middlesbrough	D	D	2	0	2	0	1	1	2	0
Hull	L	L	1	0	0	1	0	1	0	0
Leicester	W	D	3	2	0	1	1	2	1	2
Brighton	L	L	3	0	1	2	2	1	1	1
Watford	D	L	2	1	1	0	2	0	2	0
Derby	W	D	2	1	0	1	2	0	1	0
Burnley	W	D	1	1	0	0	1	0	1	0
Leeds	L	L	2	1	0	1	1	1	1	1
Ipswich	W	L	2	2	0	0	2	0	2	0
Millwall	L	D	2	1	0	1	1	1	0	1
Crystal Palace	W	L	2	1	1	0	1	1	2	0
Peterborough										
Nottm Forest	L	W	2	0	0	2	1	1	1	0
Bristol City	W	W	2	1	0	1	1	1	0	1
Barnsley	L	L	2	0	0	2	2	0	2	0
Charlton	-	-	1	0	0	1	1	0	1	0
Sheffield Weds	-	-	2	1	1	0	1	1	2	0
Huddersfield	-	-	2	2	0	0	2	0	1	1

Season	Division	Pos	P	W	D	L	F	A	GD	Pts
2011-12	Champ	18	46	13	11	22	67	77	-10	50
2010-11	League 1	4	46	23	10	13	106	75	31	79
2009-10	Champ	24	46	8	10	28	46	80	-34	34

Sheff Weds

Nickname: The Owls
Colours: Blue and White
Ground: Hillsborough (39,812)
Tel: 0871-995-1867   www.swfc.co.uk

FIRST Norwich, then Southampton, now Sheffield Wednesday? The Owls hope to make it three successive seasons in which a former top-flight side has won successive promotions to bounce back from the third tier to the Premier League.

They have plenty in their favour. Milan Mandaric has a proven track record in rousing the Football League's sleeping giants and manager Dave Jones has yet to make a false step, winning ten and drawing three of his 13 games in charge.

Longest run without loss/win: 14/3
High – low league position 2-9
Clean sheets: 16 **Yellow cards:** 76 **Red cards:** 2
Average attendance: 21,336 **Players used:** 34
Leading Scorer: G Madine 18 (4,14)
Key stat: Of the five clubs he's managed, Jones has won promotion with Wednesday, Wolves and Stockport and twice took Cardiff to the play-offs

	11-12 H	A	P	W	D	L	OV	UN	BS	CS
Bolton	-	-	0	0	0	0	0	0	0	0
Blackburn	-	-	0	0	0	0	0	0	0	0
Wolves	-	-	3	0	1	2	2	1	2	0
Birmingham	-	-	2	0	1	1	1	1	1	0
Blackpool	-	-	3	2	1	0	1	2	2	1
Cardiff	-	-	4	3	1	0	1	3	1	3
Middlesbrough	-	-	1	0	0	1	1	0	1	0
Hull	-	-	2	1	0	1	1	1	1	1
Leicester	-	-	3	2	0	1	1	2	1	1
Brighton	-	-	1	1	0	0	0	1	0	1
Watford	-	-	3	2	0	1	1	2	1	1
Derby	-	-	3	0	1	2	1	2	1	1
Burnley	-	-	3	1	1	1	1	2	2	0
Leeds	-	-	1	0	0	1	0	1	0	0
Ipswich	-	-	4	1	1	2	1	3	1	2
Millwall	-	-	0	0	0	0	0	0	0	0
Crystal Palace	-	-	4	2	2	0	3	1	3	1
Peterborough	-	-	2	1	0	1	2	0	2	0
Nottm Forest	-	-	2	1	1	0	0	2	1	1
Bristol City	-	-	3	0	1	2	0	3	0	1
Barnsley	-	-	4	2	1	1	2	2	2	1
Charlton	L	D	4	1	2	1	2	2	2	1
Sheffield Weds										
Huddersfield	D	W	2	0	1	1	1	1	1	0

Season	Division	Pos	P	W	D	L	F	A	GD	Pts
2011-12	League 1	2	46	28	9	9	81	48	33	93
2010-11	League 1	15	46	16	10	20	67	67	0	58
2009-10	Champ	22	46	11	14	21	49	69	-20	47

Watford

Nickname: The Hornets
Colours: Yellow and Red
Ground: Vicarage Road (17,477)
Tel: 0844-856-1881   www.watfordfc.co.uk

THINGS looked bleak for Watford last term as they finished 2010-11 in poor form, lost manager Malky Mackay and sold star duo Danny Graham and Will Buckley.

However, following a slow start, the Hornets again proved greater than the sum of their parts, even flirting with the play-offs.

Things are even brighter following a takeover by the Pozzo family. Replacing Sean Dyche with Gianfranco Zola will ruffle feathers but the Pozzos have a proven track record of success in club ownership.

Longest run without loss/win: 8/5
High – low league position 11-22
Clean sheets: 10 **Yellow cards:** 69 **Red cards:** 3
Average attendance: 12,704 **Players used:** 32
Leading Scorer: T Deeney 11 (2,11)
Key stat: Following a slow bedding-in period for Dyche, Watford averaged 1.64 points per game from October 29 onwards – play-off form

	11-12 H A	Last six seasons at home P	W	D	L	OV	UN	BS	CS
Bolton	- -	1	0	0	1	0	1	0	0
Blackburn	- -	1	1	0	0	1	0	1	0
Wolves	- -	2	1	0	1	2	0	1	1
Birmingham	D L	2	0	1	1	1	1	1	0
Blackpool	L D	4	0	2	2	2	2	3	0
Cardiff	D D	5	1	3	1	4	1	4	0
Middlesbrough	W L	4	3	1	0	2	2	3	1
Hull	D L	3	1	1	1	1	2	2	1
Leicester	W L	4	3	1	0	3	1	3	1
Brighton	W D	1	1	0	0	0	1	0	1
Watford									
Derby	L W	4	2	0	2	2	2	1	1
Burnley	W D	4	2	0	2	4	0	3	1
Leeds	D W	2	0	1	1	0	2	1	0
Ipswich	W W	5	5	0	0	4	1	4	1
Millwall	W W	2	2	0	0	1	1	1	1
Crystal Palace	L L	5	1	1	3	1	4	2	1
Peterborough	W D	2	1	0	1	1	1	1	0
Nottm Forest	L D	4	1	2	1	1	3	2	1
Bristol City	D W	5	1	1	3	4	1	4	1
Barnsley	W D	5	3	1	1	2	3	2	2
Charlton	- -	3	1	2	0	1	2	2	1
Sheffield Weds	- -	3	2	1	0	3	0	3	0
Huddersfield	- -	0	0	0	0	0	0	0	0

Season	Division	Pos	P	W	D	L	F	A	GD	Pts
2011-12	Champ	11	46	16	16	14	56	64	-8	64
2010-11	Champ	14	46	16	13	17	77	71	6	61
2009-10	Champ	16	46	14	12	20	61	68	-7	54

Wolves

Nickname: Wolves
Colours: Gold and Black
Ground: Molineux (27,828)
Tel: 0871-222-2220   www.wolves.co.uk

THERE were very few positives to take out of 2011-12, with the team underperforming, the suits making a hash of sacking Mick McCarthy and Terry Connor not even coming close to saving his beloved side.

The start of the off-season showed more promise though, as Stale Solbakken looks a neat appointment. The Norwegian may need a season to settle in his first managerial position in Britain but, while he struggled at Cologne, an excellent record at Copenhagen deserves respect.

Longest run without loss/win: 3/14
High – low league position 13-20
Clean sheets: 4 **Yellow cards:** 65 **Red cards:** 4
Average attendance: 25,682 **Players used:** 32
Leading Scorer: S Fletcher 12 (1,11)
Key stat: Solbakken won five Danish titles in six years with Copenhagen and got them to the last 16 of the Champions League in 2010-11

	11-12 H A	Last six seasons at home P	W	D	L	OV	UN	BS	CS
Bolton	L D	3	1	0	2	3	0	3	0
Blackburn	L W	3	0	1	2	1	2	2	0
Wolves									
Birmingham	- -	4	1	1	2	1	3	2	1
Blackpool	- -	3	3	0	0	2	1	1	2
Cardiff	- -	3	1	1	1	3	0	2	1
Middlesbrough	- -	0	0	0	0	0	0	0	0
Hull	- -	3	1	1	1	1	2	2	0
Leicester	- -	2	0	1	1	1	1	2	0
Brighton	- -	0	0	0	0	0	0	0	0
Watford	- -	2	1	0	1	2	0	2	0
Derby	- -	2	1	0	1	1	1	0	1
Burnley	- -	4	3	0	1	2	2	2	2
Leeds	- -	1	1	0	0	0	1	0	1
Ipswich	- -	3	1	2	0	0	3	1	2
Millwall	- -	0	0	0	0	0	0	0	0
Crystal Palace	- -	3	1	1	1	2	1	2	0
Peterborough	- -	0	0	0	0	0	0	0	0
Nottm Forest	- -	1	1	0	0	1	0	1	0
Bristol City	- -	2	1	1	0	0	2	1	1
Barnsley	- -	3	3	0	0	0	3	0	3
Charlton	- -	2	2	0	0	1	1	1	1
Sheffield Weds	- -	3	2	1	0	3	0	3	0
Huddersfield	- -	0	0	0	0	0	0	0	0

Season	Division	Pos	P	W	D	L	F	A	GD	Pts
2011-12	Prem	20	38	5	10	23	40	82	-42	25
2010-11	Prem	17	38	11	7	20	46	66	-20	40
2009-10	Prem	15	38	9	11	18	32	56	-24	38

SOUTHAMPTON: blasted their way back to the top flight thanks to 85-goal haul

Top scorers 2011-12		P	W	D	L	F	GFA	PGA	Pts
1	Southampton (2)	46	26	10	10	85	1.85	1.9	88
2	West Ham (3)	46	24	14	8	81	1.76	1.9	86
3	Blackpool (5)	46	20	15	11	79	1.72	1.6	75
4	Birmingham (4)	46	20	16	10	78	1.70	1.7	76
5	Reading (1)	46	27	8	11	69	1.50	1.9	89
6	Ipswich (15)	46	17	10	19	69	1.50	1.3	61
7	Peterborough (18)	46	13	11	22	67	1.46	1.1	50
8	Cardiff (6)	46	19	18	9	66	1.43	1.6	75
9	Leicester (9)	46	18	12	16	66	1.43	1.4	66
10	Leeds (14)	46	17	10	19	65	1.41	1.3	61
11	Burnley (13)	46	17	11	18	61	1.33	1.3	62
12	Watford (11)	46	16	16	14	56	1.22	1.4	64
13	Millwall (16)	46	15	12	19	55	1.20	1.2	57
14	Middlesbro (7)	46	18	16	12	52	1.13	1.5	70
15	Brighton (10)	46	17	15	14	52	1.13	1.4	66
16	Derby (12)	46	18	10	18	50	1.09	1.4	64
17	Portsmouth (22)	46	13	11	22	50	1.09	1.1	50
18	Barnsley (21)	46	13	9	24	49	1.07	1.0	48
19	Nottm Forest (19)	46	14	8	24	48	1.04	1.1	50
20	Hull (8)	46	19	11	16	47	1.02	1.5	68
21	C Palace (17)	46	13	17	16	46	1.00	1.2	56
22	Bristol C (20)	46	12	13	21	44	0.96	1.1	49
23	Doncaster (24)	46	8	12	26	43	0.93	0.8	36
24	Coventry (23)	46	9	13	24	41	0.89	0.9	40

Best defence 2011-12		P	W	D	L	F	GAA	PGA	Pts
1	Reading (1)	46	27	8	11	41	0.89	1.9	89
2	Hull (8)	46	19	11	16	44	0.96	1.5	68
3	Southampton (2)	46	26	10	10	46	1.00	1.9	88
4	West Ham (3)	46	24	14	8	48	1.04	1.9	86
5	Birmingham (4)	46	20	16	10	51	1.11	1.7	76
6	Middlesbro (7)	46	18	16	12	51	1.11	1.5	70
7	C Palace (17)	46	13	17	16	51	1.11	1.2	56
8	Brighton (10)	46	17	15	14	52	1.13	1.4	66
9	Cardiff (6)	46	19	18	9	53	1.15	1.6	75
10	Leicester (9)	46	18	12	16	55	1.20	1.4	66
11	Millwall (16)	46	15	12	19	57	1.24	1.2	57
12	Derby (12)	46	18	10	18	58	1.26	1.4	64
13	Burnley (13)	46	17	11	18	58	1.26	1.3	62
14	Blackpool (5)	46	20	15	11	59	1.28	1.6	75
15	Portsmouth (22)	46	13	11	22	59	1.28	1.1	50
16	Nottm Forest (19)	46	14	8	24	63	1.37	1.1	50
17	Watford (11)	46	16	16	14	64	1.39	1.4	64
18	Coventry (23)	46	9	13	24	65	1.41	0.9	40
19	Leeds (14)	46	17	10	19	68	1.48	1.3	61
20	Bristol C (20)	46	12	13	21	68	1.48	1.1	49
21	Barnsley (21)	46	13	9	24	74	1.61	1.0	48
22	Ipswich (15)	46	17	10	19	77	1.67	1.3	61
23	Peterborough (18)	46	13	11	22	77	1.67	1.1	50
24	Doncaster (24)	46	8	12	26	80	1.74	0.8	36

Clean sheets 2011-12

		P	CS	%
1	Reading (1)	46	20	43.5
2	Hull (8)	46	18	39.1
3	Southampton (2)	46	18	39.1
4	West Ham (3)	46	17	37.0
5	C Palace (17)	46	17	37.0
6	Brighton (10)	46	16	34.8
7	Millwall (16)	46	16	34.8
8	Cardiff (6)	46	15	32.6
9	Middlesbro (7)	46	15	32.6
10	Birmingham (4)	46	14	30.4
11	Leicester (9)	46	14	30.4
12	Blackpool (5)	46	13	28.3
13	Derby (12)	46	12	26.1
14	Burnley (13)	46	12	26.1
15	Ipswich (15)	46	12	26.1
16	Portsmouth (22)	46	12	26.1
17	Nottm Forest (19)	46	12	26.1
18	Leeds (14)	46	10	21.7
19	Watford (11)	46	10	21.7
20	Coventry (23)	46	9	19.6
21	Bristol C (20)	46	9	19.6
22	Barnsley (21)	46	8	17.4
23	Doncaster (24)	46	8	17.4
24	Peterborough (18)	46	4	8.7

First to score 2011-12

		P	FS	%
1	Cardiff (6)	46	29	63.0
2	Birmingham (4)	46	29	63.0
3	Southampton (2)	46	28	60.9
4	West Ham (3)	46	26	56.5
5	Middlesbro (7)	46	25	54.3
6	Hull (8)	46	24	52.2
7	Reading (1)	46	24	52.2
8	Burnley (13)	46	23	50.0
9	Brighton (10)	46	22	47.8
10	C Palace (17)	46	22	47.8
11	Millwall (16)	46	22	47.8
12	Ipswich (15)	46	21	45.7
13	Leicester (9)	46	21	45.7
14	Derby (12)	46	20	43.5
15	Barnsley (21)	46	19	41.3
16	Blackpool (5)	46	19	41.3
17	Bristol C (20)	46	19	41.3
18	Nottm Forest (19)	46	19	41.3
19	Leeds (14)	46	18	39.1
20	Watford (11)	46	18	39.1
21	Coventry (23)	46	18	39.1
22	Doncaster (24)	46	15	32.6
23	Portsmouth (22)	46	15	32.6
24	Peterborough (18)	46	15	32.6

Top scorers 2011-12

		Goals
R Lambert	Southampton	27
R Vaz Te	West Ham	20
B Sharp	Southampton	19
R McCormack	Leeds	18
C Austin	Burnley	16
M Fryatt	Hull	16
M King	Birmingham	16
K Phillips	Blackpool	16
D Henderson	Millwall	15
D Nugent	Leicester	15
J Rodriguez	Burnley	15
M Chopra	Ipswich	14
C Cole	West Ham	14
M Emnes	Middlesbro	14
C Burke	Birmingham	13
R Snodgrass	Leeds	13
S Davies	Derby	12
A Keogh	Millwall	12
A Le Fondre	Reading	12
K Nolan	West Ham	12

Record when keeping a clean sheet 2011-12

		P	W	D	L	F	GFA	PGA	Pts
1	Peterborough (18)	4	4	0	0	6	1.50	3.0	12
2	Southampton (2)	18	17	1	0	40	2.22	2.9	52
3	Reading (1)	20	18	2	0	30	1.50	2.8	56
4	Blackpool (5)	13	11	2	0	28	2.15	2.7	35
5	Ipswich (15)	12	10	2	0	18	1.50	2.7	32
6	West Ham (3)	17	14	3	0	32	1.88	2.6	45
7	Birmingham (4)	14	11	3	0	27	1.93	2.6	36
8	Leeds (14)	10	8	2	0	17	1.70	2.6	26
9	Coventry (23)	9	7	2	0	11	1.22	2.6	23
10	Brighton (10)	16	12	4	0	21	1.31	2.5	40
11	Derby (12)	12	9	3	0	14	1.17	2.5	30
12	Burnley (13)	12	9	3	0	17	1.42	2.5	30
13	Leicester (9)	14	10	4	0	22	1.57	2.4	34
14	Hull (8)	18	12	6	0	18	1.00	2.3	42
15	C Palace (17)	17	11	6	0	16	0.94	2.3	39
16	Millwall (16)	16	10	6	0	22	1.38	2.3	36
17	Cardiff (6)	15	10	5	0	16	1.07	2.3	35
18	Middlesbro (7)	15	10	5	0	13	0.87	2.3	35
19	Portsmouth (22)	12	8	4	0	15	1.25	2.3	28
20	Nottm Forest (19)	12	8	4	0	13	1.08	2.3	28
21	Barnsley (21)	8	5	3	0	9	1.13	2.3	18
22	Watford (11)	10	6	4	0	11	1.10	2.2	22
23	Bristol C (20)	9	5	4	0	7	0.78	2.1	19
24	Doncaster (24)	8	4	4	0	6	0.75	2.0	16

Record when first to score 2011-12

		P	W	D	L	F	GFA	PGA	Pts
1	Reading (1)	24	22	1	1	43	8	2.8	67
2	Southampton (2)	28	23	4	1	69	18	2.6	73
3	West Ham (3)	26	19	5	2	54	18	2.4	62
4	Portsmouth (22)	15	11	3	1	28	10	2.4	36
5	Leicester (9)	21	15	3	3	43	18	2.3	48
6	Derby (12)	20	14	4	2	34	17	2.3	46
7	Blackpool (5)	19	13	5	1	43	13	2.3	44
8	Barnsley (21)	19	13	4	2	38	23	2.3	43
9	Middlesbro (7)	25	15	9	1	39	19	2.2	54
10	Brighton (10)	22	15	4	3	36	17	2.2	49
11	Millwall (16)	22	15	4	3	47	20	2.2	49
12	Watford (11)	18	11	7	0	35	18	2.2	40
13	Leeds (14)	18	12	3	3	39	24	2.2	39
14	Cardiff (6)	29	17	9	3	52	31	2.1	60
15	Burnley (13)	23	14	6	3	45	19	2.1	48
16	Nottm Forest (19)	19	12	2	5	31	20	2.0	38
17	Birmingham (4)	29	16	8	5	58	32	1.9	56
18	Hull (8)	24	14	4	6	32	22	1.9	46
19	Ipswich (15)	21	13	1	7	39	30	1.9	40
20	Bristol C (20)	19	11	3	5	30	22	1.9	36
21	Peterborough (18)	15	8	4	3	26	20	1.9	28
22	C Palace (17)	22	10	9	3	30	18	1.8	39
23	Coventry (23)	18	8	4	6	24	20	1.6	28
24	Doncaster (24)	15	6	2	7	23	24	1.3	20

Key *Number in brackets refers to final league finishing position. Points do not include any deductions but league positions do. GFA: Goals for average per match, GAA: Goals against average per match, PGA: Average points gained per match, CS: clean sheet, FS: first to score*

Don't bank on Blades to bounce back up

IT was inevitable that Sheffield United would head the betting as soon as Steve Simonsen missed his penalty in that amazing shootout against Huddersfield in May, *writes Dylan Hill.*

No team in the last 20 years has reached 90 points in the third tier without going up and the division looks weaker without Charlton, Sheffield Wednesday and Huddersfield this season.

However, there are sound reasons to oppose Danny Wilson's side.

Most obvious is the end-of-season slump after Ched Evans was jailed. Evans struck 35 goals in 42 games and without him United won just one of their last six matches, scoring five goals.

Defeat at Wembley could take its toll too. Huddersfield were the first team in eight seasons from the bottom two divisions to lose a play-off final and win promotion the next year. Even then last season's ante-post title favourites took six points fewer.

Wilson will be aware of that impact – he led Swindon to the play-off final in 2010 and they went down the following year, a month after he'd left – and that shows a worrying trend of struggling to maintain initial success at Sheffield Wednesday, MK Dons and Hartlepool.

History suggests that if a relegated team fails to come straight back up it's harder the second time around, as 15 teams have spent a second season in League 1 after relegation in the last seven years and nine gained fewer points.

Finally, League 1 is never as easy for big clubs as the market thinks – no outright favourite has won for 18 years.

The best title bet are **MK Dons**, who took 80 points last year, despite going off the boil when automatic promotion was beyond them.

The Dons are heading in the right direction under Karl Robinson. They took just three more points than in Robinson's first year but improved their previously suspect away form and upped their goal difference by 30.

Coventry could benefit from some stability and look best of the relegated clubs, with striker **Cody McDonald** a decent bet to be leading goalscorer. McDonald looked ready for this level two years ago when banging in 25 goals for Gillingham and should benefit from a clearer run with injuries in his second campaign at the Ricoh Arena.

Doncaster may be worth backing to be relegated. Only two Championship teams in seven seasons have gone down with such a measly haul and one of those was at least partly down to a ten-point deduction.

League 1 winner						
	b365	Btfrd	Hills	Lads	Pwr	StJms
Sheffield Utd	11-2	6	6	6	6	11-2
MK Dons	9	8	7	9	9	9
Swindon	9	10	8	10	10	8
Coventry	12	11	12	10	11	12
Preston	11	10	12	12	10	10
Doncaster	14	14	12	12	11	14
Bournemouth	11	14	16	14	11	14
Brentford	12	14	14	16	16	16
Notts County	14	16	9	12	16	14
Crawley	16	16	12	14	16	14
Portsmouth	20	16	9	12	14	20
Stevenage	25	20	20	16	20	20
Carlisle	28	25	25	18	25	20
Colchester	33	28	33	28	33	33
Scunthorpe	28	25	33	33	33	33
Tranmere	40	33	25	25	33	25
Crewe	50	50	33	40	40	33
Shrewsbury	50	33	33	33	25	33
Hartlepool	50	40	66	40	66	25
Oldham	66	50	66	40	40	40
Bury	66	66	80	50	80	66
Leyton Orient	66	50	80	50	66	50
Yeovil	66	66	80	50	66	50
Walsall	100	50	100	66	66	66

Win or each-way. See individual bookmakers for terms

Bournemouth

Nickname: The Cherries
Colours: Red and Black
Ground: Seward Stadium (9,776)
Tel: 01202-726-300   www.afcb.co.uk

THINGS finally look rosy for the Cherries financially but there were still some worrying developments off the pitch.

Their Russian investor's wife gave a half-time team talk while chairman Eddie Mitchell gave an X-rated rant on national radio and banned the local newspaper.

Bournemouth won just three of their last 17 matches, during which time the unlucky Lee Bradbury was sacked. Paul Groves stepped up from within but may find it tough to make his mark.

Longest run without loss/win: 6/7
High – low league position 8-23
Clean sheets: 14 **Yellow cards:** 54 **Red cards:** 1
Average attendance: 5,881 **Players used:** 39
Leading Scorer: W Thomas 11 (4,10)
Key stat: Bournemouth scored more than two goals in just three matches

	11-12 H A	Last six seasons at home P	W	D	L	OV	UN	BS	CS
Portsmouth	- -	0	0	0	0	0	0	0	0
Coventry	- -	0	0	0	0	0	0	0	0
Doncaster	- -	2	1	0	1	0	2	0	1
Sheffield United	L L	1	0	0	1	0	1	0	0
MK Dons	L D	2	1	0	1	1	1	1	0
Stevenage	L D	1	0	0	1	0	1	0	0
Notts County	W L	4	2	1	1	3	1	3	0
Carlisle	D L	4	1	1	2	1	3	2	1
Brentford	W D	4	3	0	1	1	3	1	2
Colchester	D D	2	0	1	1	1	1	2	0
Bournemouth									
Tranmere	W D	4	3	0	1	3	1	3	1
Hartlepool	L D	3	1	0	2	1	2	1	1
Bury	L L	3	1	0	2	2	1	2	1
Preston	W W	1	1	0	0	0	1	0	1
Oldham	D L	4	2	1	1	3	1	1	2
Yeovil	D W	4	2	1	1	0	4	0	3
Scunthorpe	W D	2	1	1	0	0	2	1	1
Walsall	L D	3	1	1	1	1	2	1	1
Leyton Orient	L W	4	2	1	1	3	1	3	1
Swindon	- -	2	1	1	0	2	0	2	0
Shrewsbury	- -	2	2	0	0	0	2	0	2
Crawley	- -	0	0	0	0	0	0	0	0
Crewe	- -	3	3	0	0	0	3	0	3

Season	Division	Pos	P	W	D	L	F	A	GD	Pts
2011-12	League 1	11	46	15	13	18	48	52	-4	58
2010-11	League 1	6	46	19	14	13	75	54	21	71
2009-10	League 2	2	46	25	8	13	61	44	17	83

Brentford

Nickname: The Bees
Colours: Red, White and Black
Ground: Griffin Park (12,763)
Tel: 0845-3456-442   www.brentfordfc.co.uk

THE BEES have been a progressive club for many years, assembling a high-quality squad under Andy Scott, who was desperately unfortunate to get the sack in 2011, and Uwe Rosler managed to continue that progress last season.

The German led Brentford to ninth and did a superb job at beating those below them. He has clearly acquired some good contacts during his time abroad and is capable of mending Brentford's weaknesses against the better teams in the division.

Longest run without loss/win: 7/7
High – low league position 4-10
Clean sheets: 16 **Yellow cards:** 62 **Red cards:** 1
Average attendance: 5,643 **Players used:** 36
Leading Scorer: G Alexander 12 (5,8)
Key stat: Brentford won just twice against top-half opposition last term

	11-12 H A	Last six seasons at home P	W	D	L	OV	UN	BS	CS
Portsmouth	- -	0	0	0	0	0	0	0	0
Coventry	- -	0	0	0	0	0	0	0	0
Doncaster	- -	1	0	0	1	1	0	0	0
Sheffield United	L L	1	0	0	1	0	1	0	0
MK Dons	D W	4	0	2	2	3	1	2	0
Stevenage	L L	1	0	0	1	0	1	0	0
Notts County	D D	4	0	4	0	0	4	2	2
Carlisle	W D	4	3	1	0	3	1	2	2
Brentford									
Colchester	D L	3	1	2	0	0	3	2	1
Bournemouth	D L	4	1	3	0	0	4	2	2
Tranmere	L D	4	2	1	1	2	2	3	0
Hartlepool	W D	3	1	2	0	1	2	1	2
Bury	W D	3	2	0	1	2	1	1	2
Preston	L W	1	0	0	1	1	0	1	0
Oldham	W W	4	1	2	1	2	2	3	1
Yeovil	W L	4	1	1	2	2	2	3	1
Scunthorpe	D D	2	0	1	1	0	2	0	1
Walsall	D W	3	0	2	1	1	2	2	1
Leyton Orient	W L	4	3	1	0	3	1	2	2
Swindon	- -	2	0	0	2	1	1	1	0
Shrewsbury	- -	2	0	2	0	0	2	2	0
Crawley	- -	0	0	0	0	0	0	0	0
Crewe	- -	1	0	0	1	1	0	0	0

Season	Division	Pos	P	W	D	L	F	A	GD	Pts
2011-12	League 1	9	46	18	13	15	63	52	11	67
2010-11	League 1	11	46	17	10	19	55	62	-7	61
2009-10	League 1	9	46	14	20	12	55	52	3	62

Bury

Nickname: The Shakers
Colours: White and Blue
Ground: Gigg Lane (11,313)
Tel: 01284-754-721   www.buryfc.co.uk

WITH the exception of Stevenage, last season's promoted clubs found life extremely tough in League 1 and Bury were the only other team to survive.

However, they took some real hammerings along the way – only two clubs outside the relegation zone had a worse goal difference – and it's a big worry that 47 goals were conceded on the road.

They were perhaps flattered by a mid-table finish and Bury boss Richard Barker will just be looking to stay up again.

Longest run without loss/win: 4/13
High – low league position 10-22
Clean sheets: 9 **Yellow cards:** 62 **Red cards:** 5
Average attendance: 3,552 **Players used:** 31
Leading Scorer: A Bishop 8 (3,7)
Key stat: Last season Bury lost a whopping ten matches by three goals or more

	11-12		Last six seasons at home							
	H	A	P	W	D	L	OV	UN	BS	CS
Portsmouth	-	-	0	0	0	0	0	0	0	0
Coventry	-	-	0	0	0	0	0	0	0	0
Doncaster	-	-	0	0	0	0	0	0	0	0
Sheffield United	L	L	1	0	0	1	1	0	0	0
MK Dons	D	L	3	0	1	2	1	2	1	1
Stevenage	L	L	2	1	0	1	2	0	1	1
Notts County	D	W	5	2	2	1	3	2	3	1
Carlisle	L	L	1	0	0	1	0	1	0	0
Brentford	D	L	3	1	1	1	1	2	2	1
Colchester	W	L	1	1	0	0	1	0	1	0
Bournemouth	W	W	3	2	0	1	1	2	0	2
Tranmere	W	L	1	1	0	0	0	1	0	1
Hartlepool	L	L	2	0	0	2	1	1	1	0
Bury										
Preston	W	D	1	1	0	0	0	1	0	1
Oldham	D	W	1	0	1	0	0	1	0	1
Yeovil	W	W	1	1	0	0	1	0	1	0
Scunthorpe	D	W	1	0	1	0	0	1	0	1
Walsall	W	W	2	1	0	1	2	0	2	0
Leyton Orient	D	L	1	0	1	0	0	1	1	0
Swindon	-	-	1	0	0	1	0	1	0	0
Shrewsbury	-	-	5	3	1	1	2	3	3	2
Crawley	-	-	0	0	0	0	0	0	0	0
Crewe	-	-	2	2	0	0	2	0	1	1

Season	Division	Pos	P	W	D	L	F	A	GD	Pts
2011-12	League 1	14	46	15	11	20	60	79	-19	56
2010-11	League 2	2	46	23	12	11	82	50	32	81
2009-10	League 2	9	46	19	12	15	54	59	-5	69

Carlisle

Nickname: Cumbrians/The Blues
Colours: Blue, White and Red
Ground: Brunton Park (17,902)
Tel: 01228-526-237   www.carlisleunited.co.uk

THE CUMBRIANS were in the hunt for a play-off place for most of the 2011-12 campaign, eventually finishing eighth, but they would do very well to achieve such a good position again.

Opposing clubs whose goal difference was much worse than the clubs around them has proved very fruitful in recent seasons – Bristol Rovers and Exeter went down in the last two seasons against that backdrop – and a negative goal difference points to Carlisle slipping down the table.

Longest run without loss/win: 9/5
High – low league position 6-13
Clean sheets: 9 **Yellow cards:** 68 **Red cards:** 2
Average attendance: 5,247 **Players used:** 26
Leading Scorer: L Miller 14 (5,12)
Key stat: Only Rochdale led fewer League 1 matches at the break last season than the Cumbrians

	11-12		Last six seasons at home							
	H	A	P	W	D	L	OV	UN	BS	CS
Portsmouth	-	-	0	0	0	0	0	0	0	0
Coventry	-	-	0	0	0	0	0	0	0	0
Doncaster	-	-	2	2	0	0	0	2	0	2
Sheffield United	W	L	1	1	0	0	1	0	1	0
MK Dons	L	W	4	3	0	1	4	0	3	1
Stevenage	W	L	1	1	0	0	0	1	0	1
Notts County	L	L	2	1	0	1	1	1	0	1
Carlisle										
Brentford	D	L	4	2	1	1	2	2	2	2
Colchester	W	D	4	3	0	1	2	2	2	1
Bournemouth	W	D	4	3	1	0	2	2	3	1
Tranmere	D	W	6	3	1	2	2	4	1	4
Hartlepool	L	L	5	3	0	2	3	2	3	1
Bury	W	W	1	1	0	0	1	0	1	0
Preston	D	D	1	0	1	0	0	1	0	1
Oldham	D	L	6	1	4	1	3	3	5	1
Yeovil	W	W	6	4	0	2	4	2	4	1
Scunthorpe	D	W	3	0	2	1	0	3	1	1
Walsall	D	D	5	1	3	1	2	3	5	0
Leyton Orient	W	W	6	3	1	2	4	2	4	1
Swindon	-	-	4	1	2	1	1	3	1	2
Shrewsbury	-	-	0	0	0	0	0	0	0	0
Crawley	-	-	0	0	0	0	0	0	0	0
Crewe	-	-	3	2	0	1	1	2	1	1

Season	Division	Pos	P	W	D	L	F	A	GD	Pts
2011-12	League 1	8	46	18	15	13	65	66	-1	69
2010-11	League 1	12	46	16	11	19	60	62	-2	59
2009-10	League 1	14	46	15	13	18	63	66	-3	58

Colchester

Nickname: The U's
Colours: Blue and White
Ground: Weston Homes Community Stadium (10,105)
Tel: 01206-755-100   www.cu-fc.com

COLCHESTER did well to secure another mid-table finish last season after chairman Robbie Cowling had warned of major budget cuts in the summer.

However, that lack of ambition hasn't gone down well with fans who were unreasonably harsh in jeering John Ward for winning just eight home matches.

It didn't help that the goals dried up – the U's went 11 matches without scoring more than once in a game until banging in four in their final home match.

Longest run without loss/win: 9/11
High – low league position 9-16
Clean sheets: 11 **Yellow cards:** 70 **Red cards:** 2
Average attendance: 3,865 **Players used:** 26
Leading Scorer: A Wordsworth 13 (9,12)
Key stat: Despite the late-season goal drought, Colchester scored four goals or more on five occasions during 2011-12

	11-12 H A	Last six seasons at home P	W	D	L	OV	UN	BS	CS
Portsmouth	- -	0	0	0	0	0	0	0	0
Coventry	- -	2	0	1	1	1	1	1	1
Doncaster	- -	0	0	0	0	0	0	0	0
Sheffield United	D L	2	0	2	0	1	1	2	0
MK Dons	L L	4	1	0	3	3	1	2	1
Stevenage	L D	1	0	0	1	1	0	1	0
Notts County	W L	2	2	0	0	2	0	2	0
Carlisle	D L	4	2	2	0	2	2	3	1
Brentford	W D	3	1	1	1	2	1	2	0
Colchester									
Bournemouth	D D	2	1	1	0	1	1	2	0
Tranmere	W D	4	2	1	1	2	2	3	0
Hartlepool	D W	4	2	2	0	1	3	3	1
Bury	W L	1	1	0	0	1	0	1	0
Preston	W W	3	3	0	0	2	1	1	2
Oldham	W D	4	3	1	0	2	2	2	2
Yeovil	D L	4	2	2	0	2	2	2	2
Scunthorpe	D D	3	0	2	1	0	3	1	1
Walsall	W L	4	3	0	1	1	3	1	2
Leyton Orient	D W	4	3	1	0	1	3	2	2
Swindon	- -	3	3	0	0	3	0	2	1
Shrewsbury	- -	0	0	0	0	0	0	0	0
Crawley	- -	0	0	0	0	0	0	0	0
Crewe	- -	1	0	0	1	0	1	0	0

Season	Division	Pos	P	W	D	L	F	A	GD	Pts
2011-12	League 1	10	46	13	20	13	61	66	-5	59
2010-11	League 1	10	46	16	14	16	57	63	-6	62
2009-10	League 1	8	46	20	12	14	64	52	12	72

Coventry

Nickname: The Sky Blues
Colours: Sky Blue
Ground: Ricoh Arena (32,604)
Tel: 0844-873-1883   www.ccfc.co.uk

THERE was something painfully pre-dictable about Coventry's relegation last term, as it followed season upon season of mediocrity in the Championship.

The only miracle was that boss Andy Thorn remained at the helm given that when he took over in March 2011, he had become the club's ninth permanent manager since Gordon Strachan left in 2001.

Constant upheaval wasn't helping but given their financial situation, it's hard to see the Sky Blues in the promotion mix.

Longest run without loss/win: 7/11
High – low league position 19-24
Clean sheets: 9 **Yellow cards:** 58 **Red cards:** 3
Average attendance: 14,684 **Players used:** 31
Leading Scorer: L Jutkiewicz 9 (3,9)
Key stat: Coventry won just two matches in which the opposition scored in last season's Championship

	11-12 H A	Last six seasons at home P	W	D	L	OV	UN	BS	CS
Portsmouth	W L	2	2	0	0	0	2	0	2
Coventry									
Doncaster	L D	4	3	0	1	1	3	1	2
Sheffield United	- -	4	1	1	2	2	2	2	1
MK Dons	- -	0	0	0	0	0	0	0	0
Stevenage	- -	0	0	0	0	0	0	0	0
Notts County	- -	0	0	0	0	0	0	0	0
Carlisle	- -	0	0	0	0	0	0	0	0
Brentford	- -	0	0	0	0	0	0	0	0
Colchester	- -	2	2	0	0	1	1	1	1
Bournemouth	- -	0	0	0	0	0	0	0	0
Tranmere	- -	0	0	0	0	0	0	0	0
Hartlepool	- -	0	0	0	0	0	0	0	0
Bury	- -	0	0	0	0	0	0	0	0
Preston	- -	5	1	2	2	3	2	3	1
Oldham	- -	0	0	0	0	0	0	0	0
Yeovil	- -	0	0	0	0	0	0	0	0
Scunthorpe	- -	3	1	2	0	1	2	3	0
Walsall	- -	0	0	0	0	0	0	0	0
Leyton Orient	- -	0	0	0	0	0	0	0	0
Swindon	- -	0	0	0	0	0	0	0	0
Shrewsbury	- -	0	0	0	0	0	0	0	0
Crawley	- -	0	0	0	0	0	0	0	0
Crewe	- -	0	0	0	0	0	0	0	0

Season	Division	Pos	P	W	D	L	F	A	GD	Pts
2011-12	Champ	23	46	9	13	24	41	65	-24	40
2010-11	Champ	18	46	14	13	19	54	58	-4	55
2009-10	Champ	19	46	13	15	18	47	64	-17	54

Crawley

Nickname: The Red Devils
Colours: Red
Ground: Broadfield Stadium (4,718)
Tel: 01293-410-000   www.crawleytownfc.com

FINANCIAL muscle saw Crawley bully their way to a second successive promotion last season and although they found it tough to finish the job, that was understandable after an outstanding FA Cup run had led to a major fixture backlog.

It's more worrying that a club with such clout allowed the prolific Matt Tubbs to join Bournemouth, then saw manager Steve Evans effectively drop a division to join Rotherham. Sean O'Driscoll looks a good appointment to replace him, however.

Longest run without loss/win: 13/7
High – low league position 1-6
Clean sheets: 13 **Yellow cards:** 62 **Red cards:** 4
Average attendance: 3,257 **Players used:** 35
Leading Scorer: T Barnett 14 (6,10)
Key stat: Crawley gained 26 points from losing positions as they won promotion from League 2

	11-12		Last six seasons at home							
	H	A	P	W	D	L	OV	UN	BS	CS
Portsmouth	-	-	0	0	0	0	0	0	0	0
Coventry	-	-	0	0	0	0	0	0	0	0
Doncaster	-	-	0	0	0	0	0	0	0	0
Sheffield United	-	-	0	0	0	0	0	0	0	0
MK Dons	-	-	0	0	0	0	0	0	0	0
Stevenage	-	-	4	2	0	2	3	1	1	1
Notts County	-	-	0	0	0	0	0	0	0	0
Carlisle	-	-	0	0	0	0	0	0	0	0
Brentford	-	-	0	0	0	0	0	0	0	0
Colchester	-	-	0	0	0	0	0	0	0	0
Bournemouth	-	-	0	0	0	0	0	0	0	0
Tranmere	-	-	0	0	0	0	0	0	0	0
Hartlepool	-	-	0	0	0	0	0	0	0	0
Bury	-	-	0	0	0	0	0	0	0	0
Preston	-	-	0	0	0	0	0	0	0	0
Oldham	-	-	0	0	0	0	0	0	0	0
Yeovil	-	-	0	0	0	0	0	0	0	0
Scunthorpe	-	-	0	0	0	0	0	0	0	0
Walsall	-	-	0	0	0	0	0	0	0	0
Leyton Orient	-	-	0	0	0	0	0	0	0	0
Swindon	L	L	1	0	0	1	1	0	0	0
Shrewsbury	W	L	1	1	0	0	1	0	1	0
Crawley										
Crewe	D	D	1	0	1	0	0	1	1	0

Season	Division	Pos	P	W	D	L	F	A	GD	Pts
2011-12	League 2	3	46	23	15	8	76	54	22	84
2010-11	Conference	1	46	31	12	3	93	30	63	105
2009-10	Conference	7	44	19	9	16	50	57	-7	66

Crewe

Nickname: The Railwaymen
Colours: Red and White
Ground: Alexandra Stadium (10,109)
Tel: 01270-213-014   www.crewealex.net

CREWE legend Dario Gradi clearly left the team in good hands when he allowed assistant boss Steve Davis to take over in November as the new man led Alex on a phenomenal run that ended in victory in the League 2 play-off final.

The Railwaymen finished only seventh but took their unbeaten run to 19 matches when beating Cheltenham at Wembley.

Star man Nick Powell has joined Man United but they have plenty more quality youngsters to boost their survival bid.

Longest run without loss/win: 16/4
High – low league position 7-19
Clean sheets: 11 **Yellow cards:** 45 **Red cards:** 4
Average attendance: 4,124 **Players used:** 25
Leading Scorer: N Powell 14 (4,11)
Key stat: Crewe conceded the most goals of the teams who finished in the promotion or play-off places of League 2

	11-12		Last six seasons at home							
	H	A	P	W	D	L	OV	UN	BS	CS
Portsmouth	-	-	0	0	0	0	0	0	0	0
Coventry	-	-	0	0	0	0	0	0	0	0
Doncaster	-	-	2	1	0	1	2	0	1	0
Sheffield United	-	-	0	0	0	0	0	0	0	0
MK Dons	-	-	1	0	1	0	1	0	1	0
Stevenage	-	-	1	0	0	1	0	1	0	0
Notts County	-	-	1	0	0	1	0	1	0	0
Carlisle	-	-	3	1	0	2	2	1	2	0
Brentford	-	-	1	1	0	0	1	0	1	0
Colchester	-	-	1	1	0	0	0	1	0	1
Bournemouth	-	-	3	1	0	2	2	1	2	1
Tranmere	-	-	3	2	1	0	2	1	3	0
Hartlepool	-	-	2	1	1	0	1	1	1	1
Bury	-	-	2	1	0	1	2	0	1	1
Preston	-	-	0	0	0	0	0	0	0	0
Oldham	-	-	3	1	0	2	3	0	2	0
Yeovil	-	-	3	2	0	1	1	2	1	2
Scunthorpe	-	-	2	1	0	1	2	0	2	0
Walsall	-	-	2	1	1	0	1	1	1	1
Leyton Orient	-	-	3	0	0	3	1	2	0	0
Swindon	W	L	3	2	1	0	0	3	0	3
Shrewsbury	D	L	3	0	1	2	2	1	2	0
Crawley	D	D	1	0	1	0	0	1	1	0
Crewe										

Season	Division	Pos	P	W	D	L	F	A	GD	Pts
2011-12	League 2	7	46	20	12	14	67	59	8	72
2010-11	League 2	10	46	18	11	17	87	65	22	65
2009-10	League 2	18	46	15	10	21	68	73	-5	55

Doncaster

Nickname: Rovers
Colours: Red and White
Ground: Keepmoat Stadium (15,231)
Tel: 01302-764-664 www.doncasterroversfc.co.uk

DONCASTER dropped from the Championship without so much as a whimper last term and the malaise stretches back even further, given that they'd ended the previous season with just one win in 19 games.

The club attempted to stop the rot by bringing in Premier League cast-offs on loans and short-term deals, but that has left Dean Saunders searching for almost an entire new team this summer.

Another struggle lies ahead and a second successive relegation is possible.

Longest run without loss/win: 5/11
High – low league position 20-24
Clean sheets: 8 **Yellow cards:** 70 **Red cards:** 4
Average attendance: 9,309 **Players used:** 41
Leading Scorer: B Sharp 10 (4,8)
Key stat: Doncaster led at half-time and full-time in just three matches as they dropped from the second tier

	11-12 H A	P	W	D	L	OV	UN	BS	CS
Portsmouth	L L	2	0	0	2	1	1	1	0
Coventry	D W	4	1	3	0	0	4	2	2
Doncaster									
Sheffield United	- -	3	1	1	1	0	3	1	1
MK Dons	- -	0	0	0	0	0	0	0	0
Stevenage	- -	0	0	0	0	0	0	0	0
Notts County	- -	0	0	0	0	0	0	0	0
Carlisle	- -	2	1	0	1	1	1	1	1
Brentford	- -	1	1	0	0	1	0	0	1
Colchester	- -	0	0	0	0	0	0	0	0
Bournemouth	- -	2	0	1	1	1	1	2	0
Tranmere	- -	2	0	2	0	0	2	0	2
Hartlepool	- -	1	1	0	0	0	1	0	1
Bury	- -	0	0	0	0	0	0	0	0
Preston	- -	3	0	2	1	0	3	2	0
Oldham	- -	2	0	2	0	0	2	2	0
Yeovil	- -	2	0	1	1	1	1	1	1
Scunthorpe	- -	3	2	1	0	3	0	2	1
Walsall	- -	1	0	0	1	1	0	1	0
Leyton Orient	- -	2	1	1	0	1	1	1	1
Swindon	- -	1	1	0	0	0	1	0	1
Shrewsbury	- -	0	0	0	0	0	0	0	0
Crawley	- -	0	0	0	0	0	0	0	0
Crewe	- -	2	2	0	0	1	1	1	1

Season	Division	Pos	P	W	D	L	F	A	GD	Pts
2011-12	Champ	24	46	8	12	26	43	80	-37	36
2010-11	Champ	21	46	11	15	20	55	81	-26	48
2009-10	Champ	12	46	15	15	16	59	58	1	60

Hartlepool

Nickname: Pools
Colours: White and Blue
Ground: Victoria Park (7,749)
Tel: 01429-272-584 www.hartlepoolunited.co.uk

NO GROUND in League 1 saw fewer goals than Victoria Park last term, with Hartlepool scoring just 21 goals at home.

Pools were more free-scoring on the road, however, gaining eight away wins as a result. And with more luck in front of goal at home, the confidence gleaned could easily have seen them improve on an already healthy mid-table position.

Among the relegation favourites for several seasons, Hartlepool now look well established in the third tier.

Longest run without loss/win: 9/5
High – low league position 3-16
Clean sheets: 14 **Yellow cards:** 53 **Red cards:** 3
Average attendance: 4,961 **Players used:** 30
Leading Scorer: A Sweeney 8 (3,7)
Key stat: Hartlepool picked up just two points when losing at half-time last term

	11-12 H A	P	W	D	L	OV	UN	BS	CS
Portsmouth	- -	0	0	0	0	0	0	0	0
Coventry	- -	0	0	0	0	0	0	0	0
Doncaster	- -	1	1	0	0	1	0	1	0
Sheffield United	L L	1	0	0	1	0	1	0	0
MK Dons	D D	5	1	1	3	2	3	2	1
Stevenage	D D	1	0	1	0	0	1	0	1
Notts County	W L	3	1	2	0	1	2	2	1
Carlisle	W W	5	2	2	1	5	0	3	1
Brentford	D L	3	1	2	0	1	2	0	3
Colchester	L D	4	3	0	1	2	2	2	1
Bournemouth	D W	3	0	3	0	1	2	2	1
Tranmere	L D	5	3	1	1	2	3	3	1
Hartlepool									
Bury	W W	2	2	0	0	1	1	0	2
Preston	L L	1	0	0	1	0	1	0	0
Oldham	L W	5	3	1	1	4	1	4	0
Yeovil	L W	5	2	2	1	1	4	2	2
Scunthorpe	L W	2	0	0	2	2	0	2	0
Walsall	D D	6	3	2	1	4	2	4	1
Leyton Orient	W D	5	2	1	2	1	4	2	1
Swindon	- -	5	0	3	2	2	3	3	0
Shrewsbury	- -	1	0	0	1	1	0	0	0
Crawley	- -	0	0	0	0	0	0	0	0
Crewe	- -	2	1	0	1	2	0	1	1

Season	Division	Pos	P	W	D	L	F	A	GD	Pts
2011-12	League 1	13	46	14	14	18	50	55	-5	56
2010-11	League 1	16	46	15	12	19	47	65	-18	57
2009-10	League 1	20	46	14	11	21	59	67	-8	50

Leyton Orient

Nickname: The O's
Colours: Red
Ground: Matchroom Stadium (9,311)
Tel: 0871-310-1881   www.leytonorient.com

LAST SEASON was a bizarre one for Leyton Orient, who picked up just three points from their first ten matches and weren't much better at the end but stayed up thanks to a storming winter run.

Russell Slade's men deserve huge credit for that recovery, but the subsequent slide – 11 defeats in their last 17 matches – doesn't bode well as the mid-season sales of Charlie Daniels and Stephen Dawson left them badly short of quality after a similar cull in the summer.

Longest run without loss/win: 9/10
High – low league position 12-24
Clean sheets: 10 **Yellow cards:** 66 **Red cards:** 7
Average attendance: 4,298 **Players used:** 39
Leading Scorer: K Lisbie 12 (5,9)
Key stat: Leyton Orient conceded three goals or more in 13 matches – including three games against relegated teams

	11-12 H A	Last six seasons at home P	W	D	L	OV	UN	BS	CS
Portsmouth	- -	0	0	0	0	0	0	0	0
Coventry	- -	0	0	0	0	0	0	0	0
Doncaster	- -	2	0	2	0	0	2	2	0
Sheffield United	D L	1	0	1	0	0	1	1	0
MK Dons	L L	4	0	1	3	4	0	3	0
Stevenage	D W	1	0	1	0	0	1	0	1
Notts County	L W	2	1	0	1	1	1	0	1
Carlisle	L L	6	0	4	2	3	3	3	2
Brentford	W L	4	3	1	0	1	3	2	2
Colchester	L D	4	2	0	2	2	2	2	0
Bournemouth	L W	4	2	1	1	3	1	3	1
Tranmere	L L	6	3	0	3	4	2	2	1
Hartlepool	D L	5	2	1	2	2	3	3	2
Bury	W D	1	1	0	0	0	1	0	1
Preston	W W	1	1	0	0	1	0	1	0
Oldham	L W	6	3	1	2	4	2	4	2
Yeovil	D D	6	1	3	2	2	4	2	3
Scunthorpe	L W	3	0	2	1	3	0	3	0
Walsall	D L	5	2	2	1	0	5	1	3
Leyton Orient									
Swindon	- -	4	2	1	1	3	1	2	2
Shrewsbury	- -	0	0	0	0	0	0	0	0
Crawley	- -	0	0	0	0	0	0	0	0
Crewe	- -	3	1	1	1	0	3	1	1

Season	Division	Pos	P	W	D	L	F	A	GD	Pts
2011-12	League 1	20	46	13	11	22	48	75	-27	50
2010-11	League 1	7	46	19	13	14	71	62	9	70
2009-10	League 1	17	46	13	12	21	53	63	-10	51

MK Dons

Nickname: The Dons
Colours: White
Ground: stadium:mk (21,189)
Tel: 01908-622-922   www.mkdons.co.uk

DONS supporters must be getting sick of the play-offs after coming up short for the fifth time in six years, but there was still plenty of optimism last season.

Karl Robinson has got the club going forward once again after several backward steps in Paul Ince's second spell in charge, and they were well clear of the chasing pack in fifth.

Despite not seriously threatening automatic promotion, the Dons were unlucky not to beat Huddersfield in the play-offs.

Longest run without loss/win: 6/5
High – low league position 2-9
Clean sheets: 16 **Yellow cards:** 74 **Red cards:** 8
Average attendance: 8,659 **Players used:** 28
Leading Scorer: D Bowditch 12 (4,10)
Key stat: MK Dons led at the break in more than half their matches last season

	11-12 H A	Last six seasons at home P	W	D	L	OV	UN	BS	CS
Portsmouth	- -	0	0	0	0	0	0	0	0
Coventry	- -	0	0	0	0	0	0	0	0
Doncaster	- -	0	0	0	0	0	0	0	0
Sheffield United	W L	1	1	0	0	0	1	0	1
MK Dons									
Stevenage	W L	1	1	0	0	0	1	0	1
Notts County	W D	4	4	0	0	4	0	2	2
Carlisle	L W	4	2	0	2	4	0	4	0
Brentford	L D	4	0	2	2	1	3	3	0
Colchester	W W	4	2	2	0	1	3	3	1
Bournemouth	D W	2	1	1	0	1	1	1	1
Tranmere	W W	4	4	0	0	1	3	0	4
Hartlepool	D D	5	2	3	0	2	3	2	3
Bury	W D	3	2	0	1	3	0	3	0
Preston	L D	1	0	0	1	0	1	0	0
Oldham	W L	4	2	2	0	2	2	1	3
Yeovil	L W	4	2	1	1	3	1	2	1
Scunthorpe	D W	2	0	1	1	0	2	0	1
Walsall	L W	5	1	2	2	0	5	2	1
Leyton Orient	W W	4	2	0	2	3	1	3	1
Swindon	- -	4	2	0	2	3	1	3	0
Shrewsbury	- -	2	2	0	0	1	1	0	2
Crawley	- -	0	0	0	0	0	0	0	0
Crewe	- -	1	0	1	0	1	0	1	0

Season	Division	Pos	P	W	D	L	F	A	GD	Pts
2011-12	League 1	5	46	22	14	10	84	47	37	80
2010-11	League 1	5	46	23	8	15	67	60	7	77
2009-10	League 1	12	46	17	9	20	60	68	-8	60

Notts County

Nickname: The Magpies
Colours: Black and White
Ground: Meadow Lane (20,280)
Tel: 0115-952-9000   www.nottscountyfc.co.uk

COUNTY missed out on the play-offs only on goal difference last season as they finally began to realise the lofty ambitions that had begun to seem laughable after the Sven-Goran Eriksson era.

There was also a change in manager following a mid-season blip, and while Martin Allen's sacking seemed harsh at the time, Keith Curle helped them to win 12 of their last 19 matches.

On that form, Notts County will have both eyes on promotion.

Longest run without loss/win: 6/8
High – low league position 4-15
Clean sheets: 14 Yellow cards: 83 Red cards: 5
Average attendance: 6,808 Players used: 34
Leading Scorer: J Hughes 13 (5,12)
Key stat: There were 80 second-half goals in Notts County's matches last season, easily the most in League 1

	11-12 H A	Last six seasons at home P	W	D	L	OV	UN	BS	CS
Portsmouth	- -	0	0	0	0	0	0	0	0
Coventry	- -	0	0	0	0	0	0	0	0
Doncaster	- -	0	0	0	0	0	0	0	0
Sheffield United	L L	1	0	0	1	1	0	1	0
MK Dons	D L	4	1	2	1	2	2	3	1
Stevenage	W W	1	1	0	0	0	1	0	1
Notts County									
Carlisle	W W	2	1	0	1	0	2	0	1
Brentford	D D	4	0	4	0	0	4	4	0
Colchester	W L	2	2	0	0	1	1	1	1
Bournemouth	W L	4	1	2	1	2	2	3	0
Tranmere	W D	2	1	0	1	1	1	1	0
Hartlepool	W L	3	2	0	1	2	1	0	2
Bury	L D	5	1	0	4	3	2	2	1
Preston	D L	1	0	1	0	0	1	0	1
Oldham	W L	2	1	0	1	0	2	0	1
Yeovil	W L	2	2	0	0	2	0	1	1
Scunthorpe	W D	1	1	0	0	1	0	1	0
Walsall	W W	3	1	1	1	2	1	3	0
Leyton Orient	L W	2	1	0	1	2	0	2	0
Swindon	- -	2	1	1	0	0	2	1	1
Shrewsbury	- -	4	1	3	0	2	2	4	0
Crawley	- -	0	0	0	0	0	0	0	0
Crewe	- -	1	1	0	0	0	1	0	1

Season	Division	Pos	P	W	D	L	F	A	GD	Pts
2011-12	League 1	7	46	21	10	15	75	63	12	73
2010-11	League 1	19	46	14	8	24	46	60	-14	50
2009-10	League 2	1	46	27	12	7	96	31	65	93

Oldham

Nickname: The Latics
Colours: Blue
Ground: Boundary Park (10,850)
Tel: 0161-624-4972   www.oldhamathletic.co.uk

PAUL DICKOV was given the Oldham job last summer due to his eagerness to work within a limited budget, and the club must have been delighted with how the appointment worked out.

Oldham stayed up with plenty to spare and reached the area final of the Johnstone's Paint Trophy and the FA Cup third round, earning a lucrative trip to Anfield.

A resulting fixture backlog saw them finish the season poorly, but they should be in mid-table again.

Longest run without loss/win: 4/8
High – low league position 11-18
Clean sheets: 9 Yellow cards: 62 Red cards: 6
Average attendance: 4,433 Players used: 32
Leading Scorer: S Kuqi 11 (4,10)
Key stat: Oldham were unbeaten when they opened the scoring last term

	11-12 H A	Last six seasons at home P	W	D	L	OV	UN	BS	CS
Portsmouth	- -	0	0	0	0	0	0	0	0
Coventry	- -	0	0	0	0	0	0	0	0
Doncaster	- -	2	1	1	0	1	1	1	1
Sheffield United	L W	1	0	0	1	0	1	0	0
MK Dons	W L	4	3	0	1	3	1	3	1
Stevenage	D L	1	0	1	0	1	0	1	0
Notts County	W L	2	2	0	0	2	0	1	1
Carlisle	W D	6	3	2	1	1	5	1	4
Brentford	L L	4	2	0	2	3	1	2	1
Colchester	D L	4	0	3	1	1	3	2	1
Bournemouth	W D	4	3	0	1	2	2	2	2
Tranmere	W L	6	3	2	1	1	5	1	4
Hartlepool	L W	5	2	0	3	3	2	1	1
Bury	L D	1	0	0	1	0	1	0	0
Preston	D D	1	0	1	0	0	1	1	0
Oldham									
Yeovil	L L	6	2	2	2	2	4	1	4
Scunthorpe	L W	3	2	0	1	2	1	1	2
Walsall	W W	5	3	1	1	2	3	3	1
Leyton Orient	L W	6	2	3	1	1	5	3	2
Swindon	- -	4	1	3	0	2	2	2	2
Shrewsbury	- -	0	0	0	0	0	0	0	0
Crawley	- -	0	0	0	0	0	0	0	0
Crewe	- -	3	2	1	0	1	2	2	1

Season	Division	Pos	P	W	D	L	F	A	GD	Pts
2011-12	League 1	16	46	14	12	20	50	66	-16	54
2010-11	League 1	17	46	13	17	16	53	60	-7	56
2009-10	League 1	16	46	13	13	20	39	57	-18	52

Portsmouth

Nickname: Pompey
Colours: Blue and White
Ground: Fratton Park (21,178)
Tel: 023-9273-1204   www.portsmouthfc.co.uk

FEW clubs have ever fallen as swiftly as Portsmouth, who suffered their second relegation in three years last season.

This time they collected enough points on the pitch to stay up but a ten-point deduction handed to the club for going into administration cost them.

However, any punters who believe they may retain enough quality to start a revival should be warned that the club's financial difficulties have seen multiple players sold off during mid-season in recent years.

Longest run without loss/win: 4/9
High – low league position 14-20
Clean sheets: 12 **Yellow cards:** 81 **Red cards:** 4
Average attendance: 15,016 **Players used:** 31
Leading Scorer: D Norris 8 (3,8)
Key stat: Portsmouth scored the first goal in just 15 matches last season

	11-12		Last six seasons at home							
	H	A	P	W	D	L	OV	UN	BS	CS
Portsmouth										
Coventry	W	L	2	1	0	1	2	0	1	0
Doncaster	W	W	2	1	0	1	2	0	2	0
Sheffield United	-	-	2	2	0	0	1	1	1	1
MK Dons	-	-	0	0	0	0	0	0	0	0
Stevenage	-	-	0	0	0	0	0	0	0	0
Notts County	-	-	0	0	0	0	0	0	0	0
Carlisle	-	-	0	0	0	0	0	0	0	0
Brentford	-	-	0	0	0	0	0	0	0	0
Colchester	-	-	0	0	0	0	0	0	0	0
Bournemouth	-	-	0	0	0	0	0	0	0	0
Tranmere	-	-	0	0	0	0	0	0	0	0
Hartlepool	-	-	0	0	0	0	0	0	0	0
Bury	-	-	0	0	0	0	0	0	0	0
Preston	-	-	1	0	1	0	0	1	1	0
Oldham	-	-	0	0	0	0	0	0	0	0
Yeovil	-	-	0	0	0	0	0	0	0	0
Scunthorpe	-	-	1	1	0	0	0	1	0	1
Walsall	-	-	0	0	0	0	0	0	0	0
Leyton Orient	-	-	0	0	0	0	0	0	0	0
Swindon	-	-	0	0	0	0	0	0	0	0
Shrewsbury	-	-	0	0	0	0	0	0	0	0
Crawley	-	-	0	0	0	0	0	0	0	0
Crewe	-	-	0	0	0	0	0	0	0	0

Season	Division	Pos	P	W	D	L	F	A	GD	Pts
2011-12	Champ	22	46	13	11	22	50	59	-9	40*
2010-11	Champ	16	46	15	13	18	53	60	-7	58
2009-10	Prem	20	38	7	7	24	34	66	-32	19

Preston

Nickname: The Lilywhites/North End
Colours: White and Navy Blue
Ground: Deepdale (23,404)
Tel: 0844-856-1964   www.pnefc.co.uk

PRESTON had unrealistic expectations last term and after sacking Phil Brown, they slipped further to win just two of their last 17 games under Graham Westley.

Financial constraints contributed to North End finishing bottom of the Championship in 2011 and with little investment Brown, had them playing roughly to par.

Westley was known for his tough approach at Stevenage and it didn't seem to go down well – he ended up complaining about players giving away team secrets.

Longest run without loss/win: 8/9
High – low league position 3-16
Clean sheets: 13 **Yellow cards:** 91 **Red cards:** 3
Average attendance: 11,429 **Players used:** 46
Leading Scorer: I Hume 9 (3,7)
Key stat: The draw/draw double result came up in 12 of Preston's matches during 2011-12

	11-12		Last six seasons at home							
	H	A	P	W	D	L	OV	UN	BS	CS
Portsmouth	-	-	1	1	0	0	0	1	0	1
Coventry	-	-	5	4	1	0	3	2	4	1
Doncaster	-	-	3	1	1	1	0	3	1	1
Sheffield United	L	L	5	3	1	1	4	1	4	1
MK Dons	D	W	1	0	1	0	0	1	1	0
Stevenage	D	D	1	0	1	0	0	1	0	1
Notts County	W	D	1	1	0	0	0	1	0	1
Carlisle	D	D	1	0	1	0	1	0	1	0
Brentford	L	W	1	0	0	1	1	0	1	0
Colchester	L	L	3	1	0	2	2	1	1	1
Bournemouth	L	L	1	0	0	1	1	0	1	0
Tranmere	W	L	1	1	0	0	1	0	1	0
Hartlepool	W	W	1	1	0	0	0	1	0	1
Bury	D	L	1	0	1	0	0	1	1	0
Preston										
Oldham	D	D	1	0	1	0	1	0	1	0
Yeovil	W	L	1	1	0	0	1	0	1	0
Scunthorpe	D	D	4	1	1	2	2	2	2	1
Walsall	D	L	1	0	1	0	0	1	0	1
Leyton Orient	L	L	1	0	0	1	0	1	0	0
Swindon	-	-	0	0	0	0	0	0	0	0
Shrewsbury	-	-	0	0	0	0	0	0	0	0
Crawley	-	-	0	0	0	0	0	0	0	0
Crewe	-	-	0	0	0	0	0	0	0	0

Season	Division	Pos	P	W	D	L	F	A	GD	Pts
2011-12	League 1	15	46	13	15	18	54	68	-14	54
2010-11	Champ	22	46	10	12	24	54	79	-25	42
2009-10	Champ	17	46	13	15	18	58	73	-15	54

Scunthorpe

Nickname: The Iron
Colours: Claret and Blue
Ground: Glanford Park (9,144)
Tel: 0871-221-1899   www.scunthorpe-united.co.uk

THIS time last year Scunthorpe looked to have a decent chance of promotion, but their backers soon knew their fate.

New manager Alan Knill clearly needed time to get his ideas across to the team because Scunthorpe endured an awful pre-season and then failed to win any of their first nine league matches.

Things improved slightly and more of a goal threat would have seen them turn a glut of draws – eight in the last 12 – into wins. Expect more this time.

Longest run without loss/win: 10/9
High – low league position 15-22
Clean sheets: 10 **Yellow cards:** 73 **Red cards:** 9
Average attendance: 4,339 **Players used:** 33
Leading Scorer: A Barcham 9 (2,7)
Key stat: During 2011-12, Scunthorpe lost more games than they won after they had been leading at half-time

	11-12 H A	Last six seasons at home P	W	D	L	OV	UN	BS	CS
Portsmouth	- -	1	0	1	0	0	1	1	0
Coventry	- -	3	2	0	1	1	2	1	1
Doncaster	- -	3	1	1	1	2	1	2	1
Sheffield United	D L	4	3	1	0	3	1	4	0
MK Dons	L D	2	0	0	2	1	1	0	0
Stevenage	D W	1	0	1	0	0	1	1	0
Notts County	D L	1	0	1	0	0	1	0	1
Carlisle	L D	3	2	0	1	3	0	2	1
Brentford	D D	2	0	2	0	0	2	1	1
Colchester	D D	3	1	2	0	2	1	2	1
Bournemouth	D L	2	1	1	0	1	1	2	0
Tranmere	W D	3	1	2	0	1	2	3	0
Hartlepool	L W	2	1	0	1	1	1	0	1
Bury	L D	1	0	0	1	1	0	1	0
Preston	D D	4	2	1	1	3	1	3	0
Oldham	L W	3	1	1	1	1	2	2	1
Yeovil	W D	3	3	0	0	1	2	1	2
Scunthorpe									
Walsall	L D	2	0	1	0	1	0	2	1
Leyton Orient	L W	3	2	0	1	3	0	3	0
Swindon	- -	1	0	1	0	1	0	1	0
Shrewsbury	- -	0	0	0	0	0	0	0	0
Crawley	- -	0	0	0	0	0	0	0	0
Crewe	- -	2	1	1	0	2	0	1	1

Season	Division	Pos	P	W	D	L	F	A	GD	Pts
2011-12	League 1	18	46	10	22	14	55	59	-4	52
2010-11	Champ	24	46	12	6	28	43	87	-44	42
2009-10	Champ	20	46	14	10	22	62	84	-22	52

Sheff Utd

Nickname: The Blades
Colours: Red and White
Ground: Bramall Lane (32,609)
Tel: 0871-995-1899   www.sufc.co.uk

DANNY WILSON did a fine job at Bramall Lane last term, accumulating 90 points and winning over those Blades fans who had been sceptical of his appointment, given his links to Sheffield Wednesday.

However, it all went wrong at the back end of the season. Top scorer Ched Evans was jailed, leaving them desperately short of firepower with the result that Wednesday pipped them to automatic promotion. They then lost a goalless play-off final to Huddersfield on penalties.

Longest run without loss/win: 9/3
High – low league position 1-7
Clean sheets: 15 **Yellow cards:** 68 **Red cards:** 4
Average attendance: 18,702 **Players used:** 30
Leading Scorer: C Evans 29 (8,22)
Key stat: Sheffield United's only two goalless draws of 2011-12 came in the play-offs

	11-12 H A	Last six seasons at home P	W	D	L	OV	UN	BS	CS
Portsmouth	- -	2	1	1	0	0	2	1	1
Coventry	- -	4	2	1	1	1	3	2	1
Doncaster	- -	3	0	2	1	1	2	2	0
Sheffield United									
MK Dons	W L	1	1	0	0	1	0	1	0
Stevenage	D L	1	0	1	0	1	0	1	0
Notts County	W W	1	1	0	0	1	0	1	0
Carlisle	W L	1	1	0	0	0	1	0	1
Brentford	W W	1	1	0	0	1	0	1	0
Colchester	W D	2	1	1	0	2	0	1	1
Bournemouth	W W	1	1	0	0	1	0	1	0
Tranmere	D D	1	0	1	0	0	1	0	0
Hartlepool	W W	1	1	0	0	1	0	1	0
Bury	W W	1	1	0	0	1	0	0	1
Preston	W W	5	4	1	0	1	4	2	3
Oldham	L W	1	0	0	1	1	0	1	0
Yeovil	W W	1	1	0	0	1	0	0	1
Scunthorpe	W D	4	1	1	2	2	2	1	1
Walsall	W L	1	1	0	0	1	0	1	0
Leyton Orient	W D	1	1	0	0	1	0	1	0
Swindon	- -	0	0	0	0	0	0	0	0
Shrewsbury	- -	0	0	0	0	0	0	0	0
Crawley	- -	0	0	0	0	0	0	0	0
Crewe	- -	0	0	0	0	0	0	0	0

Season	Division	Pos	P	W	D	L	F	A	GD	Pts
2011-12	League 1	3	46	27	9	10	92	51	41	90
2010-11	Champ	23	46	11	9	26	44	79	-35	42
2009-10	Champ	8	46	17	14	15	62	55	7	65

Shrewsbury

Nickname: The Shrews
Colours: Blue and Amber
Ground: Greenhous Meadow (9,875)
Tel: 01743-289-177   www.shrewsburytown.com

SHREWSBURY gained a richly deserved promotion from League 2 last term, after a history of near misses. They failed to go up automatically by a single point in 2010-11 and then lost in the play-offs for the second time in three years.

Graham Turner has done well in his second spell in charge of the Shrews but, having been in the promotion mix for so long, their level is obvious and they are likely to be in the relegation fight given the record of last season's promoted clubs.

Longest run without loss/win: 9/3
High – low league position 2-6
Clean sheets: 18 **Yellow cards:** 62 **Red cards:** 5
Average attendance: 5,769 **Players used:** 25
Leading Scorer: J Collins 14 (8,12)
Key stat: Shrewsbury failed to score in just eight matches last term

	11-12 H A	Last six seasons at home P	W	D	L	OV	UN	BS	CS
Portsmouth	- -	0	0	0	0	0	0	0	0
Coventry	- -	0	0	0	0	0	0	0	0
Doncaster	- -	0	0	0	0	0	0	0	0
Sheffield United	- -	0	0	0	0	0	0	0	0
MK Dons	- -	2	1	1	0	2	0	2	0
Stevenage	- -	1	1	0	0	0	1	0	1
Notts County	- -	4	2	1	1	1	3	1	2
Carlisle	- -	0	0	0	0	0	0	0	0
Brentford	- -	2	0	0	2	1	1	1	0
Colchester	- -	0	0	0	0	0	0	0	0
Bournemouth	- -	2	2	0	0	1	1	1	1
Tranmere	- -	0	0	0	0	0	0	0	0
Hartlepool	- -	1	0	1	0	0	1	1	0
Bury	- -	5	1	1	3	2	3	2	1
Preston	- -	0	0	0	0	0	0	0	0
Oldham	- -	0	0	0	0	0	0	0	0
Yeovil	- -	0	0	0	0	0	0	0	0
Scunthorpe	- -	0	0	0	0	0	0	0	0
Walsall	- -	1	0	1	0	0	1	1	0
Leyton Orient	- -	0	0	0	0	0	0	0	0
Swindon	W L	2	1	0	1	2	0	2	0
Shrewsbury									
Crawley	W L	1	1	0	0	1	0	1	0
Crewe	W D	3	2	0	1	0	3	0	2

Season	Division	Pos	P	W	D	L	F	A	GD	Pts
2011-12	League 2	2	46	26	10	10	66	41	25	88
2010-11	League 2	4	46	22	13	11	72	49	23	79
2009-10	League 2	12	46	17	12	17	55	54	1	63

Stevenage

Nickname: The Boro
Colours: White and Red
Ground: Lamex Stadium (6,722)
Tel: 01438-223223   www.stevenagefc.com

BORO had a fantastic season in 2011-12 given they had only escaped from League 2 via the play-offs. They got close to Wembley once again as they were just five minutes away from taking Sheffield United to extra-time in the play-off semi-final.

Graham Westley was behind Stevenage's success and his move to Preston was a blow, but they showed enough under Gary Smith, winning four of their last five matches to edge into the top six, to suggest they can hold their own again.

Longest run without loss/win: 11/7
High – low league position 6-15
Clean sheets: 15 **Yellow cards:** 68 **Red cards:** 4
Average attendance: 3,559 **Players used:** 28
Leading Scorer: S Laird 8 (1,8)
Key stat: Stevenage lost the second half just seven times last term

	11-12 H A	Last six seasons at home P	W	D	L	OV	UN	BS	CS
Portsmouth	- -	0	0	0	0	0	0	0	0
Coventry	- -	0	0	0	0	0	0	0	0
Doncaster	- -	0	0	0	0	0	0	0	0
Sheffield United	W D	1	1	0	0	1	0	1	0
MK Dons	W L	1	1	0	0	1	0	1	0
Stevenage									
Notts County	L L	1	0	0	1	0	1	0	0
Carlisle	W L	1	1	0	0	0	1	0	1
Brentford	W W	1	1	0	0	1	0	1	0
Colchester	D W	1	0	1	0	0	1	0	1
Bournemouth	D W	1	0	1	0	0	1	0	1
Tranmere	W L	1	1	0	0	1	0	1	0
Hartlepool	D D	1	0	1	0	1	0	1	0
Bury	W W	2	1	1	0	2	0	1	1
Preston	D D	1	0	1	0	0	1	1	0
Oldham	W D	1	1	0	0	0	1	0	1
Yeovil	D W	1	0	1	0	0	1	0	1
Scunthorpe	L D	1	0	0	1	1	0	1	0
Walsall	D D	1	0	1	0	0	1	0	1
Leyton Orient	L D	1	0	0	1	0	1	0	0
Swindon	- -	0	0	0	0	0	0	0	0
Shrewsbury	- -	1	0	1	0	0	1	1	0
Crawley	- -	4	2	1	1	2	2	3	1
Crewe	- -	1	0	1	0	0	1	1	0

Season	Division	Pos	P	W	D	L	F	A	GD	Pts
2011-12	League 1	6	46	18	19	9	69	44	25	73
2010-11	League 2	6	46	18	15	13	62	45	17	69
2009-10	Conference	1	44	30	9	5	79	24	55	99

Swindon

Nickname: The Robins
Colours: Red and White
Ground: County Ground (14,983)
Tel: 0871-876-1879   www.swindontownfc.co.uk

A TOP-HALF finish had become the norm for League 2 champions stepping up a level until Chesterfield came along, and there have been few more impressive winners of the division than Swindon.

The Robins romped to the third-tier title under rookie boss Paolo Di Canio, who did a magnificent job in his first season at the County Ground and seems likely to prove a big success as a manager. Given a strong start, holding on to him might be their biggest concern this season.

Longest run without loss/win: 10/4
High – low league position 1-14
Clean sheets: 26 Yellow cards: 64 Red cards: 2
Average attendance: 8,411 Players used: 39
Leading Scorer: A Connell 11 (3,9) P Benson 11 (4,9)
Key stat: Swindon conceded just 18 second-half goals in 2011-12, scoring 44

| | 11-12 | | Last six seasons at home | | | | | | | |
	H	A	P	W	D	L	OV	UN	BS	CS
Portsmouth	-	-	0	0	0	0	0	0	0	0
Coventry	-	-	0	0	0	0	0	0	0	0
Doncaster	-	-	1	0	0	1	1	0	1	0
Sheffield United	-	-	0	0	0	0	0	0	0	0
MK Dons	-	-	4	1	2	1	1	3	2	1
Stevenage	-	-	0	0	0	0	0	0	0	0
Notts County	-	-	2	0	1	1	1	1	2	0
Carlisle	-	-	4	1	2	1	1	3	2	1
Brentford	-	-	2	1	1	0	1	1	2	0
Colchester	-	-	3	1	1	1	2	1	3	0
Bournemouth	-	-	2	1	0	1	2	0	2	0
Tranmere	-	-	4	3	1	0	2	2	1	3
Hartlepool	-	-	5	1	1	3	1	4	2	0
Bury	-	-	1	1	0	0	1	0	1	0
Preston	-	-	0	0	0	0	0	0	0	0
Oldham	-	-	4	3	0	1	2	2	1	2
Yeovil	-	-	4	1	0	3	2	2	2	0
Scunthorpe	-	-	1	1	0	0	1	0	1	0
Walsall	-	-	5	1	3	1	2	3	3	1
Leyton Orient	-	-	4	1	2	1	2	2	3	0
Swindon										
Shrewsbury	W	L	2	2	0	0	2	0	2	0
Crawley	W	W	1	1	0	0	1	0	0	1
Crewe	W	L	3	1	2	0	1	2	1	2

Season	Division	Pos	P	W	D	L	F	A	GD	Pts
2011-12	League 2	1	46	29	6	11	75	32	43	93
2010-11	League 1	24	46	9	14	23	50	72	-22	41
2009-10	League 1	5	46	22	16	8	73	57	16	82

Tranmere

Nickname: The Rovers
Colours: White
Ground: Prenton Park (16,151)
Tel: 0871-221-2001   www.tranmererovers.co.uk

TRANMERE'S season turned on its head when Ronnie Moore returned for a third spell in charge in March.

Moore's previous stint at Prenton Park had gone well prior to his ludicrous sacking in 2009 and he again got Rovers going by leading them to six wins in their final 13 matches.

Injuries had played a big part in their poor form under Les Parry – they had won just one of his last 20 matches – and they should continue to progress.

Longest run without loss/win: 6/12
High – low league position 7-19
Clean sheets: 17 Yellow cards: 66 Red cards: 4
Average attendance: 5,130 Players used: 29
Leading Scorer: L Akins 5 (1,4) J Labadie 5 (2,5) J Cassidy 5 (1,4)
Key stat: Tranmere won just twice against opponents who finished in the top half of the table

| | 11-12 | | Last six seasons at home | | | | | | | |
	H	A	P	W	D	L	OV	UN	BS	CS
Portsmouth	-	-	0	0	0	0	0	0	0	0
Coventry	-	-	0	0	0	0	0	0	0	0
Doncaster	-	-	2	1	0	1	0	2	0	1
Sheffield United	D	D	1	0	1	0	0	1	1	0
MK Dons	L	L	4	1	1	2	1	3	2	0
Stevenage	W	L	1	1	0	0	1	0	0	1
Notts County	D	L	2	0	1	1	0	2	1	0
Carlisle	L	D	6	3	1	2	3	3	3	2
Brentford	D	W	4	2	1	1	3	1	2	1
Colchester	D	L	4	1	2	1	1	3	2	2
Bournemouth	D	L	4	2	1	1	2	2	1	2
Tranmere										
Hartlepool	D	W	5	2	2	1	1	4	2	2
Bury	W	L	1	1	0	0	0	1	0	1
Preston	W	L	1	1	0	0	1	0	1	0
Oldham	W	L	6	2	0	4	1	5	1	2
Yeovil	D	L	6	3	2	1	3	3	4	1
Scunthorpe	D	L	3	1	1	1	0	3	1	1
Walsall	W	W	5	2	2	1	4	1	4	1
Leyton Orient	W	W	6	3	2	1	3	3	3	3
Swindon	-	-	4	2	0	2	2	2	2	1
Shrewsbury	-	-	0	0	0	0	0	0	0	0
Crawley	-	-	0	0	0	0	0	0	0	0
Crewe	-	-	3	2	1	0	0	3	1	2

Season	Division	Pos	P	W	D	L	F	A	GD	Pts
2011-12	League 1	12	46	14	14	18	49	53	-4	56
2010-11	League 1	18	46	15	11	20	53	60	-7	56
2009-10	League 1	19	46	14	9	23	45	72	-27	51

Walsall

Nickname: The Saddlers
Colours: Red and White
Ground: Banks's Stadium (10,989)
Tel: 01922-622-791   www.saddlers.co.uk

WALSALL'S survival by seven points last term wasn't as impressive as when Dean Smith had kept them up against the odds in the previous campaign having taken over mid-season.

Even so, Smith continues to do an excellent job on a limited budget and Walsall would have done better last season with just a little more firepower – they struggled to kill teams off and were hamstrung by 20 draws. It won't take much for the Saddlers to climb the table.

Longest run without loss/win: 6/8
High – low league position 14-21
Clean sheets: 11 **Yellow cards:** 52 **Red cards:** 7
Average attendance: 4,274 **Players used:** 25
Leading Scorer: J Macken 7 (5,7) A Nicholls 7 (3,7)
Key stat: Walsall dropped 29 points from winning positions last term

	11-12		Last six seasons at home							
	H	A	P	W	D	L	OV	UN	BS	CS
Portsmouth	-	-	0	0	0	0	0	0	0	
Coventry	-	-	0	0	0	0	0	0	0	
Doncaster	-	-	1	0	1	0	0	1	0	
Sheffield United	W	L	1	1	0	0	1	0	1	0
MK Dons	L	W	5	1	1	3	3	2	2	1
Stevenage	D	D	1	0	1	0	0	1	1	0
Notts County	L	L	3	1	0	2	2	1	1	0
Carlisle	D	D	5	2	3	0	3	2	5	0
Brentford	L	D	3	2	0	1	2	1	2	0
Colchester	W	L	4	3	0	1	1	3	1	2
Bournemouth	D	W	3	0	1	2	2	1	2	0
Tranmere	L	L	5	2	0	3	3	2	3	0
Hartlepool	D	D	6	3	2	1	4	2	4	2
Bury	L	L	2	0	0	2	1	1	1	0
Preston	W	D	1	1	0	0	0	1	0	1
Oldham	L	L	5	1	1	3	3	2	2	1
Yeovil	D	L	5	2	1	2	0	5	1	2
Scunthorpe	D	W	2	1	1	0	2	0	2	0
Walsall										
Leyton Orient	W	D	5	1	2	2	1	4	1	2
Swindon	-	-	5	1	2	2	3	2	4	0
Shrewsbury	-	-	1	1	0	0	0	1	0	1
Crawley	-	-	0	0	0	0	0	0	0	0
Crewe	-	-	2	0	2	0	0	2	2	0

Season	Division	Pos	P	W	D	L	F	A	GD	Pts
2011-12	League 1	19	46	10	20	16	51	57	-6	50
2010-11	League 1	20	46	12	12	22	56	75	-19	48
2009-10	League 1	10	46	16	14	16	60	63	-3	62

Yeovil

Nickname: The Glovers
Colours: Green and White
Ground: Huish Park (9,565)
Tel: 01935-423-662   www.ytfc.net

GARY JOHNSON has had plenty of ups and downs since his first terrific spell at Yeovil ended in 2005, but his return to Huish Park proved the catalyst for a strong finish last season.

The top half of the table was the aim for the Glovers given their generous backing, but two wins and 13 points in the first 18 matches had them in trouble.

Johnson, though, picked up 33 points in 22 games after arriving in January and that isn't far off play-off form.

Longest run without loss/win: 5/10
High – low league position 12-24
Clean sheets: 8 **Yellow cards:** 87 **Red cards:** 8
Average attendance: 3,984 **Players used:** 39
Leading Scorer: A Williams 16 (3,12)
Key stat: Yeovil gained 24 points from losing positions last season

	11-12		Last six seasons at home							
	H	A	P	W	D	L	OV	UN	BS	CS
Portsmouth	-	-	0	0	0	0	0	0	0	
Coventry	-	-	0	0	0	0	0	0	0	
Doncaster	-	-	2	2	0	0	1	1	1	
Sheffield United	L	L	1	0	0	1	0	1	0	0
MK Dons	L	W	4	2	1	1	0	4	0	3
Stevenage	L	D	1	0	0	1	0	0	0	0
Notts County	W	L	2	2	0	0	1	1	1	1
Carlisle	L	L	6	4	1	1	4	2	4	1
Brentford	W	L	4	4	0	0	1	3	1	3
Colchester	W	D	4	2	0	2	2	2	2	0
Bournemouth	L	D	4	1	2	1	3	1	3	1
Tranmere	W	D	6	4	1	1	2	4	3	2
Hartlepool	L	W	5	2	0	3	3	2	2	1
Bury	L	L	1	0	0	1	0	1	0	0
Preston	W	L	1	1	0	0	1	0	1	0
Oldham	W	W	6	3	3	0	3	3	3	3
Yeovil										
Scunthorpe	D	L	3	0	1	2	2	1	2	0
Walsall	W	D	5	1	2	2	2	3	4	0
Leyton Orient	D	D	6	2	3	1	4	2	4	1
Swindon	-	-	4	1	1	2	1	3	1	1
Shrewsbury	-	-	0	0	0	0	0	0	0	0
Crawley	-	-	0	0	0	0	0	0	0	0
Crewe	-	-	3	2	0	1	2	1	1	1

Season	Division	Pos	P	W	D	L	F	A	GD	Pts
2011-12	League 1	17	46	14	12	20	59	80	-21	54
2010-11	League 1	14	46	16	11	19	56	66	-10	59
2009-10	League 1	15	46	13	14	19	55	59	-4	53

Top scorers 2011-12

		P	W	D	L	F	GFA	PGA	Pts
1	Sheff Utd (3)	46	27	9	10	92	2.00	2.0	90
2	MK Dons (5)	46	22	14	10	84	1.83	1.7	80
3	Charlton (1)	46	30	11	5	82	1.78	2.2	101
4	Sheff Wed (2)	46	28	9	9	81	1.76	2.0	93
5	Huddersfield (4)	46	21	18	7	79	1.72	1.8	81
6	Notts Co (7)	46	21	10	15	75	1.63	1.6	73
7	Stevenage (6)	46	18	19	9	69	1.50	1.6	73
8	Carlisle (8)	46	18	15	13	65	1.41	1.5	69
9	Wycombe (21)	46	11	10	25	65	1.41	0.9	43
10	Brentford (9)	46	18	13	15	63	1.37	1.5	67
11	Colchester (10)	46	13	20	13	61	1.33	1.3	59
12	Bury (14)	46	15	11	20	60	1.30	1.2	56
13	Yeovil (17)	46	14	12	20	59	1.28	1.2	54
14	Chesterfield (22)	46	10	12	24	56	1.22	0.9	42
15	Scunthorpe (18)	46	10	22	14	55	1.20	1.1	52
16	Preston (15)	46	13	15	18	54	1.17	1.2	54
17	Walsall (19)	46	10	20	16	51	1.11	1.1	50
18	Hartlepool (13)	46	14	14	18	50	1.09	1.2	56
19	Oldham (16)	46	14	12	20	50	1.09	1.2	54
20	Tranmere (12)	46	14	14	18	49	1.07	1.2	56
21	Bournemouth (11)	46	15	13	18	48	1.04	1.3	58
22	Leyton Orient (20)	46	13	11	22	48	1.04	1.1	50
23	Rochdale (24)	46	8	14	24	47	1.02	0.8	38
24	Exeter (23)	46	10	12	24	46	1.00	0.9	42

Best defence 2011-12

		P	W	D	L	F	GAA	PGA	Pts
1	Charlton (1)	46	30	11	5	36	0.78	2.2	101
2	Stevenage (6)	46	18	19	9	44	0.96	1.6	73
3	Huddersfield (4)	46	21	18	7	47	1.02	1.8	81
4	MK Dons (5)	46	22	14	10	47	1.02	1.7	80
5	Sheff Wed (2)	46	28	9	9	48	1.04	2.0	93
6	Sheff Utd (3)	46	27	9	10	51	1.11	2.0	90
7	Brentford (9)	46	18	13	15	52	1.13	1.5	67
8	Bournemouth (11)	46	15	13	18	52	1.13	1.3	58
9	Tranmere (12)	46	14	14	18	53	1.15	1.2	56
10	Hartlepool (13)	46	14	14	18	55	1.20	1.2	56
11	Walsall (19)	46	10	20	16	57	1.24	1.1	50
12	Scunthorpe (18)	46	10	22	14	59	1.28	1.1	52
13	Notts Co (7)	46	21	10	15	63	1.37	1.6	73
14	Carlisle (8)	46	18	15	13	66	1.43	1.5	69
15	Colchester (10)	46	13	20	13	66	1.43	1.3	59
16	Oldham (16)	46	14	12	20	66	1.43	1.2	54
17	Preston (15)	46	13	15	18	68	1.48	1.2	54
18	Leyton Orient (20)	46	13	11	22	75	1.63	1.1	50
19	Exeter (23)	46	10	12	24	75	1.63	0.9	42
20	Bury (14)	46	15	11	20	79	1.72	1.2	56
21	Yeovil (17)	46	14	12	20	80	1.74	1.2	54
22	Chesterfield (22)	46	10	12	24	81	1.76	0.9	42
23	Rochdale (24)	46	8	14	24	81	1.76	0.8	38
24	Wycombe (21)	46	11	10	25	88	1.91	0.9	43

CHRIS POWELL: defensive overhaul at Charlton helped the Addicks take the title

Clean sheets 2011-12

		P	CS	%
1	Charlton (1)	46	20	43.5
2	Tranmere (12)	46	17	37.0
3	MK Dons (5)	46	16	34.8
4	Brentford (9)	46	16	34.8
5	Sheff Wed (2)	46	16	34.8
6	Huddersfield (4)	46	16	34.8
7	Sheff Utd (3)	46	15	32.6
8	Stevenage (6)	46	15	32.6
9	Notts Co (7)	46	14	30.4
10	Hartlepool (13)	46	14	30.4
11	Bournemouth (11)	46	14	30.4
12	Preston (15)	46	13	28.3
13	Walsall (19)	46	11	23.9
14	Colchester (10)	46	11	23.9
15	Rochdale (24)	46	10	21.7
16	Scunthorpe (18)	46	10	21.7
17	Leyton Orient (20)	46	10	21.7
18	Bury (14)	46	9	19.6
19	Exeter (23)	46	9	19.6
20	Oldham (16)	46	9	19.6
21	Carlisle (8)	46	9	19.6
22	Yeovil (17)	46	8	17.4
23	Chesterfield (22)	46	8	17.4
24	Wycombe (21)	46	4	8.7

First to score 2011-12

		P	FS	%
1	Charlton (1)	46	32	69.6
2	Huddersfield (4)	46	32	69.6
3	Sheff Wed (2)	46	29	63.0
4	MK Dons (5)	46	27	58.7
5	Notts Co (7)	46	27	58.7
6	Sheff Utd (3)	46	26	56.5
7	Tranmere (12)	46	24	52.2
8	Brentford (9)	46	23	50.0
9	Leyton Orient (20)	46	23	50.0
10	Preston (15)	46	21	45.7
11	Walsall (19)	46	21	45.7
12	Stevenage (6)	46	21	45.7
13	Colchester (10)	46	21	45.7
14	Bournemouth (11)	46	20	43.5
15	Chesterfield (22)	46	20	43.5
16	Hartlepool (13)	46	19	41.3
17	Bury (14)	46	17	37.0
18	Carlisle (8)	46	17	37.0
19	Scunthorpe (18)	46	17	37.0
20	Oldham (16)	46	16	34.8
21	Wycombe (21)	46	16	34.8
22	Yeovil (17)	46	15	32.6
23	Exeter (23)	46	12	26.1
24	Rochdale (24)	46	12	26.1

Top scorers 2011-12

		Goals
J Rhodes	Huddersfield	36
C Evans	Sheff Utd	29
B Wright-Phillips	Charlton	22
S Beavon	Wycombe	21
G Madine	Sheff Wed	18
A Williams	Yeovil	16
L Miller	Carlisle	14
J Hughes	Notts Co	13
L Novak	Huddersfield	13
L Williamson	Sheff Utd	13
A Wordsworth	Colchester	13
F Zoko	Carlisle	13
G Alexander	Brentford	12
D Bowditch	MK Dons	12
J Jackson	Charlton	12
Y Kermorgant	Charlton	12
K Lisbie	Leyton Orient	12
R Lowe	Sheff Wed	12
C Donaldson	Brentford	11
S Gillespie	Colchester	11

Record when keeping a clean sheet 2011-12

		P	W	D	L	F	GFA	PGA	Pts
1	Charlton (1)	20	20	0	0	40	2.00	3.0	60
2	Sheff Utd (3)	15	15	0	0	33	2.20	3.0	45
3	Huddersfield (4)	16	15	1	0	34	2.13	2.9	46
4	MK Dons (5)	16	14	2	0	31	1.94	2.8	44
5	Sheff Wed (2)	16	14	2	0	27	1.69	2.8	44
6	Notts Co (7)	14	11	3	0	20	1.43	2.6	36
7	Leyton Orient (20)	10	8	2	0	13	1.30	2.6	26
8	Chesterfield (22)	8	6	2	0	11	1.38	2.5	20
9	Wycombe (21)	4	3	1	0	9	2.25	2.5	10
10	Tranmere (12)	17	12	5	0	21	1.24	2.4	41
11	Bournemouth (11)	14	10	4	0	16	1.14	2.4	34
12	Brentford (9)	16	10	6	0	24	1.50	2.3	36
13	Colchester (10)	11	7	4	0	11	1.00	2.3	25
14	Bury (14)	9	6	3	0	10	1.11	2.3	21
15	Oldham (16)	9	6	3	0	8	0.89	2.3	21
16	Stevenage (6)	15	8	7	0	15	1.00	2.1	31
17	Hartlepool (13)	14	8	6	0	18	1.29	2.1	30
18	Preston (15)	13	7	6	0	9	0.69	2.1	27
19	Walsall (19)	11	6	5	0	8	0.73	2.1	23
20	Yeovil (17)	8	4	4	0	4	0.50	2.0	16
21	Exeter (23)	9	4	5	0	10	1.11	1.9	17
22	Carlisle (8)	9	4	5	0	7	0.78	1.9	17
23	Rochdale (24)	10	4	6	0	6	0.60	1.8	18
24	Scunthorpe (18)	10	2	8	0	2	0.20	1.4	14

Record when first to score 2011-12

		P	W	D	L	F	GFA	PGA	Pts
1	Charlton (1)	32	27	5	0	66	16	2.7	86
2	Sheff Wed (2)	29	25	1	3	61	21	2.6	76
3	Stevenage (6)	21	17	4	0	51	15	2.6	55
4	Sheff Utd (3)	26	20	5	1	59	17	2.5	65
5	Carlisle (8)	17	12	5	0	37	18	2.4	41
6	Oldham (16)	16	11	5	0	29	14	2.4	38
7	MK Dons (5)	27	19	6	2	62	23	2.3	63
8	Notts Co (7)	27	19	4	4	53	23	2.3	61
9	Brentford (9)	23	17	3	3	51	20	2.3	54
10	Huddersfield (4)	32	19	13	0	67	28	2.2	70
11	Hartlepool (13)	19	12	5	2	38	17	2.2	41
12	Bury (14)	17	11	2	4	35	23	2.1	35
13	Bournemouth (11)	20	12	5	3	30	14	2.0	41
14	Preston (15)	21	12	5	4	35	25	2.0	41
15	Exeter (23)	12	7	3	2	27	16	2.0	24
16	Colchester (10)	21	11	7	3	42	27	1.9	40
17	Wycombe (21)	16	9	3	4	40	22	1.9	30
18	Yeovil (17)	15	8	4	3	25	19	1.9	28
19	Tranmere (12)	24	13	5	6	37	22	1.8	44
20	Leyton Orient (20)	23	11	6	6	32	26	1.7	39
21	Scunthorpe (18)	17	7	6	4	27	23	1.6	27
22	Walsall (19)	21	7	10	4	32	28	1.5	31
23	Chesterfield (22)	20	8	6	6	35	28	1.5	30
24	Rochdale (24)	12	5	3	4	18	19	1.5	18

Key *Number in brackets refers to final league finishing position. Points do not include any deductions but league positions do. GFA: Goals for average per match, GAA: Goals against average per match, PGA: Average points gained per match, CS: clean sheet, FS: first to score*

Richards can fire the Spireites to glory

LEAGUE 2 has all the makings of being a tight and compact division and it looks unlikely that there will be a team as dominant as last season's champions Swindon, *writes Andy Dietz.*

Paolo Di Canio's title winners finished with 93 points – a figure only bettered by the MK Dons side of 2007-08 in the last decade – and a tally in the mid 80s might be enough this time.

One team capable of running away with things, at least in the eyes of the bookies, are Rotherham. They blew out as favourites in 2009-10, but are half that price at 7-2 after chairman Tony Stewart lured Steve Evans, on the brink of promotion with Crawley, to manage the side in their first season at an impressive new stadium back in their own town.

Short-priced favourites don't have a great record in this division, though. Crawley last season and Peterborough in 2007-08 were just as skinny and failed to land the odds so it might better to back a double-figure team each-way.

This brings us to Rotherham's neighbours **Chesterfield**, who are 12-1 and have course-and-distance form having won the division in 2010-11.

It's surprising to see them back so soon, but they failed to replace top striker Craig Davies last season, who moved on after spearheading their title challenge.

Manager John Sheridan will hope new recruit **Marc Richards** can fill the void. He passed a century of career league goals last season and his past performances at this level for Port Vale offer plenty of promise.

His league goals tally in the last three seasons – 16 last term, 17 in 2010-11 and 19 in 2009-10 – makes him a player to consider in the top goalscorer market.

Of the other title contenders, there has been a sustained gamble on new boys Fleetwood, who have a similar profile to Crawley 12 months ago. However, they look too short at 7-1, having been 10-1 when the betting opened.

Southend and Cheltenham are tempting in the promotion betting if they keep the core of last season's squads and shake off the play-off hangovers.

At the other end of the table, **Barnet** are a strong fancy to finally drop down and **Dagenham & Redbridge**, who rallied late to avoid a second successive relegation last season, look the team most likely to join them.

They have a well-respected manager in John Still, but the Daggers have a regressive profile and, with average attendances around the 2,000 mark, must continually sell their best players to remain afloat.

League 2 winner	b365	Btfrd	Hills	Lads	Pwr	StJms
Rotherham	10-3	**7-2**	**7-2**	3	**7-2**	**7-2**
Fleetwood	13-2	5	**7**	6	**13-2**	**7**
Chesterfield	11	12	11	10	**12**	**12**
Bristol Rovers	14	12	14	14	**16**	10
Oxford	14	**14**	11	12	12	10
Southend	**16**	14	12	14	**16**	12
Gillingham	18	**20**	**20**	18	**20**	16
Northampton	20	20	14	**20**	**20**	14
Torquay	**20**	**20**	10	14	**20**	12
Bradford	20	20	20	20	20	20
Plymouth	25	25	25	22	22	14
Cheltenham	25	20	12	14	**25**	20
Exeter	25	25	25	20	22	20
Rochdale	25	20	20	20	22	20
Wycombe	22	**25**	**25**	16	20	14
Port Vale	40	33	**40**	33	33	25
York	33	**40**	25	25	25	22
Aldershot	33	33	14	25	25	**33**
Wimbledon	50	**66**	**66**	50	50	40
Dagenham & R	**66**	50	**66**	50	50	50
Burton	66	66	**80**	50	50	33
Accrington	80	66	**100**	50	50	40
Morecambe	66	66	**100**	50	66	50
Barnet	80	80	**100**	66	66	66

Win or each-way. See individual bookmakers for terms

Accrington

Nickname: Stanley
Colours: Red, White and Black
Ground: The Crown Ground (5,070)
Tel: 0871-434-1968   www.accringtonstanley.co.uk

FOR the first time in 13 years Accy go into a season without John Coleman at the helm and they may find it tough under the new regime.

Former player coach Paul Cook has big shoes to fill and a record of three wins in 18 games doesn't inspire confidence.

There's been a shake-up in the board-room as well after chairman Ilyas Khan, who helped saved the club from extinction three year ago, quit. These changes are likely to have a detrimental effect.

Longest run without loss/win: 10/7
High – low league position 8-19
Clean sheets: 8 Yellow cards: 70 Red cards: 8
Average attendance: 1,785 Players used: 38
Leading Scorer: P Amond 7 (1,6)
Key stat: Accrington have yet to keep a clean sheet under Paul Cook's management

	11-12		Last six seasons at home							
	H	A	P	W	D	L	OV	UN	BS	CS
Wycombe	-	-	4	1	1	2	1	3	2	0
Chesterfield	-	-	4	3	1	0	2	2	2	2
Exeter	-	-	1	1	0	0	1	0	1	0
Rochdale	-	-	4	0	1	3	3	1	4	0
Southend	L	D	2	1	0	1	2	0	2	0
Torquay	W	L	4	4	0	0	2	2	2	2
Cheltenham	L	L	3	1	0	2	2	1	1	1
Gillingham	W	D	3	2	0	1	2	1	2	0
Oxford	L	D	2	0	1	1	0	2	0	1
Rotherham	D	L	5	1	1	3	3	2	4	0
Aldershot	W	D	4	2	1	1	2	2	2	1
Port Vale	D	L	4	2	1	1	3	1	2	2
Bristol Rovers	W	L	2	1	1	0	1	1	2	0
Accrington										
Morecambe	D	W	5	3	2	0	2	3	4	1
Wimbledon	W	W	1	1	0	0	1	0	1	0
Burton	W	W	3	2	0	1	2	1	2	0
Bradford	W	D	5	3	0	2	2	3	1	3
Dagenham & R	W	L	4	2	1	1	1	3	0	3
Northampton	W	D	3	2	0	1	3	0	2	0
Plymouth	L	D	1	0	0	1	1	0	0	0
Barnet	L	D	6	3	1	2	3	3	3	1
Fleetwood	-	-	0	0	0	0	0	0	0	0
York	-	-	0	0	0	0	0	0	0	0

Season	Division	Pos	P	W	D	L	F	A	GD	Pts
2011-12	League 2	14	46	14	15	17	54	66	-12	57
2010-11	League 2	5	46	18	19	9	73	55	18	73
2009-10	League 2	15	46	18	7	21	62	74	-12	61

Aldershot

Nickname: The Shots
Colours: Red and Blue
Ground: EBB Stadium (6,835)
Tel: 01252-320-211   www.theshots.co.uk

BRICK by brick, Dean Holdsworth is building solid foundations at Aldershot and his side could be set for a play-off challenge.

The Shots kept 15 clean sheets last term and, while captain and defensive lynchpin Darren Jones has left, there's plenty of potential in a vibrant squad.

Eradicating patchy form will be crucial. Although they broke a 60-year-old club record by winning six straight league games earlier this year, there were a few damaging losing streaks along the way.

Longest run without loss/win: 7/6
High – low league position 10-19
Clean sheets: 15 Yellow cards: 64 Red cards: 4
Average attendance: 2,865 Players used: 41
Leading Scorer: D Hylton 13 (7,11)
Key stat: The Shots had four losing runs of four games or more in the league last season

	11-12		Last six seasons at home							
	H	A	P	W	D	L	OV	UN	BS	CS
Wycombe	-	-	2	1	1	0	1	1	1	1
Chesterfield	-	-	3	1	1	1	0	3	1	1
Exeter	-	-	3	3	0	0	1	2	1	2
Rochdale	-	-	2	0	1	1	1	1	2	0
Southend	W	W	2	2	0	0	0	2	0	2
Torquay	L	L	4	1	0	3	1	3	0	1
Cheltenham	W	L	3	2	0	1	1	2	1	1
Gillingham	L	L	3	1	1	1	2	1	3	0
Oxford	L	D	4	1	1	2	2	2	2	1
Rotherham	D	L	4	1	2	1	3	1	2	1
Aldershot										
Port Vale	L	L	4	1	1	2	2	2	3	1
Bristol Rovers	W	W	1	1	0	0	0	1	0	1
Accrington	D	L	4	2	2	0	2	2	3	1
Morecambe	W	L	5	3	0	2	2	3	2	1
Wimbledon	D	W	1	0	1	0	0	1	1	0
Burton	W	W	5	3	0	2	2	3	2	2
Bradford	W	W	4	4	0	0	1	3	1	3
Dagenham & R	D	W	4	0	2	2	2	2	4	0
Northampton	L	L	3	1	1	1	1	2	2	0
Plymouth	D	L	1	0	1	0	0	1	0	1
Barnet	W	L	4	3	1	0	2	2	2	2
Fleetwood	-	-	0	0	0	0	0	0	0	0
York	-	-	2	1	0	1	0	2	0	1

Season	Division	Pos	P	W	D	L	F	A	GD	Pts
2011-12	League 2	11	46	19	9	18	54	52	2	66
2010-11	League 2	14	46	14	19	13	54	54	0	61
2009-10	League 2	6	46	20	12	14	69	56	13	72

Barnet

Nickname: The Bees
Colours: Amber and Black
Ground: Underhill (6,023)
Tel: 020-8441-6932   www.barnetfc.com

SURELY Barnet have used up all of their lives after a third consecutive final-day escape from relegation.

The Bees' latest Houdini act saw them defeat Burton in their last game to secure safety at the expense of Hereford, and while they've shown survival skills Bear Grylls would be proud of, sooner or later their struggles will catch up with them.

With a huge void left by the departure of 18-goal Izale McLeod, this could be the season they fall.

Longest run without loss/win: 5/9
High – low league position 17-23
Clean sheets: 10 **Yellow cards:** 70 **Red cards:** 3
Average attendance: 2,266 **Players used:** 35
Leading Scorer: I McLeod 18 (7,14)
Key stat: Barnet gained 14 points from a possible 57 in their final 19 games of last season

	11-12 H	A	Last six seasons at home P	W	D	L	OV	UN	BS	CS
Wycombe	-	-	4	2	1	1	2	2	3	0
Chesterfield	-	-	4	1	1	2	3	1	3	0
Exeter	-	-	1	0	0	1	0	1	0	0
Rochdale	-	-	4	3	1	0	2	0	2	2
Southend	L	L	2	0	0	2	1	1	0	0
Torquay	L	L	4	0	1	3	1	3	1	0
Cheltenham	D	L	3	1	2	0	2	1	3	0
Gillingham	D	L	3	0	2	1	3	0	3	0
Oxford	L	L	2	0	1	1	1	1	1	0
Rotherham	D	D	5	2	1	2	1	4	2	2
Aldershot	W	L	4	2	0	2	4	0	2	1
Port Vale	L	W	4	1	1	2	2	2	2	2
Bristol Rovers	W	W	2	1	1	0	0	2	1	1
Accrington	D	W	6	2	2	2	4	2	4	2
Morecambe	L	W	5	1	1	3	1	4	2	1
Wimbledon	W	D	1	1	0	0	1	0	0	1
Burton	L	W	3	0	2	1	2	2	1	0
Bradford	L	L	5	2	1	2	4	1	3	0
Dagenham & R	D	L	4	2	2	0	2	2	3	1
Northampton	L	W	3	1	1	1	2	1	2	1
Plymouth	W	D	1	1	0	0	0	1	0	1
Barnet										
Fleetwood	-	-	0	0	0	0	0	0	0	0
York	-	-	0	0	0	0	0	0	0	0

Season	Division	Pos	P	W	D	L	F	A	GD	Pts
2011-12	League 2	22	46	12	10	24	52	79	-27	46
2010-11	League 2	22	46	12	12	22	58	77	-19	48
2009-10	League 2	21	46	12	12	22	47	63	-16	48

Bradford

Nickname: The Bantams
Colours: Claret and Amber
Ground: Coral Windows Stadium (25,136)
Tel: 0871-978-1911   www.bradfordcityfc.co.uk

POSITIVE vibes emanating from Valley Parade could signal an improvement after another season of underachievement.

Back-to-back 18th-place finishes will have done little to appease success-starved supporters, but their side showed signs of getting their act together with three victories in their final six games.

Resources have been made available for a concerted push for promotion and although big budgets have been blown before, the early signings offer promise.

Longest run without loss/win: 5/6
High – low league position 18-22
Clean sheets: 9 **Yellow cards:** 67 **Red cards:** 6
Average attendance: 10,491 **Players used:** 40
Leading Scorer: J Hanson 13 (3,11)
Key stat: Bradford lost 14 away games in the league – only relegated Macclesfield fared worse on the road

	11-12 H	A	Last six seasons at home P	W	D	L	OV	UN	BS	CS
Wycombe	-	-	3	2	0	1	0	3	0	2
Chesterfield	-	-	5	4	0	1	2	3	1	3
Exeter	-	-	1	1	0	0	1	0	1	0
Rochdale	-	-	3	1	0	2	2	1	1	1
Southend	W	W	2	1	0	1	0	2	0	1
Torquay	W	W	3	2	0	1	0	2	0	2
Cheltenham	L	L	4	1	2	1	2	2	3	0
Gillingham	D	D	4	2	2	0	3	1	3	1
Oxford	W	D	2	2	0	0	2	0	1	1
Rotherham	L	L	6	3	1	2	5	1	5	1
Aldershot	L	L	4	3	0	1	4	0	3	1
Port Vale	D	L	5	1	2	2	0	5	1	2
Bristol Rovers	D	L	1	0	1	0	1	0	1	0
Accrington	D	L	5	0	4	1	1	4	4	0
Morecambe	D	D	5	3	1	1	2	3	1	3
Wimbledon	L	L	1	0	0	1	1	0	1	0
Burton	D	D	3	0	3	0	0	3	3	0
Bradford										
Dagenham & R	L	L	4	0	2	2	1	3	2	0
Northampton	W	W	4	2	1	1	2	2	3	1
Plymouth	D	L	1	0	1	0	0	1	1	0
Barnet	W	W	5	2	2	1	4	1	5	0
Fleetwood	-	-	0	0	0	0	0	0	0	0
York	-	-	0	0	0	0	0	0	0	0

Season	Division	Pos	P	W	D	L	F	A	GD	Pts
2011-12	League 2	18	46	12	14	20	54	59	-5	50
2010-11	League 2	18	46	15	7	24	43	68	-25	52
2009-10	League 2	14	46	16	14	16	59	62	-3	62

Bristol Rovers

Nickname: Pirates
Colours: Blue and White
Ground: Memorial Stadium (11,626)
Tel: 0117-909-6648   www.bristolrovers.co.uk

THE play-offs should be the minimum target as the Pirates aim to kick on from last season's mid-table finish.

A crumb of comfort from a poor season was the time it gave Mark McGhee to assess the players at his disposal – having taken over in January, McGhee will have had one eye on next term and will know the areas of his squad that need work.

If Rovers are to make a serious impact, they will need to find a solution to their poor away form.

Longest run without loss/win: 5/8
High – low league position 12-19
Clean sheets: 12 **Yellow cards:** 83 **Red cards:** 2
Average attendance: 6,035 **Players used:** 32
Leading Scorer: M Harrold 16 (7,13)
Key stat: Rovers have won one of their last ten away games – and they only won five on the road all season

	11-12		Last six seasons at home							
	H	A	P	W	D	L	OV	UN	BS	CS
Wycombe	-	-	2	0	0	2	2	0	2	0
Chesterfield	-	-	0	0	0	0	0	0	0	0
Exeter	-	-	2	1	0	1	0	2	0	1
Rochdale	-	-	2	1	1	0	1	1	1	1
Southend	W	D	4	3	1	0	2	2	3	1
Torquay	L	D	2	1	0	1	1	1	1	1
Cheltenham	L	W	3	2	0	1	2	1	2	1
Gillingham	D	L	3	1	2	0	2	1	3	0
Oxford	D	L	1	0	1	0	0	1	0	1
Rotherham	W	W	1	1	0	0	1	0	1	0
Aldershot	L	L	1	0	0	1	0	1	0	0
Port Vale	L	L	2	1	0	1	2	0	1	0
Bristol Rovers										
Accrington	W	L	2	2	0	0	2	0	1	1
Morecambe	W	W	1	1	0	0	1	0	1	0
Wimbledon	W	W	1	1	0	0	1	0	1	0
Burton	W	L	1	1	0	0	1	0	1	0
Bradford	W	D	1	1	0	0	1	0	1	0
Dagenham & R	W	L	2	1	0	1	0	2	0	1
Northampton	W	L	3	2	1	0	2	2	1	1
Plymouth	L	D	2	0	0	2	2	0	2	0
Barnet	L	L	2	1	0	1	0	2	0	1
Fleetwood	-	-	0	0	0	0	0	0	0	0
York	-	-	0	0	0	0	0	0	0	0

Season	Division	Pos	P	W	D	L	F	A	GD	Pts
2011-12	League 2	13	46	15	12	19	60	70	-10	57
2010-11	League 1	22	46	11	12	23	48	82	-34	45
2009-10	League 1	11	46	19	5	22	59	70	-11	62

Burton Albion

Nickname: The Brewers
Colours: Yellow and Black
Ground: Pirelli Stadium (6,912)
Tel: 01283-565938   www.burtonalbionfc.co.uk

STEERING clear of relegation is the aim for Burton but they could find themselves involved in another struggle.

For the past two seasons, they've been battling at the wrong end of the table and new boss Gary Rowett has been charged with turning things round.

He managed three wins in 11 games during his spell as caretaker and his inexperience is a worry, as is his team's leaky defence. Rowett must learn the ropes quickly if his side are to beat the drop.

Longest run without loss/win: 4/16
High – low league position 4-17
Clean sheets: 8 **Yellow cards:** 77 **Red cards:** 5
Average attendance: 2,805 **Players used:** 31
Leading Scorer: C Zola 12 (3,12) B Kee 12 (4,9)
Key stat: Burton's 81 goals conceded last season was the worst in League 2 and they shipped an average of over two goals a game on the road

	11-12		Last six seasons at home							
	H	A	P	W	D	L	OV	UN	BS	CS
Wycombe	-	-	1	0	0	1	1	0	1	0
Chesterfield	-	-	2	1	1	0	1	1	1	0
Exeter	-	-	2	1	1	0	1	1	1	1
Rochdale	-	-	1	1	0	0	0	1	0	1
Southend	L	W	2	1	0	1	1	1	1	0
Torquay	L	D	5	1	1	3	3	2	3	0
Cheltenham	L	L	3	1	0	2	1	2	1	1
Gillingham	W	L	2	1	1	0	0	2	1	1
Oxford	D	D	5	0	2	3	2	3	3	1
Rotherham	D	W	3	0	1	2	1	2	2	0
Aldershot	L	L	5	2	0	3	4	1	3	1
Port Vale	D	L	3	1	2	0	0	3	1	2
Bristol Rovers	W	L	1	1	0	0	1	0	1	0
Accrington	L	L	3	0	1	2	0	3	1	0
Morecambe	W	D	4	4	0	0	4	0	4	0
Wimbledon	W	L	1	1	0	0	1	0	1	0
Burton										
Bradford	D	D	3	1	2	0	2	1	2	1
Dagenham & R	D	D	3	0	1	2	0	3	1	0
Northampton	L	W	3	1	1	1	1	2	2	0
Plymouth	W	L	1	1	0	0	1	0	1	0
Barnet	L	W	3	1	0	2	2	1	2	1
Fleetwood	-	-	0	0	0	0	0	0	0	0
York	-	-	3	2	0	1	3	0	3	0

Season	Division	Pos	P	W	D	L	F	A	GD	Pts
2011-12	League 2	17	46	14	12	20	54	81	-27	54
2010-11	League 2	19	46	12	15	19	56	70	-14	51
2009-10	League 2	13	46	17	11	18	71	71	0	62

Cheltenham

Nickname: The Robins
Colours: Red and White
Ground: Abbey Business Stadium (7,133)
Tel: 01242-573-558   www.ctfc.com

LAST year's surprise package have the right blend to hit the promotion mix again.

Having dominated play-off winners Crewe for long periods of the final, the Robins can feel a little aggrieved at having to prepare for another season in League 2.

But if Mark Yates, the fourth-tier manager of the year for many, can keep the core of his improving squad together, his men can replicate last term's achievements.

Finding a top striker to complement his excellent wingers would be a big boost.

Longest run without loss/win: 10/7
High – low league position 1-15
Clean sheets: 16 **Yellow cards:** 56 **Red cards:** 2
Average attendance: 3,425 **Players used:** 25
Leading Scorer: D Duffy 11 (3,8) K Mohamed 11 (5,11)
Key stat: Cheltenham had a W15, D5, L4 record against teams who finished in the bottom half of the table last season

	11-12 H	A	P	W	D	L	OV	UN	BS	CS
Wycombe	-	-	1	0	0	1	1	0	1	0
Chesterfield	-	-	3	0	1	2	1	2	0	1
Exeter	-	-	0	0	0	0	0	0	0	0
Rochdale	-	-	1	0	0	1	1	0	1	0
Southend	W	L	4	1	2	1	1	3	1	2
Torquay	L	D	3	0	2	1	1	2	2	0
Cheltenham										
Gillingham	L	L	4	1	1	2	2	2	2	1
Oxford	D	W	2	0	2	0	0	2	1	1
Rotherham	W	L	4	2	2	0	0	4	2	2
Aldershot	W	L	3	1	0	2	2	1	2	1
Port Vale	W	W	5	2	2	1	0	5	1	3
Bristol Rovers	L	W	3	2	0	1	1	2	1	1
Accrington	W	W	3	1	1	1	2	1	3	0
Morecambe	L	L	3	1	1	1	1	2	2	1
Wimbledon	D	L	1	0	1	0	0	1	0	1
Burton	W	W	3	2	0	1	1	2	1	1
Bradford	W	W	4	2	0	2	4	0	3	1
Dagenham & R	W	W	2	1	1	0	1	1	2	0
Northampton	D	W	6	1	3	2	2	4	3	1
Plymouth	W	W	1	1	0	0	1	0	1	0
Barnet	W	D	3	2	1	0	1	-2	2	1
Fleetwood	-	-	0	0	0	0	0	0	0	0
York	-	-	0	0	0	0	0	0	0	0

Season	Division	Pos	P	W	D	L	F	A	GD	Pts
2011-12	League 2	6	46	23	8	15	66	50	16	77
2010-11	League 2	17	46	13	13	20	56	77	-21	52
2009-10	League 2	22	46	10	18	18	54	71	-17	48

Chesterfield

Nickname: Spireites
Colours: Blue and White
Ground: the b2net Stadium (10,300)
Tel: 01246-209-765   www.chesterfield-fc.co.uk

IT'S back to the drawing board for the 2010-11 champions after their stay in League 1 lasted a solitary season.

The Spireites looked like a club on the up having gained promotion in their first campaign at the b2net Stadium, but they never got to grips with League 1 and were in the drop slots from October onwards.

On the plus side, John Sheridan knows what it takes to get out of this division and he has landed a major coup persuading striker Marc Richards to join.

Longest run without loss/win: 4/17
High – low league position 14-24
Clean sheets: 8 **Yellow cards:** 39 **Red cards:** 0
Average attendance: 6,530 **Players used:** 36
Leading Scorer: L Clarke 9 (3,7)
Key stat: Chesterfield have just won ten games in all competitions since the turn of the year

	11-12 H	A	P	W	D	L	OV	UN	BS	CS
Wycombe	W	L	4	3	0	1	2	2	1	2
Chesterfield										
Exeter	L	L	2	1	0	1	1	1	1	0
Rochdale	W	D	4	3	0	1	3	1	2	2
Southend	-	-	1	1	0	0	1	0	1	0
Torquay	-	-	2	2	0	0	0	2	0	2
Cheltenham	-	-	3	3	0	0	1	2	0	3
Gillingham	-	-	3	1	0	2	1	2	1	0
Oxford	-	-	1	0	0	1	1	0	1	0
Rotherham	-	-	5	3	0	2	2	3	1	2
Aldershot	-	-	3	1	1	1	2	1	2	0
Port Vale	-	-	4	3	0	1	3	1	1	2
Bristol Rovers	-	-	0	0	0	0	0	0	0	0
Accrington	-	-	4	3	1	0	2	2	3	1
Morecambe	-	-	4	0	2	2	2	2	3	0
Wimbledon	-	-	0	0	0	0	0	0	0	0
Burton	-	-	2	1	0	1	2	0	2	0
Bradford	-	-	5	1	3	1	2	3	3	1
Dagenham & R	-	-	3	0	3	0	1	2	3	0
Northampton	-	-	3	2	1	0	1	2	1	2
Plymouth	-	-	0	0	0	0	0	0	0	0
Barnet	-	-	4	2	1	1	1	3	2	1
Fleetwood	-	-	0	0	0	0	0	0	0	0
York	-	-	0	0	0	0	0	0	0	0

Season	Division	Pos	P	W	D	L	F	A	GD	Pts
2011-12	League 1	22	46	10	12	24	56	81	-25	42
2010-11	League 2	1	46	24	14	8	85	51	34	86
2009-10	League 2	8	46	21	7	18	61	62	-1	70

Dagenham & R

Nickname: Daggers
Colours: Red and White
Ground: LB Barking & Dagenham Stadium (6,070)
Tel: 020-8592-1549   www.daggers.co.uk

THE Daggers flirted with relegation for large chunks of last season and their supporters might have to cope with more anxious moments this time round.

Conference football seemed a distinct possibility for John Still's men, with a run of 14 defeats in 15 league games the low point of a dismal end to 2011.

They reached safety by going unbeaten in nine of their last ten games, but that hasn't stopped a clear-out of the ageing squad and new blood is much needed.

Longest run without loss/win: 8/10
High – low league position 11-24
Clean sheets: 9 **Yellow cards:** 47 **Red cards:** 7
Average attendance: 2,091 **Players used:** 40
Leading Scorer: B Woodall 11 (4,9)
Key stat: The shot-shy Daggers averaged only 1.08 goals per league game last season. Only Plymouth and relegated Macclesfield were worse

	11-12 H A	Last six seasons at home P	W	D	L	OV	UN	BS	CS
Wycombe	- -	2	0	1	1	1	1	1	0
Chesterfield	- -	3	2	0	1	3	0	1	1
Exeter	- -	3	1	1	1	2	1	3	0
Rochdale	- -	4	1	1	2	2	2	3	0
Southend	L D	1	0	0	1	1	0	1	0
Torquay	D L	2	1	1	0	1	1	2	0
Cheltenham	L L	2	0	0	2	1	1	0	0
Gillingham	W W	2	2	0	0	1	1	1	1
Oxford	L L	2	0	0	2	0	2	0	0
Rotherham	W L	4	1	1	2	1	3	2	0
Aldershot	L D	4	2	0	2	4	0	4	0
Port Vale	L W	3	0	2	1	1	2	3	0
Bristol Rovers	W L	2	1	0	1	2	0	0	1
Accrington	W L	4	2	1	1	3	1	3	1
Morecambe	L W	5	2	1	2	2	3	3	1
Wimbledon	L L	1	0	0	1	0	1	0	0
Burton	D D	3	2	1	0	2	1	2	1
Bradford	W W	4	3	0	1	3	1	2	2
Dagenham & R									
Northampton	L L	2	0	0	2	0	2	0	0
Plymouth	L D	2	0	0	2	1	1	1	0
Barnet	W D	4	3	1	0	2	2	2	2
Fleetwood	- -	0	0	0	0	0	0	0	0
York	- -	1	1	0	0	1	0	1	0

Season	Division	Pos	P	W	D	L	F	A	GD	Pts
2011-12	League 2	19	46	14	8	24	50	72	-22	50
2010-11	League 1	21	46	12	11	23	52	70	-18	47
2009-10	League 2	7	46	20	12	14	69	58	11	72

Exeter

Nickname: The Grecians
Colours: Black and White
Ground: St James Park (8,830)
Tel: 01392-411-243   www.exetercityfc.co.uk

AFTER three seasons in League 1 the Grecians are back in the basement but they will be hoping to bounce back at the first attempt. A lack of goals cost them dear last term and strengthening their striking options is a must.

One fillip for their fans is the prospect of facing Devon rivals Torquay and Plymouth and it will be interesting to see which out of the three fares best. Local bragging rights aside, Exeter have enough about them to finish in the top ten.

Longest run without loss/win: 6/9
High – low league position 17-24
Clean sheets: 9 **Yellow cards:** 52 **Red cards:** 4
Average attendance: 4,474 **Players used:** 35
Leading Scorer: D Nardiello 9 (4,7)
Key stat: Exeter had the worst scoring record in League 1, managing just 46 goals

	11-12 H A	Last six seasons at home P	W	D	L	OV	UN	BS	CS
Wycombe	L L	3	1	1	1	1	2	2	1
Chesterfield	W W	2	1	0	1	2	0	2	0
Exeter									
Rochdale	W L	3	3	0	0	2	1	2	1
Southend	- -	1	1	0	0	1	0	1	0
Torquay	- -	1	1	0	0	1	0	1	0
Cheltenham	- -	0	0	0	0	0	0	0	0
Gillingham	- -	2	1	1	0	1	1	1	1
Oxford	- -	2	2	0	0	1	1	1	1
Rotherham	- -	1	0	1	0	0	1	1	0
Aldershot	- -	3	1	2	0	1	2	2	1
Port Vale	- -	1	1	0	0	0	1	0	1
Bristol Rovers	- -	2	1	1	0	1	1	1	1
Accrington	- -	1	1	0	0	1	0	1	0
Morecambe	- -	2	1	1	0	1	1	1	1
Wimbledon	- -	0	0	0	0	0	0	0	0
Burton	- -	2	1	0	1	2	0	1	1
Bradford	- -	1	1	0	0	1	0	1	0
Dagenham & R	- -	3	3	0	0	3	0	3	0
Northampton	- -	0	0	0	0	0	0	0	0
Plymouth	- -	1	1	0	0	0	1	0	1
Barnet	- -	1	1	0	0	1	0	1	0
Fleetwood	- -	0	0	0	0	0	0	0	0
York	- -	2	0	2	0	0	2	2	0

Season	Division	Pos	P	W	D	L	F	A	GD	Pts
2011-12	League 1	23	46	10	12	24	46	75	-29	42
2010-11	League 1	8	46	20	10	16	66	73	-7	70
2009-10	League 1	18	46	11	18	17	48	60	-12	51

Fleetwood

Nickname: The Cod Army/Trawlermen
Colours: Red and White
Ground: Highbury Stadium (5,092)
Tel: 01253-775-080   www.fleetwoodtownfc.com

LIKE Crawley 12 months earlier, runaway Conference champions Fleetwood bring financial muscle to the party and are among the front-runners for promotion.

The club's sizeable war chest has been swelled by the sale of star striker Jamie Vardy and early signings show ambition.

The Cod Army have enjoyed a meteoric rise, having plied their trade in the ninth tier of English football as recently as 2005. That momentum can continue with a play-off place a realistic target.

Longest run without loss/win: 29/4
High – low league position 1-8
Clean sheets: 15 **Yellow cards:** 93 **Red cards:** 5
Average attendance: 2,264 **Players used:** 37
Leading Scorer: J Vardy 31 (4,20)
Key stat: Fleetwood scored a staggering 102 goals in the Conference last season

Team	11-12 H	A	P	W	D	L	OV	UN	BS	CS
Wycombe	-	-	0	0	0	0	0	0	0	0
Chesterfield	-	-	0	0	0	0	0	0	0	0
Exeter	-	-	0	0	0	0	0	0	0	0
Rochdale	-	-	0	0	0	0	0	0	0	0
Southend	-	-	0	0	0	0	0	0	0	0
Torquay	-	-	0	0	0	0	0	0	0	0
Cheltenham	-	-	0	0	0	0	0	0	0	0
Gillingham	-	-	0	0	0	0	0	0	0	0
Oxford	-	-	0	0	0	0	0	0	0	0
Rotherham	-	-	0	0	0	0	0	0	0	0
Aldershot	-	-	0	0	0	0	0	0	0	0
Port Vale	-	-	0	0	0	0	0	0	0	0
Bristol Rovers	-	-	0	0	0	0	0	0	0	0
Accrington	-	-	0	0	0	0	0	0	0	0
Morecambe	-	-	0	0	0	0	0	0	0	0
Wimbledon	-	-	1	0	1	0	0	1	1	0
Burton	-	-	0	0	0	0	0	0	0	0
Bradford	-	-	0	0	0	0	0	0	0	0
Dagenham & R	-	-	0	0	0	0	0	0	0	0
Northampton	-	-	0	0	0	0	0	0	0	0
Plymouth	-	-	0	0	0	0	0	0	0	0
Barnet	-	-	0	0	0	0	0	0	0	0
Fleetwood										
York	D	W	2	1	1	0	1	1	1	1

Season	Division	Pos	P	W	D	L	F	A	GD	Pts
2011-12	Conference	1	46	31	10	5	102	48	54	103
2010-11	Conference	5	46	22	12	12	68	42	26	78
2009-10	Conf North	2	40	15	4	1	58	21	42	85

Gillingham

Nickname: The Gills
Colours: Blue and White
Ground: Priestfield (11,440)
Tel: 01634-300-000   gillinghamfootballclub.co.uk

THE GILLS are pinning their hopes on a change of manager to provide the fresh impetus needed to get out of the division.

A second season of just missing the play-offs cost Andy Hessenthaler his position as manager, although he stays on as director of football.

A host of players have departed, paving the way for new man, Martin Allen, to craft his own team. Key positions must be filled and the challenge is to hit the right blend without curbing their attacking verve.

Longest run without loss/win: 6/6
High – low league position 5-13
Clean sheets: 13 **Yellow cards:** 80 **Red cards:** 7
Average attendance: 5,146 **Players used:** 31
Leading Scorer: Kedwell 12 (4,9) Whelpdale 12 (3,11)
Key stat: Gillingham were League 2's highest scorers in 2011-12 with 79 goals

Team	11-12 H	A	P	W	D	L	OV	UN	BS	CS
Wycombe	-	-	3	1	1	1	1	2	2	0
Chesterfield	-	-	3	2	0	1	2	1	1	3
Exeter	-	-	2	2	0	0	1	1	0	2
Rochdale	-	-	1	0	1	0	0	1	1	0
Southend	L	L	4	1	2	1	2	2	2	2
Torquay	W	W	2	1	1	0	0	2	1	1
Cheltenham	W	W	4	2	2	0	1	3	2	2
Gillingham										
Oxford	W	D	2	1	1	0	0	2	0	2
Rotherham	D	L	4	3	1	0	2	2	1	3
Aldershot	W	W	3	2	1	0	2	1	2	1
Port Vale	D	L	5	3	1	1	3	2	3	2
Bristol Rovers	W	D	3	3	0	0	2	1	2	1
Accrington	D	L	3	2	1	0	1	2	2	1
Morecambe	W	L	3	2	1	0	1	2	1	2
Wimbledon	L	L	1	0	0	1	1	0	1	0
Burton	W	L	2	2	0	0	1	1	1	1
Bradford	D	D	4	2	1	1	0	4	0	3
Dagenham & R	L	L	2	1	0	1	2	0	2	0
Northampton	W	D	4	2	0	2	1	3	1	1
Plymouth	W	W	1	1	0	0	1	0	0	1
Barnet	W	D	3	1	0	2	2	1	2	0
Fleetwood	-	-	0	0	0	0	0	0	0	0
York	-	-	0	0	0	0	0	0	0	0

Season	Division	Pos	P	W	D	L	F	A	GD	Pts
2011-12	League 2	8	46	20	10	16	79	62	17	70
2010-11	League 2	8	46	17	17	12	67	57	10	68
2009-10	League 1	21	46	12	14	20	48	64	-16	50

Morecambe

Nickname: The Shrimps
Colours: Red and White
Ground: Globe Arena (6,400)
Tel: 01524-411-797   www.morecambefc.com

A LIMP finish to last season doesn't bode well for Morecambe and they rate as one of the main contenders for relegation.

Jim Bentley's first taste of management began brightly, with the 6-0 thumping of title favourites Crawley an obvious bright spot in some excellent early form.

But the longer the season went on, the worse results became and if it wasn't for their blistering start, the Shrimps could have been dragged into trouble as the squad looks light on quality and depth.

Longest run without loss/win: 8/7
High – low league position 1-15
Clean sheets: 11 **Yellow cards:** 53 **Red cards:** 1
Average attendance: 2,141 **Players used:** 26
Leading Scorer: K Ellison 15 (4,14)
Key stat: Morecambe ended the season in poor form, with just one win in their last nine games

	11-12 H A	Last six seasons at home P	W	D	L	OV	UN	BS	CS
Wycombe	- -	3	0	1	2	1	2	0	1
Chesterfield	- -	4	0	3	1	1	3	3	0
Exeter	- -	2	0	2	0	1	1	2	0
Rochdale	- -	3	0	3	0	1	2	3	0
Southend	W D	2	2	0	0	1	1	1	1
Torquay	L D	3	2	0	1	2	1	2	1
Cheltenham	W W	3	2	1	0	1	2	2	1
Gillingham	W L	3	1	1	1	1	2	2	0
Oxford	D W	3	0	1	2	2	1	0	1
Rotherham	D L	5	2	2	1	3	2	3	2
Aldershot	W L	5	4	1	0	1	4	2	3
Port Vale	D W	4	2	2	0	0	4	1	3
Bristol Rovers	L L	1	0	0	1	1	0	1	0
Accrington	L D	5	0	1	4	3	2	4	0
Morecambe									
Wimbledon	L D	1	0	0	1	1	0	1	0
Burton	D L	4	2	1	1	3	1	3	0
Bradford	D D	5	2	2	1	2	3	3	1
Dagenham & R	L W	5	2	1	2	2	3	3	2
Northampton	L W	3	0	0	3	3	0	3	0
Plymouth	D D	1	0	1	0	1	0	1	0
Barnet	L W	5	2	2	1	3	2	3	1
Fleetwood	- -	0	0	0	0	0	0	0	0
York	- -	1	0	0	1	1	0	1	0

Season	Division	Pos	P	W	D	L	F	A	GD	Pts
2011-12	League 2	15	46	14	14	18	63	57	6	56
2010-11	League 2	20	46	13	12	21	54	73	-19	51
2009-10	League 2	4	46	20	13	13	73	64	9	73

Northampton

Nickname: The Cobblers
Colours: Claret and White
Ground: Sixfields (7,300)
Tel: 01604-683-700   www.ntfc.co.uk

HAVING been stuck in a rut for two seasons, it's hard to imagine there will be a sudden upturn in Northampton's fortunes.

They never got going in a wretched 2011-12 and only began to pull clear of the relegation places after Aidy Boothroyd arrived. The manager is a big name at this level and has had a positive impact.

Although he can attract talented players, he might have to contend with a period of consolidation at a club that has suffered a couple of difficult years.

Longest run without loss/win: 4/13
High – low league position 14-24
Clean sheets: 9 **Yellow cards:** 71 **Red cards:** 4
Average attendance: 4,809 **Players used:** 44
Leading Scorer: A Akinfenwa 18 (4,16)
Key stat: Northampton averaged just over a point per game at home last term

	11-12 H A	Last six seasons at home P	W	D	L	OV	UN	BS	CS
Wycombe	- -	1	0	1	0	0	1	1	0
Chesterfield	- -	3	1	1	1	1	2	1	2
Exeter	- -	0	0	0	0	0	0	0	0
Rochdale	- -	1	0	0	1	1	0	1	0
Southend	L D	4	1	0	3	3	1	3	0
Torquay	D L	3	0	3	0	1	2	1	2
Cheltenham	L D	6	4	1	1	4	2	5	1
Gillingham	D L	4	2	2	0	2	2	3	1
Oxford	W L	2	2	0	0	2	0	2	0
Rotherham	D D	4	2	2	0	3	1	3	1
Aldershot	W W	3	1	1	1	2	1	2	0
Port Vale	L L	5	1	2	2	2	3	3	1
Bristol Rovers	W L	3	1	1	1	1	2	1	1
Accrington	D L	3	1	2	0	1	2	0	3
Morecambe	L W	3	1	1	1	1	2	1	1
Wimbledon	W W	1	1	0	0	0	1	0	1
Burton	L W	3	0	1	2	2	1	3	0
Bradford	L L	4	1	2	1	2	2	2	2
Dagenham & R	W W	2	2	0	0	1	1	1	1
Northampton									
Plymouth	D L	1	0	1	0	0	1	0	1
Barnet	L W	3	0	1	2	2	1	2	1
Fleetwood	- -	0	0	0	0	0	0	0	0
York	- -	0	0	0	0	0	0	0	0

Season	Division	Pos	P	W	D	L	F	A	GD	Pts
2011-12	League 2	20	46	12	12	22	56	79	-23	48
2010-11	League 2	16	46	11	19	16	63	71	-8	52
2009-10	League 2	11	46	18	13	15	62	53	9	67

Oxford Utd

Nickname: The U's
Colours: Yellow and Blue
Ground: The Kassam Stadium (12,500)
Tel: 01865-337500   www.oufc.co.uk

A CRUCIAL campaign awaits the U's after they relinquished a play-off berth in the final strides of last season.

Having been well placed for much of the campaign, they capitulated at the business end of the season and slipped down the table into ninth place.

Chris Wilder will need to galvanise his squad and if he doesn't get the desired response he could start to feel the pinch. With a big budget and sizeable support the pressure is on to win promotion.

Longest run without loss/win: 8/7
High – low league position 3-14
Clean sheets: 16 Yellow cards: 82 Red cards: 5
Average attendance: 7,451 Players used: 36
Leading Scorer: J Constable 11 (4,8)
Key stat: Oxford finished last season tamely after failing to win in their final seven games

	11-12		Last six seasons at home							
	H	A	P	W	D	L	OV	UN	BS	CS
Wycombe	-	-	1	0	1	0	1	0	1	0
Chesterfield	-	-	1	0	1	0	0	1	0	1
Exeter	-	-	2	1	1	0	1	1	1	1
Rochdale	-	-	0	0	0	0	0	0	0	0
Southend	L	L	2	0	0	2	0	2	0	0
Torquay	D	D	4	0	2	2	2	2	2	0
Cheltenham	L	D	2	0	1	1	1	1	2	0
Gillingham	D	L	2	0	1	1	0	2	0	1
Oxford										
Rotherham	W	L	2	2	0	0	2	0	2	0
Aldershot	D	W	4	1	1	2	1	3	2	1
Port Vale	W	L	2	2	0	0	2	0	2	0
Bristol Rovers	W	D	1	1	0	0	1	0	0	1
Accrington	D	W	2	0	2	0	0	2	1	1
Morecambe	L	D	3	1	1	1	2	1	1	2
Wimbledon	W	W	2	2	0	0	0	2	0	2
Burton	D	D	5	2	2	1	4	1	2	2
Bradford	D	L	2	1	1	0	1	1	2	0
Dagenham & R	W	W	2	1	1	0	2	0	2	0
Northampton	W	L	2	2	0	0	1	1	1	1
Plymouth	W	D	1	1	0	0	1	0	1	0
Barnet	W	W	2	2	0	0	2	0	2	0
Fleetwood	-	-	0	0	0	0	0	0	0	0
York	-	-	4	3	1	0	1	3	2	2

Season	Division	Pos	P	W	D	L	F	A	GD	Pts
2011-12	League 2	9	46	17	17	12	59	48	11	68
2010-11	League 2	12	46	17	12	17	58	60	-2	63
2009-10	Conference	3	44	25	11	8	64	31	33	86

Plymouth

Nickname: The Pilgrims
Colours: Green and White
Ground: Home Park (16,388)
Tel: 01752-562-561   www.pafc.co.uk

PLYMOUTH will be aiming to put a dismal few years behind them and start afresh.

Financial difficulties wrecked pre-season plans last term and, when they finally left administration in October, the primary objective was maintaining their league status.

Chairman James Brent, who effectively prevented Plymouth from going under, is promising a more entertaining brand of football, while manager Carl Fletcher has agreed to stay and should be able to oversee a rise up the table.

Longest run without loss/win: 6/9
High – low league position 21-24
Clean sheets: 9 Yellow cards: 83 Red cards: 7
Average attendance: 6,915 Players used: 34
Leading Scorer: S Walton 8 (4,7)
Key stat: Plymouth had the second worst scoring record in League 2 last season

	11-12		Last six seasons at home							
	H	A	P	W	D	L	OV	UN	BS	CS
Wycombe	-	-	0	0	0	0	0	0	0	0
Chesterfield	-	-	0	0	0	0	0	0	0	0
Exeter	-	-	1	1	0	0	0	1	0	1
Rochdale	-	-	1	0	0	1	0	1	0	0
Southend	D	L	2	1	0	1	0	2	0	0
Torquay	L	L	1	0	0	1	1	0	1	0
Cheltenham	L	L	1	0	0	1	1	0	1	0
Gillingham	L	L	1	0	0	1	0	1	0	0
Oxford	D	L	1	0	1	0	0	1	1	0
Rotherham	L	L	1	0	0	1	1	0	1	0
Aldershot	W	D	1	1	0	0	0	1	0	1
Port Vale	L	L	1	0	0	1	0	1	0	0
Bristol Rovers	D	W	2	1	1	0	1	1	2	0
Accrington	D	W	1	0	1	0	1	0	1	0
Morecambe	D	D	1	0	1	0	0	1	1	0
Wimbledon	L	W	1	0	0	1	0	1	0	0
Burton	W	L	1	1	0	0	1	0	1	0
Bradford	W	D	1	1	0	0	1	0	1	0
Dagenham & R	D	W	2	1	1	0	1	1	1	1
Northampton	W	D	1	1	0	0	1	0	1	0
Plymouth										
Barnet	D	L	1	0	1	0	0	1	0	1
Fleetwood	-	-	0	0	0	0	0	0	0	0
York	-	-	0	0	0	0	0	0	0	0

Season	Division	Pos	P	W	D	L	F	A	GD	Pts
2011-12	League 2	21	46	10	16	20	47	64	-17	46
2010-11	League 1	23	46	15	7	24	51	74	-23	42*
2009-10	Champ	23	46	11	8	27	43	68	-25	41

Port Vale

Nickname: The Valiants
Colours: White and Black
Ground: Vale Park (19,148)
Tel: 01782-655-800   www.port-vale.co.uk

VALE'S short-term priority must be getting their finances in order after several months in administration – as we went to press, Keith Ryder's takeover bid was being looked at by the Football League.

A ten-point deduction put paid to any play-off aspirations last term and rebuilding might come before any lofty ambitions.

The worry for the coming season is the loss of a number of established players, while plans for fresh recruits are on hold until the new ownership deal is finalised.

Longest run without loss/win: 8/4
High – low league position 7-14
Clean sheets: 14 Yellow cards: 76 Red cards: 4
Average attendance: 4,820 Players used: 30
Leading Scorer: M Richards 17 (11,16)
Key stat: 60.87 per cent of Vale's league games last season featured three goals or more

	11-12 H A	Last six seasons at home P	W	D	L	OV	UN	BS	CS
Wycombe	- -	2	1	1	0	1	1	2	0
Chesterfield	- -	4	1	1	2	2	2	3	0
Exeter	- -	1	0	0	1	1	0	1	0
Rochdale	- -	2	1	1	0	1	1	2	0
Southend	L L	3	0	1	2	2	1	3	0
Torquay	D L	3	0	2	1	2	1	2	1
Cheltenham	L L	5	1	2	2	2	3	3	1
Gillingham	W D	5	3	1	1	3	2	3	2
Oxford	W L	2	1	0	1	2	0	1	1
Rotherham	W W	5	2	1	2	2	3	2	3
Aldershot	W W	4	2	2	0	1	3	1	3
Port Vale									
Bristol Rovers	W W	2	1	1	0	0	2	1	1
Accrington	W D	4	2	1	1	2	2	2	1
Morecambe	L D	4	2	0	2	3	1	2	0
Wimbledon	L L	1	0	0	1	1	0	1	0
Burton	W D	3	3	0	0	3	0	2	1
Bradford	W D	5	3	0	2	3	2	3	0
Dagenham & R	L W	3	1	0	2	1	2	1	0
Northampton	W W	5	2	2	1	3	2	3	2
Plymouth	W W	1	1	0	0	0	1	0	1
Barnet	L W	4	0	2	2	1	3	1	2
Fleetwood	- -	0	0	0	0	0	0	0	0
York	- -	0	0	0	0	0	0	0	0

Season	Division	Pos	P	W	D	L	F	A	GD	Pts
2011-12	League 2	12	46	20	9	17	68	60	8	59*
2010-11	League 2	11	46	17	14	15	54	49	5	65
2009-10	League 2	10	46	17	17	12	61	50	11	68

Rochdale

Nickname: The Dale
Colours: Blue and Black
Ground: Spotland (10,149)
Tel: 0844-826-1907   www.rochdaleafc.co.uk

DALE are back in the division they know best and can make their presence felt in the top half of the table.

He might not have been able to keep them in League 1 but manager John Coleman is a shrewd operator at this level and capable of assembling a strong team.

The chairman put the cost of relegation at £500,000 and there will be plenty of comings and goings over the next few months but if the new arrivals bed in, Rochdale should have a good season.

Longest run without loss/win: 3/9
High – low league position 17-24
Clean sheets: 10 Yellow cards: 50 Red cards: 3
Average attendance: 3,109 Players used: 40
Leading Scorer: A Grimes 8 (0,6)
Key stat: Rochdale have finished in the top ten in their last four seasons in League 2

	11-12 H A	Last six seasons at home P	W	D	L	OV	UN	BS	CS
Wycombe	W L	4	1	0	3	1	3	1	0
Chesterfield	D L	4	1	1	2	2	2	3	0
Exeter	W L	3	1	1	1	2	1	2	0
Rochdale									
Southend	- -	0	0	0	0	0	0	0	0
Torquay	- -	2	2	0	0	1	1	1	1
Cheltenham	- -	1	0	0	1	0	1	0	0
Gillingham	- -	1	0	0	1	0	1	0	0
Oxford	- -	0	0	0	0	0	0	0	0
Rotherham	- -	3	2	0	1	3	0	2	1
Aldershot	- -	2	2	0	0	1	1	1	1
Port Vale	- -	2	1	1	0	0	2	0	2
Bristol Rovers	- -	2	1	0	1	1	1	1	0
Accrington	- -	4	3	0	1	4	0	4	0
Morecambe	- -	3	2	1	0	1	2	2	1
Wimbledon	- -	0	0	0	0	0	0	0	0
Burton	- -	1	0	0	1	0	1	0	0
Bradford	- -	3	2	0	1	3	0	2	1
Dagenham & R	- -	4	3	0	1	2	2	2	1
Northampton	- -	1	1	0	0	0	1	0	1
Plymouth	- -	1	0	1	0	0	1	0	0
Barnet	- -	4	3	0	1	3	1	2	1
Fleetwood	- -	0	0	0	0	0	0	0	0
York	- -	0	0	0	0	0	0	0	0

Season	Division	Pos	P	W	D	L	F	A	GD	Pts
2011-12	League 1	24	46	8	14	24	47	81	-34	38
2010-11	League 1	9	46	18	14	14	63	55	8	68
2009-10	League 2	3	46	25	7	14	82	48	34	82

Rotherham

Nickname: The Millers
Colours: Red and White
Ground: New York Stadium (12,021)
Tel: 0844-414-0733   www.themillers.co.uk

AFTER five years of trying, the Millers are going all out to gain an elusive promotion.

Managers have come and gone in that time and although chairman Tony Stewart wanted to open the gates to the New York Stadium with his side in League 1, his determination remains undiminished.

Stewart sold his ambition for the club to Steve Evans, who left Crawley on the brink of promotion, and with a lot of the key elements in place, Rotherham have been cut to 7-2 (from 5-1) for the title.

Longest run without loss/win: 5/9
High – low league position 2-14
Clean sheets: 12 **Yellow cards:** 48 **Red cards:** 5
Average attendance: 3,498 **Players used:** 32
Leading Scorer: L Grabban 18 (9,14)
Key stat: Despite their mid-table finish, Rotherham scored first in 58.6 per cent of their league matches

	11-12		Last six seasons at home							
	H	A	P	W	D	L	OV	UN	BS	CS
Wycombe	-	-	3	0	2	1	1	2	2	1
Chesterfield	-	-	5	4	0	1	3	2	2	2
Exeter	-	-	1	0	0	1	0	1	0	0
Rochdale	-	-	3	1	1	1	3	0	3	0
Southend	L	W	2	0	0	2	2	0	1	0
Torquay	L	D	3	1	1	1	1	2	2	0
Cheltenham	W	L	4	2	1	1	2	2	2	2
Gillingham	W	D	4	3	0	1	2	2	1	2
Oxford	W	L	2	2	0	0	1	1	1	1
Rotherham										
Aldershot	W	D	4	2	1	1	1	3	1	3
Port Vale	L	L	5	2	0	3	3	2	2	2
Bristol Rovers	L	L	1	0	0	1	0	1	0	0
Accrington	W	D	5	3	1	1	0	5	0	4
Morecambe	W	D	5	3	1	1	3	2	3	1
Wimbledon	W	W	1	1	0	0	0	1	0	1
Burton	L	D	3	0	2	1	2	1	2	0
Bradford	W	W	6	2	2	2	3	3	3	2
Dagenham & R	W	L	4	3	1	0	2	2	3	1
Northampton	D	D	4	1	2	1	2	2	3	1
Plymouth	W	W	1	1	0	0	0	1	0	1
Barnet	D	D	5	2	2	1	3	2	2	3
Fleetwood	-	-	0	0	0	0	0	0	0	0
York	-	-	0	0	0	0	0	0	0	0

Season	Division	Pos	P	W	D	L	F	A	GD	Pts
2011-12	League 2	10	46	18	13	15	67	63	4	67
2010-11	League 2	9	46	17	15	14	75	60	15	66
2009-10	League 2	5	46	21	10	15	55	52	3	73

Southend

Nickname: The Shrimpers
Colours: Blue
Ground: Roots Hall (12,163)
Tel: 01702-304-050   www.southendunited.co.uk

OF THOSE sides who missed out on promotion last season, Southend's story is probably the most agonising.

Having fallen short of third by one point they then crashed out of the play-offs and were left to reflect on an abandoned game in December when they were leading ten-man Aldershot as the floodlights failed.

They lost the rescheduled fixture and although Paul Sturrock will have to dust down his troops, there is no reason why they can't make their presence felt again.

Longest run without loss/win: 12/4
High – low league position 1-12
Clean sheets: 17 **Yellow cards:** 75 **Red cards:** 4
Average attendance: 5,965 **Players used:** 33
Leading Scorer: M Bilel 13 (4,9)
Key stat: Southend ended the regular season in top form, gaining five wins in their last seven games of 2011-12

	11-12		Last six seasons at home							
	H	A	P	W	D	L	OV	UN	BS	CS
Wycombe	-	-	2	1	1	0	1	0	2	0
Chesterfield	-	-	1	0	0	1	1	0	1	0
Exeter	-	-	1	0	1	0	0	1	0	1
Rochdale	-	-	0	0	0	0	0	0	0	0
Southend										
Torquay	W	D	2	2	0	0	2	0	2	0
Cheltenham	W	L	4	2	1	1	3	1	2	2
Gillingham	W	W	4	3	1	0	2	2	1	3
Oxford	W	W	2	2	0	0	2	0	2	0
Rotherham	L	W	2	1	0	1	0	2	0	1
Aldershot	L	L	2	0	1	1	0	2	0	1
Port Vale	W	W	3	1	1	1	2	1	2	1
Bristol Rovers	D	L	4	2	1	1	1	3	2	1
Accrington	D	W	2	0	2	0	1	1	2	0
Morecambe	D	L	2	0	1	1	1	1	2	0
Wimbledon	W	W	1	1	0	0	0	1	0	1
Burton	L	W	2	0	1	1	0	2	1	0
Bradford	L	L	2	1	0	1	1	1	0	1
Dagenham & R	D	W	1	0	1	0	0	1	1	0
Northampton	D	W	4	1	3	0	1	3	3	1
Plymouth	W	D	2	1	1	0	0	2	1	1
Barnet	W	W	2	2	0	0	2	0	1	1
Fleetwood	-	-	0	0	0	0	0	0	0	0
York	-	-	0	0	0	0	0	0	0	0

Season	Division	Pos	P	W	D	L	F	A	GD	Pts
2011-12	League 2	4	46	25	8	13	77	48	29	83
2010-11	League 2	13	46	16	13	17	62	56	6	61
2009-10	League 1	23	46	10	13	23	51	72	-21	43

Torquay

Nickname: The Gulls
Colours: Yellow and Blue
Ground: Plainmoor (6,283)
Tel: 01803-328-666   www.torquayunited.com

THE play-offs have proved a hurdle too far for Torquay in each of the last two seasons and they will do well to make them for a third year in a row.

Expectations were at a similar level 12 months ago and the Gulls overachieved again, finishing fifth after a managerial change had been forced on them last summer. Martin Ling kept up the good work started by Paul Buckle, but he might be pressed into rebuilding with his star players attracting plenty of suitors.

Longest run without loss/win: 9/8
High – low league position 2-18
Clean sheets: 20 **Yellow cards:** 63 **Red cards:** 4
Average attendance: 2,869 **Players used:** 23
Leading Scorer: L Mansell 12 (4,11) R Howe 12 (4,11)
Key stat: Torquay kept 20 clean sheets in 46 regular season games last season

	11-12		Last six seasons at home							
	H	A	P	W	D	L	OV	UN	BS	CS
Wycombe	-	-	2	1	1	0	1	1	0	2
Chesterfield	-	-	2	1	1	0	0	2	0	2
Exeter	-	-	1	1	0	0	0	1	0	1
Rochdale	-	-	2	2	0	0	1	1	0	2
Southend	D	L	2	0	2	0	0	2	1	1
Torquay										
Cheltenham	D	W	3	2	1	0	3	0	2	1
Gillingham	L	L	2	0	1	1	1	1	2	0
Oxford	D	D	4	1	2	1	2	2	3	1
Rotherham	D	W	3	0	2	1	1	2	2	0
Aldershot	W	W	4	1	1	2	1	3	2	1
Port Vale	W	D	3	1	1	1	2	1	2	1
Bristol Rovers	D	W	2	0	2	0	1	1	1	1
Accrington	W	L	4	2	1	1	1	3	1	2
Morecambe	D	W	3	1	2	0	2	1	3	0
Wimbledon	W	L	1	1	0	0	1	0	0	1
Burton	D	W	5	2	1	2	4	1	4	1
Bradford	L	L	3	1	0	2	2	1	2	1
Dagenham & R	W	D	2	1	1	0	0	2	0	2
Northampton	W	D	3	3	0	0	1	2	0	3
Plymouth	W	W	1	1	0	0	1	0	1	0
Barnet	W	W	4	1	2	1	0	4	2	1
Fleetwood	-	-	0	0	0	0	0	0	0	0
York	-	-	2	0	2	0	0	2	1	1

Season	Division	Pos	P	W	D	L	F	A	GD	Pts
2011-12	League 2	5	46	23	12	11	63	50	13	81
2010-11	League 2	7	46	17	18	11	74	53	21	68*
2009-10	League 2	17	46	14	15	17	64	55	9	57

Wimbledon

Nickname: The Dons, The Wombles
Colours: Blue and Yellow
Ground: Kingsmeadow (5,194)
Tel: 020-8547-3528   www.afcwimbledon.co.uk

THE Wombles took the step up to league football in their stride and can consolidate their position in League 2.

All eyes were on the newcomers this time last year and they didn't disappoint, racking up plenty of points early on.

Much of that good early work was undone by a run of 12 league games without a win that ran from mid-October into the new year, and since the start of 2012 their form has been streaky, but they can stay out of trouble.

Longest run without loss/win: 4/12
High – low league position 3-17
Clean sheets: 6 **Yellow cards:** 52 **Red cards:** 2
Average attendance: 4292 **Players used:** 31
Leading Scorer: J Midson 18 (5,15)
Key stat: Wimbledon lost eight of their last 14 games last season

	11-12		Last six seasons at home							
	H	A	P	W	D	L	OV	UN	BS	CS
Wycombe	-	-	0	0	0	0	0	0	0	0
Chesterfield	-	-	0	0	0	0	0	0	0	0
Exeter	-	-	0	0	0	0	0	0	0	0
Rochdale	-	-	0	0	0	0	0	0	0	0
Southend	L	L	1	0	0	1	1	0	1	0
Torquay	W	L	1	1	0	0	0	1	0	1
Cheltenham	W	D	1	1	0	0	1	0	1	0
Gillingham	W	W	1	1	0	0	1	0	1	0
Oxford	L	L	2	0	0	2	0	2	0	0
Rotherham	L	L	1	0	0	1	1	0	1	0
Aldershot	L	D	1	0	0	1	1	0	1	0
Port Vale	W	W	1	1	0	0	1	0	1	0
Bristol Rovers	L	L	1	0	0	1	1	0	1	0
Accrington	L	L	1	0	0	1	0	1	0	0
Morecambe	D	W	1	0	1	0	0	1	1	0
Wimbledon										
Burton	W	L	1	1	0	0	1	0	0	1
Bradford	W	W	1	1	0	0	1	0	1	0
Dagenham & R	W	W	1	1	0	0	1	0	1	0
Northampton	L	L	1	0	0	1	1	0	0	0
Plymouth	L	W	1	0	0	1	1	0	1	0
Barnet	D	L	1	0	1	0	0	1	1	0
Fleetwood	-	-	1	1	0	0	0	1	0	1
York	-	-	2	1	0	1	0	2	0	1

Season	Division	Pos	P	W	D	L	F	A	GD	Pts
2011-12	League 2	16	46	15	9	22	62	78	-16	54
2010-11	Conference	2	46	27	9	10	83	47	36	90
2009-10	Conference	8	44	18	10	16	61	47	14	64

Wycombe

Nickname: The Chairboys
Colours: Sky and Navy Blue
Ground: Adams Park (10,000)
Tel: 01494-443-085   www.wwfc.com

THE CHAIRBOYS have become the yo-yo club of the lower leagues and at first glance they look obvious candidates for a swift return back to League 1.

Scratch a little deeper and their claims do not appear quite as bright, with a change of ownership potentially limiting their prospects in the short term.

A supporters trust has recently taken over and has scrapped the youth academy to save money. At present, other teams appear much more settled.

Longest run without loss/win: 7/8
High – low league position 19-24
Clean sheets: 4 **Yellow cards:** 80 **Red cards:** 2
Average attendance: 4,843 **Players used:** 37
Leading Scorer: S Beavon 21 (5,16)
Key stat: Wycombe's 88 goals conceded made for the worst defensive record in League 1 last season, seven worse than rock-bottom Rochdale

	11-12 H	A	Last six seasons at home P	W	D	L	OV	UN	BS	CS
Wycombe										
Chesterfield	W	L	4	2	1	1	2	2	3	1
Exeter	W	W	3	1	2	0	2	1	3	0
Rochdale	W	L	4	1	1	2	1	3	1	1
Southend	-	-	2	1	1	0	1	1	2	0
Torquay	-	-	2	1	0	1	1	1	1	1
Cheltenham	-	-	1	1	0	0	1	0	1	0
Gillingham	-	-	3	3	0	0	1	2	0	3
Oxford	-	-	1	0	1	0	0	1	0	1
Rotherham	-	-	3	2	1	0	0	3	0	3
Aldershot	-	-	2	1	1	0	2	0	1	1
Port Vale	-	-	2	1	1	0	1	1	2	0
Bristol Rovers	-	-	2	1	0	1	1	1	1	0
Accrington	-	-	4	1	1	2	2	2	3	0
Morecambe	-	-	3	2	1	0	0	3	1	2
Wimbledon	-	-	0	0	0	0	0	0	0	0
Burton	-	-	1	1	0	0	1	0	1	0
Bradford	-	-	3	3	0	0	1	2	1	2
Dagenham & R	-	-	2	1	0	1	1	1	1	0
Northampton	-	-	1	0	1	0	1	0	1	0
Plymouth	-	-	0	0	0	0	0	0	0	0
Barnet	-	-	4	1	3	0	1	3	3	1
Fleetwood	-	-	0	0	0	0	0	0	0	0
York	-	-	0	0	0	0	0	0	0	0

Season	Division	Pos	P	W	D	L	F	A	GD	Pts
2011-12	League 1	21	46	11	10	25	65	88	-23	43
2010-11	League 2	3	46	22	14	10	69	50	19	80
2009-10	League 1	22	46	10	15	21	56	76	-20	45

York

Nickname: Minstermen
Colours: Red, White and Blue
Ground: Bootham Crescent (8,105)
Tel: 01904-624-447   yorkcityfootballclub.co.uk

AS MANY teams have done before them, the Conference play-off winners should have no problem making the step up to League 2.

Having ended their eight-year league hiatus at Wembley, York will carry all-important momentum into the new season.

A fast start would ease any nerves at Bootham Crescent, but the gap between League 2 and the Conference is closing all the time and York can provide further evidence of that with a solid showing.

Longest run without loss/win: 12/4
High – low league position 3-14
Clean sheets: 17 **Yellow cards:** 63 **Red cards:** 4
Average attendance: 3,117 **Players used:** 29
Leading Scorer: J Walker 18 (3,15)
Key stat: York gained more points on their travels than they did at home during their promotion campaign

	11-12 H	A	Last six seasons at home P	W	D	L	OV	UN	BS	CS
Wycombe	-	-	0	0	0	0	0	0	0	0
Chesterfield	-	-	0	0	0	0	0	0	0	0
Exeter	-	-	2	1	1	0	1	1	1	1
Rochdale	-	-	0	0	0	0	0	0	0	0
Southend	-	-	0	0	0	0	0	0	0	0
Torquay	-	-	2	0	0	2	1	1	1	0
Cheltenham	-	-	0	0	0	0	0	0	0	0
Gillingham	-	-	0	0	0	0	0	0	0	0
Oxford	-	-	4	1	2	1	0	4	1	2
Rotherham	-	-	0	0	0	0	0	0	0	0
Aldershot	-	-	2	2	0	0	0	2	0	2
Port Vale	-	-	0	0	0	0	0	0	0	0
Bristol Rovers	-	-	0	0	0	0	0	0	0	0
Accrington	-	-	0	0	0	0	0	0	0	0
Morecambe	-	-	1	0	0	1	1	0	1	0
Wimbledon	-	-	2	2	0	0	2	0	1	1
Burton	-	-	3	1	1	1	2	1	2	1
Bradford	-	-	0	0	0	0	0	0	0	0
Dagenham & R	-	-	1	0	0	1	1	0	1	0
Northampton	-	-	0	0	0	0	0	0	0	0
Plymouth	-	-	0	0	0	0	0	0	0	0
Barnet	-	-	0	0	0	0	0	0	0	0
Fleetwood	L	D	2	1	0	1	0	2	0	1
York										

Season	Division	Pos	P	W	D	L	F	A	GD	Pts
2011-12	Conference	4	46	23	14	9	81	45	36	83
2010-11	Conference	8	46	19	14	13	55	50	5	71
2009-10	Conference	5	44	22	12	10	62	35	27	78

Top scorers 2011-12

		P	W	D	L	F	GFA	PGA	Pts
1	Gillingham (8)	46	20	10	16	79	1.72	1.5	70
2	Southend (4)	46	25	8	13	77	1.67	1.8	83
3	Crawley (3)	46	23	15	8	76	1.65	1.8	84
4	Swindon (1)	46	29	6	11	75	1.63	2.0	93
5	Port Vale (12)	46	20	9	17	68	1.48	1.5	69
6	Crewe (7)	46	20	12	14	67	1.46	1.6	72
7	Rotherham (10)	46	18	13	15	67	1.46	1.5	67
8	Shrewsbury (2)	46	26	10	10	66	1.43	1.9	88
9	Cheltenham (6)	46	23	8	15	66	1.43	1.7	77
10	Torquay (5)	46	23	12	11	63	1.37	1.8	81
11	Morecambe (15)	46	14	14	18	63	1.37	1.2	56
12	Wimbledon (16)	46	15	9	22	62	1.35	1.2	54
13	Bristol R (13)	46	15	12	19	60	1.30	1.2	57
14	Oxford (9)	46	17	17	12	59	1.28	1.5	68
15	Northampton (20)	46	12	12	22	56	1.22	1.0	48
16	Aldershot (11)	46	19	9	18	54	1.17	1.4	66
17	Accrington (14)	46	14	15	17	54	1.17	1.2	57
18	Burton (17)	46	14	12	20	54	1.17	1.2	54
19	Bradford (18)	46	12	14	20	54	1.17	1.1	50
20	Barnet (22)	46	12	10	24	52	1.13	1.0	46
21	Dag & Red (19)	46	14	8	24	50	1.09	1.1	50
22	Hereford (23)	46	10	14	22	50	1.09	1.0	44
23	Plymouth (21)	46	10	16	20	47	1.02	1.0	46
24	Macclesfield (24)	46	8	13	25	39	0.85	0.8	37

Best defence 2011-12

		P	W	D	L	F	GFA	PGA	Pts
1	Swindon (1)	46	29	6	11	32	0.70	2.0	93
2	Shrewsbury (2)	46	26	10	10	41	0.89	1.9	88
3	Southend (4)	46	25	8	13	48	1.04	1.8	83
4	Oxford (9)	46	17	17	12	48	1.04	1.5	68
5	Torquay (5)	46	23	12	11	50	1.09	1.8	81
6	Cheltenham (6)	46	23	8	15	50	1.09	1.7	77
7	Aldershot (11)	46	19	9	18	52	1.13	1.4	66
8	Crawley (3)	46	23	15	8	54	1.17	1.8	84
9	Morecambe (15)	46	14	14	18	57	1.24	1.2	56
10	Crewe (7)	46	20	12	14	59	1.28	1.6	72
11	Bradford (18)	46	12	14	20	59	1.28	1.1	50
12	Port Vale (12)	46	20	9	17	60	1.30	1.5	69
13	Gillingham (8)	46	20	10	16	62	1.35	1.5	70
14	Rotherham (10)	46	18	13	15	63	1.37	1.5	67
15	Plymouth (21)	46	10	16	20	64	1.39	1.0	46
16	Macclesfield (24)	46	8	13	25	64	1.39	0.8	37
17	Accrington (14)	46	14	15	17	66	1.43	1.2	57
18	Bristol R (13)	46	15	12	19	70	1.52	1.2	57
19	Hereford (23)	46	10	14	22	70	1.52	1.0	44
20	Dag & Red (19)	46	14	8	24	72	1.57	1.1	50
21	Wimbledon (16)	46	15	9	22	78	1.70	1.2	54
22	Northampton (20)	46	12	12	22	79	1.72	1.0	48
23	Barnet (22)	46	12	10	24	79	1.72	1.0	46
24	Burton (17)	46	14	12	20	81	1.76	1.2	54

GILLINGHAM: unlucky to miss out on promotion after top scoring in League 2

Clean sheets 2011-12

		P	CS	%
1	Swindon (1)	46	26	56.5
2	Torquay (5)	46	20	43.5
3	Shrewsbury (2)	46	18	39.1
4	Southend (4)	46	17	37.0
5	Oxford (9)	46	16	34.8
6	Cheltenham (6)	46	16	34.8
7	Aldershot (11)	46	15	32.6
8	Port Vale (12)	46	14	30.4
9	Crawley (3)	46	13	28.3
10	Gillingham (8)	46	13	28.3
11	Bristol R (13)	46	12	26.1
12	Rotherham (10)	46	12	26.1
13	Crewe (7)	46	11	23.9
14	Morecambe (15)	46	11	23.9
15	Barnet (22)	46	10	21.7
16	Hereford (23)	46	10	21.7
17	Macclesfield (24)	46	10	21.7
18	Bradford (18)	46	9	19.6
19	Plymouth (21)	46	9	19.6
20	Dag & Red (19)	46	9	19.6
21	Northampton (20)	46	9	19.6
22	Burton (17)	46	8	17.4
23	Accrington (14)	46	8	17.4
24	Wimbledon (16)	46	6	13.0

First to score 2011-12

		P	FS	%
1	Swindon (1)	46	29	63.0
2	Southend (4)	46	27	58.7
3	Rotherham (10)	46	27	58.7
4	Crewe (7)	46	26	56.5
5	Torquay (5)	46	26	56.5
6	Shrewsbury (2)	46	26	56.5
7	Port Vale (12)	46	25	54.3
8	Cheltenham (6)	46	25	54.3
9	Oxford (9)	46	24	52.2
10	Aldershot (11)	46	24	52.2
11	Gillingham (8)	46	24	52.2
12	Crawley (3)	46	22	47.8
13	Hereford (23)	46	22	47.8
14	Morecambe (15)	46	21	45.7
15	Bristol R (13)	46	20	43.5
16	Northampton (20)	46	19	41.3
17	Barnet (22)	46	18	39.1
18	Burton (17)	46	17	37.0
19	Dag & Red (19)	46	17	37.0
20	Accrington (14)	46	17	37.0
21	Bradford (18)	46	16	34.8
22	Plymouth (21)	46	16	34.8
23	Wimbledon (16)	46	16	34.8
24	Macclesfield (24)	46	13	28.3

Top scorers 2011-12

		Goals
A Akinfenwa	Northampton	18
L Grabban	Rotherham	18
I McLeod	Barnet	18
J Midson	Wimbledon	18
M Richards	Port Vale	17
M Harrold	Bristol R	16
K Ellison	Morecambe	15
T Barnett	Crawley	14
J Collins	Shrewsbury	14
N Powell	Crewe	14
M Bilel	Southend	13
J Hanson	Bradford	13
D Hylton	Aldershot	13
R Howe	Torquay	12
D Kedwell	Gillingham	12
B Kee	Burton	12
G Madjo	Aldershot	12
L Mansell	Torquay	12
M Tubbs	Crawley	12
C Whelpdale	Gillingham	12

Record when keeping a clean sheet 2011-12

		P	W	D	L	F	GFA	PGA	Pts
1	Crewe (7)	11	11	0	0	16	1.45	3.0	33
2	Swindon (1)	26	23	3	0	51	1.96	2.8	72
3	Shrewsbury (2)	18	16	2	0	23	1.28	2.8	50
4	Southend (4)	17	15	2	0	35	2.06	2.8	47
5	Dag & Red (19)	9	8	1	0	14	1.56	2.8	25
6	Burton (17)	8	7	1	0	9	1.13	2.8	22
7	Aldershot (11)	15	13	2	0	19	1.27	2.7	41
8	Port Vale (12)	14	12	2	0	25	1.79	2.7	38
9	Rotherham (10)	12	10	2	0	16	1.33	2.7	32
10	Torquay (5)	20	16	4	0	24	1.20	2.6	52
11	Morecambe (15)	11	9	2	0	22	2.00	2.6	29
12	Cheltenham (6)	16	12	4	0	24	1.50	2.5	40
13	Crawley (3)	13	10	3	0	18	1.38	2.5	33
14	Oxford (9)	16	11	5	0	21	1.31	2.4	38
15	Gillingham (8)	13	9	4	0	16	1.23	2.4	31
16	Barnet (22)	10	7	3	0	16	1.60	2.4	24
17	Hereford (23)	10	7	3	0	11	1.10	2.4	24
18	Bradford (18)	9	6	3	0	12	1.33	2.3	21
19	Accrington (14)	8	5	3	0	12	1.50	2.3	18
20	Wimbledon (16)	6	4	2	0	10	1.67	2.3	14
21	Plymouth (21)	9	5	4	0	9	1.00	2.1	19
22	Northampton (20)	9	5	4	0	7	0.78	2.1	19
23	Bristol R (13)	12	6	6	0	8	0.67	2.0	24
24	Macclesfield (24)	10	5	5	0	12	1.20	2.0	20

Record when first to score 2011-12

		P	W	D	L	F	GFA	PGA	Pts
1	Swindon (1)	29	26	2	1	64	9	2.8	80
2	Southend (4)	27	23	4	0	63	17	2.7	73
3	Torquay (5)	26	22	3	1	44	12	2.7	69
4	Shrewsbury (2)	26	22	3	1	48	14	2.7	69
5	Cheltenham (6)	25	21	2	2	55	21	2.6	65
6	Aldershot (11)	24	19	2	3	44	17	2.5	59
7	Crawley (3)	22	16	4	2	44	16	2.4	52
8	Bristol R (13)	20	15	3	2	47	22	2.4	48
9	Accrington (14)	17	12	4	1	35	16	2.4	40
10	Crewe (7)	26	18	7	1	49	22	2.3	61
11	Oxford (9)	24	16	8	0	45	16	2.3	56
12	Gillingham (8)	24	17	3	4	56	26	2.3	54
13	Port Vale (12)	25	17	3	5	49	21	2.2	54
14	Rotherham (10)	27	17	6	4	51	31	2.1	57
15	Morecambe (15)	21	13	6	2	41	17	2.1	45
16	Burton (17)	17	10	6	1	30	17	2.1	36
17	Wimbledon (16)	16	10	4	2	37	22	2.1	34
18	Plymouth (21)	16	9	6	1	29	17	2.1	33
19	Dag & Red (19)	17	10	4	3	26	16	2.0	34
20	Bradford (18)	16	9	4	3	29	17	1.9	31
21	Hereford (23)	22	10	9	3	36	24	1.8	39
22	Northampton (20)	19	10	4	5	31	25	1.8	34
23	Barnet (22)	18	9	3	6	31	21	1.7	30
24	Macclesfield (24)	13	6	4	3	24	14	1.7	22

Key *Number in brackets refers to final league finishing position. Points do not include any deductions but league positions do. GFA: Goals for average per match, GAA: Goals against average per match, PGA: Average points gained per match, CS: clean sheet, FS: first to score*

Improving Mansfield primed for promotion

WITH the Blue Square BET Premier lacking a big-spending Crawley or Fleetwood there is an open look to the betting this year, *writes Danny Hayes.*

Luton have adopted their position at the head of the market for the fourth consecutive season but it looks risky taking short odds about a side beaten in the play-offs for the last three seasons.

An inability to turn draws into wins ultimately cost Gary Brabin his position as Luton manager towards the end of last season but there was an immediate turnaround in fortunes under Paul Buckle as the Hatters won five of their last six league games, keeping five clean sheets, before losing to York in the play-off final.

Buckle has strengthened the front line, getting Scott Rendell from Wycombe and signing Jon Shaw, who scored 35 times for Gateshead last year. However, the loss of influential captain Keith Keane is a blow and it may be the play-offs again.

The side to be with are **Mansfield**, who finished last season in impressive form.

Manager Paul Cox overhauled his squad last summer and it took them a while to gel but things clicked for the Stags in the second half of the season. They won 12 of their final 14 games to finish third and were unlucky to lose out to play-off winners York in the semi-finals.

Cox is one of the few managers able to strengthen his squad over the summer, with the signings of experienced defenders George Pilkington and Lee Beevers likely to make them very difficult to beat

this season. Allied to an already strong squad and with goals in plentiful supply through Matt Green, there is every reason to believe Mansfield will carry on from where they left off last season.

Also towards the head of the betting are Wrexham, who did remarkably well to stay with Fleetwood for so long last season, a performance that was all the more meritorious for having lost manager Dean Saunders early in the season and considering their efforts came against a backdrop of financial insecurity.

Their points tally of 98 would have been enough to win the league in most years but those early exertions told late on as they lost out to Luton in the play-offs. However, they have lost players over the summer and, having been unable to replace them thus far, Wrexham look likely to come up short again.

If there is to be a side to follow Crawley's and Fleetwood's blueprint and buy themselves league status then Forest Green look the most likely.

They finished tenth last year and have had the rare luxury in the Conference of bringing in more players than they have sold. But their squad still lacks a bit of quality and, with the bookies having already latched onto their chances, they don't represent much value.

At a bigger price, **Newport** could go well. The appointment of Anthony Hudson didn't work out last term but Justin Edinburgh steadied the ship and they pulled off some decent results in the second half of the season, even reaching the FA Trophy final, where they lost to York. They are 50-1 outright but take Blue Square's 6-1 about a top-five finish.

The teams coming down from League 2, Hereford and Macclesfield, are likely to find the transition difficult. The Bulls should fare best of the pair as they have kept most of the side who were only relegated on the final day last season. But the gap between League 2 and the Conference is closing every season and their squad is by no means certain to make a quick return to the Football League.

Macclesfield, on the other hand, could

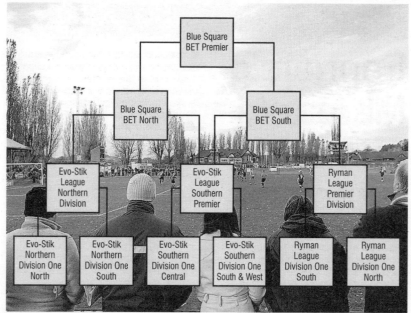

THE NON-LEAGUE PYRAMID: Step 1 (Blue Square BET Premier) down to Step 4

be in for a long season. They won just eight games last term and have seen a jaw-dropping 22 players depart over the summer. The Silkmen could find them-

Blue Square BET Premier winner						
	b365	Btfrd	Hills	Lads	Pwr	StJms
Luton	5-2	**3**	5-2	**3**	**3**	**3**
Mansfield	5	5	5	5	5	5
Wrexham	**7**	5	5	5	5	11-2
Forest Green	9	7	**9**	7	17-2	8
Grimsby	8	**9**	**9**	**9**	15-2	8
Cambridge	12	12	**16**	12	14	**16**
Kidderminster	16	14	12	14	14	**20**
Hereford	25	20	14	10	14	20
Macclesfield	22	20	14	14	**22**	**22**
Stockport	33	28	**33**	**33**	25	25
Lincoln	40	33	33	**40**	35	25
Newport	33	40	33	33	**55**	50
Gateshead	50	**66**	**66**	50	45	**66**
Woking	66	40	40	66	**70**	66
Alfreton	50	66	40	50	**70**	66
Southport	**66**	**66**	**66**	40	30	25
Braintree	200	200	200	100	100	**200**
Barrow	150	150	**200**	80	175	150
Dartford	100	**200**	**200**	150	175	150
Ebbsfleet	200	200	**250**	150	175	200
Nuneaton	**250**	**250**	**250**	150	225	200
Tamworth	**250**	**250**	**250**	150	225	200
Hyde	200	200	100	66	**250**	200
Telford	200	250	**500**	200	250	150
Win or each-way. See individual bookmakers for terms						

selves nearer the relegation dogfight than the play-offs.

Telford and Tamworth are also likely to be involved in the relegation battle. Both only narrowly avoided relegation last term and have seen their squads depleted over the summer.

Barrow did remarkably well to finish comfortably in mid-table last year but they have the smallest squad in the Conference – just nine players registered at time of going to press – and their reliance on free signings and the loan market could be their downfall over a long season. Back them to go down.

Of the newly promoted sides Woking are fancied by many to go well. They re-built the squad after they were relegated to the Conference South in 2009 and then strolled to that title last year. With much of the same squad still in place, a mid-table berth is the least they should expect.

Dartford and Hyde should have no problem coping with the higher level but Nuneaton only just scraped into the Conference North play-offs last year and this is a big step up for them.

Rangers' fall leaves punters in limbo

SCOTTISH football always used to be regarded as boring by a proportion of the football betting community, *writes Ian Wilkerson.*

It was simply a case of heads or tails. Rangers and Celtic might have been of interest when they faced each other but they were mainly regarded as a couple of odds-on shots to stick onto the end of your Saturday afternoon acca.

But we are about to embark on a campaign the like of which Scotland has never seen as the catastrophic financial problems at Ibrox have led to Rangers losing their place in the SPL.

Their demotion is likely to have an effect on each of the 41 other clubs in the SPL and Scottish Football League.

Purse strings will need to be tightened, squads are likely to change dramatically and, as a consequence, it is difficult to form any strong opinions about what is likely to happen.

Well, you could say Celtic should win the SPL but odds of 1-33 about a successful defence are hardly likely to get the pulse racing in anticipation of the new campaign.

While fans and TV viewers are likely to be interested in how Rangers adapt to life wherever they happen to wash up, for the football punter there will be other SPL markets for them to get their teeth into.

The race in the 'without Celtic' market will be a hot one, even though the decline in Scotland's Uefa coefficient means that only the winners will gain a place in the Champions League.

Motherwell have the chance to join Europe's top table this season and it will be interesting to see how they get on.

Dundee United will know that only a dismal start to the season prevented them from finishing third last term after they ended the season like a train. They are the Everton of the SPL and need to hit the ground running.

And Hearts, now under the stewardship of John McGlynn, need to build on their Scottish Cup win if they are to make a challenge.

Hibs and Aberdeen have been dismal over the last couple of seasons and there will be plenty of scope for improvement, but if fans come out in their numbers after voicing their dismay at the idea of Rangers remaining in the top flight, that can only help.

However, financial hardship is likely to be just around the corner and it will be the clubs who are best able to cope with it who should prosper. Exactly who that might be is likely to become clearer as the big kick-off approaches.

The SFL will also be affected and Dundee will be desperate to gain Rangers' place in the top flight after trying in vain to gain promotion in the last few seasons.

Partick may be able to push for the Division One title, last season's Division Three champions **Alloa** look capable of mounting a challenge for a successive title and **Peterhead** could brush themselves down from a disappointing campaign last term to take the basement division.

That is if Rangers aren't in Division Three. I'm afraid we will just have to wait and see.

Aberdeen

Nickname: The Dons
Colours: Red
Ground: Pittodrie (22,474)
Tel: 01224-650-400   www.afc.co.uk

THE DONS have finished ninth in the last three seasons and should really be showing more than that in what has not been a particularly strong league.

The goalscoring burden fell upon Scott Vernon last term as he scored 11 goals in the league with no one else contributing more than three. Celtic's Niall McGinn has been brought in to help out and, along with Rory Fallon, their strikers are decent.

They must surely be able to improve under the wise management of Craig Brown.

Longest run without loss/win: 9/7
High - low league position 6-12
Clean sheets: 11 **Yellow cards:** 65 **Red cards:** 5
Average attendance: 8,418 **Players used:** 32
Leading Scorer: S Vernon 11 (5,9)
Key stat: The Dons scored 14 away goals last season – the lowest total in the SPL

| | 11-12 | | Last five seasons at home | | | | | | | |
	H	A	P	W	D	L	OV	UN	BS	CS
Celtic	LD	L	11	1	2	8	8	3	8	0
Motherwell	L	LL	8	2	2	4	5	3	5	2
Dundee Utd	WW	W	11	5	3	3	7	4	8	1
Hearts	D	LL	11	2	5	4	1	10	3	5
St Johnstone	DD	W	6	1	2	3	2	4	2	2
Kilmarnock	DD	LD	11	6	3	2	6	5	4	6
St Mirren	DD	LD	10	6	3	1	3	7	3	6
Aberdeen										
Inverness CT	WL	LW	9	4	2	3	2	7	4	3
Hibernian	WL	DD	11	6	1	4	8	3	8	1
Ross County			0	0	0	0	0	0	0	0
Club 12										

Season	Division	Pos	P	W	D	L	F	A	GD	Pts
2011-12	SPL	9	38	9	14	15	36	44	-8	41
2010-11	SPL	9	38	11	5	22	39	59	-20	38
2009-10	SPL	9	38	10	11	17	36	52	-16	41

2011-12 SPL appearances (ten most regular starters)

	P	G	Y	R
A Considine	36	3	8	1
S Vernon	34 (1)	11	2	0
K Arnason	31 (2)	3	8	0
R Jack	30 (1)	3	4	2
F Fyvie	26 (1)	1	5	1
I Osbourne	22 (1)	0	4	0
R McArdle	20 (5)	0	4	0
J Brown	20	0	0	0
Y Mawene	19 (3)	2	5	0
R Fallon	18 (4)	2	3	1

Celtic

Nickname: The Bhoys
Colours: Green and White
Ground: Celtic Park (60,832)
Tel: 0871-226-1888   www.celticfc.net

RANGERS' demise means Celtic's main concern now will be complacency.

There were no such problems in winning the league last season even though Rangers set the early pace to establish a five-point lead, which the Bhoys eclipsed before the new year. But they were unable to win either cup, losing to Kilmarnock in the League Cup final and Hearts in the semi-final of the Scottish Cup.

They are 1-33 title favourites but it would be a mistake to think they'll win every week.

Longest run without loss/win: 21/2
High - low league position 1-3
Clean sheets: 25 **Yellow cards:** 34 **Red cards:** 5
Average attendance: 13,105 **Players used:** 32
Leading Scorer: G Hooper 24 (7,15)
Key stat: Celtic picked up over the backend of last season, winning a whopping 24 of their final 27 SPL games

| | 11-12 | | Last five seasons at home | | | | | | | |
	H	A	P	W	D	L	OV	UN	BS	CS
Celtic										
Motherwell	WW	WW	12	10	1	1	6	6	2	9
Dundee Utd	WW	WL	11	6	5	0	7	4	8	3
Hearts	WW	LW	12	9	2	1	8	4	4	8
St Johnstone	LWW	W	6	5	0	1	2	4	1	4
Kilmarnock	W	DW	9	7	2	0	5	4	4	5
St Mirren	W	WW	9	8	1	0	5	4	3	6
Aberdeen	W	WD	10	10	0	0	6	4	3	7
Inverness CT	WW	W	7	6	1	0	4	3	2	5
Hibernian	D	WW	11	8	2	1	7	4	8	3
Ross County			0	0	0	0	0	0	0	0
Club 12										

Season	Division	Pos	P	W	D	L	F	A	GD	Pts
2011-12	SPL	1	38	30	3	5	84	21	63	93
2010-11	SPL	2	38	29	5	4	85	22	63	92
2009-10	SPL	2	38	25	6	7	75	39	36	81

2011-12 SPL appearances (ten most regular starters)

	P	G	Y	R
G Hooper	34 (3)	24	1	0
F Forster	33	0	1	0
J Ledley	31 (1)	7	1	0
C Mulgrew	29 (1)	8	3	1
A Matthews	25 (2)	0	0	0
A Stokes	25 (9)	12	2	0
V Wanyama	24 (5)	4	2	1
J Forrest	23 (6)	7	1	0
S Ki	21 (9)	6	3	0
G Samaras	20 (6)	4	1	0

Dundee Utd

Nickname: The Terrors
Colours: Orange and Black
Ground: Tannadice Park (14,223)
Tel: 01382-833-166   www.dundeeunitedfc.co.uk

THE TERRORS won just three of their opening SPL 13 games last season and that slow start put paid to their chances of claiming third spot, even though they finished just three points behind Motherwell.

Eight wins at Tannadice were not enough but they have got some excellent forward options. Jon Daly was close to grabbing the golden boot last year, and there were excellent performances from Johnny Russell and Gary Mackay-Steven among others. They can go well again.

Longest run without loss/win: 9/5
High - low league position 4-10
Clean sheets: 13 **Yellow cards:** 48 **Red cards:** 1
Average attendance: 9,398 **Players used:** 25
Leading Scorer: J Daly 19 (5,16)
Key stat: The Terrors' 19 away games featured 69 goals – an average of 3.63 a game

	11-12 H	A	Last five seasons at home P	W	D	L	OV	UN	BS	CS
Celtic	LW	LL	12	2	3	7	5	7	7	1
Motherwell	LD	DW	12	5	4	3	4	8	4	6
Dundee Utd										
Hearts	WD	WW	10	7	1	2	4	6	3	5
St Johnstone	D	DWW	4	2	2	0	1	3	1	3
Kilmarnock	DW	D	9	4	4	1	2	7	3	5
St Mirren	DD	D	10	5	3	2	3	7	5	4
Aberdeen	L	LL	9	6	1	2	6	3	6	2
Inverness CT	WW	W	9	5	2	2	5	4	5	2
Hibernian	W	DW	12	5	5	2	4	8	4	6
Ross County			0	0	0	0	0	0	0	0
Club 12										

Season	Division	Pos	P	W	D	L	F	A	GD	Pts
2011-12	SPL	4	38	16	11	11	62	50	12	59
2010-11	SPL	4	38	17	10	11	55	50	5	61
2009-10	SPL	3	38	17	12	9	55	47	8	63

2011-12 SPL appearances (ten most regular starters)

	P	G	Y	R
J Rankin	38	4	5	0
D Pernis	38	0	0	0
P Dixon	37	3	7	0
J Daly	35 (1)	19	3	0
S Robertson	34 (3)	6	2	0
J Russell	33 (4)	9	2	1
W Flood	30 (2)	1	5	0
G Gunning	29 (2)	2	2	0
S Dillon	26 (2)	0	3	0
G Mackay-Steven	24 (7)	4	3	0

Hearts

Nickname: Jambos
Colours: Claret and White
Ground: Tynecastle (17,420)
Tel: 0871-663-1874   www.heartsfc.co.uk

WHILE Hearts celebrated winning the Scottish Cup last season, their league campaign was a disappointment and new manager John McGlynn will be looking to improve on a fifth-placed finish.

Bottom side Dunfermline won as many games on the road as the Jambos but they will look to improve on that with a much-changed squad.

Top goalscorer Rudi Skacel is a big loss, but their young players should be able to improve on last term's finish.

Longest run without loss/win: 5/5
High - low league position 3-6
Clean sheets: 13 **Yellow cards:** 71 **Red cards:** 4
Average attendance: 10,996 **Players used:** 29
Leading Scorer: R Skacel 12 (3,9)
Key stat: The Jambos didn't have a single home league draw last season

	11-12 H	A	Last five seasons at home P	W	D	L	OV	UN	BS	CS
Celtic	WL	LL	11	4	2	5	6	5	6	2
Motherwell	WL	LL	11	5	2	4	5	6	5	3
Dundee Utd	LL	LD	12	4	4	4	5	7	3	6
Hearts										
St Johnstone	LW	LL	5	2	1	2	2	3	3	2
Kilmarnock	L	DD	11	4	1	6	3	8	3	3
St Mirren	WW	D	11	7	2	2	5	6	6	3
Aberdeen	WW	D	9	5	2	2	6	3	4	3
Inverness CT	W	DL	8	6	1	1	4	4	5	3
Hibernian	WW	W	11	7	2	2	2	9	2	7
Ross County			0	0	0	0	0	0	0	0
Club 12										

Season	Division	Pos	P	W	D	L	F	A	GD	Pts
2011-12	SPL	5	38	15	7	16	45	43	2	52
2010-11	SPL	3	38	18	9	11	53	45	8	63
2009-10	SPL	7	38	13	9	16	35	46	-11	48

2011-12 SPL appearances (ten most regular starters)

	P	G	Y	R
M Zaliukas	36	1	7	1
A Webster	31	4	9	0
I Black	28 (1)	2	10	2
J Hamill	28 (1)	2	6	1
A Mrowiec	27 (2)	0	2	0
R McGowan	23 (5)	2	4	0
D Templeton	20 (7)	1	2	0
M Kello	20	0	0	0
S Elliott	19 (7)	3	0	0
R Skacel	19 (10)	12	5	0

Hibernian

Nickname: The Hibees
Colours: Green and White
Ground: Easter Road (17,458)
Tel: 0131-661-2159   www.hibs.co.uk

IT was a pretty dismal campaign for Hibernian. They flirted with relegation until the closing weeks of the season and won just two of their 19 league games at Easter Road. They also had to cope with the disappointment of being thrashed by Hearts in the Scottish Cup final.

Manager Pat Fenlon still has a lot to prove and although he is bringing in plenty of fresh blood, it is difficult to see them challenging for a place in the top six in 2012-13.

Longest run without loss/win: 4/9
High - low league position 9-11
Clean sheets: 6 **Yellow cards:** 84 **Red cards:** 2
Average attendance: 5,897 **Players used:** 35
Leading Scorer: G O'Connor 12 (5,11)
Key stat: Hibernian scored 17 home goals last season – the lowest total in the SPL

	11-12		Last five seasons at home							
	H	A	P	W	D	L	OV	UN	BS	CS
Celtic	LL	D	11	3	2	6	5	6	3	2
Motherwell	LD	L	10	5	2	3	2	8	4	3
Dundee Utd	DL	L	9	2	4	3	7	2	8	0
Hearts	L	LL	10	1	5	4	4	6	7	1
St Johnstone	WL	L	6	2	2	2	4	2	4	2
Kilmarnock	DL	LW	11	6	2	3	5	6	6	3
St Mirren	LD	WL	10	6	2	2	4	6	5	4
Aberdeen	DD	LW	12	2	8	2	6	6	7	5
Inverness CT	D	WWL	7	4	2	1	1	6	3	4
Hibernian										
Ross County			0	0	0	0	0	0	0	0
Club 12										

Season	Division	Pos	P	W	D	L	F	A	GD	Pts
2011-12	SPL	11	38	8	9	21	40	67	-27	33
2010-11	SPL	10	38	10	7	21	39	61	-22	37
2009-10	SPL	4	38	15	9	14	58	55	3	54

2011-12 SPL appearances (ten most regular starters)

	P	G	Y	R
P Hanlon	35	2	6	0
G Stack	30	0	2	0
I Osbourne	29 (1)	1	6	0
G O'Connor	27 (6)	12	8	0
L Stevenson	27 (2)	0	6	1
I Sproule	26 (8)	3	7	0
L Griffiths	24 (6)	8	7	0
S O'Hanlon	22	2	4	0
D Wotherspoon	20 (10)	0	6	0
D Stephens	14 (3)	0	5	0

Inverness CT

Nickname: Caley
Colours: Blue and Red
Ground: Caledonian Stadium (7,500)
Tel: 01463-222-880   www.caleythistleonline.com

TAKING just one win from their first nine games was a poor start for Inverness, but Hibs and Dunfermline were so dire during the course of 2011-12 that Caley weren't in much danger of being relegated.

The departure of Jonny Hayes to Aberdeen is a blow and Terry Butcher is still trying to sign new players to bolster his squad before the big kick-off.

It would probably be considered a good season if they avoid being embroiled in the relegation scrap.

Longest run without loss/win: 5/6
High - low league position 9-12
Clean sheets: 8 **Yellow cards:** 68 **Red cards:** 7
Average attendance: 6,054 **Players used:** 28
Leading Scorer: G Tade 9 (5,8)
Key stat: Thistle won just one of their final eight home matches of last season

	11-12		Last five seasons at home							
	H	A	P	W	D	L	OV	UN	BS	CS
Celtic	L	LL	8	2	2	4	4	4	5	1
Motherwell	L	LW	8	2	0	6	6	2	4	2
Dundee Utd	L	LL	7	1	2	4	3	4	3	2
Hearts	DW	L	8	2	3	3	3	5	4	2
St Johnstone	L	LD	3	1	1	1	0	3	1	1
Kilmarnock	WD	WL	8	5	1	2	7	1	7	1
St Mirren	WD	WW	10	5	2	3	6	4	6	4
Aberdeen	WL	LW	8	2	1	5	4	4	4	1
Inverness CT										
Hibernian	LLW	D	10	6	2	2	3	7	3	6
Ross County			2	1	0	1	2	0	1	1
Club 12										

Season	Division	Pos	P	W	D	L	F	A	GD	Pts
2011-12	SPL	10	38	10	9	19	42	60	-18	39
2010-11	SPL	5	38	14	11	13	52	44	8	53
2009-10	Div 1	1	36	21	10	5	72	32	40	73

2011-12 SPL appearances (ten most regular starters)

	P	G	Y	R
R Foran	37	2	11	0
G Tansey	33 (3)	4	6	1
R Esson	33	0	0	0
G Tade	30 (6)	9	2	0
R Tokely	28 (1)	1	5	1
J Hayes	25 (1)	7	1	1
G Shinnie	25 (1)	1	6	0
K Gillet	25	0	4	0
N Ross	18 (11)	2	1	0
R Golobart	18 (4)	2	5	0

Kilmarnock

Nickname: Killie
Colours: Blue and White
Ground: Rugby Park (18,128)
Tel: 01563-545-300   www.kilmarnockfc.co.uk

KILLIE'S away form cost them a top-six finish last season and they posted a full return from just four of their matches away from Rugby Park.

The League Cup victory over Celtic was a massive boost but they need to build on that and provide assistance for striker Paul Heffernan. Whether they are able to retain the services of manager Kenny Shiels' son Dean or not, they should have enough to at least match last season's seventh-placed finish.

Longest run without loss/win: 4/6
High - low league position 5-8
Clean sheets: 11 **Yellow cards:** 56 **Red cards:** 3
Average attendance: 6,994 **Players used:** 36
Leading Scorer: D Shiels 13 (5,11)
Key stat: Killie won three and drew one of their seven matches against the Old Firm last term, including their League Cup final victory

	11-12		Last five seasons at home							
	H	A	P	W	D	L	OV	UN	BS	CS
Celtic	DL	L	11	1	1	9	9	2	7	1
Motherwell	DW	D	9	3	2	4	3	6	2	4
Dundee Utd	D	DL	10	3	4	3	4	6	6	3
Hearts	DD	W	10	2	5	3	4	6	5	4
St Johnstone	LD	L	6	2	2	2	4	2	5	1
Kilmarnock										
St Mirren	WL	LL	11	5	3	3	4	7	6	3
Aberdeen	WD	DD	10	5	2	3	3	7	5	4
Inverness CT	LW	LD	10	4	3	3	7	3	9	1
Hibernian	WL	DW	9	5	2	2	5	4	7	1
Ross County			0	0	0	0	0	0	0	0
Club 12										

Season	Division	Pos	P	W	D	L	F	A	GD	Pts
2011-12	SPL	7	38	11	14	13	44	61	-17	47
2010-11	SPL	6	38	13	10	15	53	55	-2	49
2009-10	SPL	11	38	8	9	21	29	51	-22	33

2011-12 SPL appearances (ten most regular starters)

	P	G	Y	R
J Fowler	34 (3)	3	9	0
D Shiels	33 (2)	13	9	1
L Kelly	33 (1)	1	5	1
C Bell	32	0	0	0
G Harkins	29 (1)	1	0	0
P Heffernan	26 (3)	11	0	0
M Sissoko	24 (3)	0	7	0
M Pascali	24	3	3	0
G Hay	20 (4)	0	4	0
R McKeown	18	1	0	0

Motherwell

Nickname: The Well/The Steelmen
Colours: Amber and Claret
Ground: Fir Park (13,742)
Tel: 01698-333-333   www.motherwellfc.co.uk

MOTHERWELL had a great season last term as they were able to benefit from Rangers' financial woes to claim a place in the Champions League qualifiers after finishing third.

They played poorly against the Glasgow giants but in the end they merited their place as the best of the rest. They won four of their opening six games last season and will want to avoid too much distraction from their European commitments so they can do the same again.

Longest run without loss/win: 6/5
High - low league position 2-5
Clean sheets: 15 **Yellow cards:** 65 **Red cards:** 5
Average attendance: 8,209 **Players used:** 22
Leading Scorer: M Higdon 14 (7,10)
Key stat: The Well scored just two goals in eight matches against the Old Firm

	11-12		Last five seasons at home							
	H	A	P	W	D	L	OV	UN	BS	CS
Celtic	LL	LL	10	1	2	7	6	4	7	1
Motherwell										
Dundee Utd	DL	WD	11	4	4	3	8	3	9	1
Hearts	WW	LW	10	5	0	5	3	7	2	4
St Johnstone	LWW	W	5	3	0	2	5	0	3	1
Kilmarnock	D	DL	11	4	2	5	4	7	4	4
St Mirren	D	WD	9	3	3	3	6	5	2	
Aberdeen	WW	W	11	5	3	3	8	5	3	
Inverness CT	WL	W	9	5	2	2	6	3	5	3
Hibernian	W	WD	10	5	1	4	7	3	7	3
Ross County			0	0	0	0	0	0	0	0
Club 12										

Season	Division	Pos	P	W	D	L	F	A	GD	Pts
2011-12	SPL	3	38	18	8	12	49	44	5	62
2010-11	SPL	7	38	13	7	18	40	60	-20	46
2009-10	SPL	5	38	13	14	11	52	54	-2	53

2011-12 SPL appearances (ten most regular starters)

	P	G	Y	R
T Hateley	38	2	4	0
D Randolph	38	0	1	0
N Law	38	4	0	0
S Hammell	37	2	5	0
M Higdon	35	14	5	0
S Jennings	33 (1)	0	7	0
K Lasley	32	4	8	2
J Murphy	32 (4)	9	2	0
S Hutchinson	29 (1)	1	10	0
T Clancy	24 (2)	0	8	1

Ross County

Nickname: County, The Staggies
Colours: Blue
Ground: Victoria Park (5,800)
Tel: 01349-860860 www.rosscountyfootballclub.co.uk

DESPITE Dunfermline's relegation in May, teams who have won promotion from the second tier have had a decent record in staying in the SPL and Ross should be able to avoid an immediate return.

They cruised to the Division One title and should have nothing to fear in the bottom half of the table at least.

Momentum should be enough to carry them away from any relegation trouble and not many teams will be looking forward to a trip to Dingwall.

Longest run without loss/win: 34/3
High - low league position: 1-4
Clean sheets: 14 Yellow cards: 62 Red cards: 5
Average attendance: 2,303 Players used: 19
Leading Scorer: C McMenamin 19 (7,15)
Key stat: Ross County lost just one league match in Division One last season

	11-12		Last five seasons at home							
	H	A	P	W	D	L	OV	UN	BS	CS
Celtic			0	0	0	0	0	0	0	0
Motherwell			0	0	0	0	0	0	0	0
Dundee Utd			0	0	0	0	0	0	0	0
Hearts			0	0	0	0	0	0	0	0
St Johnstone			4	0	3	1	2	2	2	2
Kilmarnock			0	0	0	0	0	0	0	0
St Mirren			0	0	0	0	0	0	0	0
Aberdeen			0	0	0	0	0	0	0	0
Inverness CT			2	1	1	0	1	1	1	1
Hibernian			0	0	0	0	0	0	0	0
Ross County			0	0	0	0	0	0	0	0
Club 12										

Season	Division	Pos	P	W	D	L	F	A	GD	Pts
2011-12	Div 1	1	36	22	13	1	72	32	40	79
2010-11	Div 1	8	36	9	14	13	30	34	-4	41
2009-10	Div 1	5	36	15	11	10	46	44	2	56

2011-12 Div 1 appearances (ten most regular starters)

	P	G	Y	R
M Fraser	36	0	0	0
G Miller	36	1	4	1
G Munro	35	2	1	0
S Boyd	34 (1)	2	4	0
C McMenamin	34	19	6	0
R Brittain	34 (1)	10	8	0
P Lawson	31 (2)	2	6	0
M Gardyne	30 (4)	13	4	0
S Kettlewell	27 (1)	5	7	1
I Vigurs	27 (3)	5	11	0

St Johnstone

Nickname: The Saints
Colours: Blue and White
Ground: McDiarmid Park (10,673)
Tel: 01738-459090 www.perthstjohnstonefc.co.uk

THE SAINTS were as short as 5-1 to finish bottom of the SPL last season but they found their shooting boots after having lost them during the 2010-11 campaign and did well to secure a top-six finish.

St Johnstone were stronger on the road than at McDiarmid Park but they took just one point from their final seven matches and will need to get that sorry run out of their system quickly.

The loss of Francisco Sandaza and Cillian Sheridan could prove a real blow.

Longest run without loss/win: 6/7
High - low league position 4-6
Clean sheets: 15 Yellow cards: 74 Red cards: 2
Average attendance: 6,084 Players used: 28
Leading Scorer: F Sandaza 14 (4,12)
Key stat: The Saints won 30 points on their travels but claimed just 20 on their own patch

	11-12		Last five seasons at home							
	H	A	P	W	D	L	OV	UN	BS	CS
Celtic	L	WLL	4	0	0	4	2	2	1	0
Motherwell	L	WLL	5	1	1	3	3	2	2	1
Dundee Utd	DLL	D	6	0	2	4	3	3	3	1
Hearts	WW	WL	5	3	1	1	2	3	2	2
St Johnstone										
Kilmarnock	W	WD	4	1	1	2	1	3	0	2
St Mirren	L	DW	5	2	2	1	2	3	2	2
Aberdeen	L	DD	5	1	2	2	1	4	2	2
Inverness CT	WD	W	4	2	1	1	1	3	0	3
Hibernian	W	LW	4	3	1	0	2	2	3	1
Ross County			4	1	3	0	1	3	1	3
Club 12										

Season	Division	Pos	P	W	D	L	F	A	GD	Pts
2011-12	SPL	6	38	14	8	16	43	50	-7	50
2010-11	SPL	8	38	11	11	16	23	43	-20	44
2009-10	SPL	8	38	12	11	15	57	61	-4	47

2011-12 SPL appearances (ten most regular starters)

	P	G	Y	R
L Craig	36	7	7	0
D MacKay	36	4	2	0
F Sandaza	28 (1)	14	6	1
J Morris	28	1	7	0
D McCracken	27 (1)	1	4	0
C Millar	26 (4)	0	4	0
S Anderson	26 (3)	1	5	0
C Davidson	26	1	3	0
P Enckelman	25	0	0	0
C Sheridan	25 (3)	4	2	1

St Mirren

Nickname: The Saints/The Buddies
Colours: Black and White
Ground: St Mirren Park (10,752)
Tel: 0141-889-2558   www.stmirren.net

THE BUDDIES played some attractive football under Danny Lennon last season and any campaign where the Paisley club don't flirt with the drop has to be considered a success.

However, there will be a great deal of disappointment at striker Nigel Hasselbaink's departure and the worry is that the financial situation at the club means Lennon has been unable to strengthen a relatively thin squad. It could prove to be a long season.

Longest run without loss/win: 5/11
High – low league position 5-9
Clean sheets: 13 **Yellow cards:** 73 **Red cards:** 3
Average attendance: 6,716 **Players used:** 24
Leading Scorer: S Thompson 13 (3,10)
Key stat: The Buddies drew ten of their 19 away games last season

	11-12		Last five seasons at home							
	H	A	P	W	D	L	OV	UN	BS	CS
Celtic	LL	L	9	1	0	8	4	5	3	1
Motherwell	LD	D	11	2	6	3	3	8	4	5
Dundee Utd	D	DD	9	0	4	5	4	5	5	1
Hearts	D	LL	8	1	4	3	3	5	5	1
St Johnstone	DL	W	6	0	4	2	2	4	3	2
Kilmarnock	WW	LW	11	5	3	3	2	9	2	6
St Mirren										
Aberdeen	WD	DD	11	4	3	4	2	9	5	2
Inverness CT	LL	LD	10	2	3	5	5	5	7	1
Hibernian	LW	WD	10	4	4	2	2	8	5	4
Ross County			0	0	0	0	0	0	0	0
Club 12										

Season	Division	Pos	P	W	D	L	F	A	GD	Pts
2011-12	SPL	8	38	9	16	13	39	51	-12	43
2010-11	SPL	11	38	8	9	21	33	57	-24	33
2009-10	SPL	10	38	7	13	18	36	49	-13	34

2011-12 SPL appearances (ten most regular starters)

	P	G	Y	R
C Samson	38	0	0	0
P McGowan	37	8	9	0
S Thompson	35 (1)	13	6	0
D van Zanten	35	0	4	0
L Mair	34	1	6	0
J Tesselaar	33	0	1	1
M McAusland	31 (1)	1	7	1
J Goodwin	31	1	12	0
N Hasselbaink	22 (12)	6	4	1
G Teale	21 (13)	0	1	0

Top scorers 2011-12

		P	W	D	L	F	GFA	PGA	Pts
1	Celtic (1)	38	30	3	5	84	2.21	2.4	93
2	Rangers (2)	38	26	5	7	77	2.03	2.2	83
3	Dundee Utd (4)	38	16	11	11	62	1.63	1.6	59
4	Motherwell (3)	38	18	8	12	49	1.29	1.6	62
5	Hearts (5)	38	15	7	16	45	1.18	1.4	52
6	Kilmarnock (7)	38	11	14	13	44	1.16	1.2	47
7	St Johnstone (6)	38	14	8	16	43	1.13	1.3	50
8	Inverness CT (10)	38	10	9	19	42	1.11	1.0	39
9	Hibernian (11)	38	8	9	21	40	1.05	0.9	33
10	Dunfermline (12)	38	5	10	23	40	1.05	0.7	25
11	St Mirren (8)	38	9	16	13	39	1.03	1.1	43
12	Aberdeen (9)	38	9	14	15	36	0.95	1.1	41

Best defence 2011-12

		P	W	D	L	F	GFA	PGA	Pts
1	Celtic (1)	38	30	3	5	21	0.55	2.4	93
2	Rangers (2)	38	26	5	7	28	0.74	2.2	83
3	Hearts (5)	38	15	7	16	43	1.13	1.4	52
4	Motherwell (3)	38	18	8	12	44	1.16	1.6	62
5	Aberdeen (9)	38	9	14	15	44	1.16	1.1	41
6	Dundee Utd (4)	38	16	11	11	50	1.32	1.6	59
7	St Johnstone (6)	38	14	8	16	50	1.32	1.3	50
8	St Mirren (8)	38	9	16	13	51	1.34	1.1	43
9	Inverness CT (10)	38	10	9	19	60	1.58	1.0	39
10	Kilmarnock (7)	38	11	14	13	61	1.61	1.2	47
11	Hibernian (11)	38	8	9	21	67	1.76	0.9	33
12	Dunfermline (12)	38	5	10	23	82	2.16	0.7	25

GARY HOOPER: the Celtic striker bagged 24 goals to top the SPL scoring charts

Clean sheets 2011-12

		P	CS	%
1	Celtic (1)	38	25	65.8
2	Rangers (2)	38	17	44.7
3	Motherwell (3)	38	15	39.5
4	St Johnstone (6)	38	15	39.5
5	Hearts (5)	38	13	34.2
6	St Mirren (8)	38	13	34.2
7	Dundee Utd (4)	38	13	34.2
8	Aberdeen (9)	38	11	28.9
9	Kilmarnock (7)	38	11	28.9
10	Inverness CT (10)	38	8	21.1
11	Dunfermline (12)	38	7	18.4
12	Hibernian (11)	38	6	15.8

First to score 2011-12

		P	FS	%
1	Celtic (1)	38	30	78.9
2	Rangers (2)	38	26	68.4
3	Motherwell (3)	38	20	52.6
4	Hearts (5)	38	17	44.7
5	Kilmarnock (7)	38	17	44.7
6	Dundee Utd (4)	38	16	42.1
7	Inverness CT (10)	38	15	39.5
8	St Mirren (8)	38	13	34.2
9	Hibernian (11)	38	13	34.2
10	Dunfermline (12)	38	13	34.2
11	Aberdeen (9)	38	12	31.6
12	St Johnstone (6)	38	11	28.9

Top scorers 2011-12

		Goals
G Hooper	Celtic	24
J Daly	Dundee Utd	19
N Jelavic	Rangers	14
M Higdon	Motherwell	14
F Sandaza	St Johnstone	14
S Thompson	St Mirren	13
A Stokes	Celtic	12
G O'Connor	Hibernian	12
D Shiels	Kilmarnock	12
R Skacel	Hearts	12
S Aluko	Rangers	12
A Kirk	Dunfermline	11
S Vernon	Aberdeen	11

Record when keeping a clean sheet 2011-12

		P	W	D	L	F	GFA	PGA	Pts
	Celtic (1)	25	24	1	0	61	2.44	2.9	73
2	Rangers (2)	17	15	2	0	40	2.35	2.8	47
3	Hearts (5)	13	10	3	0	24	1.85	2.5	33
4	Dundee Utd (4)	13	10	3	0	21	1.62	2.5	33
5	Dunfermline (12)	7	5	2	0	9	1.29	2.4	17
6	Motherwell (3)	15	10	5	0	17	1.13	2.3	35
7	Inverness CT (10)	8	5	3	0	6	0.75	2.3	18
8	St Johnstone (6)	15	8	7	0	17	1.13	2.1	31
9	Kilmarnock (7)	11	6	5	0	8	0.73	2.1	23
10	St Mirren (8)	13	5	8	0	8	0.62	1.8	23
11	Aberdeen (9)	11	4	7	0	8	0.73	1.7	19
12	Hibernian (11)	6	2	4	0	5	0.83	1.7	10

Record when first to score 2011-12

		P	W	D	L	F	GFA	PGA	Pts
1	Celtic (1)	30	29	1	0	75	6	2.9	88
2	Rangers (2)	26	23	1	2	66	15	2.7	70
3	St Johnstone (6)	11	10	0	1	22	10	2.7	30
4	Dundee Utd (4)	16	13	2	1	36	10	2.6	41
5	Hearts (5)	17	14	1	2	38	11	2.5	43
6	Motherwell (3)	20	15	2	3	38	17	2.4	47
7	Aberdeen (9)	12	7	4	1	24	13	2.1	25
8	Kilmarnock (7)	17	8	7	2	31	24	1.8	31
9	Inverness CT (10)	15	8	3	4	21	17	1.8	27
10	St Mirren (8)	13	6	5	2	21	14	1.8	23
11	Hibernian (11)	13	5	4	4	27	24	1.5	19
12	Dunfermline (12)	13	5	2	6	20	21	1.3	17

Key *Number in brackets refers to final league finishing position. Points do not include any deductions but league positions do. GFA: Goals for average per match, GAA: Goals against average per match, PGA: Average points gained per match, CS: clean sheet, FS: first to score*

Cowdenbeath

Nickname: The Blue Brazil   Ground: Central Park
www.cowdenbeathfc.com

THE Blue Brazil did well to bounce back up after acquitting themselves well in Division One two seasons ago only to fall into the play-off place.

If they can be as strong at home as last season – just one defeat on their own patch – they can avoid another relegation scrap.

	11-12 H	A	Last five seasons at home P	W	D	L	OV	UN	BS	CS
Dunfermline			2	0	0	2	1	1	0	0
Dundee			2	1	0	1	2	0	2	0
Falkirk			2	0	1	1	1	1	1	1
Hamilton			0	0	0	0	0	0	0	0
Livingston			0	0	0	0	0	0	0	0
Partick			2	1	1	0	1	1	2	0
Raith			6	1	0	5	5	1	4	1
Morton			4	0	2	2	2	2	3	0
Cowdenbeath										
Dumbarton	DW	WW	6	3	3	0	2	4	2	4

Season	Division	Pos	P	W	D	L	F	A	GD	Pts
2011-12	Div 2	1	36	20	11	5	68	29	39	71
2010-11	Div 1	9	36	9	8	19	41	72	-31	35
2009-10	Div 2	3	36	16	11	9	60	41	19	59

Dundee

Nickname: The Dark Blues   Ground: Dens Park
www.dundeefc.co.uk

The perennial bridesmaids could yet benefit from the Rangers situation but they are likely challengers in the second tier.

The big spending days at Dens Park appear to be over and if they can show more steel at home – just seven wins last term – they should be a real force.

	11-12 H	A	Last five seasons at home P	W	D	L	OV	UN	BS	CS
Dunfermline			8	3	5	0	2	6	4	4
Dundee										
Falkirk	WW	LD	4	4	0	0	2	2	2	2
Hamilton	LD	WL	6	1	4	1	1	5	2	3
Livingston	WW	LW	8	5	2	1	4	4	2	5
Partick	LL	WD	12	7	3	2	5	7	2	8
Raith	WD	WW	6	4	2	0	4	3	3	4
Morton	LL	WW	10	6	2	2	3	7	4	4
Cowdenbeath			2	1	1	0	2	0	1	1
Dumbarton			0	0	0	0	0	0	0	0

Season	Division	Pos	P	W	D	L	F	A	GD	Pts
2011-12	Div 1	2	36	15	10	11	53	43	10	55
2010-11	Div 1	6	36	19	12	5	54	34	20	44*
2009-10	Div 1	2	36	16	13	7	48	34	14	61

Dumbarton

Nickname: The SonsGround: Dumbarton Stadium
www.dumbartonfootballclub.com

AFTER battling their way through the play-offs to make it to the second tier, the priority for the Sons has to be staying in the division.

Having conceded 61 goals in finishing third in Division Two last season, they will need to tighten up defensively if they are to survive.

	11-12 H	A	Last five seasons at home P	W	D	L	OV	UN	BS	CS
Dunfermline			0	0	0	0	0	0	0	0
Dundee			0	0	0	0	0	0	0	0
Falkirk			0	0	0	0	0	0	0	0
Hamilton			0	0	0	0	0	0	0	0
Livingston			2	0	0	2	2	0	1	0
Partick			0	0	0	0	0	0	0	0
Raith			0	0	0	0	0	0	0	0
Morton			0	0	0	0	0	0	0	0
Cowdenbeath	LL	DL	6	2	1	3	4	2	3	0
Dumbarton										

Season	Division	Pos	P	W	D	L	F	A	GD	Pts
2011-12	Div 2	3	36	17	7	12	61	61	0	58
2010-11	Div 2	7	36	11	7	18	52	70	-18	40
2009-10	Div 2	6	36	14	6	16	49	58	-9	48

Dunfermline

Nickname: The ParsGround: East End Park
www.dafc.co.uk

COULD yet be handed their place in the SPL back but must improve on dismal home form to be among the challengers in Div One.

They posted just one success on their home patch last term and anything other than promotion would be regarded as a disappointment.

	11-12 H	A	Last five seasons at home P	W	D	L	OV	UN	BS	CS
Dunfermline										
Dundee			8	2	3	3	2	6	4	1
Falkirk			4	1	1	2	3	1	1	1
Hamilton			2	0	1	1	1	1	1	0
Livingston			4	1	1	2	2	2	2	1
Partick			8	3	3	2	6	3	4	
Raith			4	2	1	1	3	1	3	0
Morton			8	5	0	3	4	4	4	2
Cowdenbeath			2	2	0	0	2	0	1	1
Dumbarton			0	0	0	0	0	0	0	0

Season	Division	Pos	P	W	D	L	F	A	GD	Pts
2011-12	SPL	12	38	5	10	23	40	82	-42	25
2010-11	Div 1	1	36	20	10	6	66	31	35	70
2009-10	Div 1	3	36	17	7	12	54	44	10	58

Falkirk

Nickname: The Bairns   **Ground: Falkirk Stadium**
www.falkirkfc.co.uk

ANOTHER club with promotion ambitions, but the potential loss of striker Farid Al Alagui would be huge after he scored 18 goals last season with the next top scorer hitting just six. They were also poor away from Falkirk Stadium last term, posting just four away wins.

| | 11-12 | | Last five seasons at home | | | | | | | |
	H	A	P	W	D	L	OV	UN	BS	CS
Dunfermline			4	2	0	2	1	3	1	2
Dundee	WD	LL	4	1	3	0	3	1	4	0
Falkirk										
Hamilton	DW	WW	6	3	1	2	3	3	2	3
Livingston	WL	DW	2	1	0	1	2	0	2	0
Partick	WD	DD	4	2	1	1	2	2	3	1
Raith	WL	LD	4	2	1	1	2	2	2	2
Morton	WL	LD	4	3	0	1	1	3	1	2
Cowdenbeath			2	2	0	0	1	1	1	1
Dumbarton			0	0	0	0	0	0	0	0

Season	Division	Pos	P	W	D	L	F	A	GD	Pts
2011-12	Div 1	3	36	13	13	10	53	48	5	52
2010-11	Div 1	3	36	17	7	12	57	41	16	58
2009-10	SPL	12	38	6	13	19	31	57	-26	31

Hamilton

Nickname: The Accies   **Ground: New Douglas Park**
www.acciesfc.co.uk

THERE is talk of tight budgets at New Douglas Park and the Accies will again be looking to blood young talent.

Last year's youthful side will have another season's experience under their belts but they will do well to challenge and another mid-table finish looks likely.

| | 11-12 | | Last five seasons at home | | | | | | | |
	H	A	P	W	D	L	OV	UN	BS	CS
Dunfermline			2	2	0	0	2	0	1	1
Dundee	LW	WD	6	3	2	1	2	4	2	4
Falkirk	LL	DL	6	0	3	3	1	5	2	1
Hamilton										
Livingston	DL	LW	6	1	4	1	1	5	3	2
Partick	WD	DL	6	2	4	0	1	5	1	5
Raith	DW	LL	2	1	1	0	2	0	2	0
Morton	LW	WW	4	3	0	1	3	1	2	2
Cowdenbeath			0	0	0	0	0	0	0	0
Dumbarton			0	0	0	0	0	0	0	0

Season	Division	Pos	P	W	D	L	F	A	GD	Pts
2011-12	Div 1	4	36	14	7	15	55	56	-1	49
2010-11	SPL	12	38	5	11	22	24	59	-35	26
2009-10	SPL	6	38	13	10	15	39	46	-7	49

Livingston

Nickname: Livi Lions   **Ground: Almondvale**
www.livingstonfc.co.uk

LIVI adapted quite well to life back in Division One after two promotions but they struggled to find any consistency – they won just five matches at Almondvale so the area for improvement is obvious.

However, Livingston kept most of the squad together and could progress.

| | 11-12 | | Last five seasons at home | | | | | | | |
	H	A	P	W	D	L	OV	UN	BS	CS
Dunfermline			4	1	1	2	2	2	3	0
Dundee	WL	LL	8	1	3	4	3	5	4	2
Falkirk	DL	LW	2	0	1	1	1	1	2	0
Hamilton	WL	DW	6	2	2	2	2	4	1	4
Livingston										
Partick	WW	LW	8	4	2	2	5	3	4	3
Raith	DW	WW	2	1	1	0	1	1	1	1
Morton	DD	LW	6	3	2	1	2	4	2	3
Cowdenbeath			0	0	0	0	0	0	0	0
Dumbarton			2	1	1	0	0	2	1	1

Season	Division	Pos	P	W	D	L	F	A	GD	Pts
2011-12	Div 1	5	36	13	9	14	56	54	2	48
2010-11	Div 2	1	36	25	7	4	79	33	46	82
2009-10	Div 3	1	36	24	6	6	63	25	38	78

Morton

Nickname: The Ton   **Ground: Cappielow Park**
www.gmfc.net

FLIRTED with the play-off place at the bottom of the table last season and won just two of their final 14 matches of the campaign.

A huge improvement is needed from Allan Moore's men if they are going to mount any sort of challenge at the top of the table.

| | 11-12 | | Last five seasons at home | | | | | | | |
	H	A	P	W	D	L	OV	UN	BS	CS
Dunfermline			8	3	1	4	4	4	4	1
Dundee	LL	WW	10	2	1	7	4	6	4	2
Falkirk	WD	LW	4	1	3	0	2	2	2	2
Hamilton	LL	WL	4	0	0	4	2	2	2	0
Livingston	WL	DD	6	1	3	2	5	1	6	0
Partick	LW	LD	10	6	1	3	2	8	2	6
Raith	DL	DL	8	3	3	2	2	6	3	4
Morton										
Cowdenbeath			4	3	0	1	3	1	1	3
Dumbarton			0	0	0	0	0	0	0	0

Season	Division	Pos	P	W	D	L	F	A	GD	Pts
2011-12	Div 1	8	36	10	12	14	40	55	-15	42
2010-11	Div 1	7	36	11	10	15	39	43	-4	43
2009-10	Div 1	8	36	11	4	21	40	65	-25	37

Partick

Nickname: The Jags **Ground: Firhill Stadium**
www.ptfc.co.uk

THE JAGS conceded just 16 home goals last season and are another team who are putting their faith in young players in 2011-12.

They have an ambitious manager in Jackie McNamara and could be the team to emerge form the pack to put in a challenge.

	11-12 H	A	P	W	D	L	OV	UN	BS	CS
Dunfermline			8	3	1	4	2	6	3	3
Dundee	LD	WW	12	2	7	3	0	12	2	7
Falkirk	DD	LD	4	1	2	1	2	2	3	1
Hamilton	DW	LD	6	2	3	1	2	4	1	4
Livingston	WL	LL	8	5	2	1	5	3	4	4
Partick										
Raith	LD	LL	6	1	3	2	2	4	2	3
Morton	WD	WL	10	6	3	1	4	6	2	7
Cowdenbeath			2	1	0	1	0	2	0	1
Dumbarton			0	0	0	0	0	0	0	0

Season	Division	Pos	P	W	D	L	F	A	GD	Pts
2011-12	Div 1	6	36	12	11	13	50	39	11	47
2010-11	Div 1	5	36	12	11	13	44	39	5	47
2009-10	Div 1	6	36	14	6	16	43	40	3	48

Raith

Nickname: The Rovers **Ground: Stark's Park**
www.raithrovers.net

JOHN MCGLYNN'S departure from the Stark's Park dugout to take charge at Hearts could have a destablising effect.

They finished the campaign strongly having lost just one of their last nine games but have plenty of work to do if they are to be among the title contenders.

	11-12 H	A	P	W	D	L	OV	UN	BS	CS
Dunfermline			4	2	0	2	3	1	3	1
Dundee	LL	LD	6	2	1	3	3	3	3	1
Falkirk	WD	LW	4	2	1	1	3	1	3	1
Hamilton	WW	DL	2	2	0	0	2	0	2	0
Livingston	LL	DL	2	0	0	2	1	1	0	0
Partick	WW	WD	6	4	1	1	2	4	2	3
Raith										
Morton	DW	DW	8	4	2	2	5	3	4	4
Cowdenbeath			6	3	1	2	5	1	5	1
Dumbarton			0	0	0	0	0	0	0	0

Season	Division	Pos	P	W	D	L	F	A	GD	Pts
2011-12	Div 1	7	36	11	11	14	46	49	-3	44
2010-11	Div 1	2	36	17	9	10	47	35	12	60
2009-10	Div 1	7	36	11	9	16	36	47	-11	42

FALKIRK: made it all the way to the semi-finals of the Scottish League Cup

Top scorers 2011-12

		P	W	D	L	F	GFA	PGA	Pts
1	Ross County (1)	36	22	13	1	72	2.00	2.2	79
2	Livingston (5)	36	13	9	14	56	1.56	1.3	48
3	Hamilton (4)	36	14	7	15	55	1.53	1.4	49
4	Dundee (2)	36	15	10	11	53	1.47	1.5	55
5	Falkirk (3)	36	13	13	10	53	1.47	1.4	52
6	Partick (6)	36	12	11	13	50	1.39	1.3	47
7	Raith (7)	36	11	11	14	46	1.28	1.2	44
8	Ayr (9)	36	9	11	16	44	1.22	1.1	38
9	Morton (8)	36	10	12	14	40	1.11	1.2	42
10	Queen of Sth (10)	36	7	11	18	38	1.06	0.9	32

Best defence 2011-12

		P	W	D	L	F	GFA	PGA	Pts
1	Ross County (1)	36	22	13	1	32	0.89	2.2	79
2	Partick (6)	36	12	11	13	39	1.08	1.3	47
3	Dundee (2)	36	15	10	11	43	1.19	1.5	55
4	Falkirk (3)	36	13	13	10	48	1.33	1.4	52
5	Raith (7)	36	11	11	14	49	1.36	1.2	44
6	Livingston (5)	36	13	9	14	54	1.50	1.3	48
7	Morton (8)	36	10	12	14	55	1.53	1.2	42
8	Hamilton (4)	36	14	7	15	56	1.56	1.4	49
9	Queen of Sth (10)	36	7	11	18	64	1.78	0.9	32
10	Ayr (9)	36	9	11	16	67	1.86	1.1	38

Clean sheets 2011-12

		P	CS	%
1	Ross County (1)	36	14	38.9
2	Falkirk (3)	36	11	30.6
3	Partick (6)	36	11	30.6
4	Morton (8)	36	10	27.8
5	Dundee (2)	36	9	25.0
6	Livingston (5)	36	9	25.0
7	Ayr (9)	36	8	22.2
8	Queen of Sth (10)	36	7	19.4
9	Hamilton (4)	36	6	16.7
10	Raith (7)	36	4	11.1

First to score 2011-12

		P	FS	%
1	Ross County (1)	36	27	75.0
2	Dundee (2)	36	21	58.3
3	Falkirk (3)	36	17	47.2
4	Partick (6)	36	17	47.2
5	Raith (7)	36	16	44.4
6	Hamilton (4)	36	15	41.7
7	Livingston (5)	36	15	41.7
8	Queen of Sth (10)	36	15	41.7
9	Morton (8)	36	13	36.1
10	Ayr (9)	36	10	27.8

Top scorers 2011-12

		Goals
C McMenamin	Ross County	19
F El Alagui	Falkirk	18
K Doolan	Partick	13
M Gardyne	Ross County	13
R Boulding	Livingston	11
P Cairney	Partick	11
R Conroy	Dundee	11
B Graham	Raith	11
M McNulty	Livingston	11
S Milne	Dundee	11

Record when keeping a clean sheet 2011-12

		P	W	D	L	F	GFA	PGA	Pts
1	Raith (7)	4	4	0	0	9	2.25	3.0	12
2	Ross County (1)	14	12	2	0	26	1.86	2.7	38
3	Hamilton (4)	6	5	1	0	11	1.83	2.7	16
4	Dundee (2)	9	7	2	0	10	1.11	2.6	23
5	Livingston (5)	9	7	2	0	16	1.78	2.6	23
6	Falkirk (3)	11	7	4	0	12	1.09	2.3	25
7	Partick (6)	11	7	4	0	21	1.91	2.3	25
8	Morton (8)	10	5	5	0	6	0.60	2.0	20
9	Ayr (9)	8	4	4	0	4	0.50	2.0	16
10	Queen of Sth (10)	7	3	4	0	4	0.57	1.9	13

Record when first to score 2011-12

		P	W	D	L	F	GFA	PGA	Pts
1	Ross County (1)	27	19	8	0	57	18	2.4	65
2	Livingston (5)	15	11	2	2	32	12	2.3	35
3	Falkirk (3)	17	11	4	2	33	21	2.2	37
4	Partick (6)	17	11	4	2	37	13	2.2	37
5	Hamilton (4)	15	10	3	2	33	15	2.2	33
6	Morton (8)	13	9	2	2	24	14	2.2	29
7	Dundee (2)	21	14	3	4	43	22	2.1	45
8	Raith (7)	16	7	7	2	30	19	1.8	28
9	Queen of Sth (10)	15	7	5	3	29	25	1.7	26
10	Ayr (9)	10	4	2	4	14	16	1.4	14

Key *Number in brackets refers to final league finishing position. Points do not include any deductions but league positions do. GFA: Goals for average per match, GAA: Goals against average per match, PGA: Average points gained per match, CS: clean sheet, FS: first to score*

Airdrie Utd

Nickname: The Diamonds **Ground: Excelsior Stadium**
www.airdriefc.com

AIRDRIE put together a great run to force their way into the play-offs last season, losing just one of their final 11 matches.

They are unlikely to keep hold of top goalscorer Ryan Donnelly but only Arbroath scored goals last term and they appear to be on the upgrade.

	11-12		Last five seasons at home							
	H	A	P	W	D	L	OV	UN	BS	CS
Ayr			6	1	3	2	3	3	3	1
Queen of Sth			6	2	3	1	0	6	1	4
Arbroath	DW	LD	2	1	1	0	1	1	1	1
Airdrie										
Stenhousemuir	WL	DW	4	2	1	1	3	1	2	1
East Fife	LW	LL	4	1	2	1	2	2	3	1
Forfar	DW	LW	4	3	1	0	3	1	2	2
Brechin	LW	DD	6	2	2	2	5	1	6	0
Albion	WW	LW	2	2	0	0	1	1	0	2
Alloa			4	1	1	2	0	4	1	1

Season	Division	Pos	P	W	D	L	F	A	GD	Pts
2011-12	Div 2	4	36	14	10	12	68	60	8	52
2010-11	Div 2	6	36	13	9	14	52	60	-8	48
2009-10	Div 1	9	36	8	9	19	41	56	-15	33

Alloa

Nickname: The Wasps **Ground: Recreation Park**
www.alloaathletic.co.uk

THE WASPS were far and away the best team in Division Three last season, eventually easing to the title by a whopping 14 points.

They suffered just one defeat on their artificial pitch and a play-off place should be the minimum aim for Paul Hartley's side.

	11-12		Last five seasons at home							
	H	A	P	W	D	L	OV	UN	BS	CS
Ayr			8	3	1	4	4	4	5	0
Queen of Sth			0	0	0	0	0	0	0	0
Arbroath			4	3	0	1	1	3	1	2
Airdrie			4	1	0	3	3	1	2	1
Stenhousemuir			4	2	0	2	3	1	3	1
East Fife			6	2	1	3	3	3	2	2
Forfar			4	3	0	1	2	2	1	2
Brechin			10	3	4	3	10	0	9	0
Albion			0	0	0	0	0	0	0	0
Alloa										

Season	Division	Pos	P	W	D	L	F	A	GD	Pts
2011-12	Div 3	1	36	23	8	5	70	39	31	77
2010-11	Div 2	9	36	9	9	18	49	71	-22	36
2009-10	Div 2	2	36	19	8	9	49	35	14	65

Albion

Nickname: The Wee Rovers **Ground: Cliftonhill**
www.albionroversfc.com

THE WEE ROVERS stayed up in their first season after winning promotion via the play-offs and maintaining their Division Two status will have to be the priority this term.

They will do well to do that if they concede more than the 44 away goals they let in last term.

	11-12		Last five seasons at home							
	H	A	P	W	D	L	OV	UN	BS	CS
Ayr			0	0	0	0	0	0	0	0
Queen of Sth			0	0	0	0	0	0	0	0
Arbroath	WD	LL	8	3	1	4	4	4	3	2
Airdrie	WL	LL	2	1	0	1	1	1	1	0
Stenhousemuir	DW	LW	8	2	3	3	5	3	7	1
East Fife	LD	LW	6	0	2	4	4	2	3	0
Forfar	WD	WL	8	3	3	2	3	5	4	3
Brechin	LL	WL	2	0	0	2	1	1	1	0
Albion										
Alloa			0	0	0	0	0	0	0	0

Season	Division	Pos	P	W	D	L	F	A	GD	Pts
2011-12	Div 2	9	36	10	7	19	43	66	-23	37
2010-11	Div 3	2	36	17	10	9	56	40	16	61
2009-10	Div 3	5	36	13	11	12	35	35	0	50

Arbroath

Nickname: Red Lichties **Ground: Gayfield Park**
www.arbroathfc.co.uk

WENT toe-to-toe with Cowdenbeath for much of last season but three wins from their final 11 games meant they had nothing left in the tank for the play-offs.

Striker Steven Doris has renewed his contract which is a massive boost, and they are right to aim to go one better.

	11-12		Last five seasons at home							
	H	A	P	W	D	L	OV	UN	BS	CS
Ayr			2	0	0	2	2	0	1	0
Queen of Sth			0	0	0	0	0	0	0	0
Arbroath										
Airdrie	WD	DL	2	1	1	0	2	0	2	0
Stenhousemuir	WL	LW	8	4	2	2	3	5	3	3
East Fife	WD	DW	10	1	3	6	5	5	5	1
Forfar	WL	DW	4	1	1	2	2	2	3	0
Brechin	DL	WD	6	1	2	3	3	3	4	2
Albion	WW	LD	8	4	2	2	5	3	5	3
Alloa			4	2	2	0	2	2	2	2

Season	Division	Pos	P	W	D	L	F	A	GD	Pts
2011-12	Div 2	2	36	17	12	7	76	51	25	63
2010-11	Div 3	1	36	20	6	10	80	61	19	66
2009-10	Div 2	9	36	10	10	16	41	55	-14	40

Ayr

Nickname: The Honest Men   Ground: Somerset Park
www.ayrunitedfc.co.uk

THE HONEST MEN were relegated after winning just two of their final ten matches and being beaten in the play-offs.

New manager Mark Roberts will have plenty of work to do if his side are to bounce straight back into Division One and it is difficult to see them doing it.

| | 11-12 | | Last five seasons at home | | | | | | | |
	H	A	P	W	D	L	OV	UN	BS	CS
Ayr										
Queen of Sth	WD	LL	4	2	1	1	1	3	1	2
Arbroath			2	2	0	0	2	0	2	0
Airdrie			6	2	2	2	3	3	5	1
Stenhousemuir			2	2	0	0	1	1	1	1
East Fife			4	2	1	1	2	2	2	1
Forfar			4	3	0	1	3	1	2	1
Brechin			8	3	2	3	4	4	5	1
Albion			0	0	0	0	0	0	0	0
Alloa			8	6	1	1	4	4	4	3

Season	Division	Pos	P	W	D	L	F	A	GD	Pts
2011-12	Div 1	9	36	9	11	16	44	67	-23	38
2010-11	Div 2	2	36	18	5	13	62	55	7	59
2009-10	Div 1	10	36	7	10	19	29	60	-31	31

Brechin

Nickname: The City   Ground: Glebe Park
www.brechincity.com

OVERS would have copped in Brechin's last 12 league games but it was a poor finish to an average campaign.

Paul McManus looks set to leave after scoring 15 goals last season and Scott Dalziel, who has been captured from East Fife, needs to hit the ground running.

| | 11-12 | | Last five seasons at home | | | | | | | |
	H	A	P	W	D	L	OV	UN	BS	CS
Ayr			8	4	1	3	3	5	2	3
Queen of Sth			0	0	0	0	0	0	0	0
Arbroath	LD	DW	6	1	2	3	2	4	3	1
Airdrie	DD	WL	6	3	2	1	4	2	6	0
Stenhousemuir	WW	DL	6	4	2	0	2	4	2	4
East Fife	LL	DD	8	4	0	4	6	2	6	1
Forfar	LW	DL	6	2	2	2	3	3	3	1
Brechin										
Albion	LW	WW	2	1	0	1	2	0	2	0
Alloa			10	6	3	1	5	5	6	4

Season	Division	Pos	P	W	D	L	F	A	GD	Pts
2011-12	Div 2	8	36	10	11	15	47	62	-15	41
2010-11	Div 2	4	36	15	12	9	63	45	18	57
2009-10	Div 2	4	36	15	9	12	50	45	5	54

East Fife

Nickname: The Fifers   Ground: New Bayview Stadium
www.eastfifefc.info

STRUGGLED to find consistency last term which meant they were an archetypal mid-table team.

Last season's top goalscorer Ryan Wal-lace has headed out of the door and it is difficult to see them making enough of an improvement to mount a serious promotion bid.

| | 11-12 | | Last five seasons at home | | | | | | | |
	H	A	P	W	D	L	OV	UN	BS	CS
Ayr			4	2	0	2	3	1	2	1
Queen of Sth			0	0	0	0	0	0	0	0
Arbroath	DL	LD	10	4	3	3	7	3	8	1
Airdrie	WW	WL	4	2	1	1	1	3	1	2
Stenhousemuir	LD	LL	10	3	5	2	4	6	6	3
East Fife										
Forfar	WW	LW	6	5	0	1	6	0	2	4
Brechin	DD	WW	8	3	4	1	3	5	4	4
Albion	WL	WD	6	2	2	2	4	2	3	3
Alloa			6	3	0	3	2	4	2	1

Season	Division	Pos	P	W	D	L	F	A	GD	Pts
2011-12	Div 2	6	36	14	6	16	55	57	-2	48
2010-11	Div 2	5	36	14	10	12	77	60	17	52
2009-10	Div 2	7	36	10	11	15	46	53	-7	41

Forfar

Nickname: The Loons   Ground: Station Park
www.forfarathletic.co.uk

LAST season was a bit of a struggle for the Loons but Dick Campbell has done plenty of business in the summer, including the impressive capture of Gavin Swankie from local rivals Arbroath.

It's easy to see them pushing up the table and avoiding a relegation battle.

| | 11-12 | | Last five seasons at home | | | | | | | |
	H	A	P	W	D	L	OV	UN	BS	CS
Ayr			4	2	1	1	2	2	3	0
Queen of Sth			0	0	0	0	0	0	0	0
Arbroath	DL	LW	4	1	1	2	2	2	3	1
Airdrie	WL	DL	4	1	0	3	4	0	4	0
Stenhousemuir	LL	WW	8	2	2	4	4	4	5	2
East Fife	WL	LL	6	2	1	3	4	2	4	1
Forfar										
Brechin	DW	WL	6	3	2	1	4	2	5	1
Albion	LW	LD	8	3	3	2	4	4	3	4
Alloa			4	1	1	2	1	3	2	0

Season	Division	Pos	P	W	D	L	F	A	GD	Pts
2011-12	Div 2	7	36	11	9	16	59	72	-13	42
2010-11	Div 2	3	36	17	8	11	50	48	2	59
2009-10	Div 3	2	36	18	9	9	59	44	15	63

Queen of Sth

Nickname: Doonhamers   Ground: Palmerston Park
www.qosfc.com

LAST season will be written off by the Doonhamers as a disaster and they need to start again after being relegated. Manager Allen 'Magic' Johnstone may have to be just that to get them back into Division One at the first attempt.

Just one away win tells its own story.

	11-12		Last five seasons at home							
	H	A	P	W	D	L	OV	UN	BS	CS
Ayr	WW	LD	4	4	0	0	3	1	2	2
Queen of Sth										
Arbroath			0	0	0	0	0	0	0	0
Airdrie			6	2	4	0	3	3	1	5
Stenhousemuir			0	0	0	0	0	0	0	0
East Fife			0	0	0	0	0	0	0	0
Forfar			0	0	0	0	0	0	0	0
Brechin			0	0	0	0	0	0	0	0
Albion			0	0	0	0	0	0	0	0
Alloa			0	0	0	0	0	0	0	0

Season	Division	Pos	P	W	D	L	F	A	GD	Pts
2011-12	Div 1	10	36	7	11	18	38	64	-26	32
2010-11	Div 1	4	36	14	7	15	54	53	1	49
2009-10	Div 1	4	36	15	11	10	53	40	13	56

Stenhousemuir

Nickname: The Warriors   Ground: Ochilview Park
www.stenhousemuirfc.com

LOST their way in the middle of last season and 11 league defeats after Christmas cost them a play-off place.

They need to get that dismal run out of their system and that could be difficult with experienced boss Davie Irons having left the club at the beginning of July.

	11-12		Last five seasons at home							
	H	A	P	W	D	L	OV	UN	BS	CS
Ayr			2	2	0	0	2	0	2	0
Queen of Sth			0	0	0	0	0	0	0	0
Arbroath	WL	LW	8	3	1	4	5	3	4	3
Airdrie	DL	LW	4	1	1	2	2	2	2	1
Stenhousemuir										
East Fife	WW	WD	10	3	3	4	3	7	6	1
Forfar	LL	WW	8	3	1	4	4	4	3	3
Brechin	DW	LL	6	1	3	2	3	3	5	1
Albion	WL	DL	8	4	1	3	5	3	3	3
Alloa			4	1	0	3	1	3	1	1

Season	Division	Pos	P	W	D	L	F	A	GD	Pts
2011-12	Div 2	5	36	15	6	15	54	49	5	51
2010-11	Div 2	8	36	10	8	18	46	59	-13	38
2009-10	Div 2	8	36	9	13	14	38	42	-4	40

GAYFIELD PARK: Scottish Cup action between Arbroath and Rangers

Top scorers 2011-12

		P	W	D	L	F	GFA	PGA	Pts
1	Arbroath (2)	36	17	12	7	76	2.11	1.8	63
2	Cowdenbeath (1)	36	20	11	5	68	1.89	2.0	71
3	Airdrie Utd (4)	36	14	10	12	68	1.89	1.4	52
4	Dumbarton (3)	36	17	7	12	61	1.69	1.6	58
5	Forfar (7)	36	11	9	16	59	1.64	1.2	42
6	East Fife (6)	36	14	6	16	55	1.53	1.3	48
7	Stenhousemuir (5)	36	15	6	15	54	1.50	1.4	51
8	Brechin (8)	36	10	11	15	47	1.31	1.1	41
9	Stirling (10)	36	9	7	20	46	1.28	0.9	34
10	Albion (9)	36	10	7	19	43	1.19	1.0	37

Best defence 2011-12

		P	W	D	L	F	GFA	PGA	Pts
1	Cowdenbeath (1)	36	20	11	5	29	0.81	2.0	71
2	Stenhousemuir (5)	36	15	6	15	49	1.36	1.4	51
3	Arbroath (2)	36	17	12	7	51	1.42	1.8	63
4	East Fife (6)	36	14	6	16	57	1.58	1.3	48
5	Airdrie Utd (4)	36	14	10	12	60	1.67	1.4	52
6	Dumbarton (3)	36	17	7	12	61	1.69	1.6	58
7	Brechin (8)	36	10	11	15	62	1.72	1.1	41
8	Albion (9)	36	10	7	19	66	1.83	1.0	37
9	Stirling (10)	36	9	7	20	70	1.94	0.9	34
10	Forfar (7)	36	11	9	16	72	2.00	1.2	42

Clean sheets 2011-12

		P	CS	%
1	Cowdenbeath (1)	36	16	44.4
2	East Fife (6)	36	10	27.8
3	Airdrie Utd (4)	36	10	27.8
4	Dumbarton (3)	36	9	25.0
5	Stenhousemuir (5)	36	9	25.0
6	Arbroath (2)	36	6	16.7
7	Albion (9)	36	5	13.9
8	Forfar (7)	36	5	13.9
9	Brechin (8)	36	5	13.9
10	Stirling (10)	36	4	11.1

First to score 2011-12

		P	FS	%
1	Stenhousemuir (5)	36	21	58.3
2	East Fife (6)	36	20	55.6
3	Cowdenbeath (1)	36	20	55.6
4	Arbroath (2)	36	19	52.8
5	Airdrie Utd (4)	36	19	52.8
6	Forfar (7)	36	18	50.0
7	Stirling (10)	36	16	44.4
8	Brechin (8)	36	15	41.7
9	Albion (9)	36	14	38.9
10	Dumbarton (3)	36	13	36.1

Top scorers 2011-12

-		Goals
S Doris	Arbroath	21
R Donnelly	Airdrie Utd	21
R Wallace	East Fife	20
M McKenzie	Cowdenbeath	18
C Templeman	Forfar	16
P McManus	Brechin	15
B Prunty	Dumbarton	14
A Rodgers	Stenhousemuir	14
S Agnew	Dumbarton	13
L Coult	Cowdenbeath	13

Record when keeping a clean sheet 2011-12

		P	W	D	L	F	GFA	PGA	Pts
1	East Fife (6)	10	10	0	0	22	2.20	3.0	30
2	Albion (9)	5	5	0	0	6	1.20	3.0	15
3	Stirling (10)	4	4	0	0	6	1.50	3.0	12
4	Airdrie Utd (4)	10	9	1	0	21	2.10	2.8	28
5	Dumbarton (3)	9	8	1	0	18	2.00	2.8	25
6	Stenhousemuir (5)	9	8	1	0	21	2.33	2.8	25
7	Arbroath (2)	6	5	1	0	9	1.50	2.7	16
8	Forfar (7)	5	4	1	0	7	1.40	2.6	13
9	Brechin (8)	5	4	1	0	5	1.00	2.6	13
10	Cowdenbeath (1)	16	12	4	0	27	1.69	2.5	40

Record when first to score 2011-12

		P	W	D	L	F	GFA	PGA	Pts
1	Cowdenbeath (1)	20	17	2	1	48	11	2.6	53
2	Dumbarton (3)	13	10	2	1	31	12	2.5	32
3	Stenhousemuir (5)	21	15	3	3	47	19	2.3	48
4	Arbroath (2)	19	12	7	0	49	22	2.3	43
5	Airdrie Utd (4)	19	13	3	3	45	18	2.2	42
6	East Fife (6)	20	13	4	3	42	18	2.1	43
7	Albion (9)	14	9	3	2	29	14	2.1	30
8	Forfar (7)	18	9	5	4	39	30	1.8	32
9	Stirling (10)	16	8	4	4	31	23	1.8	28
10	Brechin (8)	15	7	5	3	26	23	1.7	26

Key *Number in brackets refers to final league finishing position. Points do not include any deductions but league positions do. GFA: Goals for average per match, GAA: Goals against average per match, PGA: Average points gained per match, CS: clean sheet, FS: first to score*

Annan

Nickname: Galabankies **Ground: Galabank**
www.annanathleticfc.com

ATHLETIC got off to a brilliant start last term, winning seven of their first ten league games, but they were unable to sustain a challenge, winning just three of their final 18 matches.

They have a new artificial pitch for this season but reaching the play-offs would be a decent effort.

	11-12 H	A	P	W	D	L	OV	UN	BS	CS
Stirling			0	0	0	0	0	0	0	0
Queens Park	WL	DL	6	3	0	3	5	1	5	0
Stranraer	LL	LL	6	3	1	2	5	1	4	1
Elgin	DD	LW	8	2	4	2	4	4	4	2
Peterhead	WL	WL	2	1	0	1	1	1	0	1
Annan										
Berwick	DD	WW	8	0	5	3	3	5	7	0
Montrose	WL	WD	8	4	2	2	6	2	6	2
Clyde	WW	DD	4	3	0	1	0	4	0	3
East Stirling	WD	LW	8	6	1	1	6	2	4	3

Season	Division	Pos	P	W	D	L	F	A	GD	Pts
2011-12	Div 3	6	36	13	10	13	53	53	0	49
2010-11	Div 3	4	36	16	11	9	58	45	13	59
2009-10	Div 3	8	36	11	10	15	41	42	-1	43

Berwick

Nickname: The Borderers **Ground: Shielfield Park**
www.berwickrangersfc.co.uk

THE WEE RANGERS struggled with inconsistency all season and were never able to post the sort of sustained run of successes that would have put them in the play-offs.

They need to improve with a much-changed squad if they are to challenge for a top-four place.

	11-12 H	A	P	W	D	L	OV	UN	BS	CS
Stirling			0	0	0	0	0	0	0	0
Queens Park	WL	DD	10	4	3	3	7	6	3	
Stranraer	DW	LW	6	3	3	0	3	3	3	3
Elgin	DD	LL	10	6	4	0	6	4	7	3
Peterhead	WL	LW	4	1	1	2	3	1	3	0
Annan	LL	DD	8	2	2	4	5	3	5	1
Berwick										
Montrose	LD	WD	10	4	1	5	4	6	4	3
Clyde	LW	WD	4	2	1	1	2	2	2	1
East Stirling	WL	WL	10	4	3	3	6	4	6	3

Season	Division	Pos	P	W	D	L	F	A	GD	Pts
2011-12	Div 3	7	36	12	12	12	61	58	3	48
2010-11	Div 3	6	36	12	13	11	62	56	6	49
2009-10	Div 3	6	36	14	8	14	46	49	-3	50

Clyde

Nickname: The Bully Wee **Ground: Broadwood**
www.clydefc.co.uk

THE misery has continued at Broadwood and while finishing second from bottom was an improvement, it was hardly a significant one.

They scored just 11 away goals last term so it is obvious where the changes have to be made and it may be a step-by-step process.

	11-12 H	A	P	W	D	L	OV	UN	BS	CS
Stirling			4	1	0	3	3	1	2	1
Queens Park	LL	LL	4	0	0	4	2	2	2	0
Stranraer	DW	DL	4	2	2	0	3	1	4	0
Elgin	LL	WD	4	0	2	2	2	2	3	0
Peterhead	WL	DD	4	2	0	2	2	2	2	1
Annan	DD	LL	4	0	2	2	0	4	1	1
Berwick	LD	WL	4	1	1	2	3	1	3	1
Montrose	WL	LL	4	2	1	1	1	3	2	2
Clyde										
East Stirling	WW	DW	4	3	0	1	3	1	2	2

Season	Division	Pos	P	W	D	L	F	A	GD	Pts
2011-12	Div 3	9	36	8	11	17	35	50	-15	35
2010-11	Div 3	10	36	8	8	20	37	67	-30	32
2009-10	Div 2	10	36	8	7	21	37	57	-20	31

East Stirling

Nickname: The Shire **Ground: Ochilview Park**
www.eaststirlingshirefc.co.uk

THE perennial wooden spooners have gone back to their old way after reaching the play-offs a couple of years ago and found themselves 11 points adrift at the foot of the table.

It's difficult to see them reach the play-offs this term – getting off the bottom would be a start.

	11-12 H	A	P	W	D	L	OV	UN	BS	CS
Stirling			0	0	0	0	0	0	0	0
Queens Park	LL	LL	8	3	0	5	5	3	4	1
Stranraer	LD	LL	8	1	2	5	4	4	5	1
Elgin	DD	LL	12	6	4	2	5	7	7	3
Peterhead	LW	LL	2	1	0	1	1	1	1	0
Annan	WL	LD	8	4	1	3	5	3	5	2
Berwick	LW	LW	10	5	1	4	5	5	3	4
Montrose	WW	LL	12	7	0	5	9	3	6	3
Clyde	DL	LL	4	1	2	1	0	4	1	2
East Stirling										

Season	Division	Pos	P	W	D	L	F	A	GD	Pts
2011-12	Div 3	10	36	6	6	24	38	88	-50	24
2010-11	Div 3	9	36	10	4	22	33	62	-29	34
2009-10	Div 3	3	36	19	4	13	50	46	4	61

Elgin

Nickname: Black & Whites   Ground: Borough Briggs
www.elgincity.com

CITY are often seen as strugglers in the bottom division but they could be a force this term.

They got to the play-offs mainly thanks to a strong home record and if they can improve on the road, where they conceded 43 goals in 18 matches, they could go well.

	11-12 H	A	Last five seasons at home P	W	D	L	OV	UN	BS	CS
Stirling			0	0	0	0	0	0	0	0
Queens Park	WD	LW	8	2	1	5	3	5	3	1
Stranraer	DL	LL	8	1	1	6	7	1	7	0
Elgin										
Peterhead	WL	WL	2	1	0	1	2	0	2	0
Annan	WL	DD	8	3	1	4	4	4	4	3
Berwick	WW	DD	10	5	1	4	8	2	7	2
Montrose	WW	LW	12	8	0	4	7	5	7	2
Clyde	LD	WW	4	0	1	3	1	3	1	0
East Stirling	WW	DD	12	7	0	5	7	5	3	5

Season	Division	Pos	P	W	D	L	F	A	GD	Pts
2011-12	Div 3	4	36	16	9	11	68	60	8	57
2010-11	Div 3	7	36	13	6	17	53	63	-10	45
2009-10	Div 3	9	36	9	7	20	45	59	-14	34

Peterhead

Nickname: The Blue Toon   Ground: Balmoor
www.peterheadfc.co.uk

THE BLUE TOON had a dismal season and never looked like justifying ante-post favouritism.

Rory McAllister, who could play at a higher level, bagged 21 league goals and a six-match unbeaten run at the end of the season suggests they could hit the ground running.

	11-12 H	A	Last five seasons at home P	W	D	L	OV	UN	BS	CS
Stirling			6	2	3	1	3	3	6	0
Queens Park	DW	DW	6	4	2	0	2	4	4	2
Stranraer	LD	LW	6	4	1	1	4	2	3	3
Elgin	LW	LW	2	1	0	1	2	0	1	1
Peterhead										
Annan	LW	LW	2	1	0	1	2	0	2	0
Berwick	WL	LW	4	3	0	1	3	1	3	1
Montrose	LW	LW	2	1	0	1	2	0	2	0
Clyde	DD	LW	4	1	3	0	0	4	1	3
East Stirling	WW	WL	2	2	0	0	0	2	0	2

Season	Division	Pos	P	W	D	L	F	A	GD	Pts
2011-12	Div 3	5	36	15	6	15	51	53	-2	51
2010-11	Div 2	10	36	5	11	20	47	76	-29	26
2009-10	Div 2	5	36	15	6	15	45	49	-4	51

Montrose

Nickname: The Gable Endies   Ground: Links Park
www.montrosefc.co.uk

IT always looked like being a long season after the Gable Endies conceded ten goals in their first two cup games of the campaign and they didn't make much of a recovery.

They were solid against the weaker teams in the section but they look unlikely challengers.

	11-12 H	A	Last five seasons at home P	W	D	L	OV	UN	BS	CS
Stirling			0	0	0	0	0	0	0	0
Queens Park	LW	LL	8	1	0	7	5	3	4	0
Stranraer	LL	DL	8	1	2	5	6	2	6	0
Elgin	WL	LL	12	6	2	4	5	7	4	5
Peterhead	WL	WL	2	1	0	1	2	0	2	0
Annan	LD	LW	8	0	4	4	3	5	5	1
Berwick	LD	WD	10	0	6	4	3	7	9	0
Montrose										
Clyde	WW	LW	4	4	0	0	4	0	2	2
East Stirling	WW	LL	12	8	0	4	7	5	3	5

Season	Division	Pos	P	W	D	L	F	A	GD	Pts
2011-12	Div 3	8	36	11	5	20	58	75	-17	38
2010-11	Div 3	8	36	10	7	19	47	61	-14	37
2009-10	Div 3	10	36	5	9	22	30	63	-33	24

Queen's Park

Nickname: The Spiders   Ground: Hampden Park
www.queensparkfc.co.uk

THE SPIDERS were runners-up to runaway winners Alloa last season and have a decent chance of going one better this time around.

Queen's Park have maintained the services of hotshot striker Jamie Longworth and there will be high hopes for a decent push for the title.

	11-12 H	A	Last five seasons at home P	W	D	L	OV	UN	BS	CS
Stirling			2	1	1	0	1	1	2	0
Queens Park										
Stranraer	WW	WW	8	2	3	3	6	2	7	1
Elgin	WL	LD	8	4	1	3	5	3	2	4
Peterhead	DL	DL	6	2	2	2	1	5	3	1
Annan	DW	LW	6	3	2	1	2	4	1	4
Berwick	DD	LW	10	5	2	3	3	7	4	4
Montrose	WW	WL	8	7	1	0	6	2	4	4
Clyde	WW	WW	4	3	0	1	3	1	0	3
East Stirling	WW	WW	8	7	0	1	3	5	3	5

Season	Division	Pos	P	W	D	L	F	A	GD	Pts
2011-12	Div 3	2	36	19	6	11	70	48	22	63
2010-11	Div 3	3	36	18	5	13	57	43	14	59
2009-10	Div 3	4	36	15	6	15	42	42	0	51

Stirling

Nickname: The Binos   **Ground: Forthbank**
www.stirlingalbionfc.co.uk

ALBION posted just four home wins in Division Two last season and that is what confirmed their second successive relegation.

Stirling will either take the basement by storm or need to steady the ship but they should be challenging for at least a play-off place.

	11-12 H	A	Last five seasons at home P	W	D	L	OV	UN	BS	CS
Stirling										
Queens Park			2	1	0	1	2	0	0	1
Stranraer			4	1	1	2	3	1	3	0
Elgin			0	0	0	0	0	0	0	0
Peterhead			6	5	1	0	3	3	3	3
Annan			0	0	0	0	0	0	0	0
Berwick			0	0	0	0	0	0	0	0
Montrose			0	0	0	0	0	0	0	0
Clyde			4	1	2	1	0	4	2	1
East Stirling			0	0	0	0	0	0	0	0

Season	Division	Pos	P	W	D	L	F	A	GD	Pts
2011-12	Div 2	10	36	9	7	20	46	70	-24	34
2010-11	Div 1	10	36	4	8	24	32	82	-50	20
2009-10	Div 2	1	36	18	11	7	68	48	20	65

Rangers

Nickname: The Gers
Colours: Blue, White and Black
Ground: Ibrox (51,082)
Tel: 0871-702-1972

THE last nine months at Ibrox have been mind-blowing and it is impossible to say what will happen to Rangers this season – at the time of going to press we don't know which division they will play in or how many players Ally McCoist will have.

Key men are leaving but younger players will see this as a chance to shine, and help get the club back on its feet again.

They had a great start before the financial problems hit last year and a good beginning will be essential to lift the gloom.

Longest run without loss/win: 9/5
High - low league position 4-10
Clean sheets: 13 **Yellow cards:** 48 **Red cards:** 1
Average attendance: 9,398 **Players used:** 25
Leading Scorer: J Daly 19 (5,16)
Key stat: Ten of Rangers' final 11 games of last season featured at least three goals

Stranraer

Nickname: The Blues   **Ground: Stair Park**
www.stranraerfc.org

THE Stair Park outfit had a season of fits and starts last season – they would go on a decent run but would then be unable to buy a win.

They held on to a play-off spot and surprised Queen's Park after five successive defeats. The Blues should be hopeful of going well again.

	11-12 H	A	Last five seasons at home P	W	D	L	OV	UN	BS	CS
Stirling			4	3	0	1	3	1	3	1
Queens Park	LL	LL	8	2	4	2	4	4	5	3
Stranraer										
Elgin	WW	DW	8	4	2	2	5	3	5	2
Peterhead	WL	WD	6	2	1	3	4	2	3	0
Annan	WW	WD	6	4	2	0	4	2	5	1
Berwick	WL	DL	6	3	1	2	5	1	6	0
Montrose	DW	WW	8	3	2	3	4	4	4	2
Clyde	DW	DL	4	3	1	0	2	2	1	3
East Stirling	WW	WD	8	6	1	1	7	1	6	2

Season	Division	Pos	P	W	D	L	F	A	GD	Pts
2011-12	Div 3	3	36	17	7	12	77	57	20	58
2010-11	Div 3	5	36	15	12	9	72	57	15	57
2009-10	Div 3	7	36	13	8	15	48	54	-6	47

RANGERS: facing uncertainty

Season	Division	Pos	P	W	D	L	F	A	GD	Pts
2011-12	SPL	2	38	26	5	7	77	28	49	73*
2010-11	SPL	1	38	30	3	5	88	29	59	93
2009-10	SPL	1	38	26	9	3	82	28	54	87

2011-12 SPL appearances (ten most regular starters)	P	G	Y	R
A McGregor	37	0	0	0
M Edu	34 (2)	3	8	1
S Davis	33	5	4	0
D Goian	33	0	10	1
C Bocanegra	29	2	7	1
L Wallace	26 (2)	2	1	0
S Whittaker	24 (1)	2	5	0
N Jelavic	21 (1)	14	2	0
S Papac	21	0	2	1
L McCulloch	20 (6)	5	4	1

BROADWOOD STADIUM: one of the venues that might soon play host to Rangers

Top scorers 2011-12

		P	W	D	L	F	GFA	PGA	Pts
1	Stranraer (3)	36	17	7	12	77	2.14	1.6	58
2	Alloa (1)	36	23	8	5	70	1.94	2.1	77
3	Queen's Park (2)	36	19	6	11	70	1.94	1.8	63
4	Elgin City (4)	36	16	9	11	68	1.89	1.6	57
5	Berwick (7)	36	12	12	12	61	1.69	1.3	48
6	Montrose (8)	36	11	5	20	58	1.61	1.1	38
7	Annan (6)	36	13	10	13	53	1.47	1.4	49
8	Peterhead (5)	36	15	6	15	51	1.42	1.4	51
9	East Stirling (10)	36	6	6	24	38	1.06	0.7	24
10	Clyde (9)	36	8	11	17	35	0.97	1.0	35

Best defence 2011-12

		P	W	D	L	F	GFA	PGA	Pts
1	Alloa (1)	36	23	8	5	39	1.08	2.1	77
2	Queen's Park (2)	36	19	6	11	48	1.33	1.8	63
3	Clyde (9)	36	8	11	17	50	1.39	1.0	35
4	Peterhead (5)	36	15	6	15	53	1.47	1.4	51
5	Annan (6)	36	13	10	13	53	1.47	1.4	49
6	Stranraer (3)	36	17	7	12	57	1.58	1.6	58
7	Berwick (7)	36	12	12	12	58	1.61	1.3	48
8	Elgin City (4)	36	16	9	11	60	1.67	1.6	57
9	Montrose (8)	36	11	5	20	75	2.08	1.1	38
10	East Stirling (10)	36	6	6	24	88	2.44	0.7	24

Clean sheets 2011-12

		P	CS	%
1	Alloa (1)	36	12	33.3
2	Peterhead (5)	36	11	30.6
3	Queen's Park (2)	36	10	27.8
4	Annan (6)	36	9	25.0
5	Clyde (9)	36	9	25.0
6	Elgin City (4)	36	7	19.4
7	Stranraer (3)	36	6	16.7
8	Berwick (7)	36	5	13.9
9	Montrose (8)	36	3	8.3
10	East Stirling (10)	36	3	8.3

First to score 2011-12

		P	FS	%
1	Elgin City (4)	36	25	69.4
2	Alloa (1)	36	24	66.7
3	Peterhead (5)	36	20	55.6
4	Queen's Park (2)	36	19	52.8
5	Annan (6)	36	18	50.0
6	Berwick (7)	36	16	44.4
7	Stranraer (3)	36	16	44.4
8	Montrose (8)	36	14	38.9
9	Clyde (9)	36	12	33.3
10	East Stirling (10)	36	12	33.3

Top scorers 2011-12

		Goals
M Boyle	Montrose	22
R McAllister	Peterhead	21
J Longworth	Queen's Park	20
S May	Alloa	19
C Gunn	Elgin	18
C Malcolm	Stranraer	15
M Moore	Stranraer	12
S Stirling	Stranraer	12
R McCord	Alloa	11
M Daly	Queen's Park	10
D Gribben	Berwick	10

Record when keeping a clean sheet 2011-12

		P	W	D	L	F	GFA	PGA	Pts
1	Alloa (1)	12	12	0	0	22	1.83	3.0	36
2	Elgin City (4)	7	7	0	0	21	3.00	3.0	21
3	Berwick (7)	5	5	0	0	12	2.40	3.0	15
4	Montrose (8)	3	3	0	0	12	4.00	3.0	9
5	East Stirling (10)	3	3	0	0	4	1.33	3.0	9
6	Peterhead (5)	11	10	1	0	18	1.64	2.8	31
7	Queen's Park (2)	10	9	1	0	26	2.60	2.8	28
8	Stranraer (3)	6	5	1	0	17	2.83	2.7	16
9	Annan (6)	9	7	2	0	14	1.56	2.6	23
10	Clyde (9)	9	6	3	0	12	1.33	2.3	21

Record when first to score 2011-12

		P	W	D	L	F	GFA	PGA	Pts
1	Alloa (1)	24	20	4	0	50	15	2.7	64
2	Queen's Park (2)	19	15	1	3	51	19	2.4	46
3	Berwick (7)	16	11	4	1	39	17	2.3	37
4	Clyde (9)	12	7	5	0	26	8	2.2	26
5	Stranraer (3)	16	10	4	2	44	19	2.1	34
6	Elgin City (4)	25	15	5	5	55	33	2.0	50
7	Peterhead (5)	20	12	1	7	35	27	1.9	37
8	Annan (6)	18	9	5	4	33	22	1.8	32
9	East Stirling (10)	12	5	4	3	18	18	1.6	19
10	Montrose (8)	14	6	3	5	29	23	1.5	21

Key *Number in brackets refers to final league finishing position. Points do not include any deductions but league positions do. GFA: Goals for average per match, GAA: Goals against average per match, PGA: Average points gained per match, CS: clean sheet, FS: first to score*

Premier League

Champions	Man City
Runners-up	Man United
Relegated	Bolton
	Blackburn
	Wolves

Championship

Champions	Reading
Runners-up	Southampton
Play-off winners	West Ham
Relegated	Portsmouth
	Coventry
	Doncaster

League 1

Champions	Charlton
Runners-up	Sheff Weds
Play-off winners	Huddersfield
Relegated	Wycombe
	Chesterfield
	Exeter
	Rochdale

League 2

Champions	Swindon
Runners-up	Shrewsbury
Third	Crawley
Play-off winners	Crewe
Relegated	Hereford
	Macclesfield

Blue Sq Premier

Champions	Fleetwood
Play-off winners	York
Relegated	Hayes & Y
	Darlington
	Bath City
	Kettering

Blue Sq North

Champions	Hyde
Play-off winners	Nuneaton
Relegated	Blyth Spartans
	Eastwood Town

Blue Sq South

Champions	Woking
Play-off winners	Dartford
Relegated	Hampton & R
	Thurrock

FA CUP FINAL: Stewart Downing heads for the corner

Community Shield

Winners	Man United
Finalists	Man City

FA Cup

Winners	Chelsea
Finalists	Liverpool

League Cup

Winners	Liverpool
Finalists	Cardiff

Football League Trophy

Winners	Chesterfield
Finalists	Swindon

FA Trophy

Winners	York
Finalists	Newport County

Scottish Premier League

Champions	Celtic
Runners-up	Rangers
Relegated	Dunfermline

Scottish Division One

Champions	Ross County
Runners-up	Dundee
Play-off winners	Dumbarton
Relegated	Ayr United
	Queen of Sth

Scottish Division Two

Champions	Cowdenbeath
Runners-up	Arbroath
Play-off winners	Albion
Relegated	Stirling

Scottish Division Three

Champions	Alloa
Runners-up	Queen's Park

Scottish Cup

Winners	Hearts
Finalists	Hibernian

Scottish League Cup

Winners	Kilmarnock
Finalists	Celtic

Scottish Challenge Cup

Winners	Falkirk
Finalists	Hamilton

Profitable teams 2011-12				Teams to swerve 2011-12			
Wigan	+£24.82	Sheff Weds	+£13.90	Wolves	-£23.25	Chesterfield	-£13.73
Charlton	+£19.00	Swindon	+£13.12	Rochdale	-£23.10	Aberdeen	-£13.07
Reading	+£18.50	Dumbarton	+£12.62	Macclesfield	-£20.80	Clyde	-£13.03
Newcastle	+£17.51	Derby	+£12.55	Scunthorpe	-£19.60	Hibernian	-£12.92
Cheltenham	+£17.23	Southend	+£12.04	Coventry	-£18.38	Preston	-£12.37
St Johnstone	+£15.87	Alloa	+£11.97	Exeter	-£16.78	Wycombe	-£12.23
Crewe	+£15.26	Ross County	+£11.73	Queen of Sth	-£14.73	Chelsea	-£11.51
Torquay	+£14.55	Blackburn	+£11.02	Dunfermline	-£13.75	Doncaster	-£11.40
		QPR	+£10.85			Portsmouth	-£11.35

Profit/loss figures based on backing each team blindly to a £1 level stake at best bookmakers' prices. League matches only

Premier League

Pos		P	W	D	L	F	A	Pts
1	Man City	38	28	5	5	93	29	89
2	Man Utd	38	28	5	5	89	33	89
3	Arsenal	38	21	7	10	74	49	70
4	Tottenham	38	20	9	9	66	41	69
5	Newcastle	38	19	8	11	56	51	65
6	Chelsea	38	18	10	10	65	46	64
7	Everton	38	15	11	12	50	40	56
8	Liverpool	38	14	10	14	47	40	52
9	Fulham	38	14	10	14	48	51	52
10	West Brom	38	13	8	17	45	52	47
11	Swansea	38	12	11	15	44	51	47
12	Norwich	38	12	11	15	52	66	47
13	Sunderland	38	11	12	15	45	46	45
14	Stoke	38	11	12	15	36	53	45
15	Wigan	38	11	10	17	42	62	43
16	Aston Villa	38	7	17	14	37	53	38
17	QPR	38	10	7	21	43	66	37
18	Bolton	38	10	6	22	46	77	36
19	Blackburn	38	8	7	23	48	78	31
20	Wolves	38	5	10	23	40	82	25

Premier League home

Pos		P	W	D	L	F	A	Pts
1	Man City	19	18	1	0	55	12	55
2	Man Utd	19	15	2	2	52	19	47
3	Tottenham	19	13	3	3	39	17	42
4	Arsenal	19	12	4	3	39	17	40
5	Chelsea	19	12	3	4	41	24	39
6	Newcastle	19	11	5	3	29	17	38
7	Fulham	19	10	5	4	36	26	35
8	Everton	19	10	3	6	28	15	33
9	Swansea	19	8	7	4	27	18	31
10	Stoke	19	7	8	4	25	20	29
11	Sunderland	19	7	7	5	26	17	28
12	Liverpool	19	6	9	4	24	16	27
13	Norwich	19	7	6	6	28	30	27
14	QPR	19	7	5	7	24	25	26
15	Wigan	19	5	7	7	22	27	22
16	West Brom	19	6	3	10	21	22	21
17	Aston Villa	19	4	7	8	20	25	19
18	Blackburn	19	6	1	12	26	33	19
19	Bolton	19	4	4	11	23	39	16
20	Wolves	19	3	3	13	19	43	12

Premier League away

Pos		P	W	D	L	F	A	Pts
1	Man Utd	19	13	3	3	37	14	42
2	Man City	19	10	4	5	38	17	34
3	Arsenal	19	9	3	7	35	32	30
4	Tottenham	19	7	6	6	27	24	27
5	Newcastle	19	8	3	8	27	34	27
6	West Brom	19	7	5	7	24	30	26
7	Chelsea	19	6	7	6	24	22	25
8	Liverpool	19	8	1	10	23	24	25
9	Everton	19	5	8	6	22	25	23
10	Wigan	19	6	3	10	20	35	21
11	Norwich	19	5	5	9	24	36	20
12	Bolton	19	6	2	11	23	38	20
13	Aston Villa	19	3	10	6	17	28	19
14	Sunderland	19	4	5	10	19	29	17
15	Fulham	19	4	5	10	12	25	17
16	Swansea	19	4	4	11	17	33	16
17	Stoke	19	4	4	11	11	33	16
18	Wolves	19	2	7	10	21	39	13
19	Blackburn	19	2	6	11	22	45	12
20	QPR	19	3	2	14	19	41	11

Championship

Pos		P	W	D	L	F	A	Pts
1	Reading	46	27	8	11	69	41	89
2	Southampton	46	26	10	10	85	46	88
3	West Ham	46	24	14	8	81	48	86
4	Birmingham	46	20	16	10	78	51	76
5	Blackpool	46	20	15	11	79	59	75
6	Cardiff	46	19	18	9	66	53	75
7	Middlesbro	46	18	16	12	52	51	70
8	Hull	46	19	11	16	47	44	68
9	Leicester	46	18	12	16	66	55	66
10	Brighton	46	17	15	14	52	52	66
11	Watford	46	16	16	14	56	64	64
12	Derby	46	18	10	18	50	58	64
13	Burnley	46	17	11	18	61	58	62
14	Leeds	46	17	10	19	65	68	61
15	Ipswich	46	17	10	19	69	77	61
16	Millwall	46	15	12	19	55	57	57
17	C Palace	46	13	17	16	46	51	56
18	Peterborough	46	13	11	22	67	77	50
19	Nottm Forest	46	14	8	24	48	63	50
20	Bristol C	46	12	13	21	44	68	49
21	Barnsley	46	13	9	24	49	74	48
22	Portsmouth	46	13	11	22	50	59	40
23	Coventry	46	9	13	24	41	65	40
24	Doncaster	46	8	12	26	43	80	36

Championship home

Pos		P	W	D	L	F	A	Pts
1	Southampton	23	16	4	3	49	18	52
2	Birmingham	23	13	9	1	37	14	48
3	Reading	23	14	5	4	36	18	47
4	Blackpool	23	13	7	3	42	21	46
5	West Ham	23	11	8	4	41	26	41
6	Brighton	23	11	8	4	36	21	41
7	Cardiff	23	11	7	5	37	29	40
8	Hull	23	12	4	7	28	22	40
9	Leicester	23	11	6	6	36	22	39
10	Derby	23	11	4	8	28	23	37
11	Ipswich	23	11	3	9	39	32	36
12	Watford	23	10	6	7	32	33	36
13	Portsmouth	23	10	5	8	30	24	35
14	Middlesbro	23	8	10	5	22	21	34
15	Peterborough	23	10	3	10	41	38	33
16	C Palace	23	7	11	5	22	19	32
17	Coventry	23	8	7	8	28	26	31
18	Barnsley	23	9	4	10	31	37	31
19	Burnley	23	7	9	7	33	27	30
20	Leeds	23	9	3	11	34	41	30
21	Millwall	23	7	7	9	27	30	28
22	Bristol C	23	7	6	10	26	32	27
23	Nottm Forest	23	6	5	12	21	32	23
24	Doncaster	23	4	8	11	22	35	20

Championship away

Pos		P	W	D	L	F	A	Pts
1	West Ham	23	13	6	4	40	22	45
2	Reading	23	13	3	7	33	23	42
3	Southampton	23	10	6	7	36	28	36
4	Middlesbro	23	10	6	7	30	30	36
5	Cardiff	23	8	11	4	29	24	35
6	Burnley	23	10	2	11	28	31	32
7	Leeds	23	8	7	8	31	27	31
8	Millwall	23	8	5	10	28	27	29
9	Blackpool	23	7	8	8	37	38	29
10	Birmingham	23	7	7	9	41	37	28
11	Hull	23	7	7	9	19	22	28
12	Watford	23	6	10	7	24	31	28
13	Leicester	23	7	6	10	30	33	27
14	Nottm Forest	23	8	3	12	27	31	27
15	Derby	23	7	6	10	22	35	27
16	Ipswich	23	6	7	10	30	45	25
17	Brighton	23	6	7	10	16	31	25
18	C Palace	23	6	6	11	24	32	24
19	Bristol C	23	5	7	11	18	36	22
20	Peterborough	23	3	8	12	26	39	17
21	Barnsley	23	4	5	14	18	37	17
22	Doncaster	23	4	4	15	21	45	16
23	Portsmouth	23	3	6	14	20	35	15
24	Coventry	23	1	6	16	13	39	9

League 1

Pos		P	W	D	L	F	A	Pts
1	Charlton	46	30	11	5	82	36	101
2	Sheff Wed	46	28	9	9	81	48	93
3	Sheff Utd	46	27	9	10	92	51	90
4	Huddersfield	46	21	18	7	79	47	81
5	MK Dons	46	22	14	10	84	47	80
6	Stevenage	46	18	19	9	69	44	73
7	Notts Co	46	21	10	15	75	63	73
8	Carlisle	46	18	15	13	65	66	69
9	Brentford	46	18	13	15	63	52	67
10	Colchester	46	13	20	13	61	66	59
11	Bournemouth	46	15	13	18	48	52	58
12	Tranmere	46	14	14	18	49	53	56
13	Hartlepool	46	14	14	18	50	55	56
14	Bury	46	15	11	20	60	79	56
15	Preston	46	13	15	18	54	68	54
16	Oldham	46	14	12	20	50	66	54
17	Yeovil	46	14	12	20	59	80	54
18	Scunthorpe	46	10	22	14	55	59	52
19	Walsall	46	10	20	16	51	57	50
20	Leyton Orient	46	13	11	22	48	75	50
21	Wycombe	46	11	10	25	65	88	43
22	Chesterfield	46	10	12	24	56	81	42
23	Exeter	46	10	12	24	46	75	42
24	Rochdale	46	8	14	24	47	81	38

League 1 home

Pos		P	W	D	L	F	A	Pts
1	Sheff Wed	23	17	4	2	48	19	55
2	Sheff Utd	23	16	4	3	54	27	52
3	Charlton	23	15	6	2	46	20	51
4	Huddersfield	23	14	6	3	35	19	48
5	Notts Co	23	13	5	5	42	29	44
6	Carlisle	23	12	7	4	41	30	43
7	MK Dons	23	12	6	5	45	22	42
8	Stevenage	23	10	10	3	36	23	40
9	Tranmere	23	9	11	3	27	16	38
10	Brentford	23	10	6	7	36	24	36
11	Colchester	23	8	11	4	38	33	35
12	Yeovil	23	10	3	10	34	41	33
13	Exeter	23	8	8	7	31	29	32
14	Oldham	23	9	5	9	26	26	32
15	Bournemouth	23	9	5	9	23	23	32
16	Bury	23	8	8	7	31	32	32
17	Walsall	23	7	9	7	27	27	30
18	Preston	23	7	9	7	30	35	30
19	Wycombe	23	7	6	10	37	38	27
20	Chesterfield	23	7	6	10	26	33	27
21	Rochdale	23	6	8	9	30	39	26
22	Scunthorpe	23	5	10	8	28	33	25
23	Hartlepool	23	6	6	11	21	22	24
24	Leyton Orient	23	6	6	11	23	34	24

League 1 away

Pos		P	W	D	L	F	A	Pts
1	Charlton	23	15	5	3	36	16	50
2	MK Dons	23	10	8	5	39	25	38
3	Sheff Utd	23	11	5	7	38	24	38
4	Sheff Wed	23	11	5	7	33	29	38
5	Huddersfield	23	7	12	4	44	28	33
6	Stevenage	23	8	9	6	33	21	33
7	Hartlepool	23	8	8	7	29	33	32
8	Brentford	23	8	7	8	27	28	31
9	Notts Co	23	8	5	10	33	34	29
10	Scunthorpe	23	5	12	6	27	26	27
11	Bournemouth	23	6	8	9	25	29	26
12	Carlisle	23	6	8	9	24	36	26
13	Leyton Orient	23	7	5	11	25	41	26
14	Preston	23	6	6	11	24	33	24
15	Colchester	23	5	9	9	23	33	24
16	Bury	23	7	3	13	29	47	24
17	Oldham	23	5	7	11	24	40	22
18	Yeovil	23	4	9	10	25	39	21
19	Walsall	23	3	11	9	24	30	20
20	Tranmere	23	5	3	15	22	37	18
21	Wycombe	23	4	4	15	28	50	16
22	Chesterfield	23	3	6	14	30	48	15
23	Rochdale	23	2	6	15	17	42	12
24	Coventry	23	2	4	17	15	46	10

League 2

Pos	Team	P	W	D	L	F	A	Pts
1	Swindon	46	29	6	11	75	32	93
2	Shrewsbury	46	26	10	10	66	41	88
3	Crawley	46	23	15	8	76	54	84
4	Southend	46	25	8	13	77	48	83
5	Torquay	46	23	12	11	63	50	81
6	Cheltenham	46	23	8	15	66	50	77
7	Crewe	46	20	12	14	67	59	72
8	Gillingham	46	20	10	16	79	62	70
9	Oxford	46	17	17	12	59	48	68
10	Rotherham	46	18	13	15	67	63	67
11	Aldershot	46	19	9	18	54	52	66
12	Port Vale	46	15	14	17	68	60	59
13	Bristol R	46	15	12	19	60	70	57
14	Accrington	46	14	15	17	54	66	57
15	Morecambe	46	14	14	18	63	57	56
16	AFC W'bledon	46	15	9	22	62	78	54
17	Burton	46	14	12	20	54	81	54
18	Bradford	46	14	8	24	54	59	50
19	Dag & Red	46	14	8	24	50	72	50
20	Northampton	46	12	12	22	56	79	48
21	Plymouth	46	10	16	20	47	64	46
22	Barnet	46	12	10	24	52	79	46
23	Hereford	46	10	14	22	50	70	44
24	Macclesfield	46	8	13	25	39	64	37

League 2 home

Pos	Team	P	W	D	L	F	A	Pts
1	Swindon	23	19	3	1	49	8	60
2	Shrewsbury	23	18	5	0	37	12	59
3	Crawley	23	14	5	4	47	25	47
4	Cheltenham	23	13	5	5	32	16	44
5	Torquay	23	12	8	3	36	23	44
6	Gillingham	23	13	4	6	44	27	43
7	Southend	23	12	6	5	36	18	42
8	Rotherham	23	12	4	7	31	22	40
9	Port Vale	23	12	3	8	38	26	39
10	Oxford	23	10	9	4	36	24	39
11	Crewe	23	11	6	6	38	28	39
12	Aldershot	23	11	5	7	26	19	38
13	Accrington	23	11	4	8	34	33	37
14	Bristol R	23	10	6	7	37	29	36
15	Bradford	23	8	9	6	34	27	33
16	Wimbledon	23	9	4	10	39	40	31
17	Burton	23	8	7	8	24	32	31
18	Dag & Red	23	9	3	11	31	35	30
19	Plymouth	23	6	9	8	23	26	27
20	Macclesfield	23	5	11	7	25	26	26
21	Morecambe	23	6	6	11	31	29	24
22	Barnet	23	6	6	11	29	39	24
23	Northampton	23	6	6	11	30	43	24
24	Hereford	23	5	5	13	23	41	20

League 2 away

Pos	Team	P	W	D	L	F	A	Pts
1	Southend	23	13	2	8	41	30	41
2	Crawley	23	9	10	4	29	29	37
3	Torquay	23	11	4	8	27	27	37
4	Swindon	23	10	3	10	26	24	33
5	Cheltenham	23	10	3	10	34	34	33
6	Crewe	23	9	6	8	29	31	33
7	Morecambe	23	8	8	7	32	28	32
8	Port Vale	23	8	6	9	30	34	30
9	Shrewsbury	23	8	5	10	29	29	29
10	Oxford	23	7	8	8	23	24	29
11	Aldershot	23	8	4	11	28	33	28
12	Gillingham	23	7	6	10	35	35	27
13	Rotherham	23	6	9	8	36	41	27
14	Hereford	23	5	9	9	27	29	24
15	Northampton	23	6	6	11	26	36	24
16	Wimbledon	23	6	5	12	23	38	23
17	Burton	23	6	5	12	30	49	23
18	Barnet	23	6	4	13	23	40	22
19	Bristol R	23	5	6	12	23	41	21
20	Accrington	23	3	11	9	20	33	20
21	Dag & Red	23	5	5	13	19	37	20
22	Plymouth	23	4	7	12	24	38	19
23	Bradford	23	4	5	14	20	32	17
24	Macclesfield	23	3	2	18	14	38	11

Blue Sq Premier

Pos	Team	P	W	D	L	F	A	Pts
1	Fleetwood	46	31	10	5	102	48	103
2	Wrexham	46	30	8	8	85	33	98
3	Mansfield	46	25	14	7	87	48	89
4	York	46	23	14	9	81	45	83
5	Luton	46	22	15	9	78	42	81
6	Kidderminster	46	22	10	14	82	63	76
7	Southport	46	21	13	12	72	69	76
8	Gateshead	46	21	11	14	69	62	74
9	Cambridge U	46	19	14	13	57	41	71
10	Forest Green	46	19	13	14	66	45	70
11	Grimsby	46	19	13	14	79	60	70
12	Braintree	46	17	11	18	76	80	62
13	Barrow	46	17	9	20	62	76	60
14	Ebbsfleet	46	14	12	20	69	84	54
15	Alfreton	46	15	9	22	62	86	54
16	Stockport	46	12	15	19	58	74	51
17	Lincoln	46	13	10	23	56	66	49
18	Tamworth	46	11	15	20	47	70	48
19	Newport Co	46	11	14	21	53	65	47
20	Telford	46	11	13	22	47	73	46
21	Hayes & Y	46	11	8	27	58	90	41
22	Darlington	46	11	13	22	47	73	36
23	Bath City	46	7	10	29	43	89	31
24	Kettering	46	8	9	29	40	100	30

Blue Sq Premier home

Pos	Team	P	W	D	L	F	A	Pts
1	Wrexham	23	16	3	4	48	17	51
2	Luton	23	15	4	4	48	15	49
3	Mansfield	23	14	6	3	50	25	48
4	Fleetwood	23	13	8	2	50	25	47
5	Barrow	23	12	6	5	39	25	42
6	Gateshead	23	11	8	4	39	26	41
7	Grimsby	23	12	4	7	51	28	40
8	York	23	11	6	6	43	24	39
9	Cambridge U	23	11	6	6	31	16	39
10	Forest Green	23	11	5	7	37	25	38
11	Braintree	23	11	5	7	39	34	38
12	Kidderminster	23	10	7	6	44	32	37
13	Telford	23	10	3	10	26	34	33
14	Southport	23	8	8	7	36	39	32
15	Stockport	23	8	7	8	35	28	31
16	Darlington	23	8	7	8	24	24	31
17	Lincoln	23	8	6	9	32	24	30
18	Tamworth	23	7	9	7	30	30	30
19	Newport Co	23	8	6	9	22	22	30
20	Alfreton	23	8	6	9	39	48	30
21	Ebbsfleet	23	7	6	10	34	39	27
22	Hayes & Y	23	5	5	13	26	41	20
23	Kettering	23	5	5	13	25	47	20
24	Bath City	23	5	4	14	27	41	19

Blue Sq Premier away

Pos	Team	P	W	D	L	F	A	Pts
1	Fleetwood	23	18	2	3	52	23	56
2	Wrexham	23	14	5	4	37	16	47
3	York	23	12	8	3	38	21	44
4	Southport	23	13	5	5	36	30	44
5	Mansfield	23	11	8	4	37	23	41
6	Kidderminster	23	12	3	8	38	31	39
7	Gateshead	23	10	3	10	30	36	33
8	Forest Green	23	8	8	7	29	20	32
9	Luton	23	7	11	5	30	27	32
10	Cambridge U	23	8	8	7	26	25	32
11	Grimsby	23	7	9	7	28	32	30
12	Ebbsfleet	23	7	6	10	35	45	27
13	Braintree	23	6	6	11	37	46	24
14	Alfreton	23	7	3	13	23	38	24
15	Hayes & Y	23	6	3	14	32	49	21
16	Stockport	23	4	8	11	23	46	20
17	Lincoln	23	5	4	14	24	42	19
18	Tamworth	23	4	6	13	17	40	18
19	Barrow	23	5	3	15	23	51	18
20	Newport Co	23	3	8	12	31	43	17
21	Darlington	23	3	6	14	23	49	15
22	Telford	23	1	10	12	21	39	13
23	Kettering	23	3	4	16	15	53	13
24	Bath City	23	2	6	15	16	48	12

Blue Square North

Pos	Team	P	W	D	L	F	A	Pts
1	Hyde	42	27	9	6	89	36	90
2	Guiseley	42	25	10	7	87	50	85
3	Halifax	42	21	11	10	80	59	74
4	Gainsborough	42	23	5	14	74	60	74
5	Nuneaton	42	22	12	8	72	40	72
6	Stalybridge	42	20	11	11	82	63	71
7	Worcester	42	18	11	13	63	58	65
8	Altrincham	42	17	10	15	90	71	61
9	Droylsden	42	16	11	15	83	86	59
10	Bishop's St.	42	17	7	18	69	74	58
11	Boston Utd	42	15	9	18	60	67	54
12	Colwyn Bay	42	15	8	19	55	70	53
13	Workington	42	14	10	18	56	61	52
14	Gloucester	42	15	7	20	53	60	52
15	Harrogate T	42	14	10	18	58	68	52
16	Histon	42	12	15	15	67	72	51
17	Corby	42	14	8	20	65	71	50
18	Vauxhall M	42	14	8	20	63	77	50
19	Solihull Moors	42	13	10	19	44	54	49
20	Hinckley Utd	42	13	9	20	75	90	48
21	Blyth Sptns	42	7	13	22	51	81	34
22	Eastwood T	42	4	8	30	37	105	20

Blue Square North home

Pos	Team	P	W	D	L	F	A	Pts
1	Hyde	21	15	5	1	55	17	50
2	Guiseley	21	15	3	3	52	24	48
3	Gainsborough	21	14	2	5	38	22	44
4	Nuneaton	21	13	4	4	35	18	43
5	Stalybridge	21	13	2	6	48	33	41
6	Worcester	21	10	7	4	31	20	37
7	Altrincham	21	10	6	5	49	31	36
8	Droylsden	21	10	6	5	46	35	36
9	Halifax	21	10	5	6	41	33	35
10	Solihull Moors	21	9	4	8	29	25	31
11	Workington	21	8	6	7	31	28	30
12	Colwyn Bay	21	9	3	9	18	19	30
13	Bishop's St.	21	8	4	9	35	30	28
14	Harrogate T	21	7	7	7	24	25	28
15	Vauxhall M	21	9	1	11	27	32	28
16	Gloucester	21	8	3	10	25	27	27
17	Boston Utd	21	6	8	7	28	29	26
18	Histon	21	5	9	7	41	41	24
19	Hinckley Utd	21	5	5	11	36	43	20
20	Blyth Sptns	21	5	5	11	30	38	20
21	Corby	21	6	1	14	33	43	19
22	Eastwood T	21	1	7	13	22	53	10

Blue Square North away

Pos	Team	P	W	D	L	F	A	Pts
1	Hyde	21	12	4	5	34	19	40
2	Halifax	21	11	6	4	39	26	39
3	Guiseley	21	10	7	4	35	26	37
4	Nuneaton	21	9	8	4	37	22	35
5	Corby	21	8	7	6	32	28	31
6	Stalybridge	21	7	9	5	34	30	30
7	Gainsborough	21	9	3	9	36	38	30
8	Bishop's St.	21	9	3	9	34	44	30
9	Boston Utd	21	9	1	11	32	38	28
10	Worcester	21	8	4	9	32	38	28
11	Hinckley Utd	21	8	4	9	39	47	28
12	Histon	21	7	6	8	26	31	27
13	Altrincham	21	7	4	10	41	40	25
14	Gloucester	21	7	4	10	28	33	25
15	Harrogate T	21	7	3	11	34	43	24
16	Colwyn Bay	21	6	5	10	37	51	23
17	Droylsden	21	6	5	10	37	51	23
18	Workington	21	6	4	11	25	33	22
19	Vauxhall M	21	5	7	9	36	45	22
20	Solihull Moors	21	4	6	11	15	29	18
21	Blyth Sptns	21	2	8	11	21	43	14
22	Eastwood T	21	3	1	17	15	52	10

Blue Square South

Pos		P	W	D	L	F	A	Pts
1	Woking	42	30	7	5	92	41	97
2	Dartford	42	26	10	6	89	40	88
3	Welling	42	24	9	9	79	47	81
4	Sutton Utd	42	20	14	8	68	53	74
5	Basingstoke	42	20	11	11	65	50	71
6	Chelmsford	42	18	13	11	67	44	67
7	Dover	42	17	15	10	62	49	66
8	Boreham W	42	17	10	15	66	58	61
9	Tonbridge	42	15	12	15	70	67	57
10	Salisbury	42	15	12	15	55	54	57
11	Dorchester	42	16	8	18	58	65	56
12	Eastleigh	42	15	9	18	57	63	54
13	Weston S-M.	42	14	9	19	58	71	51
14	Truro City	42	13	9	20	65	80	48
15	Staines	42	12	10	20	53	63	46
16	Farnborough	42	15	6	21	52	79	46
17	Bromley	42	10	15	17	52	66	45
18	Eastbourne	42	12	9	21	54	69	45
19	Havant & W	42	11	11	20	64	75	44
20	Maidenhead	42	11	10	21	49	74	43
21	Hampton & R	42	10	12	20	53	69	42
22	Thurrock	42	6	8	28	33	84	26

Blue Square South home

Pos		P	W	D	L	F	A	Pts
1	Dartford	21	15	4	2	52	19	49
2	Woking	21	15	4	2	43	18	49
3	Welling	21	14	6	1	42	18	48
4	Sutton Utd	21	12	6	3	39	24	42
5	Boreham W	21	11	5	5	43	26	38
6	Basingstoke	21	10	6	5	35	29	36
7	Eastleigh	21	10	5	6	36	25	35
8	Tonbridge	21	10	4	7	41	34	34
9	Salisbury	21	9	4	8	27	21	31
10	Weston S-M.	21	8	6	7	34	35	30
11	Chelmsford	21	8	5	8	33	25	29
12	Dover	21	8	5	8	26	24	29
13	Havant & W	21	7	6	8	39	34	27
14	Farnborough	21	9	0	12	21	32	27
15	Eastbourne	21	7	4	10	29	33	25
16	Dorchester	21	7	4	10	30	37	25
17	Truro City	21	7	3	11	33	37	24
18	Bromley	21	4	10	7	23	24	22
19	Staines	21	4	6	11	25	39	18
20	Maidenhead	21	4	6	11	25	41	18
21	Hampton & R	21	3	7	11	22	39	16
22	Thurrock	21	2	7	12	13	36	13

Blue Square South away

Pos		P	W	D	L	F	A	Pts
1	Woking	21	15	3	3	49	23	48
2	Dartford	21	11	6	4	37	21	39
3	Chelmsford	21	10	8	3	34	19	38
4	Dover	21	10	7	4	36	25	37
5	Basingstoke	21	10	6	5	30	21	35
6	Welling	21	10	3	8	37	29	33
7	Sutton Utd	21	8	8	5	29	29	32
8	Dorchester	21	9	4	8	28	28	31
9	Staines	21	8	4	9	28	24	28
10	Hampton & R	21	7	5	9	31	30	26
11	Salisbury	21	6	8	7	28	33	26
12	Maidenhead	21	7	4	10	24	33	25
13	Truro City	21	6	6	9	32	43	24
14	Farnborough	21	6	6	9	31	47	24
15	Tonbridge	21	5	8	8	29	33	23
16	Boreham W	21	6	5	10	23	32	23
17	Bromley	21	6	5	10	29	42	23
18	Weston S-M.	21	6	3	12	24	36	21
19	Eastbourne	21	5	5	11	25	36	20
20	Eastleigh	21	5	2	11	21	38	19
21	Havant & W	21	4	5	12	25	41	17
22	Thurrock	21	4	3	14	20	48	13

Scottish Premier League

Pos		P	W	D	L	F	A	Pts
1	Celtic	38	30	3	5	84	21	93
2	Rangers*	38	26	5	7	77	28	73
3	Motherwell	38	18	8	12	49	44	62
4	Dundee Utd	38	16	11	11	62	50	59
5	Hearts	38	15	7	16	45	43	52
6	St Johnstone	38	14	8	16	43	50	50
7	Kilmarnock	38	11	14	13	44	61	47
8	St Mirren	38	9	16	13	39	51	43
9	Aberdeen	38	9	14	15	36	44	41
10	Inverness CT	38	10	9	19	42	60	39
11	Hibernian	38	8	9	21	40	67	33
12	Dunfermline	38	5	10	23	40	82	25

Scottish Premier League home

Pos		P	W	D	L	F	A	Pts
1	Celtic	19	17	1	1	41	6	52
2	Rangers	19	12	5	2	38	14	41
3	Hearts	19	11	0	8	30	19	33
4	Dundee Utd	19	8	6	5	27	16	30
5	Motherwell	19	9	3	7	27	24	30
6	Kilmarnock	20	7	7	6	29	35	28
7	Aberdeen	19	6	8	5	22	16	26
8	St Mirren	19	6	6	7	23	25	24
9	Inverness CT	19	5	5	9	19	27	20
10	St Johnstone	19	6	2	10	20	30	20
11	Hibernian	19	2	7	10	17	30	13
12	Dunfermline	19	1	7	11	22	44	10

Scottish Premier League away

Pos	P		W	D	L	F	A	Pts
1	Rangers	19	14	0	5	39	14	42
2	Celtic	19	13	2	4	43	15	41
3	Motherwell	19	9	5	5	22	20	32
4	St Johnstone	20	8	6	6	23	20	30
5	Dundee Utd	19	8	5	6	35	34	29
6	Hibernian	19	6	2	11	23	37	20
7	Hearts	19	4	7	8	15	24	19
8	Inverness CT	19	5	4	10	23	33	19
9	St Mirren	19	3	10	6	16	26	19
10	Kilmarnock	18	4	7	7	15	26	19
11	Aberdeen	19	3	6	10	14	28	15
12	Dunfermline	19	4	3	12	18	38	15

Scottish Div One

Pos		P	W	D	L	F	A	Pts
1	Ross County	36	22	13	1	72	32	79
2	Dundee	36	15	10	11	53	43	55
3	Falkirk	36	13	13	10	53	48	52
4	Hamilton	36	14	7	15	55	56	49
5	Livingston	36	13	9	14	56	54	48
6	Partick	36	12	11	13	50	39	47
7	Raith	36	11	11	14	46	49	44
8	Morton	36	10	12	14	40	55	42
9	Ayr	36	9	11	16	44	67	38
10	Queen of Sth	36	7	11	18	38	64	32

Scottish Div One home

Pos		P	W	D	L	F	A	Pts
1	Ross County	18	11	7	0	40	14	40
2	Falkirk	18	9	6	3	29	21	33
3	Partick	18	7	6	5	27	16	27
4	Hamilton	18	8	3	7	33	30	27
5	Dundee	18	7	5	6	25	20	26
6	Raith	18	7	4	7	24	21	25
7	Queen of Sth	18	6	5	7	21	31	23
8	Ayr	18	5	7	6	22	25	22
9	Livingston	18	5	6	7	26	29	21
10	Morton	18	5	5	8	24	29	20

Scottish Div One away

Pos		P	W	D	L	F	A	Pts
1	Ross County	18	11	6	1	32	18	39
2	Dundee	18	8	5	5	28	23	29
3	Livingston	18	8	3	7	30	25	27
4	Hamilton	18	6	4	8	22	26	22
5	Morton	18	5	7	6	16	26	22
6	Partick	18	5	5	8	23	23	20
7	Falkirk	18	4	7	7	24	27	19
8	Raith	18	4	7	7	22	28	19
9	Ayr	18	4	4	10	22	42	16
10	Queen of Sth	18	1	6	11	17	33	9

Scottish Div Two

Pos		P	W	D	L	F	A	Pts
1	Cowdenbeath	36	20	11	5	68	29	71
2	Arbroath	36	17	12	7	76	51	63
3	Dumbarton	36	17	7	12	61	61	58
4	Airdrie Utd	36	14	10	12	68	60	52
5	Stenh'semuir	36	15	6	15	54	49	51
6	East Fife	36	14	6	16	55	57	48
7	Forfar	36	11	9	16	59	72	42
8	Brechin	36	10	11	15	47	62	41
9	Albion	36	10	7	19	43	66	37
10	Stirling	36	9	7	20	46	70	34

Scottish Div Two home

Pos		P	W	D	L	F	A	Pts
1	Cowdenbeath	18	13	4	1	37	10	43
2	Arbroath	18	10	5	3	44	23	35
3	Dumbarton	18	10	2	6	30	30	32
4	Airdrie Utd	18	9	4	5	43	30	31
5	Stenh'semuir	18	9	2	7	32	23	29
6	East Fife	18	7	4	7	27	29	25
7	Albion	18	6	6	6	25	22	24
8	Forfar	18	6	5	7	33	34	23
9	Brechin	18	6	6	7	24	30	21
10	Stirling	18	4	5	9	22	29	17

Scottish Div Two away

Pos		P	W	D	L	F	A	Pts
1	Cowdenbeath	18	7	7	4	31	19	28
2	Arbroath	18	7	7	4	32	28	28
3	Dumbarton	18	7	5	6	31	31	26
4	East Fife	18	7	2	9	28	28	23
5	Stenh'semuir	18	6	4	8	22	26	22
6	Airdrie Utd	18	5	6	7	25	30	21
7	Brechin	18	5	5	8	23	32	20
8	Forfar	18	5	4	9	26	38	19
9	Stirling	18	5	2	11	24	41	17
10	Albion	18	4	1	13	18	44	13

Scottish Div Three

Pos		P	W	D	L	F	A	Pts
1	Alloa	36	23	8	5	70	39	77
2	Queen's Park	36	16	9	11	70	48	63
3	Stranraer	36	17	7	12	77	57	58
4	Elgin City	36	16	9	11	68	60	57
5	Peterhead	36	15	8	13	53	51	53
6	Annan	36	13	10	13	53	53	49
7	Berwick	36	12	12	12	61	63	48
8	Montrose	36	11	5	20	58	75	38
9	Clyde	36	8	11	17	35	50	35
10	East Stirling	36	6	6	24	38	88	24

Scottish Div Three home

Pos		P	W	D	L	F	A	Pts
1	Alloa	18	13	4	1	43	13	43
2	Elgin City	18	11	3	4	43	17	36
3	Queen's Park	18	10	4	4	41	17	34
4	Stranraer	18	10	2	6	43	33	32
5	Annan	18	7	5	6	28	26	26
6	Peterhead	18	7	5	6	25	23	26
7	Montrose	18	7	3	8	34	33	24
8	Berwick	18	6	5	7	30	28	23
9	Clyde	18	5	5	8	24	23	20
10	East Stirling	18	5	4	9	24	33	19

Scottish Div Three away

Pos		P	W	D	L	F	A	Pts
1	Alloa	18	10	4	4	27	26	34
2	Queen's Park	18	9	2	7	29	31	29
3	Stranraer	18	7	5	6	34	24	26
4	Berwick	18	6	7	5	31	30	25
5	Peterhead	18	8	1	9	26	30	25
6	Annan	18	6	5	7	25	27	23
7	Elgin City	18	5	6	7	25	43	21
8	Clyde	18	3	6	9	11	27	15
9	Montrose	18	4	2	12	24	42	14
10	East Stirling	18	1	2	15	14	55	5

Premier League results 2011-12

	Arsenal	Aston Villa	Blackburn	Bolton	Chelsea	Everton	Fulham	Liverpool	Man City	Man Utd	Newcastle	Norwich	QPR	Stoke	Sunderland	Swansea	Tottenham	West Brom	Wigan	Wolves
Arsenal	*	3-0	7-1	3-0	0-0	1-0	1-1	0-2	1-0	1-2	2-1	3-3	1-0	3-1	2-1	1-0	5-2	3-0	1-2	1-1
Aston Villa	1-2	*	3-1	1-2	2-4	1-1	1-0	0-2	0-1	0-1	1-1	3-2	2-2	1-1	0-0	0-2	1-1	1-2	2-0	0-0
Blackburn	4-3	1-1	*	1-2	0-1	0-1	3-1	2-3	0-4	0-2	0-2	2-0	3-2	1-2	2-0	4-2	1-2	1-2	0-1	1-2
Bolton	0-0	1-2	1-2	*	1-5	0-2	0-3	3-1	2-3	0-5	0-2	1-2	2-1	5-0	0-2	1-1	1-4	2-2	1-2	1-1
Chelsea	3-5	1-3	2-1	3-0	*	3-1	1-1	1-2	2-1	3-3	0-2	3-1	6-1	1-0	1-0	4-1	0-0	2-1	2-1	3-0
Everton	0-1	2-2	1-1	1-2	2-0	*	4-0	0-2	1-0	0-1	3-1	1-1	0-1	0-1	4-0	1-0	1-0	2-0	3-1	2-1
Fulham	2-1	0-0	1-1	2-0	1-1	1-3	*	1-0	2-2	0-5	5-2	2-1	6-0	2-1	2-1	0-3	1-3	1-1	2-1	5-0
Liverpool	1-2	1-1	1-1	3-1	4-1	3-0	0-1	*	1-1	1-1	3-1	1-1	1-0	0-0	1-1	0-0	0-0	0-1	1-2	2-1
Man City	1-0	4-1	3-0	2-0	2-1	2-0	3-0	1-1	*	1-0	3-1	5-1	3-2	3-0	3-3	4-0	3-2	4-0	3-0	3-1
Man Utd	8-2	4-0	2-3	3-0	3-1	4-4	1-0	1-2	1-6	*	1-1	2-0	2-0	2-0	1-0	2-0	3-0	2-0	5-0	4-1
Newcastle	0-0	2-1	3-1	2-0	0-3	2-1	2-1	2-0	0-2	3-0	*	1-0	1-0	3-0	1-1	0-0	2-2	2-3	1-0	2-2
Norwich	1-2	2-0	3-3	2-0	0-0	2-2	1-1	0-3	1-6	1-2	4-2	*	2-1	1-1	2-1	3-1	0-2	0-1	1-1	2-1
QPR	2-1	1-1	1-1	0-4	1-0	1-1	0-1	3-2	2-3	0-2	0-0	1-2	*	1-0	2-3	3-0	1-0	1-1	3-1	2-1
Stoke	1-1	1-1	3-1	2-2	0-0	1-1	2-0	1-0	1-1	1-1	1-3	1-0	2-3	*	0-1	2-0	2-1	1-2	2-2	2-1
Sunderland	1-2	2-2	2-1	2-2	1-2	0-2	0-0	1-0	1-0	0-1	0-1	3-0	3-1	4-0	*	2-0	0-0	2-2	1-2	0-0
Swansea	3-2	0-0	3-0	3-0	1-1	2-0	2-0	1-0	1-0	1-3	0-2	2-3	1-1	2-0	0-0	*	1-1	3-0	0-0	4-4
Tottenham	2-1	2-0	2-0	3-0	1-1	0-1	2-0	4-0	1-5	1-2	5-0	1-2	3-1	1-1	1-0	3-1	*	1-0	3-1	1-1
West Brom	2-3	0-0	3-0	2-1	1-0	1-1	0-0	0-2	0-0	1-0	1-3	1-2	1-0	0-1	4-0	1-2	1-3	*	1-2	2-0
Wigan	0-4	0-0	3-3	1-3	1-1	1-1	0-2	0-0	0-1	1-0	4-0	1-1	2-0	2-0	1-4	0-2	1-2	1-1	*	3-2
Wolves	0-3	2-3	0-2	2-3	1-2	0-0	2-0	0-3	0-2	0-5	1-2	2-2	0-3	1-2	2-1	2-2	0-2	1-5	3-1	*

	Barnsley	Birmingham	Blackpool	Brighton	Bristol C	Burnley	C Palace	Cardiff	Coventry	Derby	Doncaster	Hull	Ipswich	Leeds	Leicester	Middlesbro	Millwall	Nottm F	Peterborough	Portsmouth	Reading	Southampton	Watford	West Ham
Barnsley	*	1-3	1-1	0-0	1-2	2-0	2-1	0-1	2-0	3-2	2-0	2-1	3-5	4-1	1-1	1-3	1-3	1-1	1-0	2-0	0-4	0-1	1-1	0-4
Birmingham	1-1	*	3-0	0-0	2-2	2-0	3-1	1-1	1-0	2-2	2-1	0-0	2-1	1-0	2-0	3-0	3-0	1-2	1-1	1-0	2-0	0-0	1-1	1-1
Blackpool	1-1	2-2	*	3-1	5-0	4-0	2-1	1-1	1-0	0-1	2-1	1-1	2-1	1-0	3-3	3-0	1-0	1-2	2-1	1-1	1-0	3-0	3-0	1-4
Brighton	2-0	1-1	3-1	*	2-0	0-1	2-1	1-1	2-1	0-1	2-1	0-0	3-0	3-3	1-0	1-1	1-0	1-2	2-1	1-1	1-0	3-0	0-0	1-1
Bristol C	2-0	0-2	1-3	0-1	*	3-1	1-3	1-2	3-1	1-1	2-1	0-0	0-3	0-3	3-2	0-1	0-1	0-0	1-1	0-0	2-3	2-0	0-2	0-1
Burnley	2-0	1-3	3-1	1-0	3-1	*	1-1	1-2	3-1	1-1	3-0	1-0	4-0	1-2	1-3	0-1	1-0	0-0	1-1	2-2	0-1	1-1	0-2	1-1
C Palace	1-0	1-0	1-1	1-0	2-0	2-0	*	1-2	1-1	1-1	1-1	1-0	1-1	1-1	1-2	0-2	0-0	5-1	1-0	0-1	0-0	1-1	2-2	2-2
Cardiff	5-3	1-0	1-3	1-1	3-1	2-2	1-2	*	2-0	2-0	3-0	0-3	1-1	1-1	1-3	2-3	1-3	0-3	3-1	3-2	3-1	0-2	4-0	2-2
Coventry	1-0	1-3	2-2	1-3	1-0	1-2	2-0	1-1	*	2-0	0-2	0-1	2-2	1-1	0-1	3-1	0-0	1-0	2-2	3-1	1-1	2-1	1-1	0-2
Derby	1-1	2-1	2-1	0-1	1-2	1-2	1-1	1-1	1-0	*	3-0	0-2	2-3	2-1	0-1	0-1	0-3	1-0	2-2	3-1	1-1	2-4	0-0	1-2
Doncaster	2-0	1-3	1-3	1-1	1-2	2-3	3-2	0-3	1-0	1-2	*	3-0	2-3	0-3	2-1	0-1	0-3	0-1	1-1	3-4	0-1	1-1	0-0	0-1
Hull	3-1	2-1	0-1	0-0	1-2	2-3	0-1	1-1	1-1	1-2	0-0	*	2-2	0-0	2-1	2-1	2-0	2-1	1-1	1-0	1-0	0-2	3-2	0-2
Ipswich	1-0	1-1	2-2	3-1	3-0	1-0	0-1	1-1	3-0	1-0	2-3	0-1	*	2-1	1-2	1-1	0-3	1-3	3-2	1-0	2-3	2-5	1-2	5-1
Leeds	1-2	1-4	0-5	1-2	2-1	2-1	3-2	1-2	1-1	0-2	3-2	4-1	3-1	*	1-2	1-1	2-0	3-7	4-1	1-1	0-1	0-1	0-2	1-1
Leicester	1-2	3-1	2-0	1-0	2-1	0-0	3-0	2-1	2-0	4-0	4-0	2-1	1-1	0-1	*	0-1	2-0	0-0	4-1	1-1	0-2	0-1	2-0	1-1
Middlesbro	2-0	3-1	2-2	2-0	1-1	0-2	0-0	0-2	1-1	2-0	0-0	1-0	0-0	0-2	2-2	*	1-1	2-0	1-1	2-2	0-2	3-2	2-0	0-2
Millwall	0-0	0-6	2-2	1-1	1-1	0-2	0-1	0-1	3-0	0-1	3-2	1-0	4-1	0-2	0-0	1-3	*	2-0	1-1	2-2	1-2	2-3	1-0	0-0
Nottm F	0-0	1-3	0-0	1-1	0-1	0-2	0-1	0-1	3-0	1-0	3-2	0-1	4-1	0-4	2-1	1-3	3-1	*	0-1	2-0	1-2	0-3	2-2	0-0
Peterborough	3-4	1-1	3-1	1-2	3-0	2-1	2-1	4-3	1-0	3-2	1-2	0-1	7-1	2-3	2-1	2-0	3-1	0-1	*	0-3	1-2	1-3	1-1	1-4
Portsmouth	2-0	4-1	1-0	1-2	0-0	1-5	2-1	1-1	2-1	1-1	3-1	2-0	0-1	0-0	1-0	1-1	0-1	3-0	2-3	*	3-1	1-3	2-2	0-2
Reading	1-2	1-0	3-1	0-1	1-0	1-0	2-2	2-1	4-0	4-0	2-0	2-1	1-0	3-1	3-1	1-3	2-2	3-0	3-2	1-0	*	1-1	4-0	3-0
Southampton	2-0	4-1	2-2	3-0	2-2	2-0	2-2	0-2	4-0	0-1	2-0	0-1	1-0	3-1	0-2	3-0	1-0	3-2	2-1	1-0	1-3	*	4-0	1-0
Watford	2-1	2-2	0-2	1-0	0-0	3-2	0-2	1-1	4-0	0-1	4-1	1-1	2-1	2-2	3-2	1-1	2-1	0-1	3-2	2-0	1-2	0-3	*	0-4
West Ham	1-0	3-3	4-0	6-0	1-2	1-1	2-2	2-2	0-2	1-2	1-1	2-1	0-1	2-2	3-2	1-1	2-1	2-1	1-0	4-3	2-4	1-1	1-1	*

	Yeovil	Wycombe	Walsall	Tranmere	Stevenage	Sheff Weds	Sheff Utd	Scunthorpe	Rochdale	Preston	Oldham	Notts Co	MK Dons	Leyton O	Huddersfield	Hartlepool	Exeter	Colchester	Chesterfield	Charlton	Carlisle	Bury	Brentford	Bournemouth
Bournemouth	0-0	2-0	0-2	2-1	1-3	2-0	0-2	2-0	1-1	1-0	0-0	2-1	0-1	1-2	2-0	1-2	2-0	1-1	0-3	0-1	1-1	1-2	1-0	*
Brentford	2-0	5-2	0-0	0-2	0-1	1-2	0-2	0-0	2-0	1-3	2-0	0-0	3-3	5-0	0-4	2-1	2-0	1-1	2-1	0-1	4-0	3-0	*	1-1
Bury	3-2	1-4	2-1	2-0	1-2	2-1	0-3	2-2	2-4	1-0	0-0	2-2	0-0	1-1	3-3	1-2	2-0	4-1	1-1	1-2	0-2	*	1-1	1-0
Carlisle	3-2	2-2	2-1	0-0	1-0	3-2	3-2	0-0	2-1	0-0	3-3	0-3	1-3	4-1	2-1	1-2	4-1	1-0	2-1	0-1	*	4-1	2-2	2-1
Charlton	3-0	2-2	1-0	0-0	2-0	1-1	3-2	2-2	2-1	5-2	1-1	2-4	2-1	4-1	2-1	1-2	4-1	1-0	2-1	*	4-0	4-1	2-0	3-0
Chesterfield	3-0	2-1	1-0	1-1	2-0	1-0	0-1	1-4	0-0	0-2	1-1	1-3	2-1	2-0	2-0	3-2	0-2	0-1	*	0-4	4-1	1-0	2-3	1-0
Colchester	2-2	4-0	1-0	4-2	1-6	1-1	1-1	1-1	0-0	3-0	4-1	1-3	1-5	1-1	0-2	2-3	2-0	*	1-2	0-2	1-1	1-0	2-1	1-1
Exeter	2-2	1-3	4-2	1-0	1-1	2-1	2-2	0-0	3-1	3-0	2-0	4-2	0-2	3-0	0-4	0-0	*	1-1	2-1	0-2	0-0	3-2	1-2	0-2
Hartlepool	1-1	1-3	1-0	0-2	0-0	2-1	2-2	0-0	3-1	1-2	2-0	1-1	0-2	3-0	0-0	*	2-0	1-1	1-2	0-4	0-0	3-2	2-1	1-1
Huddersfield	2-2	1-3	1-1	2-0	1-1	0-1	2-2	0-0	2-2	3-1	1-0	2-1	1-1	2-2	*	0-0	3-0	1-3	1-1	0-4	1-2	1-0	3-0	0-1
Leyton O	4-2	1-3	0-1	0-1	0-0	1-1	0-1	1-3	0-1	0-1	1-3	0-3	0-3	*	1-3	1-1	3-0	0-1	1-1	3-0	1-2	1-0	2-0	1-3
MK Dons	2-2	4-3	0-0	2-1	1-5	2-2	2-5	0-2	2-0	0-0	5-0	3-0	*	4-1	1-1	2-2	3-0	2-4	6-2	1-1	2-0	2-1	3-1	2-2
Notts Co	1-0	1-1	0-0	0-1	1-1	0-2	2-4	1-0	0-1	1-1	3-2	*	3-2	2-0	1-1	0-1	1-0	2-1	0-3	1-3	0-3	2-4	0-2	2-1
Oldham	0-0	2-0	0-1	0-2	1-0	0-1	2-5	0-0	2-0	0-0	*	3-2	2-1	1-2	1-0	3-2	2-1	2-4	1-0	1-2	0-0	1-3	0-2	3-3
Preston	2-1	2-0	2-1	3-1	1-1	0-0	1-1	0-0	0-1	*	3-3	2-0	2-1	0-1	1-1	2-2	1-0	2-2	2-3	3-1	0-0	3-0	1-3	1-3
Rochdale	3-1	3-0	0-0	0-2	1-5	0-0	2-5	1-0	*	1-1	2-0	2-0	1-1	2-3	2-2	3-0	1-0	2-2	0-0	2-2	1-0	4-2	0-0	1-0
Scunthorpe	4-0	3-0	3-2	4-2	1-1	2-2	1-1	*	3-0	1-0	2-3	2-1	1-0	2-3	2-2	3-1	3-0	0-0	2-0	0-0	1-2	0-0	0-0	1-1
Sheff Utd	2-1	4-1	3-2	1-1	0-1	2-2	*	2-1	3-0	2-0	2-3	2-1	2-1	3-1	2-2	2-2	3-2	2-2	4-1	3-0	1-2	2-0	0-0	1-1
Sheff Weds	3-0	3-0	3-2	4-2	2-2	*	1-0	3-2	3-0	1-2	3-0	2-1	4-2	1-0	0-3	3-0	4-4	3-0	4-1	2-0	1-0	4-1	2-0	3-0
Stevenage	0-1	2-2	2-2	1-1	*	5-1	1-0	2-1	3-0	2-0	3-0	2-1	0-0	1-0	2-2	3-1	3-0	0-0	3-1	2-0	1-2	2-0	2-0	2-1
Tranmere	0-0	2-0	0-0	*	3-0	1-2	1-1	2-1	0-0	1-0	0-1	0-1	0-2	1-0	1-1	1-0	2-0	0-0	3-2	1-1	1-1	2-4	0-1	0-0
Walsall	2-0	2-0	*	0-1	1-1	2-1	1-0	2-2	0-0	1-0	0-1	0-1	0-2	1-0	1-1	0-0	1-2	2-0	3-2	2-2	1-1	2-4	0-2	2-2
Wycombe	2-3	*	2-0	2-1	0-1	1-2	1-0	1-1	3-0	3-4	2-2	3-4	1-1	4-2	0-6	5-0	3-1	0-0	3-2	2-2	1-1	0-2	0-1	2-2
Yeovil	*	1-0	2-1	2-1	0-6	2-3	0-1	2-2	3-1	2-1	3-1	1-0	0-1	2-2	2-0	0-1	2-2	3-2	3-2	2-3	0-3	1-3	2-1	1-3

Home \ Away	Wimbledon	Torquay	Swindon	Southend	Shrewsbury	Rotherham	Port Vale	Plymouth	Oxford Utd	Northampton	Morecambe	Macclesfield	Hereford	Gillingham	Dagenham	Crewe	Crawley	Cheltenham	Burton	Bristol R	Bradford	Barnet	Aldershot	Accrington
Accrington	2-1	3-1	0-2	1-2	1-1	1-1	2-2	0-4	0-2	2-1	1-1	4-0	2-1	4-3	3-0	0-2	0-1	0-1	2-1	2-1	1-0	0-3	3-2	*
Aldershot	1-1	0-1	2-1	2-0	1-0	2-2	1-1	0-0	0-3	0-1	1-0	1-2	1-0	1-2	2-2	3-1	0-1	1-0	2-0	2-2	1-0	4-1	*	0-0
Barnet	4-0	0-1	0-1	1-2	1-2	1-1	1-1	2-1	0-3	1-2	0-2	2-1	1-1	2-2	2-2	2-0	1-2	2-2	3-6	2-0	0-4	*	2-1	0-0
Bradford	1-2	4-0	0-0	2-0	3-1	2-3	1-1	2-3	0-2	1-2	0-2	1-0	1-0	2-2	0-1	3-0	1-2	0-1	1-1	2-2	*	4-2	1-2	1-1
Bristol R	1-0	1-2	1-1	1-0	1-0	5-2	0-3	2-3	0-0	2-1	2-2	0-0	1-1	2-2	2-0	2-5	0-0	1-3	7-1	*	2-1	0-2	0-1	5-1
Burton	3-2	1-0	2-0	0-2	1-1	1-1	1-1	2-1	0-0	2-2	3-2	1-0	0-2	1-0	1-1	1-0	0-0	0-2	*	2-1	2-2	1-2	0-4	0-2
Cheltenham	0-0	1-4	1-0	3-0	0-0	1-0	2-0	2-1	0-1	0-1	1-2	2-0	0-3	0-3	2-1	1-0	3-1	*	2-0	2-1	3-1	2-0	2-0	4-1
Crawley	1-1	0-1	0-3	3-0	2-1	3-0	3-2	2-0	0-0	2-2	1-2	1-0	0-0	1-2	3-1	0-1	*	4-2	3-0	4-1	3-1	1-0	2-2	1-1
Crewe	3-3	0-1	2-0	1-3	3-0	1-2	1-1	2-1	4-1	3-1	1-1	2-0	0-3	1-2	4-1	*	3-1	1-0	3-2	0-2	3-1	1-0	2-0	2-0
Dagenham	0-2	0-3	3-1	1-2	0-1	3-2	1-1	3-2	0-0	0-1	1-1	2-0	1-0	1-2	*	2-1	1-1	1-0	3-2	4-0	1-0	3-1	2-5	2-1
Gillingham	3-4	1-1	1-2	2-3	0-1	0-0	2-1	3-0	0-1	4-3	1-1	2-0	5-4	*	2-1	3-4	0-1	0-5	3-1	4-1	0-0	3-1	1-0	1-1
Hereford	2-1	2-0	2-0	0-2	0-2	2-3	0-0	1-1	0-1	0-0	0-3	0-4	*	1-6	1-0	0-1	1-1	1-1	2-3	1-2	2-0	1-0	0-2	1-1
Macclesfield	4-0	3-2	0-1	1-0	0-1	0-0	2-1	0-0	1-1	3-1	1-1	*	2-2	0-0	2-1	2-2	2-2	1-3	0-2	0-0	1-0	0-0	0-1	1-1
Morecambe	1-2	1-2	0-1	2-5	2-7	3-3	2-1	2-0	0-1	1-2	*	1-0	0-1	2-3	1-2	1-2	6-0	3-1	2-3	3-2	1-3	0-1	1-2	0-0
Northampton	1-0	0-0	1-2	0-2	2-0	1-1	0-2	1-0	0-1	*	0-2	2-0	1-3	0-1	0-1	0-1	0-1	2-3	2-3	3-2	1-3	1-2	3-1	1-1
Oxford Utd	1-0	2-2	2-0	0-0	1-0	1-1	5-1	5-1	*	2-0	1-2	1-1	2-2	0-0	2-1	0-1	1-1	1-3	2-1	3-0	2-2	2-1	1-1	1-1
Plymouth	0-2	1-0	0-1	0-4	2-3	1-4	0-2	*	1-1	4-1	4-1	2-0	1-0	2-1	0-1	0-1	1-1	1-2	2-1	2-1	1-0	0-0	1-0	2-2
Port Vale	1-2	0-0	1-2	2-3	2-3	2-0	*	0-2	1-1	3-0	0-4	4-2	1-0	3-2	0-1	1-1	2-2	1-0	3-0	1-0	3-0	3-2	1-2	1-0
Rotherham	1-0	0-1	0-2	0-4	1-1	*	2-0	1-0	3-0	3-0	3-2	1-0	1-0	2-0	3-1	1-1	1-2	1-0	2-1	1-0	1-0	2-2	2-0	4-1
Shrewsbury	0-0	2-0	2-1	2-1	*	2-3	1-0	1-1	2-2	3-1	3-2	1-0	3-1	0-2	2-1	1-1	2-1	1-0	0-1	1-1	0-1	3-0	1-1	1-0
Southend	2-0	4-1	1-4	*	1-1	3-1	1-0	2-0	2-1	1-1	1-1	2-0	2-0	2-5	1-0	3-0	2-1	4-0	2-2	0-0	0-0	3-0	0-1	2-2
Swindon	2-1	2-0	*	2-0	3-0	2-1	5-0	1-0	1-2	1-0	3-0	1-0	3-3	3-0	4-0	3-0	3-0	1-0	2-2	0-0	0-0	4-0	3-0	2-0
Torquay	4-0	*	1-0	0-0	2-1	3-2	1-2	3-1	1-2	1-0	3-0	3-0	2-0	2-1	3-1	2-2	1-3	2-2	4-0	2-3	3-1	1-0	1-0	1-0
Wimbledon	*	2-0	1-1	1-4	3-1	1-2	3-2	1-2	0-2	0-3	1-1	2-1	1-1	2-1	3-1	1-3	2-5	4-1	4-0	2-3	3-1	1-1	1-2	0-2

Blue Sq Bet Premier results 2011-12

	York	Wrexham	Telford	Tamworth	Stockport	Southport	Newport Co	Mansfield	Luton	Lincoln	Kidderminstr	Kettering	Hayes & Y	Grimsby	Gateshead	Forest G	Fleetwood	Ebbsfleet	Darlington	Cambridge U	Braintree	Bath	Barrow	Alfreton
Alfreton	0-2	1-4	0-0	5-2	6-1	0-0	3-2	3-6	1-0	1-3	0-2	1-1	3-2	2-5	1-1	1-6	1-4	2-2	3-1	2-1	0-1	2-1	2-1	*
Barrow	0-0	3-1	2-1	1-1	1-0	2-2	3-2	2-3	1-0	1-3	3-1	3-0	3-1	2-2	1-2	1-1	4-0	1-1	3-0	3-2	0-4	0-1	*	1-0
Bath	0-1	0-2	3-1	0-2	0-2	1-2	3-2	1-1	1-1	2-1	1-2	0-1	0-1	2-2	4-2	0-2	1-4	2-3	2-0	1-3	1-1	*	0-1	0-3
Braintree	0-1	0-0	2-1	3-1	2-2	0-0	1-0	1-1	3-1	1-0	1-4	2-1	0-3	5-0	3-1	1-5	1-2	2-3	3-1	3-2	*	3-3	1-1	1-2
Cambridge U	0-1	1-1	1-0	0-1	2-2	3-0	1-1	1-2	1-1	2-0	1-2	2-0	2-1	0-1	0-1	1-1	2-0	2-0	2-0	*	2-0	2-0	3-2	3-0
Darlington	2-2	2-4	1-0	2-0	0-1	0-3	2-0	0-2	1-1	3-1	1-0	3-1	3-1	0-0	0-1	0-0	0-1	0-2	*	2-0	1-0	2-2	0-1	1-1
Ebbsfleet	1-2	0-5	3-2	3-0	2-1	1-2	1-1	0-3	0-2	2-3	3-3	1-0	3-1	3-1	0-1	1-1	1-3	*	1-3	0-0	1-1	3-0	1-2	1-2
Fleetwood	1-1	1-1	2-1	3-0	2-1	2-2	1-4	2-3	3-0	2-2	5-2	3-0	1-0	2-1	3-1	0-0	*	6-2	0-0	0-0	1-1	3-0	1-2	4-0
Forest G	0-0	1-0	2-1	3-1	1-1	2-3	1-1	1-1	3-0	0-2	1-1	1-0	1-3	0-1	3-1	*	1-3	6-2	0-0	0-0	0-0	3-0	4-1	4-1
Gateshead	3-2	1-4	3-0	1-1	2-0	2-3	2-3	3-0	3-0	3-3	2-1	2-1	2-0	1-0	*	2-1	0-2	3-1	1-1	1-1	2-2	1-0	5-2	2-0
Grimsby	2-3	1-3	2-0	1-1	7-0	2-3	0-4	1-3	0-5	3-3	1-2	0-0	3-0	*	2-0	2-0	1-3	4-3	1-2	2-1	1-2	6-0	5-2	5-2
Hayes & Y	2-4	0-2	1-0	0-2	1-2	0-2	0-4	1-3	2-2	1-2	1-3	1-0	*	3-0	2-0	1-0	1-3	1-2	3-2	0-0	1-2	1-1	1-1	3-1
Kettering	1-5	0-1	2-1	2-2	1-0	1-1	2-0	0-5	0-5	1-0	0-1	*	6-1	2-1	2-3	1-1	0-2	2-2	3-1	0-0	2-1	1-1	1-2	0-2
Kidderminstr	1-1	0-2	2-2	4-0	1-3	2-0	3-2	0-3	1-1	2-1	*	0-1	3-5	1-1	3-1	1-1	3-1	2-2	3-1	0-1	5-4	4-1	1-2	3-1
Lincoln	0-2	0-1	0-0	4-0	5-0	2-0	0-2	1-0	1-1	*	0-1	0-2	3-5	1-2	1-0	1-1	4-2	3-0	5-0	3-1	3-1	2-0	5-1	0-1
Luton	1-2	1-1	1-1	3-0	5-0	5-1	5-0	0-0	*	1-1	1-3	2-0	4-0	1-1	4-0	1-1	4-2	1-0	2-0	1-2	4-1	2-0	5-1	1-0
Mansfield	1-1	2-0	3-2	1-2	2-1	1-3	5-0	*	1-0	2-1	0-3	3-0	3-2	2-1	4-0	0-0	3-2	0-1	3-2	1-2	4-1	2-0	7-0	3-2
Newport Co	2-1	0-1	0-0	1-2	5-0	0-3	*	1-0	0-1	1-3	1-3	0-0	4-0	0-0	4-0	0-0	4-0	3-3	0-1	1-0	3-4	2-1	2-2	1-0
Southport	1-1	0-1	3-2	2-0	5-0	*	1-1	1-0	0-1	2-2	1-2	3-3	1-2	1-2	1-3	1-3	1-1	3-3	0-0	5-2	0-4	2-1	2-1	2-1
Stockport	1-1	1-0	2-2	0-1	*	0-1	1-1	1-0	0-1	4-0	1-2	1-0	0-1	1-1	2-0	0-1	1-1	1-1	2-0	1-2	3-1	1-1	2-1	0-0
Tamworth	2-1	1-2	0-2	*	2-0	0-1	2-2	1-2	1-1	0-1	2-1	4-0	2-0	1-1	2-0	2-0	0-3	0-2	1-0	2-2	1-0	4-0	2-3	2-2
Telford	0-0	1-0	*	1-0	2-2	0-1	0-0	0-0	0-2	1-2	2-1	3-1	4-1	0-0	2-1	2-0	1-2	1-0	0-0	1-2	6-2	1-0	2-0	1-0
Wrexham	0-3	*	4-0	3-0	2-0	2-0	0-0	1-3	2-0	2-0	2-3	7-0	2-0	2-2	2-1	1-2	2-1	2-2	2-1	2-2	6-2	1-0	2-0	0-1
York	*	0-0	0-1	0-0	2-1	1-2	1-1	2-2	3-0	2-0	0-1	2-0	2-0	2-1	2-1	1-0	2-2	0-1	1-2	2-2	3-2	1-0	3-1	0-1

	Altrincham	B Stortford	Blyth Sp	Boston	Colwyn Bay	Corby	Droylsden	Eastwood	Gainsborough	Gloucester	Guiseley	Halifax	Harrogate	Hinckley	Histon	Hyde	Nuneaton	Solihull M	Stalybridge	Vauxhall M	Worcester	Workington
Altrincham	*	0-2	1-1	1-1	1-6	1-3	3-1	1-6	2-0	1-1	3-2	2-4	3-2	1-4	2-3	2-1	2-1	2-0	5-1	2-2	3-0	1-2
B Stortford	1-0	*	3-3	0-1	4-1	6-1	2-2	3-4	4-2	0-1	4-1	0-1	1-1	1-3	0-2	0-1	2-0	3-1	2-3	4-3	2-1	1-1
Blyth Sp	1-1	3-1	*	1-0	0-2	1-2	3-3	0-0	2-0	4-0	3-0	1-3	0-0	1-3	2-1	0-1	2-3	2-2	1-1	1-2	1-2	0-3
Boston	1-1	0-2	1-1	*	2-2	1-1	2-1	2-1	2-0	4-2	5-0	1-2	0-0	2-2	1-1	0-2	0-0	2-2	3-2	1-2	2-3	2-1
Colwyn Bay	1-6	4-1	0-2	3-2	*	0-2	1-2	4-0	2-0	1-2	1-0	0-2	4-0	2-0	2-1	0-1	1-6	0-0	2-0	0-0	0-2	1-0
Corby	1-3	6-1	4-0	1-2	1-0	*	5-2	3-3	1-3	0-1	0-1	2-4	2-2	0-5	2-3	0-4	0-2	0-3	1-2	1-0	2-3	3-3
Droylsden	3-1	2-2	3-3	2-1	1-2	5-2	*	3-3	1-2	1-2	2-0	2-1	1-1	2-3	2-3	2-3	2-1	1-0	3-3	5-2	2-3	1-1
Eastwood	1-6	3-4	0-0	2-2	0-1	1-4	2-1	*	1-6	2-1	2-2	2-2	2-3	2-5	2-3	0-4	0-5	1-1	0-1	2-4	2-3	3-3
Gainsborough	2-0	4-2	2-0	1-3	2-0	1-0	2-0	1-2	*	1-4	2-0	2-2	0-1	0-3	3-2	2-3	0-5	1-1	0-1	2-4	2-2	0-3
Gloucester	1-1	0-2	4-0	1-3	0-1	0-0	1-3	2-0	0-2	*	1-0	0-1	1-0	2-1	0-1	0-2	1-2	1-0	1-2	1-1	3-1	2-0
Guiseley	3-2	0-1	5-0	2-1	2-0	3-0	4-3	1-2	2-0	3-2	*	3-4	3-1	3-0	2-2	3-2	1-1	0-0	2-2	1-5	4-1	2-1
Halifax	2-4	0-1	3-0	3-2	1-1	2-1	2-1	1-2	2-1	3-4	0-0	*	3-1	6-1	4-0	3-2	0-1	2-1	1-1	4-1	2-1	3-1
Harrogate	3-2	1-1	0-0	0-2	4-0	6-2	0-0	2-1	2-1	2-0	0-1	0-0	*	2-1	0-0	0-3	1-1	1-1	1-1	1-5	0-2	0-1
Hinckley	1-4	1-3	1-3	1-2	3-1	0-3	1-1	4-0	3-0	2-3	2-1	3-2	1-2	*	0-3	0-0	1-2	1-2	5-5	1-2	2-3	4-2
Histon	2-3	2-3	2-2	1-3	0-0	1-1	5-5	3-0	1-1	4-3	2-2	1-4	4-0	2-3	*	1-1	1-1	3-0	0-1	3-3	1-5	2-0
Hyde	2-1	5-0	1-0	4-1	3-2	2-2	4-0	4-1	3-1	0-0	0-1	1-0	3-2	4-0	4-0	*	1-1	3-0	1-1	4-2	2-1	4-0
Nuneaton	2-1	2-0	2-2	2-0	1-1	2-0	2-1	4-0	0-1	0-0	1-1	1-0	2-0	2-5	3-2	2-0	*	0-1	1-2	2-1	3-0	2-1
Solihull M	2-0	3-1	2-2	1-0	1-0	3-1	2-0	0-2	5-3	1-0	0-1	1-2	5-1	1-2	0-2	1-0	0-0	*	1-1	2-3	0-0	2-0
Stalybridge	5-1	2-3	2-0	3-0	0-4	2-2	1-3	2-1	4-0	2-2	0-3	2-1	3-2	4-2	2-0	1-3	4-1	0-0	*	4-2	2-0	1-3
Vauxhall M	2-2	4-3	2-1	0-4	1-0	2-1	1-1	1-2	3-1	0-2	1-1	1-3	0-1	1-2	1-1	0-2	1-2	2-0	1-0	*	3-2	0-1
Worcester	3-0	2-1	2-1	3-0	0-1	0-2	0-2	1-0	2-1	2-1	2-2	1-1	3-2	1-1	1-1	2-2	1-1	2-1	0-0	2-0	*	0-1
Workington	1-2	1-1	2-0	1-2	3-1	1-1	3-1	3-0	0-2	3-0	1-3	1-2	2-1	3-1	0-0	0-3	1-1	1-1	2-5	2-1	0-0	*

	Basingstoke	Boreham Wood	Bromley	Chelmsford	Dartford	Dorchester	Dover	Eastbourne	Eastleigh	Farnborough	Hampton	Havant & W	Maidenhead	Salisbury	Staines	Sutton Utd	Thurrock	Tonbridge	Truro City	Welling	Weston SM	Woking
Basingstoke	*	1-1	1-0	1-1	3-2	1-0	1-1	3-0	1-0	4-3	2-2	3-2	1-3	2-2	1-1	1-2	3-1	0-2	2-1	0-1	4-1	0-3
Boreham Wood	1-1	*	2-1	1-3	3-1	2-2	4-2	1-1	6-1	4-0	2-1	0-1	1-0	1-1	0-2	1-1	2-1	4-2	1-2	2-1	3-0	1-2
Bromley	1-3	4-0	*	1-0	1-2	0-0	0-1	1-3	0-0	1-1	1-2	0-0	0-1	2-2	1-1	3-0	0-0	2-2	1-1	1-1	1-0	2-4
Chelmsford	0-1	0-0	6-1	*	0-0	0-0	2-3	1-0	3-0	2-2	1-0	3-1	2-0	2-3	0-1	2-3	1-0	2-2	0-1	1-2	3-2	2-3
Dartford	4-1	2-2	3-1	0-0	*	1-1	3-1	2-1	3-0	3-0	2-1	3-1	2-1	0-3	0-3	6-1	6-0	3-1	1-2	1-0	1-1	2-3
Dorchester	2-1	0-1	1-1	1-2	1-0	*	1-1	0-3	1-3	3-3	2-1	3-6	4-0	0-3	0-3	0-0	3-0	3-1	2-3	3-2	1-3	0-1
Dover	0-0	0-2	4-1	1-2	1-0	4-0	*	1-1	2-0	0-0	0-1	1-1	2-2	1-1	0-4	0-2	3-1	0-0	3-1	0-1	1-0	0-3
Eastbourne	0-2	3-2	5-0	1-3	0-1	1-4	2-2	*	3-0	1-1	2-0	1-1	2-2	1-3	0-1	0-0	2-1	1-2	2-2	0-3	1-2	2-1
Eastleigh	0-2	2-0	0-2	1-1	2-2	0-1	2-3	2-1	*	0-1	1-1	3-2	4-1	1-1	2-1	4-0	3-2	1-2	3-1	3-0	2-1	0-0
Farnborough	1-0	4-0	2-1	1-3	1-2	1-2	0-2	1-0	1-3	*	0-2	1-0	0-3	1-0	1-0	0-3	0-2	3-2	2-1	1-4	0-1	0-1
Hampton	0-2	0-1	1-2	0-4	1-3	0-2	2-2	3-1	0-4	1-1	*	3-3	0-0	1-2	3-2	0-0	0-2	1-1	4-3	0-2	3-1	1-1
Havant & W	0-1	2-4	1-2	2-3	1-4	3-3	0-1	3-1	0-4	5-0	2-2	*	2-1	2-1	3-2	2-2	3-0	1-1	4-1	1-2	1-1	3-4
Maidenhead	1-1	0-3	3-3	1-1	1-1	0-1	1-4	1-0	4-3	3-4	0-2	2-0	*	0-1	1-1	4-0	4-0	0-4	1-3	0-4	1-3	0-1
Salisbury	1-1	0-2	0-2	0-1	1-2	0-1	0-1	3-0	2-0	1-3	4-2	4-1	0-2	*	1-0	3-1	1-1	2-0	2-1	0-0	0-0	2-0
Staines	0-2	2-1	4-1	1-1	1-4	0-2	0-3	1-2	2-2	1-2	1-4	1-1	0-0	0-1	*	3-1	2-3	1-1	1-1	4-2	2-1	0-1
Sutton Utd	1-0	2-1	1-1	3-2	0-1	3-1	0-0	2-2	2-0	2-0	2-2	2-0	0-0	5-0	1-0	*	1-1	0-1	2-2	4-3	3-2	0-5
Thurrock	1-2	1-0	1-1	0-2	0-3	2-0	0-4	1-4	1-3	0-1	0-2	0-0	1-1	1-1	1-2	0-1	*	0-0	1-1	1-4	0-3	1-1
Tonbridge	2-3	1-1	1-1	0-0	0-1	2-1	2-3	5-1	4-0	1-5	1-0	1-2	1-0	3-1	3-2	1-4	3-2	*	3-0	1-1	3-0	3-6
Truro City	2-5	2-1	1-2	0-2	0-1	2-1	1-0	0-2	2-1	8-2	3-3	0-1	1-2	2-2	2-1	0-3	3-0	2-0	*	2-3	0-1	1-4
Welling	1-1	2-0	2-1	1-1	3-2	3-0	0-0	3-0	0-1	1-0	2-1	3-1	4-0	4-3	1-1	0-0	1-0	3-2	5-1	*	2-0	3-2
Weston SM	2-1	4-1	0-3	1-2	0-4	0-2	1-1	1-1	2-1	5-2	1-2	3-1	4-2	2-0	2-1	0-0	2-2	2-2	0-1	2-0	*	0-3
Woking	1-0	0-0	3-2	1-1	1-0	4-1	3-1	3-1	1-0	1-0	2-1	3-0	0-2	0-0	0-1	4-1	5-1	2-1	3-3	2-1	4-1	*

Scottish Premier League results 2011-12

(home) \ (away)	Aberdeen	Celtic	Dundee Utd	Dunfermline	Hearts	Hibernian	Inverness	Kilmarnock	Motherwell	Rangers	St Johnstone	St Mirren
Aberdeen	* *	1-1 0-1	3-1 3-1	1-0 4-0	0-0	1-0 1-2	2-1 0-1	0-0 2-2	1-2	1-2	0-0 0-0	2-2 0-0
Celtic	2-1	*	5-1 2-1	2-1 2-0	1-0 5-0	0-0	1-0 2-0	2-1	1-0 4-0	1-0 3-0	0-1 2-0	1-0 5-0
Dundee Utd	1-2	0-1 1-0	*	0-1 3-0	1-0 2-2	3-1	3-1 3-0	1-1 4-0	1-1 1-3	2-1 0-1	0-0	1-1 0-0
Dunfermline	3-3 3-0	0-3	1-4	*	1-0 0-2	2-3 2-0	3-3 1-1	1-1 1-2	2-4 0-2	1-4 0-4	0-3	1-1 0-0
Hearts	3-0 3-0	2-0 0-4	0-2 0-1	4-0	*	2-0 2-0	2-1	0-1	2-0 0-1	0-2 0-3	1-2 2-0	5-2 2-0
Hibernian	0-0 0-0	0-2 0-5	0-2 3-3	0-1 4-0	1-3	*	1-1	1-1 0-1	0-1 1-1	0-2	2-3 3-2	1-2 0-0
Inverness	2-1 0-2	0-2	2-3	1-1 0-0	1-0 1-1	0-1 2-3	*	2-1 1-1	2-3	0-2 1-4	0-1	0-2 2-1
Kilmarnock	2-0 1-1	0-6 3-3	1-1	0-3 3-2	1-0 0-0	1-3 4-1	3-6 4-3	*	2-3	1-0	0-0 1-2	2-1 0-2
Motherwell	1-0 1-0	1-2 0-3	0-0 0-2	3-1	1-0 3-0	4-3	0-1 3-0	0-0	*	0-3 1-2	3-2 0-3	1-1
Rangers	1-2	4-2 3-2	3-1 5-0	2-1	1-1 1-2	4-0 1-0	2-1	0-1 2-0	3-0 0-0	*	0-0	3-1 1-1
St Johnstone	1-2	0-2	3-3 1-5	0-1 3-1	2-1 2-0	3-1	0-0 2-0	2-0	0-3	1-2 0-2	*	0-1
St Mirren	1-1 1-0	0-2 0-2	2-2	2-1 4-4	0-0	2-3 1-0	1-2 0-1	4-2 3-0	0-1 0-0	2-1	0-3 0-0	*

Scottish Division One results 2011-12

(home) \ (away)	Ayr	Dundee	Falkirk	Hamilton	Livingston	Morton	Partick	Queen of Sth	Raith	Ross County
Ayr	*	3-2 1-3	2-2 1-0	1-2 2-2	3-1	0-0	1-3	1-1	2-1 1-1	1-3 2-3
Dundee	1-1	*	3-1 4-2	2-2 0-1	3-0 1-0	0-1	0-3	1-1	1-1 1-0	1-2 1-1
Falkirk	0-0	2-1 1-1	*	3-0 0-0	2-5 4-3	1-0	2-1	3-0	2-3 2-0	1-1 2-0
Hamilton	3-2	1-6 3-1	0-1	*	1-1	4-3 0-1	2-2 3-1	3-0 3-1	2-2 4-0	5-1 0-2
Livingston	0-1	4-2 2-3	1-2 1-1	1-0 0-4	*	0-0	3-1 1-0	2-2 2-1	1-1 1-3	1-3 0-3
Morton	3-1	0-2 1-2	0-0 3-2	1-0 0-2	2-1 1-3	*	1-0 1-2	2-1 1-0	1-1 0-1	1-1 0-2
Partick	4-0	0-1 0-0	1-1 2-2	1-1 2-0	2-1 2-3	0-0	*	0-5	1-0 1-3	1-1 0-1
Queen of Sth	4-1	1-1 0-0	0-0 1-5	1-2 1-0	0-4 0-2	2-1	0-5	*	1-3 1-0	0-1 3-5
Raith	2-2	0-1 0-1	1-0 2-2	2-1 3-2	0-3 1-0	1-1	4-1 5-0	3-1	*	1-1 0-1
Ross County	1-1	3-0 1-1	2-1 3-1	5-1 1-0	3-0 1-1	0-0	2-2	2-0 2-1	4-2 1-1	*

Scottish Division Two results 2011-12

	Airdrie	Albion	Arbroath	Brechin	Cowdenbeath	Dumbarton	East Fife	Forfar	Stenhousemuir	Stirling
Airdrie	*	1-0	4-0	4-1	1-5	3-0	2-0	3-0	0-3	4-1
Albion	0-1	*	6-1	1-2	3-3	1-1	1-1	1-0	1-1	0-1
Arbroath	3-1	6-2	*	1-1	1-1	2-0	3-0	0-1	0-2	4-2
Brechin	1-1	2-1	1-4	*	2-2	3-3	1-3	2-1	2-0	1-2
Cowdenbeath	2-0	1-0	2-1	3-1	*	4-1	0-4	2-0	0-0	4-1
Dumbarton	2-1	1-2	2-1	1-0	0-4	*	4-0	1-1	0-2	1-5
East Fife	2-0	4-0	2-0	1-1	0-1	0-6	*	4-0	1-3	1-0
Forfar	3-2	1-2	0-2	4-1	2-2	0-2	1-4	*	2-3	4-3
Stenhousemuir	0-3	1-2	3-0	2-1	3-1	1-2	3-2	2-3	*	4-0
Stirling	1-4	2-2	3-0	2-3	0-2	1-2	1-0	2-4	3-1	*

Scottish Division Three results 2011-12

	Alloa	Annan	Berwick	Clyde	E Stirling	Elgin	Montrose	Peterhead	Queen's Park	Stranraer
Alloa	*	1-0	0-1	2-2	5-1	8-1	2-0	2-1	1-0	3-1
Annan	2-0	*	1-1	1-0	2-2	1-1	2-1	0-3	5-2	1-3
Berwick	5-0	1-3	*	0-2	4-2	3-3	2-2	2-1	1-4	2-2
Clyde	1-1	1-1	1-4	*	3-0	0-2	1-0	2-1	1-2	2-1
E Stirling	1-3	1-0	2-1	0-1	*	2-2	2-1	0-2	1-2	2-2
Elgin	3-0	1-2	4-1	4-0	2-0	*	3-0	6-3	2-0	1-1
Montrose	1-1	1-1	1-1	3-5	3-1	3-0	*	6-1	3-1	0-6
Peterhead	0-1	2-3	3-2	1-0	1-0	3-0	2-1	*	2-1	1-1
Queen's Park	1-2	2-0	1-1	3-0	5-1	6-0	5-0	1-1	*	2-0
Stranraer	2-3	4-2	2-1	1-0	6-0	5-2	3-1	0-3	2-3	*

X = Score draw = 0-0 draw v = Void match * = Pools panel

Pools No	August 6 13 20 27	September 3 10 17 24	October 1 8 15 22 29	November 5 12 19 26	December 3 10 17 26 31	January 7 14 21 28	February 4 11 18 25	March 3 10 17 24 31	April 7 14 21 28	May 5 12	0	X
1											2	8
2											4	5
3											3	7
4											3	11
5											3	10
6											5	9
7											3	10
8											7	7
9											2	6
10											3	6
11											6	9
12											5	8
13											5	6
14											3	7
15											2	6
16											2	6
17											-	4
18											7	8
19											2	4
20											3	5
21											3	10
22											2	9

FA Cup first round
November 11 2011
Cambridge U ...... 2-2 ...... Wrexham
November 12 2011
AFC Totton ...... 8-1 ...... Bradford PA
Alfreton ...... 0-4 ...... Carlisle
Barrow ...... 1-2 ...... Rotherham
Blyth Sptns ...... 0-2 ...... Gateshead
Bournemouth ...... 3-3 ...... Gillingham
Bradford ...... 1-0 ...... Rochdale
Brentford ...... 1-0 ...... Basingstoke
Bristol R ...... 3-1 ...... Corby
Bury ...... 0-2 ...... Crawley
Chelmsford ...... 4-0 ...... Telford
Chesterfield ...... 1-3 ...... Torquay
Crewe ...... 1-4 ...... Colchester
Dagenham & R ...... 1-1 ...... Bath City
E Thurrock ...... 0-3 ...... Macclesfield
Exeter ...... 1-1 ...... Walsall
Fleetwood ...... 2-0 ...... Wycombe
Hartlepool ...... 0-1 ...... Stevenage
Hereford ...... 0-3 ...... Yeovil
Hinckley Utd ...... 2-2 ...... Tamworth
Leyton Orient ...... 3-0 ...... Bromley
Luton ...... 1-0 ...... Northampton
MK Dons ...... 6-0 ...... Nantwich Town
Maidenhead ...... 1-1 ...... Aldershot
Newport Co ...... 0-1 ...... Shrewsbury
Notts Co ...... 4-1 ...... Accrington
Oldham ...... 3-1 ...... Burton
Plymouth ...... 3-3 ...... Stourbridge
Port Vale ...... 0-0 ...... Grimsby
Preston ...... 0-0 ...... Southend
Redbridge ...... 0-0 ...... Oxford C
Salisbury ...... 3-1 ...... Arlesey
Sheff Utd ...... 3-0 ...... Oxford
Southport ...... 1-2 ...... Barnet
Sutton Utd ...... 1-0 ...... Kettering
Swindon ...... 4-1 ...... Huddersfield
Tranmere ...... 0-1 ...... Cheltenham
Wimbledon ...... 0-0 ...... Scunthorpe
November 13 2011
Halifax ...... 0-4 ...... Charlton
Morecambe ...... 1-2 ...... Sheff Wed

FA Cup first-round replays
November 22 2011
Aldershot ...... 2-0 ...... Maidenhead
Gillingham ...... 3-2 ...... Bournemouth
Grimsby ...... 1-0 ...... Port Vale
Oxford C ...... 1-2 ...... Redbridge
Scunthorpe ...... 0-1 ...... Wimbledon
Southend ...... 1-0 ...... Preston
Stourbridge ...... 2-0 ...... Plymouth
Tamworth ...... 1-0 ...... Hinckley Utd
Wrexham ...... 2-1 ...... Cambridge U
November 23 2011
Bath City ...... 1-3 ...... Dagenham & R
Walsall ...... 3-2 ...... Exeter

FA Cup second round
December 2 2011
Fleetwood ...... 2-2 ...... Yeovil
December 3 2011
Barnet ...... 1-3 ...... MK Dons
Bradford ...... 3-1 ...... Wimbledon
Brentford ...... 0-1 ...... Wrexham
Charlton ...... 2-0 ...... Carlisle
Chelmsford ...... 1-1 ...... Macclesfield
Colchester ...... 0-1 ...... Swindon

Crawley ...... 5-0 ...... Redbridge
Dagenham & R ...... 1-1 ...... Walsall
Gateshead ...... 1-2 ...... Tamworth
Leyton Orient ...... 0-1 ...... Gillingham
Luton ...... 2-4 ...... Cheltenham
Salisbury ...... 0-0 ...... Grimsby
Sheff Utd ...... 3-2 ...... Torquay
Sheff Wed ...... 1-0 ...... Aldershot
Shrewsbury ...... 2-1 ...... Rotherham
Southend ...... 1-1 ...... Oldham
Stourbridge ...... 0-3 ...... Stevenage
December 4 2011
AFC Totton ...... 1-6 ...... Bristol R
Sutton Utd ...... 0-2 ...... Notts Co

FA Cup second-round replays
December 13 2011
Grimsby ...... 2-3 ...... Salisbury
Oldham ...... 1-0 ...... Southend
Walsall ...... 0-0 ...... Dagenham & R
Yeovil ...... 0-2 ...... Fleetwood
December 14 2011
Macclesfield ...... 1-0 ...... Chelmsford

FA Cup third round
January 6 2012
Liverpool ...... 5-1 ...... Oldham
January 7 2012
Barnsley ...... 2-4 ...... Swansea
Birmingham ...... 0-0 ...... Wolves
Brighton ...... 1-1 ...... Wrexham
Bristol R ...... 1-3 ...... Aston Villa
Coventry ...... 1-2 ...... Southampton
Crawley ...... 1-0 ...... Bristol C
Dagenham & R ...... 0-0 ...... Millwall
Derby ...... 1-0 ...... C Palace
Doncaster ...... 0-2 ...... Notts Co
Everton ...... 2-0 ...... Tamworth
Fleetwood ...... 1-5 ...... Blackpool
Fulham ...... 4-0 ...... Charlton
Gillingham ...... 1-3 ...... Stoke
Hull ...... 3-1 ...... Ipswich
MK Dons ...... 1-1 ...... QPR
Macclesfield ...... 2-2 ...... Bolton
Middlesbrough ...... 1-0 ...... Shrewsbury
Newcastle ...... 2-1 ...... Blackburn
Norwich ...... 4-1 ...... Burnley
Nottm Forest ...... 0-0 ...... Leicester
Reading ...... 0-1 ...... Stevenage
Sheff Utd ...... 3-1 ...... Salisbury
Swindon ...... 2-1 ...... Wigan
Tottenham ...... 3-0 ...... Cheltenham
Watford ...... 4-2 ...... Bradford
West Brom ...... 4-2 ...... Cardiff
January 8 2012
Chelsea ...... 4-0 ...... Portsmouth
Man City ...... 2-3 ...... Man Utd
Peterborough ...... 0-2 ...... Sunderland
Sheff Wed ...... 1-0 ...... West Ham
January 9 2012
Arsenal ...... 1-0 ...... Leeds

FA Cup third-round replays
January 17 2012
Bolton ...... 2-0 ...... Macclesfield
Leicester ...... 4-0 ...... Nottm Forest
Millwall ...... 5-0 ...... Dagenham & R
QPR ...... 1-0 ...... MK Dons
January 18 2012
Wolves ...... 0-1 ...... Birmingham

Wrexham ....1-1...........................Brighton

FA Cup fourth round
January 27 2012
Everton............................2-1..............................Fulham
Watford............................0-1...........................Tottenham
January 28 2012
Blackpool........................1-1........................Sheff Wed
Bolton.............................2-1...........................Swansea
Brighton ....1-0.........................Newcastle
Derby ....0-2...............................Stoke
Hull................................0-1...........................Crawley
Leicester ....2-0..........................Swindon
Liverpool ....2-1...........................Man Utd
Millwall ....1-1....................Southampton
QPR................................0-1...........................Chelsea
Sheff Utd ....0-4......................Birmingham
Stevenage ....1-0..........................Notts Co
West Brom ....1-2...........................Norwich
January 29 2012
Arsenal............................3-2......................Aston Villa
Sunderland ....1-1....................Middlesbrough

FA Cup fourth-round replays
February 7 2012
Sheff Wed ....0-3..........................Blackpool
Southampton...................2-3.............................Millwall
February 8 2012
Middlesbrough ....1-2.........................Sunderland

FA Cup fifth round
February 18 2012
Chelsea ....1-1......................Birmingham
Everton............................2-0..........................Blackpool
Millwall ....0-2.............................Bolton
Norwich ....1-2..........................Leicester
Sunderland ....2-0............................Arsenal
February 19 2012
Crawley ....0-2...............................Stoke
Liverpool ....6-1...........................Brighton
Stevenage ....0-0.........................Tottenham

FA Cup fifth-round replays
March 6 2012
Birmingham.....................0-2...........................Chelsea
March 7 2012
Tottenham ....3-1.........................Stevenage

FA Cup sixth round
March 17 2012
Everton............................1-1.......................Sunderland
March 18 2012
Chelsea ....5-2..........................Leicester
Liverpool ....2-1...............................Stoke

FA Cup sixth round-replays
March 27 2012
Sunderland ....0-2............................Everton
Tottenham ....3-1.............................Bolton

FA Cup semi-finals
April 14 2012
Liverpool ....2-1............................Everton
April 15 2012
Tottenham ....1-5...........................Chelsea

FA Cup final
May 5 2012
Chelsea ....2-1..........................Liverpool

League Cup qualifying round
July 29 2011
Crawley ....3-2......................Wimbledon

League Cup first round
August 9 2011
Accrington ....0-2......................Scunthorpe
Barnsley..........................0-2.......................Morecambe
Bournemouth...................5-0...............Dagenham & R
Brighton ....1-0..........................Gillingham
Burnley............................6-3..............................Burton
Bury ....3-1...........................Coventry
Cheltenham ....1-4..........................MK Dons
Derby ....2-3.....................Shrewsbury
Doncaster ....3-0.........................Tranmere
Exeter.............................2-0...............................Yeovil
Hartlepool ....1-1.........................Sheff Utd
Hereford ....1-0..........................Brentford
Hull................................0-2.......................Macclesfield
Ipswich...........................1-2.....................Northampton
Leeds ....3-2...........................Bradford
Nottm Forest ....3-3...........................Notts Co
Oldham ....1-1.............................Carlisle
Plymouth ....0-1.............................Millwall
Port Vale.........................2-4.....................Huddersfield
Portsmouth......................0-1...............................Barnet
Preston...........................3-2...............................Crewe
Rochdale ....3-2......................Chesterfield
Rotherham ....1-4..........................Leicester
Southampton....................4-1............................Torquay
Southend ....1-1.................Leyton Orient
Stevenage ....3-4.....................Peterborough
Walsall ....0-3....................Middlesbrough
Wycombe.........................3-3.......................Colchester
August 10 2011
Oxford ....1-3.............................Cardiff
August 11 2011
Sheff Wed ....0-0..........................Blackpool
August 23 2011
Bristol R ....1-1...........................Watford
C Palace..........................2-0...........................Crawley
Charlton..........................2-1...........................Reading
August 24 2011
Bristol C ....0-1..........................Swindon
West Ham ....1-2.........................Aldershot

League Cup second round
August 23 2011
Aston Villa ....2-0...........................Hereford
Bournemouth...................1-4.......................West Brom
Brighton ....1-0.......................Sunderland
Burnley............................3-2..............................Barnet
Bury ....2-4..........................Leicester
Cardiff ....5-3.....................Huddersfield
Doncaster ....1-2..............................Leeds
Millwall ....2-0.......................Morecambe
Northampton...................0-4............................Wolves
Norwich ....0-4..........................MK Dons
QPR................................0-2.........................Rochdale
Shrewsbury ....3-1.........................Swansea
Wycombe.........................1-4..................Nottm Forest
August 24 2011
Blackburn........................3-1........................Sheff Wed
Bolton.............................2-1......................Macclesfield
Everton............................3-1..........................Sheff Utd
Exeter.............................1-3..........................Liverpool
Peterborough...................0-2....................Middlesbrough

August 25 2011
Scunthorpe ....1-2 ....Newcastle
August 30 2011
Aldershot ....2-0.............................Carlisle
Leyton Orient ....3-2............................Bristol R
Swindon..........................1-3....................Southampton
September 13 2011
C Palace..........................2-1 ....Wigan
Charlton ....0-2 ....Preston

League Cup third round
September 20 2011
Aldershot ....2-1 ....Rochdale
Arsenal............................3-1 ....Shrewsbury
Aston Villa ....0-2 ....Bolton
Blackburn........................3-2....................Leyton Orient
Burnley............................2-1 ....MK Dons
C Palace...........................2-1 ....Middlesbrough
Leeds ....0-3 ....Man Utd
Nottm Forest ....3-4 ....Newcastle
Stoke ....0-0 ....Tottenham
Stoke won 7-6 on penalties
Wolves ....5-0 ....Millwall
September 21 2011
Brighton ....1-2 ....Liverpool
Cardiff ....2-2 ....Leicester
Chelsea ....0-0 ....Fulham
Chelsea won 4-3 on penalties
Everton............................2-1 ....West Brom
Man City..........................2-0 ....Birmingham
Southampton...................2-1 ....Preston

League Cup fourth round
October 25 2011
Aldershot ....0-3 ....Man Utd
Arsenal............................2-1 ....Bolton
C Palace...........................2-0 ....Southampton
Cardiff ....1-0 ....Burnley
October 26 2011
Blackburn........................4-3 ....Newcastle
Everton............................1-2 ....Chelsea
Stoke ....1-2 ....Liverpool
Wolves ....2-5 ....Man City

League Cup quarter-finals
November 29 2011
Arsenal............................0-1 ....Man City
Cardiff ....2-0 ....Blackburn
Chelsea ....0-2 ....Liverpool
November 30 2011
Man Utd...........................1-2 ....C Palace

League Cup semi-finals
January 10 2012
C Palace...........................1-0 ....Cardiff
January 11 2012
Man City..........................0-1 ....Liverpool
January 24 2012
Cardiff ....1-0 ....C Palace
Cardiff won 3-1 on penalties
January 25 2012
Liverpool ....2-2 ....Man City
Liverpool won 3-2 on aggregate

League Cup final
February 26 2012
Liverpool ....2-2 ....Cardiff
Liverpool won 3-2 on penalties

JP Trophy Southern Section first round
August 30 2011
Bournemouth...................4-1...........................Hereford
Cheltenham ....2-1 ....Torquay
Colchester ....1-3 ....Barnet
Exeter..............................1-1 ....Plymouth
MK Dons ....3-3 ....Brentford
Southend ....1-0 ....Crawley
September 6 2011
Wycombe.........................3-1 ....Bristol R
September 7 2011
Leyton Orient...................1-1 ....Dagenham & R

JP Trophy Southern Section second round
October 4 2011
Aldershot ....1-2 ....Oxford
Bournemouth...................3-2 ....Yeovil
Dagenham & R ....1-3 ....Southend
Exeter..............................1-2 ....Swindon
Gillingham ....1-3 ....Barnet
Wimbledon ....2-2 ....Stevenage
Wycombe.........................1-3 ....Cheltenham
October 5 2011
Charlton ....0-3 ....Brentford

JP Trophy Southern Section quarter-finals
November 8 2011
Brentford ....6-0...................Bournemouth
Cheltenham ....0-2 ....Barnet
Oxford ....0-1 ....Southend
Swindon..........................1-1 ....Wimbledon
Swindon won 3-1 on penalties

JP Trophy Southern Section semi-finals
December 6 2011
Southend ....1-2 ....Swindon
Barnet ....0-0 ....Brentford
Barnet won 5-3 on penalties

JP Trophy Southern Section final
January 10 2012
Barnet ....1-1 ....Swindon
February 7 2012
Swindon..........................1-0 ....Barnet
Swindon won 2-1 on aggregate

JP Trophy Northern Section first Round
August 30 2011
Bradford ....0-0 ....Sheff Wed
Burton ....1-2 ....Sheff Utd
Bury ....0-0 ....Crewe
Northampton ....1-2 ....Huddersfield
Scunthorpe ....2-0 ....Hartlepool
Tranmere ....1-1 ....Port Vale
Walsall.............................2-1 ....Shrewsbury
September 6 2011
Accrington ....3-2.............................Carlisle

JP Trophy Northern Section second round
October 4 2011
Huddersfield ....2-2.............................Bradford
Morecambe ....2-2 ....Preston
Notts Co...........................1-3 ....Chesterfield
Rochdale ....1-1 ....Walsall
Rotherham ....1-2 ....Sheff Utd
Scunthorpe ....0-1 ....Oldham

October 5 2011
Crewe................................1-0....................Macclesfield

JP Trophy Northern Section quarter-finals
November 8 2011
Oldham ....3-1 ....Crewe
Rochdale ....1-1 ....Preston
Preston won 4-2 on penalties

November 9 2011
Chesterfield ....4-3 ....Tranmere

JP Trophy Northern Section semi-finals
December 6 2011
Oldham ....2-0....................Bradford
Preston...........................1-1 ....Chesterfield
Chesterfield won 4-2 on penalties

JP Trophy Northern Section final
January 18 2012
Chesterfield ....2-1 ....Oldham
January 30 2012
Oldham ....0-1 ....Chesterfield
Chesterfield won 3-1 on aggregate

Johnstone's Paint Trophy final
March 25 2012
Chesterfield ....2-0..........................Swindon

FA Trophy first round
December 10 2011
Alfreton.............................4-0......................Southport
Barrow ....3-2 ....Harrogate T
Boreham W ....0-1 ....Cambridge U
Boston Utd.......................2-1 ....Hyde
Brackley...........................0-3 ....Dartford
Carshalton ....5-0 ....Bishop's St.
Chelmsford ....2-3 ....Bath City
Colwyn Bay ....1-3 ....Lincoln
Didcot Town ....0-1 ....Basingstoke
Droylsden ....2-1 ....Mansfield
E Thurrock ....2-1 ....Welling
Gateshead.......................3-2 ....Kettering
Gosport Bor ....0-1 ....Braintree
Grimsby ....3-0 ....Darlington
Guiseley ....2-0 ....FC Utd
Hampton & R....................2-0 ....Hayes & Y
Hornchurch ....0-0 ....Farnborough
Luton ....2-0 ....Swindon Sup.
Newport Co ....0-0 ....Forest Green
Northwich.........................3-1 ....Fleetwood
Nth Ferriby ....1-5 ....Chester
Salisbury ....4-1 ....Lowestoft T
Staines............................0-0 ....Maidenhead
Stockport ....2-2 ....Stalybridge
Truro City ....2-5 ....Ebbsfleet
Vauxhall M ....4-4 ....Kidderminster
Wealdstone ....5-0 ....Uxbridge
Weymouth ....2-1 ....Chippenham
Worksop...........................1-0 ....Tamworth
Wrexham ....1-2 ....Hinckley Utd
York ....2-2 ....Solihull Moors
December 11 2011
Nuneaton.........................0-2 ....Telford

FA Trophy first-round replays
December 13 2011
Forest Green ....0-2 ....Newport Co
Kidderminster ....2-0 ....Vauxhall M
Maidenhead.....................1-2 ....Staines
Solihull Moors ....0-3 ....York
Stalybridge......................2-1 ....Stockport

December 14 2011
Farnborough ....2-3 ....Hornchurch

FA Trophy second round
January 14 2012
Bath City ....1-0 ....Basingstoke
Cambridge U ....4-1 ....Telford
Dartford ....4-2 ....Boston Utd
E Thurrock ....1-1 ....Hampton & R
Ebbsfleet ....3-2 ....Chester
Gateshead ....2-2 ....Braintree
Grimsby ....4-0 ....Hornchurch
Guiseley ....2-0 ....Stalybridge
Kidderminster ....5-1 ....Droylsden
Lincoln ....0-0 ....Carshalton
Northwich.........................0-0 ....Staines
Salisbury ....2-6 ....York
Wealdstone ....2-1 ....Barrow
Weymouth ....0-6 ....Alfreton
January 17 2012
Braintree ....1-1 ....Gateshead
January 18 2012
Hinckley Utd ....0-0 ....Luton

FA Trophy second-round replays
January 18 2012
Carshalton ....3-1 ....Lincoln
January 23 2012
Luton ....3-0 ....Hinckley Utd
January 24 2012
Worksop...........................1-3 ....Newport Co
January 31 2012
Hampton & R....................4-1 ....E Thurrock

FA Trophy third round
February 7 2012
Bath City ....1-2 ....Grimsby
Kidderminster ....1-2 ....Luton
Newport Co ....4-0 ....Carshalton
February 14 2012
Dartford ....2-2 ....Wealdstone
Gateshead ....2-1 ....Alfreton
Northwich.........................4-1 ....Hampton & R
York ....1-0 ....Ebbsfleet

FA Trophy third-round replays
February 21 2012
Cambridge U ....1-0 ....Guiseley
Wealdstone ....1-0 ....Dartford

FA Trophy fourth round
February 25 2012
Cambridge U ....1-2 ....Wealdstone
Grimsby ....0-1 ....York
Luton ....2-0 ....Gateshead
Northwich.........................2-3 ....Newport Co

FA Trophy semi-finals
March 10 2012
Newport Co ....3-1 ....Wealdstone
York ....1-0 ....Luton
March 17 2012
Luton ....1-1 ....York
York won 2-1 on aggregate
Wealdstone ....0-0 ....Newport Co
Newport won 3-1 on aggregate

FA Trophy final
May 12 2012
Newport Co ....0-2 ....York

Scottish Cup first round
September 24 2011

Rothes ....0-3 ....Clachnacuddin
Edinburgh City................3-0 ....Brora Rangers
Nairn County ....2-1 ....Selkirk
Fraserburgh ....4-3 ....Civil Service
Wigtown & B ....2-0 ....Preston Athletic
Lossiemouth ....1-2 ....Auchinleck
Huntly..............................6-1 ....Newton Stewart
Forres Mechanics ....2-2 ....Irvine
Dalbeattie Star ....1-6 ....Inverurie Locos
Wick ....9-1 ....Coldstream
Glasgow University ....0-4 ....Cove Rangers
Vale of Leithen ....1-0 ....Girvan
Gala Fairydean ....8-1 ....Hawick Royal
Culter ....4-0 ....Burntisland
Edinburgh University ....0-3 ....Whitehill Welfare
St Cuthbert Wanderers ....0-2.............................Keith

October 1 2011

Fort William ....0-4 ....Boness United

Scottish Cup first-round replay
October 1 2011

Irvine ....6-3 ....Forres Mechanics

Scottish Cup second round
October 22 2011

Alloa ....2-2 ....Annan
Auchinleck.......................8-1 ....Threave Rovers
Boness Utd ....2-1 ....Whitehill W
Clachnacuddin ....1-1 ....Inverurie Locos
Culter ....0-2 ....Spartans
Deveronvale....................4-0 ....Berwick
Edinburgh C ....0-1 ....Irvine
Fraserburgh ....0-0 ....Elgin City
Gala Fairydean ....5-2 ....Golspie
Huntly..............................0-3 ....Queen's Park
Montrose ....2-1 ....Clyde
Peterhead ....2-0 ....Nairn County
Vale of Leithen ....3-2 ....Cove Rangers
Wick Academy ....0-1 ....Keith
Wigtown & B ....0-9 ....Stranraer

October 23 2011

East Stirling ....1-1 ....Buckie Thistle

Scottish Cup second-round replays
October 29 2011

Annan...............................2-0 ....Alloa
Buckie Thistle ....2-4 ....East Stirling
Elgin City ....5-2 ....Fraserburgh
Inverurie Locos ....3-2 ....Clachnacuddin

Scottish Cup third round
November 19 2011

Airdrie Utd.......................11-0 ....Gala Fairydean
Auchinleck.......................3-1 ....Vale of Leithen
Ayr ....2-2 ....Montrose
Boness Utd ....0-3 ....Cowdenbeath
Brechin.............................3-0 ....Dumbarton
Culter ....1-1 ....Partick
East Fife...........................5-0 ....East Stirling
Elgin City ....1-1 ....Queen's Park
Inverurie Locos ....2-4 ....Peterhead
Irvine ....0-6 ....Livingston
Keith ....0-1 ....Arbroath

Morton ....5-1 ....Deveronvale
Ross County ....4-0 ....Albion
Stenhousemuir ....4-0 ....Annan
Stirling ....1-2 ....Dundee
Stranraer ....1-1 ....Forfar

Scottish Cup third-round replays
November 22 2011

Montrose ....1-2 ....Ayr

November 26 2011

Forfar ....3-0 ....Stranraer
Partick ....4-0 ....Culter
Queen's Park ....3-1 ....Elgin City

Scottish Cup fourth round
January 7 2012

Airdrie Utd ....2-6 ....Dundee Utd
Cowdenbeath ....2-3 ....Hibernian
Dundee ....1-1 ....Kilmarnock
Falkirk ....2-0 ....East Fife
Forfar ....0-4 ....Aberdeen
Hearts ....1-0 ....Auchinleck
Inverness CT ....1-1 ....Dunfermline
Livingston........................1-2 ....Ayr
Motherwell ....4-0 ....Queen's Park
Partick ....0-1 ....Queen of Sth
Raith ....1-2 ....Morton
Ross County ....7-0 ....Stenhousemuir
St Johnstone ....2-1 ....Brechin
St Mirren ....0-0 ....Hamilton

January 8 2012

Arbroath ....0-4 ....Rangers
Peterhead ....0-3 ....Celtic

Scottish Cup fourth-round replays
January 17 2012

Hamilton...........................0-1 ....St Mirren
Kilmarnock......................2-1 ....Dundee

January 18 2012

Dunfermline ....1-3 ....Inverness CT

Scottish Cup fifth round
February 4 2012

Aberdeen ....1-1 ....Queen of Sth
Hibernian ....1-0 ....Kilmarnock
Inverness CT ....0-2 ....Celtic
Motherwell ....6-0 ....Morton
St Mirren ....1-1 ....Ross County

February 5 2012

Hearts ....1-1 ....St Johnstone
Rangers ....0-2 ....Dundee Utd

Scottish Cup fifth-round replays
February 14 2012

Queen of Sth ....1-2 ....Aberdeen
Ross County ....1-2 ....St Mirren
St Johnstone ....1-2 ....Hearts

February 15 2012

Ayr ....2-1 ....Falkirk

Scottish Cup quarter-finals
March 10 2012

Ayr ....0-2 ....Hibernian
Hearts ....2-2 ....St Mirren

March 11 2012

Dundee Utd ....0-4 ....Celtic
Motherwell ....1-2.........................Aberdeen

Scottish Cup quarter-final replay
March 21 2012

St Mirren ....0-2 ....Hearts

Scottish Cup semi-finals
April 14 2012

Aberdeen ....1-2 ....Hibernian
April 15 2012

Celtic ....1-2 ....Hearts

Scottish Cup final
May 19 2012

Hibernian ....1-5 ....Hearts

Scottish League Cup first round
July 30 2011

Airdrie Utd ....5-0 ....Stirling
Albion................................2-4 ....Falkirk
Alloa.................................0-3 ....Morton
Annan................................1-2.................Dunfermline
Brechin..............................2-4 ....Clyde
Cowdenbeath ....2-2 ....Stenhousemuir
Dumbarton.........................0-4 ....Dundee
East Fife............................2-1 ....Elgin City
East Stirling ....0-3 ....Ayr
Forfar ....2-0 ....Peterhead
Livingston..........................6-0............................Arbroath
Montrose ....1-4.................................Raith
Partick ....1-3 ....Berwick
Queen of Sth ....2-1 ....Stranraer
Ross County ....2-1....................Queen's Park

Scottish League Cup second round
August 23 2011

Aberdeen ....1-0 ....Dundee
Airdrie Utd ....2-0.................................Raith
East Fife............................2-1 ....Dunfermline
Hamilton............................1-2 ....Ross County
Hibernian ....5-0 ....Berwick
Morton ....3-4 ....St Mirren
Queen of Sth ....3-0 ....Forfar
August 24 2011

Ayr ....1-0 ....Inverness CT
Clyde ....0-4 ....Motherwell
Falkirk ....3-1 ....Stenhousemuir
St Johnstone ....3-0 ....Livingston

Scottish League Cup third round
September 20 2011

Aberdeen ....3-3............................East Fife
East Fife won 4-3 on penalties
Airdrie Utd ....0-2 ....Dundee Utd
Kilmarnock........................5-0 ....Queen of Sth
Motherwell ....2-2 ....Hibernian
Hibernian won 7-6 on penalties
St Johnstone ....0-2 ....St Mirren
September 21 2011

Ayr ....1-1 ....Hearts
Ayr won 4-1 on penalties
Falkirk ....3-2 ....Rangers
Ross County ....0-2 ....Celtic

Scottish League Cup quarter-finals
October 25 2011

Dundee Utd ....2-2 ....Falkirk
Falkirk won 5-4 on penalties
Kilmarnock........................2-0............................East Fife
St Mirren ....0-1 ....Ayr
October 26 2011

Hibernian ....1-4 ....Celtic

Scottish League Cup semi-finals
January 28 2012

Ayr ....0-1......................Kilmarnock
January 29 2012

Falkirk ....1-3 ....Celtic

Scottish League Cup final
March 18 2012

Celtic ....0-1......................Kilmarnock

Scottish Challenge Cup first round
July 23 2011

Airdrie Utd ....0-5 ....Livingston
Albion................................0-2 ....Annan
Arbroath ....1-2 ....Dundee
Ayr ....2-0 ....Queen of Sth
Brechin..............................1-2 ....Falkirk
Clyde ....2-2 ....Berwick
Deveronvale ....1-3 ....Stirling
Forfar ....1-1 ....Buckie Thistle
Montrose ....1-6...........................East Fife
Partick ....2-1 ....Stenhousemuir
Peterhead ....2-2..................................Alloa
Queen's Park ....0-2 ....Hamilton
Raith ....2-1 ....Cowdenbeath
Ross County ....1-2 ....Elgin City
Stranraer ....0-8 ....Morton
July 24 2011

Dumbarton.........................3-2 ....East Stirling

Scottish Challenge Cup second round
August 9 2011

Annan................................4-2 ....Peterhead
Ayr ....3-0.................................Raith
Dumbarton.........................0-2 ....Berwick
East Fife............................2-0 ....Elgin City
Falkirk ....1-0 ....Dundee
Forfar ....0-5 ....Morton
Hamilton............................1-0 ....Partick
Livingston..........................5-0 ....Stirling

Scottish Challenge Cup quarter-finals
September 4 2011

Ayr ....0-1 ....Annan
Berwick ....1-2 ....Livingston
East Fife............................1-4 ....Falkirk
Hamilton............................2-1 ....Morton

Scottish Challenge Cup semi-finals
October 9 2011

Annan................................0-3 ....Falkirk
Hamilton............................1-0 ....Livingston

Scottish Challenge Cup final
April 1 2012

Falkirk ....1-0 ....Hamilton

No substitute for hard work and a rational approach to punting

BETTING requires a rational numerical approach if you are to have any hope of coming out ahead of the game. Add to that dedication, hard work, intelligence and more than your fair share of luck and then – and only then – might you just be in with a shot at profitability, *writes Alex Deacon*.

Bringing all that together as well as holding down a day job and keeping your relationships and sanity intact is a gargantuan effort even if it's a rewarding and fascinating exercise.

Of course, there are shortcuts you can take but it goes without saying that the less you put into working on your betting the less you almost certainly will take out of it. It also goes without saying that one of the best shortcuts is simply to go to your newsagent every Tuesday morning and pick up the latest edition of the *Racing & Football Outlook* where you will find, among the many excellent and insightful articles, my unique ratings and forecasts. Taking pride of place in the various techniques that I employ are the league points forecasts which at any point in the season provide an accurate forecast of who will win each of the English leagues along with the forecasted odds with which to go and find that all important value.

Given some of the uncertainty that we see at the start of this season in many of the competitions that will kick off in August it's frequently the case that the best policy is to simply stand back and wait for a few games to be played before getting involved. Of course, the tradition when betting in the outright markets

makes it seemingly compulsory for tipsters to have to tip a team at the start and for punters to establish their betting portfolio before a ball has been kicked.

This is patently ridiculous and might have made sense when betting across turf accountant counters with bits of paper in the last century but in the second decade of the 21st century, this should not be considered the optimum way to actually win money on these markets over the course of the season.

However it's definitely the case that a rational and academic approach to betting can sometimes be a little dull and, whisper it, joyless. So, to that end I'm considering changing my overly rational, odds-based approach into something a little more easy going.

One area of uncertainty going into the start of the season has been around the participation of Rangers in the Scottish league. While I know many Gers fans have had their fair share of sleepless nights over the fate of their club, I have sought to reassure them that, through the insights provided to me by the ever-reliable Old Moore's Almanack, it seems Rangers are destined to be good score-draw material for August. That's what the Almanack's Pools advice says, anyway, and if conclusive proof were needed that all's well that ends well at Ibrox, this is it.

And against that backdrop and as a counter to simply placing a bet before a ball has been kicked, I think it's as useful and a lot more fun to look to the world of the likes of Old Moore for some of my early season thinking.

You may scoff but, having looked into

LAST RESORT: when computers stop working – perhaps the year 2038 problem will prove more destructive than the Millennium Bug – it might be crystal balls all round

this a little, I have come to the opinion that it's definitely significant that the Full Moon of August 21 corresponds with the start of a full midweek programme of Football League action.

Quite what forces were present inside the 'computer' that creates the fixture list I'm not sure, but I think this could well serve as an indicator for those looking to have a bit more information before placing some outright bets.

Further research over the summer also makes me feel that there is a real connection there with what we see at the next Full Moon on September 19 and the fact that Blackburn entertain Barnsley. I think we're seeing a pattern around what could happen in the Championship. It's also clearly important bearing in mind Blackburn's Indian ownership that the night of the 19th is also an important date in the Hindu calendar and the festival of Ganesh Chaturthi.

It's clearly too early to make a call on whether Blackburn can make a return to the Premier League at the first time of asking, but with these sort of early indications and alignments, those looking at taking some of the 16-1 that you can get about Rovers might well find themselves with an excellent trading opportunity come the start of autumn.

LEAGUE tables are, quite simply, one of the most deceptive tools a punter can employ in making selections each week, showing as they do the state of a competition at any given point in time, *writes Alex deacon.*

In their usual format they reveal nothing as to the quality of the opponents each side has met until then. That's where the *Outlook Index* comes in, showing as it does the relative strength of each side determined by the results of over 90,000 matches and weighted by the strength of the opposition.

Detailed 60-match form is also given for each side so that trends in any side's playing strength can be readily identified. Each week of the football season, the *Outlook* prints updated *Index* ratings along with True Odds, forecasted league tables and our analysis to help your football betting.

Premier League 2011-12

	Current	1-6	7-12	13-18	19-24	25-30	31-36	37-42	43-48	49-54	55-60	Home	Away	Trend
Man Utd	941	943	948	936	946	942	946	936	937	947	948	979	915	-1
Man City	939	929	932	934	936	936	922	908	904	911	908	958	885	5
Arsenal	905	907	908	892	906	894	886	905	920	920	914	931	886	1
Chelsea	894	900	897	906	914	914	921	925	922	914	916	956	870	-5
Tottenham	892	890	904	918	916	914	900	895	899	906	902	938	851	-6
Newcastle	888	894	880	880	877	888	872	858	862	868	863	914	860	2
Everton	883	879	871	866	871	878	885	888	887	878	882	894	832	7
Fulham	873	871	863	860	857	854	862	868	861	853	846	916	806	6
Wigan	866	853	833	828	833	827	847	846	840	836	838	887	864	18
Liverpool	865	868	880	898	906	903	896	898	890	881	880	937	862	-10
West Brom	853	856	856	848	850	852	849	858	847	834	842	855	849	0
Sunderland	850	858	861	859	839	840	841	845	852	870	868	886	820	-4
Norwich	848	847	851	853	843	840	833	827	820	813	812	856	836	0
Stoke	847	852	852	855	856	847	855	854	850	857	858	897	817	-4
Aston Villa	845	850	854	862	862	868	877	868	864	865	867	860	852	-6
Swansea	843	839	846	840	828	826	818	808	808	812	806	886	804	2
Bolton	838	833	827	827	818	829	838	853	865	857	867	858	847	7
QPR	832	826	812	819	828	832	824	822	826	822	811	870	806	8
Blackburn	818	824	834	827	822	832	840	844	845	858	861	858	818	-6
Wolves	802	802	814	824	832	832	848	842	841	834	833	823	827	-7

Championship 2011-12

	Current	1-6	7-12	13-18	19-24	25-30	31-36	37-42	43-48	49-54	55-60	Home	Away	Trend
Reading	851	852	841	830	820	807	806	802	819	824	803	865	841	7
West Ham	836	828	831	830	829	836	826	828	824	839	838	841	838	5
Southampton	830	832	832	813	811	822	814	811	795	779	767	862	812	3
Birmingham	827	824	818	830	823	819	831	822	832	850	852	907	802	3
Blackpool	822	820	815	825	816	815	811	821	829	823	827	854	811	2
Cardiff	817	809	803	816	824	825	814	818	823	817	818	825	816	5
Leicester	800	800	800	798	796	805	809	804	800	801	812	837	800	1
Watford	799	798	789	780	778	771	765	772	779	789	793	838	800	7
Middlesbrough	799	800	806	807	819	817	818	824	810	792	781	828	820	-4
Hull	798	794	810	811	805	801	804	799	802	808	808	816	812	-3
Millwall	797	783	770	770	777	784	783	790	799	800	786	831	812	15
Burnley	792	794	789	803	801	786	791	792	795	795	809	821	816	-2
Ipswich	792	795	796	783	769	773	793	786	786	792	781	833	814	2
Brighton	788	793	803	796	782	786	784	797	782	789	782	843	781	-5
Derby	782	782	778	776	778	766	779	778	765	768	764	817	795	2
Nottm Forest	780	779	771	763	767	786	789	798	809	800	821	827	802	6
Leeds	779	785	792	794	800	810	807	800	796	802	811	811	813	-7
Bristol City	779	768	757	766	773	776	763	781	786	796	787	826	799	10
Crystal Palace	769	776	790	784	783	780	783	773	766	766	768	845	784	-9
Portsmouth	765	770	770	782	789	786	780	787	791	800	805	831	783	-6
Peterborough	759	761	761	764	774	769	770	767	762	763	762	814	766	-2
Coventry	752	763	755	750	749	753	767	768	772	770	765	826	774	-3
Barnsley	747	753	764	778	784	787	781	775	767	770	774	815	770	-11
Doncaster	738	739	751	749	752	746	746	743	754	761	771	800	785	-5

League 1 2011-12

	Current	1-6	7-12	13-18	19-24	25-30	31-36	37-42	43-48	49-54	55-60	Home	Away	Trend
Charlton	783	778	776	783	773	766	751	737	719	720	728	823	784	4
Sheffield Weds	778	769	752	752	758	755	744	726	719	718	722	822	773	13
Huddersfield	759	763	774	777	780	792	790	783	784	771	760	814	753	-7
Sheffield Utd	759	764	753	771	768	758	756	766	760	750	751	832	764	-2
MK Dons	750	748	755	759	762	759	759	766	752	755	735	782	770	-2
Stevenage	746	732	734	739	738	724	704	710	704	710	698	753	742	8
Notts County	742	734	728	716	704	718	724	705	700	695	714	792	753	11
Brentford	732	736	726	722	726	729	731	735	726	730	723	772	744	2
Carlisle	727	736	739	736	736	723	720	719	714	721	726	787	728	-6
Bournemouth	722	715	713	728	732	718	706	707	727	736	752	781	750	3
Colchester	718	721	730	723	722	725	730	726	725	723	728	806	722	-4
Scunthorpe	714	721	716	718	714	722	727	726	742	742	748	779	772	-2
Walsall	712	711	711	696	696	692	701	711	714	710	704	792	732	4
Tranmere	712	714	706	700	710	720	722	720	716	708	712	807	722	3
Hartlepool	712	711	712	714	705	713	722	724	710	710	722	777	759	1
Yeovil	712	716	725	709	702	703	702	714	719	715	708	764	748	-2
Preston	710	710	710	716	728	730	752	764	751	755	739	790	745	-2
Bury	709	706	696	709	718	712	703	705	710	704	706	771	740	3
Oldham	708	699	710	718	715	719	714	711	705	704	712	765	758	1
Wycombe	701	711	706	690	695	694	702	710	715	702	705	763	740	-1
Leyton Orient	700	702	717	730	734	727	720	714	739	742	756	754	748	-10
Chesterfield	694	695	697	690	678	682	695	698	701	710	710	762	718	1
Exeter	690	688	699	709	706	716	708	724	738	724	721	784	703	-4
Rochdale	677	686	694	696	695	699	709	713	723	733	719	773	718	-9

League 2 2011-12

	Current	1-6	7-12	13-18	19-24	25-30	31-36	37-42	43-48	49-54	55-60	Home	Away	Trend
Swindon	728	736	733	730	706	699	687	680	686	694	698	809	724	-1
Shrewsbury	722	727	718	719	713	716	714	713	709	698	693	806	714	1
Crawley	710	714	711	712	726	734	724	715	714	705	701	751	700	-2
Crewe	709	705	691	684	672	669	671	668	668	668	668	763	730	11
Torquay	706	721	719	714	701	691	684	699	695	698	689	750	726	-7
Southend	704	694	696	699	710	716	702	681	682	679	686	759	744	5
Aldershot	696	690	688	680	662	675	676	678	680	688	676	739	730	8
Cheltenham	684	677	687	696	702	688	666	655	645	654	667	741	726	-1
Rotherham	684	679	670	675	679	681	678	692	677	676	686	749	709	6
Gillingham	684	678	687	680	694	692	691	690	693	700	696	776	693	1
Oxford	680	692	702	693	693	689	692	682	678	680	680	748	687	-10
Port Vale	679	674	675	679	675	676	681	676	673	681	688	745	707	3
Bristol Rovers	674	677	675	674	658	671	682	689	694	699	685	765	708	1
Dagenham & R	668	661	647	646	647	644	666	688	693	697	703	737	700	11
Plymouth	664	670	663	662	661	658	669	680	710	710	708	759	705	0
Accrington	662	671	675	684	695	680	682	692	701	698	686	758	671	-10
Bradford	661	657	660	664	660	644	646	649	652	656	662	756	695	1
Northampton	659	662	660	642	638	648	666	664	668	661	672	736	716	3
Wimbledon	658	651	659	662	662	675	685	678	675	664	672	706	678	1
Morecambe	652	660	660	660	666	678	678	676	661	667	668	712	717	-5
Hereford	652	639	651	652	654	657	657	658	664	672	670	718	732	4
Burton	646	650	646	666	684	692	684	677	664	650	654	739	690	-6
Barnet	643	636	645	654	652	644	644	654	655	641	635	732	691	0
Macclesfield	619	628	641	644	666	673	674	666	664	660	671	745	690	-13

Stronger at home*		Stronger away*		Hot		Not	
Fulham	110	East Fife	24	Peterhead	2.18%	Macclesfield	-2.10%
Birmingham	105	Stirling	21	Wigan	2.08%	Stranraer	-2.08%
Shrewsbury	92	Raith	20	Airdrie Utd	1.97%	Brechin	-1.77%
Cowdenbeath	89	Livingston	19	Millwall	1.88%	Accrington	-1.51%
Accrington	87	Dunfermline	18	Raith	1.67%	Barnsley	-1.47%
Tottenham	87	Hereford	14	Sheff Weds	1.67%	Oxford	-1.47%

Difference between Home and Away ratings

Conference 2011-12

	Current	1-6	7-12	13-18	19-24	25-30	31-36	37-42	43-48	49-54	55-60	Home	Away	Trend
Fleetwood	711	724	718	708	695	686	682	667	666	654	649	686	721	-3
Mansfield	693	680	668	651	640	641	649	638	628	632	631	728	680	18
Wrexham	693	692	703	702	701	692	681	689	674	663	670	717	704	-3
York	681	670	670	670	670	674	668	664	662	661	661	709	676	8
Luton	667	656	668	680	674	674	674	679	678	682	690	726	647	1
Kidderminster	658	660	652	666	671	665	670	670	666	676	667	687	664	-1
Grimsby	650	656	661	658	638	625	633	629	633	634	646	696	673	-4
Southport	647	649	657	650	657	653	632	613	612	609	606	664	680	-3
Forest Green	647	648	641	635	638	620	614	613	616	615	620	707	648	4
Cambridge	646	643	641	649	660	659	646	630	630	625	624	679	656	1
Gateshead	639	636	640	647	644	641	644	642	624	630	632	704	635	0
Alfreton	639	638	619	605	601	601	621	631	-	-	-	650	650	12
Stockport	627	616	610	599	598	614	626	634	635	631	627	721	656	12
Braintree	627	635	632	625	627	642	654	642	-	-	-	663	628	-2
Ebbsfleet	620	625	630	630	625	627	616	620	620	620	620	672	653	-5
Newport County	618	622	617	615	614	615	616	629	643	633	630	658	632	0
Barrow	613	614	638	634	630	632	622	625	618	628	622	696	612	-9
Lincoln	610	608	605	610	614	614	613	616	636	654	666	691	659	2
Telford	610	610	609	610	615	621	637	631	-	-	-	664	606	0
Darlington	600	599	606	627	646	645	644	654	654	642	646	686	638	-7
Tamworth	599	607	614	614	621	636	628	625	610	607	620	679	637	-8
Hayes & Y	598	600	596	591	599	607	614	616	623	613	599	641	643	1
Bath City	588	584	582	590	597	590	596	613	636	649	645	649	616	2
Kettering	575	583	593	604	610	621	618	626	636	634	635	642	632	-11

Scottish Premier League 2011-12

	Current	1-6	7-12	13-18	19-24	25-30	31-36	37-42	43-48	49-54	55-60	Home	Away	Trend
Celtic	902	904	905	901	888	882	894	896	898	898	892	938	876	0
Rangers	890	888	889	900	914	917	908	900	890	893	894	920	889	-2
Dundee Utd	845	836	827	814	818	816	829	829	826	809	815	848	811	12
Motherwell	817	816	820	812	821	814	808	800	797	796	802	814	805	1
Hearts	807	807	802	810	806	816	812	825	841	852	838	833	778	1
Kilmarnock	794	791	793	796	800	794	804	799	799	795	794	820	790	1
St Johnstone	790	800	800	802	802	804	794	794	791	798	791	786	794	-7
Inverness CT	781	776	787	789	782	784	787	793	783	790	808	786	793	-1
St Mirren	776	777	775	777	772	769	770	760	759	758	765	822	773	1
Aberdeen	772	773	779	776	766	768	764	769	780	779	766	833	763	-1
Hibernian	760	760	757	757	764	772	767	779	794	776	783	808	783	1
Dunfermline	740	742	744	748	756	762	772	758	742	741	748	761	779	-3

Scottish Division One 2011-12

	Current	1-6	7-12	13-18	19-24	25-30	31-36	37-42	43-48	49-54	55-60	Home	Away	Trend
Ross County	779	773	760	748	750	725	710	700	698	691	705	775	778	12
Dundee	740	748	748	751	746	738	758	762	766	759	743	798	734	-5
Hamilton	726	729	725	728	731	749	758	756	756	770	772	765	754	-1
Falkirk	719	720	742	745	740	736	732	743	741	746	750	782	726	-9
Raith	719	706	698	699	702	715	722	729	733	735	732	736	756	12
Partick	715	709	711	712	714	715	710	709	710	705	698	773	729	3
Livingston	711	715	709	717	721	722	719	712	703	692	678	731	750	-2
Morton	698	700	699	706	704	711	706	710	709	702	693	738	741	-2
Queen Of Sth	688	695	694	695	702	706	708	705	712	720	724	758	707	-4
Ayr	686	685	690	677	677	672	668	666	668	678	684	760	707	2

Scottish Division Two 2011-12

	Current	1-6	7-12	13-18	19-24	25-30	31-36	37-42	43-48	49-54	55-60	Home	Away	Trend
Cowdenbeath	682	683	686	687	682	678	670	667	660	656	661	757	668	-1
Airdrie Utd	660	642	638	640	648	661	656	656	672	689	694	723	684	13
Dumbarton	654	645	657	648	630	622	621	626	632	618	607	703	674	5
Arbroath	649	652	664	652	645	639	620	623	626	619	613	694	676	-3
East Fife	641	650	642	644	646	647	653	649	634	621	616	678	702	-3
Stenhousemuir	634	629	628	636	644	640	630	621	614	606	607	688	684	2
Forfar	634	625	623	630	631	644	646	644	638	644	639	690	667	6
Brechin	622	632	642	648	640	643	655	654	669	672	670	698	661	-11
Stirling	611	611	617	619	624	639	647	640	653	662	673	664	685	-3
Albion	605	608	593	601	613	592	595	593	584	585	590	692	638	2

Scottish Division Three 2011-12

	Current	1-6	7-12	13-18	19-24	25-30	31-36	37-42	43-48	49-54	55-60	Home	Away	Trend
Alloa	639	643	634	636	624	625	620	627	634	645	662	715	671	2
Queen's Park	606	609	616	611	603	603	605	600	604	587	566	671	664	-3
Peterhead	596	585	579	570	561	570	591	610	619	642	632	678	656	13
Elgin	588	582	589	574	568	571	564	552	565	570	557	659	634	5
Stranraer	578	594	596	604	597	598	584	586	590	594	596	669	622	-12
Berwick	577	574	570	580	579	567	567	577	577	563	578	654	637	2
Annan	564	566	577	589	600	611	600	595	591	584	584	638	619	-8
Montrose	550	543	535	544	544	544	544	541	534	544	544	640	614	7
Clyde	544	542	544	554	568	569	569	565	563	562	568	647	635	-2
East Stirling	520	523	527	521	523	526	545	545	543	560	572	649	573	-2

Spanish Primera Liga 2011-12

	Current	1-6	7-12	13-18	19-24	25-30	31-36	37-42	43-48	49-54	55-60	Home	Away	Trend
Real Madrid	1028	1024	1018	1017	1011	1006	998	1002	1003	1005	1012	1018	1033	6
Barcelona	1008	1011	1007	1001	1006	1010	1011	1014	1027	1026	1026	1039	987	1
Valencia	932	934	938	946	962	966	964	956	962	969	962	967	925	-5
Atl Madrid	931	921	920	925	918	920	924	921	917	910	918	966	896	7
Real Mallorca	924	914	908	902	901	894	892	903	912	916	926	964	897	11
Malaga	921	920	924	909	910	914	916	907	887	877	876	958	900	2
Osasuna	915	912	918	914	920	914	912	904	894	889	885	980	868	0
Real Sociedad	914	908	902	905	896	882	894	891	883	902	896	964	883	7
Levante	914	915	919	914	927	936	924	914	906	885	867	944	898	-2
Real Zaragoza	912	897	886	877	882	904	912	911	903	897	896	950	886	16
Seville	910	913	910	904	922	934	940	931	930	923	930	941	903	0
Real Betis	907	906	898	900	897	898	921	908	916	911	905	945	917	4
Getafe	906	913	912	906	900	888	888	892	894	907	924	950	886	-2
Villarreal	905	909	902	912	900	911	918	929	941	946	959	984	884	-1
Ath Bilbao	904	912	910	919	914	915	903	912	919	924	921	948	885	-6
Granada	901	906	903	910	912	906	910	-	-	-	-	932	901	-3
Sp Gijon	892	891	888	890	899	899	890	906	906	890	880	940	880	1
Espanyol	889	895	907	910	901	898	890	896	902	915	925	950	873	-8
Rayo Vallecano	885	888	904	903	896	899	894	891	894	900	906	920	902	-7
Racing Santander	866	875	890	906	901	895	899	909	908	909	900	894	912	-14

Italian Serie A 2011-12

	Current	1-6	7-12	13-18	19-24	25-30	31-36	37-42	43-48	49-54	55-60	Home	Away	Trend
Juventus	924	918	900	900	892	886	872	867	861	863	877	997	940	12
Milan	921	921	924	918	920	919	911	920	918	910	908	976	964	0
Napoli	881	880	891	880	882	886	890	888	896	888	882	1004	889	-1
Inter	876	877	874	888	899	886	897	916	917	923	918	987	914	-3
Parma	874	856	839	843	838	840	837	835	820	820	832	948	871	19
Udinese	873	862	872	882	893	885	882	871	877	869	848	966	893	1
Lazio	870	866	878	883	882	883	871	866	870	870	872	926	917	-3
Roma	864	866	873	886	884	886	889	891	896	902	909	973	906	-6
Bologna	848	840	834	822	811	805	792	803	844	844	832	903	794	11
Atalanta	847	852	851	844	845	843	841	830	828	822	828	938	860	-1
Chievo	844	843	843	840	842	837	842	833	828	836	828	919	893	2
Fiorentina	843	841	833	842	843	848	857	861	854	846	843	930	879	3
Catania	842	850	859	847	845	856	846	838	829	826	836	927	832	-6
Novara	837	833	837	836	851	865	888	-	-	-	-	897	873	1
Siena	834	840	833	820	821	830	822	822	826	821	820	907	892	2
Genoa	832	830	839	849	849	852	852	846	848	847	849	948	836	-4
Cagliari	832	833	836	842	834	835	843	833	848	849	839	938	858	-2
Palermo	829	837	846	855	848	860	863	861	854	872	882	963	858	-10
Lecce	815	826	816	803	784	784	785	786	774	766	751	873	775	1
Cesena	799	810	809	822	833	833	842	860	865	876	889	876	873	-10

SPAIN: with three major tournament wins in a row they sure do a good podium

French Ligue 1 2011-12														
	Current	1-6	7-12	13-18	19-24	25-30	31-36	37-42	43-48	49-54	55-60	Home	Away	Trend
Lille	943	940	932	936	941	941	935	936	932	929	926	953	890	5
Montpellier	934	922	916	908	898	885	882	872	884	892	893	924	888	13
Paris St-G	930	921	924	926	911	912	892	892	893	894	894	936	879	6
Bordeaux	915	901	896	896	883	878	883	880	884	888	893	936	882	13
Lyon	910	917	910	912	919	922	923	918	924	922	919	944	870	-2
Rennes	895	898	892	895	898	896	888	881	892	904	892	909	877	0
Evian TG	888	896	889	881	887	882	897	900	-	-	-	886	892	-1
Marseille	882	882	900	930	920	912	919	934	939	927	921	905	866	-12
St Etienne	880	890	892	898	889	878	875	874	878	878	879	901	874	-8
Toulouse	878	890	900	889	891	886	881	869	863	870	877	905	864	-9
Nancy	876	881	873	866	867	864	869	871	871	862	869	903	868	2
Nice	876	868	865	855	857	863	861	869	869	861	864	932	843	9
Sochaux	872	862	860	855	873	886	893	886	864	855	856	902	847	8
Brest	867	857	868	880	876	868	873	872	871	886	899	910	850	1
Ajaccio	866	860	863	855	835	840	847	848	834	841	834	907	842	6
Valenciennes	865	867	873	872	871	868	868	878	875	874	865	924	820	-3
Dijon	855	861	872	869	873	877	888	894	-	-	-	877	870	-8
Caen	853	860	856	856	862	878	875	868	860	859	846	890	854	-3
Lorient	850	857	854	864	878	889	883	884	885	884	882	895	831	-6
Auxerre	848	853	852	856	870	884	890	895	886	883	894	896	833	-4

German Bundesliga 2011-12														
	Current	1-6	7-12	13-18	19-24	25-30	31-36	37-42	43-48	49-54	55-60	Home	Away	Trend
B Dortmund	982	974	965	953	945	934	945	954	959	957	947	980	941	12
B Munich	957	952	944	946	947	951	940	934	934	934	936	983	909	7
Schalke	918	916	917	918	902	888	884	899	903	905	895	938	895	2
B Leverkusen	916	904	918	919	925	934	933	940	928	926	921	921	908	2
Stuttgart	914	911	893	889	906	904	904	894	885	885	898	932	897	9
B M'gladbach	910	907	920	914	900	890	877	853	849	848	857	939	884	-1
Augsburg	898	889	878	874	871	872	884	-	-	-	-	918	888	12
Hannover	893	896	899	897	904	909	904	904	896	895	878	955	845	-3
Freiburg	888	882	860	857	856	860	866	869	881	879	871	914	878	14
Nuremberg	886	882	882	872	876	888	886	897	889	868	871	904	896	5
Wolfsburg	884	887	879	877	873	876	881	874	884	892	901	922	869	2
Mainz	880	885	888	886	885	896	909	894	895	905	917	900	880	-4
Hamburg	878	878	884	890	878	868	882	893	899	899	904	908	898	-2
Hoffenheim	871	884	878	875	879	886	878	883	889	889	891	899	884	-5
Werder Bremen	868	880	894	901	904	906	898	898	892	901	916	926	858	-15
Cologne	852	859	870	880	887	885	880	879	872	858	852	902	861	-11
Hertha Berlin	852	852	856	870	884	883	870	868	863	866	872	876	899	-5
Kaiserslautern	837	841	856	869	873	872	884	873	860	866	860	883	864	-11

International Outlook Index (Europe only)

	Current	1-6	7-12	13-18	19-24	25-30	31-36	37-42	43-48	49-54	55-60	Home	Away	Trend
Spain	981	976	967	956	948	957	950	937	925	932	934	974	948	4
Germany	975	974	963	957	954	949	946	950	949	936	929	950	961	3
Holland	950	969	971	966	955	946	943	947	950	941	931	994	932	-9
England	945	943	941	941	938	935	937	939	935	935	934	967	922	2
Italy	939	934	929	932	940	951	953	948	941	936	931	1018	913	4
Portugal	933	922	921	923	916	922	930	929	935	945	940	976	893	6
Croatia	926	924	924	926	929	927	924	916	926	922	918	936	918	1
Sweden	910	907	908	906	908	915	920	919	919	915	915	956	901	2
Russia	906	909	906	916	914	901	899	894	894	898	899	948	884	-1
France	904	907	909	923	936	937	957	965	962	954	957	939	906	-1
Denmark	904	902	894	905	899	902	904	893	903	902	901	914	911	3
Czech Republic	903	902	900	903	919	927	924	932	933	933	930	911	909	1
Greece	897	898	892	893	892	899	907	899	891	889	888	904	888	1
Serbia	888	892	902	911	898	903	912	915	925	928	925	924	895	-3
Norway	885	889	878	883	878	884	884	879	892	884	898	916	891	0
Rep of Ireland	885	892	887	888	884	882	884	888	894	899	905	956	869	-2
Romania	884	886	896	903	915	914	903	899	904	906	914	940	879	-2
Ukraine	883	888	882	881	894	892	898	890	888	894	897	924	863	-1
Switzerland	883	882	892	888	882	881	872	869	867	862	865	922	869	-1
Scotland	876	875	881	892	891	883	880	891	890	892	882	938	848	0
Turkey	875	878	888	896	904	893	904	901	897	897	903	891	859	-3
Poland	860	866	882	888	891	884	889	882	875	883	894	931	872	-5
Bosnia-Hz	859	857	847	852	835	846	847	846	841	828	832	886	844	3
Slovakia	858	868	869	868	855	855	860	856	858	851	853	900	868	-5
Israel	857	857	858	866	864	858	850	836	834	832	829	901	798	0
Slovenia	854	855	860	854	846	842	850	869	874	875	880	885	868	-1
Hungary	853	847	835	830	828	834	841	837	844	844	848	900	854	5
Bulgaria	852	864	876	876	871	863	858	862	870	863	857	925	834	-8
Belgium	850	850	846	864	866	873	886	895	897	904	903	914	840	1
Finland	847	847	855	861	856	849	850	847	843	836	827	886	813	-1
Austria	843	846	855	850	852	854	857	867	875	871	877	918	818	-3
Wales	832	817	826	832	830	829	829	844	850	835	840	861	837	6
Lithuania	830	842	840	851	830	828	833	831	830	836	846	870	840	-5
Latvia	824	822	828	821	819	816	824	826	830	811	802	864	842	0
Northern Ireland	823	834	840	828	827	824	811	810	820	822	828	896	807	-6
Montenegro	822	830	817	804	-	-	-	-	-	-	-	845	806	-1
Belarus	816	821	820	811	802	809	805	800	802	804	793	856	794	-2
Estonia	815	808	802	789	786	783	792	789	786	778	776	834	828	5
Armenia	810	802	786	786	800	792	791	793	801	800	799	854	805	7
Georgia	803	812	806	817	824	827	836	844	852	855	854	872	820	-3
Macedonia	800	803	811	812	803	804	804	809	807	818	828	846	810	-2
Cyprus	798	806	808	809	803	802	806	816	823	830	822	833	775	-4
Albania	796	802	806	812	820	819	820	812	809	802	806	872	782	-3
Moldova	782	785	789	793	798	793	799	800	800	806	810	840	787	-2
Iceland	764	798	804	807	815	821	830	845	844	842	836	860	766	-18
Azerbaijan	759	758	753	750	758	759	762	766	762	762	759	819	752	2
Kazakhstan	751	752	756	760	758	752	748	752	758	755	762	792	738	-1
Liechtenstein	742	738	739	744	742	736	736	737	742	747	755	792	759	2
Faroe Islands	742	740	740	735	737	744	753	760	767	769	769	794	781	1
Malta	718	719	724	728	734	734	725	726	729	736	740	790	751	-1
Andorra	703	706	715	723	735	748	756	761	759	772	779	747	765	-3
Luxembourg	702	696	697	696	682	682	688	697	704	709	717	745	742	3
San Marino	669	672	676	681	686	691	696	700	706	710	715	701	719	-2

So-called bankers are rarely value bets

LITERALLY central to the RFO's presentation of fixtures are our exclusive form figures, *writes Figaro*.

Now approaching the 20th anniversary of their first appearance in the paper, they assess the home form of the home side and the away form of the visitors, taking the last six matches into account, plus the form of their opponents at the time of each game and the margins of defeat or victory, so a couple of sliding scales are at work.

We have 25 year's worth of data to check on how they have performed too so the tables on the facing page draw on some pretty fat samples that show you exactly that – one for English and Scottish league games since the 1987-88 season on their own and another devoted only to cup ties in that period.

At the same time, I thought it would be interesting to look at the connection between actual results and the relative league positions at the time games were played over the past 25 seasons.

In all four tables, the percentage occurrence of each possible result is given for a different band of games (defined in each case in the first column) and the number in brackets after the percentages indicates the total games where that particular result has occurred.

You can see with just a quick glance how even in the (inevitably less frequently occur-

ring) extreme bands at the top and bottom of each table, the sample being examined is substantial.

In some ways, all four tables highlight the same thing. For example, the richest seam in which Treble Chance players should do their mining is matches where the away side is slightly ahead of their hosts either in terms of relative form or in terms of relative league position.

The other point all the tables prove is just how elusive bankers can be. If we ignore the top band of the table dealing with Scottish League games (it no longer applies because the divisions are too small), there's no profile of game that produces more than two home wins every three games.

The Scottish record is a little distorted by the omnipotence of Celtic and Rangers, but if I had to pick out one stat to highlight here ahead of all others it would that in the English League over the last 25 seasons, games where the home side has been 17 or more places higher than their visitors in the league table have finished as home wins only 62.03 per cent of the time.

That means the theoretical odds against the home win in such cases are 8-13. Any quote below that (which is probably all of them!) may not represent value. That's why with our *Soccer Betting Hotline* bankers of the day, we always try to find some additional angle to give us an edge on the rare occasions that we use such games.

It is also why bookmakers are delighted with the tens of thousands of punters whose main bet is accumulators based around such teams.

The other crucial point worth stressing here is just how up-and-down the numbers are in the table devoted to cup ties. Form does not go straight out of the window in cup games, but it certainly sits on the window sill feeling adventurous.

LIVERPOOL: not home bankers

Relative Outlook form and actual results In all English and Scottish league games since the 1987-88 season

Outlook form	Home win	Away win	Score draw	0-0 draw	Any draw
Away 33+ higher	27.15% (60)	52.94% (117)	10.86% (24)	9.05% (20)	19.91% (44)
Away 28-32 higher	25.53% (97)	47.37% (180)	20.53% (78)	6.58% (25)	27.11% (103)
Away 23-27 higher	28.50% (303)	46.85% (498)	18.81% (200)	5.83% (62)	24.65% (262)
Away 18-22 higher	31.50% (818)	41.28% (1072)	19.14% (497)	8.09% (210)	27.22% (707)
Away 13-17 higher	35.15% (1687)	37.70% (1809)	18.59% (892)	8.56% (411)	27.15% (1303)
Away 8-12 higher	38.81% (3097)	33.85% (2701)	19.37% (1546)	7.97% (636)	27.34% (2182)
Away 3-7 higher	41.50% (4433)	30.44% (3252)	19.79% (2114)	8.27% (883)	28.06% (2997)
Sides within 2 points	44.23% (5237)	28.19% (3338)	19.54% (2314)	8.04% (952)	27.58% (3266)
Home 3-7 higher	47.47% (5158)	25.09% (2726)	19.54% (2123)	7.91% (859)	27.44% (2982)
Home 8-12 higher	50.99% (4265)	22.65% (1895)	18.74% (1568)	7.62% (637)	26.36% (2205)
Home 13-17 higher	53.38% (2789)	20.65% (1079)	18.39% (961)	7.58% (396)	25.97% (1357)
Home 18-22 higher	56.82% (1620)	19.01% (542)	16.56% (472)	7.61% (217)	24.17% (689)
Home 23-27 higher	62.17% (761)	17.16% (210)	15.03% (184)	5.64% (69)	20.67% (253)
Home 28-32 higher	62.78% (280)	15.25% (68)	16.82% (75)	5.16% (23)	21.97% (98)
Home 33+ higher	60.46% (211)	17.48% (61)	14.61% (51)	7.45% (26)	22.06% (77)
Total games 68,889					

Relative league positions and actual results In all English league games since the 1987-88 season

League positions	Home win	Away win	Score draw	0-0 draw	Any draw
Home 17+ higher	62.03% (1196)	14.32% (276)	16.96% (327)	6.69% (129)	23.65% (456)
Home 13-16 higher	58.25% (1794)	17.50% (539)	17.40% (536)	6.85% (211)	24.25% (747)
Home 9-12 higher	55.33% (2568)	18.92% (878)	18.14% (842)	7.61% (353)	25.75% (1195)
Home 5-8 higher	51.14% (3308)	21.80% (1410)	19.08% (1234)	7.98% (516)	27.06% (1750)
Home 1-4 higher	47.48% (3891)	24.56% (2013)	19.44% (1593)	8.52% (698)	27.96% (2291)
Away 1-4 higher	42.47% (3646)	28.76% (2469)	20.13% (1728)	8.64% (742)	28.77% (2470)
Away 5-8 higher	41.33% (2804)	30.97% (2101)	19.09% (1295)	8.61% (584)	27.70% (1879)
Away 9-12 higher	37.16% (1897)	33.83% (1727)	20.65% (1054)	8.36% (427)	29.01% (1481)
Away 13-16 higher	34.99% (1154)	37.20% (1227)	19.59% (646)	8.22% (271)	27.80% (917)
Away 17+ higher	31.51% (674)	41.05% (878)	19.64% (420)	7.81% (167)	27.44% (587)
Total games 50,223					

Relative league positions and actual results In all Scottish league games since the 1987-88 season

League positions	Home win	Away win	Score draw	0-0 draw	Any draw
Home 13-16 higher	91.67% (11)	0% (0)	0% (0)	8.33% (1)	8.33% (1)
Home 9-12 higher	66.52% (312)	13.22% (62)	14.50% (68)	5.76% (27)	20.26% (95)
Home 5-8 higher	59.03% (1615)	18.27% (500)	17.11% (468)	5.59% (153)	22.70% (621)
Home 1-4 higher	48.78% (2907)	25.08% (1495)	18.83% (1122)	7.32% (436)	26.14% (1558)
Away 1-4 higher	35.52% (2156)	38.05% (2309)	19.01% (1154)	7.41% (450)	26.43% (1604)
Away 5-8 higher	26.95% (783)	47.33% (1375)	18.07% (525)	7.64% (222)	25.71% (747)
Away 9-12 higher	19.32% (97)	55.98% (281)	16.93% (85)	7.77% (39)	24.70% (124)
Away 13-16 higher	23.08% (3)	61.54% (8)	15.38% (2)	0% (0)	15.38% (2)
Total games 18,666					

Relative Outlook form and actual results in all English and Scottish cup games since the 1987-88 season

League positions	Home win	Away win	Score draw	0-0 draw	Any draw
Away 33+ higher	41.22% (61)	39.86% (59)	16.22% (24)	2.70% (4)	18.92% (28)
Away 28-32 higher	43.14% (44)	41.18% (42)	11.76% (12)	3.92% (4)	15.69% (16)
Away 23-27 higher	34.43% (73)	42.45% (90)	17.45% (37)	5.66% (12)	23.11% (49)
Away 18-22 higher	39.42% (162)	42.09% (173)	15.33% (63)	3.16% (13)	18.49% (76)
Away 13-17 higher	42.17% (272)	38.29% (247)	14.11% (91)	5.43% (35)	19.53% (126)
Away 8-12 higher	42.87% (499)	36.94% (430)	14.18% (165)	6.01% (70)	20.19% (235)
Away 3-7 higher	44.34% (690)	34.90% (543)	14.59% (227)	6.17% (96)	20.76% (323)
Sides within 2 points	49.94% (827)	30.50% (505)	14.55% (241)	5.01% (83)	19.57% (324)
Home 3-7 higher	48.17% (763)	31.63% (501)	14.27% (226)	5.93% (94)	20.20% (320)
Home 8-12 higher	50.09% (581)	30.69% (356)	13.79% (160)	5.43% (63)	19.22% (223)
Home 13-17 higher	52.17% (372)	28.89% (206)	13.74% (98)	5.19% (37)	18.93% (135)
Home 18-22 higher	51.84% (211)	27.52% (112)	14.99% (61)	5.65% (23)	20.64% (84)
Home 23-27 higher	52.44% (118)	28.89% (65)	12.00% (27)	6.67% (15)	18.67% (42)
Home 28-32 higher	54.55% (60)	29.09% (32)	10.00% (11)	6.36% (7)	16.36% (18)
Home 33+ higher	55.13% (86)	32.05% (50)	8.97% (14)	3.85% (6)	12.82% (20)
Total games 10,249					

Back Malaga to move closer to the big two

IF YOU thought Malaga was only good for sun, sea and sand, think again. The area, famed for housing Brit expats on the Costa del Sol, is also home to one of Spain's most-improved football teams and they are worth backing to finish best of the rest in La Liga this term, *writes Derek Guldberg*.

Malaga have certainly had a chequered history. They were first promoted to the Spanish top flight in 1949, only to be wound up and relaunched in 1992.

Nowadays though, Malaga are definitely on the upgrade. The Andalusian outfit finished fourth in Primera Liga in 2011-12, having finished 11th the season before, and landed a Champions League spot in the process.

Their recent success has coincided with the arrival

of Sheikh Abdullah Al-Thani of the Qatari royal family, who became the club's owner in June 2010. High-profile purchases and infrastructure improvements quickly followed and Malaga secured their highest ever league finishing position last term as a result.

Traditionally, Valencia have made third spot their own – they've finished there three years running – but the Bats' reign is under threat, and Malaga could be about to upstage the old guard.

In France, the bet of the season comes courtesy of Paddy Power, who are offering 13-8 about **Lyon** finishing in the top three. Les Gones have had a tough time of it in recent years. They won the title seven years running up until 2008 but since then Lyon have failed to finish top of the pile, with four different sides landing the silverware instead.

Cash-rich Paris Saint-Germain are the obvious favourites after going close last time out, but at around 1-2 they're too short for me and it makes sense to trust in Remi Garde improving Lyon's position instead.

After all, they finished fourth last term, so only need to rise one place to see us collect, and their boss is clearly taking Lyon back in the right direction, having won the French Cup with them in his first season in charge. It's also easy to imagine the defending champions, Montpellier, and third-placed Lille going backwards next season as both have lost key men over the summer.

In Germany, Borussia Dortmund upset the applecart by retaining the Bundesliga trophy. Bayern Munich are odds-on to wrestle the title back from Dortmund, but that's a short price about a Munich side who won nothing last season and blew up big-time on their

MANUEL PELLEGRINI: Malaga's boss

NERVOUS: Hamburg supporters could be facing another edgy campaign

own patch against Chelsea in the Champions League final.

The German relegation market is far more attractive than a bet on who'll win the league at this stage. Only two sides go down automatically, with the third-bottom team facing a play-off for survival, but whichever way you cut it, **Hamburg** could be in trouble this season.

Hamburg had a tough time of it last season, finishing 15th – just one place and five points above the play-off spot – which is quite a downward spiral, given that they had finished seventh and eighth in the two previous seasons.

Worse still is that they scored just two goals in their final five league games of last season, despite the fact they were fighting a relegation battle. Hamburg didn't score more than once in a single league game from the end of January 2012 onwards either.

A change of manager in the autumn didn't help much and more of the same could see Hamburg, the only team to have played in every season of the Bundesliga since it was founded in 1963,

drop out of the top flight at a big price.

Serie A went to the wire too, where Juventus won the Scudetto. Although they remained unbeaten all season, a feat that hadn't been achieved for 20 years, the Black and Whites drew 15 of 38 fixtures, allowing **AC Milan** to finish within four points of the ultimately triumphant Bianconeri.

The Old Lady might not have things all her own way this year, with both Milan outfits bound to be there or thereabouts. The Milanese dominance of Serie A stretched back for six consecutive years before Juve finally brought it to an end.

Inter are currently struggling financially and finished way off the pace last season, but AC Milan look good at 11-5 to win the title.

The Rossoneri are in a period of transition after parting company with a number of big names, including Filippo Inzaghi, Mark van Bommel and Alessandro Nesta, but their price is unlikely to get much bigger as the campaign unfolds – it's probably wise to get involved sooner rather than later.

Ath Bilbao

Ground: San Mames

	11-12 H A	Last six seasons at home P	W	D	L	OV	UN	BS	CS
Real Madrid	L L	6	1	0	5	4	2	2	1
Barcelona	D L	6	0	3	3	3	5	0	
Valencia	L D	6	3	0	3	5	1	4	1
Malaga	W L	4	2	2	0	2	2	3	1
Atl Madrid	W L	6	2	0	4	4	2	3	2
Levante	W L	4	4	0	0	2	2	1	3
Osasuna	W L	4	1	1	2	2	4	1	4
Real Mallorca	W D	6	4	0	2	4	2	3	3
Seville	W W	6	3	0	3	3	3	2	3
Ath Bilbao									
Getafe	D D	6	3	2	1	2	4	1	4
Real Sociedad	W W	3	2	1	0	1	2	2	1
Real Betis	L L	4	1	1	2	2	2	2	2
Espanyol	D L	6	4	2	0	3	3	4	2
Rayo Vallecano	D W	1	0	1	0	0	1	1	0
Real Zaragoza	W L	5	2	3	0	2	3	3	2
Granada	L D	1	0	0	1	0	1	0	0
Deportivo		5	1	2	2	2	3	3	1
Celta de Vigo		1	0	0	1	0	1	0	0
Real Valladolid		3	3	0	0	0	3	0	3

Season	Division	Pos	P	W	D	L	F	A	GD	Pts
2011-12	La Liga	10	38	12	13	13	49	52	-3	49
2010-11	La Liga	6	38	18	4	16	59	55	4	58
2009-10	La Liga	8	38	15	9	14	50	53	-3	54

Atl Madrid

Ground: Vicente Calderon

	11-12 H A	Last six seasons at home P	W	D	L	OV	UN	BS	CS
Real Madrid	L L	6	0	1	5	4	2	5	0
Barcelona	L L	6	3	0	3	6	0	5	0
Valencia	D L	6	3	1	2	2	4	2	3
Malaga	W D	4	2	0	2	3	1	1	1
Atl Madrid									
Levante	W L	4	4	0	0	3	1	2	2
Osasuna	D W	6	4	1	1	2	4	1	5
Real Mallorca	D L	6	2	4	0	1	5	4	2
Seville	D D	6	3	2	1	4	2	4	1
Ath Bilbao	W L	6	3	0	3	3	3	3	2
Getafe	W L	6	4	1	1	2	4	1	4
Real Sociedad	D W	3	1	2	0	1	2	2	1
Real Betis	L D	4	1	1	2	1	3	1	2
Espanyol	W L	6	3	0	3	6	0	5	1
Rayo Vallecano	W W	1	1	0	0	1	0	1	0
Real Zaragoza	W L	5	4	0	1	3	2	2	2
Granada	W D	1	1	0	0	0	1	0	1
Deportivo		5	5	0	0	2	3	1	4
Celta de Vigo		1	0	0	1	1	0	1	0
Real Valladolid		3	2	0	1	3	0	3	0

Season	Division	Pos	P	W	D	L	F	A	GD	Pts
2011-12	La Liga	5	38	15	11	12	53	46	7	56
2010-11	La Liga	7	38	17	7	14	62	53	9	58
2009-10	La Liga	9	38	13	8	17	57	61	-4	47

Barcelona

Ground: Camp Nou

	11-12 H A	Last six seasons at home P	W	D	L	OV	UN	BS	CS
Real Madrid	L W	6	3	1	2	3	3	2	3
Barcelona									
Valencia	W D	6	5	1	0	5	1	3	3
Malaga	W W	4	4	0	0	4	0	3	1
Atl Madrid	W W	6	5	1	0	5	1	3	3
Levante	W W	4	4	0	0	3	1	2	2
Osasuna	W L	6	5	0	1	2	4	0	5
Real Mallorca	W W	6	4	1	1	4	2	4	2
Seville	D W	6	5	1	0	5	1	2	4
Ath Bilbao	W D	6	6	0	0	4	2	3	3
Getafe	W L	6	4	2	0	3	3	3	3
Real Sociedad	W D	3	3	0	0	2	1	1	2
Real Betis	W D	4	3	1	0	3	1	3	1
Espanyol	W D	6	3	2	1	3	3	2	4
Rayo Vallecano	W W	1	1	0	0	1	0	0	1
Real Zaragoza	W W	5	5	0	0	4	1	3	2
Granada	W W	1	1	0	0	1	0	1	0
Deportivo		5	4	1	0	4	1	2	3
Celta de Vigo		1	1	0	0	1	0	1	0
Real Valladolid		3	3	0	0	3	0	1	2

Season	Division	Pos	P	W	D	L	F	A	GD	Pts
2011-12	La Liga	2	38	28	7	3	114	29	85	91
2010-11	La Liga	1	38	30	6	2	95	21	74	96
2009-10	La Liga	1	38	31	6	1	98	24	74	99

Celta de Vigo

Ground: Balaidos

	11-12 H A	Last six seasons at home P	W	D	L	OV	UN	BS	CS
Real Madrid		1	0	0	1	1	0	1	0
Barcelona		1	0	0	1	1	0	1	0
Valencia		1	1	0	0	1	0	1	0
Malaga		1	0	0	1	1	0	1	0
Atl Madrid		1	0	0	1	1	0	1	0
Levante		3	0	2	1	2	1	3	0
Osasuna		1	0	0	1	0	1	0	0
Real Mallorca		1	0	0	1	1	0	0	0
Seville		1	0	0	1	1	0	1	0
Ath Bilbao		1	0	1	0	0	1	1	0
Getafe		1	1	0	0	1	0	1	0
Real Sociedad		4	0	3	1	0	4	1	2
Real Betis		3	1	2	0	1	2	3	0
Espanyol		1	0	0	1	1	0	1	0
Rayo Vallecano		3	0	3	0	0	3	0	3
Real Zaragoza		2	1	1	0	0	2	1	1
Granada		1	0	1	0	0	1	0	0
Deportivo	L L	2	1	0	1	1	1	1	1
Celta de Vigo									
Real Valladolid	D W	2	0	1	1	1	1	2	0

Season	Division	Pos	P	W	D	L	F	A	GD	Pts
2011-12	Segunda	2	42	26	7	9	83	37	46	85
2010-11	Segunda	6	42	17	16	9	62	43	19	67
2009-10	Segunda	12	42	13	13	16	38	44	-6	52

Deportivo

Ground: Riazor

	11-12 H A	P	W	D	L	OV	UN	BS	CS
						Last six seasons at home			
Real Madrid		5	3	1	1	2	3	2	3
Barcelona		5	1	2	2	2	3	3	1
Valencia		5	0	2	3	2	3	3	1
Malaga		3	3	0	0	1	2	0	3
Atl Madrid		5	2	0	3	3	2	2	1
Levante		3	1	1	1	0	3	0	2
Osasuna		5	2	2	1	1	4	1	4
Real Mallorca		5	3	2	0	1	4	2	3
Seville		5	2	1	2	4	1	4	1
Ath Bilbao		5	4	0	1	4	1	3	1
Getafe		5	1	3	1	2	3	4	1
Real Sociedad		2	2	0	0	1	1	1	1
Real Betis		3	1	1	1	0	3	1	1
Espanyol		5	3	1	1	2	3	1	4
Rayo Vallecano		0	0	0	0	0	0	0	0
Real Zaragoza		4	1	2	1	1	3	2	1
Granada		0	0	0	0	0	0	0	0
Deportivo									
Celta de Vigo	W W	2	1	0	1	1	1	1	0
Real Valladolid	D D	4	2	1	1	1	3	2	1

Season	Division	Pos	P	W	D	L	F	A	GD	Pts
2011-12	Segunda	1	42	29	4	9	76	45	31	91
2010-11	La Liga	18	38	10	13	15	31	47	-16	43
2009-10	La Liga	10	38	13	8	17	35	49	-14	47

Espanyol

Ground: Conella-El Prat

	11-12 H A	P	W	D	L	OV	UN	BS	CS
						Last six seasons at home			
Real Madrid	L L	6	1	0	5	3	3	1	0
Barcelona	D L	6	1	3	2	3	3	5	1
Valencia	W L	6	3	2	1	3	3	2	3
Malaga	L L	4	3	0	1	3	1	2	2
Atl Madrid	W L	6	3	1	2	5	1	4	1
Levante	L L	4	2	1	1	2	2	3	1
Osasuna	L L	6	3	1	2	2	4	2	3
Real Mallorca	W L	6	3	2	1	4	2	5	1
Seville	D D	6	2	1	3	3	3	4	1
Ath Bilbao	W D	6	6	0	0	4	2	4	2
Getafe	W D	6	3	1	2	2	4	3	2
Real Sociedad	D D	3	2	1	0	2	1	2	1
Real Betis	W D	4	2	1	1	2	2	2	2
Espanyol									
Rayo Vallecano	W W	1	1	0	0	1	0	1	0
Real Zaragoza	L L	5	2	1	2	3	2	3	1
Granada	W L	1	1	0	0	0	0	1	0
Deportivo		5	4	0	1	2	3	2	3
Celta de Vigo		1	1	0	0	1	0	1	0
Real Valladolid		3	1	1	1	0	3	1	1

Season	Division	Pos	P	W	D	L	F	A	GD	Pts
2011-12	La Liga	14	38	12	10	16	46	56	-10	46
2010-11	La Liga	8	38	15	4	19	46	55	-9	49
2009-10	La Liga	11	38	11	11	16	29	46	-17	44

Getafe

Ground: Alfonso Perez

	11-12 H A	P	W	D	L	OV	UN	BS	CS
						Last six seasons at home			
Real Madrid	L L	6	2	0	4	3	3	3	1
Barcelona	W L	6	2	1	3	1	5	2	2
Valencia	W L	6	3	1	2	5	1	3	2
Malaga	L L	4	1	0	3	3	1	3	0
Atl Madrid	W L	6	2	2	2	3	3	5	1
Levante	D W	4	2	2	0	2	2	3	1
Osasuna	D D	6	4	1	1	3	3	2	3
Real Mallorca	L W	6	4	1	1	5	1	3	3
Seville	W L	6	4	1	1	3	3	3	2
Ath Bilbao	D D	6	2	4	0	1	5	2	4
Getafe									
Real Sociedad	W D	3	2	0	1	1	2	0	2
Real Betis	W D	4	1	3	0	0	4	2	2
Espanyol	D L	6	0	3	3	1	5	4	0
Rayo Vallecano	L L	1	0	0	1	0	1	0	0
Real Zaragoza	L D	5	0	3	2	1	4	2	1
Granada	W L	1	1	0	0	0	1	0	0
Deportivo		5	2	1	2	2	3	2	2
Celta de Vigo		1	1	0	0	0	1	0	1
Real Valladolid		3	2	0	1	1	2	0	2

Season	Division	Pos	P	W	D	L	F	A	GD	Pts
2011-12	La Liga	11	38	12	11	15	40	51	-11	47
2010-11	La Liga	16	38	12	8	18	49	60	-11	44
2009-10	La Liga	6	38	17	7	14	58	48	10	58

Granada

Ground: Nuevo Los Carmenes

	11-12 H A	P	W	D	L	OV	UN	BS	CS
						Last six seasons at home			
Real Madrid	L L	1	0	0	1	1	0	1	0
Barcelona	L L	1	0	0	1	0	1	0	0
Valencia	L L	1	0	0	1	0	1	0	0
Malaga	W L	1	1	0	0	1	0	1	0
Atl Madrid	D L	1	0	1	0	0	1	0	1
Levante	W L	1	1	0	0	1	0	1	0
Osasuna	D L	1	0	1	0	0	1	1	0
Real Mallorca	D D	1	0	1	0	1	0	1	0
Seville	L W	1	0	0	1	1	0	0	0
Ath Bilbao	D W	1	0	1	0	1	0	1	0
Getafe	W L	1	1	0	0	0	1	0	1
Real Sociedad	W L	1	1	0	0	1	0	1	0
Real Betis	L W	2	1	0	1	1	1	0	1
Espanyol	W L	1	1	0	0	0	1	0	1
Rayo Vallecano	L L	2	0	1	1	1	1	2	0
Real Zaragoza	W L	1	1	0	0	0	1	0	1
Granada									
Deportivo		0	0	0	0	0	0	0	0
Celta de Vigo		1	0	1	0	0	1	1	0
Real Valladolid		1	0	0	1	0	1	0	0

Season	Division	Pos	P	W	D	L	F	A	GD	Pts
2011-12	La Liga	17	38	12	6	20	35	56	-21	42
2010-11	Segunda	5	42	18	14	10	71	47	24	68
2009-10	Segunda B4	1	38	23	7	8	74	37	37	76

Levante

Ground: Ciutat de Valencia

	11-12		Last six seasons at home							
	H	A	P	W	D	L	OV	UN	BS	CS
Real Madrid	W	L	4	1	1	2	1	3	1	2
Barcelona	L	L	4	0	2	2	2	2	4	0
Valencia	L	D	4	1	0	3	2	2	2	0
Malaga	W	L	2	2	0	0	2	0	1	1
Atl Madrid	W	L	4	2	0	2	1	3	0	2
Levante										
Osasuna	L	L	4	2	0	2	3	1	3	0
Real Mallorca	D	L	4	0	3	1	1	3	2	1
Seville	W	D	4	1	0	3	2	2	2	1
Ath Bilbao	W	L	4	1	1	2	3	1	2	2
Getafe	L	D	4	2	1	1	2	2	3	1
Real Sociedad	W	W	5	4	0	1	2	3	2	2
Real Betis	W	W	4	3	1	0	2	2	3	1
Espanyol	W	W	4	2	2	0	1	3	2	2
Rayo Vallecano	L	W	3	2	0	1	2	1	2	1
Real Zaragoza	D	L	5	2	2	1	3	2	3	2
Granada	W	L	1	1	0	0	1	0	1	0
Deportivo			3	1	0	2	1	2	1	1
Celta de Vigo			3	1	1	1	2	2		1
Real Valladolid			1	0	0	1	1	0	0	0

Season	Division	Pos	P	W	D	L	F	A	GD	Pts
2011-12	La Liga	6	38	16	7	15	54	50	4	55
2010-11	La Liga	14	38	12	9	17	41	52	-11	45
2009-10	Segunda	3	42	19	14	9	63	45	18	71

Malaga

Ground: La Rosaleda

	11-12		Last six seasons at home							
	H	A	P	W	D	L	OV	UN	BS	CS
Real Madrid	L	D	4	0	1	3	2	2	2	0
Barcelona	L	L	4	0	0	4	3	1	3	0
Valencia	W	L	4	1	0	3	1	3	1	1
Malaga										
Atl Madrid	D	L	4	1	2	1	2	2	1	2
Levante	W	L	2	2	0	0	0	2	0	2
Osasuna	D	D	4	1	2	1	1	3	3	0
Real Mallorca	W	W	4	3	1	0	3	1	3	1
Seville	W	L	4	1	1	2	4	0	4	0
Ath Bilbao	W	L	4	1	3	0	0	4	2	2
Getafe	W	W	4	3	1	0	3	1	3	1
Real Sociedad	D	L	3	0	1	2	1	2	2	0
Real Betis	L	D	2	0	1	1	0	2	1	0
Espanyol	W	W	4	4	0	0	3	1	2	2
Rayo Vallecano	W	L	1	1	0	0	1	0	1	0
Real Zaragoza	W	D	3	1	1	1	2	1	3	0
Granada	W	L	1	1	0	0	1	0	0	1
Deportivo			3	0	3	0	0	3	1	2
Celta de Vigo			1	0	1	0	0	1	1	0
Real Valladolid			3	1	1	1	1	2	1	1

Season	Division	Pos	P	W	D	L	F	A	GD	Pts
2011-12	La Liga	4	38	17	7	14	54	53	1	58
2010-11	La Liga	11	38	13	7	18	54	68	-14	46
2009-10	La Liga	17	38	7	16	15	42	48	-6	37

Osasuna

Ground: El Sadar

	11-12		Last six seasons at home							
	H	A	P	W	D	L	OV	UN	BS	CS
Real Madrid	L	L	6	2	1	3	4	2	4	2
Barcelona	W	L	6	1	3	2	3	3	3	2
Valencia	D	L	6	2	3	1	1	5	3	3
Malaga	D	D	4	1	2	1	3	1	3	1
Atl Madrid	L	D	6	2	1	3	4	2	3	2
Levante	W	W	4	3	1	0	2	2	3	1
Osasuna										
Real Mallorca	D	D	6	3	2	1	3	3	3	2
Seville	D	L	6	1	4	1	1	5	2	3
Ath Bilbao	W	L	6	3	2	1	3	4	4	2
Getafe	D	D	6	1	3	2	1	5	1	3
Real Sociedad	W	D	3	3	0	0	1	2	1	2
Real Betis	W	L	4	2	0	2	2	2	2	0
Espanyol	W	W	6	4	0	2	2	4	1	4
Rayo Vallecano	D	L	1	0	1	0	0	1	0	1
Real Zaragoza	W	D	5	3	2	0	2	3	1	4
Granada	W	D	1	1	0	0	1	0	1	0
Deportivo			5	2	2	1	2	3	2	2
Celta de Vigo			1	0	0	1	0	1	0	0
Real Valladolid			3	0	3	0	2	1	3	0

Season	Division	Pos	P	W	D	L	F	A	GD	Pts
2011-12	La Liga	7	38	13	15	10	44	61	-17	54
2010-11	La Liga	9	38	13	8	17	45	46	-1	47
2009-10	La Liga	12	38	11	10	17	37	46	-9	43

R Vallecano

Ground: Campo de Vallecas

	11-12		Last six seasons at home							
	H	A	P	W	D	L	OV	UN	BS	CS
Real Madrid	L	L	1	0	0	1	0	1	0	0
Barcelona	L	L	1	0	0	1	1	0	1	0
Valencia	L	L	1	0	0	1	1	0	1	0
Malaga	W	L	1	1	0	0	0	1	0	1
Atl Madrid	L	L	1	0	0	1	0	1	0	0
Levante	L	W	3	0	2	1	1	2	1	2
Osasuna	W	D	1	1	0	0	1	0	0	1
Real Mallorca	L	L	1	0	0	1	1	0	1	0
Seville	W	L	1	1	0	0	1	0	1	0
Ath Bilbao	L	D	1	0	0	1	1	0	1	0
Getafe	W	W	1	1	0	0	0	1	0	1
Real Sociedad	W	L	3	2	1	0	3	0	2	1
Real Betis	W	W	3	2	1	0	2	1	1	2
Espanyol	L	L	1	0	0	1	0	1	0	0
Rayo Vallecano										
Real Zaragoza	D	W	2	0	2	0	1	1	1	1
Granada	W	W	2	1	1	0	0	2	1	1
Deportivo			0	0	0	0	0	0	0	0
Celta de Vigo			3	1	0	2	3	0	3	0
Real Valladolid			1	1	0	0	1	0	0	1

Season	Division	Pos	P	W	D	L	F	A	GD	Pts
2011-12	La Liga	15	38	13	4	21	53	73	-20	43
2010-11	Segunda	2	42	23	10	9	73	48	25	79
2009-10	Segunda	11	42	13	14	15	67	58	9	53

Real Betis

Ground: Benito Villamarin

	11-12 H A	P	W	D	L	OV	UN	BS	CS
		Last six seasons at home							
Real Madrid	L L	4	1	0	3	3	1	3	0
Barcelona	D L	4	1	3	0	3	1	4	0
Valencia	W L	4	2	0	2	4	0	4	0
Malaga	D W	2	0	1	1	1	1	1	1
Atl Madrid	D W	4	0	1	3	1	3	1	0
Levante	L L	4	2	0	2	2	2	1	1
Osasuna	W L	4	1	1	2	2	2	0	2
Real Mallorca	W L	4	3	0	1	2	2	0	3
Seville	D W	4	0	3	1	0	4	1	2
Ath Bilbao	W W	4	2	0	2	3	1	2	1
Getafe	D L	4	1	2	1	2	2	3	0
Real Sociedad	L D	3	1	0	2	1	2	1	1
Real Betis									
Espanyol	D L	4	0	4	0	1	3	4	0
Rayo Vallecano	L L	3	2	0	1	2	1	1	1
Real Zaragoza	W W	3	2	1	0	2	1	3	0
Granada	L W	2	1	0	1	2	0	2	0
Deportivo		3	0	1	2	1	2	1	0
Celta de Vigo		3	1	2	0	0	3	2	1
Real Valladolid		3	1	2	0	1	2	3	0

Season	Division	Pos	P	W	D	L	F	A	GD	Pts
2011-12	La Liga	13	38	13	8	17	47	56	-9	47
2010-11	Segunda	1	42	25	8	9	85	44	41	83
2009-10	Segunda	4	42	19	14	9	61	38	23	71

Real Madrid

Ground: Santiago Bernabeu

	11-12 H A	P	W	D	L	OV	UN	BS	CS
		Last six seasons at home							
Real Madrid									
Barcelona	L W	6	2	1	3	3	3	4	1
Valencia	D W	6	4	1	1	2	4	2	4
Malaga	D W	4	3	1	0	2	2	2	2
Atl Madrid	W W	6	4	2	0	3	3	5	1
Levante	W L	4	3	0	1	2	2	2	1
Osasuna	W W	6	6	0	0	3	3	3	3
Real Mallorca	W W	6	5	0	1	4	2	4	2
Seville	W W	6	5	0	1	5	1	4	2
Ath Bilbao	W W	6	6	0	0	6	0	5	1
Getafe	W W	6	4	1	1	3	3	3	2
Real Sociedad	W W	3	3	0	0	2	1	2	1
Real Betis	W W	4	3	1	0	2	2	2	2
Espanyol	W W	6	5	1	0	6	0	3	3
Rayo Vallecano	W W	1	1	0	0	1	0	1	0
Real Zaragoza	W W	5	4	0	1	3	2	2	3
Granada	W W	1	1	0	0	1	0	1	0
Deportivo		5	5	0	0	4	1	4	1
Celta de Vigo		1	0	0	1	1	0	1	0
Real Valladolid		3	3	0	0	2	1	1	2

Season	Division	Pos	P	W	D	L	F	A	GD	Pts
2011-12	La Liga	1	38	32	4	2	121	32	89	100
2010-11	La Liga	2	38	29	5	4	102	33	69	92
2009-10	La Liga	2	38	31	3	4	102	35	67	96

Real Mallorca

Ground: Iberostar Stadium

	11-12 H A	P	W	D	L	OV	UN	BS	CS
		Last six seasons at home							
Real Madrid	L L	6	0	2	4	3	3	3	1
Barcelona	L L	6	1	0	5	3	3	2	0
Valencia	D D	6	2	1	3	3	3	4	0
Malaga	L L	4	1	2	1	1	3	2	1
Atl Madrid	W D	6	4	1	1	3	3	3	3
Levante	W D	4	4	0	0	3	1	2	2
Osasuna	D D	6	4	2	0	2	4	4	2
Real Mallorca									
Seville	D L	6	0	4	2	3	3	3	3
Ath Bilbao	D L	6	2	3	1	2	4	3	3
Getafe	L W	6	5	0	1	4	2	4	2
Real Sociedad	W L	3	2	1	0	1	2	1	2
Real Betis	W L	4	2	2	0	1	3	2	2
Espanyol	W L	6	4	1	1	2	4	1	4
Rayo Vallecano	W W	1	1	0	0	0	1	0	1
Real Zaragoza	W W	5	5	0	0	3	2	3	2
Granada	D D	1	0	1	0	0	1	0	1
Deportivo		5	2	3	0	0	5	1	4
Celta de Vigo		1	0	1	0	1	0	1	0
Real Valladolid		3	3	0	0	2	1	1	2

Season	Division	Pos	P	W	D	L	F	A	GD	Pts
2011-12	La Liga	8	38	14	10	14	42	46	-4	52
2010-11	La Liga	17	38	12	8	18	41	56	-15	44
2009-10	La Liga	5	38	18	8	12	59	44	15	62

Real Sociedad

Ground: Anoeta

	11-12 H A	P	W	D	L	OV	UN	BS	CS
		Last six seasons at home							
Real Madrid	L L	3	0	0	3	2	1	2	0
Barcelona	D L	3	1	1	1	2	1	2	0
Valencia	W W	3	1	0	2	1	2	1	1
Malaga	W D	3	2	0	1	1	2	1	1
Atl Madrid	L D	3	1	0	2	2	1	1	1
Levante	L L	5	2	2	1	2	3	4	1
Osasuna	D L	3	2	1	0	1	2	1	2
Real Mallorca	W L	3	3	0	0	1	2	1	2
Seville	W L	3	1	0	2	2	1	2	1
Ath Bilbao	L L	3	1	0	2	1	2	1	1
Getafe	D L	3	0	3	0	0	3	1	2
Real Sociedad									
Real Betis	D W	3	1	2	0	0	3	1	2
Espanyol	D D	3	1	2	0	0	3	1	2
Rayo Vallecano	W L	3	2	1	0	1	2	1	2
Real Zaragoza	W L	4	2	1	1	3	1	3	1
Granada	W L	1	1	0	0	0	1	0	1
Deportivo		2	1	0	1	1	1	0	1
Celta de Vigo		4	2	2	0	2	2	3	1
Real Valladolid		0	0	0	0	0	0	0	0

Season	Division	Pos	P	W	D	L	F	A	GD	Pts
2011-12	La Liga	12	38	12	11	15	46	52	-6	47
2010-11	La Liga	15	38	14	3	21	49	66	-17	45
2009-10	Segunda	1	42	20	14	8	53	37	16	74

Real Vallodolid

Ground: Jose Zorrilla

	11-12		Last six seasons at home							
	H	A	P	W	D	L	OV	UN	BS	CS
Real Madrid			3	1	1	1	1	2	2	1
Barcelona			3	0	1	2	1	2	1	0
Valencia			3	0	0	3	1	2	1	0
Malaga			3	1	1	1	1	2	2	1
Atl Madrid			3	1	1	2	1	2	0	
Levante			1	1	0	0	0	1	0	1
Osasuna			3	0	2	1	1	2	1	2
Real Mallorca			3	1	1	1	2	1	2	1
Seville			3	2	1	0	2	1	2	1
Ath Bilbao			3	1	1	3	0	3	0	
Getafe			3	1	2	0	0	3	0	3
Real Sociedad			0	0	0	0	0	0	0	0
Real Betis			3	1	1	1	2	1	2	
Espanyol			3	1	2	0	1	2	2	1
Rayo Vallecano			1	0	1	0	1	0	1	0
Real Zaragoza			2	1	1	0	1	1	2	0
Granada			1	0	0	1	1	0	1	0
Deportivo	D	D	4	2	2	0	3	1	1	3
Celta de Vigo	L	D	2	1	0	1	2	0	2	0
Real Valladolid										

Season	Division	Pos	P	W	D	L	F	A	GD	Pts
2011-12	Segunda	3	42	23	13	6	69	37	32	82
2010-11	Segunda	7	42	19	9	14	65	51	14	66
2009-10	La Liga	18	38	7	15	16	37	62	-25	36

Real Zaragoza

Ground: La Romareda

	11-12		Last six seasons at home							
	H	A	P	W	D	L	OV	UN	BS	CS
Real Madrid	L	L	5	0	2	3	5	0	4	0
Barcelona	L	L	5	1	0	4	3	2	3	1
Valencia	L	W	5	2	1	2	3	2	1	2
Malaga	D	L	3	1	1	1	1	2	1	2
Atl Madrid	W	L	5	3	1	1	1	4	2	2
Levante	W	D	5	4	1	0	3	2	2	3
Osasuna	D	L	5	1	1	3	3	2	4	0
Real Mallorca	L	L	5	2	2	1	2	3	3	1
Seville	L	L	5	3	0	2	3	2	3	1
Ath Bilbao	W	L	5	4	0	1	3	2	3	2
Getafe	D	W	5	3	2	0	3	2	4	1
Real Sociedad	W	L	4	3	1	0	3	1	3	1
Real Betis	L	L	3	1	0	2	2	1	1	0
Espanyol	W	W	5	4	1	0	3	2	2	3
Rayo Vallecano	L	D	2	0	0	2	2	0	2	0
Real Zaragoza										
Granada	W	L	1	1	0	0	0	1	0	1
Deportivo			4	2	2	0	0	4	1	3
Celta de Vigo			2	2	0	0	1	1	0	2
Real Valladolid			2	0	0	2	2	0	2	0

Season	Division	Pos	P	W	D	L	F	A	GD	Pts
2011-12	La Liga	16	38	12	7	19	36	61	-25	43
2010-11	La Liga	13	38	12	9	17	40	53	-13	45
2009-10	La Liga	14	38	10	11	17	46	64	-18	41

Seville

Ground: Ramon Sanchez

	11-12		Last six seasons at home							
	H	A	P	W	D	L	OV	UN	BS	CS
Real Madrid	L	L	6	3	0	3	5	1	5	1
Barcelona	L	D	6	1	2	3	3	3	4	0
Valencia	W	W	6	5	1	0	3	3	1	5
Malaga	W	L	4	1	2	1	2	2	2	1
Atl Madrid	D	D	6	4	1	1	4	2	5	1
Levante	D	L	4	3	1	0	3	1	3	1
Osasuna	W	D	6	5	1	0	1	5	2	4
Real Mallorca	W	D	6	3	0	3	5	1	5	1
Seville										
Ath Bilbao	L	L	6	4	1	1	5	1	4	2
Getafe	W	L	6	3	0	3	4	2	3	2
Real Sociedad	W	L	3	2	1	0	1	2	1	2
Real Betis	L	D	4	2	0	2	4	0	3	1
Espanyol	D	D	6	2	2	2	3	3	3	3
Rayo Vallecano	W	L	1	1	0	0	1	0	1	0
Real Zaragoza	W	W	5	5	0	0	5	0	3	2
Granada	L	W	1	0	0	1	1	0	1	0
Deportivo			5	2	2	1	4	1	4	3
Celta de Vigo			1	1	0	0	0	1	0	1
Real Valladolid			3	2	1	0	1	2	2	1

Season	Division	Pos	P	W	D	L	F	A	GD	Pts
2011-12	La Liga	9	38	13	11	14	48	47	1	50
2010-11	La Liga	5	38	17	7	14	62	61	1	58
2009-10	La Liga	4	38	19	6	13	65	49	16	63

Valencia

Ground: Mestalla

	11-12		Last six seasons at home							
	H	A	P	W	D	L	OV	UN	BS	CS
Real Madrid	L	D	6	1	0	5	5	1	4	1
Barcelona	D	L	6	1	3	2	4	2	3	1
Valencia										
Malaga	W	L	4	3	1	0	1	3	2	2
Atl Madrid	W	D	6	4	2	0	4	2	5	1
Levante	D	W	4	1	3	0	1	3	1	3
Osasuna	W	D	6	5	1	0	4	2	1	5
Real Mallorca	D	D	6	2	2	2	5	1	4	1
Seville	L	L	6	3	0	3	3	3	3	2
Ath Bilbao	D	W	6	3	2	1	2	4	3	2
Getafe	W	L	6	6	0	0	4	2	4	2
Real Sociedad	L	L	3	1	1	1	2	1	1	1
Real Betis	W	L	4	4	0	0	4	0	3	1
Espanyol	W	L	6	5	0	1	5	1	5	1
Rayo Vallecano	W	W	1	1	0	0	1	0	1	0
Real Zaragoza	L	W	5	3	1	1	2	3	3	2
Granada	W	W	1	1	0	0	0	1	0	1
Deportivo			5	4	1	0	3	2	2	3
Celta de Vigo			1	1	0	0	0	1	0	1
Real Valladolid			3	2	0	1	2	1	2	1

Season	Division	Pos	P	W	D	L	F	A	GD	Pts
2011-12	La Liga	3	38	17	10	11	59	44	15	61
2010-11	La Liga	3	38	21	8	9	64	44	20	71
2009-10	La Liga	3	38	21	8	9	59	40	19	71

Atalanta

Ground: Atleti Azzurri D'Italia

	11-12		Last six seasons at home							
	H	A	P	W	D	L	OV	UN	BS	CS
Juventus	L	L	4	0	0	4	3	1	2	0
Milan	L	L	5	2	1	2	1	4	2	1
Udinese	D	D	5	1	3	1	2	3	1	4
Lazio	L	L	5	3	1	1	2	3	1	3
Napoli	D	W	4	2	1	1	2	2	3	0
Inter	D	D	5	1	3	1	1	4	4	0
Roma	W	L	5	3	0	2	5	0	4	1
Parma	D	W	4	2	2	0	1	3	3	1
Bologna	W	L	3	1	1	1	0	3	1	1
Chievo	W	D	4	2	0	2	0	4	0	2
Catania	D	L	5	1	4	0	0	5	2	3
Atalanta										
Fiorentina	W	D	5	2	2	1	4	1	4	1
Siena	L	D	6	3	2	1	3	3	3	3
Cagliari	W	L	5	3	2	0	3	2	3	2
Palermo	W	L	5	1	2	2	3	2	4	1
Genoa	W	D	4	2	1	1	0	4	1	2
Pescara			1	1	0	0	0	1	0	1
Torino			4	2	1	1	3	1	3	1
Sampdoria			4	3	0	1	3	1	3	0

Season	Division	Pos	P	W	D	L	F	A	GD	Pts
2011-12	Serie A	12	38	13	13	12	41	43	-2	46*
2010-11	Serie B	1	42	22	13	7	61	35	26	79
2009-10	Serie A	18	38	9	8	21	37	53	-16	35

Bologna

Ground: Renato Dall'Ara

	11-12		Last six seasons at home							
	H	A	P	W	D	L	OV	UN	BS	CS
Juventus	D	D	5	0	2	3	2	3	3	1
Milan	D	D	4	0	2	2	3	1	2	1
Udinese	L	L	4	2	0	2	4	0	3	0
Lazio	L	W	4	2	0	2	3	1	3	0
Napoli	W	D	5	2	0	3	2	3	2	1
Inter	L	W	4	0	1	3	3	1	3	1
Roma	L	D	4	0	1	3	0	4	1	0
Parma	D	L	3	1	2	0	1	2	1	2
Bologna										
Chievo	D	W	5	2	2	1	3	2	3	1
Catania	W	W	4	3	1	0	1	3	2	2
Atalanta	W	L	3	1	1	1	2	1	2	0
Fiorentina	W	L	4	1	2	1	1	3	3	1
Siena	W	D	3	2	0	1	2	1	2	1
Cagliari	W	D	4	1	1	2	1	3	1	1
Palermo	L	L	4	2	1	1	2	2	3	1
Genoa	W	L	5	3	1	1	3	2	4	1
Pescara			1	1	0	0	1	0	1	0
Torino			1	1	0	0	1	0	1	0
Sampdoria			3	1	2	0	1	2	2	1

Season	Division	Pos	P	W	D	L	F	A	GD	Pts
2011-12	Serie A	9	38	13	12	13	41	43	-2	51
2010-11	Serie A	16	38	11	12	15	35	52	-17	42*
2009-10	Serie A	17	38	10	12	16	42	55	-13	42

Cagliari

Ground: Is Arenas

	11-12		Last six seasons at home							
	H	A	P	W	D	L	OV	UN	BS	CS
Juventus	L	D	5	1	0	4	2	3	2	1
Milan	L	L	6	0	2	4	3	3	3	1
Udinese	D	D	6	2	2	2	3	3	2	2
Lazio	L	L	6	2	0	4	2	4	1	2
Napoli	D	L	5	2	2	1	2	3	2	2
Inter	D	L	6	1	2	3	3	3	4	0
Roma	W	W	6	3	3	0	5	1	6	0
Parma	D	L	5	1	4	0	0	5	2	3
Bologna	D	L	4	2	2	0	1	3	3	1
Chievo	D	L	5	2	1	2	2	3	2	2
Catania	W	W	6	3	2	1	3	3	2	3
Atalanta	W	L	5	4	0	1	1	4	0	4
Fiorentina	D	D	6	2	2	2	3	3	3	2
Siena	D	L	5	2	2	1	2	3	2	3
Cagliari										
Palermo	W	L	6	4	1	1	3	3	3	2
Genoa	W	L	5	3	0	2	3	2	2	1
Pescara			0	0	0	0	0	0	0	0
Torino			3	1	2	0	1	2	0	3
Sampdoria			5	3	1	1	1	4	0	4

Season	Division	Pos	P	W	D	L	F	A	GD	Pts
2011-12	Serie A	15	38	10	13	15	37	46	-9	43
2010-11	Serie A	14	38	12	9	17	44	51	-7	45
2009-10	Serie A	16	38	11	11	16	56	58	-2	44

Catania

Ground: Angelo Massimino

	11-12		Last six seasons at home							
	H	A	P	W	D	L	OV	UN	BS	CS
Juventus	D	L	5	0	3	2	2	3	3	0
Milan	D	L	6	0	3	3	0	6	3	0
Udinese	L	L	6	3	1	2	0	6	1	3
Lazio	W	D	6	4	1	1	2	4	3	3
Napoli	W	D	5	3	2	0	3	2	3	2
Inter	W	D	6	2	0	4	4	2	4	0
Roma	D	D	6	2	3	1	2	4	5	0
Parma	D	D	5	3	2	0	2	3	2	3
Bologna	L	L	4	1	1	2	1	3	2	1
Chievo	L	L	5	2	1	2	2	3	3	2
Catania										
Atalanta	W	D	5	2	2	1	1	4	1	4
Fiorentina	W	D	6	2	1	3	0	6	0	4
Siena	D	W	5	0	4	1	2	3	2	2
Cagliari	L	L	6	4	0	2	3	3	3	1
Palermo	W	D	6	5	0	1	3	3	2	4
Genoa	W	L	5	4	1	0	2	3	1	4
Pescara			0	0	0	0	0	0	0	0
Torino			3	1	1	1	2	1	3	0
Sampdoria			5	4	0	1	2	3	2	3

Season	Division	Pos	P	W	D	L	F	A	GD	Pts
2011-12	Serie A	11	38	11	15	12	47	52	-5	48
2010-11	Serie A	13	38	12	10	16	40	52	-12	46
2009-10	Serie A	13	38	10	15	13	44	45	-1	45

Chievo

Ground: Marc'Antonio Bentegodi

	11-12 H A	Last six seasons at home P	W	D	L	OV	UN	BS	CS
Juventus	D D	4	1	2	1	0	4	1	2
Milan	L L	5	0	0	5	2	3	2	0
Udinese	D L	5	1	2	2	1	4	2	2
Lazio	L D	5	0	0	5	3	2	2	0
Napoli	W L	4	3	0	1	2	2	2	2
Inter	L L	5	1	1	3	2	3	2	0
Roma	D L	5	0	3	2	2	3	2	1
Parma	L L	4	1	2	1	1	3	1	3
Bologna	L D	5	1	3	1	0	5	2	2
Chievo									
Catania	W W	5	3	2	0	3	2	5	0
Atalanta	D L	4	0	4	0	1	3	3	1
Fiorentina	W W	5	2	0	3	1	4	1	1
Siena	D L	4	0	1	3	1	3	2	0
Cagliari	W D	5	2	3	0	1	4	2	3
Palermo	W D	5	3	1	1	0	5	0	4
Genoa	W W	4	2	1	1	2	2	2	1
Pescara		0	0	0	0	0	0	0	0
Torino		2	1	1	0	1	1	1	1
Sampdoria		4	0	3	1	1	3	3	1

Season	Division	Pos	P	W	D	L	F	A	GD	Pts
2011-12	Serie A	10	38	12	13	13	35	45	-10	49
2010-11	Serie A	11	38	11	13	14	38	40	-2	46
2009-10	Serie A	14	38	12	8	18	37	42	-5	44

Fiorentina

Ground: Artemio Franchi

	11-12 H A	Last six seasons at home P	W	D	L	OV	UN	BS	CS
Juventus	L L	5	0	3	2	2	3	3	1
Milan	D W	6	0	2	4	3	3	3	1
Udinese	W L	6	5	0	1	5	1	5	1
Lazio	L L	6	3	1	2	2	4	2	4
Napoli	L D	5	2	1	2	2	3	2	1
Inter	D L	6	0	3	3	3	3	3	2
Roma	W W	6	2	3	1	4	2	3	2
Parma	W D	5	4	0	1	3	2	2	3
Bologna	W L	4	2	1	1	3	2	2	3
Chievo	L L	5	3	0	2	2	3	2	2
Catania	D L	6	5	1	0	5	1	3	3
Atalanta	D L	5	3	2	0	4	1	4	1
Fiorentina									
Siena	W D	5	4	1	0	2	3	2	3
Cagliari	D D	6	5	1	0	2	4	2	4
Palermo	D L	6	2	1	3	2	4	2	3
Genoa	W D	5	5	0	0	2	3	1	4
Pescara		0	0	0	0	0	0	0	0
Torino		3	3	0	0	2	1	2	1
Sampdoria		5	3	2	0	2	3	2	3

Season	Division	Pos	P	W	D	L	F	A	GD	Pts
2011-12	Serie A	13	38	11	13	14	37	43	-6	46
2010-11	Serie A	9	38	12	15	11	49	44	5	51
2009-10	Serie A	11	38	13	8	17	48	47	1	47

Genoa

Ground: Luigi Ferraris

	11-12 H A	Last six seasons at home P	W	D	L	OV	UN	BS	CS
Juventus	D D	6	1	3	2	2	4	3	1
Milan	L L	5	2	1	2	1	4	1	2
Udinese	W L	5	4	0	1	4	1	3	2
Lazio	W W	5	1	1	3	2	3	2	1
Napoli	W L	6	4	1	1	3	3	3	2
Inter	L L	5	0	1	4	1	4	1	0
Roma	W L	5	4	0	1	4	1	4	0
Parma	D L	4	2	2	0	3	1	3	1
Bologna	W L	5	3	1	1	3	2	3	2
Chievo	L L	4	1	1	2	2	2	2	1
Catania	W L	5	4	1	0	2	3	2	3
Atalanta	D L	4	2	2	0	2	2	3	1
Fiorentina	D L	5	1	4	0	3	2	4	1
Siena	L W	4	2	0	2	3	1	3	1
Cagliari	W L	5	4	0	1	3	2	3	1
Palermo	W L	5	3	2	0	2	3	2	3
Genoa									
Pescara		1	1	0	0	1	0	0	1
Torino		2	2	0	0	2	0	0	2
Sampdoria		4	3	0	1	3	1	2	1

Season	Division	Pos	P	W	D	L	F	A	GD	Pts
2011-12	Serie A	17	38	11	9	18	50	69	-19	42
2010-11	Serie A	10	38	14	9	15	45	47	-2	51
2009-10	Serie A	9	38	14	9	15	57	61	-4	51

Inter

Ground: San Siro

	11-12 H A	Last six seasons at home P	W	D	L	OV	UN	BS	CS
Juventus	L L	5	2	1	2	2	3	2	3
Milan	W W	6	5	0	1	4	2	4	1
Udinese	L W	6	3	2	1	2	4	4	1
Lazio	W L	6	6	0	0	4	2	3	3
Napoli	L L	5	4	0	1	5	0	4	0
Inter									
Roma	D L	6	1	4	1	3	3	5	1
Parma	W L	5	5	0	0	3	2	2	3
Bologna	L W	4	3	0	1	4	0	2	1
Chievo	W W	5	5	0	0	3	2	3	2
Catania	D L	6	5	1	0	5	1	5	1
Atalanta	D D	5	4	1	0	4	1	4	1
Fiorentina	W D	6	6	0	0	2	4	2	4
Siena	W W	5	4	1	0	4	1	3	2
Cagliari	W D	6	5	1	0	3	3	3	3
Palermo	D L	6	3	3	0	6	0	6	0
Genoa	W W	5	3	2	0	3	2	3	2
Pescara		0	0	0	0	0	0	0	0
Torino		3	2	1	0	2	1	1	2
Sampdoria		5	2	3	0	1	4	2	3

Season	Division	Pos	P	W	D	L	F	A	GD	Pts
2011-12	Serie A	6	38	17	7	14	58	55	3	58
2010-11	Serie A	2	38	23	7	8	69	42	27	76
2009-10	Serie A	1	38	24	10	4	75	34	41	82

Juventus

Ground: Juventus Stadium

	11-12 H	A	P	W	D	L	OV	UN	BS	CS
Juventus										
Milan	W	D	5	3	0	2	3	2	2	1
Udinese	W	D	5	3	0	2	2	3	2	2
Lazio	W	W	5	4	1	0	3	2	4	1
Napoli	W	D	5	3	1	1	3	2	2	3
Inter	W	W	5	3	2	0	1	4	3	2
Roma	W	D	5	3	1	1	2	3	2	3
Parma	W	D	4	2	0	2	4	0	3	1
Bologna	D	D	5	2	2	1	2	3	4	0
Chievo	D	D	4	1	3	0	2	2	3	1
Catania	W	D	5	1	3	1	3	2	5	0
Atalanta	W	W	4	3	1	0	3	1	3	1
Fiorentina	W	W	5	2	2	1	2	3	4	1
Siena	D	W	4	2	2	0	1	3	1	3
Cagliari	D	W	5	2	2	1	2	3	4	1
Palermo	W	W	5	2	0	3	4	1	2	2
Genoa	D	D	6	5	1	0	5	1	5	1
Pescara			1	1	0	0	0	1	0	1
Torino			2	1	1	0	0	2	0	2
Sampdoria			4	1	3	0	2	2	3	1

Season	Division	Pos	P	W	D	L	F	A	GD	Pts
2011-12	Serie A	1	38	23	15	0	68	20	48	84
2010-11	Serie A	7	38	15	13	10	57	47	10	58
2009-10	Serie A	7	38	16	7	15	55	56	-1	55

Lazio

Ground: Olimpico

	11-12 H	A	P	W	D	L	OV	UN	BS	CS
Juventus	L	L	5	0	1	4	1	4	2	0
Milan	W	D	6	1	2	3	3	3	3	2
Udinese	D	L	6	3	1	2	5	1	4	1
Lazio										
Napoli	W	D	5	3	1	1	2	3	3	1
Inter	W	L	6	2	1	3	3	3	3	0
Roma	W	W	6	4	0	2	5	1	4	1
Parma	W	L	5	3	1	1	1	4	1	4
Bologna	L	W	4	2	1	1	2	2	2	2
Chievo	D	W	5	0	4	1	1	4	2	2
Catania	D	L	6	3	2	1	1	5	3	2
Atalanta	W	W	5	4	0	1	1	4	0	4
Fiorentina	W	W	6	3	1	2	1	5	1	3
Siena	D	L	5	2	3	0	1	4	3	2
Cagliari	W	W	6	3	1	2	3	3	3	2
Palermo	D	L	6	2	2	2	2	4	3	3
Genoa	L	L	5	2	1	2	3	2	4	1
Pescara			0	0	0	0	0	0	0	0
Torino			3	1	2	0	1	2	2	1
Sampdoria			5	4	1	0	1	4	2	3

Season	Division	Pos	P	W	D	L	F	A	GD	Pts
2011-12	Serie A	4	38	18	8	12	56	47	9	62
2010-11	Serie A	5	38	20	6	12	55	39	16	66
2009-10	Serie A	12	38	11	13	14	39	43	-4	46

Milan

Ground: San Siro

	11-12 H	A	P	W	D	L	OV	UN	BS	CS
Juventus	D	L	5	1	3	1	2	3	3	2
Milan										
Udinese	D	W	6	3	2	1	5	1	6	0
Lazio	D	L	6	2	4	0	3	3	5	1
Napoli	D	L	5	3	2	0	2	3	2	3
Inter	L	L	6	3	0	3	4	2	2	2
Roma	W	W	6	2	0	4	4	2	4	0
Parma	W	W	5	4	1	0	2	3	2	3
Bologna	D	D	4	2	1	1	1	3	2	2
Chievo	W	W	5	5	0	0	3	2	2	3
Catania	W	D	6	3	3	0	3	3	3	3
Atalanta	W	W	5	4	0	1	3	2	2	3
Fiorentina	L	D	6	3	2	1	1	5	2	4
Siena	W	W	5	4	1	0	2	3	1	4
Cagliari	W	W	6	6	0	0	5	1	4	2
Palermo	W	W	6	4	0	2	4	2	2	2
Genoa	W	W	5	4	1	0	1	4	2	3
Pescara			0	0	0	0	0	0	0	0
Torino			3	1	2	0	1	2	1	2
Sampdoria			5	4	0	1	4	1	1	4

Season	Division	Pos	P	W	D	L	F	A	GD	Pts
2011-12	Serie A	2	38	24	8	6	74	33	41	80
2010-11	Serie A	1	38	24	10	4	65	24	41	82
2009-10	Serie A	3	38	20	10	8	60	39	21	70

Napoli

Ground: San Paolo

	11-12 H	A	P	W	D	L	OV	UN	BS	CS
Juventus	D	L	6	4	2	0	5	1	5	1
Milan	W	D	5	2	2	1	4	1	4	1
Udinese	W	D	5	2	2	1	3	2	3	2
Lazio	D	L	5	1	3	1	2	3	2	2
Napoli										
Inter	W	W	5	3	2	0	0	5	1	4
Roma	L	D	5	1	1	3	3	2	2	1
Parma	L	W	4	2	0	2	2	2	2	2
Bologna	D	L	5	3	2	0	2	3	4	1
Chievo	W	L	4	3	0	1	2	2	1	3
Catania	D	L	5	4	1	0	1	4	1	4
Atalanta	L	D	4	2	1	1	1	3	1	3
Fiorentina	D	W	5	2	2	1	2	3	2	3
Siena	W	D	4	3	1	0	2	2	2	2
Cagliari	W	D	5	2	2	1	3	2	3	1
Palermo	W	W	5	4	1	0	1	4	1	4
Genoa	W	L	6	2	2	2	2	4	3	2
Pescara			1	1	0	0	0	1	0	1
Torino			2	0	1	1	1	1	2	0
Sampdoria			4	4	0	0	1	3	0	4

Season	Division	Pos	P	W	D	L	F	A	GD	Pts
2011-12	Serie A	5	38	16	13	9	66	46	20	61
2010-11	Serie A	3	38	21	7	10	59	39	20	70
2009-10	Serie A	6	38	15	14	9	50	43	7	59

Palermo

Ground: Renzo Barbera

	11-12 H A	P	W	D	L	OV	UN	BS	CS
Juventus	L L	5	3	0	2	2	3	2	1
Milan	L L	6	4	1	1	4	2	3	2
Udinese	D L	6	3	2	1	2	4	3	2
Lazio	W D	6	3	1	2	4	2	3	1
Napoli	L L	5	4	0	1	5	0	5	0
Inter	W D	6	1	2	3	3	3	4	1
Roma	L L	6	2	1	3	4	2	4	0
Parma	L D	5	2	1	2	4	1	5	0
Bologna	W W	4	4	0	0	4	0	4	0
Chievo	D L	5	2	2	1	4	1	4	1
Catania	D L	6	3	2	1	3	3	4	1
Atalanta	W L	5	3	1	1	3	2	3	2
Fiorentina	W D	6	3	1	2	3	3	3	3
Siena	W L	5	4	0	1	2	3	2	3
Cagliari	W L	6	4	1	1	5	1	5	1
Palermo									
Genoa	W L	5	3	1	1	3	2	3	2
Pescara		0	0	0	0	0	0	0	0
Torino		3	2	1	0	1	2	1	2
Sampdoria		5	2	2	1	2	3	2	2

Season	Division	Pos	P	W	D	L	F	A	GD	Pts
2011-12	Serie A	16	38	11	10	17	52	62	-10	43
2010-11	Serie A	8	38	17	5	16	58	63	-5	56
2009-10	Serie A	5	38	18	11	9	59	47	12	65

Parma

Ground: Ennio Tardini

	11-12 H A	P	W	D	L	OV	UN	BS	CS
Juventus	D L	4	1	2	1	2	2	2	2
Milan	L L	5	1	1	3	0	5	0	2
Udinese	W L	5	3	1	1	2	3	1	3
Lazio	W L	5	1	2	2	3	2	4	0
Napoli	L W	4	0	1	3	3	1	4	0
Inter	W L	5	2	1	2	2	3	3	1
Roma	L L	5	0	1	4	3	2	1	1
Parma									
Bologna	W D	3	2	1	0	1	2	1	2
Chievo	W W	4	2	2	0	2	2	2	2
Catania	D D	5	2	3	0	3	2	4	1
Atalanta	L D	4	2	0	2	3	1	3	1
Fiorentina	D L	5	1	3	1	2	3	4	1
Siena	W W	4	3	1	0	2	2	2	2
Cagliari	W D	5	2	1	2	3	2	3	1
Palermo	D W	5	3	2	0	2	3	2	3
Genoa	W D	4	2	1	1	2	2	3	1
Pescara		0	0	0	0	0	0	0	0
Torino		2	2	0	0	0	2	0	2
Sampdoria		4	2	0	2	1	3	1	2

Season	Division	Pos	P	W	D	L	F	A	GD	Pts
2011-12	Serie A	8	38	15	11	12	54	53	1	56
2010-11	Serie A	12	38	11	13	14	39	47	-8	46
2009-10	Serie A	8	38	14	10	14	46	51	-5	52

Pescara

Ground: Adriatico

	11-12 H A	P	W	D	L	OV	UN	BS	CS
Juventus		1	0	0	1	0	1	0	0
Milan		0	0	0	0	0	0	0	0
Udinese		0	0	0	0	0	0	0	0
Lazio		0	0	0	0	0	0	0	0
Napoli		1	0	0	1	0	1	0	0
Inter		0	0	0	0	0	0	0	0
Roma		0	0	0	0	0	0	0	0
Parma		0	0	0	0	0	0	0	0
Bologna		1	0	0	1	0	1	0	0
Chievo		0	0	0	0	0	0	0	0
Catania		1	0	0	1	0	1	0	0
Atalanta		0	0	0	0	0	0	0	0
Fiorentina		0	0	0	0	0	0	0	0
Siena		1	0	1	0	0	0	1	0
Cagliari		0	0	0	0	0	0	0	0
Palermo		0	0	0	0	0	0	0	0
Genoa		1	1	0	0	1	0	1	0
Pescara									
Torino	W L	2	2	0	0	0	2	0	2
Sampdoria	W W	1	1	0	0	0	1	0	1

Season	Division	Pos	P	W	D	L	F	A	GD	Pts
2011-12	Serie B	1	42	26	5	11	90	55	35	83
2010-11	Serie B	13	42	14	11	17	44	48	-4	53
2009-10	Pro 1B	2	34	15	13	6	39	25	14	58

Roma

Ground: Olimpico

	11-12 H A	P	W	D	L	OV	UN	BS	CS
Juventus	D L	5	0	2	3	3	2	4	0
Milan	L L	6	1	4	1	3	3	4	2
Udinese	W L	6	5	1	0	4	2	5	1
Lazio	L L	6	4	1	1	2	4	2	4
Napoli	D W	5	1	3	1	3	2	4	0
Inter	W D	6	3	0	3	4	2	2	2
Roma									
Parma	W W	5	4	1	0	3	2	1	4
Bologna	D W	4	2	2	0	3	1	4	0
Chievo	W D	5	3	2	0	0	5	1	4
Catania	D D	6	5	1	0	4	2	3	3
Atalanta	W L	5	5	0	0	4	1	4	1
Fiorentina	L L	6	5	0	1	4	2	4	2
Siena	D L	5	4	1	0	2	3	2	3
Cagliari	L L	6	5	0	1	4	2	3	3
Palermo	W W	6	5	0	1	4	2	3	3
Genoa	W L	5	5	0	0	4	1	2	3
Pescara		0	0	0	0	0	0	0	0
Torino		3	2	0	1	2	1	2	0
Sampdoria		5	4	0	1	3	2	2	3

Season	Division	Pos	P	W	D	L	F	A	GD	Pts
2011-12	Serie A	7	38	16	8	14	60	54	6	56
2010-11	Serie A	6	38	18	9	11	59	52	7	63
2009-10	Serie A	2	38	24	8	6	68	41	27	80

Sampdoria

Ground: Luigi Ferraris

	11-12 H A	P	W	D	L	OV	UN	BS	CS
Juventus		4	1	3	0	1	3	1	3
Milan		5	2	2	1	3	2	4	0
Udinese		5	2	3	0	4	1	3	2
Lazio		5	4	1	0	2	3	2	3
Napoli		4	2	1	1	2	2	2	2
Inter		5	1	2	2	0	5	2	1
Roma		5	1	2	2	4	1	3	1
Parma		4	2	1	1	2	2	2	1
Bologna		3	3	0	0	2	1	2	1
Chievo		4	2	2	0	2	2	2	2
Catania		5	3	2	0	2	3	2	3
Atalanta		4	4	0	0	2		1	3
Fiorentina		5	2	2	1	2	3	2	2
Siena		4	2	2	0	2	2	2	2
Cagliari		5	0	4	1	1	4	4	0
Palermo		5	1	2	2	3	3	3	1
Genoa		4	1	1	2	0	4	0	2
Pescara	L L	1	0	0	1	1	0	1	0
Torino	L L	4	2	1	1	2	2	2	2
Sampdoria									

Season	Division	Pos	P	W	D	L	F	A	GD	Pts
2011-12	Serie B	6	42	17	16	9	53	34	19	67
2010-11	Serie A	18	38	8	12	18	33	49	-16	36
2009-10	Serie A	4	38	19	10	9	49	41	8	67

Siena

Ground: Artemio Franchi

	11-12 H A	P	W	D	L	OV	UN	BS	CS
Juventus	L D	4	1	0	3	1	3	0	1
Milan	L L	5	0	1	4	4	1	5	0
Udinese	W L	5	2	3	0	2	3	4	1
Lazio	W D	5	3	2	0	2	3	3	2
Napoli	D L	4	1	3	0	1	3	3	1
Inter	L L	5	0	0	5	3	2	3	0
Roma	W D	5	3	0	2	3	2	2	3
Parma	L L	4	1	2	1	1	3	2	1
Bologna	D L	3	1	2	0	0	3	2	1
Chievo	W D	4	2	1	1	2	2	2	1
Catania	L D	5	1	3	1	1	4	4	0
Atalanta	D W	6	2	3	1	1	5	3	2
Fiorentina	D L	5	2	2	1	1	4	2	3
Siena									
Cagliari	W D	5	3	2	0	1	4	1	4
Palermo	W L	5	2	2	1	3	2	4	1
Genoa	L W	4	0	2	2	0	4	0	2
Pescara		1	1	0	0	1	0	1	0
Torino		4	2	2	0	1	3	1	3
Sampdoria		4	0	1	3	2	2	2	1

Season	Division	Pos	P	W	D	L	F	A	GD	Pts
2011-12	Serie A	14	38	11	11	16	45	45	0	44
2010-11	Serie B	2	42	21	14	7	67	35	32	77
2009-10	Serie A	19	38	7	10	21	40	67	-27	31

Torino

Ground: Olimpico di Torino

	11-12 H A	P	W	D	L	OV	UN	BS	CS
Juventus		2	0	0	2	0	2	0	0
Milan		3	0	1	2	1	2	1	0
Udinese		3	1	0	2	1	2	1	1
Lazio		3	0	1	2	2	1	1	1
Napoli		2	2	0	0	1	1	1	1
Inter		3	0	0	3	2	1	2	0
Roma		3	0	1	2	1	2	1	1
Parma		2	0	2	0	1	1	2	0
Bologna		1	0	1	0	0	1	1	0
Chievo		2	1	1	0	0	2	1	1
Catania		3	2	1	0	1	2	2	1
Atalanta		4	2	0	2	3	1	3	1
Fiorentina		3	0	0	3	1	2	1	0
Siena		4	1	2	1	1	3	3	1
Cagliari		3	2	0	1	0	3	0	2
Palermo		3	2	1	0	1	2	1	2
Genoa		2	0	1	1	1	1	2	0
Pescara	W L	2	2	0	0	2	0	2	0
Torino									
Sampdoria	W W	4	3	0	1	2	2	2	2

Season	Division	Pos	P	W	D	L	F	A	GD	Pts
2011-12	Serie B	2	42	24	11	7	57	28	29	83
2010-11	Serie B	8	42	15	13	14	49	48	1	58
2009-10	Serie B	5	42	19	11	12	53	36	17	68

Udinese

Ground: Friuli

	11-12 H A	P	W	D	L	OV	UN	BS	CS
Juventus	D L	5	2	1	2	4	1	2	2
Milan	L D	6	2	1	3	3	3	2	2
Udinese									
Lazio	W D	6	2	3	1	4	2	5	1
Napoli	D L	5	2	2	1	4	1	3	1
Inter	L W	6	1	2	3	3	3	3	2
Roma	W L	6	3	0	3	4	2	4	1
Parma	W L	5	2	2	1	4	1	4	0
Bologna	W W	4	2	2	0	0	4	2	2
Chievo	W D	5	3	1	1	2	3	2	2
Catania	W W	6	4	1	1	3	3	4	1
Atalanta	D D	5	2	1	2	3	2	2	3
Fiorentina	W L	6	5	0	1	3	3	3	2
Siena	W L	5	5	0	0	4	1	3	2
Cagliari	D D	6	3	2	1	3	3	4	1
Palermo	W D	6	4	1	1	4	2	5	1
Genoa	W L	5	2	1	2	2	3	2	2
Pescara		0	0	0	0	0	0	0	0
Torino		3	3	0	0	1	2	1	2
Sampdoria		5	3	1	1	2	3	3	2

Season	Division	Pos	P	W	D	L	F	A	GD	Pts
2011-12	Serie A	3	38	18	10	10	52	35	17	64
2010-11	Serie A	4	38	20	6	12	65	43	22	66
2009-10	Serie A	15	38	11	11	16	54	59	-5	44

Ajaccio

Ground: Francois COTY

	11-12 H	A	P	W	D	L	OV	UN	BS	CS
Montpellier	L	L	4	1	0	3	3	1	2	0
Paris SG	L	L	1	0	0	1	1	0	1	0
Lille	L	L	1	0	0	1	1	0	1	0
Lyon	D	D	1	0	1	0	0	1	1	0
Bordeaux	L	D	1	0	0	1	0	1	0	0
Rennes	W	L	1	1	0	0	0	1	0	1
St Etienne	D	L	1	0	1	0	0	1	1	0
Toulouse	L	W	1	0	0	1	0	1	0	0
Evian TG	D	L	2	1	1	0	0	2	1	1
Marseille	W	L	1	1	0	0	0	1	0	1
Nancy	D	D	1	0	1	0	0	1	0	1
Valenciennes	W	W	1	1	0	0	1	0	1	0
Nice	D	L	1	0	1	0	0	1	1	0
Sochaux	W	W	1	1	0	0	1	0	1	0
Brest	D	D	5	1	4	0	1	4	3	2
Ajaccio										
Lorient	D	L	1	0	1	0	0	1	1	0
Bastia			4	0	1	3	1	3	2	0
Reims			4	3	1	0	3	1	2	2
Troyes			3	2	1	0	1	2	2	2

Season	Division	Pos	P	W	D	L	F	A	GD	Pts
2011-12	Ligue 1	16	38	9	14	15	40	61	-21	41
2010-11	Ligue 2	2	38	17	13	8	45	37	8	64
2009-10	Ligue 2	13	38	13	9	16	41	42	-1	48

Bastia

Ground: Armand Cesari

	11-12 H	A	P	W	D	L	OV	UN	BS	CS
Montpellier			3	2	1	0	0	3	1	2
Paris SG			0	0	0	0	0	0	0	0
Lille			0	0	0	0	0	0	0	0
Lyon			0	0	0	0	0	0	0	0
Bordeaux			0	0	0	0	0	0	0	0
Rennes			0	0	0	0	0	0	0	0
St Etienne			0	0	0	0	0	0	0	0
Toulouse			0	0	0	0	0	0	0	0
Evian TG			0	0	0	0	0	0	0	0
Marseille			0	0	0	0	0	0	0	0
Nancy			0	0	0	0	0	0	0	0
Valenciennes			0	0	0	0	0	0	0	0
Nice			0	0	0	0	0	0	0	0
Sochaux			0	0	0	0	0	0	0	0
Brest			4	2	1	1	2	2	2	1
Ajaccio			4	3	0	1	2	2	2	1
Lorient			0	0	0	0	0	0	0	0
Bastia										
Reims	W	L	4	2	1	1	2	2	2	2
Troyes	W	L	3	3	0	0	2	1	2	1

Season	Division	Pos	P	W	D	L	F	A	GD	Pts
2011-12	Ligue 2	1	38	21	8	9	61	36	25	71
2010-11	National	1	40	27	10	3	81	24	57	91
2009-10	Ligue 2	20	38	10	9	19	40	48	-8	39

Bordeaux

Ground: Chaban-Delmas

	11-12 H	A	P	W	D	L	OV	UN	BS	CS
Montpellier	D	L	3	1	2	0	0	2	2	1
Paris SG	D	D	6	4	2	0	2	4	1	5
Lille	D	W	6	1	4	1	2	4	4	1
Lyon	W	L	6	3	1	2	3	3	3	3
Bordeaux										
Rennes	W	L	6	3	2	1	2	4	2	4
St Etienne	L	W	6	4	1	1	2	4	3	3
Toulouse	W	L	6	5	0	1	3	3	3	3
Evian TG	D	D	1	0	1	0	0	1	0	1
Marseille	W	D	6	2	4	0	2	4	5	1
Nancy	W	D	6	5	0	1	4	2	3	3
Valenciennes	W	W	6	4	1	1	4	2	5	0
Nice	L	L	6	4	1	1	4	2	3	3
Sochaux	W	W	6	5	0	1	2	4	0	5
Brest	D	W	2	0	1	1	0	2	1	0
Ajaccio	D	W	1	0	1	0	0	1	1	0
Lorient	W	D	6	4	2	0	2	4	3	3
Bastia			0	0	0	0	0	0	0	0
Reims			0	0	0	0	0	0	0	0
Troyes			1	1	0	0	1	0	1	0

Season	Division	Pos	P	W	D	L	F	A	GD	Pts
2011-12	Ligue 1	5	38	16	13	9	53	41	12	61
2010-11	Ligue 1	7	38	12	15	11	43	42	1	51
2009-10	Ligue 1	6	38	19	7	12	58	40	18	64

Brest

Ground: Francis-Le Ble

	11-12 H	A	P	W	D	L	OV	UN	BS	CS
Montpellier	D	L	5	1	3	1	2	3	1	3
Paris SG	L	L	2	0	1	1	1	1	1	0
Lille	W	L	2	1	0	1	2	0	2	0
Lyon	D	D	2	0	2	0	0	2	2	0
Bordeaux	L	D	2	0	0	2	1	1	1	0
Rennes	L	D	2	1	0	1	0	2	0	1
St Etienne	D	L	2	1	1	0	1	1	1	1
Toulouse	D	D	2	0	1	1	0	2	0	1
Evian TG	D	W	1	0	1	0	0	1	0	0
Marseille	W	D	2	1	1	0	0	2	0	2
Nancy	L	L	2	1	0	1	1	1	1	0
Valenciennes	W	D	2	2	0	0	0	2	0	2
Nice	W	D	2	1	1	0	0	2	0	2
Sochaux	W	L	2	1	1	0	0	2	1	1
Brest										
Ajaccio	D	D	5	0	1	4	1	4	2	0
Lorient	W	L	2	1	1	0	1	1	1	1
Bastia			4	4	0	0	4	0	2	2
Reims			3	2	1	0	1	2	0	3
Troyes			2	1	1	0	1	1	1	1

Season	Division	Pos	P	W	D	L	F	A	GD	Pts
2011-12	Ligue 1	15	38	8	17	13	31	38	-7	41
2010-11	Ligue 1	16	38	11	13	14	36	43	-7	46
2009-10	Ligue 2	2	38	20	7	11	53	34	19	67

Evian TG

Ground: Parc des Sports d'Annecy

	11-12 H A	P	W	D	L	OV	UN	BS	CS
Montpellier	W D	1	1	0	0	1	0	1	0
Paris SG	D L	1	0	1	0	1	0	1	0
Lille	L D	1	0	0	1	1	0	0	0
Lyon	L L	1	0	0	1	1	0	1	0
Bordeaux	D D	1	0	1	0	0	1	0	1
Rennes	L L	1	0	0	1	1	0	1	0
St Etienne	L W	1	0	0	1	1	0	1	0
Toulouse	W L	1	1	0	0	1	0	1	0
Evian TG									
Marseille	W L	1	1	0	0	0	1	0	1
Nancy	W D	1	1	0	0	0	1	0	1
Valenciennes	W W	1	1	0	0	0	1	0	1
Nice	W D	1	1	0	0	0	1	0	1
Sochaux	L D	1	0	0	1	1	0	1	0
Brest	L D	1	0	0	1	0	1	0	0
Ajaccio	W D	2	1	1	0	1	1	2	0
Lorient	W W	1	1	0	0	1	0	1	0
Bastia		0	0	0	0	0	0	0	0
Reims		1	0	0	1	1	0	1	0
Troyes		1	1	0	0	1	0	0	1

Season	Division	Pos	P	W	D	L	F	A	GD	Pts
2011-12	Ligue 1	9	38	13	11	14	54	55	-1	50
2010-11	Ligue 2	1	38	18	13	7	63	41	22	67
2009-10	National	1	38	25	7	6	61	28	33	82

Lille

Ground: Lille Metropole

	11-12 H A	P	W	D	L	OV	UN	BS	CS
Montpellier	L L	3	2	0	1	2	1	2	0
Paris SG	W D	6	3	3	0	2	4	2	4
Lille									
Lyon	W L	6	3	1	2	3	3	4	1
Bordeaux	L D	6	3	2	1	3	3	4	2
Rennes	W D	6	4	2	0	2	4	3	3
St Etienne	W W	6	4	2	0	5	1	2	4
Toulouse	W D	6	3	2	1	3	3	5	1
Evian TG	D W	1	0	1	0	0	1	1	0
Marseille	W L	6	3	1	2	4	2	5	1
Nancy	W D	6	5	0	1	5	1	4	1
Valenciennes	W D	6	5	0	1	4	2	1	4
Nice	D W	6	1	5	0	1	5	5	1
Sochaux	D W	6	4	2	0	2	4	3	3
Brest	W L	2	2	0	0	1	1	1	1
Ajaccio	W W	1	1	0	0	1	0	1	0
Lorient	D W	6	2	3	1	2	4	4	2
Bastia		0	0	0	0	0	0	0	0
Reims		0	0	0	0	0	0	0	0
Troyes		1	1	0	0	1	0	0	1

Season	Division	Pos	P	W	D	L	F	A	GD	Pts
2011-12	Ligue 1	3	38	21	11	6	72	39	33	74
2010-11	Ligue 1	1	38	21	13	4	68	36	32	76
2009-10	Ligue 1	4	38	21	7	10	72	40	32	70

Lorient

Ground: Stade du Moustoir

	11-12 H A	P	W	D	L	OV	UN	BS	CS
Montpellier	W L	3	1	2	0	2	1	2	1
Paris SG	L W	6	1	2	3	1	5	3	1
Lille	L D	6	2	3	1	2	4	4	1
Lyon	L L	6	2	1	3	3	3	3	2
Bordeaux	D L	6	3	1	2	2	4	3	2
Rennes	L L	6	1	2	3	1	5	2	2
St Etienne	W L	6	3	3	0	3	3	2	4
Toulouse	D D	6	2	3	1	0	6	1	4
Evian TG	L L	1	0	0	1	1	0	0	0
Marseille	W L	6	2	1	3	6	0	6	0
Nancy	W D	6	4	2	0	2	4	2	4
Valenciennes	W L	6	4	1	1	3	3	4	2
Nice	W L	6	2	2	2	2	4	2	3
Sochaux	D D	6	2	2	2	3	3	5	1
Brest	W L	2	2	0	0	1	1	1	1
Ajaccio	W D	1	1	0	0	0	1	0	1
Lorient									
Bastia		0	0	0	0	0	0	0	0
Reims		0	0	0	0	0	0	0	0
Troyes		1	0	1	0	0	1	0	1

Season	Division	Pos	P	W	D	L	F	A	GD	Pts
2011-12	Ligue 1	17	38	9	12	17	35	49	-14	39
2010-11	Ligue 1	11	38	12	13	13	46	48	-2	49
2009-10	Ligue 1	7	38	16	10	12	54	42	12	58

Lyon

Ground: Stade de Gerland

	11-12 H A	P	W	D	L	OV	UN	BS	CS
Montpellier	W L	3	2	0	1	3	0	3	0
Paris SG	D L	6	3	3	0	5	1	5	1
Lille	W L	6	3	3	0	4	2	6	0
Lyon									
Bordeaux	W L	6	3	1	2	4	2	4	1
Rennes	L D	6	0	5	1	1	5	5	1
St Etienne	W W	6	3	2	1	1	5	3	2
Toulouse	W L	6	5	1	0	4	2	4	2
Evian TG	W W	1	1	0	0	1	0	1	0
Marseille	W D	6	2	3	1	3	3	4	2
Nancy	W L	6	6	0	0	4	2	3	3
Valenciennes	W L	6	4	2	0	2	4	3	3
Nice	L W	6	3	2	1	2	4	3	3
Sochaux	W L	6	4	1	1	4	2	4	1
Brest	D D	2	1	1	0	0	2	1	1
Ajaccio	D D	1	0	1	0	0	1	1	0
Lorient	W W	6	5	1	0	2	4	2	4
Bastia		0	0	0	0	0	0	0	0
Reims		0	0	0	0	0	0	0	0
Troyes		1	1	0	0	0	1	0	1

Season	Division	Pos	P	W	D	L	F	A	GD	Pts
2011-12	Ligue 1	4	38	19	7	12	64	51	13	64
2010-11	Ligue 1	3	38	17	13	8	61	40	21	64
2009-10	Ligue 1	2	38	20	12	6	64	38	26	72

Marseille

Ground: Stade Velodrome

	11-12 H	A	P	W	D	L	OV	UN	BS	CS
Montpellier	L	L	3	2	0	1	3	0	2	1
Paris SG	W	L	6	4	1	1	4	2	4	2
Lille	W	L	6	3	1	2	4	2	4	2
Lyon	D	L	6	2	2	2	5	1	6	0
Bordeaux	D	L	6	3	2	1	3	3	3	3
Rennes	L	W	6	3	2	1	2	4	1	4
St Etienne	D	D	6	5	1	0	3	3	3	3
Toulouse	L	D	6	1	3	2	4	2	4	1
Evian TG	W	L	1	1	0	0	0	1	0	1
Marseille										
Nancy	W	W	6	4	1	1	4	2	3	2
Valenciennes	D	D	6	3	3	0	3	3	4	2
Nice	W	D	6	5	0	1	4	2	3	2
Sochaux	D	L	6	4	1	1	5	1	4	1
Brest	D	L	2	1	1	0	1	1	1	1
Ajaccio	W	L	1	1	0	0	0	1	0	1
Lorient	W	L	6	2	2	2	2	4	3	2
Bastia			0	0	0	0	0	0	0	0
Reims			0	0	0	0	0	0	0	0
Troyes			1	1	0	0	1	0	1	0

Season	Division	Pos	P	W	D	L	F	A	GD	Pts
2011-12	Ligue 1	10	38	12	12	14	45	41	4	48
2010-11	Ligue 1	2	38	18	14	6	62	39	23	68
2009-10	Ligue 1	1	38	23	9	6	69	36	33	78

Montpellier

Ground: Stade de la Mosson

	11-12 H	A	P	W	D	L	OV	UN	BS	CS
Montpellier										
Paris SG	L	D	3	0	2	1	1	2	2	0
Lille	W	W	3	3	0	0	0	3	0	3
Lyon	W	L	3	1	0	2	1	2	1	1
Bordeaux	W	D	3	2	0	1	0	3	0	2
Rennes	W	W	3	2	0	1	2	1	1	1
St Etienne	W	D	3	2	0	1	2	1	2	1
Toulouse	D	W	3	1	2	0	0	3	2	1
Evian TG	D	L	1	0	1	0	1	0	1	0
Marseille	W	W	3	2	0	1	1	2	1	2
Nancy	W	L	3	1	0	2	1	2	1	1
Valenciennes	W	L	3	3	0	0	2	1	2	1
Nic e	W	W	3	2	1	0	0	3	1	2
Sochaux	W	W	3	3	0	0	1	2	1	2
Brest	W	D	5	3	2	0	2	3	2	3
Ajaccio	W	W	4	3	0	1	3	1	2	2
Lorient	W	L	3	3	0	0	3	0	2	1
Bastia			3	3	0	0	3	0	2	1
Reims			3	1	2	0	1	2	1	2
Troyes			2	2	0	0	2	0	0	2

Season	Division	Pos	P	W	D	L	F	A	GD	Pts
2011-12	Ligue 1	1	38	25	7	6	68	34	34	82
2010-11	Ligue 1	14	38	12	11	15	32	43	-11	47
2009-10	Ligue 1	5	38	20	9	9	50	40	10	69

Nancy

Ground: Marcel Picot

	11-12 H	A	P	W	D	L	OV	UN	BS	CS
Montpellier	W	L	3	1	1	1	1	2	1	2
Paris SG	W	W	6	3	2	1	2	4	2	3
Lille	D	L	6	1	2	3	2	4	2	2
Lyon	W	L	6	1	1	4	2	4	2	1
Bordeaux	D	L	6	3	2	1	3	3	2	3
Rennes	D	D	6	0	3	3	3	3	2	3
St Etienne	W	L	6	2	1	3	2	4	3	1
Toulouse	L	L	6	2	2	2	2	4	1	3
Evian TG	D	L	1	0	1	0	0	1	1	0
Marseille	L	L	6	1	1	4	4	2	4	1
Nancy										
Valenciennes	D	L	6	3	3	0	0	6	2	4
Nice	W	D	6	5	0	1	4	2	2	4
Sochaux	L	L	6	3	2	1	3	3	5	1
Brest	W	W	2	1	0	1	1	1	1	0
Ajaccio	D	D	1	0	1	0	1	0	1	0
Lorient	D	L	6	3	2	1	2	4	2	3
Bastia			0	0	0	0	0	0	0	0
Reims			0	0	0	0	0	0	0	0
Troyes			1	1	0	0	1	0	1	0

Season	Division	Pos	P	W	D	L	F	A	GD	Pts
2011-12	Ligue 1	11	38	11	12	15	38	48	-10	45
2010-11	Ligue 1	13	38	13	9	16	43	48	-5	48
2009-10	Ligue 1	12	38	13	9	16	46	53	-7	48

Nice

Ground: Stade du Ray

	11-12 H	A	P	W	D	L	OV	UN	BS	CS
Montpellier	L	L	3	0	0	3	1	2	0	0
Paris SG	D	L	6	4	1	1	2	4	1	4
Lille	L	D	6	1	2	3	1	5	2	1
Lyon	L	W	6	1	2	3	5	1	5	1
Bordeaux	W	W	6	3	3	0	4	2	5	1
Rennes	W	L	6	1	3	2	1	5	4	1
St Etienne	L	W	6	4	1	1	4	2	4	1
Toulouse	D	D	6	2	2	2	0	6	2	2
Evian TG	D	L	1	0	1	0	1	0	1	0
Marseille	D	L	6	2	1	3	2	4	3	1
Nancy	D	L	6	2	3	1	2	4	4	2
Valenciennes	W	L	6	5	1	0	1	5	1	5
Nice										
Sochaux	D	L	6	1	5	0	0	6	2	4
Brest	D	L	2	0	2	0	0	2	1	1
Ajaccio	W	D	1	1	0	0	1	0	0	1
Lorient	W	L	6	5	0	1	2	4	1	5
Bastia			0	0	0	0	0	0	0	0
Reims			0	0	0	0	0	0	0	0
Troyes			1	1	0	0	1	0	0	1

Season	Division	Pos	P	W	D	L	F	A	GD	Pts
2011-12	Ligue 1	13	38	10	12	16	39	46	-7	42
2010-11	Ligue 1	17	38	11	13	14	33	48	-15	46
2009-10	Ligue 1	15	38	11	11	16	41	57	-16	44

Paris SG

Ground: Parc des Princes

	11-12 H	A	P	W	D	L	OV	UN	BS	CS
Montpellier	D	W	3	0	2	1	3	0	3	0
Paris SG										
Lille	D	L	6	3	3	0	2	4	2	4
Lyon	W	D	6	3	2	1	1	5	3	3
Bordeaux	D	D	6	2	1	3	2	4	3	1
Rennes	W	D	6	2	2	2	2	4	2	3
St Etienne	W	W	6	4	1	1	3	3	3	2
Toulouse	W	W	6	3	1	2	3	3	3	2
Evian TG	W	D	1	1	0	0	1	0	1	0
Marseille	W	L	6	2	1	3	5	1	5	0
Nancy	L	L	6	1	4	1	2	4	3	2
Valenciennes	W	W	6	2	3	1	5	1	5	0
Nice	W	D	6	2	2	2	3	3	3	2
Sochaux	W	W	6	4	2	0	4	2	4	2
Brest	W	W	2	2	0	0	1	1	1	1
Ajaccio	W	W	1	1	0	0	1	0	1	0
Lorient	L	W	6	1	1	4	4	2	3	1
Bastia			0	0	0	0	0	0	0	0
Reims			0	0	0	0	0	0	0	0
Troyes			1	1	0	0	1	0	1	0

Season	Division	Pos	P	W	D	L	F	A	GD	Pts
2011-12	Ligue 1	2	38	23	10	5	75	41	34	79
2010-11	Ligue 1	4	38	15	15	8	56	41	15	60
2009-10	Ligue 1	13	38	12	11	15	50	46	4	47

Reims

Ground: Auguste Delaune

	11-12 H	A	P	W	D	L	OV	UN	BS	CS
Montpellier			3	2	0	1	3	0	2	0
Paris SG			0	0	0	0	0	0	0	0
Lille			0	0	0	0	0	0	0	0
Lyon			0	0	0	0	0	0	0	0
Bordeaux			0	0	0	0	0	0	0	0
Rennes			0	0	0	0	0	0	0	0
St Etienne			0	0	0	0	0	0	0	0
Toulouse			0	0	0	0	0	0	0	0
Evian TG			1	0	0	1	1	0	1	0
Marseille			0	0	0	0	0	0	0	0
Nancy			0	0	0	0	0	0	0	0
Valenciennes			0	0	0	0	0	0	0	0
Nice			0	0	0	0	0	0	0	0
Sochaux			0	0	0	0	0	0	0	0
Brest			3	2	1	0	1	2	1	2
Ajaccio			4	1	2	1	2	2	3	1
Lorient			0	0	0	0	0	0	0	0
Bastia	W	L	4	2	1	1	1	3	2	2
Reims										
Troyes	W	L	4	1	1	2	0	4	0	2

Season	Division	Pos	P	W	D	L	F	A	GD	Pts
2011-12	Ligue 2	2	38	18	11	9	54	37	17	65
2010-11	Ligue 2	10	38	12	13	13	53	51	2	49
2009-10	National	3	38	21	8	9	63	30	33	71

Rennes

Ground: Stade de la Route de Lorient

	11-12 H	A	P	W	D	L	OV	UN	BS	CS
Montpellier	L	L	3	1	0	2	1	2	0	1
Paris SG	D	L	6	5	1	0	0	6	1	5
Lille	D	L	6	1	3	2	4	2	6	0
Lyon	D	W	6	2	2	2	2	4	3	2
Bordeaux	W	L	6	2	2	2	2	4	2	3
Rennes										
St Etienne	D	L	6	3	3	0	0	6	1	5
Toulouse	L	L	6	4	1	1	4	2	4	1
Evian TG	W	W	1	1	0	0	1	0	1	0
Marseille	L	W	6	1	2	3	3	3	4	0
Nancy	D	D	6	0	4	2	0	6	3	1
Valenciennes	D	L	6	3	2	1	1	5	1	4
Nice	W	L	6	4	2	0	2	4	3	3
Sochaux	W	W	6	4	0	2	3	3	3	2
Brest	D	W	2	1	1	0	1	1	2	0
Ajaccio	W	L	1	1	0	0	1	0	1	0
Lorient	W	W	6	5	0	1	3	3	3	3
Bastia			0	0	0	0	0	0	0	0
Reims			0	0	0	0	0	0	0	0
Troyes			1	0	1	0	0	1	1	0

Season	Division	Pos	P	W	D	L	F	A	GD	Pts
2011-12	Ligue 1	6	38	17	9	12	53	44	9	60
2010-11	Ligue 1	6	38	15	11	12	38	35	3	56
2009-10	Ligue 1	9	38	14	11	13	52	41	11	53

Saint-Etienne

Ground: Geoffroy-Guichard

	11-12 H	A	P	W	D	L	OV	UN	BS	CS
Montpellier	D	L	3	2	1	0	1	2	1	2
Paris SG	L	L	6	2	2	2	0	6	1	3
Lille	L	L	6	2	2	2	4	2	5	1
Lyon	L	L	6	0	1	5	2	4	3	0
Bordeaux	L	W	6	1	3	2	3	3	4	1
Rennes	W	D	6	2	1	3	4	2	2	3
St Etienne										
Toulouse	D	W	6	2	3	1	3	3	3	2
Evian TG	L	W	1	0	0	1	0	1	0	0
Marseille	D	D	6	1	3	2	2	4	2	3
Nancy	W	L	6	4	2	0	2	4	1	5
Valenciennes	W	W	6	4	1	1	3	3	2	3
Nice	L	W	6	1	1	4	2	4	2	1
Sochaux	W	L	6	4	1	1	3	3	3	3
Brest	W	D	2	2	0	0	1	1	1	1
Ajaccio	W	D	1	1	0	0	1	0	1	0
Lorient	W	L	6	3	0	3	3	3	3	2
Bastia			0	0	0	0	0	0	0	0
Reims			0	0	0	0	0	0	0	0
Troyes			1	1	0	0	1	0	1	0

Season	Division	Pos	P	W	D	L	F	A	GD	Pts
2011-12	Ligue 1	7	38	16	9	13	49	45	4	57
2010-11	Ligue 1	10	38	12	13	13	46	47	-1	49
2009-10	Ligue 1	17	38	10	10	18	27	45	-18	40

Sochaux

Ground: Auguste Bonal

	11-12 H A	P	W	D	L	OV	UN	BS	CS
		Last six seasons at home							
Montpellier	L L	3	0	1	2	1	2	1	1
Paris SG	L L	6	2	1	3	4	2	5	0
Lille	L D	6	1	4	1	1	5	3	2
Lyon	W L	6	1	0	5	3	3	2	0
Bordeaux	L L	6	1	2	3	3	3	3	1
Rennes	L L	6	3	2	1	3	3	2	4
St Etienne	W L	6	4	1	1	2	4	3	2
Toulouse	W L	6	3	0	3	4	2	3	2
Evian TG	D W	1	0	1	0	0	1	1	0
Marseille	W D	6	4	0	2	2	4	2	3
Nancy	W W	6	4	2	0	2	4	4	2
Valenciennes	D L	6	3	2	1	2	4	4	2
Nice	W D	6	5	1	0	1	5	1	5
Sochaux									
Brest	W L	2	2	0	0	2	0	2	0
Ajaccio	L L	1	0	0	1	0	1	0	0
Lorient	D D	6	2	4	0	0	6	4	2
Bastia		0	0	0	0	0	0	0	0
Reims		0	0	0	0	0	0	0	0
Troyes		1	1	0	0	0	1	0	1

Season	Division	Pos	P	W	D	L	F	A	GD	Pts
2011-12	Ligue 1	14	38	11	9	18	40	60	-20	42
2010-11	Ligue 1	5	38	17	7	14	60	43	17	58
2009-10	Ligue 1	16	38	11	8	19	28	52	-24	41

Toulouse

Ground: Stadium de Toulouse

	11-12 H A	P	W	D	L	OV	UN	BS	CS
		Last six seasons at home							
Montpellier	L D	3	0	0	3	0	3	0	0
Paris SG	L L	6	2	1	3	3	3	4	1
Lille	D L	6	2	3	1	0	6	1	4
Lyon	W L	6	4	2	0	1	5	0	6
Bordeaux	W L	6	4	0	2	4	2	3	2
Rennes	W W	6	3	2	1	2	4	2	4
St Etienne	L D	6	3	0	3	2	4	2	1
Toulouse									
Evian TG	W L	1	1	0	0	1	0	1	0
Marseille	D W	6	1	4	1	1	5	1	4
Nancy	W W	6	3	3	0	2	4	2	4
Valenciennes	W L	6	3	2	1	2	4	1	4
Nice	D D	6	1	4	1	1	5	3	2
Sochaux	W L	6	3	0	3	3	3	3	2
Brest	D D	2	1	1	0	0	2	0	2
Ajaccio	L W	1	0	0	1	0	1	0	0
Lorient	D D	6	1	4	1	1	5	2	3
Bastia		0	0	0	0	0	0	0	0
Reims		0	0	0	0	0	0	0	0
Troyes		1	0	1	0	0	1	1	0

Season	Division	Pos	P	W	D	L	F	A	GD	Pts
2011-12	Ligue 1	8	38	15	11	12	37	34	3	56
2010-11	Ligue 1	8	38	14	8	16	38	36	2	50
2009-10	Ligue 1	14	38	12	11	15	36	36	0	47

Troyes

Ground: Stade de l'Aube

	11-12 H A	P	W	D	L	OV	UN	BS	CS
		Last six seasons at home							
Montpellier		2	1	0	1	2	0	2	0
Paris SG		1	0	1	0	0	1	1	0
Lille		1	0	1	0	0	1	1	0
Lyon		1	1	0	0	0	1	0	1
Bordeaux		1	1	0	0	0	1	0	1
Rennes		1	0	1	0	1	0	1	0
St Etienne		1	1	0	0	1	0	1	0
Toulouse		1	0	0	1	1	0	1	0
Evian TG		1	0	1	0	0	1	1	0
Marseille		1	0	1	0	0	1	1	0
Nancy		1	0	1	0	0	1	0	1
Valenciennes		1	0	0	1	1	0	1	0
Nice		1	1	0	0	0	1	0	1
Sochaux		1	0	0	1	0	1	0	0
Brest		2	1	0	1	1	1	1	1
Ajaccio		3	2	0	1	1	2	0	2
Lorient		1	1	0	0	0	1	0	1
Bastia	W L	3	2	0	1	1	2	1	2
Reims	W L	4	4	0	0	2	2	2	2
Troyes									

Season	Division	Pos	P	W	D	L	F	A	GD	Pts
2011-12	Ligue 2	3	38	17	13	8	45	35	10	64
2010-11	Ligue 2	16	38	13	7	18	35	45	-10	46
2009-10	National	2	38	19	14	5	64	31	33	71

Valenciennes

Ground: Stade du Hainaut

	11-12 H A	P	W	D	L	OV	UN	BS	CS
		Last six seasons at home							
Montpellier	W L	3	1	1	1	0	3	1	1
Paris SG	L L	6	1	2	3	4	2	4	2
Lille	D L	6	2	3	1	1	5	1	4
Lyon	W L	6	3	2	1	3	3	3	3
Bordeaux	L L	6	3	1	2	4	2	4	2
Rennes	W D	6	4	1	1	2	4	1	4
St Etienne	L L	6	4	1	1	1	5	2	4
Toulouse	W L	6	3	1	2	3	3	3	2
Evian TG	L L	1	0	0	1	0	1	0	0
Marseille	D D	6	3	2	1	4	2	5	1
Nancy	W D	6	2	2	2	1	5	3	2
Valenciennes									
Nice	W L	6	4	0	2	3	3	3	2
Sochaux	W D	6	2	4	0	3	3	4	2
Brest	D L	2	1	1	0	1	1	0	2
Ajaccio	L L	1	0	0	1	0	1	0	0
Lorient	W L	6	3	3	0	2	4	1	5
Bastia		0	0	0	0	0	0	0	0
Reims		0	0	0	0	0	0	0	0
Troyes		1	1	0	0	1	0	1	0

Season	Division	Pos	P	W	D	L	F	A	GD	Pts
2011-12	Ligue 1	12	38	12	7	19	40	50	-10	43
2010-11	Ligue 1	12	38	10	18	10	45	41	4	48
2009-10	Ligue 1	10	38	14	10	14	50	50	0	52

Augsburg

Ground: SGL arena

	11-12 H A	Last six seasons at home P W D L OV UN BS CS
B Dortmund	D L	1 0 1 0 0 1 0 1
B Munich	L L	1 0 0 1 1 0 1 0
Schalke	D L	1 0 1 0 0 1 1 0
B M'gladbach	W D	2 1 0 1 0 2 0 1
B Leverkusen	L L	1 0 0 1 1 0 1 0
Stuttgart	L L	1 0 0 1 1 0 1 0
Hannover	D D	1 0 1 0 0 1 0 1
Wolfsburg	W W	1 1 0 0 0 1 0 1
Werder Bremen	D D	1 0 1 0 0 1 1 0
Nuremberg	D L	2 0 2 0 0 2 0 2
Hoffenheim	L D	2 0 1 1 1 1 1 0
Freiburg	D L	4 1 2 1 2 2 3 1
Mainz	W W	3 2 0 1 2 1 2 0
Augsburg		
Hamburg	W D	1 1 0 0 0 1 0 1
Greuther Furth		5 2 3 0 1 4 2 3
E Frankfurt		0 0 0 0 0 0 0 0
Fortuna Dusseldorf		2 2 0 0 1 1 1 1

Season	Division	Pos	P	W	D	L	F	A	GD	Pts
2011-12	Bund	14	34	8	14	12	36	49	-13	38
2010-11	2.Bund	2	34	19	8	7	58	27	31	65
2009-10	2.Bund	3	34	17	11	6	60	40	20	62

B Leverkusen

Ground: BayArena

	11-12 H A	Last six seasons at home P W D L OV UN BS CS
B Dortmund	D L	6 1 3 2 4 2 5 1
B Munich	W L	6 1 2 3 1 5 3 1
Schalke	L L	6 4 0 2 2 4 2 2
B M'gladbach	L D	5 3 0 2 4 1 3 2
B Leverkusen		
Stuttgart	D W	6 4 1 1 6 0 4 2
Hannover	W D	6 5 0 1 2 4 0 5
Wolfsburg	W L	6 4 2 0 4 2 4 2
Werder Bremen	W D	6 1 3 2 1 5 2 2
Nuremberg	L W	5 3 1 1 3 2 1 3
Hoffenheim	W W	4 4 0 0 2 2 2 2
Freiburg	L W	3 1 1 1 2 1 2 0
Mainz	W L	4 2 1 1 2 2 3 0
Augsburg	W W	1 1 0 0 1 0 1 0
Hamburg	D D	6 1 3 2 4 2 6 0
Greuther Furth		0 0 0 0 0 0 0 0
E Frankfurt		5 2 2 1 3 2 3 1
Fortuna Dusseldorf		0 0 0 0 0 0 0 0

Season	Division	Pos	P	W	D	L	F	A	GD	Pts
2011-12	Bund	5	34	15	9	10	52	44	8	54
2010-11	Bund	2	34	20	8	6	64	44	20	68
2009-10	Bund	4	34	15	14	5	65	38	27	59

B Munich

Ground: Allianz Arena

	11-12 H A	Last six seasons at home P W D L OV UN BS CS
B Dortmund	L L	6 4 0 2 4 2 3 2
B Munich		
Schalke	W W	6 3 2 1 1 5 3 2
B M'gladbach	L L	5 3 1 1 2 3 3 1
B Leverkusen	W L	6 5 1 0 5 1 4 2
Stuttgart	W W	6 5 0 1 5 1 5 1
Hannover	W L	6 5 0 1 5 1 2 3
Wolfsburg	W W	6 6 0 0 5 1 4 2
Werder Bremen	W W	6 1 4 1 2 4 5 1
Nuremberg	W W	5 4 1 0 4 1 1 4
Hoffenheim	W D	4 4 0 0 3 1 2 2
Freiburg	W D	3 3 0 0 3 0 2 1
Mainz	D L	4 2 1 1 3 1 2 2
Augsburg	W W	1 1 0 0 1 0 1 0
Hamburg	W D	6 3 2 1 4 2 3 3
Greuther Furth		0 0 0 0 0 0 0 0
E Frankfurt		5 4 1 0 3 2 2 3
Fortuna Dusseldorf		0 0 0 0 0 0 0 0

Season	Division	Pos	P	W	D	L	F	A	GD	Pts
2011-12	Bund	2	34	23	4	7	77	22	55	73
2010-11	Bund	3	34	19	8	7	81	40	41	65
2009-10	Bund	1	34	20	10	4	72	31	41	70

B Dortmund

Ground: Signal Iduna Park

	11-12 H A	Last six seasons at home P W D L OV UN BS CS
B Dortmund		
B Munich	W W	6 3 2 1 2 4 3 3
Schalke	W W	6 2 2 2 2 4 2 3
B M'gladbach	W D	5 5 0 0 3 2 2 3
B Leverkusen	W D	6 3 1 2 3 3 3 2
Stuttgart	D D	6 2 3 1 3 3 4 1
Hannover	W L	6 3 2 1 5 1 6 0
Wolfsburg	W W	6 3 2 1 2 4 3 3
Werder Bremen	W W	6 5 0 1 2 4 1 4
Nuremberg	W W	5 3 2 0 1 4 0 5
Hoffenheim	W L	4 1 3 0 1 3 3 1
Freiburg	W W	3 3 0 0 2 1 0 3
Mainz	W W	4 1 3 0 1 3 3 1
Augsburg	W D	1 1 0 0 1 0 0 1
Hamburg	W W	6 5 0 1 2 4 1 4
Greuther Furth		0 0 0 0 0 0 0 0
E Frankfurt		5 3 1 1 3 2 3 2
Fortuna Dusseldorf		0 0 0 0 0 0 0 0

Season	Division	Pos	P	W	D	L	F	A	GD	Pts
2011-12	Bund	1	34	25	6	3	80	25	55	81
2010-11	Bund	1	34	23	6	5	67	22	45	75
2009-10	Bund	5	34	16	9	9	54	42	12	57

B M'gladbach

Ground: Stadion im BORUSSIA-PARK

	11-12 H A	Last six seasons at home P	W	D	L	OV	UN	BS	CS
B Dortmund	D L	5	2	2	1	0	5	2	2
B Munich	W W	5	1	4	0	3	2	5	0
Schalke	W L	5	4	0	1	2	3	1	3
B M'gladbach									
B Leverkusen	D W	5	0	2	3	3	2	4	0
Stuttgart	D W	5	0	2	3	2	3	3	1
Hannover	W L	5	3	0	2	4	1	4	0
Wolfsburg	W D	5	2	1	2	4	1	4	0
Werder Bremen	W D	5	3	1	1	5	0	4	1
Nuremberg	W L	4	2	2	0	1	3	2	2
Hoffenheim	L L	5	1	2	2	2	3	2	2
Freiburg	D L	4	1	2	1	1	3	2	2
Mainz	W W	5	2	1	2	1	4	2	2
Augsburg	D L	2	1	1	0	1	1	1	1
Hamburg	D W	5	2	1	2	2	3	3	1
Greuther Furth		1	1	0	0	1	0	0	1
E Frankfurt		4	1	1	2	2	2	2	1
Fortuna Dusseldorf		0	0	0	0	0	0	0	0

Season	Division	Pos	P	W	D	L	F	A	GD	Pts
2011-12	Bund	4	34	17	9	8	49	24	25	60
2010-11	Bund	16	34	10	6	18	48	65	-17	36
2009-10	Bund	12	34	10	9	15	43	60	-17	39

E Frankfurt

Ground: Commerzbank-Arena

	11-12 H A	Last six seasons at home P	W	D	L	OV	UN	BS	CS
B Dortmund		5	1	3	1	0	5	3	1
B Munich		5	2	1	2	3	2	4	1
Schalke		5	0	2	3	4	1	4	1
B M'gladbach		4	2	0	2	2	2	2	1
B Leverkusen		5	3	0	2	4	1	3	0
Stuttgart		5	0	1	4	4	1	2	0
Hannover		5	3	1	1	3	2	1	3
Wolfsburg		5	1	2	2	3	2	3	1
Werder Bremen		5	2	1	2	2	3	2	2
Nuremberg		4	1	2	1	2	2	3	1
Hoffenheim		3	0	1	2	2	1	2	0
Freiburg		2	1	0	1	1	1	1	0
Mainz		3	2	1	0	1	2	1	2
Augsburg		0	0	0	0	0	0	0	0
Hamburg		5	1	2	2	4	1	5	0
Greuther Furth	D W	1	0	1	0	0	1	0	1
E Frankfurt									
Fortuna Dusseldorf	D D	1	0	1	0	0	1	1	0

Season	Division	Pos	P	W	D	L	F	A	GD	Pts
2011-12	2.Bund	2	34	20	8	6	76	33	43	68
2010-11	Bund	17	34	9	7	18	31	49	-18	34
2009-10	Bund	10	34	12	10	12	47	54	-7	46

F Dusseldorf

Ground: Esprit Arena

	11-12 H A	Last six seasons at home P	W	D	L	OV	UN	BS	CS
B Dortmund		0	0	0	0	0	0	0	0
B Munich		0	0	0	0	0	0	0	0
Schalke		0	0	0	0	0	0	0	0
B M'gladbach		0	0	0	0	0	0	0	0
B Leverkusen		0	0	0	0	0	0	0	0
Stuttgart		0	0	0	0	0	0	0	0
Hannover		0	0	0	0	0	0	0	0
Wolfsburg		0	0	0	0	0	0	0	0
Werder Bremen		0	0	0	0	0	0	0	0
Nuremberg		0	0	0	0	0	0	0	0
Hoffenheim		0	0	0	0	0	0	0	0
Freiburg		0	0	0	0	0	0	0	0
Mainz		0	0	0	0	0	0	0	0
Augsburg		2	1	1	0	0	2	1	1
Hamburg		0	0	0	0	0	0	0	0
Greuther Furth	W D	3	2	1	0	1	2	1	2
E Frankfurt	D D	1	0	1	0	0	1	1	0
Fortuna Dusseldorf									

Season	Division	Pos	P	W	D	L	F	A	GD	Pts
2011-12	2.Bund	3	34	16	14	4	64	35	29	62
2010-11	2.Bund	7	34	16	5	13	49	39	10	53
2009-10	2.Bund	4	34	17	8	9	48	31	17	59

Freiburg

Ground: MAGE SOLAR Stadion

	11-12 H A	Last six seasons at home P	W	D	L	OV	UN	BS	CS
B Dortmund	L L	3	1	0	2	3	0	3	0
B Munich	D L	3	0	1	2	2	1	2	1
Schalke	W L	3	1	1	1	2	1	2	1
B M'gladbach	W D	4	3	0	1	3	1	1	3
B Leverkusen	L W	3	0	0	3	1	2	0	0
Stuttgart	L L	3	1	0	2	2	1	2	0
Hannover	D D	3	0	2	1	2	1	3	0
Wolfsburg	W L	3	3	0	0	2	1	1	2
Werder Bremen	D L	3	0	1	2	3	0	2	0
Nuremberg	D W	4	1	2	1	2	2	3	0
Hoffenheim	D D	4	2	1	1	2	2	2	1
Freiburg									
Mainz	L L	5	2	1	2	1	4	2	2
Augsburg	W D	4	4	0	0	0	4	0	4
Hamburg	L W	3	1	1	1	1	2	2	1
Greuther Furth		3	1	2	0	2	1	2	1
E Frankfurt		2	0	1	1	0	2	0	1
Fortuna Dusseldorf		0	0	0	0	0	0	0	0

Season	Division	Pos	P	W	D	L	F	A	GD	Pts
2011-12	Bund	12	34	10	10	14	45	61	-16	40
2010-11	Bund	9	34	13	5	16	41	50	-9	44
2009-10	Bund	14	34	9	8	17	35	59	-24	35

Greuther Furth

Ground: Trolli Arena

	11-12 H A	P	W	D	L	OV	UN	BS	CS
B Dortmund		0	0	0	0	0	0	0	0
B Munich		0	0	0	0	0	0	0	0
Schalke		0	0	0	0	0	0	0	0
B M'gladbach		1	0	0	1	1	0	1	0
B Leverkusen		0	0	0	0	0	0	0	0
Stuttgart		0	0	0	0	0	0	0	0
Hannover		0	0	0	0	0	0	0	0
Wolfsburg		0	0	0	0	0	0	0	0
Werder Bremen		0	0	0	0	0	0	0	0
Nuremberg		1	0	1	0	0	0	1	0
Hoffenheim		1	1	0	0	1	0	1	0
Freiburg		3	0	3	0	0	3	2	1
Mainz		2	1	0	1	1	1	0	1
Augsburg		5	3	1	1	4	1	5	0
Hamburg		0	0	0	0	0	0	0	0
Greuther Furth									
E Frankfurt	L D	1	0	0	1	1	0	1	0
Fortuna Dusseldorf	D L	3	1	2	0	1	2	3	0

Season	Division	Pos	P	W	D	L	F	A	GD	Pts
2011-12	2.Bund	1	34	20	10	4	73	27	46	70
2010-11	2.Bund	4	34	17	10	7	47	27	20	61
2009-10	2.Bund	11	34	12	8	14	51	50	1	44

Hamburg

Ground: Imtech Arena

	11-12 H A	P	W	D	L	OV	UN	BS	CS
B Dortmund	L L	6	4	1	1	4	2	4	2
B Munich	D L	6	2	3	1	1	5	3	3
Schalke	L L	6	1	2	3	4	2	5	0
B M'gladbach	L D	5	1	2	2	1	4	3	1
B Leverkusen	D D	6	2	3	1	2	4	3	3
Stuttgart	L W	6	4	0	2	5	1	4	1
Hannover	W D	6	2	4	0	1	5	2	4
Wolfsburg	D L	6	1	3	2	3	3	5	1
Werder Bremen	L L	6	3	1	2	4	2	4	1
Nuremberg	W D	5	3	2	0	1	4	1	4
Hoffenheim	W L	4	3	1	0	1	3	1	3
Freiburg	L W	3	1	0	2	1	2	1	1
Mainz	D D	4	0	2	2	2	2	2	1
Augsburg	D L	1	0	1	0	0	1	1	0
Hamburg									
Greuther Furth		0	0	0	0	0	0	0	0
E Frankfurt		5	4	1	0	2	3	2	3
Fortuna Dusseldorf		0	0	0	0	0	0	0	0

Season	Division	Pos	P	W	D	L	F	A	GD	Pts
2011-12	Bund	15	34	8	12	14	35	57	-22	36
2010-11	Bund	8	34	12	9	13	46	52	-6	45
2009-10	Bund	7	34	13	13	8	56	41	15	52

Hannover

Ground: AWD Arena

	11-12 H A	P	W	D	L	OV	UN	BS	CS
B Dortmund	W L	6	3	2	1	5	1	5	0
B Munich	W L	6	3	0	3	5	1	3	1
Schalke	D L	6	2	2	2	3	3	4	1
B M'gladbach	W L	5	4	0	1	3	2	3	1
B Leverkusen	D L	6	1	4	1	2	4	2	3
Stuttgart	W L	6	3	2	1	4	2	4	2
Hannover									
Wolfsburg	W L	6	2	2	2	3	3	2	2
Werder Bremen	W L	6	3	1	2	5	1	6	0
Nuremberg	W W	5	3	0	2	4	1	3	1
Hoffenheim	W D	4	2	0	2	2	2	2	1
Freiburg	D D	3	2	1	0	2	1	1	2
Mainz	D D	4	2	2	0	0	4	2	2
Augsburg	D D	1	0	1	0	0	1	0	0
Hamburg	D L	6	2	3	1	3	3	3	2
Greuther Furth		0	0	0	0	0	0	0	0
E Frankfurt		5	3	2	0	3	2	5	0
Fortuna Dusseldorf		0	0	0	0	0	0	0	0

Season	Division	Pos	P	W	D	L	F	A	GD	Pts
2011-12	Bund	7	34	12	12	10	41	45	-4	48
2010-11	Bund	4	34	19	3	12	49	45	4	60
2009-10	Bund	15	34	9	6	19	43	67	-24	33

Hoffenheim

Ground: WIRSOL Rhein Neckar Arena

	11-12 H A	P	W	D	L	OV	UN	BS	CS
B Dortmund	W L	4	3	0	1	2	2	2	2
B Munich	D L	4	0	3	1	2	2	3	1
Schalke	D L	4	1	3	0	0	4	2	2
B M'gladbach	W W	5	4	1	0	3	2	3	2
B Leverkusen	L L	4	0	1	3	3	1	2	0
Stuttgart	L L	4	0	2	2	2	2	3	1
Hannover	D L	4	2	2	0	3	1	2	2
Wolfsburg	W W	4	2	0	2	4	0	4	0
Werder Bremen	L D	4	1	1	2	2	2	2	1
Nuremberg	L W	3	1	1	1	2	1	2	1
Hoffenheim									
Freiburg	D D	4	1	2	1	0	4	2	1
Mainz	D W	4	1	1	2	1	3	2	1
Augsburg	D W	2	1	1	0	1	1	1	1
Hamburg	W L	4	3	1	0	3	1	1	3
Greuther Furth		1	1	0	0	1	0	0	1
E Frankfurt		3	2	1	0	1	2	2	1
Fortuna Dusseldorf		0	0	0	0	0	0	0	0

Season	Division	Pos	P	W	D	L	F	A	GD	Pts
2011-12	Bund	11	34	10	11	13	41	47	-6	41
2010-11	Bund	11	34	11	10	13	50	50	0	43
2009-10	Bund	11	34	11	9	14	44	42	2	42

Mainz

Ground: Coface Arena

	11-12 H A	P	W	D	L	OV	UN	BS	CS
B Dortmund	L L	4	2	0	2	1	3	1	2
B Munich	W D	4	2	0	2	4	0	3	0
Schalke	L D	4	0	1	3	2	2	1	1
B M'gladbach	L L	5	4	0	1	3	2	1	3
B Leverkusen	W L	4	1	1	2	2	2	2	1
Stuttgart	W L	4	2	2	0	1	3	2	2
Hannover	D D	4	1	1	2	1	3	2	1
Wolfsburg	D D	4	0	1	3	1	3	1	1
Werder Bremen	L W	4	0	1	3	3	1	4	0
Nuremberg	W D	5	5	0	0	3	2	2	3
Hoffenheim	L D	4	2	1	1	3	1	3	0
Freiburg	W W	5	2	2	1	3	2	4	1
Mainz									
Augsburg	L L	3	0	2	1	0	3	2	0
Hamburg	D D	4	0	3	1	0	4	1	2
Greuther Furth		2	0	0	2	1	1	1	0
E Frankfurt		3	1	2	0	2	1	2	1
Fortuna Dusseldorf		0	0	0	0	0	0	0	0

Season	Division	Pos	P	W	D	L	F	A	GD	Pts
2011-12	Bund	13	34	9	12	13	47	51	-4	39
2010-11	Bund	5	34	18	4	12	52	39	13	58
2009-10	Bund	9	34	12	11	11	36	42	-6	47

Nuremberg

Ground: easyCredit-Stadion

	11-12 H A	P	W	D	L	OV	UN	BS	CS
B Dortmund	L L	5	1	1	3	1	4	2	1
B Munich	L L	5	1	3	1	1	4	3	1
Schalke	W L	5	2	1	2	3	2	3	1
B M'gladbach	W L	4	3	0	1	0	4	0	3
B Leverkusen	L W	5	3	0	2	4	1	4	1
Stuttgart	D L	5	2	1	2	4	1	4	0
Hannover	L L	5	2	1	2	4	1	4	0
Wolfsburg	L L	5	2	1	2	2	3	3	1
Werder Bremen	D W	5	0	2	3	3	2	4	0
Nuremberg									
Hoffenheim	L W	3	0	1	2	1	2	1	1
Freiburg	L D	4	1	0	3	2	2	2	1
Mainz	D L	5	1	4	0	1	4	2	3
Augsburg	W D	2	2	0	0	1	1	1	1
Hamburg	D L	5	1	2	2	1	4	1	2
Greuther Furth		1	1	0	0	1	0	1	0
E Frankfurt		4	2	2	0	3	1	3	1
Fortuna Dusseldorf		0	0	0	0	0	0	0	0

Season	Division	Pos	P	W	D	L	F	A	GD	Pts
2011-12	Bund	10	34	12	6	16	38	49	-11	42
2010-11	Bund	6	34	13	8	13	47	45	2	47
2009-10	Bund	16	34	8	7	19	32	58	-26	31

Schalke

Ground: VELTINS-Arena

	11-12 H A	P	W	D	L	OV	UN	BS	CS
B Dortmund	L L	6	3	1	2	5	1	6	0
B Munich	L L	6	1	1	4	3	3	3	1
Schalke									
B M'gladbach	W L	5	4	1	0	3	2	3	2
B Leverkusen	W W	6	1	2	3	2	4	3	1
Stuttgart	W L	6	4	1	1	5	1	5	1
Hannover	W D	4	4	1	1	4	2	3	3
Wolfsburg	W L	6	3	1	2	4	2	3	3
Werder Bremen	W W	6	4	1	1	2	4	1	4
Nuremberg	W L	5	4	1	0	2	3	2	3
Hoffenheim	W D	4	2	0	2	2	2	2	1
Freiburg	W L	3	2	0	1	1	2	1	1
Mainz	D W	4	2	1	1	2	2	2	2
Augsburg	W D	1	1	0	0	1	0	1	0
Hamburg	W W	6	1	2	3	3	3	4	0
Greuther Furth		0	0	0	0	0	0	0	0
E Frankfurt		5	4	1	0	1	4	2	3
Fortuna Dusseldorf		0	0	0	0	0	0	0	0

Season	Division	Pos	P	W	D	L	F	A	GD	Pts
2011-12	Bund	3	34	20	4	10	74	44	30	64
2010-11	Bund	14	34	11	7	16	38	44	-6	40
2009-10	Bund	2	34	19	8	7	53	31	22	65

Stuttgart

Ground: Mercedes-Benz-Arena

	11-12 H A	P	W	D	L	OV	UN	BS	CS
B Dortmund	D D	6	2	1	3	5	1	6	0
B Munich	L L	6	2	2	2	4	2	4	2
Schalke	W L	6	4	1	1	4	2	2	4
B M'gladbach	L D	5	4	0	1	3	2	1	3
B Leverkusen	L D	6	3	0	3	3	3	2	2
Stuttgart									
Hannover	W L	6	5	0	1	3	3	2	3
Wolfsburg	W L	6	4	2	0	4	2	5	1
Werder Bremen	W L	6	5	0	1	5	1	4	1
Nuremberg	W D	5	2	1	2	3	2	1	3
Hoffenheim	W W	4	2	2	0	2	2	3	1
Freiburg	W W	3	2	0	1	2	1	2	0
Mainz	W L	4	3	1	0	2	2	2	2
Augsburg	W W	1	1	0	0	1	0	1	0
Hamburg	L W	6	4	0	2	3	3	2	4
Greuther Furth		0	0	0	0	0	0	0	0
E Frankfurt		5	3	1	1	3	2	4	1
Fortuna Dusseldorf		0	0	0	0	0	0	0	0

Season	Division	Pos	P	W	D	L	F	A	GD	Pts
2011-12	Bund	6	34	15	8	11	63	46	17	53
2010-11	Bund	12	34	12	6	16	60	59	1	42
2009-10	Bund	6	34	15	10	9	51	41	10	55

Werder Bremen

Ground: Weserstadion

	11-12 H A	Last six seasons at home P	W	D	L	OV	UN	BS	CS
B Dortmund	L L	6	2	2	2	2	4	3	2
B Munich	L L	6	1	1	4	5	1	4	1
Schalke	L L	6	1	2	3	2	4	4	0
B M'gladbach	D L	5	2	3	0	3	2	3	2
B Leverkusen	D L	6	2	3	1	4	2	5	0
Stuttgart	W L	6	3	2	1	4	2	4	2
Hannover	W L	6	4	2	0	4	2	3	3
Wolfsburg	W L	6	3	1	2	4	2	4	0
Werder Bremen									
Nuremberg	L D	5	3	0	2	2	3	2	2
Hoffenheim	D W	4	3	1	0	2	2	3	1
Freiburg	W D	3	3	0	0	3	0	2	1
Mainz	L W	4	2	0	2	2	2	0	2
Augsburg	D D	1	0	1	0	0	0	1	0
Hamburg	W W	6	4	1	1	2	4	3	2
Greuther Furth		0	0	0	0	0	0	0	0
E Frankfurt		5	2	1	2	4	1	3	2
Fortuna Dusseldorf		0	0	0	0	0	0	0	0

Season	Division	Pos	P	W	D	L	F	A	GD	Pts
2011-12	Bund	9	34	11	9	14	49	58	-9	42
2010-11	Bund	13	34	10	11	13	47	61	-14	41
2009-10	Bund	3	34	17	10	7	71	40	31	61

Spanish Primera Liga winner (top 12 in the betting)

	b365	Btfrd	Hills	Lads	Pwr	StJms
Real Madrid	4-6	4-5	4-5	4-5	8-11	4-6
Barcelona	5-4	11-10	1	21-20	6-5	6-5
Malaga	50	50	50	66	80	66
Atl Madrid	66	50	80	66	80	80
Valencia	66	66	66	66	80	80
Seville	100	100	100	150	125	100
Ath Bilbao	150	100	100	66	125	100
Levante	500	750	750	750	750	2000
Osasuna	1500	1000	1000	1000	1000	1500
Real Betis	1000	500	500	750	750	1000
Real Mallorca	1000	750	1000	1000	1000	1500
Espanyol	500	500	500	500	750	500

Win/each-way. See bookies for terms. Others available

French Ligue 1 winner (top 12 in the betting)

	b365	Btfrd	Hills	Lads	Pwr	StJms
Paris Saint-G	1-2	4-7	8-15	-	4-7	8-13
Lille	11-2	5	5	-	5	9-2
Lyon	7	7	7	-	8	7
Marseille	9	9	9	-	9	8
Bordeaux	14	16	16	-	16	16
Montpellier	16	16	16	-	18	15
Rennes	40	33	40	-	33	40
St Etienne	66	50	66	-	50	66
Toulouse	66	80	80	-	90	80
Lorient	200	250	250	-	250	250
Nancy	200	250	250	-	250	250
Bastia	400	500	250	-	250	500

Win/each-way. See bookies for terms. Others available

Wolfsburg

Ground: Volkswagen Arena

	11-12 H A	Last six seasons at home P	W	D	L	OV	UN	BS	CS
B Dortmund	L L	6	2	0	4	5	1	2	2
B Munich	L L	6	2	2	2	2	4	3	2
Schalke	W L	6	3	3	0	5	1	6	0
B M'gladbach	D L	5	4	1	0	3	2	2	3
B Leverkusen	W L	6	3	0	3	6	0	6	0
Stuttgart	W L	6	5	1	0	2	4	2	4
Hannover	W L	6	5	0	1	5	1	5	1
Wolfsburg									
Werder Bremen	W L	6	2	2	2	3	3	4	1
Nuremberg	W W	5	2	1	2	4	1	5	0
Hoffenheim	L L	4	2	1	1	4	0	2	2
Freiburg	W L	3	2	1	0	3	0	3	0
Mainz	D D	4	1	2	1	4	0	4	0
Augsburg	L L	1	0	0	1	1	0	1	0
Hamburg	W D	6	3	1	2	3	3	3	2
Greuther Furth		0	0	0	0	0	0	0	0
E Frankfurt		5	1	4	0	4	1	5	0
Fortuna Dusseldorf		0	0	0	0	0	0	0	0

Season	Division	Pos	P	W	D	L	F	A	GD	Pts
2011-12	Bund	8	34	13	5	16	47	60	-13	44
2010-11	Bund	15	34	9	11	14	43	48	-5	38
2009-10	Bund	8	34	14	8	12	64	58	6	50

Italian Serie A winner (top 12 in the betting)

	b365	Btfrd	Hills	Lads	Pwr	StJms
Juventus	6-4	6-4	6-4	13-8	6-4	11-8
Milan	2	15-8	7-4	2	21-10	2
Inter	9-2	4	4	13-5	4	4
Napoli	14	16	16	18	16	14
Roma	20	14	16	12	16	16
Lazio	20	20	25	28	25	20
Udinese	20	28	25	50	25	25
Fiorentina	66	80	100	250	125	100
Genoa	250	200	200	300	275	250
Palermo	150	200	200	300	325	200
Parma	80	150	100	80	125	150
Sampdoria	250	500	500	300	500	500

Win/each-way. See bookies for terms. Others available

German Bundesliga winner (top 12 in the betting)

	b365	Btfrd	Hills	Lads	Pwr	StJms
B Munich	4-5	4-5	5-6	4-5	5-6	5-6
B Dortmund	13-8	6-4	5-4	6-4	8-5	6-5
Schalke	16	12	16	12	16	20
Stuttgart	25	25	25	33	35	50
B M'gladbach	33	33	40	33	45	80
B Leverkusen	25	33	33	25	35	50
Wolfsburg	66	80	50	66	55	66
Hannover	66	80	66	66	70	66
Werder Bremen	50	50	100	66	80	150
Hamburg	80	66	100	66	125	200
Hoffenheim	100	100	150	100	125	200
Mainz	150	200	250	150	275	250

Win/each-way. See bookies for terms. Others available

Uefa Association Coefficients

Current Ranking		2007-08	2008-09	2009-10	2010-11	2011-12	Total Points	Change in position	Change in coefficient	Clubs in Europe
1	England	17.875	15	17.928	18.357	15.25	84.41	=	-1.375	8
2	Spain	13.875	13.312	17.928	18.214	20.857	84.186	=	+1.857	7
3	Germany	13.5	12.687	18.083	15.666	15.25	75.186	=	+5.75	6
4	Italy	10.25	11.375	15.428	11.571	11.357	59.981	=	-0.571	7
5	Portugal	7.928	6.785	10	18.8	11.833	55.346	+1	+3.75	6
6	France	6.928	11	15	10.75	10.5	54.178	-1	+0.5	6
7	Russia	11.25	9.75	6.166	10.916	9.75	47.832	=	+3.125	6
8	Holland	5	6.333	9.416	11.166	13.6	45.515	+1	+5.386	5
9	Ukraine	4.875	16.625	5.8	10.083	7.75	45.133	-1	+1.25	6
10	Greece	7.5	6.5	7.9	7.6	7.6	37.1	+1	+2.934	5
11	Turkey	9.75	7	7.6	4.6	5.1	34.05	-1	-1	5
12	Belgium	4.5	4.5	8.7	4.6	10.1	32.4	+1	+5.4	5
13	Denmark	5.125	8.2	4.4	6.7	3.1	27.525	-1	-3.025	5
14	Switzerland	6.25	2.9	5.75	5.9	6	26.8	+2	+1.9	5
15	Austria	3	2.25	9.375	4.375	7.125	26.125	+4	+5.425	4
16	Cyprus	2.666	6.333	4.25	3.125	9.125	25.499	+4	+7.375	4
17	Israel	2.375	1.75	7.25	4.625	6	22	=	0	4
18	Scotland	10.25	1.875	2.666	3.6	2.75	21.141	-3	-4	4
19	Czech Rep	5.125	2.375	4.1	3.5	5.25	20.35	-1	-0.5	4
20	Poland	1.666	5	2.125	4.5	6.625	19.916	+4	+4	4
21	Croatia	3.666	4.333	3	4.125	3.75	18.874	+1	+2.75	4
22	Romania	2.6	2.642	6.083	3.166	4.333	18.824	-8	-7	6
23	Belarus	1.833	4	3.375	5.875	3.125	18.208	=	+2.125	4
24	Sweden	5.4	2.5	2.5	2.6	2.9	15.9	+4	+1.775	5
25	Slovakia	2.166	4.833	2.5	3	2.375	14.874	=	+0.375	4
26	Norway	5.4	2.5	2.1	2.375	2.3	14.675	=	+0.3	5
27	Serbia	2.625	3	3	3.5	2.125	14.25	=	0	4
28	Bulgaria	2.75	2.25	3.125	4.625	1.5	14.25	-7	-3.625	4
29	Hungary	1	1	2.75	2.75	2.25	9.75	+3	+1.25	4
30	Finland	2.625	1.833	1.375	1.8	1.5	9.133	=	+0.167	4
31	Georgia	1	1.166	1.75	1.875	2.875	8.666	+5	+1.709	4
32	Bosnia-Hz	1.833	1.833	1.75	1.875	1.125	8.416	-3	-0.708	4
33	Rep of Ireland	1	2.5	1.375	1	1.5	7.375	-2	-1.333	4
34	Slovenia	0.666	1.333	1.375	1.5	2.25	7.124	+4	+1	4
35	Lithuania	1.5	2.5	1.25	0.625	1	6.875	-1	-0.833	4
36	Moldova	1.333	0.666	2.125	2.125	0.5	6.749	-3	-1	4
37	Azerbaijan	0.666	0.666	1.5	2	1.375	6.207	=	+0.042	4
38	Latvia	1.333	1.166	2.25	0.5	0.625	5.874	-3	-1.541	4
39	Macedonia	1.666	0.5	0.5	1.375	1.625	5.666	=	+0.459	4
40	Kazakhstan	0.75	0.833	1.25	0.875	1.625	5.333	+1	+0.959	4
41	Iceland	1.166	1.166	1.25	0.375	1.375	5.332	-1	+0.375	4
42	Montenegro	0.5	0.5	1.125	1.75	0.5	4.375	+1	+0.5	4
43	Liechtenstein	0.5	0	1	0.5	2	4	-1	0	1
44	Albania	0.5	0.666	1	0.875	0.875	3.916	=	+0.042	4
45	Malta	0	0	0.75	1.5	0.833	3.083	+3	+0.667	3
46	Wales	0.666	0.333	0.25	0.875	0.625	2.749	=	-0.041	4
47	Estonia	0.833	0.333	0.875	0.25	0.375	2.666	-2	-1.125	4
48	N Ireland	0.5	0.333	0.125	1.125	0.5	2.583	+1	+0.334	4
49	Luxembourg	0.333	0	0.25	0.625	1.125	2.333	+2	+0.959	4
50	Armenia	1.333	0	0.5	0.25	0.125	2.208	-3	-0.375	4
51	Faroe Islands	0.333	0.333	0	0.25	0.5	1.416	-1	0	4
52	Andorra	0.5	0	0.5	0	0	1	=	0	4
53	San Marino	0.25	0	0.5	0.166	0	0.916	=	0	3

Uefa's country coefficients are calculated using the performances of each FA's clubs in the last five Europa League/Uefa Cup and Champions League seasons and are used to determine the number of places allocated to each country and seedings in Uefa's club tournaments.

Teams are awarded two points for a win and one for a draw – half that in qualifying and play-off rounds – with an extra point awarded for each round from the last 16 of the Champions League onwards or the quarter-finals of the Europa League. Four additional points are awarded for reaching the group stage of the Champions League and a further four for qualifying for the knockout rounds.

The country coefficient is the total of the average points for each nation in each of the last five seasons. For example, England's teams have average 17.875, 15, 17.928, 18.357 and 15.25 over the last five seasons – add them together and you get 84.41, England's current association coefficient.

Domestic league tables for the top-rated associations are shown on the facing page.

Spanish Primera Liga 2011-12

		P	W	D	L	F	A	GD	Pts
1	Real Madrid	38	32	4	2	121	32	89	100
2	Barcelona	38	28	7	3	114	29	85	91
3	Valencia	38	17	10	11	59	44	15	61
4	Malaga	38	17	7	14	54	53	1	58
5	Atl Madrid	38	15	11	12	53	46	7	56
6	Levante	38	16	7	15	54	50	4	55
7	Osasuna	38	13	15	10	44	61	-17	54
8	Mallorca	38	14	10	14	42	46	-4	52
9	Seville	38	13	11	14	48	47	1	50
10	Ath Bilbao	38	12	13	13	49	52	-3	49
11	Getafe	38	12	11	15	40	51	-11	47
12	Real Sociedad	38	12	11	15	46	52	-6	47
13	Real Betis	38	13	8	17	47	56	-9	47
14	Espanyol	38	12	10	16	46	56	-10	46
15	Rayo Vallecano	38	13	4	21	53	73	-20	43
16	Real Zaragoza	38	12	7	19	36	61	-25	43
17	Granada	38	12	6	20	35	56	-21	42
18	Villarreal	38	9	14	15	39	53	-14	41
19	Sp Gijon	38	10	7	21	42	69	-27	37
20	Racing Santander	38	4	15	19	28	63	-35	27

German Bundesliga 2011-12

		P	W	D	L	F	A	GD	Pts
1	B Dortmund	34	25	6	3	80	25	55	81
2	B Munich	34	23	4	7	77	22	55	73
3	Schalke	34	20	4	10	74	44	30	64
4	B M'gladbach	34	17	9	8	49	24	25	60
5	B Leverkusen	34	15	9	10	52	44	8	54
6	Stuttgart	34	15	8	11	63	46	17	53
7	Hannover	34	12	12	10	41	45	-4	48
8	Wolfsburg	34	13	5	16	47	60	-13	44
9	Werder Bremen	34	11	9	14	49	58	-9	42
10	Nuremburg	34	12	6	16	38	49	-11	42
11	Hoffenheim	34	10	11	13	41	47	-6	41
12	Freiburg	34	10	10	14	45	61	-16	40
13	Mainz	34	9	12	13	47	51	-4	39
14	Augsburg	34	8	14	12	36	49	-13	38
15	Hamburg	34	8	12	14	35	57	-22	36
16	Hertha	34	7	10	17	38	64	-26	31
17	Cologne	34	8	6	20	39	75	-36	30
18	Kaiserslautern	34	4	11	19	24	54	-30	23

Italian Serie A 2011-12

		P	W	D	L	F	A	GD	Pts
1	Juventus	38	23	15	0	68	20	48	84
2	Milan	38	24	8	6	74	33	41	80
3	Udinese	38	18	10	10	52	35	17	64
4	Lazio	38	18	8	12	56	47	9	62
5	Napoli	38	16	13	9	66	46	20	61
6	Inter	38	17	7	14	58	55	3	58
7	Roma	38	16	8	14	60	54	6	56
8	Parma	38	15	11	12	54	53	1	56
9	Bologna	38	13	12	13	41	43	-2	51
10	Chievo	38	12	13	13	35	45	-10	49
11	Catania	38	11	15	12	47	52	-5	48
12	Atalanta	38	13	13	12	41	43	-2	46
13	Fiorentina	38	11	13	14	37	43	-6	46
14	Siena	38	11	11	16	45	45	0	44
15	Cagliari	38	10	13	15	37	46	-9	43
16	Palermo	38	11	10	17	52	62	-10	43
17	Genoa	38	11	9	18	50	69	-19	42
18	Lecce	38	8	12	18	40	56	-16	36
19	Novara	38	7	11	20	35	65	-30	32
20	Cesena	38	4	10	24	24	60	-36	22

Portuguese Primeira Liga 2011-12

		P	W	D	L	F	A	GD	Pts
1	Porto	30	23	6	1	69	19	50	75
2	Benfica	30	21	6	3	66	27	39	69
3	Sporting Braga	30	19	5	6	59	29	30	62
4	Sporting CP	30	18	5	7	47	26	21	59
5	Maritimo	30	14	8	8	41	38	3	50
6	Vitoria Guimaraes	30	14	3	13	40	40	0	45
7	Nacional	30	13	5	12	48	50	-2	44
8	Olhanense	30	9	12	9	36	38	-2	39
9	Gil Vicente	30	8	10	12	31	42	-11	34
10	Pacos de Ferreira	30	8	7	15	35	53	-18	31
11	Vitoria Setubal	30	8	6	16	24	49	-25	30
12	Academica	30	7	8	15	27	38	-11	29
13	Beira-Mar	30	8	5	17	26	38	-12	29
14	Rio Ave	30	7	7	16	33	42	-9	28
15	Feirense	30	5	9	16	27	49	-22	24
16	Uniao de Leiria	30	5	4	21	25	56	-31	19

French Ligue 1 2011-12

		P	W	D	L	F	A	GD	Pts
1	Montpellier	38	25	7	6	68	34	34	82
2	PSG	38	23	10	5	75	41	34	79
3	Lille	38	21	11	6	72	39	33	74
4	Lyon	38	19	7	12	64	51	13	64
5	Bordeaux	38	16	13	9	53	41	12	61
6	Rennes	38	17	9	12	53	44	9	60
7	Saint-Etienne	38	16	9	13	49	45	4	57
8	Toulouse	38	15	11	12	37	34	3	56
9	Evian TG	38	13	11	14	54	55	-1	50
10	Marseille	38	12	12	14	45	41	4	48
11	Nancy	38	11	12	15	38	48	-10	45
12	Valenciennes	38	12	7	19	40	50	-10	43
13	Nice	38	10	12	16	39	46	-7	42
14	Sochaux	38	11	9	18	40	60	-20	42
15	Brest	38	8	17	13	31	38	-7	41
16	Ajaccio	38	9	14	15	40	61	-21	41
17	Lorient	38	9	12	17	35	49	-14	39
18	Caen	38	9	11	18	39	59	-20	38
19	Dijon	38	9	9	20	38	63	-25	36
20	Auxerre	38	7	13	18	46	57	-11	34

Russian Premier League (top half of split) 2011-12

		P	W	D	L	F	A	GD	Pts
1	Zenit	44	24	16	4	85	40	45	88
2	Spartak Moscow	44	21	12	11	68	48	20	75
3	CSKA Moskva	44	16	9	72	47	25	73
4	Dinamo Moscow	44	20	12	12	66	50	16	72
5	Anzhi	44	19	13	12	54	42	12	70
6	Rubin Kazan	44	17	17	10	55	41	14	68
7	Lok Moscow	44	18	12	14	59	48	11	66
8	Kuban Krasnodar	44	15	16	13	50	45	5	61

Dutch Eredivise 2011-12

		P	W	D	L	F	A	GD	Pts
1	Ajax	34	23	7	4	93	36	57	76
2	Feyenoord	34	21	7	6	70	37	33	70
3	PSV	34	21	6	7	87	47	40	69
4	AZ	34	19	8	7	64	35	29	65
5	Heerenveen	34	18	10	6	79	59	20	64
6	Twente	34	17	9	8	82	46	36	60
7	Vitesse	34	15	8	11	48	43	5	53
8	NEC	34	13	6	15	42	45	-3	45
9	RKC Waalwijk	34	13	6	15	40	49	-9	45
10	Roda JC	34	14	2	18	55	70	-15	44
11	Utrecht	34	11	10	13	55	58	-3	43
12	Heracles	34	11	7	16	52	62	-10	40
13	NAC Breda	34	10	8	16	45	54	-9	38
14	Groningen	34	10	7	17	41	61	-20	37
15	ADO Den Haag	34	8	8	18	38	67	-29	32
16	VVV	34	9	4	21	42	78	-36	31
17	De Graafschap	34	6	6	22	36	74	-38	24
18	Excelsior	34	4	7	23	28	76	-48	19

Champions League first qualifying round
June 8 2011
Santa Coloma ....0-2 ....Dudelange
Tre Fiori ....0-3 ....Valletta
July 5 2011
Dudelange ....2-0 ....Santa Coloma
Aggregate score 4-0
July 6 2011
Valletta ....2-1 ....Tre Fiori
Aggregate score 5-1

Champions League second qualifying round
July 12 2011
Pyunik ....0-4 ....Plzen
Valletta ....2-3 ....Ekranas
Mogren.............................1-2 ....Litex
Maribor.............................2-0 ....Dudelange
Slovan Bratislava ....2-0 ....Tobol
Shamrock Rovers ....1-0.................................Flora
July 13 2011
Zestafoni ....3-0 ....Dacia
M Haifa.............................5-1 ....Borac
Malmo ....2-0 ....HB
Bangor..............................0-3 ....HJK
Skenderbeu ....0-2 ....APOEL
Dinamo Zagreb ....3-0 ....Neftci
Sturn ....2-0 ....Videoton
Skonto ....0-1 ....Wisla
Partizan ....4-0.............................Shkendija
Rosenborg.........................5-0.............................Breidablik
Linfield ....1-1 ....BATE
July 19 2011
Flora..................................0-0 ....Shamrock Rovers
Aggregate score 0-1
Dudelange ....1-3 ....Maribor
Aggregate score 1-5
Tobol ....1-1 ....Slovan Bratislava
Aggregate score 1-3
Neftci ....0-0 ....Dinamo Zagreb
Aggregate score 0-3
Ekranas ....1-0 ....Valletta
Aggregate score 4-2
HJK.....................................10-0 ....Bangor
Aggregate score 13-0
BATE ....2-0 ....Linfield
Aggregate score 3-1
Litex ....3-0 ....Mogren
Aggregate score 5-1
HB ....1-1 ....Malmo
Aggregate score 1-3
Plzen ....5-1 ....Pyunik
Aggregate score 9-1
Wisla ....2-0 ....Skonto
Aggregate score 3-0
Shkendija............................0-1 ....Partizan
Aggregate score 0-5
APOEL ....4-0 ....Skenderbeu
Aggregate score 6-0
July 20 2011
Dacia ....2-0 ....Zestafoni
Aggregate score 2-3
Videoton..............................3-2 ....Sturm
Aggregate score 3-4
Borac ....3-2 ....M Haifa
Aggregate score 4-7
Breidablik............................2-0 ....Rosenborg
Aggregate score 2-5

Champions League third qualifying round
July 26 2011
Zestafoni ....1-1 ....Sturm
Ekranas ....0-0 ....BATE
APOEL ....0-0..............Slovan Bratislava
Litex ....1-2 ....Wisla
Dynamo Kiev ....0-2 ....Rubin
Genk ....2-1 ....Partizan
Rangers ....0-1 ....Malmo
Twente ....2-0 ....Vaslui
July 27 2011
HJK ....1-2 ....Dinamo Zagreb
Copenhagen ....1-0 ....Shamrock Rovers
OB ....1-1 ....Panathinaikos
M Haifa...............................2-1 ....Maribor
Standard Liege ....1-1 ....Zurich
Rosenborg..........................0-1 ....Plzen
Benfica...............................2-0 ....Trabzonspor
August 2 2011
BATE ....3-1 ....Ekranas
Aggregate score 3-1
Shamrock Rovers ....0-2 ....Copenhagen
Aggregate score 0-3
Panathinaikos ....3-4 ....OB
Aggregate score 4-5
August 3 2011
Rubin ....2-1 ....Dynamo Kiev
Aggregate score 4-1
Malmo ....1-1 ....Rangers
Aggregate score 2-1
Vaslui ....0-0 ....Twente
Aggregate score 0-2
Slovan Bratislava ....0-2 ....APOEL
Aggregate score 0-2
Plzen ....3-2 ....Rosenborg
Aggregate score 4-2
Zurich..................................1-0 ....Standard Liege
Aggregate score 2-1
Wisla ....3-1 ....Litex
Aggregate score 5-2
Sturm ....1-0 ....Zestafoni
Aggregate score 2-1
Maribor................................1-1 ....M Haifa
Aggregate score 2-3
Dinamo Zagreb ....1-0 ....HJK
Aggregate score 3-1
Partizan ....1-1 ....Genk
Aggregate score 2-3
Trabzonspor.......................1-1 ....Benfica
Aggregate score 1-3

Champions League play-off round
August 16 2011
Copenhagen ....1-3 ....Plzen
BATE ....1-1 ....Sturm
Twente ....2-2 ....Benfica
Arsenal...............................1-0 ....Udinese
Lyon ....3-1 ....Rubin
August 17 2011
Wisla ....1-0 ....APOEL
M Haifa...............................2-1 ....Genk
Dinamo Zagreb ....4-1 ....Malmo
OB ....1-0 ....Villarreal
Bayern ....2-0...................................Zurich
August 23 2011
APOEL ....3-1 ....Wisla

Aggregate score 3-2
Genk ....2-1 ....M Haifa
Aggregate score 3-3 Genk won 4-1 on penalties
Malmo ....2-0 ....Dinamo Zagreb
Aggregate score 3-4
Villarreal ....3-0 ....OB
Aggregate score 3-1
Zurich..............................0-1 ....Bayern
Aggregate score 0-3

August 24 2011
Rubin ....1-1 ....Lyon
Aggregate score 2-4
Plzen ....2-1 ....Copenhagen
Aggregate score 5-2
Sturm ....0-2 ....BATE
Aggregate score 1-3
Benfica...........................3-1 ....Twente
Aggregate score 5-3
Udinese ....1-2 ....Arsenal
Aggregate score 1-3

Group A

	P	W	D	L	F	A	+/-	Pts
1 Bayern	6	4	1	1	11	6	5	13
2 Napoli	6	3	2	1	10	6	4	11
3 Man City	6	3	1	2	9	6	3	10
4 Villarreal	6	0	0	6	2	14	-12	0

Group B

	P	W	D	L	F	A	+/-	Pts
1 Inter Milan	6	3	1	2	8	7	1	10
2 CSKA Moscow	6	2	2	2	9	8	1	8
3 Trabzonspor	6	1	4	1	3	5	-2	7
4 Lille	6	1	3	2	6	6	0	6

Group C

	P	W	D	L	F	A	+/-	Pts
1 Benfica	6	3	3	0	8	4	4	12
2 Basel	6	3	2	1	11	10	1	11
3 Man United	6	2	3	1	11	8	3	9
4 Otelul	6	0	0	6	3	11	-8	0

Group D

	P	W	D	L	F	A	+/-	Pts
1 Real Madrid	6	6	0	0	19	2	17	18
2 Lyon	6	2	2	2	9	7	2	8
3 Ajax	6	2	2	2	6	6	0	8
4 Dinamo Zagreb	6	0	0	6	3	22	-19	0

Group E

	P	W	D	L	F	A	+/-	Pts
1 Chelsea	6	3	2	1	13	4	9	11
2 Leverkusen	6	3	1	2	8	8	0	10
3 Valencia	6	2	2	2	12	7	5	8
4 Genk	6	0	3	3	2	16	-14	3

Group F

	P	W	D	L	F	A	+/-	Pts
1 Arsenal	6	3	2	1	7	6	1	11
2 Marseille	6	3	1	2	7	4	3	10
3 Olympiacos	6	3	0	3	8	6	2	9
4 Dortmund	6	1	1	4	6	12	-6	4

Group G

	P	W	D	L	F	A	+/-	Pts
1 APOEL	6	2	3	1	6	6	0	9
2 Zenit	6	2	3	1	7	5	2	9
3 Porto	6	2	2	2	7	7	0	8
4 Shakhtar Donetsk	6	1	2	3	6	8	-2	5

Group H

	P	W	D	L	F	A	+/-	Pts
1 Barcelona	6	5	1	0	20	4	16	16
2 Milan	6	2	3	1	11	8	3	9
3 Plzen	6	1	2	3	4	11	-7	5
4 BATE	6	0	2	4	2	14	-12	2

Champions League group stage matchday 1
September 13 2011
Chelsea ....2-0 ....Leverkusen
Genk ....0-0 ....Valencia
Olympiacos ....0-1 ....Marseille
Dortmund........................1-1 ....Arsenal
Porto ....2-1 ....Shakhtar Donetsk
APOEL ....2-1 ....Zenit
Barcelona........................2-2 ....Milan
Plzen ....1-1 ....BATE

September 14 2011
Man City..........................1-1 ....Napoli
Villarreal ....0-2 ....Bayern
Lille..................................2-2..................CSKA Moscow
Inter Milan ....0-1 ....Trabzonspor
Basel ....2-1 ....Otelul
Benfica.............................1-1 ....Man United
Dinamo Zagreb ....0-1 ....Real Madrid
Ajax ....0-0 ....Lyon

Champions League group stage matchday 2
September 27 2011
Bayern.............................2-0 ....Man City
Napoli...............................2-0 ....Villarreal
CSKA Moscow................2-3 ....Inter Milan
Trabzonspor....................1-1 ....Lille
Man United ....3-3 ....Basel
Otelul ....0-1 ....Benfica
Lyon ....2-0 ....Dinamo Zagreb
Real Madrid.....................3-0 ....Ajax

September 28 2011
Valencia ....1-1 ....Chelsea
Leverkusen ....2-0 ....Genk
Arsenal............................2-1 ....Olympiacos
Marseille..........................3-0 ....Dortmund
Zenit ....3-1 ....Porto
Shakhtar Donetsk ....1-1 ....APOEL
BATE ....0-5 ....Barcelona
Milan ....2-0 ....Plzen

Champions League group stage matchday 3
October 18 2011
Napoli...............................1-1 ....Bayern
Man City...........................2-1 ....Villarreal
CSKA Moscow................3-0 ....Trabzonspor
Lille...................................0-1 ....Inter Milan
Otelul ....0-2 ....Man United
Basel ....0-2 ....Benfica
Real Madrid ....4-0 ....Lyon
Dinamo Zagreb ....0-2 ....Ajax

October 19 2011
Leverkusen ....2-1 ....Valencia
Chelsea ....5-0 ....Genk
Marseille..........................0-1 ....Arsenal
Olympiacos ....3-1 ....Dortmund
Shakhtar Donetsk ....2-2..................................Zenit
Porto ....1-1 ....APOEL
Milan ....2-0 ....BATE
Barcelona........................2-0 ....Plzen

Champions League group stage matchday 4
November 1 2011
Valencia ....3-1 ....Leverkusen
Genk ....1-1 ....Chelsea
Arsenal ....0-0 ....Marseille
Dortmund ....1-0 ....Olympiacos
Zenit ....1-0 ....Shakhtar Donetsk
APOEL ....2-1 ....Porto
BATE ....1-1 ....Milan
Plzen ....0-4 ....Barcelona

November 2 2011
Bayern ....3-2 ....Napoli
Villarreal ....0-3 ....Man City
Trabzonspor ....0-0 ....CSKA Moscow
Inter Milan ....2-1 ....Lille
Man United ....2-0 ....Otelul
Benfica ....1-1 ....Basel
Lyon ....0-2 ....Real Madrid
Ajax ....4-0 ....Dinamo Zagreb

Champions League group stage matchday 5
November 22 2011
Napoli ....2-1 ....Man City
Bayern ....3-1 ....Villarreal
CSKA Moscow ....0-2 ....Lille
Trabzonspor ....1-1 ....Inter Milan
Otelul ....2-3 ....Basel
Man United ....2-2 ....Benfica
Real Madrid ....6-2 ....Dinamo Zagreb
Lyon ....0-0 ....Ajax

November 23 2011
Leverkusen ....2-1 ....Chelsea
Valencia ....7-0 ....Genk
Marseille ....0-1 ....Olympiacos
Arsenal ....2-1 ....Dortmund
Zenit ....0-0 ....APOEL
Shakhtar Donetsk ....0-2 ....Porto
BATE ....0-1 ....Plzen
Milan ....2-3 ....Barcelona

Champions League group stage matchday 6
December 6 2011
Chelsea ....3-0 ....Valencia
Genk ....1-1 ....Leverkusen
Olympiacos ....3-1 ....Arsenal
Dortmund ....2-3 ....Marseille
Porto ....0-0 ....Zenit
APOEL ....0-2 ....Shakhtar Donetsk
Barcelona ....4-0 ....BATE
Plzen ....2-2 ....Milan

December 7 2011
Man City ....2-0 ....Bayern
Villarreal ....0-2 ....Napoli
Lille ....0-0 ....Trabzonspor
Inter Milan ....1-2 ....CSKA Moscow
Basel ....2-1 ....Man United
Benfica ....1-0 ....Otelul
Dinamo Zagreb ....1-7 ....Lyon
Ajax ....0-3 ....Real Madrid

Champions League round of 16
February 14 2012
Lyon ....1-0 ....APOEL
Leverkusen ....1-3 ....Barcelona

February 15 2012
Zenit ....3-2 ....Benfica
Milan ....4-0 ....Arsenal

February 21 2012
CSKA Moscow ....1-1 ....Real Madrid
Napoli ....3-1 ....Chelsea
Marseille ....1-0 ....Inter Milan

February 22 2012
Basel ....1-0 ....Bayern

March 6 2012
Benfica ....2-0 ....Zenit
Aggregate score 4-3
Arsenal ....3-0 ....Milan
Aggregate score 3-4

March 7 2012
APOEL ....1-0 ....Lyon
Aggregate score 1-1 APOEL won 4-3 on penalties
Barcelona ....7-1 ....Leverkusen
Aggregate score 10-2

March 13 2012
Inter Milan ....2-1 ....Marseille
Aggregate score 2-2 Marseille won on away goals
Bayern ....7-0 ....Basel
Aggregate score 7-1

March 14 2012
Chelsea ....4-1 ....Napoli
Aggregate score 5-4 Chelsea won after extra time
Real Madrid ....4-1 ....CSKA Moscow
Aggregate score 5-2

Champions League quarter finals
March 27 2012
APOEL ....0-3 ....Real Madrid
Benfica ....0-1 ....Chelsea

March 28 2012
Marseille ....0-2 ....Bayern
Milan ....0-0 ....Barcelona

April 3 2012
Barcelona ....3-1 ....Milan
Aggregate score 3-1
Bayern ....2-0 ....Marseille
Aggregate score 4-0

April 4 2012
Chelsea ....2-1 ....Benfica
Aggregate score 3-1
Real Madrid ....5-2 ....APOEL
Aggregate score 8-2

Champions League semi-finals
April 17 2012
Bayern ....2-1 ....Real Madrid

April 18 2012
Chelsea ....1-0 ....Barcelona

April 24 2012
Barcelona ....2-2 ....Chelsea
Aggregate score 2-3

April 25 2012
Real Madrid ....2-1 ....Bayern
Aggregate score 3-3 Bayern won 3-1 on penalties

Champions League final
May 19 2012
Bayern ....1-1 ....Chelsea
Chelsea won 4-3 on penalties

Europa League first qualifying round
June 30 2011

Banants	0-1	Metalurgi Rustavi
Olimpik-Suvalan	1-1	Minsk
Banga	0-4	Qarabag
Trans	1-4	Rabotnicki
Rad	6-0	Tre Penne
Daugava	0-5	Tromso
Elfsborg	4-0	Fola
Honka	0-0	Kalju
Varazdin	5-1	Lusitans
Ferencvaros	3-0	Ulisses
UE Santa Coloma	0-1	Paks
Aalesund	4-1	Neath
Dinamo Tbilisi	2-0	Milsami-Ursidos
Spartak Trnava	3-0	Zeta
IF	1-3	KR
IBV	1-0	St Patrick's
Kaerjeng	1-1	Hacken
TNS	1-1	Cliftonville
Fulham	3-0	NSI
Jagiellonia	1-0	Irtysh
Birkirkara	0-1	Vllaznia
Renova	2-1	Glentoran
Koper	1-1	Shakhter
Siroki Brijeg	0-0	Olimpija Ljubljana
Buducnost Podgorica	1-3	Flamurtari

7 July 2011

Shakhter	2-1	Koper
Aggregate score 3-2		
Metalurgi Rustavi	1-1	Banants
Aggregate score 2-1		
Irtysh	2-0	Jagiellonia
Aggregate score 2-1		
Ulisses	0-2	Ferencvaros
Aggregate score 0-5		
Flamurtari	1-2	Buducnost Podgorica
Aggregate score 4-3		
Milsami-Ursidos	1-3	Dinamo Tbilisi
Aggregate score 1-5		
Zeta	2-1	Spartak Trnava
Aggregate score 2-4		
Qarabag	3-0	Banga
Aggregate score 7-0		
Fola	1-1	Elfsborg
Aggregate score 1-5		
Kalju	0-2	Honka
Aggregate score 0-2		
Lusitans	0-1	Varazdin
Aggregate score 1-6		
Tromso	2-1	Daugava
Aggregate score 7-1		
Hacken	5-1	Kaerjeng
Aggregate score 6-2		
Vllaznia	1-1	Birkirkara
Aggregate score 2-1		
Minsk	2-1	Olimpik-Suvalan
Aggregate score 3-2		
NSI	0-0	Fulham
Aggregate score 0-3		
Paks	4-0	UE Santa Coloma
Aggregate score 5-0		
Neath	0-2	Aalesund
Aggregate score 1-6		
Rabotnicki	3-0	Trans
Aggregate score 7-1		
Olimpija Ljubljana	3-0	Siroki Brijeg

Aggregate score 3-0		
Tre Penne	1-3	Rad
Aggregate score 1-9		
St Patrick's	2-0	IBV
Aggregate score 2-1		
Cliftonville	0-1	TNS
Aggregate score 1-2		
Glentoran	2-1	Renova
Aggregate score 3-3 Glentoran won 3-2 on penalties		
KR	5-1	IF
Aggregate score 8-2		

Europa League second qualifying round
July 14 2011

Shakhter	2-1	St Patrick's
Metalurgi Rustavi	1-1	Irtysh
Slask	1-0	Dundee United
Rad	0-1	Olympiacos Volou
KuPS	1-0	Gaz Metan
Flamurtari	0-2	Jablonec
Iskra-Stal	1-1	Varazdin
Tauras	2-3	Den Haag
Rudar Pljevlja	0-3	Austria Vienna
TPS	0-1	Westerlo
Sant Julia	0-2	Bnei Yehuda
Minsk	1-1	Gaziantepspor
Orebro	0-0	Sarajevo
Shakhtyor	0-1	Ventspils
Valerenga	1-0	Mika
Ferencvaros	2-1	Aalesund
Hacken	1-0	Honka
Anorthosis	3-0	Gagra
Floriana	0-8	AEK Larnaca
M Tel Aviv	3-1	Xazar Lankaran
Llanelli	2-1	Dinamo Tbilisi
Suduva	1-1	Elfsborg
Olimpija Ljubljana	2-0	Bohemians
Differdange	0-0	Levadia
Tirana	0-0	Spartak Trnava
TNS	1-3	Midtjylland
Vaduz	0-2	Vojvodina
EB/Streymur	1-1	Qarabag
Paks	1-1	Tromso
Kecskemet	1-1	Aktobe
Zeljeznicar	1-0	Sheriff
Juvenes/Dogana	0-1	Rabotnicki
Liepajas Metalurgs	1-4	Salzburg
Vllaznia	0-0	Thun
Metalurg Skopje	0-0	Lokomotiv Sofia
Glentoran	0-2	Vorskla
Crusaders	1-3	Fulham
Domzale	1-2	Split
KR	3-0	Zilina
FH	1-1	Nacional

July 21 2011

Irtysh	0-2	Metalurgi Rustavi
Aggregate score 1-3		
Mika	0-1	Valerenga
Aggregate score 0-2		
Gaz Metan	2-0	KuPS
Aggregate score 2-1		
Vojvodina	1-3	Vaduz
Aggregate score 3-3		

July 21 2011

Ventspils	3-2	Shakhtyor
Aggregate score 4-2		

Xazar Lankaran ....0-0.................M Tel Aviv
Aggregate score 1-3
Levadia ....0-1 ....Differdange
Aggregate score 0-1
Elfsborg ....3-0....................Suduva
Aggregate score 4-1
Sheriff..............................0-0....................Zeljeznicar
Aggregate score 0-1
Aktobe ....0-0....................Kecskemet
Aggregate score 1-1 Aktobe won on away goals
Honka ....0-2....................Hacken
Aggregate score 0-3
Qarabag...........................0-0 ....EB/Streymur
Aggregate score 1-1 Qarabag won on away goals
Bnei Yehuda.....................2-0....................Sant Julia
Aggregate score 4-0
Varazdin ....3-1 ....Iskra-Stal
Aggregate score 4-2
Vorskla............................3-0....................Glentoran
Aggregate score 5-0
Sarajevo ....2-0....................Orebro
Aggregate score 2-0
Dinamo Tbilisi ....5-0....................Llanelli
Aggregate score 6-2
AEK Larnaca ....1-0....................Floriana
Aggregate score 9-0
Spartak Trnava.................3-1....................Tirana
Aggregate score 3-1
Aalesund ....3-1....................Ferencvaros
Aggregate score 4-3 Aalesund won after extra time
Salzburg...........................0-0 ....Liepajas Metalurgs
Aggregate score 4-1
Gagra...............................2-0....................Anorthosis
Aggregate score 2-3
Tromso............................0-3....................Paks
Aggregate score 1-4
Midtjylland ....5-2....................TNS
Aggregate score 8-3
Lokomotiv Sofia...............3-2 ....Metalurg Skopje
Aggregate score 3-2
Zilina................................2-0 ....KR
Aggregate score 2-3
Thun................................2-1....................Vllaznia
Aggregate score 2-1
Gaziantepspor ....4-1....................Minsk
Aggregate score 5-2
Den Haag.........................2-0....................Tauras
Aggregate score 5-2
Rabotnicki ....3-0.............Juvenes/Dogana
Aggregate score 4-0
Jablonec ....5-1....................Flamurtari
Aggregate score 7-1
Olympiacos Volou ....1-1....................Rad
Aggregate score 2-1
Westerlo..........................0-0....................TPS
Aggregate score 1-0
Fulham.............................4-0....................Crusaders
Aggregate score 7-1
Split ....3-1....................Domzale
Aggregate score 5-2
Bohemians......................1-1 ....Olimpija Ljubljana
Aggregate score 1-3
Dundee United ....3-2 ....Slask
Aggregate score 3-3 Slask won on away goals
St Patrick's......................2-0....................Shakhter
Aggregate score 3-2
Nacional..........................2-0....................FH
Aggregate score 3-1

Austria Vienna ....2-0....................Rudar Pljevlja
Aggregate score 5-0

Europa League third qualifying round
July 26 2011
Bnei Yehuda.....................1-0....................Helsingborg
July 28 2011
Slask ....0-0....................Lokomotiv Sofia
AEK Larnaca ....3-0....................Mlada Boleslav
Ventspils...........................1-2....................Crvena Zvezda
Alania...............................1-1....................Aktobe
Karpaty............................2-0....................St Patrick's
Olimpija Ljubljana ....1-1....................Austria Vienna
Aalesund ....4-0....................Elfsborg
Metalurgi Rustavi ....2-5....................Rennes
Salzburg...........................1-0....................Senica
Anorthosis ....0-2....................Rabotnicki
Sparta Prague ....5-0....................Sarajevo
Vorskla.............................0-0....................Sligo
Valerenga ....0-2....................PAOK
Young Boys ....3-1....................Westerlo
Bursaspor ....2-1....................Gomel
H Tel Aviv ....4-0....................Vaduz
Omonia ....3-0....................Den Haag
Split ....0-0....................Fulham
Levski..............................2-1....................Spartak Trnava
AZ...................................2-0....................Jablonec
Gaziantepspor ....0-1....................Legia
Dinamo Bucharest............2-2....................Varazdin
Differdange ....0-3....................Olympiacos Volou
Paks ....1-1....................Hearts
Zeljeznicar ....0-2....................M Tel Aviv
Club Brugge ....4-1....................Qarabag
Mainz ....1-1....................Gaz Metan
Palermo ....2-2....................Thun
Stoke ....1-0....................Hajduk Split
Nacional...........................3-0....................Hacken
Atl Madrid........................2-1....................Stromsgodset
Midtjylland ....0-0....................Vitoria SC
Ried ....2-0....................Brondby
KR...................................1-4....................Dinamo Tbilisi

August 4 2011
Mlada Boleslav ....2-2 ....AEK Larnaca
Aggregate score 2-5
Varazdin ....1-2....................Dinamo Bucharest
Aggregate score 3-4
Aktobe ....1-1....................Alania
Aggregate score 2-2 Alania won 4-2 on penalties
Elfsborg ....1-1....................Aalesund
Aggregate score 1-5
Qarabag...........................1-0....................Club Brugge
Aggregate score 2-4
Stromsgodset ....0-2....................Atl Madrid
Aggregate score 1-4
Sligo................................0-2....................Vorskla
Aggregate score 0-2
Gomel ....1-3....................Bursaspor
Aggregate score 2-5
Legia ....0-0....................Gaziantepspor
Aggregate score 1-0
Rennes.............................2-0....................Metalurgi Rustavi
Aggregate score 7-2
Spartak Trnava.................2-1....................Levski
Aggregate score 3-3 Spartak Trnava won 5-4 on penalties
Dinamo Tbilisi ....2-0 ....KR
Aggregate score 6-1

Senica ....0-3 ....Salzburg
Aggregate score 0-4
Gaz Metan ....1-1 ....Mainz
Aggregate score 2-2 Gaz Metan won 4-3 on penalties
Helsingborg ....3-0 ....Bnei Yehuda
Aggregate score 3-1
Hajduk Split ....0-1 ....Stoke
Aggregate score 0-2
Hacken..............................2-1..........................Nacional
Aggregate score 2-4
Brondby ....4-2 ....Ried
Aggregate score 4-4 Ried won on away goals
M Tel Aviv.........................6-0 ....Zeljeznicar
Aggregate score 8-0
Thun..................................1-1 ....Palermo
Aggregate score 3-3 Thun won on away goals
Lokomotiv Sofia................0-0 ....Slask
Aggregate score 0-0 Slask won 4-3 on penalties
Westerlo ....0-2 ....Young Boys
Aggregate score 1-5
Vaduz ....2-1 ....H Tel Aviv
Aggregate score 2-5
Den Haag..........................1-0 ....Omonia
Aggregate score 1-3
Olympiacos Volou ....3-0 ....Differdange
Aggregate score 6-0
Rabotnicki ....1-2 ....Anorthosis
Aggregate score 3-2
PAOK ....3-0..........................Valerenga
Aggregate score 5-0
Crvena Zvezda.................7-0 ....Ventspils
Aggregate score 9-1
Jablonec ....1-1 ....AZ
Aggregate score 1-3
Fulham ....2-0 ....Split
Aggregate score 2-0
St Patrick's.......................1-3 ....Karpaty
Aggregate score 1-5
Hearts ....4-1 ....Paks
Aggregate score 5-2
Sarajevo...........................0-2 ....Sparta Prague
Aggregate score 0-7
Austria Vienna ....3-2 ....Olimpija Ljubljana
Aggregate score 4-3
Vitoria SC.........................2-1 ....Midtjylland
Aggregate score 2-1

Europa League play-off round
August 18 2011

Legia ....2-2 ....Spartak Moscow
Ekranas ....1-0 ....H Tel Aviv
Lokomotiv Moscow ....2-0 ....Spartak Trnava
Vaslui ....2-0 ....Sparta Prague
Zestafoni ....3-3 ....Club Brugge
HJK ....2-0 ....Schalke
Litex ....1-2 ....Dynamo Kiev
Vorskla ....2-1..........Dinamo Bucharest
Aalesund ....2-1 ....AZ
Omonia ....2-1 ....Salzburg
Austria Vienna ....3-1 ....Gaz Metan
M Tel Aviv.........................3-0 ....Panathinaikos
Steaua ....2-0 ....CSKA Sofia
Thun..................................0-1 ....Stoke
Besiktas ....3-0........................Alania
Bursaspor ....1-2 ....Anderlecht
PAOK ....2-0 ....Karpaty
Nordsjaelland ....0-0...........................Sporting

Slask ....1-3 ....Rapid Bucharest
Standard Liege ....1-0....................Helsingborg
Metalist.............................0-0............................Sochaux
Fulham ....3-0 ....Dnipro
Hannover ....2-1 ....Seville
Crvena Zvezda.................1-2 ....Rennes
Shamrock Rovers ....1-1 ....Partizan
Rosenborg ....0-0 ....AEK Larnaca
Slovan Bratislava ....1-0 ....Roma
Differdange ....0-4 ....PSG
Hearts ....0-5 ....Tottenham
Maribor.............................2-1 ....Rangers
Nacional............................0-0 ....Birmingham
AEK ....1-0 ....Dinamo Tbilisi
Ath Bilbao ....0-0 ....Trabzonspor
Lazio ....6-0 ....Rabotnicki
Celtic ....3-0 (f)..........................Sion
Ried ....0-0 ....PSV
Atl Madrid.........................2-0..........................Vitoria SC
Braga ....0-0 ....Young Boys

August 25 2011

Dinamo Bucharest............2-3 ....Vorskla
Aggregate score 3-5
Spartak Moscow ....2-3 ....Legia
Aggregate score 4-5
Rennes...............................4-0 ....Crvena Zvezda
Aggregate score 6-1
PSV ....5-0 ....Ried
Aggregate score 5-0
Alania ....2-0 ....Besiktas
Aggregate score 2-3
AEK Larnaca ....2-1 ....Rosenborg
Aggregate score 2-1
Spartak Trnava.................1-1 ....Lokomotiv Moscow
Aggregate score 1-3
Dynamo Kiev ....1-0 ....Litex
Aggregate score 3-1
Gaz Metan ....1-0 ....Austria Vienna
Aggregate score 2-3
Dinamo Tbilisi ....1-1 ....AEK
Aggregate score 1-2 AEK won after extra time
H Tel Aviv ....4-0 ....Ekranas
Aggregate score 4-1
CSKA Sofia ....1-1 ....Steaua
Aggregate score 1-3
Young Boys ....2-2 ....Braga
Aggregate score 2-2 Braga won on away goals
Rapid Bucharest ....1-1 ....Slask
Aggregate score 4-2
Sparta Prague ....1-0 ....Vaslui
Aggregate score 1-2
Panathinaikos ....2-1............M Tel Aviv
Aggregate score 2-4
Helsingborg ....1-3 ....Standard Liege
Aggregate score 1-4
Schalke ....6-1 ....HJK
Aggregate score 6-3
Vitoria SC..........................0-4 ....Atl Madrid
Aggregate score 0-6
Partizan ....1-2 ....Shamrock Rovers
Aggregate score 2-3 Shamrock won after extra time
Anderlecht ....2-2 ....Bursaspor
Aggregate score 4-3
Trabzonspor ....- ....Ath Bilbao
Match cancelled
Rangers ....1-1 ....Maribor

Aggregate score 2-3
Dnipro ....1-0.............................Fulham
Aggregate score 1-3
Sion ....0-3 (f) ....Celtic
Aggregate score 0-6
Club Brugge ....2-0 ....Zestafoni
Aggregate score 5-3
Sochaux..........................0-4 ....Metalist
Aggregate score 0-4
Roma ....1-1 ....Slovan Bratislava
Aggregate score 1-2
Rabotnicki ....1-3 ....Lazio
Aggregate score 1-9
Birmingham ....3-0............................Nacional
Aggregate score 3-0
Stoke ....4-1...............................Thun
Aggregate score 5-1
AZ....................................6-0............................Aalesund
Aggregate score 7-2
PSG ....2-0........................Differdange
Aggregate score 6-0
Karpaty............................1-1 ....PAOK
Aggregate score 1-3
Tottenham ....0-0 ....Hearts
Aggregate score 5-0
Salzburg............................1-0 ....Omonia
Aggregate score 2-2 Salzburg won on away goals
Seville.................................1-1 ....Hannover
Aggregate score 2-3
Sporting ....2-1 ....Nordsjaelland
Aggregate score 2-1

Group A

	P	W	D	L	F	A	GD	Pts
1 PAOK	6	3	3	0	10	6	4	12
2 Rubin Kazan	6	3	2	1	11	5	6	11
3 Tottenham	6	3	1	2	9	4	5	10
4 Shamrock Rovers	6	0	0	6	4	19	-15	0

Group B

	P	W	D	L	F	A	GD	Pts
1 Standard Liege	6	4	2	0	9	1	8	14
2 Hannover	6	3	2	1	9	7	2	11
3 Copenhagen	6	1	2	3	5	9	-4	5
4 Vorskla Poltava	6	0	2	4	4	10	-6	2

Group C

	P	W	D	L	F	A	GD	Pts
1 PSV	6	5	1	0	13	5	8	16
2 Legia Warsaw	6	3	0	3	7	9	-2	9
3 Hapoel Tel Aviv	6	2	1	3	10	9	1	7
4 Rapid Bucharest	6	1	0	5	5	12	-7	3

Group D

	P	W	D	L	F	A	GD	Pts
1 Sporting	6	4	0	2	8	4	4	12
2 Lazio	6	2	3	1	7	5	2	9
3 Vaslui	6	1	3	2	5	8	-3	6
4 Zurich	6	1	2	3	5	8	-3	5

Group E

	P	W	D	L	F	A	GD	Pts
1 Besiktas	6	4	0	2	13	7	6	12
2 Stoke	6	3	2	1	10	7	3	11
3 Dynamo Kiev	6	1	4	1	7	7	0	7
4 Maccabi Tel Aviv	6	0	2	4	8	17	-9	2

Group F

	P	W	D	L	F	A	GD	Pts
1 Ath Bilbao	6	4	1	1	11	8	3	13
2 Salzburg	6	3	1	2	11	8	3	10
3 Paris Saint-Germain	6	3	1	2	8	7	1	10
4 Slovan Bratislava	6	0	1	5	4	11	-7	1

Group G

	P	W	D	L	F	A	GD	Pts
1 Metalist Kharkiv	6	4	2	0	15	6	9	14
2 AZ	6	1	5	0	10	7	3	8
3 Austria Vienna	6	2	2	2	10	11	-1	8
4 Malmo	6	0	1	5	4	15	-11	1

Group H

	P	W	D	L	F	A	GD	Pts
1 Club Brugge	6	3	2	1	12	9	3	11
2 Braga	6	3	2	1	12	6	6	11
3 Birmingham	6	3	1	2	8	8	0	10
4 Maribor	6	0	1	5	6	15	-9	1

Group I

	P	W	D	L	F	A	GD	Pts
1 Atl Madrid	6	4	1	1	11	4	7	13
2 Udinese	6	2	3	1	6	7	-1	9
3 Celtic	6	1	3	2	6	7	-1	6
4 Rennes	6	0	3	3	5	10	-5	3

Group J

	P	W	D	L	F	A	GD	Pts
1 Schalke	6	4	2	0	13	2	11	14
2 Steaua Bucharest	6	2	2	2	9	11	-2	8
3 Maccabi Haifa	6	2	0	4	10	12	-2	6
4 AEK Larnaca	6	1	2	3	4	11	-7	5

Group K

	P	W	D	L	F	A	GD	Pts
1 Twente	6	4	1	1	14	7	7	13
2 Wisla Krakow	6	3	0	3	8	13	-5	9
3 Fulham	6	2	2	2	9	6	3	8
4 OB	6	1	1	4	9	14	-5	4

Group L

	P	W	D	L	F	A	GD	Pts
1 Anderlecht	6	6	0	0	18	5	13	18
2 Lokomotiv Moscow	6	4	0	2	14	11	3	12
3 AEK Athens	6	1	0	5	8	15	-7	3
4 Sturm Graz	6	1	0	5	5	14	-9	3

Europa League group stage matchday 1
September 15 2011

PAOK ....0-0 ....Tottenham
Shamrock Rovers ....0-3 ....Rubin
Hannover ....0-0 ....Standard Liege
Copengahen ....1-0...............................Vorskla
H Tel Aviv ....0-1 ....Rapid Bucharest
PSV ....1-0 ....Legia
Zurich ....0-2 ....Sporting
Lazio ....2-2 ....Vaslui
Dynamo Kiev ....1-1 ....Stoke
Besiktas ....5-1.......................M Tel Aviv
Slovan Bratislava ....1-2 ....Ath Bilbao
PSG ....3-1 ....Salzburg
AZ..4-1 ....Malmo
Austria Vienna ....1-2 ....Metalist
Club Brugge ....2-0 ....Maribor
Birmingham ....1-3 ....Braga

Udinese	2-1	Rennes
Atl Madrid	2-0	Celtic
M Haifa	1-0	AEK Larnaca
Steaua	0-0	Schalke
Wisla	1-3	OB
Fulham	1-1	Twente
Sturm	1-2	Lokomotiv Moscow
Anderlecht	4-1	AEK

Europa League group stage matchday 2
September 29 2011

Rubin	2-2	PAOK
Tottenham	3-1	Shamrock Rovers
Vorskla	1-2	Hannover
Standard Liege	3-0	Copengahen
Legia	3-2	H Tel Aviv
Rapid Bucharest	1-3	PSV
Vaslui	2-2	Zurich
Sporting	2-1	Lazio
M Tel Aviv	1-1	Dynamo Kiev
Stoke	2-1	Besiktas
Salzburg	3-0	Slovan Bratislava
Ath Bilbao	2-0	PSG
Metalist	1-1	AZ
Malmo	1-2	Austria Vienna
Braga	1-2	Club Brugge
Maribor	1-2	Birmingham
Celtic	1-1	Udinese
Rennes	1-1	Atl Madrid
Schalke	3-1	M Haifa
AEK Larnaca	1-1	Steaua
Twente	4-1	Wisla
OB	0-2	Fulham
Lokomotiv Moscow	0-2	Anderlecht
AEK	1-2	Sturm

Europa League group stage matchday 3
October 20 2011

Tottenham	1-0	Rubin
PAOK	2-1	Shamrock Rovers
Standard Liege	0-0	Vorskla
Hannover	2-2	Copengahen
Rapid Bucharest	0-1	Legia
H Tel Aviv	0-1	PSV
Sporting	2-0	Vaslui
Zurich	1-1	Lazio
Stoke	3-0	M Tel Aviv
Dynamo Kiev	1-0	Besiktas
Ath Bilbao	2-2	Salzburg
Slovan Bratislava	0-0	PSG
Malmo	1-4	Metalist
AZ	2-2	Austria Vienna
Maribor	1-1	Braga
Club Brugge	1-2	Birmingham
Rennes	1-1	Celtic
Udinese	2-0	Atl Madrid
AEK Larnaca	0-5	Schalke
M Haifa	5-0	Steaua
OB	1-4	Twente
Wisla	1-0	Fulham
Lokomotiv Moscow	3-1	AEK

Europa League group stage matchday 4
November 3 2011

Sturm	0-2	Anderlecht
Rubin	1-0	Tottenham

Shamrock Rovers	1-3	PAOK
Vorskla	1-3	Standard Liege
Copengahen	1-2	Hannover
Legia	3-1	Rapid Bucharest
PSV	3-3	H Tel Aviv
Vaslui	1-0	Sporting
Lazio	1-0	Zurich
M Tel Aviv	1-2	Stoke
Besiktas	1-0	Dynamo Kiev
Salzburg	0-1	Ath Bilbao
PSG	1-0	Slovan Bratislava
Metalist	3-1	Malmo
Austria Vienna	2-2	AZ
Braga	5-1	Maribor
Birmingham	2-2	Club Brugge
Celtic	3-1	Rennes
Atl Madrid	4-0	Udinese
Schalke	0-0	AEK Larnaca
Steaua	4-2	M Haifa
Twente	3-2	OB
Fulham	4-1	Wisla
AEK	1-3	Lokomotiv Moscow
Anderlecht	3-0	Sturm

Europa League group stage matchday 5
November 30 2011

Rubin	4-1	Shamrock Rovers
Tottenham	1-2	PAOK
Standard Liege	2-0	Hannover
Vorskla	1-1	Copengahen
Rapid Bucharest	1-3	H Tel Aviv
Legia	0-3	PSV
Malmo	0-0	AZ
Metalist	4-1	Austria Vienna
Maribor	3-4	Club Brugge
Braga	1-0	Birmingham
Rennes	0-0	Udinese
Celtic	0-1	Atl Madrid

December 1 2011

Sporting	2-0	Zurich
Vaslui	0-0	Lazio
Stoke	1-1	Dynamo Kiev
M Tel Aviv	2-3	Besiktas
Ath Bilbao	2-1	Slovan Bratislava
Salzburg	2-0	PSG
AEK Larnaca	2-1	M Haifa
Schalke	2-1	Steaua
OB	1-2	Wisla
Twente	1-0	Fulham
Lokomotiv Moscow	3-1	Sturm
AEK	1-2	Anderlecht

Europa League group stage matchday 6
December 14 2011

Zurich	2-0	Vaslui
Lazio	2-0	Sporting
Dynamo Kiev	3-3	M Tel Aviv
Besiktas	3-1	Stoke
Slovan Bratislava	2-3	Salzburg
PSG	4-2	Ath Bilbao
M Haifa	0-3	Schalke
Steaua	3-1	AEK Larnaca
Wisla	2-1	Twente
Fulham	2-2	OB
Sturm	1-3	AEK

Anderlecht ....5-3 ....Lokomotiv Moscow

December 15 2011

PAOK ....1-1 ....Rubin
Shamrock Rovers ....0-4 ....Tottenham
Hannover ....3-1 ....Vorskla
Copengahen ....0-1 ....Standard Liege
H Tel Aviv ....2-0 ....Legia
PSV ....2-1 ....Rapid Bucharest
AZ ....1-1 ....Metalist
Austria Vienna ....2-0 ....Malmo
Club Brugge ....1-1 ....Braga
Birmingham ....1-0 ....Maribor
Udinese ....1-1 ....Celtic
Atl Madrid..........................3-1 ....Rennes

Europa League round of 32
February 14 2012

Rubin ....0-1 ....Olympiacos
Braga ....0-2 ....Besiktas

February 16 2012

Lokomotiv Moscow ....2-1 ....Ath Bilbao
Ajax ....0-2 ....Man United
Salzburg..............................0-4 ....Metalist
AZ ....1-0 ....Anderlecht
Lazio ....1-3 ....Atl Madrid
Plzen ....1-1 ....Schalke
Legia ....2-2 ....Sporting
Porto ....1-2 ....Man City
Stoke ....0-1 ....Valencia
Steaua ....0-1 ....Twente
Wisla ....1-1 ....Standard Liege
Udinese ....0-0 ....PAOK
Trabzonspor.......................1-2 ....PSV
Hannover ....2-1 ....Club Brugge

February 22 2012

Man City.............................4-0 ....Porto
Aggregate score 6-1

February 23 2012

Ath Bilbao ....1-0 ....Lokomotiv Moscow
Aggregate score 2-2 Ath Bilbao won on away goals
Valencia ....1-0 ....Stoke
Aggregate score 2-0
Twente ....1-0 ....Steaua
Aggregate score 2-0
Standard Liege ....0-0 ....Wisla
Aggregate score 1-1 Standard Liege won on away goals
PAOK ....0-3 ....Udinese
Aggregate score 0-3
PSV ....4-1 ....Trabzonspor
Aggregate score 6-2
Club Brugge ....0-1 ....Hannover
Aggregate score 1-3
Man United ....1-2 ....Ajax
Aggregate score 3-2
Metalist...............................4-1 ....Salzburg
Aggregate score 8-1
Olympiacos ....1-0 ....Rubin
Aggregate score 2-0
Anderlecht ....0-1 ....AZ
Aggregate score 0-2
Atl Madrid...........................1-0 ....Lazio
Aggregate score 4-1
Schalke ....3-1 ....Plzen
Aggregate score 4-2 Schalke won after extra time
Besiktas ....0-1 ....Braga
Aggregate score 2-1

Sporting ....1-0 ....Legia
Aggregate score 3-2

Europa League round of 16
March 8 2012

Metalist...............................0-1 ....Olympiacos
Sporting ....1-0 ....Man City
Twente ....1-0 ....Schalke
Atl Madrid...........................3-1 ....Besiktas
Standard Liege ....2-2 ....Hannover
Valencia ....4-2 ....PSV
AZ..2-0 ....Udinese
Man United ....2-3 ....Ath Bilbao

March 15

Hannover ....4-0 ....Standard Liege
Aggregate score 6-2
PSV ....1-1 ....Valencia
Aggregate score 3-5
Udinese ....2-1 ....AZ
Aggregate score 2-3
Ath Bilbao ....2-1 ....Man United
Aggregate score 5-3
Olympiacos ....1-2 ....Metalist
Aggregate score 2-2 Metalist won on away goals
Man City.............................3-2 ....Sporting
Aggregate score 3-3 Sporting won on away goals
Schalke ....4-1 ....Twente
Aggregate score 4-2

March 15 2012

Besiktas ....0-3 ....Atl Madrid
Aggregate score 1-6

Europa League quarter-finals
March 29 2012

AZ..2-1 ....Valencia
Schalke ....2-4 ....Ath Bilbao
Sporting ....2-1 ....Metalist
Atl Madrid...........................2-1 ....Hannover

April 5 2012

Valencia ....4-0 ....AZ
Aggregate score 5-2
Ath Bilbao ....2-2 ....Schalke
Aggregate score 6-4
Metalist...............................1-1 ....Sporting
Aggregate score 2-3
Hannover ....1-2 ....Atl Madrid
Aggregate score 2-4

Europa League semi-finals
April 19 2012

Atl Madrid...........................4-2 ....Valencia
Sporting ....2-1 ....Ath Bilbao

April 26 2012

Valencia ....0-1 ....Atl Madrid
Aggregate score 2-5
Ath Bilbao ....3-1 ....Sporting
Aggregate score 4-3

Europa League final
May 9 2012

Atl Madrid..........................3-0 ....Ath Bilbao

Euro 2012 qualifying Group A

	P	W	D	L	F	A	GD	Pts
1 Germany	10	10	0	0	34	7	27	30
2 Turkey	10	5	2	3	13	11	2	17
3 Belgium	10	4	3	3	21	15	6	15
4 Austria	10	3	3	4	16	17	-1	12
5 Azerbaijan	10	2	1	7	10	26	-16	7
6 Kazakhstan	10	1	1	8	6	24	-18	4

September 3 2010
Kazakhstan ....0-3 ....Turkey
Belgium ....0-1 ....Germany

September 7 2010
Turkey ....3-2 ....Belgium
Austria ....2-0 ....Kazakhstan
Germany ....6-1 ....Azerbaijan

October 8 2010
Kazakhstan ....0-2 ....Belgium
Austria ....3-0 ....Azerbaijan
Germany ....3-0 ....Turkey

October 12 2010
Azerbaijan ....1-0 ....Turkey
Kazakhstan ....0-3 ....Germany
Belgium ....4-4 ....Austria

March 25 2011
Austria ....0-2 ....Belgium

March 26 2011
Germany ....4-0 ....Kazakhstan

March 29 2011
Turkey ....2-0 ....Austria
Belgium ....4-1 ....Azerbaijan

June 3 2011
Kazakhstan ....2-1 ....Azerbaijan
Austria ....1-2 ....Germany
Belgium ....1-1 ....Turkey

June 7 2011
Azerbaijan ....1-3 ....Germany

September 2 2011
Azerbaijan ....1-1 ....Belgium
Turkey ....2-1 ....Kazakhstan
Germany ....6-2 ....Austria

September 6 2011
Azerbaijan ....3-2 ....Kazakhstan
Austria ....0-0 ....Turkey

October 7 2011
Azerbaijan ....1-4 ....Austria
Belgium ....4-1 ....Kazakhstan
Turkey ....1-3 ....Germany

October 11 2011
Kazakhstan ....0-0 ....Austria
Germany ....3-1 ....Belgium
Turkey ....1-0 ....Azerbaijan

Euro 2012 qualifying Group B

	P	W	D	L	F	A	GD	Pts
1 Russia	10	7	2	1	17	4	13	23
2 Rep of Ireland	10	6	3	1	15	7	8	21
3 Armenia	10	5	2	3	22	10	12	17
4 Slovakia	10	4	3	3	7	10	-3	15
5 Macedonia	10	2	2	6	8	14	-6	8
6 Andorra	10	0	0	10	1	25	-24	0

3 September 2010
Armenia ....0-1 ....Rep of Ireland
Andorra ....0-2 ....Russia
Slovakia ....1-0.........................Macedonia

September 7 2010
Russia ....0-1 ....Slovakia
Macedonia.....................2-2 ....Armenia
Rep of Ireland ....3-1 ....Andorra

October 8 2010
Armenia ....3-1 ....Slovakia
Andorra ....0-2 ....Macedonia
Rep of Ireland ....2-3 ....Russia

October 12 2010
Armenia ....4-0 ....Andorra
Macedonia.....................0-1 ....Russia
Slovakia ....1-1 ....Rep of Ireland

March 26 2011
Armenia ....0-0 ....Russia
Andorra ....0-1 ....Slovakia
Rep of Ireland ....2-1 ....Macedonia

June 4 2011
Russia ....3-1 ....Armenia
Slovakia ....1-0 ....Andorra
Macedonia.....................0-2 ....Rep of Ireland

September 2 2011
Andorra ....0-3 ....Armenia
Russia ....1-0.........................Macedonia
Rep of Ireland ....0-0 ....Slovakia

September 6 2011
Russia ....0-0 ....Rep of Ireland
Macedonia.....................1-0 ....Andorra
Slovakia ....0-4 ....Armenia

October 7 2011
Armenia ....4-1 ....Macedonia
Slovakia ....0-1 ....Russia
Andorra ....0-2 ....Rep of Ireland

October 11 2011
Rep of Ireland ....2-1 ....Armenia
Russia ....6-0 ....Andorra
Macedonia.....................1-1 ....Slovakia

Euro 2012 qualifying Group C

	P	W	D	L	F	A	GD	Pts
1 Italy	10	8	2	0	20	2	18	26
2 Estonia	10	5	1	4	15	14	1	16
3 Serbia	10	4	3	3	13	12	1	15
4 Slovenia	10	4	2	4	11	7	4	14
5 N Ireland	10	2	3	5	9	13	-4	9
6 Faroe Islands	10	1	1	8	6	26	-20	4

August 11 2010
Estonia ....2-1 ....Faroe Islands

September 3 2010
Faroe Islands ....0-3 ....Serbia
Estonia...........................1-2 ....Italy
Slovenia ....0-1 ....N Ireland

September 7 2010
Serbia.............................1-1 ....Slovenia
Italy ....5-0...................Faroe Islands

October 8 2010
Serbia.............................1-3 ....Estonia
Slovenia ....5-1...................Faroe Islands
N Ireland ....0-0 ....Italy

October 12 2010
Faroe Islands ....1-1 ....N Ireland
Estonia...........................0-1 ....Slovenia
Italy ....3-0 ....Serbia

March 25 2011
Serbia.................2-1 ....N Ireland
Slovenia.............0-1 ....Italy
March 29 2011
Estonia...............1-1 ....Serbia
N Ireland ....0-0 ....Slovenia
June 3 2011
Faroe Islands ....0-2 ....Slovenia
Italy ....3-0 ....Estonia
June 7 2011
Faroe Islands ....2-0 ....Estonia
August 10 2011
N Ireland ....4-0 ....Faroe Islands
September 2 2011
Slovenia ....1-2 ....Estonia
Faroe Islands ....0-1 ....Italy
N Ireland ....0-1 ....Serbia
September 6 2011
Serbia.................3-1 ....Faroe Islands
Estonia...............4-1 ....N Ireland
Italy ....1-0 ....Slovenia
October 7 2011
Serbia.................1-1 ....Italy
N Ireland ....1-2 ....Estonia
October 11 2011
Italy ....3-0 ....N Ireland
Slovenia ....1-0 ....Serbia

Euro 2012 qualifying Group D

	P	W	D	L	F	A	GD	Pts
1 France	10	6	3	1	15	4	11	21
2 Bosnia-Hz	10	6	2	2	17	8	9	20
3 Romania	10	3	5	2	13	9	4	14
4 Belarus	10	3	4	3	8	7	1	13
5 Albania	10	2	3	5	7	14	-7	9
6 Luxembourg	10	1	1	8	3	21	-18	4

September 3 2010
Romania.............1-1 ....Albania
Luxembourg ....0-3 ....Bosnia-Hz
France ....0-1 ....Belarus
September 7 2010
Belarus..............0-0 ....Romania
Albania...............1-0 ....Luxembourg
Bosnia-Hz ....0-2 ....France
October 8 2010
Luxembourg ....0-0 ....Belarus
Albania...............1-1 ....Bosnia-Hz
October 9 2010
France ....2-0 ....Romania
October 12 2010
Belarus..............2-0 ....Albania
France ....2-0 ....Luxembourg
March 25 2011
Luxembourg ....0-2 ....France
March 26 2011
Bosnia-Hz ....2-1 ....Romania
Albania...............1-0 ....Belarus
March 29 2011
Romania.............3-1 ....Luxembourg
June 3 2011
Romania.............3-0 ....Bosnia-Hz
Belarus..............1-1 ....France
June 7 2011
Belarus..............2-0 ....Luxembourg

Bosnia-Hz ....2-0 ....Albania
September 2 2011
Belarus..............0-2 ....Bosnia-Hz
Luxembourg ....0-2 ....Romania
Albania...............1-2 ....France
September 6 2011
Luxembourg ....2-1 ....Albania
Bosnia-Hz ....1-0.............................Belarus
Romania.............0-0 ....France
October 7 2011
Bosnia-Hz ....5-0 ....Luxembourg
Romania.............2-2 ....Belarus
France ....3-0 ....Albania
October 11 2011
Albania...............1-1 ....Romania
France ....1-1 ....Bosnia-Hz

Euro 2012 qualifying Group E

	P	W	D	L	F	A	GD	Pts
1 Holland	10	9	0	1	37	8	29	27
2 Sweden	10	8	0	2	31	11	20	24
3 Hungary	10	6	1	3	22	14	8	19
4 Finland	10	3	1	6	16	16	0	10
5 Moldova	10	3	0	7	12	16	-4	9
6 San Marino	10	0	0	10	0	53	-53	0

September 3 2010
Moldova.............2-0 ....Finland
Sweden ....2-0 ....Hungary
San Marino ....0-5 ....Holland
September 7 2010
Sweden ....6-0 ....San Marino
Hungary ....2-1 ....Moldova
Holland ....2-1 ....Finland
October 8 2010
Hungary ....8-0 ....San Marino
Moldova.............0-1 ....Holland
October 12 2010
Finland ....1-2 ....Hungary
Holland ....4-1 ....Sweden
San Marino ....0-2 ....Moldova
November 17 2010
Finland ....8-0 ....San Marino
March 25 2011
Hungary ....0-4 ....Holland
March 29 2011
Sweden ....2-1 ....Moldova
Holland ....5-3 ....Hungary
June 3 2011
Moldova.............1-4 ....Sweden
San Marino ....0-1 ....Finland
June 7 2011
Sweden ....5-0 ....Finland
San Marino ....0-3 ....Hungary
September 2 2011
Finland ....4-1 ....Moldova
Hungary ....2-1 ....Sweden
Holland ....11-0 ....San Marino
September 6 2011
Finland ....0-2 ....Holland
Moldova.............0-2 ....Hungary
San Marino ....0-5 ....Sweden
October 7 2011
Finland ....1-2 ....Sweden
Holland ....1-0 ....Moldova

October 11 2011

Moldova ....4-0 ....San Marino
Sweden ....3-2 ....Holland
Hungary ....0-0 ....Finland

Euro 2012 qualifying Group F

	P	W	D	L	F	A	GD	Pts
1 Greece	10	7	3	0	14	5	9	24
2 Croatia	10	7	1	2	18	7	11	22
3 Israel	10	5	1	4	13	11	2	16
4 Latvia	10	3	2	5	9	12	-3	11
5 Georgia	10	2	4	4	7	9	-2	10
6 Malta	10	0	1	9	4	21	-17	1

September 2 2010

Israel ....3-1 ....Malta

September 3 2010

Latvia ....0-3 ....Croatia
Greece ....1-1 ....Georgia

September 7 2010

Georgia ....0-0 ....Israel
Malta ....0-2 ....Latvia
Croatia ....0-0 ....Greece

October 8 2010

Georgia ....1-0 ....Malta
Greece ....1-0 ....Latvia

October 9 2010

Israel ....1-2 ....Croatia

October 12 2010

Latvia ....1-1 ....Georgia
Greece ....2-1 ....Israel

November 17 2010

Croatia ....3-0 ....Malta

March 26 2011

Georgia ....1-0 ....Croatia
Israel ....2-1 ....Latvia
Malta ....0-1 ....Greece

March 29 2011

Israel ....1-0 ....Georgia

June 3 2011

Croatia ....2-1 ....Georgia

June 4 2011

Latvia ....1-2 ....Israel
Greece ....3-1 ....Malta

September 2 2011

Israel ....0-1 ....Greece
Malta ....1-3 ....Croatia
Georgia ....0-1 ....Latvia

September 6 2011

Croatia ....3-1 ....Israel
Latvia ....1-1 ....Greece
Malta ....1-1 ....Georgia

October 7 2011

Latvia ....2-0 ....Malta
Greece ....2-0 ....Croatia

October 11 2011

Georgia ....1-2 ....Greece
Malta ....0-2 ....Israel
Croatia ....2-0 ....Latvia

Euro 2012 qualifying Group G

	P	W	D	L	F	A	GD	Pts
1 England	8	5	3	0	17	5	12	18
2 Montenegro	8	3	3	2	7	7	0	12
3 Switzerland	8	3	2	3	12	10	2	11
4 Wales	8	3	0	5	6	10	-4	9
5 Bulgaria	8	1	2	5	3	13	-10	5

September 3 2010

Montenegro ....1-0 ....Wales
England ....4-0 ....Bulgaria

September 7 2010

Bulgaria ....0-1 ....Montenegro
Switzerland ....1-3 ....England

October 8 2010

Wales ....0-1 ....Bulgaria
Montenegro ....1-0 ....Switzerland

October 12 2010

Switzerland ....4-1 ....Wales
England ....0-0 ....Montenegro

March 26 2011

Wales ....0-2 ....England
Bulgaria ....0-0 ....Switzerland

June 4 2011

England ....2-2 ....Switzerland
Montenegro ....1-1 ....Bulgaria

September 2 2011

Bulgaria ....0-3 ....England
Wales ....2-1 ....Montenegro

September 6 2011

Switzerland ....3-1 ....Bulgaria
England ....1-0 ....Wales

October 7 2011

Wales ....2-0 ....Switzerland
Montenegro ....2-2 ....England

October 11 2011

Bulgaria ....0-1 ....Wales
Switzerland ....2-0 ....Montenegro

Euro 2012 qualifying Group H

	P	W	D	L	F	A	GD	Pts
1 Denmark	8	6	1	1	15	6	9	19
2 Portugal	8	5	1	2	21	12	9	16
3 Norway	8	5	1	2	10	7	3	16
4 Iceland	8	1	1	6	6	14	-8	4
5 Cyprus	8	0	2	6	7	20	-13	2

September 3 2010

Iceland ....1-2 ....Norway
Portugal ....4-4 ....Cyprus

September 7 2010

Denmark ....1-0 ....Iceland
Norway ....1-0 ....Portugal

October 8 2010

Cyprus ....1-2 ....Norway
Portugal ....3-1 ....Denmark

October 12 2010

Denmark ....2-0 ....Cyprus
Iceland ....1-3 ....Portugal

March 26 2011

Cyprus ....0-0 ....Iceland
Norway ....1-1 ....Denmark

June 4 2011

Iceland ....0-2 ....Denmark
Portugal ....1-0 ....Norway

September 2 2011

Norway ....1-0 ....Iceland
Cyprus ....0-4 ....Portugal

September 6 2011

Denmark ....2-0 ....Norway
Iceland ....1-0 ....Cyprus

October 7 2011
Cyprus ....1-4 ....Denmark
Portugal ....5-3 ....Iceland
October 11 2011
Norway...........................3-1 ....Cyprus
Denmark ....2-1 ....Portugal

Euro 2012 qualifying Group I

	P	W	D	L	F	A	GD	Pts
1 Spain	8	8	0	0	26	6	20	24
2 Czech Republic	8	4	1	3	12	8	4	13
3 Scotland	8	3	2	3	9	10	-1	11
4 Lithuania	8	1	2	5	4	13	-9	5
5 Liechtenstein	8	1	1	6	3	17	-14	4

September 3 2010
Lithuania ....0-0 ....Scotland
Liechtenstein ....0-4 ....Spain
September 7 2010
Czech Republic ....0-1 ....Lithuania
Scotland...........................2-1 ....Liechtenstein
October 8 2010
Czech Republic ....1-0 ....Scotland
Spain ....3-1 ....Lithuania
October 12 2010
Liechtenstein ....0-2 ....Czech Republic
Scotland...........................2-3 ....Spain
March 25 2011
Spain ....2-1 ....Czech Republic
March 29 2011
Czech Republic ....2-0 ....Liechtenstein
Lithuania ....1-3 ....Spain
June 3 2011
Liechtenstein ....2-0 ....Lithuania
September 2 2011
Lithuania ....0-0 ....Liechtenstein
September 3 2011
Scotland...........................2-2 ....Czech Republic
September 6 2011
Scotland...........................1-0 ....Lithuania
Spain ....6-0 ....Liechtenstein
October 7 2011
Czech Republic ....0-2 ....Spain
October 8 2011
Liechtenstein ....0-1 ....Scotland
October 11 2011
Spain ....3-1 ....Scotland
Lithuania ....1-4 ....Czech Republic

Euro 2012 qualifying play-offs
November 11 2011
Bosnia-Hz ....0-0 ....Portugal
Turkey ....0-3 ....Croatia
Czech Republic ....2-0 ....Montenegro
Estonia ....0-4 ....Rep of Ireland
November 15 2011
Croatia ....0-0 ....Turkey
Aggregate score 3-0
Montenegro ....0-1 ....Czech Republic
Aggregate score 3-0
Rep of Ireland ....1-1 ....Estonia
Aggregate score 5-1
Portugal ....6-2 ....Bosnia-Hz
Aggregate score 6-2

Euro 2012 Group A

	P	W	D	L	F	A	GD	Pts
1 Czech Republic	3	2	0	1	4	5	-1	6
2 Greece	3	1	1	1	3	3	0	4
3 Russia	3	1	1	1	5	3	2	4
4 Poland	3	0	2	1	2	3	-1	2

June 8 2012
Poland ....1-1 ....Greece
Russia ....4-1 ....Czech Rep
June 12 2012
Greece ....1-2 ....Czech Rep
Poland ....1-1 ....Russia
June 16 2012
Greece ....1-0 ....Russia
Poland ....0-1 ....Czech Rep

Euro 2012 Group B

	P	W	D	L	F	A	GD	Pts
1 Germany	3	3	0	0	5	2	3	9
2 Portugal	3	2	0	1	5	4	1	6
3 Denmark	3	1	0	2	4	5	-1	3
4 Holland	3	0	0	3	2	5	-3	0

June 9 2012
Holland ....0-1 ....Denmark
Germany ....1-0 ....Portugal
June 13 2012
Denmark ....2-3 ....Portugal
Holland ....1-2 ....Germany
June 17 2012
Portugal ....2-1 ....Holland
Denmark ....1-2 ....Germany

Euro 2012 Group C

	P	W	D	L	F	A	GD	Pts
1 Spain	3	2	1	0	6	1	5	7
2 Italy	3	1	2	0	4	2	2	5
3 Croatia	3	1	1	1	4	3	1	4
4 Rep of Ireland	3	0	0	3	1	9	-8	0

June 10 2012
Spain ....1-1 ....Italy
Rep of Ireland ....1-3 ....Croatia
June 14 2012
Italy ....1-1 ....Croatia
Spain ....4-0 ....Rep of Ireland
June 18 2012
Croatia ....0-1 ....Spain
Italy ....2-0 ....Rep of Ireland

Euro 2012 Group D

	P	W	D	L	F	A	GD	Pts
1 England	3	2	1	0	5	3	2	7
2 France	3	1	1	1	3	3	0	4
3 Ukraine	3	1	0	2	2	4	-2	3
4 Sweden	3	1	0	2	5	5	0	3

June 11 2012
France ....1-1 ....England
Ukraine............................2-1 ....Sweden
June 15 2012
Ukraine............................0-2 ....France
Sweden ....2-3 ....England
June 19 2012
Sweden ....2-0 ....France
England ....1-0 ....Ukraine

Euro 2012 quarter-finals
June 21 2012
Czech Republic ....0-1 ....Portugal
June 22 2012
Germany ....4-2 ....Greece
June 23 2012
Spain ....2-0 ....France
June 24 2012
England ....0-0 ....Italy
Italy won 4-2 on penalties

Euro 2012 semi-finals
June 27 2012
Portugal ....0-0 ....Spain
Spain won 4-2 on penalties
June 28 2012
Germany ....1-2 ....Italy

Euro 2012 final
July 1 2012
Spain ....4-0 ....Italy

World Cup qualifying European Group A fixtures
Sept 7 2012 Croatia v Macedonia, Sept 8 2012 Scotland v Serbia, Sept 11 2012 Scotland v Macedonia, Belgium v Croatia, Serbia v Wales, Oct 12 2012 Wales v Scotland, Serbia v Belgium, Macedonia v Croatia, Oct 16 2012 Belgium v Scotland, Macedonia v Serbia, Croatia v Wales, Mar 22 2012 Croatia v Serbia, Scotland v Wales, Macedonia v Belgium, Mar 26 2012 Wales v Croatia, Serbia v Scotland, Belgium v Macedonia, Jun 7 2012 Belgium v Serbia, Croatia v Scotland, Sept 6 2012 Macedonia v Wales, Serbia v Croatia, Scotland v Belgium, Sept 10 2012 Macedonia v Scotland, Wales v Serbia, Oct 11 2012 Wales v Macedonia, Croatia v Belgium, Oct 15 2012 Scotland v Croatia, Belgium v Wales, Serbia v Macedonia

World Cup qualifying European Group B fixtures
Sept 7 2012 Malta v Armenia, Bulgaria v Italy, Sept 8 2012 Denmark v Czech Rep, Sept 11 2012 Italy v Malta, Bulgaria v Armenia, Oct 12 2012 Bulgaria v Denmark, Czech Rep v Malta, Armenia v Italy, Oct 16 2012 Italy v Denmark, Czech Rep v Bulgaria, Mar 22 2012 Czech Rep v Denmark, Bulgaria v Malta, Mar 26 2012 Malta v Italy, Denmark v Bulgaria, Armenia v Czech Rep, Jun 7 2012 Armenia v Malta, Jun 8 2012 Czech Rep v Italy, Jun 11 2012 Denmark v Armenia, Sept 6 2012 Czech Rep v Armenia, Italy v Bulgaria, Malta v Czech Rep, Sept 10 2012 Malta v Bulgaria, Italy v Czech Rep, Armenia v Denmark, Oct 11 2012 Malta v Czech Rep, Denmark v Italy, Armenia v Bulgaria, Oct 15 2012 Italy v Armenia, Denmark v Malta, Bulgaria v Czech Rep

World Cup qualifying European Group C fixtures
Sept 7 2012 Germany v Faroe Islands, Kazakhstan v Rep of Ireland, Sept 11 2012 Sweden v Kazakhstan, Austria v Germany, Oct 12 2012 Rep of Ireland v Germany, Kazakhstan v Austria, Faroe Islands v Sweden, Oct 16 2012 Germany v Sweden, Faroe Islands v Rep of Ireland, Austria v Kazakhstan, Mar 22 2012 Kazakhstan v Germany, Sweden v Rep of Ireland, Austria v Faroe Islands, Mar 26 2012 Rep of Ireland v Austria, Germany v Kazakhstan, Jun 7 2012 Austria v Sweden, Rep of Ireland v Faroe Islands, Jun 11 2012 Sweden v Faroe Islands, Sept 6 2012 Kazakhstan v Faroe Islands, Germany v Austria, Rep of Ireland v Sweden, Sept 10 2012 Kazakhstan v Sweden, Austria v Rep of Ireland, Faroe Islands v Germany, Oct 11 2012 Sweden v Austria, Germany v Rep of Ireland, Faroe Islands v Kazakhstan, Oct 15 2012 Rep of Ireland v Kazakhstan, Faroe Islands v Austria, Sweden v Germany

World Cup qualifying European Group D fixtures
Sept 7 2012 Andorra v Hungary, Estonia v Romania, Holland v Turkey, Sept 11 2012 Hungary v Holland, Romania v Andorra, Turkey v Estonia, Oct 12 2012 Estonia v Hungary, Holland v Andorra, Turkey v Romania, Oct 16 2012 Hungary v Turkey, Andorra v Estonia, Romania v Holland, Mar 22 2012 Holland v Estonia, Andorra v Turkey, Hungary v Romania, Mar 26 2012 Holland v Romania, Estonia v Andorra, Turkey v Hungary, Sept 6 2012 Romania v Hungary, Turkey v Andorra, Estonia v Holland, Sept 10 2012 Andorra v Holland, Romania v Turkey, Hungary v Estonia, Oct 11 2012 Holland v Hungary, Andorra v Romania, Estonia v Turkey, Oct 15 2012 Turkey v Holland, Romania v Estonia, Hungary v Andorra

World Cup qualifying European Group E fixtures
Sept 7 2012 Albania v Cyprus, Iceland v Norway, Slovenia v Switzerland, Sept 11 2012 Norway v Slovenia, Cyprus v Iceland, Switzerland v Albania, Oct 12 2012 Slovenia v Cyprus, Albania v Iceland, Switzerland v Norway, Oct 16 2012 Albania v Slovenia, Cyprus v Norway, Iceland v Switzerland, Mar 22 2012 Slovenia v Iceland, Switzerland v Cyprus, Norway v Albania, Jun 7 2012 Cyprus v Switzerland, Albania v Norway, Iceland v Slovenia, Sept 6 2012 Slovenia v Albania, Switzerland v Iceland, Norway v Cyprus, Sept 10 2012 Iceland v Albania, Cyprus v Slovenia, Norway v Switzerland, Oct 11 2012 Albania v Switzerland, Iceland v Cyprus, Slovenia v Norway, Oct 15 2012 Norway v Iceland, Cyprus v Albania, Switzerland v Slovenia

World Cup qualifying European Group F fixtures
Sept 7 2012 Russia v N Ireland, Luxembourg v Portugal, Azerbaijan v Israel, Sept 11 2012 Israel v Russia, Portugal v Azerbaijan, N Ireland v Luxembourg, Oct 12 2012 Russia v Portugal, Luxembourg v Israel, Oct 16 2012 Russia v Azerbaijan, Portugal v N Ireland, Israel v Luxembourg, 11 14 2012 N Ireland v Azerbaijan, Mar 22 2012 Luxembourg v Azerbaijan, N Ireland v Russia, Israel v Portugal, Mar 26 2012 Azerbaijan v Portugal, N Ireland v Israel, Jun 7 2012 Portugal v Russia, Azerbaijan v Luxembourg, Sept 6 2012 Russia v Luxembourg, N Ireland v Portugal, Israel v Azerbaijan, Sept 10 2012 Russia v Israel, Luxembourg v N Ireland, Oct 11 2012 Azerbaijan v N Ireland, Portugal v Israel, Luxembourg v Russia, Oct 15 2012 Azerbaijan v Russia, Israel v N Ireland, Portugal v Luxembourg, ,

World Cup qualifying European Group G fixtures
Sept 7 2012 Latvia v Greece, Lithuania v Slovakia, Liechtenstein v Bosnia-Hz, Sept 11 2012 Greece v Lithuania, Bosnia-Hz v Latvia, Slovakia v Liechtenstein, Oct 12 2012 Slovakia v Latvia, Liechtenstein v Lithuania, Greece v Bosnia-Hz, Oct 16 2012 Latvia v Liechtenstein, Bosnia-Hz v Lithuania, Slovakia v Greece, Mar 22 2012 Bosnia-Hz v Greece, Liechtenstein v Latvia, Slovakia v Lithuania, Jun 7 2012 Lithuania v Greece, Latvia v Bosnia-Hz, Liechtenstein v Slovakia, Sept 6 2012 Latvia v Lithuania, Bosnia-Hz v Slovakia, Liechtenstein v Greece, Sept 10 2012 Greece v Latvia, Lithuania v Liechtenstein, Slovakia v Bosnia-Hz, Oct 11 2012 Greece v Slovakia, Bosnia-Hz v Liechtenstein, Lithuania v Latvia, Oct 15 2012 Greece v Liechtenstein, Lithuania v Bosnia-Hz, Latvia v Slovakia

World Cup qualifying European Group H fixtures
Sept 7 2012 Moldova v England, Montenegro v Poland, Sept 11 2012 Poland v Moldova, England v Ukraine, San Marino v Montenegro, Oct 12 2012 England v San Marino, Moldova v Ukraine, Oct 16 2012 Poland v England, Ukraine v Montenegro, San Marino v Moldova, 11 14 2012 Montenegro v San Marino, Mar 22 2012 Moldova v Montenegro, San Marino v England, Poland v Ukraine, Mar 26 2012 Poland v San Marino, Montenegro v England, Ukraine v Moldova, Jun 7 2012 Moldova v Poland, Montenegro v Ukraine, Sept 6 2012 Ukraine v San Marino, England v Moldova, Poland v Montenegro, Sept 10 2012 San Marino v Poland, Ukraine v England, Oct 11 2012 Ukraine v Poland, Moldova v San Marino, England v Montenegro, Oct 15 2012 Montenegro v Moldova, San Marino v Ukraine, England v Poland

World Cup qualifying European Group I fixtures
Sept 7 2012 Georgia v Belarus, Finland v France, Sept 11 2012 France v Belarus, Georgia v Spain, Oct 12 2012 Belarus v Spain, Finland v Georgia, Oct 16 2012 Belarus v Georgia, Spain v France, Mar 22 2012 France v Georgia, Spain v Finland, Mar 26 2012 France v Spain, Jun 7 2012 Finland v Belarus, Jun 11 2012 Belarus v Finland, Sept 6 2012 Georgia v Finland, Sept 10 2012 Georgia v Finland, Belarus v France, Oct 11 2012 Spain v Belarus, Oct 15 2012 France v Finland, Spain v Georgia

How to read the results

Alongside each fixture are the results for the corresponding league match over the last six seasons. The most recent result (ie 2011-12) is on the right. The final figure on each fixture line is, from left to right the number of home wins, draws and away wins between the two sides dating back to 1988-89.

Where Scottish clubs have met more than once in the same season each result is divided by an oblique stroke, the most recent of the matches appearing to the right.

Please note that Sky/ESPN television coverage and weather conditions will cause alterations to the fixture list.

The Scottish Premier League will also split into top and bottom six sections later in the season. These fixtures cover the period until that split.

The Scottish Football League had not voted on which division Rangers would play in for the 2012-13 season as we went to press, and the Scottish Premier League await that decision before allocating the 'Club12' position to either Dunfermline or Dundee.

Readers who want an updated fixture list should contact RFO at rfo@rfoutlook.com and we will email a new PDF version.

Home team Away team	Six-season fixture record, latest result at right						Since 1988 – HW D AW
SATURDAY 4TH AUGUST 2012							
SCOTTISH PREMIER LEAGUE							
Celtic v Aberdeen	1-0/2-1	3-0/1-0	3-2/2-0	3-0	9-0/1-0	2-1	(35-04-06)
Hearts v St Johnstone	-	-	-	1-2	1-1/1-0	1-2/2-0	(08-08-06)
Kilmarnock v Club 12	-	-	-	-	-	-	(None)
Ross County v Motherwell	-	-	-	-	-	-	(None)
St Mirren v Inverness	1-1/0-1	2-1/1-1	2-0/1-2	-	1-2/3-3	1-2/0-1	(04-06-08)
SUNDAY 5TH AUGUST 2012							
SCOTTISH PREMIER LEAGUE							
Dundee Utd v Hibernian	0-3/0-0	0-0/1-1/1-1	2-0/2-2	1-0/0-2	1-0/3-0	3-1	(16-16-10)
SATURDAY 11TH AUGUST 2012							
SCOTTISH PREMIER LEAGUE							
Aberdeen v Ross County	-	-	-	-	-	-	(None)
Celtic v Dundee Utd	2-2	3-0/0-0	2-2/2-1	1-1/1-0	1-1/4-1	5-1/2-1	(31-11-02)
Club 12 v St Mirren	-	-	-	-	-	-	(None)
Hibernian v Hearts	2-2/0-1	1-1	1-1/1-0	1-1/1-2	0-2/2-2	1-3	(12-17-14)

Home team / Away team	\	\	Six-season fixture record, latest result at right	\	\	Since 1988 – HW D AW	
Inverness v Kilmarnock	3-4	3-1/3-0	3-1/2-1	-	1-3	2-1/1-1	(05-03-04)
Motherwell v St Johnstone	-	-	-	1-3	4-0	0-3/3-2/5-1	(12-05-07)

SCOTTISH DIVISION ONE

Cowdenbeath v Dunfermline	-	-	-	-	0-4/0-1	-	(00-00-03)
Dundee v Dumbarton	-	-	-	-	-	-	(01-01-00)
Morton v Livingston	-	2-2/1-1	1-2/2-2	-	-	2-1/1-3	(09-06-06)
Partick v Falkirk	-	-	-	-	1-0/1-2	2-2/1-1	(09-06-08)
Raith v Hamilton	-	-	-	-	-	3-2/2-1	(08-07-04)

SCOTTISH DIVISION TWO

Airdrie v Arbroath	-	-	-	-	-	3-3/2-0	(04-01-01)
Alloa v East Fife	-	-	0-3/0-1	0-0/2-0	3-2/1-3	-	(06-05-06)
Ayr v Stenhsmuir	-	-	-	-	2-0/4-3	-	(03-01-02)
Brechin v Albion	-	-	-	-	-	1-4/2-1	(11-01-05)
Queen of Sth v Forfar	-	-	-	-	-	-	(06-03-06)

SCOTTISH DIVISION THREE

Berwick v Elgin	3-1/0-0	-	1-1/2-1	2-0/2-1	6-2/4-0	1-1/3-3	(07-05-00)
E Stirling v Queen's Park	2-1/0-2	-	-	1-0/0-3	0-1/3-2	1-3/1-2	(16-07-16)
Montrose v Clyde	-	-	-	-	8-1/3-1	4-0/5-0	(04-01-02)
Peterhead v Stranraer	5-2/5-0	-	4-0/1-0	-	-	1-3/1-1	(05-01-02)
Stirling v Annan	-	-	-	-	-	-	(None)

CONFERENCE

Barrow v Telford	-	4-0	-	-	-	2-1	(05-01-00)
Braintree v Hyde	-	-	-	-	-	-	(None)
Dartford v Tamworth	-	-	-	-	-	-	(None)
Forest G v Cambridge U	1-1	3-1	2-2	1-1	1-1	2-1	(03-04-00)
Hereford v Macclesfield	1-0	0-1	-	0-2	2-2	0-4	(01-01-03)
Lincoln v Kidderminstr	-	-	-	-	-	0-1	(02-02-02)
Luton v Gateshead	-	-	-	2-1	2-2	5-1	(02-01-00)
Mansfield v Newport Co	-	-	-	-	3-3	5-0	(01-01-00)
Nuneaton v Ebbsfleet	-	-	-	-	-	-	(01-00-01)
Southport v Grimsby	-	-	-	-	2-2	1-2	(00-01-01)
Stockport v Alfreton	-	-	-	-	-	0-0	(00-01-00)
Wrexham v Woking	-	-	1-1	-	-	-	(00-01-00)

TUESDAY 14TH AUGUST 2012

CONFERENCE

Alfreton v Southport	-	1-2	2-0	1-1	-	0-0	(02-02-02)
Cambridge U v Lincoln	-	-	-	-	-	2-0	(03-03-03)
Ebbsfleet v Braintree	-	-	-	-	0-0	1-1	(01-02-00)
Gateshead v Mansfield	-	-	-	1-3	1-1	3-0	(01-01-01)
Grimsby v Stockport	0-1	1-1	-	-	-	7-0	(05-03-03)
Hyde v Barrow	1-1	2-1	-	-	-	-	(05-05-04)
Kidderminstr v Luton	-	-	-	1-2	3-3	1-2	(00-01-03)
Macclesfield v Wrexham	2-0	3-2	-	-	-	-	(03-00-02)
Newport Co v Nuneaton	-	-	-	-	-	-	(00-01-01)
Tamworth v Hereford	-	-	-	-	-	-	(00-01-02)
Telford v Forest G	-	-	-	-	-	2-0	(04-01-02)
Woking v Dartford	-	-	-	-	2-2	1-0	(01-01-00)

FRIDAY 17TH AUGUST 2012

CHAMPIONSHIP

Cardiff v Huddersfield	-	-	-	-	-	-	(02-02-02)

SATURDAY 18TH AUGUST 2012

PREMIER LEAGUE

Fixture							
Arsenal v Sunderland	-	3-2	0-0	2-0	0-0	2-1	(09-03-00)
Fulham v Norwich	-	-	-	-	-	2-1	(03-01-00)
Newcastle v Tottenham	3-1	3-1	2-1	-	1-1	2-2	(10-06-03)
QPR v Swansea	-	-	1-0	1-1	4-0	3-0	(03-01-00)
Reading v Stoke	-	-	-	-	-	-	(09-04-02)
West Brom v Liverpool	-	-	0-2	-	2-1	0-2	(01-00-05)
West Ham v Aston Villa	1-1	2-2	0-1	2-1	1-2	-	(05-09-04)

CHAMPIONSHIP

Fixture							
Barnsley v Middlesboro	-	-	-	2-1	2-0	1-3	(04-02-02)
Birmingham v Charlton	-	-	3-2	-	-	-	(04-04-03)
Burnley v Bolton	-	-	-	1-1	-	-	(00-02-02)
C Palace v Watford	-	0-2	0-0	3-0	3-2	4-0	(07-02-05)
Derby v Sheff Weds	1-0	-	3-0	3-0	-	-	(07-03-01)
Hull v Brighton	-	-	-	-	-	0-0	(05-05-04)
Ipswich v Blackburn	-	-	-	-	-	-	(06-02-01)
Leeds v Wolves	0-1	-	-	-	-	-	(03-01-01)
Leicester v Peterborough	-	-	4-0	1-1	-	1-1	(02-02-01)
Millwall v Blackpool	0-0	-	-	-	-	2-2	(03-03-00)
Nottm F v Bristol C	1-0	-	3-2	1-1	1-0	0-1	(04-02-01)

LEAGUE 1

Bury v Brentford	-	1-2	1-0	-	-	1-1	(03-04-04)
Crawley v Scunthorpe	-	-	-	-	-	-	(None)
Crewe v Notts Co	-	-	-	0-1	-	-	(02-01-02)
Hartlepool v Swindon	0-1	1-1	3-3	0-1	2-2	-	(02-04-02)
MK Dons v Oldham	-	-	6-2	0-0	0-0	5-0	(05-03-01)
Portsmouth v Bournemouth	-	-	-	-	-	-	(02-00-00)
Preston v Colchester	1-0	0-3	-	-	-	2-4	(05-00-03)
Sheff Utd v Shrewsbury	-	-	-	-	-	-	(None)
Stevenage v Carlisle	-	-	-	-	-	1-0	(02-00-00)
Tranmere v Leyton O	3-0	1-1	0-0	2-1	1-2	2-0	(06-02-01)
Walsall v Doncaster	-	1-1	-	-	-	-	(04-02-02)
Yeovil v Coventry	-	-	-	-	-	-	(None)

LEAGUE 2

Fixture							
Wimbledon v Chesterfield	-	-	-	-	-	-	(None)
Bristol R v Oxford Utd	-	-	-	-	-	0-0	(07-04-02)
Cheltenham v Dagenham	-	-	-	1-1	-	2-1	(01-01-00)
Exeter v Morecambe	1-0	-	2-2	-	-	-	(03-02-00)
Fleetwood v Torquay	-	-	-	-	-	-	(None)
Gillingham v Bradford	1-0	-	0-2	-	2-0	0-0	(05-01-02)
Plymouth v Aldershot	-	-	-	-	-	1-0	(01-00-00)
Port Vale v Barnet	-	-	0-0	0-2	0-0	1-2	(01-02-02)
Rochdale v Northampton	-	-	-	1-0	-	-	(04-05-03)
Rotherham v Burton	-	-	-	2-2	3-3	0-1	(00-02-01)
Southend v Accrington	-	-	-	-	1-1	2-2	(00-02-00)
York v Wycombe	-	-	-	-	-	-	(04-01-00)

SCOTTISH PREMIER LEAGUE

Fixture							
Dundee Utd v Club 12	-	-	-	-	-	-	(None)
Hearts v Inverness	4-1/1-0	2-3/1-0	1-0/3-2	-	1-1	2-1	(07-02-02)
Kilmarnock v Motherwell	1-2	0-1	1-0/0-0	0-3	0-1/3-1	0-0/2-0	(14-05-14)
Ross County v Celtic	-	-	-	-	-	-	(None)

Home team Away team	Six-season fixture record, latest result at right					Since 1988 – HW D AW	
St Johnstone v Aberdeen	-	-	-	1-0/1-1	0-1/0-0	1-2	(06-07-10)
St Mirren v Hibernian	1-0/1-1	2-1	0-0/1-1	1-1	1-0/0-1	2-3/1-0	(08-06-07)

SCOTTISH DIVISION ONE

Dumbarton v Cowdenbeath	-	-	2-1/1-1	0-3/2-1	-	0-4/0-2	(10-06-08)
Dunfermline v Partick	-	1-0/1-1	1-0/0-1	3-1/1-2	0-0/0-0	-	(07-04-02)
Falkirk v Raith	-	-	-	-	0-0/2-1	2-0/2-3	(17-02-06)
Hamilton v Morton	-	1-0/3-0	-	-	-	1-2/4-3	(11-06-06)
Livingston v Dundee	2-3/1-3	0-2/1-1	1-2/0-1	-	-	4-2/2-3	(03-05-08)

SCOTTISH DIVISION TWO

Albion v Alloa	-	-	-	-	-	-	(07-04-05)
Arbroath v Ayr	-	-	0-3/1-3	-	-	-	(02-02-04)
East Fife v Queen of Sth	-	-	-	-	-	-	(08-01-07)
Forfar v Airdrie	-	-	-	-	1-2/1-2	3-2/2-3	(02-04-06)
Stenhsmuir v Brechin	-	-	-	1-1/1-2	0-0/1-3	1-1/2-1	(09-07-06)

SCOTTISH DIVISION THREE

Annan v Berwick	-	-	1-2/1-1	1-1/0-1	1-1/2-3	2-2/1-1	(00-05-03)
Clyde v Peterhead	-	-	-	1-3/3-1	-	2-0/0-1	(02-00-02)
Elgin v Stirling	-	-	-	-	-	-	(01-01-04)
Queen's Park v Montrose	1-1/5-0	-	-	3-2/3-0	1-0/4-1	3-1/5-0	(16-11-09)
Stranraer v E Stirling	-	2-1/2-1	-	1-2/2-2	4-1/2-0	6-0/4-1	(11-04-04)

CONFERENCE

Alfreton v Hereford	-	-	-	-	-	-	(None)
Cambridge U v Southport	2-2	-	-	-	0-0	3-0	(02-02-00)
Ebbsfleet v Wrexham	-	-	1-0	0-1	-	0-5	(01-00-02)
Gateshead v Forest G	-	-	-	3-1	1-1	1-0	(02-01-00)
Grimsby v Nuneaton	-	-	-	-	-	-	(None)
Hyde v Luton	-	-	-	-	-	-	(None)
Kidderminstr v Mansfield	-	-	2-0	3-1	1-3	0-3	(04-01-03)
Macclesfield v Dartford	-	-	-	-	-	-	(None)
Newport Co v Lincoln	-	-	-	-	-	1-0	(01-00-00)
Tamworth v Stockport	-	-	-	-	-	1-1	(00-01-00)
Telford v Braintree	-	-	-	-	-	1-0	(01-00-00)
Woking v Barrow	-	-	1-0	-	-	-	(01-00-01)

SUNDAY 19TH AUGUST 2012

PREMIER LEAGUE

Man City v Southampton	-	-	-	-	-	-	(03-03-05)
Wigan v Chelsea	2-3	0-2	0-1	3-1	0-6	1-1	(01-01-05)

MONDAY 20TH AUGUST 2012

PREMIER LEAGUE

Everton v Man Utd	2-4	0-1	1-1	3-1	3-3	0-1	(04-05-15)

TUESDAY 21ST AUGUST 2012

CHAMPIONSHIP

Blackpool v Leeds	-	-	-	-	-	1-0	(01-00-00)
Bolton v Derby	-	1-0	-	-	-	-	(02-01-02)
Brighton v Cardiff	-	-	-	-	-	2-2	(03-03-04)
Bristol C v C Palace	-	1-1	1-0	1-0	1-1	2-2	(03-04-00)

Home team	Away team	Six-season fixture record, latest result at right						Since 1988 – HW D AW
Charlton v Leicester		-	2-0	-	-	-	-	(06-02-02)
Huddersfield v Nottm F		1-1	1-1	-	-	-	-	(02-03-01)
Middlesboro v Burnley		-	-	-	-	2-1	0-2	(02-00-01)
Peterborough v Millwall		-	-	1-0	-	-	0-3	(01-03-02)
Sheff Weds v Birmingham		0-3	-	1-1	-	-	-	(01-01-02)
Watford v Ipswich		-	2-0	2-1	2-1	2-1	2-1	(08-03-04)
Wolves v Barnsley		2-0	1-0	2-0	-	-	-	(07-06-02)

LEAGUE 1

Home team	Away team							Since 1988 – HW D AW
Bournemouth v MK Dons		-	-	-	-	3-2	0-1	(02-00-02)
Brentford v Yeovil		1-2	-	-	1-1	1-2	2-0	(02-01-02)
Carlisle v Tranmere		1-0	0-1	1-2	3-0	2-0	0-0	(03-02-02)
Colchester v Portsmouth		-	-	-	-	-	-	(None)
Coventry v Sheff Utd		-	0-1	1-2	3-2	0-0	-	(05-03-05)
Doncaster v Bury		-	-	-	-	-	-	(01-00-04)
Leyton O v Stevenage		-	-	-	-	-	0-0	(00-01-00)
Notts Co v Hartlepool		0-1	-	-	-	3-0	3-0	(04-00-01)
Oldham v Walsall		-	0-2	3-2	1-0	1-1	2-1	(06-03-02)
Scunthorpe v Crewe		2-2	-	3-0	-	-	-	(03-03-00)
Shrewsbury v Preston		-	-	-	-	-	-	(03-00-02)
Swindon v Crawley		-	-	-	-	-	3-0	(01-00-00)

LEAGUE 2

Home team	Away team							Since 1988 – HW D AW
Accrington v Port Vale		-	-	2-0	1-2	3-0	2-2	(02-01-01)
Aldershot v Exeter		3-2	2-0	1-0	-	-	-	(06-00-00)
Barnet v Bristol R		1-1	-	-	-	-	2-0	(01-02-01)
Bradford v Fleetwood		-	-	-	-	-	-	(None)
Burton v Wimbledon		-	-	-	-	-	3-2	(01-00-00)
Chesterfield v Rochdale		-	3-4	3-0	2-0	-	2-1	(04-04-03)
Dagenham v Plymouth		-	-	-	-	0-1	2-3	(00-00-02)
Morecambe v York		1-3	-	-	-	-	-	(02-00-01)
Northampton v Rotherham		3-0	-	-	3-1	2-2	1-1	(02-02-04)
Oxford Utd v Southend		-	-	-	-	0-2	0-2	(05-00-05)
Torquay v Cheltenham		-	-	-	3-0	2-1	2-2	(03-02-03)
Wycombe v Gillingham		-	-	1-0	3-0	1-0	-	(05-02-01)

WEDNESDAY 22ND AUGUST 2012

CHAMPIONSHIP

Home team	Away team							Since 1988 – HW D AW
Blackburn v Hull		-	-	1-1	1-0	-	-	(03-02-00)

FRIDAY 24TH AUGUST 2012

CHAMPIONSHIP

Home team	Away team							Since 1988 – HW D AW
Bolton v Nottm F		-	-	-	-	-	-	(02-02-00)

SATURDAY 25TH AUGUST 2012

PREMIER LEAGUE

Home team	Away team							Since 1988 – HW D AW
Aston Villa v Everton		1-1	2-0	3-3	2-2	1-0	1-1	(13-10-01)
Chelsea v Newcastle		1-0	2-1	0-0	-	2-2	0-2	(11-06-01)
Man Utd v Fulham		5-1	2-0	3-0	3-0	2-0	1-0	(10-00-01)
Norwich v QPR		1-0	3-0	0-1	-	1-0	2-1	(12-03-03)
Southampton v Wigan		-	-	-	-	-	-	(None)
Sunderland v Reading		-	2-1	-	-	-	-	(03-01-02)
Swansea v West Ham		-	-	-	-	-	-	(None)
Tottenham v West Brom		-	-	1-0	-	2-2	1-0	(04-02-00)

Home team	Away team	Six-season fixture record, latest result at right					Since 1988 – HW D AW

CHAMPIONSHIP

Home team v Away team						
Blackburn v Leicester	-	-	-	-	-	(05-02-03)
Blackpool v Ipswich	-	1-1	0-1	1-0	2-0	(02-01-01)
Brighton v Barnsley	-	-	-	-	2-0	(04-01-01)
Bristol C v Cardiff	-	1-0	1-1	0-6	3-0	1-2	(05-03-02)
Charlton v Hull	-	1-1	-	-	-	(01-01-00)
Huddersfield v Burnley	-	-	-	-	-	(00-02-01)
Middlesboro v C Palace	-	-	-	1-1	2-1	0-0	(02-02-02)
Peterborough v Leeds	-	-	2-0	-	2-3	(01-00-01)
Sheff Weds v Millwall	-	-	-	-	-	(02-02-02)
Watford v Birmingham	-	-	0-1	-	2-2	(04-04-01)
Wolves v Derby	0-1	-	3-0	-	-	(03-03-04)

LEAGUE 1

Bournemouth v Preston	-	-	-	-	1-0	(05-01-02)
Brentford v Crewe	0-4	-	-	-	-	(03-00-04)
Carlisle v Portsmouth	-	-	-	-	-	(None)
Colchester v Sheff Utd	-	2-2	-	-	1-1	(00-02-00)
Coventry v Bury	-	-	-	-	-	(None)
Doncaster v Crawley	-	-	-	-	-	(None)
Leyton O v Hartlepool	-	2-4	1-0	1-3	1-0	1-1	(10-03-04)
Notts Co v Walsall	1-2	-	-	-	1-1	2-1	(06-01-01)
Oldham v Stevenage	-	-	-	-	1-1	(00-01-00)
Scunthorpe v Yeovil	1-0	-	2-0	-	2-1	(05-00-01)
Shrewsbury v Tranmere	-	-	-	-	-	(01-00-01)
Swindon v MK Dons	2-1	-	1-1	0-0	0-1	(02-02-03)

LEAGUE 2

Accrington v Exeter	-	-	2-1	-	-	(01-01-02)
Aldershot v Cheltenham	-	-	-	4-1	0-2	1-0	(02-00-01)
Barnet v York	-	-	-	-	-	(04-00-02)
Bradford v Wimbledon	-	-	-	-	1-2	(00-00-01)
Burton v Fleetwood	-	-	-	-	-	(None)
Chesterfield v Rotherham	2-1	0-2	1-0	0-1	5-0	-	(04-02-03)
Dagenham v Gillingham	-	-	2-0	-	2-1	(02-00-00)
Morecambe v Port Vale	-	-	1-1	1-0	1-0	0-0	(02-02-00)
Northampton v Southend	-	0-1	2-3	-	2-1	2-5	(03-02-04)
Oxford Utd v Plymouth	-	-	-	-	5-1	(04-02-01)
Torquay v Rochdale	1-0	-	-	5-0	-	(11-03-04)
Wycombe v Bristol R	0-1	-	-	2-1	-	(04-04-03)

SCOTTISH PREMIER LEAGUE

Club 12 v Ross County	-	-	-	-	-	(None)
Hibernian v St Johnstone	-	-	-	3-0/1-1	0-0/1-2	3-2/2-3	(08-07-06)
Inverness v Celtic	1-1/1-2	3-2	1-2/0-0	-	0-1/3-2	0-2	(02-03-06)
Kilmarnock v Dundee Utd	0-0/1-0	2-1/1-2	2-0	0-2/4-4	1-2/1-1	1-1	(13-09-09)
Motherwell v St Mirren	0-0/2-3	1-1	2-1/0-2	2-0	3-1/0-1	1-1	(10-05-04)

SCOTTISH DIVISION ONE

Cowdenbeath v Hamilton	-	-	-	-	-	(03-01-04)
Dundee v Dunfermline	-	1-1/0-0	0-0/1-0	1-0/3-2	2-2/1-1	-	(08-09-08)
Morton v Falkirk	-	-	-	-	0-0/2-2	3-2/0-0	(04-07-10)
Partick v Dumbarton	-	-	-	-	-	(02-00-00)
Raith v Livingston	-	-	-	-	-	0-1/0-3	(07-01-06)

SCOTTISH DIVISION TWO

Airdrie v Stenhsmuir	-	-	-	-	1-0/2-2	5-2/0-3	(06-01-01)
Alloa v Arbroath	-	-	2-1/2-0	0-1/1-0	-	-	(13-08-09)
Ayr v Forfar	5-0/3-1	-	-	-	0-1/3-1	-	(08-05-03)

Home team — Away team	Six-season fixture record, latest result at right						Since 1988 – HW D AW
Brechin v East Fife	-	-	2-1/2-1	3-2/1-0	1-3/2-3	0-2/1-3	(14-04-06)
Queen of Sth v Albion	-	-	-	-	-	-	(01-01-04)

SCOTTISH DIVISION THREE

Home team — Away team							Since 1988 – HW D AW
Berwick v Stranraer	-	-	-	1-0/1-0	2-2/3-3	2-2/1-0	(13-06-08)
E Stirling v Elgin	2-1/0-2	3-1/0-0	5-2/1-0	1-1/2-0	0-2/2-1	1-1/2-2	(10-05-09)
Montrose v Annan	-	-	1-1/0-3	0-0/1-2	1-1/0-1	2-3/1-1	(00-04-04)
Peterhead v Queen's Park	-	1-0/1-0	4-1/1-1	-	-	1-1/2-1	(08-05-01)
Stirling v Clyde	-	0-2/1-1	-	1-1/1-0	-	-	(03-04-07)

CONFERENCE

Home team — Away team							Since 1988 – HW D AW
Barrow v Alfreton	1-1	2-1	-	-	-	1-0	(04-02-02)
Braintree v Newport Co	2-1	0-0	3-2	1-2	-	1-0	(03-01-01)
Dartford v Kidderminstr	-	-	-	-	-	-	(None)
Forest G v Woking	2-3	2-1	0-2	-	-	-	(03-03-05)
Hereford v Ebbsfleet	-	-	-	-	-	-	(02-02-00)
Lincoln v Macclesfield	2-1	3-1	1-0	0-0	2-1	-	(09-04-01)
Luton v Telford	-	-	-	-	-	1-1	(00-01-00)
Mansfield v Hyde	-	-	-	-	-	-	(None)
Nuneaton v Cambridge U	-	-	-	-	-	-	(None)
Southport v Tamworth	1-0	2-2	0-1	-	2-1	1-1	(02-03-01)
Stockport v Gateshead	-	-	-	-	-	0-1	(00-00-01)
Wrexham v Grimsby	3-0	0-0	-	-	2-0	2-2	(03-03-03)

SUNDAY 26TH AUGUST 2012

PREMIER LEAGUE

Home team — Away team							Since 1988 – HW D AW
Liverpool v Man City	1-0	1-0	1-1	2-2	3-0	1-1	(11-06-01)
Stoke v Arsenal	-	-	2-1	1-3	3-1	1-1	(02-01-01)

SCOTTISH PREMIER LEAGUE

Home team — Away team							Since 1988 – HW D AW
Aberdeen v Hearts	1-3/1-0	1-1/0-1	1-0/0-0	1-1/0-1	0-1/0-0	0-0	(17-13-15)

MONDAY 27TH AUGUST 2012

CONFERENCE

Home team — Away team							Since 1988 – HW D AW
Alfreton v Nuneaton	0-3	1-3	-	-	3-2	-	(03-00-02)
Cambridge U v Dartford	-	-	-	-	-	-	(None)
Ebbsfleet v Luton	-	-	-	1-6	-	2-2	(00-01-01)
Gateshead v Lincoln	-	-	-	-	-	3-3	(00-01-00)
Grimsby v Mansfield	1-1	1-0	-	-	7-2	0-0	(05-02-00)
Hyde v Southport	-	1-3	1-1	1-1	-	-	(02-03-03)
Kidderminstr v Forest G	2-2	1-0	1-1	2-1	1-0	1-0	(04-04-01)
Macclesfield v Barrow	-	-	-	-	-	-	(02-00-01)
Newport Co v Hereford	-	-	-	-	-	-	(None)
Tamworth v Wrexham	-	-	-	2-1	1-1	1-2	(01-01-01)
Telford v Stockport	-	-	-	-	-	1-1	(00-01-00)

TUESDAY 28TH AUGUST 2012

CONFERENCE

Home team — Away team							Since 1988 – HW D AW
Woking v Braintree	-	-	-	0-0	0-1	-	(00-01-01)

SATURDAY 1ST SEPTEMBER 2012

PREMIER LEAGUE

Home team — Away team							Since 1988 – HW D AW
Chelsea v Reading	2-2	1-0	-	-	-	-	(01-01-00)

Home team v Away team							Since 1988 – HW D AW
Man City v QPR	-	-	-	-	-	3-2	(05-03-03)
Newcastle v Aston Villa	3-1	0-0	2-0	-	6-0	2-1	(12-04-03)
Swansea v Sunderland	-	-	-	-	-	0-0	(00-01-00)
Tottenham v Norwich	-	-	-	-	-	1-2	(06-01-02)
West Brom v Everton	-	-	1-2	-	1-0	0-1	(03-00-03)
West Ham v Fulham	3-3	2-1	3-1	2-2	1-1	-	(03-04-01)
Wigan v Stoke	-	-	0-0	1-1	2-2	2-0	(05-05-03)

CHAMPIONSHIP

Home team v Away team							Since 1988 – HW D AW
Barnsley v Bristol C	-	3-0	0-0	2-3	4-2	1-2	(08-02-05)
Birmingham v Peterborough	-	-	-	-	-	1-1	(02-03-00)
Burnley v Brighton	-	-	-	-	-	1-0	(03-02-02)
C Palace v Sheff Weds	1-2	2-1	1-1	0-0	-	-	(06-06-01)
Derby v Watford	-	-	1-0	2-0	4-1	1-2	(07-03-04)
Hull v Bolton	-	-	0-1	1-0	-	-	(02-00-02)
Ipswich v Huddersfield	-	-	-	-	-	-	(04-00-01)
Leeds v Blackburn	-	-	-	-	-	-	(06-05-01)
Leicester v Blackpool	-	0-1	-	2-1	-	2-0	(02-00-01)
Millwall v Middlesboro	-	-	-	-	2-3	1-3	(02-03-02)
Nottm F v Charlton	-	-	0-0	-	-	-	(03-03-01)

LEAGUE 1

Home team v Away team							Since 1988 – HW D AW
Bury v Notts Co	0-1	2-1	2-0	3-3	-	2-2	(05-04-04)
Crawley v Leyton O	-	-	-	-	-	-	(None)
Crewe v Coventry	-	-	-	-	-	-	(03-00-01)
Hartlepool v Scunthorpe	-	-	2-3	-	-	1-2	(05-02-07)
MK Dons v Carlisle	-	-	3-1	3-4	3-2	1-2	(02-00-02)
Portsmouth v Oldham	-	-	-	-	-	-	(03-02-01)
Sheff Utd v Bournemouth	-	-	-	-	-	2-1	(02-00-00)
Stevenage v Shrewsbury	-	-	-	-	1-1	-	(01-01-00)
Tranmere v Colchester	-	-	3-4	1-1	1-0	0-0	(01-08-01)
Walsall v Brentford	-	-	-	2-1	3-2	0-1	(05-02-03)
Yeovil v Doncaster	1-0	2-1	-	-	-	-	(04-03-02)

LEAGUE 2

Home team v Away team							Since 1988 – HW D AW
Wimbledon v Dagenham	-	-	-	-	-	2-1	(01-00-00)
Bristol R v Morecambe	-	-	-	-	-	2-1	(01-00-00)
Cheltenham v Accrington	-	-	-	1-1	1-2	4-1	(01-01-01)
Exeter v Burton	3-0	1-4	-	-	-	-	(03-00-02)
Fleetwood v Aldershot	-	-	-	-	-	-	(None)
Gillingham v Chesterfield	2-1	-	2-1	-	0-2	-	(07-02-06)
Plymouth v Northampton	-	-	-	-	-	4-1	(03-01-01)
Port Vale v Torquay	-	-	-	2-2	1-2	0-0	(00-02-02)
Rochdale v Barnet	0-2	3-0	3-1	2-1	-	-	(05-06-03)
Rotherham v Bradford	4-1	1-1	0-2	1-2	0-0	3-0	(07-04-04)
Southend v Wycombe	-	-	-	1-1	3-2	-	(01-01-02)
York v Oxford Utd	1-0	0-1	0-0	1-1	-	-	(03-03-03)

SCOTTISH PREMIER LEAGUE

Home team v Away team							Since 1988 – HW D AW
Aberdeen v St Mirren	2-0	4-0/1-1	2-0	1-0/2-1	2-0/0-1	2-2/0-0	(14-05-01)
Celtic v Hibernian	2-1/1-0	1-1/2-0	4-2/3-1	1-2/3-2	2-1/3-1	0-0	(27-12-04)
Motherwell v Inverness	1-4/1-0	2-1/3-1	3-2/2-2	-	0-0	3-0/0-1	(05-02-05)
Ross County v Kilmarnock	-	-	-	-	-	-	(None)
St Johnstone v Dundee Utd	-	-	-	2-3/0-1	0-0	3-3/1-5/0-2	(05-09-12)

SCOTTISH DIVISION ONE

Home team v Away team							Since 1988 – HW D AW
Dundee v Cowdenbeath	-	-	-	-	3-0/2-2	-	(01-01-00)
Dunfermline v Raith	-	-	-	0-2/2-1	2-2/2-1	-	(06-03-05)
Falkirk v Livingston	-	-	-	-	-	4-3/2-5	(06-04-03)

Home team	Away team						Since 1988 – HW D AW	
Morton v Dumbarton	-	-	-	-	-	-	(09-03-02)
Partick v Hamilton	3-1/0-2	0-3/3-0	-	-	-	1-1/2-0	(05-07-05)

SCOTTISH DIVISION TWO

Airdrie v Ayr	-	0-0/0-2	-	3-1/1-1	2-2/0-5	-	(08-11-05)
Brechin v Alloa	2-0/2-3	0-0/0-0	3-1/1-0	2-1/1-1	3-1/3-2	-	(11-03-06)
East Fife v Albion	2-2/1-3	4-0/0-0	-	-	-	2-0/1-2	(10-09-06)
Queen of Sth v Arbroath	-	-	-	-	-	-	(07-04-04)
Stenhsmuir v Forfar	-	4-0/2-0	1-1/0-1	-	3-0/0-1	2-3/1-2	(09-04-10)

SCOTTISH DIVISION THREE

Berwick v E Stirling	2-2/2-0	-	2-1/1-2	0-1/2-2	3-0/1-1	4-2/0-2	(13-06-08)
Clyde v Annan	-	-	-	-	0-2/0-2	0-0/1-1	(00-02-02)
Peterhead v Montrose	-	-	-	-	-	2-3/2-1	(08-02-02)
Stirling v Queen's Park	-	-	0-3/4-0	-	-	08-03-04)
Stranraer v Elgin	-	3-3/0-0	-	0-2/2-1	2-1/1-2	1-0/5-2	(06-02-02)

CONFERENCE

Barrow v Kidderminstr	-	-	1-0	1-0	2-1	3-1	(06-00-02)
Braintree v Tamworth	-	-	-	-	-	3-1	(01-00-00)
Dartford v Alfreton	-	-	-	-	-	-	(None)
Forest G v Hyde	-	-	-	-	-	-	(None)
Hereford v Grimsby	0-1	2-0	-	0-1	-	-	(02-00-03)
Lincoln v Ebbsfleet	-	-	-	-	-	3-0	(01-00-00)
Luton v Macclesfield	-	-	1-0	-	-	-	(01-01-01)
Mansfield v Woking	-	-	0-1	-	-	-	(00-00-01)
Nuneaton v Gateshead	-	-	-	-	-	-	(None)
Southport v Telford	-	1-1	1-1	3-0	-	3-2	(07-04-03)
Stockport v Cambridge U	-	-	-	-	-	0-1	(03-01-01)
Wrexham v Newport Co	-	-	-	-	1-0	0-0	(01-01-00)

SUNDAY 2ND SEPTEMBER 2012

PREMIER LEAGUE

Liverpool v Arsenal	4-1	1-1	4-4	1-2	1-1	1-2	(11-06-07)
Southampton v Man Utd	-	-	-	-	-	-	(06-02-09)

CHAMPIONSHIP

Cardiff v Wolves	4-0	2-3	1-2	-	-	-	(01-03-02)

LEAGUE 1

Preston v Swindon	-	-	-	-	-	-	(None)

SCOTTISH PREMIER LEAGUE

Hearts v Club 12	-	-	-	-	-	-	(None)

TUESDAY 4TH SEPTEMBER 2012

CONFERENCE

Barrow v Grimsby	-	-	-	-	0-2	2-2	(00-01-01)
Braintree v Kidderminstr	-	-	-	-	-	1-4	(00-00-01)
Dartford v Newport Co	-	-	-	-	-	-	(None)
Forest G v Ebbsfleet	0-1	2-2	1-4	0-0	-	3-1	(02-03-04)
Hereford v Woking	-	-	-	-	-	-	(03-02-04)
Lincoln v Alfreton	-	-	-	-	-	0-1	(00-00-01)
Luton v Cambridge U	-	-	-	2-2	2-0	0-1	(03-02-01)
Mansfield v Tamworth	-	-	-	0-0	0-1	2-1	(01-01-01)
Nuneaton v Telford	-	2-0	-	-	0-0	-	(02-03-01)
Southport v Gateshead	-	-	2-3	-	5-1	1-3	(05-03-02)

Home team v Away team							
Stockport v Macclesfield	1-1	2-0	-	-	1-4	-	(02-01-01)
Wrexham v Hyde	-	-	-	-	-	-	(None)

SATURDAY 8TH SEPTEMBER 2012

LEAGUE 1

Brentford v Colchester	-	-	-	1-0	1-1	1-1	(05-04-01)
Bury v Preston	-	-	-	-	-	1-0	(03-04-03)
Coventry v Stevenage	-	-	-	-	-	-	(None)
Crawley v Portsmouth	-	-	-	-	-	-	(None)
Crewe v Tranmere	1-1	4-3	2-1	-	-	-	(06-02-03)
Doncaster v Oldham	1-1	1-1	-	-	-	-	(01-03-00)
Hartlepool v Carlisle	-	2-2	2-2	4-1	0-4	4-0	(07-04-04)
Notts Co v Shrewsbury	1-1	2-1	2-2	1-1	-	-	(04-05-01)
Scunthorpe v Sheff Utd	-	3-2	-	3-1	3-2	1-1	(03-01-00)
Swindon v Leyton O	-	1-1	0-1	3-2	2-2	-	(01-02-01)
Walsall v MK Dons	0-0	-	0-3	2-1	1-2	0-2	(04-03-03)
Yeovil v Bournemouth	0-0	2-1	-	-	2-2	1-3	(01-03-01)

LEAGUE 2

Accrington v Bradford	-	0-2	2-3	2-0	3-0	1-0	(03-00-02)
Barnet v Gillingham	-	-	2-2	-	1-2	2-2	(03-02-02)
Bristol R v Aldershot	-	-	-	-	-	0-1	(00-00-01)
Morecambe v Fleetwood	-	-	-	-	-	-	(03-01-02)
Northampton v Wimbledon	-	-	-	-	-	1-0	(01-00-00)
Oxford Utd v Exeter	1-0	2-2	-	-	-	-	(01-02-01)
Port Vale v Rotherham	1-3	-	0-0	1-2	1-0	2-0	(05-01-03)
Rochdale v Burton	-	-	-	1-2	-	-	(00-00-01)
Southend v Dagenham	-	-	-	-	-	1-1	(00-01-00)
Torquay v Plymouth	-	-	-	-	-	3-1	(01-02-03)
Wycombe v Cheltenham	-	-	-	-	2-1	-	(02-04-02)
York v Chesterfield	-	-	-	-	-	-	(01-02-06)

CONFERENCE

Alfreton v Luton	-	-	-	-	-	0-0	(00-01-00)
Cambridge U v Wrexham	-	-	2-0	2-0	1-3	1-1	(03-04-05)
Ebbsfleet v Mansfield	-	-	2-2	2-1	-	0-3	(01-01-01)
Gateshead v Dartford	-	-	-	-	-	-	(None)
Grimsby v Forest G	-	-	-	-	1-1	2-1	(01-01-00)
Hyde v Hereford	-	-	-	-	-	-	(None)
Kidderminstr v Southport	2-0	-	-	-	3-4	2-0	(06-02-03)
Macclesfield v Braintree	-	-	-	-	-	-	(None)
Newport Co v Stockport	-	-	-	-	-	1-1	(00-01-00)
Tamworth v Barrow	-	0-0	-	3-0	2-2	2-3	(01-02-01)
Telford v Lincoln	-	-	-	-	-	1-2	(00-00-01)
Woking v Nuneaton	-	-	-	-	-	-	(01-02-01)

THURSDAY 13TH SEPTEMBER 2012

LEAGUE 1

Leyton O v Brentford	1-1	-	-	2-1	1-0	2-0	(05-02-03)

FRIDAY 14TH SEPTEMBER 2012

CHAMPIONSHIP

Brighton v Sheff Weds	-	-	-	-	2-0	-	(02-01-02)
Charlton v C Palace	-	2-0	1-0	-	-	-	(04-03-01)

SATURDAY 15TH SEPTEMBER 2012

PREMIER LEAGUE

Home v Away							
Arsenal v Southampton	-	-	-	-	-	-	(12-05-00)
Aston Villa v Swansea	-	-	-	-	-	0-2	(00-00-01)
Fulham v West Brom	-	-	2-0	-	3-0	1-1	(06-04-00)
Man Utd v Wigan	3-1	4-0	1-0	5-0	2-0	5-0	(07-00-00)
Norwich v West Ham	-	-	-	-	-	-	(03-02-00)
QPR v Chelsea	-	-	-	-	-	1-0	(04-03-01)
Stoke v Man City	-	-	1-0	1-1	1-1	1-1	(03-03-02)
Sunderland v Liverpool	-	0-2	0-1	1-0	0-2	1-0	(03-01-08)

CHAMPIONSHIP

Home v Away							
Barnsley v Blackpool	-	2-1	0-1	1-0	-	1-3	(05-01-02)
Bolton v Watford	1-0	-	-	-	-	-	(04-00-01)
Bristol C v Blackburn	-	-	-	-	-	-	(02-00-00)
Burnley v Peterborough	-	-	-	-	-	1-1	(03-02-01)
Cardiff v Leeds	1-0	-	-	-	2-1	1-1	(03-02-00)
Huddersfield v Derby	-	-	-	-	-	-	(00-00-01)
Hull v Millwall	-	-	-	-	0-1	2-0	(01-02-01)
Middlesboro v Ipswich	-	-	-	3-1	1-3	0-0	(02-05-03)
Nottm F v Birmingham	-	-	1-1	-	-	1-3	(03-02-02)
Wolves v Leicester	1-2	1-1	-	-	-	-	(05-05-02)

LEAGUE 1

Home v Away							
Bournemouth v Hartlepool	-	2-0	-	-	0-1	1-2	(03-04-03)
Carlisle v Swindon	-	3-0	1-1	0-1	0-0	-	(01-02-02)
Colchester v Doncaster	-	-	-	-	-	-	(07-01-02)
MK Dons v Yeovil	-	-	3-0	2-2	3-2	0-1	(02-02-01)
Oldham v Notts Co	-	-	-	-	3-0	3-2	(05-02-04)
Portsmouth v Walsall	-	-	-	-	-	-	(02-02-00)
Preston v Crawley	-	-	-	-	-	-	(None)
Sheff Utd v Bury	-	-	-	-	-	4-0	(04-00-00)
Shrewsbury v Scunthorpe	-	-	-	-	-	-	(02-03-03)
Stevenage v Crewe	-	-	-	-	1-1	-	(00-01-00)
Tranmere v Coventry	-	-	-	-	-	-	(None)

LEAGUE 2

Home v Away							
Wimbledon v Rochdale	-	-	-	-	-	-	(None)
Aldershot v Morecambe	0-1	-	0-2	4-1	2-1	1-0	(04-02-02)
Bradford v Barnet	-	1-1	3-3	2-1	1-3	4-2	(03-02-01)
Burton v Oxford Utd	1-2	1-2	0-1	-	0-0	1-1	(00-02-03)
Cheltenham v Southend	-	1-1	0-0	-	0-2	3-0	(03-04-02)
Chesterfield v Wycombe	-	2-0	0-1	-	4-1	4-0	(08-01-04)
Dagenham v Accrington	-	1-3	0-0	3-1	-	2-1	(02-01-04)
Exeter v York	1-1	1-1	-	-	-	-	(05-02-04)
Fleetwood v Northampton	-	-	-	-	-	-	(None)
Gillingham v Bristol R	-	3-2	-	1-0	-	4-1	(04-02-02)
Plymouth v Port Vale	-	-	-	-	-	0-2	(05-00-03)
Rotherham v Torquay	-	-	-	1-1	3-1	0-1	(03-02-02)

SCOTTISH PREMIER LEAGUE

Home v Away							
Club 12 v Motherwell	-	-	-	-	-	-	(None)
Dundee Utd v Ross County	-	-	-	-	-	-	(16-10-08)
Hibernian v Kilmarnock	2-2/0-1	4-1/2-0	2-4	1-0/1-0	2-1/2-1	1-1/0-1	(16-10-08)
Inverness v Aberdeen	1-1	1-2/3-4	0-3	-	2-0/0-2	2-1/0-2	(02-02-08)
St Johnstone v Celtic	-	-	-	1-4	0-3/0-1	0-2	(06-03-12)
St Mirren v Hearts	2-2	1-3/1-1	0-1	2-1/1-1	0-2	0-0	(03-07-07)

SCOTTISH DIVISION ONE

Home v Away							Since 1988
Cowdenbeath v Morton	1-2/1-1	-	-	-	2-2/0-2	-	(00-04-04)
Dumbarton v Dunfermline	-	-	-	-	-	-	(00-01-05)
Hamilton v Falkirk	-	-	1-1/0-1	0-0/2-2	-	0-1/0-1	(03-07-07)
Livingston v Partick	2-2/0-1	0-4/1-0	3-1/2-4	-	-	2-1/3-1	(08-07-05)
Raith v Dundee	-	-	-	2-2/1-0	1-2/2-1	0-1/0-1	(04-06-05)

SCOTTISH DIVISION TWO

Home v Away							Since 1988
Albion v Airdrie	-	-	-	-	-	7-2/0-1	(01-00-03)
Alloa v Stenhsmuir	-	-	-	1-4/2-1	1-0/1-2	-	(09-02-07)
Arbroath v East Fife	1-1/1-3	2-3/0-1	0-1/0-2	0-1/2-2	-	3-0/2-2	(07-06-12)
Ayr v Queen of Sth	-	-	-	0-1/3-0	-	1-0/1-1	(05-04-04)
Forfar v Brechin	1-2/3-2	-	-	-	1-1/2-1	0-0/4-1	(08-04-05)

SCOTTISH DIVISION THREE

Home v Away							Since 1988
Annan v Stranraer	-	-	-	1-0/3-2	2-2/2-1	0-3/1-3	(03-01-02)
E Stirling v Stirling	-	-	-	-	-	-	(01-03-06)
Elgin v Peterhead	-	-	-	-	-	6-1/1-2	(04-01-07)
Montrose v Berwick	0-1/1-2	-	1-1/1-1	1-3/1-1	1-1/1-1	3-5/1-1	(03-09-15)
Queen's Park v Clyde	-	-	-	-	0-1/4-0	3-0/3-0	(04-00-03)

CONFERENCE

Home v Away							Since 1988
Barrow v Newport Co	-	-	-	-	2-1	3-1	(02-00-00)
Cambridge U v Telford	-	-	-	-	-	1-0	(01-00-00)
Dartford v Hereford	-	-	-	-	-	-	(None)
Forest G v Alfreton	-	-	-	-	-	4-1	(01-00-00)
Gateshead v Tamworth	-	-	5-1	1-1	3-1	1-1	(02-02-00)
Kidderminstr v Grimsby	-	-	-	-	3-2	1-1	(01-01-01)
Lincoln v Hyde	-	-	-	-	-	-	(None)
Luton v Wrexham	-	-	-	1-0	1-1	0-1	(04-02-04)
Mansfield v Braintree	-	-	-	-	-	4-1	(01-00-00)
Nuneaton v Macclesfield	-	-	-	-	-	-	(None)
Southport v Ebbsfleet	2-2	-	-	-	-	3-3	(01-03-00)
Stockport v Woking	-	-	-	-	-	-	(None)

SUNDAY 16TH SEPTEMBER 2012

PREMIER LEAGUE

Home v Away							Since 1988
Reading v Tottenham	3-1	0-1	-	-	-	-	(01-00-01)

MONDAY 17TH SEPTEMBER 2012

PREMIER LEAGUE

Home v Away							Since 1988
Everton v Newcastle	3-0	3-1	2-2	-	0-1	3-1	(10-04-05)

TUESDAY 18TH SEPTEMBER 2012

CHAMPIONSHIP

Home v Away							Since 1988
Birmingham v Bolton	-	1-0	-	1-2	2-1	-	(10-02-03)
Blackburn v Barnsley	-	-	-	-	-	-	(04-01-02)
Blackpool v Middlesboro	-	-	-	2-0	-	3-0	(02-00-00)
C Palace v Nottm F	-	-	1-2	1-1	0-3	0-3	(04-06-05)
Derby v Charlton	-	-	1-0	-	-	-	(05-04-02)
Ipswich v Wolves	0-1	3-0	0-2	-	-	-	(06-03-05)
Leeds v Hull	0-0	-	-	-	2-2	4-1	(04-02-00)
Millwall v Cardiff	-	-	-	-	3-3	0-0	(01-05-00)

Home team v Away team						Since 1988 – H W D A W	
Peterborough v Bristol C	-	-	-	0-1	-	3-0	(04-02-05)
Watford v Brighton	-	-	-	-	-	1-0	(03-03-02)

LEAGUE 1

Bournemouth v Brentford	1-0	-	0-1	-	3-1	1-0	(10-03-04)
Carlisle v Crewe	0-2	1-0	4-2	-	-	-	(04-00-04)
Colchester v Crawley	-	-	-	-	-	-	(None)
Leyton O v Yeovil	0-0	0-0	0-1	2-0	1-5	2-2	(02-03-03)
MK Dons v Notts Co	3-2	3-0	-	-	2-1	3-0	(05-00-00)
Oldham v Scunthorpe	1-0	-	3-0	-	-	1-2	(02-02-01)
Portsmouth v Swindon	-	-	-	-	-	-	(05-02-03)
Preston v Hartlepool	-	-	-	-	-	1-0	(03-00-02)
Sheff Utd v Doncaster	-	-	0-1	1-1	2-2	-	(00-02-01)
Shrewsbury v Coventry	-	-	-	-	-	-	(None)
Stevenage v Walsall	-	-	-	-	-	0-0	(00-01-00)
Tranmere v Bury	-	-	-	-	-	2-0	(02-01-03)

LEAGUE 2

Wimbledon v Torquay	-	-	-	-	-	2-0	(01-00-00)
Aldershot v Barnet	-	-	1-1	4-0	1-0	4-1	(03-02-01)
Bradford v Morecambe	-	1-0	4-0	2-0	0-1	2-2	(03-01-01)
Cheltenham v Oxford Utd	-	-	-	-	1-1	0-0	(01-03-02)
Chesterfield v Accrington	-	4-2	1-1	1-0	5-2	-	(03-01-00)
Dagenham v Northampton	-	-	-	0-1	-	0-1	(00-00-02)
Exeter v Wycombe	-	-	1-0	1-1	-	1-3	(01-01-01)
Fleetwood v Port Vale	-	-	-	-	-	-	(None)
Gillingham v Southend	-	1-1	-	3-0	0-0	1-2	(02-03-03)
Plymouth v Bristol R	-	-	-	-	3-1	1-1	(02-05-02)
Rotherham v Rochdale	-	2-4	2-2	2-1	-	-	(03-03-02)

WEDNESDAY 19TH SEPTEMBER 2012

CHAMPIONSHIP

Leicester v Burnley	0-1	0-1	-	-	4-0	0-0	(01-02-04)
Sheff Weds v Huddersfield	-	-	-	-	0-2	4-4	(01-01-02)

LEAGUE 2

Burton v York	1-2	4-3	2-1	-	-	-	(02-01-02)

FRIDAY 21ST SEPTEMBER 2012

CHAMPIONSHIP

Blackburn v Middlesboro	2-1	1-1	1-1	-	-	-	(06-06-03)

SATURDAY 22ND SEPTEMBER 2012

PREMIER LEAGUE

Chelsea v Stoke	-	-	2-1	7-0	2-0	1-0	(05-00-00)
Newcastle v Norwich	-	-	-	-	-	1-0	(03-01-01)
Southampton v Aston Villa	-	-	-	-	-	-	(07-04-06)
Swansea v Everton	-	-	-	-	-	0-2	(00-00-01)
Tottenham v QPR	-	-	-	-	-	3-1	(05-03-01)
West Brom v Reading	-	-	-	3-1	-	-	(07-01-00)
West Ham v Sunderland	-	3-1	2-0	1-0	0-3	-	(10-01-03)

Home team	Away team	Six-season fixture record, latest result at right						Since 1988 – HW D AW
Wigan v Fulham		0-0	1-1	0-0	1-1	1-1	0-2	(05-08-04)

CHAMPIONSHIP

Home team	Away team							Since 1988
Birmingham v Barnsley		2-0	-	2-0	-	-	1-1	(06-04-02)
Blackpool v Huddersfield		3-1	-	-	-	-	-	(03-04-03)
C Palace v Cardiff		1-2	0-0	0-2	1-2	1-0	1-2	(03-01-04)
Derby v Burnley		1-0	-	1-1	-	2-4	1-2	(04-02-03)
Ipswich v Charlton		-	2-0	1-1	-	-	-	(06-02-02)
Leeds v Nottm F		-	1-1	-	-	4-1	3-7	(06-02-03)
Leicester v Hull		0-1	0-2	-	-	1-1	2-1	(03-01-04)
Millwall v Brighton		0-1	3-0	0-1	1-1	-	1-1	(04-02-04)
Peterborough v Wolves		-	-	-	-	-	-	(00-00-02)
Sheff Weds v Bolton		-	-	-	-	-	-	(02-00-01)
Watford v Bristol C		-	1-2	2-4	2-0	1-3	2-2	(05-04-04)

LEAGUE 1

Home team	Away team							Since 1988
Brentford v Oldham		2-2	-	-	1-1	1-3	2-0	(05-06-01)
Bury v MK Dons		0-2	1-5	-	-	-	0-0	(00-01-02)
Coventry v Carlisle		-	-	-	-	-	-	(None)
Crawley v Tranmere		-	-	-	-	-	-	(None)
Crewe v Leyton O		0-4	0-2	0-2	-	-	-	(02-01-04)
Doncaster v Stevenage		-	-	-	-	-	-	(01-03-01)
Hartlepool v Shrewsbury		0-3	-	-	-	-	-	(04-02-02)
Notts Co v Portsmouth		-	-	-	-	-	-	(01-01-02)
Scunthorpe v Colchester		-	3-3	3-0	-	-	1-1	(06-05-02)
Swindon v Bournemouth		-	4-1	-	-	1-2	-	(04-03-03)
Walsall v Preston		-	-	-	-	-	1-0	(06-03-01)
Yeovil v Sheff Utd		-	-	-	-	-	0-1	(00-00-01)

LEAGUE 2

Home team	Away team							Since 1988
Accrington v Aldershot		-	-	0-1	2-1	0-0	3-2	(04-02-01)
Barnet v Rotherham		-	2-0	2-0	0-1	1-4	1-1	(05-02-03)
Bristol R v Fleetwood		-	-	-	-	-	-	(None)
Morecambe v Plymouth		-	-	-	-	-	2-2	(00-01-00)
Northampton v Chesterfield		1-0	-	-	0-0	1-2	-	(04-04-05)
Oxford Utd v Bradford		-	-	-	-	2-1	1-1	(05-02-02)
Port Vale v Gillingham		2-0	2-1	1-3	-	0-0	2-1	(04-02-01)
Rochdale v Dagenham		-	1-0	0-2	3-1	3-2	-	(03-00-01)
Southend v Exeter		-	-	-	-	0-0	-	(03-03-02)
Torquay v Burton		-	1-2	2-1	2-3	1-0	2-2	(02-01-02)
Wycombe v Wimbledon		-	-	-	-	-	-	(None)
York v Cheltenham		-	-	-	-	-	-	(00-00-04)

SCOTTISH PREMIER LEAGUE

Home team	Away team							Since 1988
Aberdeen v Motherwell		2-1	1-2/1-1	2-0	0-0/0-3	1-2	1-2	(17-15-10)
Celtic v Club 12		-	-	-	-	-	-	(None)
Dundee Utd v Hearts		0-1	4-1	3-0/0-1	2-0/1-0	2-0/2-1	1-0/2-2	(16-13-13)
Hibernian v Inverness		2-0	1-0/2-0	1-2	-	1-1/2-0	1-1	(05-02-03)
Kilmarnock v St Mirren		1-1	0-0/1-0	0-1/2-1	1-2/1-1	2-1/2-0	2-1/0-2	(07-03-04)
Ross County v St Johnstone		2-2/1-1	-	1-2/2-2	-	-	-	(03-05-04)

SCOTTISH DIVISION ONE

Home team	Away team							Since 1988
Dumbarton v Hamilton		-	-	-	-	-	-	(04-03-07)
Dunfermline v Livingston		-	0-4/1-1	1-2/1-0	-	-	-	(09-04-05)
Falkirk v Dundee		-	-	-	-	3-3/2-2	2-1/1-1	(04-07-01)
Morton v Raith		2-0/1-0	-	-	5-0/1-1	0-1/0-0	1-1/1-3	(10-07-10)
Partick v Cowdenbeath		-	-	-	-	1-0/0-1	-	(01-00-01)

SCOTTISH DIVISION TWO

Home team v Away team							
Albion v Stenhsmuir	2-5/2-1	1-1/3-3	1-2/1-2	-	-	1-1/1-0	(04-07-10)
Alloa v Airdrie	-	0-6/1-2	-	-	2-3/1-0	-	(03-00-06)
Arbroath v Forfar	-	3-4/1-1	-	-	-	4-1/0-1	(02-09-08)
Brechin v Queen of Sth	-	-	-	-	-	-	(04-05-05)
East Fife v Ayr	-	-	3-0/0-1	-	2-3/3-2	-	(03-01-02)

SCOTTISH DIVISION THREE

Annan v Peterhead	-	-	-	-	-	2-0/0-3	(01-00-01)
Berwick v Stirling	-	-	-	-	-	-	(03-08-02)
E Stirling v Clyde	-	-	-	-	0-0/2-0	1-1/0-1	(03-02-02)
Elgin v Queen's Park	1-2/0-3	-	-	0-1/0-1	4-2/0-1	2-0/1-1	(05-05-08)
Stranraer v Montrose	-	1-0/0-2	-	2-0/0-2	1-2/2-2	4-4/3-1	(11-02-05)

CONFERENCE

Alfreton v Kidderminstr	-	-	-	-	-	0-2	(00-00-01)
Braintree v Stockport	-	-	-	-	-	2-2	(00-01-00)
Ebbsfleet v Barrow	-	-	1-0	1-4	-	1-2	(01-00-02)
Grimsby v Luton	-	-	2-2	-	2-0	0-1	(05-02-02)
Hereford v Cambridge U	-	-	-	-	-	-	(03-00-02)
Hyde v Nuneaton	3-2	2-0	-	-	1-1	1-1	(03-02-00)
Macclesfield v Forest G	-	-	-	-	-	-	(None)
Newport Co v Southport	-	-	-	-	2-0	0-3	(01-00-01)
Tamworth v Lincoln	-	-	-	-	-	4-0	(01-00-00)
Telford v Mansfield	-	-	-	-	-	0-0	(00-01-00)
Woking v Gateshead	-	-	-	-	-	-	(03-02-01)
Wrexham v Dartford	-	-	-	-	-	-	(None)

SUNDAY 23RD SEPTEMBER 2012

PREMIER LEAGUE

Liverpool v Man Utd	0-1	0-1	2-1	2-0	3-1	1-1	(10-05-09)
Man City v Arsenal	1-0	1-3	3-0	4-2	0-3	1-0	(05-02-11)

TUESDAY 25TH SEPTEMBER 2012

CONFERENCE

Braintree v Dartford	-	-	-	-	1-1	-	(00-01-00)
Cambridge U v Kidderminstr	1-1	0-3	2-1	2-0	1-2	1-2	(02-02-06)
Ebbsfleet v Woking	1-0	1-1	2-0	-	1-1	-	(04-04-00)
Grimsby v Gateshead	-	-	-	-	2-2	2-0	(01-01-00)
Hereford v Forest G	-	-	-	-	-	-	(05-03-00)
Hyde v Alfreton	2-1	0-2	1-1	1-5	1-5	-	(03-01-04)
Lincoln v Nuneaton	-	-	-	-	-	-	(None)
Macclesfield v Mansfield	2-3	0-0	-	-	-	-	(03-03-03)
Southport v Stockport	-	-	-	-	-	5-0	(01-00-00)
Tamworth v Luton	-	-	-	1-1	3-1	1-3	(01-01-01)
Telford v Newport Co	-	-	-	-	-	2-1	(01-00-00)
Wrexham v Barrow	-	-	1-1	0-0	1-1	2-0	(01-03-00)

FRIDAY 28TH SEPTEMBER 2012

LEAGUE 2

Cheltenham v Morecambe	-	-	-	2-0	1-1	1-2	(03-01-01)

SATURDAY 29TH SEPTEMBER 2012

PREMIER LEAGUE

Home v Away							Since 1988
Arsenal v Chelsea	1-1	1-0	1-4	0-3	3-1	0-0	(13-06-04)
Everton v Southampton	-	-	-	-	-	-	(12-03-02)
Fulham v Man City	1-3	3-3	1-1	1-2	1-4	2-2	(02-06-04)
Man Utd v Tottenham	1-0	1-0	5-2	3-1	2-0	3-0	(19-04-01)
Norwich v Liverpool	-	-	-	-	-	0-3	(02-03-04)
Reading v Newcastle	1-0	2-1	-	1-2	-	-	(02-00-01)
Stoke v Swansea	-	-	-	-	-	2-0	(03-01-01)
Sunderland v Wigan	-	2-0	1-2	1-1	4-2	1-2	(02-03-03)

CHAMPIONSHIP

Home v Away							Since 1988
Barnsley v Ipswich	1-0	4-1	1-2	2-1	1-1	3-5	(06-02-06)
Bolton v C Palace	-	-	-	-	-	-	(05-02-00)
Brighton v Birmingham	-	-	-	-	-	1-1	(01-01-01)
Bristol C v Leeds	-	-	-	-	0-2	0-3	(00-00-02)
Burnley v Millwall	-	-	-	-	0-3	1-3	(05-03-04)
Cardiff v Blackpool	-	3-1	2-0	1-1	-	1-3	(03-08-03)
Charlton v Blackburn	1-0	-	-	-	-	-	(04-02-04)
Huddersfield v Watford	-	-	-	-	-	-	(02-00-01)
Hull v Peterborough	-	-	-	-	-	1-0	(03-02-03)
Middlesboro v Leicester	-	-	-	0-1	3-3	0-0	(05-04-04)
Wolves v Sheff Weds	2-2	2-1	4-1	-	-	-	(03-04-01)

LEAGUE 1

Home v Away							Since 1988
Bournemouth v Walsall	-	1-1	-	-	3-0	0-2	(03-05-03)
Carlisle v Crawley	-	-	-	-	-	-	(01-00-00)
Colchester v Hartlepool	-	-	1-1	2-0	3-2	1-1	(06-03-04)
Leyton O v Doncaster	1-1	1-1	-	-	-	-	(04-02-01)
MK Dons v Crewe	-	-	2-2	-	-	-	(02-02-00)
Oldham v Coventry	-	-	-	-	-	-	(01-01-01)
Portsmouth v Scunthorpe	-	-	-	-	2-0	-	(01-00-00)
Preston v Yeovil	-	-	-	-	-	4-3	(01-00-00)
Sheff Utd v Notts Co	-	-	-	-	-	2-1	(01-01-02)
Shrewsbury v Swindon	1-2	-	-	-	-	2-1	(01-00-03)
Stevenage v Bury	-	-	-	-	3-3	3-0	(01-01-00)
Tranmere v Brentford	3-1	-	-	1-0	0-3	2-2	(08-02-02)

LEAGUE 2

Home v Away							Since 1988
Wimbledon v Accrington	-	-	-	-	-	0-2	(00-00-01)
Aldershot v York	0-2	2-0	-	-	-	-	(03-00-01)
Bradford v Port Vale	2-0	-	0-1	0-0	0-2	1-1	(07-03-03)
Burton v Northampton	-	-	-	3-2	1-1	0-1	(01-01-01)
Chesterfield v Torquay	-	-	-	1-0	1-0	-	(07-02-00)
Dagenham v Wycombe	-	2-2	0-1	-	-	-	(00-01-02)
Exeter v Bristol R	-	-	-	1-0	2-2	-	(03-02-00)
Fleetwood v Barnet	-	-	-	-	-	-	(None)
Gillingham v Rochdale	-	-	1-1	-	-	-	(03-04-01)
Plymouth v Southend	2-1	-	-	-	-	2-2	(02-03-03)
Rotherham v Oxford Utd	-	-	-	-	2-1	1-0	(04-01-00)

SCOTTISH PREMIER LEAGUE

Home v Away							Since 1988
Aberdeen v Hibernian	2-1/2-2	3-1/2-1	1-2/2-1	0-2	4-2/0-1	1-0/1-2	(23-07-14)
Club 12 v St Johnstone	-	-	-	-	-	-	(None)
Hearts v Kilmarnock	0-2/1-0	1-1/0-2	1-2/3-1	1-0/1-0	0-3/0-2	0-1	(19-08-08)
Inverness v Dundee Utd	0-0/1-0	0-3/1-1	1-3	-	0-2	2-3	(02-04-05)

Home team — Away team							Since 1988 – HW D AW
Motherwell v Celtic	1-1	1-4/1-2	2-4/1-1	2-3	0-1/2-0	1-2/0-3	(09-15-21)
St Mirren v Ross County	-	-	-	-	-	-	(06-03-01)

SCOTTISH DIVISION ONE

Cowdenbeath v Falkirk	-	-	-	-	0-0/1-2	-	(00-01-01)
Dundee v Morton	-	2-1/2-0	1-0/0-0	1-0/3-1	2-1/1-1	0-1/0-1	(11-05-04)
Hamilton v Dunfermline	-	2-1/3-0	-	-	-	-	(04-02-04)
Livingston v Dumbarton	-	-	-	-	2-0/1-1	-	(04-03-01)
Raith v Partick	-	-	-	1-1/1-0	4-0/0-2	2-0/2-1	(11-08-06)

SCOTTISH DIVISION TWO

Airdrie v East Fife	-	-	-	-	1-1/2-2	1-3/2-0	(02-05-01)
Ayr v Brechin	1-2/1-1	2-1/0-3	1-1/4-2	-	0-2/2-0	-	(08-03-06)
Forfar v Albion	-	1-0/1-4	0-0/4-0	2-2/1-1	-	0-2/4-0	(11-05-02)
Queen of Sth v Alloa	-	-	-	-	-	-	(03-04-07)
Stenhsmuir v Arbroath	1-2/1-2	1-0/0-3	-	3-0/1-1	-	2-0/1-3	(14-03-08)

CONFERENCE

Alfreton v Braintree	-	-	-	-	-	0-1	(00-00-01)
Barrow v Cambridge U	-	-	0-2	0-1	1-2	1-3	(00-00-04)
Dartford v Hyde	-	-	-	-	-	-	(None)
Forest G v Lincoln	-	-	-	-	-	0-2	(00-00-01)
Gateshead v Telford	4-3	-	1-1	-	-	3-0	(03-03-06)
Kidderminstr v Macclesfield	-	-	-	-	-	-	(04-04-06)
Luton v Southport	-	-	-	-	6-0	5-1	(02-00-00)
Mansfield v Hereford	4-1	0-1	-	-	-	-	(04-01-02)
Newport Co v Grimsby	-	-	-	-	2-1	0-0	(01-01-00)
Nuneaton v Wrexham	-	-	-	-	-	-	(None)
Stockport v Ebbsfleet	-	-	-	-	-	1-1	(00-01-00)
Woking v Tamworth	0-2	-	-	-	-	-	(03-00-01)

SUNDAY 30TH SEPTEMBER 2012

PREMIER LEAGUE

Aston Villa v West Brom	-	-	2-1	-	2-1	1-2	(03-02-01)

CHAMPIONSHIP

Nottm F v Derby	-	-	1-3	3-2	5-2	1-2	(05-06-02)

MONDAY 1ST OCTOBER 2012

PREMIER LEAGUE

QPR v West Ham	-	-	-	-	-	-	(04-02-00)

TUESDAY 2ND OCTOBER 2012

CHAMPIONSHIP

Barnsley v Peterborough	-	-	-	2-2	-	1-0	(03-01-03)
Bolton v Leeds	-	-	-	-	-	-	(01-00-04)
Brighton v Ipswich	-	-	-	-	-	3-0	(03-04-01)
Bristol C v Millwall	1-0	-	-	-	0-3	1-0	(05-04-03)
Burnley v Sheff Weds	1-1	1-1	2-4	-	-	-	(01-02-04)
Cardiff v Birmingham	2-0	-	1-2	-	-	1-0	(02-00-03)
Charlton v Watford	0-0	2-2	2-3	-	-	-	(04-03-02)
Huddersfield v Leicester	-	-	2-3	-	-	-	(01-00-01)
Hull v Blackpool	-	2-2	-	-	-	0-1	(04-02-02)
Wolves v C Palace	1-1	0-3	2-1	-	-	-	(05-02-05)

Home team v Away team							Since 1988

LEAGUE 1

	1	2	3	4	5	6	Since 1988
Brentford v Shrewsbury	-	1-1	1-1	-	-	-	(03-05-01)
Bury v Carlisle	-	-	-	-	-	0-2	(03-01-03)
Coventry v MK Dons	-	-	-	-	-	-	(06-06-03)
Crawley v Bournemouth	-	-	-	-	-	-	(None)
Crewe v Oldham	2-1	1-4	0-3	-	-	-	(01-00-03)
Doncaster v Preston	-	-	0-2	1-1	1-1	-	(01-04-01)
Hartlepool v Sheff Utd	-	-	-	-	-	0-1	(00-00-01)
Notts Co v Stevenage	-	-	-	-	-	1-0	(01-00-00)
Scunthorpe v Tranmere	1-1	-	1-1	-	-	4-2	(01-02-02)
Swindon v Colchester	-	-	1-3	1-1	2-1	-	(04-03-02)
Walsall v Leyton O	-	0-0	0-2	2-2	0-2	1-0	(01-02-03)
Yeovil v Portsmouth	-	-	-	-	-	-	(None)

LEAGUE 2

	1	2	3	4	5	6	Since 1988
Accrington v Rotherham	-	0-1	1-3	2-1	2-3	1-1	(01-01-03)
Barnet v Exeter	-	-	0-1	-	-	-	(04-03-04)
Morecambe v Chesterfield	-	1-1	2-2	0-1	1-1	-	(00-03-01)
Northampton v Gillingham	1-1	4-0	-	-	2-1	1-1	(05-05-03)
Oxford Utd v Wimbledon	-	-	-	2-0	-	1-0	(02-00-00)
Port Vale v Dagenham	-	-	0-1	3-1	-	0-1	(01-00-02)
Rochdale v Bradford	-	2-1	3-0	1-3	-	-	(02-00-01)
Southend v Burton	-	-	-	-	1-1	0-1	(00-01-01)
Torquay v Aldershot	-	1-2	-	1-1	0-1	1-0	(01-01-02)
Wycombe v Plymouth	-	-	-	-	-	-	(03-01-01)
York v Fleetwood	-	-	-	-	1-0	0-1	(01-00-01)

WEDNESDAY 3RD OCTOBER 2012

CHAMPIONSHIP

	1	2	3	4	5	6	Since 1988
Middlesboro v Derby	-	1-0	-	2-0	2-1	2-0	(08-02-03)
Nottm F v Blackburn	-	-	-	-	-	-	(01-02-04)

LEAGUE 2

	1	2	3	4	5	6	Since 1988
Bristol R v Cheltenham	-	2-0	3-2	-	-	1-3	(03-01-03)

SATURDAY 6TH OCTOBER 2012

PREMIER LEAGUE

	1	2	3	4	5	6	Since 1988
Chelsea v Norwich	-	-	-	-	-	3-1	(03-02-03)
Liverpool v Stoke	-	-	0-0	4-0	2-0	0-0	(02-02-00)
Man City v Sunderland	-	1-0	1-0	4-3	5-0	3-3	(08-02-01)
Swansea v Reading	-	-	2-0	0-0	1-0	-	(05-02-03)
Tottenham v Aston Villa	2-1	4-4	1-2	0-0	2-1	2-0	(11-07-06)
West Brom v QPR	3-3	5-1	-	2-2	-	1-0	(05-03-01)
West Ham v Arsenal	1-0	0-1	0-2	2-2	0-3	-	(02-06-10)
Wigan v Everton	0-2	1-2	1-0	0-1	1-1	1-1	(01-03-03)

CHAMPIONSHIP

	1	2	3	4	5	6	Since 1988
Birmingham v Huddersfield	-	-	-	-	-	-	(05-03-02)
Blackburn v Wolves	-	-	-	3-1	3-0	1-2	(04-02-03)
Blackpool v Charlton	-	5-3	2-0	-	-	-	(02-00-00)
C Palace v Burnley	2-2	5-0	0-0	-	0-0	2-0	(03-05-02)
Derby v Brighton	-	-	-	-	-	0-1	(03-01-01)
Ipswich v Cardiff	3-1	1-1	1-2	2-0	2-0	3-0	(06-02-01)
Leeds v Barnsley	2-2	-	-	-	3-3	1-2	(02-02-02)
Leicester v Bristol C	-	0-0	-	1-3	2-1	1-2	(04-02-02)

Home team / Away team	Six-season fixture record, latest result at right						Since 1988 – HW D AW
Millwall v Bolton	-	-	-	-	-	-	(01-00-01)
Peterborough v Nottm F	-	-	-	1-2	-	0-1	(00-00-03)
Sheff Weds v Hull	1-2	1-0	-	-	-	-	(02-01-02)
Watford v Middlesboro	2-0	-	-	1-1	3-1	2-1	(05-02-03)

LEAGUE 1

Home team / Away team							Since 1988
Brentford v Crawley	-	-	-	-	-	-	(None)
Bury v Swindon	0-1	-	-	-	-	-	(03-00-02)
Coventry v Bournemouth	-	-	-	-	-	-	(None)
Crewe v Hartlepool	-	3-1	0-0	-	-	-	(02-01-00)
Doncaster v Shrewsbury	-	-	-	-	-	-	(01-01-01)
Leyton O v Sheff Utd	-	-	-	-	-	1-1	(00-01-00)
MK Dons v Portsmouth	-	-	-	-	-	-	(01-02-00)
Notts Co v Tranmere	-	-	-	-	0-1	3-2	(05-02-02)
Oldham v Preston	-	-	-	-	-	1-1	(01-01-02)
Stevenage v Scunthorpe	-	-	-	-	-	1-2	(00-00-01)
Walsall v Carlisle	-	1-1	2-1	2-2	2-1	1-1	(05-05-02)
Yeovil v Colchester	-	-	0-2	0-1	4-2	3-2	(03-01-03)

LEAGUE 2

Home team / Away team							Since 1988
Accrington v Rochdale	1-1	1-2	1-3	2-4	-	-	(00-01-03)
Aldershot v Chesterfield	-	-	1-1	1-0	0-2	-	(01-01-01)
Bristol R v Northampton	-	1-1	1-0	-	-	2-1	(04-04-03)
Cheltenham v Fleetwood	-	-	-	-	-	-	(None)
Dagenham v Bradford	-	1-4	3-0	2-1	-	1-0	(03-00-01)
Exeter v Port Vale	-	-	1-0	-	-	-	(01-02-00)
Morecambe v Burton	0-1	-	-	3-2	2-1	2-2	(06-01-01)
Oxford Utd v Gillingham	-	-	-	-	0-1	0-0	(00-01-02)
Plymouth v Wimbledon	-	-	-	-	-	0-2	(00-00-01)
Southend v Barnet	-	-	-	-	2-1	3-0	(03-00-02)
Wycombe v Torquay	2-0	-	-	-	1-3	-	(01-01-02)
York v Rotherham	-	-	-	-	-	-	(02-04-01)

SCOTTISH PREMIER LEAGUE

Home team / Away team							Since 1988
Celtic v Hearts	2-1/1-3	5-0/3-0	1-1/0-0	2-1/2-0	3-0/4-0	1-0/5-0	(30-13-05)
Hibernian v Club 12	-	-	-	-	-	-	(None)
Inverness v Ross County	-	-	-	1-3/3-0	-	-	(07-06-03)
Kilmarnock v Aberdeen	1-0/1-2	0-1/3-1	1-2	1-1/2-0	2-0	2-0/1-1	(20-07-08)
Motherwell v Dundee Utd	2-3	5-3/2-2	1-1/2-1	2-2/2-3	2-1/2-1	0-0/0-2	(19-11-15)
St Johnstone v St Mirren	-	-	-	1-0/2-2	2-1/0-0	0-1	(12-08-05)

SCOTTISH DIVISION ONE

Home team / Away team							Since 1988
Dundee v Hamilton	1-1/1-0	1-0/1-1	-	-	-	0-1/2-2	(09-06-04)
Falkirk v Dunfermline	1-0/1-0	-	-	-	0-1/1-2	-	(07-02-05)
Morton v Partick	-	4-2/0-0	2-0/0-1	0-2/1-0	2-0/1-0	1-2/1-0	(14-04-05)
Livingston v Cowdenbeath	-	-	-	-	-	-	(03-01-01)
Raith v Dumbarton	-	-	-	-	-	-	(05-01-00)

SCOTTISH DIVISION TWO

Home team / Away team							Since 1988
Airdrie v Queen of Sth	2-2/0-3	-	2-0/2-0	1-1/0-1	-	-	(06-03-03)
Arbroath v Brechin	-	-	1-2/0-0	1-4/1-0	-	1-1/2-3	(03-05-08)
Ayr v Albion	-	-	-	-	-	-	(01-00-01)
Forfar v Alloa	0-2/0-2	-	-	-	1-1/3-1	-	(11-07-05)
Stenhsmuir v East Fife	0-1/3-5	2-1/0-1	-	1-1/1-1	1-1/0-2	2-1/1-0	(11-09-11)

SCOTTISH DIVISION THREE

Home team / Away team							Since 1988
Clyde v Elgin	-	-	-	-	1-1/3-3	1-2/0-2	(00-02-00)
Montrose v E Stirling	1-0/4-0	3-1/2-0	3-0/0-2	0-3/0-1	0-2/3-0	2-1/3-1	(26-07-09)
Peterhead v Berwick	-	4-3/9-2	-	-	-	1-0/1-2	(03-00-01)

Home team v Away team							Since 1988
Queen's Park v Annan	-	-	-	0-0/3-2	3-0/0-1	0-0/2-0	(03-02-01)
Stirling v Stranraer	3-3/0-2	-	3-2/1-2	-	-	-	(07-06-05)

CONFERENCE

Home team v Away team							Since 1988
Braintree v Barrow	-	-	-	-	-	1-0	(01-00-00)
Cambridge U v Mansfield	-	-	2-1	3-2	1-5	1-2	(06-01-04)
Ebbsfleet v Kidderminstr	1-3	5-4	1-1	0-0	-	3-3	(01-03-02)
Grimsby v Dartford	-	-	-	-	-	-	(None)
Hereford v Stockport	0-2	0-1	0-1	-	3-0	-	(02-01-04)
Hyde v Gateshead	-	-	2-5	-	-	-	(06-01-02)
Lincoln v Luton	-	-	0-0	-	-	1-1	(00-03-01)
Macclesfield v Alfreton	-	-	-	-	-	-	(None)
Southport v Nuneaton	-	2-2	-	-	-	-	(03-02-01)
Tamworth v Newport Co	-	-	-	-	3-2	2-1	(04-02-00)
Telford v Woking	-	-	-	-	-	-	(05-03-04)
Wrexham v Forest G	-	-	1-1	1-0	2-1	1-2	(02-01-01)

SUNDAY 7TH OCTOBER 2012

PREMIER LEAGUE

Home team v Away team							Since 1988
Newcastle v Man Utd	2-2	1-5	1-2	-	0-0	3-0	(04-06-09)
Southampton v Fulham	-	-	-	-	-	-	(01-03-00)

TUESDAY 9TH OCTOBER 2012

CONFERENCE

Home team v Away team							Since 1988
Alfreton v Grimsby	-	-	-	-	-	2-5	(00-00-01)
Barrow v Southport	-	1-0	-	-	1-1	2-2	(02-04-02)
Dartford v Telford	-	-	-	-	-	-	(None)
Forest G v Tamworth	2-0	-	-	2-4	4-0	3-1	(05-01-02)
Gateshead v Macclesfield	-	-	-	-	-	-	(03-02-01)
Kidderminstr v Hyde	-	-	-	-	-	-	(None)
Luton v Braintree	-	-	-	-	-	3-1	(01-00-00)
Mansfield v Lincoln	2-4	1-3	-	-	-	2-1	(05-05-05)
Newport Co v Ebbsfleet	-	-	-	-	-	0-1	(00-00-03)
Nuneaton v Hereford	-	-	-	-	-	-	(01-00-03)
Stockport v Wrexham	5-2	2-1	-	-	-	1-0	(06-02-05)
Woking v Cambridge U	0-1	0-0	0-1	-	-	-	(00-01-03)

SATURDAY 13TH OCTOBER 2012

LEAGUE 1

Home team v Away team							Since 1988
Bournemouth v Leyton O	5-0	3-1	-	-	1-1	1-2	(05-03-02)
Carlisle v Notts Co	-	-	-	-	1-0	0-3	(02-01-01)
Colchester v Stevenage	-	-	-	-	-	1-6	(00-00-01)
Crawley v Bury	-	-	-	-	-	-	(None)
Hartlepool v Doncaster	-	2-1	-	-	-	-	(05-02-03)
Portsmouth v Crewe	-	-	-	-	-	-	(02-00-03)
Preston v MK Dons	-	-	-	-	-	1-1	(01-03-01)
Scunthorpe v Brentford	1-1	-	-	-	-	0-0	(00-04-01)
Sheff Utd v Oldham	-	-	-	-	-	2-3	(06-01-01)
Swindon v Coventry	-	-	-	-	-	-	(01-00-00)
Tranmere v Yeovil	2-1	2-1	1-1	2-1	0-1	0-0	(04-02-01)

LEAGUE 2

Home team v Away team							Since 1988
Wimbledon v Cheltenham	-	-	-	-	-	4-1	(01-00-00)

Home team	Away team	Six-season fixture record, latest result at right						Since 1988 – HW D AW
Barnet v Plymouth		-	-	-	-	-	2-0	(02-03-01)
Bradford v York		-	-	-	-	-	-	(00-03-00)
Burton v Bristol R		-	-	-	-	-	2-1	(01-00-00)
Chesterfield v Dagenham		-	1-1	1-1	2-2	-	-	(00-03-00)
Fleetwood v Wycombe		-	-	-	-	-	-	(None)
Gillingham v Aldershot		-	-	4-4	-	2-1	1-0	(02-01-00)
Northampton v Exeter		-	-	-	-	-	-	(03-01-00)
Rochdale v Morecambe		-	1-0	1-1	4-1	-	-	(02-01-00)
Rotherham v Southend		-	-	-	-	1-2	0-4	(00-02-04)
Torquay v Accrington		0-2	-	-	2-1	0-0	1-0	(02-01-01)

CONFERENCE

Home team	Away team							Since 1988 – HW D AW
Barrow v Dartford		-	-	-	-	-	-	(None)
Ebbsfleet v Alfreton		-	-	-	-	-	1-2	(00-00-01)
Gateshead v Cambridge U		-	-	-	2-0	2-3	1-1	(01-01-01)
Hereford v Braintree		-	-	-	-	-	-	(None)
Hyde v Tamworth		-	1-2	1-2	-	-	-	(00-00-02)
Luton v Nuneaton		-	-	-	-	-	-	(None)
Macclesfield v Newport Co		-	-	-	-	-	-	(None)
Mansfield v Forest G		-	-	3-0	1-0	3-1	1-0	(04-00-00)
Stockport v Kidderminstr		-	-	-	-	-	2-1	(01-00-00)
Telford v Grimsby		-	-	-	-	-	0-0	(00-01-00)
Woking v Southport		1-1	-	-	-	-	-	(05-04-03)
Wrexham v Lincoln		2-1	1-0	-	-	-	2-0	(06-03-02)

SUNDAY 14TH OCTOBER 2012

LEAGUE 1

Home team	Away team							Since 1988 – HW D AW
Shrewsbury v Walsall		1-1	-	-	-	-	-	(01-03-03)

MONDAY 15TH OCTOBER 2012

LEAGUE 2

Home team	Away team							Since 1988 – HW D AW
Port Vale v Oxford Utd		-	-	-	-	1-2	3-0	(07-00-02)

FRIDAY 19TH OCTOBER 2012

CHAMPIONSHIP

Home team	Away team							Since 1988 – HW D AW
Sheff Weds v Leeds		0-1	-	-	-	-	-	(02-04-05)

LEAGUE 2

Home team	Away team							Since 1988 – HW D AW
Barnet v Northampton		-	-	-	0-0	4-1	1-2	(05-02-03)

SATURDAY 20TH OCTOBER 2012

PREMIER LEAGUE

Home team	Away team							Since 1988 – HW D AW
Fulham v Aston Villa		1-1	2-1	3-1	0-2	1-1	0-0	(03-06-02)
Liverpool v Reading		2-0	2-1	-	-	-	-	(02-00-00)
Man Utd v Stoke		-	-	5-0	4-0	2-1	2-0	(04-00-00)
Norwich v Arsenal		-	-	-	-	-	1-2	(00-06-03)
Swansea v Wigan		-	-	-	-	-	0-0	(04-02-02)
Tottenham v Chelsea		2-1	4-4	1-0	2-1	1-1	1-1	(03-09-11)
West Brom v Man City		-	-	2-1	-	0-2	0-0	(05-01-05)
West Ham v Southampton		-	-	-	-	-	1-1	(07-02-04)

CHAMPIONSHIP

Home team v Away team							Since 1988 – HW D AW
Birmingham v Leicester	1-1	-	-	-	-	2-0	(01-02-04)
Bolton v Bristol C	-	-	-	-	-	-	(03-01-01)
Brighton v Middlesboro	-	-	-	-	-	1-1	(01-02-01)
Burnley v Blackpool	-	2-2	2-0	-	-	3-1	(07-03-02)
Charlton v Barnsley	-	1-1	1-3	-	-	-	(03-06-01)
C Palace v Millwall	-	-	-	-	0-1	0-0	(03-02-04)
Derby v Blackburn	-	1-2	-	-	-	-	(03-01-02)
Huddersfield v Wolves	-	-	-	-	-	-	(05-01-01)
Hull v Ipswich	2-5	3-1	-	-	1-0	2-2	(04-03-01)
Nottm F v Cardiff	-	-	0-1	0-0	2-1	0-1	(01-02-03)
Watford v Peterborough	-	-	-	0-1	-	3-2	(02-01-02)

LEAGUE 1

Home team v Away team							Since 1988 – HW D AW
Bournemouth v Tranmere	2-0	2-1	-	-	1-2	2-1	(04-02-03)
Colchester v Carlisle	-	-	5-0	2-1	1-1	1-1	(05-04-01)
Coventry v Notts Co	-	-	-	-	-	-	(01-00-00)
Doncaster v Brentford	3-0	-	-	-	-	-	(01-02-00)
Hartlepool v Crawley	-	-	-	-	-	-	(None)
MK Dons v Stevenage	-	-	-	-	-	1-0	(01-00-00)
Oldham v Leyton O	3-3	2-0	1-1	2-0	1-1	0-1	(02-03-01)
Portsmouth v Shrewsbury	-	-	-	-	-	-	(01-00-00)
Preston v Sheff Utd	-	3-1	0-0	2-1	3-1	2-4	(07-03-02)
Swindon v Scunthorpe	-	-	4-2	-	-	-	(01-01-00)
Walsall v Crewe	-	1-1	1-1	-	-	-	(04-05-02)
Yeovil v Bury	-	-	-	-	-	1-3	(01-00-02)

LEAGUE 2

Home team v Away team							Since 1988 – HW D AW
Aldershot v Rotherham	-	-	0-1	3-0	2-2	2-2	(01-02-01)
Bradford v Cheltenham	2-2	-	-	1-1	3-1	0-1	(01-02-01)
Bristol R v Torquay	1-0	-	-	-	-	1-2	(02-02-02)
Exeter v Chesterfield	-	-	1-6	-	-	2-1	(02-01-02)
Fleetwood v Wimbledon	-	-	-	-	1-1	-	(00-01-00)
Gillingham v Burton	-	-	-	-	1-0	3-1	(02-00-00)
Morecambe v Southend	-	-	-	-	2-1	1-0	(02-00-00)
Oxford Utd v Accrington	-	-	-	-	0-0	1-1	(00-02-00)
Plymouth v Rochdale	-	-	-	-	0-1	-	(02-02-02)
Port Vale v Wycombe	-	-	1-1	-	2-1	-	(01-04-01)
York v Dagenham	2-3	-	-	-	-	-	(00-02-01)

SCOTTISH PREMIER LEAGUE

Home team v Away team							Since 1988 – HW D AW
Club 12 v Inverness	-	-	-	-	-	-	(None)
Dundee Utd v Aberdeen	3-1	1-0/3-0	2-1/1-1	0-1	3-1/3-1	1-2	(16-17-09)
Hearts v Motherwell	4-1	1-2	3-2/2-1	1-0/0-2	0-2/0-0/3-3	2-0/0-1	(25-13-08)
Ross County v Hibernian	-	-	-	-	-	-	(None)
St Johnstone v Kilmarnock	-	-	-	0-1	0-3/0-0	2-0	(05-06-07)
St Mirren v Celtic	1-3	1-5/0-1	1-3	0-2/4-0	0-1	0-2/0-2	(02-01-15)

SCOTTISH DIVISION ONE

Home team v Away team							Since 1988 – HW D AW
Cowdenbeath v Raith	1-2/1-5	1-0/1-4	-	-	1-2/0-3	-	(02-01-07)
Dumbarton v Falkirk	-	-	-	-	-	-	(00-00-02)
Dunfermline v Morton	-	0-1/2-0	0-1/2-1	3-1/4-1	2-0/1-3	-	(11-02-05)
Hamilton v Livingston	1-1/3-0	1-1/3-1	-	-	-	1-1/0-1	(07-06-02)
Partick v Dundee	3-1/2-1	1-1/1-0	0-0/1-1	0-2/0-1	1-0/0-0	0-1/0-0	(10-08-10)

SCOTTISH DIVISION TWO

Home team v Away team							Since 1988 – HW D AW
Albion v Arbroath	1-3/0-3	5-2/0-2	-	-	0-2/3-0	1-0/1-1	(05-05-16)
Alloa v Ayr	0-1/1-1	2-1/1-2	0-2/3-2	-	4-1/0-1	-	(04-05-09)

Home team	Away team	Six-season fixture record, latest result at right					Since 1988 – HW D AW	
Brechin v Airdrie		-	4-2/2-1	-	-	3-1/1-2	1-1/1-1	(03-05-06)
East Fife v Forfar		-	3-0/3-0	-	-	1-3/3-0	4-3/4-0	(12-03-04)
Queen of Sth v Stenhsmuir		-	-	-	-	-	-	(09-03-10)

SCOTTISH DIVISION THREE

Berwick v Clyde		-	-	-	-	2-1/1-1	0-2/3-0	(04-03-06)
E Stirling v Peterhead		-	-	-	-	-	0-2/6-3	(03-01-08)
Elgin v Annan		-	-	1-2/0-1	1-1/1-0	2-0/2-3	3-0/1-2	(03-01-04)
Stirling v Montrose		-	-	-	-	-	-	(07-05-02)
Stranraer v Queen's Park		-	-	0-0/2-2	1-1/0-0	1-0/2-1	2-3/2-3	(10-06-05)

SUNDAY 21ST OCTOBER 2012

PREMIER LEAGUE

QPR v Everton		-	-	-	-	-	1-1	(05-03-01)
Sunderland v Newcastle		-	1-1	2-1	-	1-1	0-1	(01-06-06)

TUESDAY 23RD OCTOBER 2012

CHAMPIONSHIP

Barnsley v C Palace		2-0	0-0	3-1	0-0	1-0	2-1	(07-05-03)
Blackpool v Nottm F		0-2	-	1-1	3-1	-	1-2	(01-02-02)
Bristol C v Burnley		-	2-2	1-2	-	2-0	3-1	(04-03-02)
Cardiff v Watford		-	1-2	2-1	3-1	4-2	1-1	(04-01-03)
Ipswich v Derby		2-1	-	2-0	1-0	0-2	1-0	(10-00-03)
Leeds v Charlton		-	-	-	0-0	-	-	(02-03-01)
Leicester v Brighton		-	-	0-0	-	-	1-0	(06-02-01)
Middlesboro v Hull		-	-	3-1	-	2-2	1-0	(04-01-00)
Millwall v Birmingham		-	-	-	-	-	0-6	(02-02-01)
Peterborough v Huddersfield		-	-	4-0	-	4-2	-	(03-01-03)
Wolves v Bolton		-	-	-	2-1	2-3	2-3	(05-01-05)

LEAGUE 1

Brentford v Coventry		-	-	-	-	-	-	(None)
Bury v Hartlepool		0-1	-	-	-	-	1-2	(01-02-03)
Carlisle v Oldham		1-1	1-0	1-1	1-2	2-2	3-3	(02-04-01)
Crawley v MK Dons		-	-	-	-	-	-	(None)
Crewe v Swindon		-	0-0	1-0	-	-	2-0	(04-01-03)
Leyton O v Colchester		-	-	2-1	0-1	4-2	0-1	(03-01-04)
Notts Co v Bournemouth		-	-	1-1	2-2	0-2	3-1	(04-02-05)
Scunthorpe v Preston		-	2-1	-	3-1	0-3	1-1	(04-02-02)
Sheff Utd v Walsall		-	-	-	-	-	3-2	(02-02-01)
Shrewsbury v Yeovil		-	-	-	-	-	-	(00-00-01)
Stevenage v Portsmouth		-	-	-	-	-	-	(None)
Tranmere v Doncaster		1-0	0-1	-	-	-	-	(01-01-03)

LEAGUE 2

Wimbledon v Bristol R		-	-	-	-	-	2-3	(00-00-01)
Accrington v York		-	-	-	-	-	-	(01-01-00)
Burton v Port Vale		-	-	-	1-0	0-0	1-1	(01-02-00)
Cheltenham v Plymouth		-	-	-	-	-	2-1	(03-01-01)
Chesterfield v Fleetwood		-	-	-	-	-	-	(None)
Dagenham v Exeter		4-1	-	1-2	-	1-1	-	(01-02-03)
Northampton v Bradford		0-0	-	-	2-2	2-0	1-3	(01-02-01)
Rochdale v Oxford Utd		-	-	-	-	-	-	(02-01-02)
Rotherham v Morecambe		-	3-1	3-2	0-0	0-1	3-2	(03-01-01)
Southend v Aldershot		-	-	-	-	0-0	0-1	(00-01-01)

Match							Record
Torquay v Gillingham	-	-	-	-	1-1	2-5	(03-02-03)
Wycombe v Barnet	1-1	0-0	1-1	-	4-2	-	(03-03-02)

WEDNESDAY 24TH OCTOBER 2012

CHAMPIONSHIP

Match							Record
Blackburn v Sheff Weds	-	-	-	-	-	-	(07-01-01)

SATURDAY 27TH OCTOBER 2012

PREMIER LEAGUE

Match							Record
Arsenal v QPR	-	-	-	-	-	1-0	(05-03-01)
Everton v Liverpool	3-0	1-2	0-2	0-2	2-0	0-2	(07-06-11)
Man City v Swansea	-	-	-	-	-	4-0	(01-00-00)
Newcastle v West Brom	-	-	2-1	2-2	3-3	2-3	(05-03-01)
Reading v Fulham	1-0	0-2	-	-	-	-	(05-00-04)
Southampton v Tottenham	-	-	-	-	-	-	(09-04-04)
Stoke v Sunderland	2-1	-	1-0	1-0	3-2	0-1	(08-00-05)
Wigan v West Ham	0-3	1-0	0-1	1-0	3-2	-	(03-01-04)

CHAMPIONSHIP

Match							Record
Barnsley v Nottm F	-	-	1-1	2-1	3-1	1-1	(06-02-01)
Blackburn v Watford	3-1	-	-	-	-	-	(03-01-02)
Blackpool v Brighton	0-0	-	-	-	-	3-1	(04-04-01)
Bristol C v Hull	-	2-1	-	-	3-0	1-1	(05-01-00)
Cardiff v Burnley	1-0	2-1	3-1	-	1-1	0-0	(08-02-02)
Ipswich v Sheff Weds	0-2	4-1	1-1	0-0	-	-	(03-02-05)
Leeds v Birmingham	3-2	-	-	-	-	1-4	(03-00-02)
Leicester v C Palace	1-1	1-0	-	2-0	1-1	3-0	(05-05-02)
Middlesboro v Bolton	5-1	0-1	1-3	-	-	-	(05-02-04)
Millwall v Huddersfield	0-0	1-2	2-1	3-1	-	-	(02-02-01)
Peterborough v Derby	-	-	-	0-3	-	3-2	(02-01-01)
Wolves v Charlton	-	2-0	2-1	-	-	-	(07-03-02)

LEAGUE 1

Match							Record
Brentford v Hartlepool	-	-	-	0-0	0-0	2-1	(06-03-00)
Bury v Walsall	1-2	-	-	-	-	2-1	(04-01-03)
Carlisle v Bournemouth	3-1	1-1	-	-	1-0	2-1	(04-01-02)
Crawley v Oldham	-	-	-	-	-	-	(None)
Crewe v Yeovil	2-3	2-0	2-0	-	-	-	(02-00-01)
Leyton O v Coventry	-	-	-	-	-	-	(None)
Notts Co v Doncaster	-	-	-	-	-	-	(01-00-00)
Scunthorpe v MK Dons	-	-	0-1	-	-	0-3	(01-00-02)
Sheff Utd v Portsmouth	1-1	-	-	-	1-0	-	(10-02-00)
Shrewsbury v Colchester	-	-	-	-	-	-	(02-00-01)
Stevenage v Swindon	-	-	-	-	-	-	(None)
Tranmere v Preston	-	-	-	-	-	2-1	(03-01-00)

LEAGUE 2

Match							Record
Wimbledon v Gillingham	-	-	-	-	-	3-1	(01-00-00)
Accrington v Bristol R	1-1	-	-	-	-	2-1	(01-01-00)
Burton v Bradford	-	-	-	1-1	3-0	2-2	(01-02-00)
Cheltenham v Exeter	-	-	-	-	-	-	(03-00-00)
Chesterfield v Barnet	-	0-1	1-1	1-0	2-1	-	(04-01-03)
Dagenham v Aldershot	2-1	-	3-1	2-5	-	2-5	(05-00-04)
Northampton v Port Vale	0-2	2-1	-	1-1	0-0	1-2	(03-02-04)
Rochdale v Fleetwood	-	-	-	-	-	-	(None)

Home team v Away team	Six-season fixture record, latest result at right						Since 1988 – HW D AW
Rotherham v Plymouth	-	-	-	-	-	1-0	(02-02-04)
Southend v York	-	-	-	-	-	-	(03-03-01)
Torquay v Morecambe	-	-	-	2-2	3-1	1-1	(01-02-00)
Wycombe v Oxford Utd	-	-	-	-	0-0	-	(03-02-02)

SCOTTISH PREMIER LEAGUE

Home team v Away team							Since 1988 – HW D AW
Aberdeen v Club 12	-	-	-	-	-	-	(None)
Celtic v Kilmarnock	4-1/2-0	0-0/1-0	3-0	3-0/3-1	1-1	2-1	(26-07-00)
Hearts v Ross County	-	-	-	-	-	-	(None)
Inverness v St Johnstone	-	-	-	-	1-1/2-0	0-1	(04-01-02)
Motherwell v Hibernian	1-6	2-1/1-0	1-4	1-3/1-0/6-6	2-3/2-0	4-3	(14-15-14)
St Mirren v Dundee Utd	1-3/0-1	0-3	0-2	0-0/1-2	1-1/1-1	2-2	(02-09-10)

SCOTTISH DIVISION ONE

Home team v Away team							Since 1988 – HW D AW
Dumbarton v Dundee	-	-	-	-	-	-	(00-00-02)
Dunfermline v Cowdenbeath	-	-	-	-	2-1/5-0/0-4-	-	(03-00-01)
Falkirk v Partick	-	-	-	-	2-3/2-0	2-1/1-1	(09-04-09)
Hamilton v Raith	-	-	-	-	-	2-2/2-1	(08-06-05)
Livingston v Morton	-	4-0/6-1	1-0/0-2	-	-	1-1/0-0	(10-05-05)

SCOTTISH DIVISION TWO

Home team v Away team							Since 1988 – HW D AW
Airdrie v Forfar	-	-	-	-	2-0/3-1	4-4/3-0	(07-05-01)
Alloa v Albion	-	-	-	-	-	-	(15-01-02)
Ayr v Arbroath	-	-	2-1/2-1	-	-	-	(04-03-01)
Brechin v Stenhsmuir	-	-	-	1-0/2-2	0-0/3-1	2-0/1-0	(10-09-03)
Queen of Sth v East Fife	-	-	-	-	-	-	(07-04-04)

SCOTTISH DIVISION THREE

Home team v Away team							Since 1988 – HW D AW
Annan v E Stirling	-	-	2-1/4-0	0-1/1-0	3-1/2-1	3-0/2-2	(06-01-01)
Clyde v Stranraer	-	-	-	-	2-2/4-2	1-1/2-1	(06-09-02)
Montrose v Elgin	2-0/0-1	0-0/3-2	1-0/3-1	1-1/0-4	0-1/1-0	3-0/2-3	(14-04-06)
Peterhead v Stirling	2-3/2-1	-	1-1/1-1	3-2/1-1	-	-	(06-06-02)
Queen's Park v Berwick	1-0/1-0/0-2	1-0/3-1	-	2-0/2-3	0-2/1-0	1-1/2-2	(13-06-10)

CONFERENCE

Home team v Away team							Since 1988 – HW D AW
Alfreton v Telford	-	0-1	3-1	4-0	0-0	0-0	(02-02-01)
Braintree v Wrexham	-	-	-	-	-	0-0	(00-01-00)
Cambridge U v Hyde	-	-	-	-	-	-	(None)
Dartford v Mansfield	-	-	-	-	-	-	(None)
Forest G v Luton	-	-	-	0-1	0-1	3-0	(01-00-02)
Grimsby v Macclesfield	1-1	1-1	0-0	1-1	-	-	(01-05-00)
Kidderminstr v Gateshead	-	-	-	3-2	2-1	2-3	(04-04-03)
Lincoln v Stockport	0-0	0-1	-	-	0-0	1-1	(01-05-02)
Newport Co v Woking	-	-	-	1-0	-	-	(01-00-00)
Nuneaton v Barrow	3-0	0-0	-	-	-	-	(02-02-00)
Southport v Hereford	-	-	-	-	-	-	(00-04-03)
Tamworth v Ebbsfleet	2-1	-	-	3-4	-	1-0	(04-00-02)

SUNDAY 28TH OCTOBER 2012

PREMIER LEAGUE

Home team v Away team							Since 1988 – HW D AW
Aston Villa v Norwich	-	-	-	-	-	3-2	(05-03-01)
Chelsea v Man Utd	0-0	2-1	1-1	1-0	2-1	3-3	(10-08-05)

FRIDAY 2ND NOVEMBER 2012

CHAMPIONSHIP

Brighton v Leeds	-	0-1	0-2	0-3	-	3-3	(03-02-03)

SATURDAY 3RD NOVEMBER 2012

PREMIER LEAGUE

Fulham v Everton	1-0	1-0	0-2	2-1	0-0	1-3	(08-01-02)
Man Utd v Arsenal	0-1	2-1	0-0	2-1	1-0	8-2	(13-07-04)
Norwich v Stoke	1-0	0-1	-	-	-	1-1	(04-03-02)
Sunderland v Aston Villa	-	1-1	1-2	0-2	1-0	2-2	(04-04-04)
Swansea v Chelsea	-	-	-	-	-	1-1	(00-01-00)
Tottenham v Wigan	3-1	4-0	0-0	9-1	0-1	3-1	(04-02-01)
West Ham v Man City	0-1	0-2	1-0	1-1	1-3	-	(06-02-04)

CHAMPIONSHIP

Birmingham v Ipswich	2-2	-	2-1	-	-	2-1	(06-03-00)
Bolton v Cardiff	-	-	-	-	-	-	(02-00-00)
Burnley v Wolves	0-1	1-3	1-0	1-2	-	-	(02-01-07)
Charlton v Middlesboro	1-3	-	-	-	-	-	(06-03-05)
C Palace v Blackburn	-	-	-	-	-	-	(01-03-03)
Derby v Blackpool	-	-	4-1	0-2	-	2-1	(02-00-01)
Huddersfield v Bristol C	2-1	-	-	-	-	-	(04-02-02)
Hull v Barnsley	2-3	3-0	-	-	2-0	3-1	(04-01-03)
Nottm F v Millwall	3-1	2-0	-	-	1-1	3-1	(05-03-03)
Sheff Weds v Peterborough	-	-	-	2-1	1-4	-	(03-00-01)
Watford v Leicester	-	1-0	-	3-3	3-2	3-2	(06-04-05)

SCOTTISH PREMIER LEAGUE

Club 12 v Hearts	-	-	-	-	-	-	(None)
Dundee Utd v Celtic	1-4/1-1	0-2/0-2	1-1/2-2	2-1/0-2	1-2/1-3	0-1/1-0	(10-08-24)
Hibernian v St Mirren	5-1	0-1/2-0	2-0	2-1/2-1	2-0/1-1	1-2/0-0	(16-03-03)
Kilmarnock v Inverness	1-1/3-2	2-2/4-1	1-2/1-0	-	1-2/1-1	3-6/4-3	(04-05-04)
Ross County v Aberdeen	-	-	-	-	-	-	(None)
St Johnstone v Motherwell	-	-	-	2-2/1-2	0-2/1-0	0-3	(08-06-08)

SUNDAY 4TH NOVEMBER 2012

PREMIER LEAGUE

Liverpool v Newcastle	2-0	3-0	3-0	-	3-0	3-1	(15-02-02)
QPR v Reading	-	-	0-0	4-1	3-1	-	(02-04-02)

MONDAY 5TH NOVEMBER 2012

PREMIER LEAGUE

West Brom v Southampton	1-1	1-1	-	-	-	-	(01-03-00)

TUESDAY 6TH NOVEMBER 2012

CHAMPIONSHIP

Birmingham v Bristol C	-	-	1-0	-	-	2-2	(02-02-02)
Bolton v Leicester	-	-	-	-	-	-	(01-02-01)

| --- | --- | --- | --- | --- | --- | --- | --- | --- |
Brighton v Peterborough			2-4	-	3-1	2-0	(04-03-03)
Burnley v Leeds	2-1	-	-	-	2-3	1-2	(01-00-04)
Charlton v Cardiff	-	3-0	2-2	-	-	-	(01-01-00)
C Palace v Ipswich	2-0	0-1	1-4	3-1	1-2	1-1	(06-06-04)
Derby v Barnsley	2-1	-	0-0	2-3	0-0	1-1	(06-04-01)
Huddersfield v Blackburn	-	-	-	-	-	-	(01-00-01)
Hull v Wolves	2-0	2-0	-	2-2	-	-	(03-01-02)
Nottm F v Middlesboro	-	-	-	1-0	1-0	2-0	(06-03-01)
Sheff Weds v Blackpool	-	2-1	1-1	2-0	-	-	(03-01-01)
Watford v Millwall	-	-	-	-	1-0	2-1	(07-01-07)

LEAGUE 1

Home team	Away team							Since 1988
Bournemouth v Shrewsbury	-	-	1-0	1-0	-	-	(06-01-02)
Colchester v Notts Co	-	-	-	-	2-1	4-2	(06-01-02)
Coventry v Crawley	-	-	-	-	-	-	(None)
Doncaster v Crewe	3-1	2-0	-	-	-	-	(02-02-02)
Hartlepool v Tranmere	-	3-1	2-1	1-0	1-1	0-2	(03-04-02)
MK Dons v Leyton O	-	-	1-2	1-0	2-3	4-1	(02-00-02)
Oldham v Bury	-	-	-	-	-	0-2	(02-01-01)
Portsmouth v Brentford	-	-	-	-	-	-	(01-00-00)
Preston v Carlisle	-	-	-	-	-	3-3	(01-01-02)
Swindon v Sheff Utd	-	-	-	-	-	-	(01-04-02)
Walsall v Scunthorpe	-	-	2-1	-	-	2-2	(05-03-00)
Yeovil v Stevenage	-	-	-	-	-	0-6	(03-03-02)

LEAGUE 2

Home team	Away team							Since 1988
Aldershot v Wycombe	-	-	3-2	-	0-0	-	(01-01-00)
Barnet v Torquay	0-1	-	-	1-1	0-3	0-1	(05-03-05)
Bradford v Chesterfield	1-0	1-0	3-2	3-0	0-1	-	(06-00-02)
Bristol R v Southend	-	1-1	4-2	4-3	-	1-0	(07-03-02)
Exeter v Wimbledon	-	-	-	-	-	-	(None)
Fleetwood v Rotherham	-	-	-	-	-	-	(None)
Gillingham v Cheltenham	2-1	0-0	-	-	1-1	1-0	(02-02-00)
Morecambe v Accrington	-	0-1	1-1	1-2	1-2	1-2	(06-01-05)
Oxford Utd v Dagenham	2-2	-	-	-	-	2-1	(01-01-00)
Plymouth v Burton	-	-	-	-	-	2-1	(01-00-00)
Port Vale v Rochdale	-	-	2-1	1-1	-	-	(01-01-00)
York v Northampton	-	-	-	-	-	-	(02-03-02)

CONFERENCE

Home team	Away team							Since 1988
Dartford v Forest G	-	-	-	-	-	-	(None)
Gateshead v Alfreton	-	-	3-0	-	-	2-0	(02-00-00)
Hereford v Luton	-	-	-	-	-	-	(None)
Hyde v Grimsby	-	-	-	-	-	-	(None)
Lincoln v Braintree	-	-	-	-	-	3-3	(00-01-00)
Macclesfield v Tamworth	-	-	-	-	-	-	(None)
Newport Co v Cambridge U	-	-	-	-	1-1	0-1	(00-01-01)
Nuneaton v Mansfield	-	-	-	-	-	-	(None)
Southport v Wrexham	-	-	-	-	0-1	0-0	(00-01-01)
Stockport v Barrow	-	-	-	-	-	3-2	(01-00-00)
Telford v Ebbsfleet	-	-	-	-	-	0-2	(01-01-01)
Woking v Kidderminstr	3-0	3-0	1-5	-	-	-	(06-02-04)

FRIDAY 9TH NOVEMBER 2012

CHAMPIONSHIP

Home team	Away team							Since 1988
Middlesboro v Sheff Weds	-	-	-	1-0	-	-	(05-01-02)

SATURDAY 10TH NOVEMBER 2012

PREMIER LEAGUE

Arsenal v Fulham	3-1	2-1	0-0	4-0	2-1	1-1	(08-03-00)
Aston Villa v Man Utd	0-3	1-4	0-0	1-1	2-2	0-1	(03-08-13)
Everton v Sunderland	-	7-1	3-0	2-0	2-0	4-0	(09-02-01)
Newcastle v West Ham	2-2	3-1	2-2	-	5-0	-	(10-06-03)
Reading v Norwich	-	-	2-0	-	3-3	-	(03-01-04)
Southampton v Swansea	-	-	2-2	-	-	-	(00-01-00)
Stoke v QPR	1-0	3-1	-	-	-	2-3	(03-01-04)
Wigan v West Brom	-	-	2-1	-	1-0	1-1	(04-01-02)

CHAMPIONSHIP

Barnsley v Huddersfield	-	-	-	-	-	-	(06-01-01)
Blackburn v Birmingham	-	2-1	-	2-1	1-1	-	(06-04-00)
Blackpool v Bolton	-	-	-	-	4-3	-	(03-01-00)
Cardiff v Hull	0-1	1-0	-	-	2-0	0-3	(06-01-04)
Ipswich v Burnley	1-1	0-0	1-1	-	1-1	1-0	(03-06-00)
Leeds v Watford	-	-	-	-	2-2	0-2	(03-02-02)
Leicester v Nottm F	-	-	-	3-0	1-0	0-0	(05-02-02)
Millwall v Derby	-	-	-	-	2-0	0-0	(07-04-02)
Peterborough v C Palace	-	-	-	1-1	-	2-1	(01-02-00)
Wolves v Brighton	-	-	-	-	-	-	(02-02-02)

LEAGUE 1

Brentford v Carlisle	0-0	-	-	3-1	2-1	4-0	(03-03-01)
Bury v Portsmouth	-	-	-	-	-	-	(01-00-01)
Coventry v Scunthorpe	-	1-1	-	2-1	1-1	-	(01-02-00)
Crewe v Colchester	-	-	2-0	-	-	-	(05-00-00)
Doncaster v Bournemouth	1-1	1-2	-	-	-	-	(01-02-01)
Leyton O v Shrewsbury	-	-	-	-	-	-	(07-00-05)
MK Dons v Sheff Utd	-	-	-	-	-	1-0	(05-03-01)
Notts Co v Crawley	-	-	-	-	-	-	(None)
Oldham v Tranmere	1-0	3-1	0-2	0-0	0-0	1-0	(05-06-03)
Stevenage v Preston	-	-	-	-	-	1-1	(00-01-00)
Walsall v Swindon	0-2	2-2	2-1	1-1	1-2	-	(04-05-02)
Yeovil v Hartlepool	-	3-1	2-3	4-0	0-2	0-1	(03-00-03)

LEAGUE 2

Accrington v Northampton	-	-	-	0-3	3-1	2-1	(02-00-01)
Aldershot v Bradford	-	-	3-2	1-0	1-0	1-0	(04-00-00)
Bristol R v Chesterfield	-	-	-	-	-	-	(05-01-00)
Cheltenham v Burton	-	-	-	0-1	2-1	2-0	(04-02-02)
Dagenham v Rotherham	-	0-2	1-1	0-1	-	3-2	(01-01-02)
Exeter v Fleetwood	-	-	-	-	-	-	(None)
Morecambe v Barnet	-	0-0	2-1	2-1	2-2	0-1	(03-04-02)
Oxford Utd v Torquay	-	3-3	0-2	-	0-2	2-2	(02-04-02)
Plymouth v Gillingham	-	-	-	-	-	0-1	(03-00-02)
Southend v Port Vale	-	1-1	-	-	1-3	3-0	(02-04-03)
Wycombe v Rochdale	1-1	0-1	0-1	-	-	3-0	(02-02-03)
York v Wimbledon	-	-	-	5-0	4-1	-	(02-00-00)

SCOTTISH PREMIER LEAGUE

Celtic v St Johnstone	-	-	-	5-2/3-0	2-0	0-1/2-0/1-0	(19-02-02)
Hibernian v Dundee Utd	2-1	2-2	2-1/1-2	1-1/2-4	2-2	3-3/0-2	(21-10-08)
Inverness v Hearts	0-0	2-1/0-3	0-1	-	1-3/1-1	1-1/1-0	(02-05-04)
Kilmarnock v Ross County	-	-	-	-	-	-	(None)

Home team / Away team			Six-season fixture record, latest result at right				Since 1988 – HW D AW
Motherwell v Club 12	-	-	-	-	-	-	(None)
St Mirren v Aberdeen	1-1/0-2	0-1	0-1/1-1	1-0/0-1	2-1/3-2	1-0/1-1	(07-04-10)

SCOTTISH DIVISION ONE

Cowdenbeath v Dumbarton	-	-	2-0/0-0	2-1/0-0	-	0-0/4-1	(10-06-08)
Dundee v Livingston	0-1/2-0	4-1/2-0	0-3/4-1	-	-	3-0/1-0	(15-02-04)
Morton v Hamilton	-	0-2/1-3	-	-	-	0-2/1-2	(06-07-10)
Partick v Dunfermline	-	1-1/0-1	1-0/2-3	2-0/1-4	0-2/2-0	-	(05-02-05)
Raith v Falkirk	-	-	-	-	2-1/1-2	1-0/2-2	(11-05-08)

SCOTTISH DIVISION TWO

Albion v Brechin	-	-	-	-	-	1-2/0-1	(02-04-10)
Arbroath v Airdrie	-	-	-	-	-	3-1/2-2	(02-02-02)
East Fife v Alloa	-	-	1-0/0-2	0-2/0-1	4-1/3-1	-	(07-04-07)
Forfar v Queen of Sth	-	-	-	-	-	-	(05-02-07)
Stenhsmuir v Ayr	-	-	-	-	3-1/2-1	-	(02-01-03)

SCOTTISH DIVISION THREE

Annan v Stirling	-	-	-	-	-	-	(None)
Clyde v Montrose	-	-	-	-	2-0/1-1	1-0/1-2	(04-01-03)
Elgin v Berwick	1-2/2-1	-	0-2/2-0	3-3/1-5	1-2/3-2	4-1/4-0	(05-02-05)
Queen's Park v E Stirling	1-3/2-1	-	-	1-0/2-0	2-0/2-0	2-0/5-1	(24-06-09)
Stranraer v Peterhead	2-1/1-1	-	0-3/0-1	-	-	2-1/0-3	(02-02-04)

CONFERENCE

Alfreton v Newport Co	-	-	-	-	-	3-2	(01-00-00)
Barrow v Lincoln	-	-	-	-	-	1-0	(01-00-00)
Braintree v Gateshead	-	-	-	-	-	3-1	(01-00-00)
Cambridge U v Macclesfield	-	-	-	-	-	-	(02-01-01)
Ebbsfleet v Hyde	-	-	-	-	-	-	(None)
Forest G v Stockport	-	-	-	-	-	1-1	(00-01-00)
Grimsby v Woking	-	-	-	-	-	-	(None)
Kidderminstr v Nuneaton	-	-	-	-	-	-	(00-00-01)
Luton v Dartford	-	-	-	-	-	-	(None)
Mansfield v Southport	-	-	-	-	2-2	1-3	(00-01-01)
Tamworth v Telford	-	0-0	0-1	-	-	2-2	(00-02-02)
Wrexham v Hereford	1-0	0-2	-	-	-	-	(02-02-03)

SUNDAY 11TH NOVEMBER 2012

PREMIER LEAGUE

Chelsea v Liverpool	1-0	0-0	0-1	2-0	0-1	1-2	(13-05-05)
Man City v Tottenham	1-2	2-1	1-2	0-1	1-0	3-2	(06-03-09)

CHAMPIONSHIP

Bristol C v Charlton	-	0-1	2-1	-	-	-	(03-01-03)

FRIDAY 16TH NOVEMBER 2012

LEAGUE 2

Barnet v Accrington	1-2	2-2	2-1	1-2	2-0	0-0	(03-03-02)

SATURDAY 17TH NOVEMBER 2012

PREMIER LEAGUE

Arsenal v Tottenham	3-0	2-1	4-4	3-0	2-3	5-2	(14-08-02)

Home team	Away team	Six-season fixture record, latest result at right						Since 1988 – HW D AW
Liverpool v Wigan		2-0	1-1	3-2	2-1	1-1	1-2	(04-02-01)
Man City v Aston Villa		0-2	1-0	2-0	3-1	4-0	4-1	(13-02-03)
Newcastle v Swansea		-	-	-	3-0	-	0-0	(01-01-00)
Norwich v Man Utd		-	-	-	-	-	1-2	(03-00-06)
QPR v Southampton		0-2	0-3	4-1	-	-	-	(06-02-04)
Reading v Everton		0-2	1-0	-	-	-	-	(01-00-01)
West Brom v Chelsea		-	-	0-3	-	1-3	1-0	(01-00-06)

CHAMPIONSHIP

Home team	Away team							
Birmingham v Hull		2-1	-	-	0-0	-	0-0	(02-04-00)
Bolton v Barnsley		-	-	-	-	-	-	(02-04-01)
Bristol C v Blackpool		2-4	1-0	0-0	2-0	-	1-3	(08-04-04)
Burnley v Charlton		-	1-0	2-1	-	-	-	(03-00-00)
Cardiff v Middlesboro		-	-	-	1-0	0-3	2-3	(01-00-02)
C Palace v Derby		2-0	-	1-0	1-0	2-2	1-1	(06-06-01)
Huddersfield v Brighton		0-3	2-1	2-2	7-1	2-1	-	(04-01-04)
Leicester v Ipswich		3-1	2-0	-	1-1	4-2	1-1	(05-06-05)
Nottm F v Sheff Weds		-	-	2-1	2-1	-	-	(06-01-06)
Peterborough v Blackburn		-	-	-	-	-	-	(None)
Watford v Wolves		-	3-0	2-3	-	-	-	(08-04-03)

LEAGUE 1

Home team	Away team							
Bournemouth v Oldham		3-2	0-3	-	-	3-0	0-0	(08-05-01)
Carlisle v Leyton O		3-1	1-0	1-3	2-2	0-1	4-1	(09-02-04)
Colchester v Bury		-	-	-	-	-	4-1	(04-02-02)
Crawley v Walsall		-	-	-	-	-	-	(None)
Hartlepool v Coventry		-	-	-	-	-	-	(None)
Portsmouth v Doncaster		-	-	-	-	2-3	3-1	(01-00-01)
Preston v Brentford		-	-	-	-	-	1-3	(06-01-01)
Scunthorpe v Notts Co		-	-	-	-	-	0-0	(01-02-01)
Sheff Utd v Stevenage		-	-	-	-	-	2-2	(00-01-00)
Shrewsbury v Crewe		-	-	-	2-0	0-1	2-0	(04-02-04)
Swindon v Yeovil		-	0-1	2-3	3-1	0-1	-	(02-00-03)
Tranmere v MK Dons		-	-	1-1	0-1	4-2	0-2	(02-01-04)

LEAGUE 2

Home team	Away team							
Wimbledon v Aldershot		-	-	-	-	-	1-2	(00-00-01)
Bradford v Exeter		-	-	4-1	-	-	-	(04-01-00)
Burton v Dagenham		0-2	-	-	0-1	-	1-1	(00-04-03)
Chesterfield v Oxford Utd		-	-	-	-	1-2	-	(01-01-01)
Fleetwood v Plymouth		-	-	-	-	-	-	(None)
Gillingham v Morecambe		-	-	5-0	-	1-1	2-0	(02-01-00)
Northampton v Wycombe		-	-	-	-	1-1	-	(02-06-01)
Port Vale v York		-	-	-	-	-	-	(01-00-00)
Rochdale v Bristol R		0-1	-	-	-	3-1	-	(03-03-01)
Rotherham v Cheltenham		2-4	-	-	0-0	6-4	1-0	(03-01-01)
Torquay v Southend		-	-	-	-	1-1	0-0	(05-03-01)

SCOTTISH PREMIER LEAGUE

Home team	Away team							
Aberdeen v Celtic		0-1/1-2	1-3/1-5	4-2/1-3	1-3/4-4	0-3	0-1/1-1	(07-16-22)
Club 12 v Hibernian		-	-	-	-	-	-	(None)
Dundee Utd v Kilmarnock		1-0	2-0	0-2/0-0	0-0	1-1/4-2	1-1/4-0	(07-16-09)
Hearts v St Mirren		0-1/1-1	0-1/3-2	2-1/1-1	1-0	3-0/3-2	2-0/5-2	(12-06-03)
Inverness v Motherwell		0-1/2-0	0-3	1-2/1-2	-	1-2/3-0	2-3	(03-01-08)
St Johnstone v Ross County		3-1/2-1	-	2-1/0-0	-	-	-	(04-07-01)

SCOTTISH DIVISION ONE

Home team	Away team							
Cowdenbeath v Dundee		-	-	-	-	2-1/1-3	-	(01-00-01)

Home team · Away team	Six-season fixture record, latest result at right					Since 1988 – HW D AW	
Dumbarton v Morton	-	-	-	-	-	-	(08-01-05)
Hamilton v Partick	1-2/2-1	2-0/0-0	-	-	-	1-0/2-2	(04-06-07)
Livingston v Falkirk	-	-	-	-	-	1-1/1-2	(04-02-06)
Raith v Dunfermline	-	-	-	1-2/1-2	2-0/2-1	-	(05-02-06)

SCOTTISH DIVISION TWO

Albion v East Fife	0-1/0-3	1-4/2-2	-	-	-	0-3/1-1	(08-04-14)
Alloa v Brechin	2-2/2-3	2-2/0-4	2-1/3-2	2-1/2-3	2-2/2-2	-	(07-07-04)
Arbroath v Queen of Sth	-	-	-	-	-	-	(06-03-07)
Ayr v Airdrie	-	1-1/1-2	-	1-1/1-4	1-0/3-1	-	(08-04-13)
Forfar v Stenhsmuir	-	0-1/1-2	1-0/4-4	-	1-1/2-0	2-3/1-2	(10-07-06)

SCOTTISH DIVISION THREE

Berwick v Annan	-	-	3-0/1-1	2-1/0-2	2-2/2-3	0-1/1-3	(02-02-04)
E Stirling v Stranraer	-	2-3/1-3	-	1-1/2-0	0-1/0-2	1-3/2-2	(02-04-13)
Montrose v Queen's Park	0-3/0-2	-	-	1-2/1-2	1-2/0-2	0-1/3-1	(13-08-14)
Peterhead v Clyde	-	-	-	2-0/0-0	-	0-0/1-1	(01-03-00)
Stirling v Elgin	-	-	-	-	-	-	(04-01-01)

CONFERENCE

Barrow v Forest G	-	-	3-1	1-1	3-0	1-1	(03-02-00)
Cambridge U v Tamworth	1-0	-	-	2-0	3-3	0-1	(03-01-01)
Dartford v Southport	-	-	-	-	-	-	(None)
Grimsby v Braintree	-	-	-	-	-	1-1	(00-01-00)
Lincoln v Hereford	1-4	2-1	-	3-1	3-1	-	(10-02-01)
Macclesfield v Ebbsfleet	-	-	-	-	-	-	(None)
Mansfield v Luton	-	-	-	0-0	0-0	1-1	(02-03-00)
Newport Co v Hyde	-	-	-	-	-	-	(None)
Nuneaton v Stockport	-	-	-	-	-	-	(None)
Telford v Kidderminstr	-	-	-	-	-	2-1	(07-05-01)
Woking v Alfreton	-	-	-	-	-	-	(None)
Wrexham v Gateshead	-	-	-	0-0	2-7	2-1	(01-01-01)

SUNDAY 18TH NOVEMBER 2012

PREMIER LEAGUE

Fulham v Sunderland	-	1-3	0-0	1-0	0-0	2-1	(05-02-01)

CHAMPIONSHIP

Millwall v Leeds	-	0-2	3-1	2-1	3-2	0-1	(03-01-03)

MONDAY 19TH NOVEMBER 2012

PREMIER LEAGUE

West Ham v Stoke	-	-	2-1	0-1	3-0	-	(03-01-02)

TUESDAY 20TH NOVEMBER 2012

LEAGUE 1

Bournemouth v Stevenage	-	-	-	-	-	1-3	(00-00-01)
Carlisle v Doncaster	1-0	1-0	-	-	-	-	(05-03-03)
Colchester v Coventry	0-0	1-5	-	-	-	-	(00-01-01)
Crawley v Yeovil	-	-	-	-	-	-	(None)
Hartlepool v Oldham	-	4-1	3-3	2-1	4-2	0-1	(04-03-01)
Portsmouth v Leyton O	-	-	-	-	-	-	(None)
Preston v Notts Co	-	-	-	-	-	2-0	(04-01-01)

Home team	Away team						Since 1988 – HW D AW	
Scunthorpe v Bury	-	-	-	-	-	1-3	(03-02-04)	
Sheff Utd v Crewe	-	-	-	-	-	-	(06-02-00)	
Shrewsbury v MK Dons	2-1	3-3	-	-	-	-	(01-01-00)	
Swindon v Brentford	-	-	-	3-2	1-1	-	(05-02-03)	
Tranmere v Walsall	-	0-0	2-1	2-3	3-3	2-1	(04-03-02)	

LEAGUE 2

Home team	Away team						Since 1988	
Wimbledon v Southend	-	-	-	-	-	1-4	(00-00-01)	
Barnet v Oxford Utd	-	-	-	-	2-2	0-2	(00-02-01)	
Bradford v Plymouth	-	-	-	-	-	1-1	(01-03-02)	
Burton v Aldershot	1-3	2-0	-	6-1	1-2	0-4	(02-00-06)	
Chesterfield v Cheltenham	1-0	-	-	1-0	3-0	-	(04-01-00)	
Fleetwood v Accrington	-	-	-	-	-	-	(01-00-02)	
Gillingham v Exeter	-	-	1-0	3-0	-	-	(04-01-00)	
Northampton v Morecambe	-	-	-	2-0	3-3	0-2	(01-01-01)	
Port Vale v Bristol R	-	1-1	-	-	-	1-0	(05-01-01)	
Rochdale v York	-	-	-	-	-	-	(05-01-04)	
Rotherham v Wycombe	-	1-1	0-0	-	3-4	-	(03-03-01)	
Torquay v Dagenham	-	-	-	0-0	-	1-0	(01-01-00)	

SATURDAY 24TH NOVEMBER 2012

PREMIER LEAGUE

Home team	Away team						Since 1988	
Aston Villa v Arsenal	0-1	1-2	2-2	0-0	2-4	1-2	(05-09-10)	
Everton v Norwich	-	-	-	-	-	1-1	(04-03-02)	
Man Utd v QPR	-	-	-	-	-	2-0	(05-03-01)	
Southampton v Newcastle	-	-	-	-	-	-	(09-03-01)	
Stoke v Fulham	-	-	0-0	3-2	0-2	2-0	(04-02-02)	
Swansea v Liverpool	-	-	-	-	-	1-0	(01-00-00)	
Tottenham v West Ham	1-0	4-0	1-0	2-0	0-0	-	(11-04-03)	
Wigan v Reading	1-0	0-0	-	-	-	-	(07-04-02)	

CHAMPIONSHIP

Home team	Away team						Since 1988	
Barnsley v Cardiff	1-2	1-1	0-1	1-0	1-2	0-1	(02-01-04)	
Blackburn v Millwall	-	-	-	-	-	-	(02-00-00)	
Blackpool v Watford	-	1-1	0-2	3-2	-	0-0	(01-04-01)	
Brighton v Bolton	-	-	-	-	-	-	(01-00-00)	
Charlton v Huddersfield	-	-	-	2-1	0-1	2-0	(05-00-02)	
Derby v Birmingham	0-1	1-2	1-1	-	-	2-1	(02-03-02)	
Hull v Burnley	2-0	2-0	-	1-4	0-1	2-3	(03-01-05)	
Ipswich v Peterborough	-	-	-	0-0	-	3-2	(01-01-00)	
Leeds v C Palace	2-1	-	-	-	2-1	3-2	(04-02-04)	
Middlesboro v Bristol C	-	-	-	0-0	1-2	1-1	(03-02-02)	
Sheff Weds v Leicester	2-1	0-2	-	2-0	-	-	(07-02-02)	
Wolves v Nottm F	-	-	5-1	-	-	-	(07-01-00)	

LEAGUE 1

Home team	Away team						Since 1988	
Brentford v Sheff Utd	-	-	-	-	-	0-2	(00-00-02)	
Bury v Bournemouth	-	-	1-0	0-3	-	1-0	(05-01-04)	
Coventry v Portsmouth	-	-	-	-	2-0	2-0	(03-00-01)	
Crewe v Crawley	-	-	-	-	-	1-1	(00-01-00)	
Doncaster v Scunthorpe	2-2	-	-	4-3	3-0	-	(06-04-05)	
Leyton O v Preston	-	-	-	-	-	2-1	(04-01-01)	
MK Dons v Colchester	-	-	1-1	2-1	1-1	1-0	(03-03-00)	
Notts Co v Swindon	1-1	-	-	-	1-0	-	(03-04-03)	
Oldham v Shrewsbury	-	-	-	-	-	-	(01-00-00)	
Stevenage v Tranmere	-	-	-	-	-	2-1	(01-00-00)	

Home team / Away team	Six-season fixture record, latest result at right						Since 1988 – HW D AW
Walsall v Hartlepool	2-0	2-2	2-3	3-1	5-2	0-0	(06-02-02)
Yeovil v Carlisle	2-1	2-1	1-1	3-1	1-0	0-3	(05-01-01)

LEAGUE 2

Home team / Away team							Since 1988 – HW D AW
Accrington v Gillingham	-	-	0-2	-	7-4	4-3	(02-00-01)
Aldershot v Port Vale	-	-	1-0	1-1	1-2	1-2	(01-01-02)
Bristol R v Bradford	-	-	-	-	-	2-1	(04-00-00)
Cheltenham v Barnet	-	-	-	5-1	1-1	2-0	(04-02-03)
Dagenham v Fleetwood	-	-	-	-	-	-	(None)
Exeter v Rotherham	-	-	1-1	-	-	-	(04-03-01)
Morecambe v Wimbledon	-	-	-	-	-	1-2	(00-00-01)
Oxford Utd v Northampton	-	-	-	-	3-1	2-0	(04-00-02)
Plymouth v Chesterfield	-	-	-	-	-	-	(02-01-02)
Southend v Rochdale	-	-	-	-	-	-	(05-03-00)
Wycombe v Burton	-	-	-	-	4-1	-	(01-00-00)
York v Torquay	-	0-1	1-2	-	-	-	(03-06-02)

SCOTTISH PREMIER LEAGUE

Home team / Away team							Since 1988 – HW D AW
Celtic v Inverness	3-0	5-0/2-1	1-0	-	2-2	2-0/1-0	(09-01-00)
Hibernian v Aberdeen	1-1/0-0	3-3/3-1	2-2/0-0	2-0/2-2	1-2/1-3	0-0/0-0	(14-15-16)
Kilmarnock v St Johnstone	-	-	-	2-1/3-2/1-2	1-1	1-2/0-0	(05-06-07)
Motherwell v Hearts	0-1/0-2	0-2/0-1	1-0	1-0/3-1	1-2	1-0/3-0	(15-09-19)
Ross County v Dundee Utd	-	-	-	-	-	-	(None)
St Mirren v Club 12	-	-	-	-	-	-	(None)

SCOTTISH DIVISION ONE

Home team / Away team							Since 1988 – HW D AW
Dundee v Raith	-	-	-	2-1/2-0	0-0/2-1	1-0/1-1	(08-06-02)
Dunfermline v Dumbarton	-	-	-	-	-	-	(05-01-00)
Falkirk v Hamilton	-	-	4-1/1-2	2-0/0-1	-	0-0/3-0	(08-05-04)
Morton v Cowdenbeath	1-0/3-0	-	-	-	1-2/3-0	-	(05-01-02)
Partick v Livingston	2-3/0-0	3-0/2-1	2-1/1-0	-	-	2-1/2-3	(08-06-07)

SCOTTISH DIVISION TWO

Home team / Away team							Since 1988 – HW D AW
Airdrie v Albion	-	-	-	-	-	4-0/1-0	(03-00-00)
Brechin v Forfar	4-2/2-2	-	-	-	0-0/0-1	0-1/2-1	(07-03-07)
East Fife v Arbroath	2-1/1-2	0-2/2-1	3-2/0-0	1-1/3-1	-	2-2/1-3	(08-06-11)
Queen of Sth v Ayr	-	-	-	2-0/3-0	-	4-1/2-1	(05-04-05)
Stenhsmuir v Alloa	-	-	-	1-0/0-2	0-1/2-3	-	(07-03-07)

SCOTTISH DIVISION THREE

Home team / Away team							Since 1988 – HW D AW
Annan v Clyde	-	-	-	-	1-0/0-2	1-0/1-0	(03-00-01)
Elgin v Stranraer	-	0-5/2-3	-	1-2/2-3	1-2/2-1	1-1/1-2	(01-02-07)
Montrose v Peterhead	-	-	-	-	-	2-1/1-3	(03-01-08)
Queen's Park v Stirling	-	-	1-1/3-1	-	-	-	(05-06-03)

SUNDAY 25TH NOVEMBER 2012

PREMIER LEAGUE

Home team / Away team							Since 1988 – HW D AW
Chelsea v Man City	3-0	6-0	1-0	2-4	2-0	2-1	(10-06-03)
Sunderland v West Brom	2-0	-	4-0	-	2-3	2-2	(05-06-03)

SCOTTISH DIVISION THREE

Home team / Away team							Since 1988 – HW D AW
E Stirling v Berwick	0-1/0-3	-	1-0/0-4	1-0/3-2	0-0/1-0	1-3/2-1	(12-04-11)

TUESDAY 27TH NOVEMBER 2012

PREMIER LEAGUE

Home team / Away team							Since 1988 – HW D AW
Aston Villa v Reading	2-1	3-1	-	-	-	-	(02-00-00)
Man Utd v West Ham	0-1	4-1	2-0	3-0	3-0	-	(16-00-02)

Home v Away							Date
Southampton v Norwich	2-1	0-1	2-0	2-2	-	-	(07-04-02)
Stoke v Newcastle	-	-	1-1	-	4-0	1-3	(02-01-01)
Sunderland v QPR	2-1	-	-	-	-	3-1	(03-02-01)
Swansea v West Brom	-	-	-	0-2	-	3-0	(01-02-01)
Tottenham v Liverpool	0-1	0-2	2-1	2-1	2-1	4-0	(11-05-08)

CHAMPIONSHIP

Home v Away							Date
Barnsley v Burnley	1-0	1-1	3-2	-	1-2	2-0	(05-02-01)
Blackpool v Birmingham	-	-	2-0	-	1-2	2-2	(02-02-01)
Brighton v Bristol C	0-2	-	-	-	-	2-0	(02-01-04)
Charlton v Peterborough	-	-	-	-	3-2	-	(02-00-01)
Derby v Cardiff	3-1	-	1-1	2-0	1-2	0-3	(03-02-03)
Hull v C Palace	1-1	2-1	-	-	1-1	0-1	(01-02-03)
Ipswich v Nottm F	-	-	2-1	1-1	0-1	1-3	(04-01-06)
Leeds v Leicester	1-2	-	1-1	-	1-2	1-2	(07-03-06)
Middlesboro v Huddersfield	-	-	-	-	-	-	(01-00-00)
Sheff Weds v Watford	-	0-1	2-0	2-1	-	-	(04-03-02)
Wolves v Millwall	-	-	-	-	-	-	(05-03-02)

WEDNESDAY 28TH NOVEMBER 2012

PREMIER LEAGUE

Home v Away							Date
Chelsea v Fulham	2-2	0-0	3-1	2-1	1-0	1-1	(07-04-00)
Everton v Arsenal	1-0	1-4	1-1	1-6	1-2	0-1	(06-07-11)
Wigan v Man City	4-0	1-1	2-1	1-1	0-2	0-1	(03-02-03)

CHAMPIONSHIP

Home v Away							Date
Blackburn v Bolton	0-1	4-1	2-2	3-0	1-0	1-2	(06-05-04)

SCOTTISH PREMIER LEAGUE

Home v Away							Date
Aberdeen v Inverness	1-1/1-1	1-0	0-2/1-0	-	1-2/1-0	2-1/0-1	(04-04-03)
Club 12 v Kilmarnock	-	-	-	-	-	-	(None)
Dundee Utd v Motherwell	1-1/1-1/0-0 1-0/2-0	-	0-4	0-1/3-0	2-0/4-0	1-3/1-1	(16-20-09)
Hearts v Celtic	2-1/1-2	1-1	0-2/1-1	2-1/1-2	2-0/0-3	2-0/0-4	(13-07-28)
Ross County v St Mirren	-	-	-	-	-	-	(05-01-04)
St Johnstone v Hibernian	-	-	-	5-1	2-0/1-1	3-1	(07-09-04)

SATURDAY 1ST DECEMBER 2012

PREMIER LEAGUE

Home v Away							Date
Arsenal v Swansea	-	-	-	-	-	1-0	(01-00-00)
Fulham v Tottenham	1-1	3-3	2-1	0-0	1-2	1-3	(05-03-03)
Liverpool v Southampton	-	-	-	-	-	-	(10-05-02)
Man City v Everton	2-1	0-2	0-1	0-2	1-2	2-0	(10-00-08)
Newcastle v Wigan	2-1	1-0	2-2	-	2-2	1-0	(04-02-00)
Norwich v Sunderland	1-0	-	-	-	-	2-1	(05-02-00)
QPR v Aston Villa	-	-	-	-	-	1-1	(05-03-01)
Reading v Man Utd	1-1	0-2	-	-	-	-	(00-01-01)
West Brom v Stoke	1-3	1-1	0-2	-	0-3	0-1	(02-05-08)
West Ham v Chelsea	1-4	0-4	0-1	1-1	1-3	-	(05-04-08)

CHAMPIONSHIP

Home v Away							Date
Birmingham v Middlesboro	-	3-0	-	-	-	3-0	(06-01-01)
Bolton v Ipswich	-	-	-	-	-	-	(02-01-01)
Bristol C v Wolves	-	0-0	2-2	-	-	-	(03-03-03)
Burnley v Blackburn	-	-	-	0-1	-	-	(00-00-02)
C Palace v Brighton	-	-	-	-	-	1-1	(02-01-01)

Home team / Away team							Since 1988 – HW D AW
Huddersfield v Leeds	-	1-0	1-0	2-2	-	-	(02-01-00)
Leicester v Derby	1-1	-	-	0-0	2-0	4-0	(07-05-05)
Millwall v Charlton	-	-	-	4-0	-	-	(07-01-01)
Nottm F v Hull	-	-	-	-	0-1	0-1	(00-00-02)
Peterborough v Blackpool	-	-	-	0-1	-	3-1	(05-03-02)
Watford v Barnsley	-	0-3	1-1	1-0	1-0	2-1	(07-05-04)

SCOTTISH DIVISION THREE

Berwick v Montrose	1-2/1-0	-	3-2/0-1	2-0/0-2	1-0/0-1	1-2/2-2	(11-09-08)
Clyde v Queen's Park	-	-	-	-	2-3/0-2	0-2/1-2	(02-00-05)
Peterhead v Elgin	-	-	-	-	-	1-3/3-0	(08-03-01)
Stirling v E Stirling	-	-	-	-	-	-	(10-01-00)
Stranraer v Annan	-	-	-	2-0/3-2	2-2/1-1	4-2/4-2	(04-02-00)

CONFERENCE

Alfreton v Cambridge U	-	-	-	-	-	2-1	(01-00-00)
Braintree v Macclesfield	-	-	-	-	-	-	(None)
Ebbsfleet v Grimsby	-	-	-	-	-	3-1	(01-00-00)
Forest G v Nuneaton	-	-	-	-	-	-	(02-01-02)
Gateshead v Newport Co	-	-	-	-	1-7	2-3	(00-00-02)
Hereford v Telford	-	-	-	-	-	-	(03-03-01)
Hyde v Woking	-	-	-	-	-	-	(None)
Kidderminstr v Wrexham	-	-	1-0	2-0	1-0	0-1	(03-00-02)
Luton v Barrow	-	-	-	1-0	0-0	5-1	(02-01-00)
Southport v Lincoln	-	-	-	-	-	2-2	(00-01-00)
Stockport v Mansfield	1-0	2-1	-	-	-	0-1	(03-01-02)
Tamworth v Dartford	-	-	-	-	-	-	(None)

SUNDAY 2ND DECEMBER 2012

CHAMPIONSHIP

Cardiff v Sheff Weds	1-2	1-0	2-0	3-2	-	-	(04-00-01)

TUESDAY 4TH DECEMBER 2012

CONFERENCE

Alfreton v Wrexham	-	-	-	-	-	1-4	(00-00-01)
Braintree v Forest G	-	-	-	-	-	1-5	(00-00-01)
Ebbsfleet v Cambridge U	2-0	2-1	1-1	1-3	-	0-0	(02-03-01)
Gateshead v Grimsby	-	-	-	-	0-0	1-0	(01-01-00)
Hereford v Mansfield	1-3	2-1	-	-	-	-	(01-01-05)
Lincoln v Woking	-	-	-	-	-	-	(None)
Macclesfield v Hyde	-	-	-	-	-	-	(None)
Newport Co v Luton	-	-	-	-	1-1	0-1	(00-01-01)
Nuneaton v Dartford	-	-	-	-	-	-	(None)
Stockport v Southport	-	-	-	-	-	0-1	(00-00-01)
Tamworth v Kidderminstr	0-0	-	-	2-1	2-2	0-0	(01-04-00)
Telford v Barrow	-	0-2	-	-	-	1-0	(03-01-02)

SATURDAY 8TH DECEMBER 2012

PREMIER LEAGUE

Arsenal v West Brom	-	-	1-0	-	2-3	3-0	(04-01-01)
Aston Villa v Stoke	-	-	2-2	1-0	1-1	1-1	(01-03-00)
Everton v Tottenham	1-2	0-0	0-0	2-2	2-1	1-0	(07-10-07)
Fulham v Newcastle	2-1	0-1	2-1	-	1-0	5-2	(07-00-03)

Home team v Away team	Six-season fixture record, latest result at right						Since 1988 – HW D AW
Man City v Man Utd	0-1	1-0	0-1	0-1	0-0	1-0	(06-04-08)
Southampton v Reading	-	-	1-1	-	-	1-3	(00-02-01)
Sunderland v Chelsea	-	0-1	2-3	1-3	2-4	1-2	(04-01-08)
Swansea v Norwich	-	-	2-1	-	3-0	2-3	(02-00-01)
West Ham v Liverpool	1-2	1-0	0-3	2-3	3-1	-	(06-04-08)
Wigan v QPR	-	-	-	-	-	2-0	(01-02-01)

CHAMPIONSHIP

Home team v Away team							Since 1988 – HW D AW
Blackburn v Cardiff	-	-	-	-	-	-	(None)
Charlton v Brighton	-	-	-	1-2	0-4	-	(01-00-03)
C Palace v Blackpool	-	0-0	0-1	4-1	-	1-1	(01-02-01)
Derby v Leeds	2-0	-	-	-	2-1	1-0	(04-04-04)
Huddersfield v Bolton	-	-	-	-	-	-	(03-02-04)
Ipswich v Millwall	-	-	-	-	2-0	0-3	(03-03-03)
Leicester v Barnsley	2-0	2-0	-	1-0	4-1	1-2	(08-02-03)
Nottm F v Burnley	-	-	1-2	-	2-0	0-2	(05-01-02)
Peterborough v Middlesboro	-	-	-	2-2	-	1-1	(01-02-00)
Sheff Weds v Bristol C	-	0-1	0-0	0-1	-	-	(02-01-03)
Watford v Hull	-	1-0	-	-	1-2	1-1	(03-02-02)
Wolves v Birmingham	2-3	-	1-1	0-1	1-0	-	(07-02-05)

LEAGUE 1

Home team v Away team							Since 1988 – HW D AW
Brentford v MK Dons	-	0-3	-	3-3	0-2	3-3	(02-02-02)
Bury v Leyton O	-	-	-	-	-	1-1	(04-03-02)
Carlisle v Sheff Utd	-	-	-	-	-	3-2	(01-00-00)
Colchester v Oldham	-	-	2-2	1-0	1-0	4-1	(05-05-02)
Coventry v Walsall	-	-	-	-	-	-	(01-02-00)
Crawley v Shrewsbury	-	-	-	-	-	2-1	(01-00-00)
Hartlepool v Stevenage	-	-	-	-	-	0-0	(00-01-00)
Preston v Crewe	-	-	-	-	-	-	(05-03-01)
Scunthorpe v Bournemouth	3-2	-	-	-	-	1-1	(02-02-01)
Swindon v Doncaster	-	1-2	-	-	-	-	(01-01-01)
Tranmere v Portsmouth	-	-	-	-	-	-	(04-03-03)
Yeovil v Notts Co	-	-	-	-	2-1	1-0	(02-00-01)

LEAGUE 2

Home team v Away team							Since 1988 – HW D AW
Barnet v Wimbledon	-	-	-	-	-	4-0	(01-00-00)
Bradford v Torquay	-	-	-	2-0	0-3	1-0	(03-01-01)
Bristol R v Dagenham	-	-	-	-	0-2	2-0	(01-00-01)
Fleetwood v Southend	-	-	-	-	-	-	(None)
Northampton v Cheltenham	2-0	2-1	4-2	2-1	1-1	2-3	(06-02-03)
Oxford Utd v Aldershot	2-0	2-3	-	-	0-1	1-1	(01-01-02)
Plymouth v York	-	-	-	-	-	-	(05-01-01)
Port Vale v Chesterfield	3-2	-	0-1	1-2	1-1	-	(06-02-02)
Rochdale v Exeter	-	-	2-2	-	0-1	3-2	(08-03-03)
Rotherham v Gillingham	3-2	-	2-0	-	0-1	3-0	(05-03-03)
Wycombe v Morecambe	-	2-0	1-1	-	2-0	-	(02-01-00)

SCOTTISH PREMIER LEAGUE

Home team v Away team							Since 1988 – HW D AW
Club 12 v Dundee Utd	-	-	-	-	-	-	(None)
Hearts v Aberdeen	0-1/1-1	4-1	1-1/2-1	0-3	5-0	3-0/3-0	(24-09-11)
Inverness v Hibernian	0-0/3-0	2-0	1-1/2-0	-	4-2/2-0	0-1/2-3/2-0	(08-02-03)
Kilmarnock v Celtic	1-2/1-2	1-2	1-3/1-2	1-0	1-2/0-4/0-2	3-3/0-6	(05-09-23)
Motherwell v Ross County	-	-	-	-	-	-	(None)
St Mirren v St Johnstone	-	-	-	1-1/1-1	1-2/0-0	0-0/0-3	(03-13-10)

SCOTTISH DIVISION ONE

Home team v Away team							Since 1988 – HW D AW
Cowdenbeath v Partick	-	-	-	-	2-1/1-1	-	(01-01-00)

Match							
Dundee v Falkirk	-	-	-	-	2-0/1-0	4-2/3-1	(07-01-03)
Hamilton v Dumbarton	-	-	-	-	-	-	(12-02-00)
Livingston v Dunfermline	-	1-1/0-2	2-3/4-2	-	-	-	(06-07-06)
Raith v Morton	1-3/2-0	-	-	3-0/1-2	1-0/2-2	1-1/5-0	(13-07-06)

SCOTTISH DIVISION TWO

Match							
Albion v Forfar	-	2-1/0-0	1-3/2-0	1-1/0-1	-	1-0/2-2	(05-04-10)
Alloa v Queen of Sth	-	-	-	-	-	-	(10-02-02)
Arbroath v Stenhsmuir	2-0/4-1	2-2/1-0	-	0-3/1-1	-	1-0/0-2	(14-06-05)
Brechin v Ayr	0-2/2-0	2-2/5-1	0-1/1-0	-	0-3/1-0	-	(07-04-07)
East Fife v Airdrie	-	-	-	-	3-3/0-1	2-0/2-0	(03-02-03)

SCOTTISH DIVISION THREE

Match							
Annan v Queen's Park	-	-	-	3-1/0-2	2-1/1-2	5-2/2-3	(03-00-03)
Berwick v Peterhead	-	1-2/2-2	-	-	-	2-1/0-1	(01-01-02)
E Stirling v Montrose	0-3/0-2	0-3/3-1	5-0/2-1	1-0/2-3	2-1/1-2	1-0/3-1	(17-06-18)
Elgin v Clyde	-	-	-	-	0-1/0-1	0-3/1-1	(00-01-03)
Stranraer v Stirling	2-1/3-1	-	1-0/2-8	-	-	-	(05-07-07)

CONFERENCE

Match							
Barrow v Hereford	-	-	-	-	-	-	(00-00-01)
Cambridge U v Gateshead	-	-	-	3-0	5-0	0-1	(02-00-01)
Dartford v Lincoln	-	-	-	-	-	-	(None)
Forest G v Macclesfield	-	-	-	-	-	-	(None)
Grimsby v Tamworth	-	-	-	-	2-2	0-0	(00-02-00)
Hyde v Telford	-	1-0	0-4	1-1	0-3	-	(01-01-02)
Kidderminstr v Newport Co	-	-	-	-	2-3	3-2	(01-00-01)
Luton v Alfreton	-	-	-	-	-	1-0	(01-00-00)
Mansfield v Ebbsfleet	-	-	2-0	3-0	-	1-0	(03-00-00)
Southport v Braintree	-	-	-	-	-	0-4	(00-00-01)
Woking v Stockport	-	-	-	-	-	-	(None)
Wrexham v Nuneaton	-	-	-	-	-	-	(None)

SUNDAY 9TH DECEMBER 2012

LEAGUE 2

Match							
Burton v Accrington	-	-	-	0-2	1-1	0-2	(01-03-03)

SATURDAY 15TH DECEMBER 2012

PREMIER LEAGUE

Match							
Chelsea v Southampton	-	-	-	-	-	-	(08-05-03)
Liverpool v Aston Villa	3-1	2-2	5-0	1-3	3-0	1-1	(14-06-04)
Man Utd v Sunderland	-	1-0	1-0	2-2	2-0	1-0	(10-02-00)
Newcastle v Man City	0-1	0-2	2-2	-	1-3	0-2	(06-02-05)
Norwich v Wigan	-	-	-	-	-	1-1	(01-01-00)
QPR v Fulham	-	-	-	-	-	0-1	(00-01-02)
Reading v Arsenal	0-4	1-3	-	-	-	-	(00-00-02)
Stoke v Everton	-	-	2-3	0-0	2-0	1-1	(01-02-01)
Tottenham v Swansea	-	-	-	-	-	3-1	(01-00-00)
West Brom v West Ham	-	-	3-2	-	3-3	-	(01-03-03)

CHAMPIONSHIP

Match							
Barnsley v Sheff Weds	0-3	0-0	2-1	1-2	-	-	(04-04-02)
Birmingham v C Palace	2-1	-	1-0	-	-	3-1	(08-01-03)
Blackpool v Blackburn	-	-	-	-	1-2	-	(00-00-01)
Bolton v Charlton	1-1	-	-	-	-	-	(05-03-02)

Home team v Away team							Since 1988 HWDAW
Brighton v Nottm F	2-1	0-2	-	-	-	1-0	(03-01-01)
Bristol C v Derby	-	-	1-1	2-1	2-0	1-1	(02-04-02)
Burnley v Watford	-	2-2	3-2	-	3-2	2-2	(08-03-02)
Cardiff v Peterborough	-	-	-	2-0	-	3-1	(03-02-03)
Hull v Huddersfield	-	-	-	-	-	-	(04-01-01)
Leeds v Ipswich	1-1	-	-	-	0-0	3-1	(04-05-03)
Middlesboro v Wolves	-	-	-	-	-	-	(05-02-00)
Millwall v Leicester	-	-	0-1	-	2-0	2-1	(06-03-02)

LEAGUE 1

Home team v Away team							Since 1988 HWDAW
Bournemouth v Colchester	-	-	-	-	1-2	1-1	(02-03-04)
Crewe v Bury	-	-	-	2-3	3-0	-	(05-01-03)
Doncaster v Coventry	-	-	1-0	0-0	1-1	1-1	(01-03-00)
Leyton O v Scunthorpe	2-2	-	2-2	-	-	1-3	(04-07-02)
MK Dons v Hartlepool	0-0	-	3-1	0-0	1-0	2-2	(04-03-00)
Notts Co v Brentford	-	1-1	1-1	-	1-1	1-1	(04-09-01)
Oldham v Swindon	-	2-2	0-0	2-2	2-0	-	(07-07-02)
Portsmouth v Preston	-	-	-	-	1-1	-	(01-01-02)
Sheff Utd v Tranmere	-	-	-	-	-	1-1	(04-03-01)
Shrewsbury v Carlisle	-	-	-	-	-	-	(04-02-03)
Stevenage v Crawley	2-3	3-1	1-1	2-0	-	-	(04-01-01)
Walsall v Yeovil	-	2-0	2-0	0-1	0-1	1-1	(02-01-03)

LEAGUE 2

Home team v Away team							Since 1988 HWDAW
Wimbledon v Rotherham	-	-	-	-	-	1-2	(00-00-01)
Accrington v Wycombe	2-1	0-2	0-1	-	1-1	-	(01-01-02)
Aldershot v Rochdale	-	-	2-4	1-1	-	-	(00-01-01)
Cheltenham v Port Vale	0-1	1-0	-	1-1	0-0	2-0	(02-02-02)
Chesterfield v Burton	-	-	-	5-2	1-2	-	(01-00-01)
Dagenham v Barnet	-	1-1	2-0	4-1	-	3-0	(06-02-00)
Exeter v Plymouth	-	-	-	-	1-0	-	(02-03-03)
Gillingham v Fleetwood	-	-	-	-	-	-	(None)
Morecambe v Oxford Utd	0-3	-	-	-	0-3	0-0	(00-01-02)
Southend v Bradford	-	-	-	-	4-0	0-1	(01-03-01)
Torquay v Northampton	-	-	-	1-0	3-0	1-0	(08-02-02)
York v Bristol R	-	-	-	-	-	-	(03-02-04)

SCOTTISH PREMIER LEAGUE

Home team v Away team							Since 1988 HWDAW
Aberdeen v Kilmarnock	3-1/3-0	2-1	1-0/0-0	1-0/1-2	0-1/5-0	2-2/0-0	(17-10-08)
Celtic v St Mirren	2-0/5-1	1-1	1-0/7-0	3-1	4-0/1-0	5-0	(15-03-01)
Dundee Utd v Inverness	3-1/1-1	0-1	2-1/1-1	-	0-4/1-0	3-1/3-0	(06-04-03)
Hibernian v Motherwell	3-1/2-0	1-0/0-2	0-1/1-1	2-0	2-1	0-1/1-1	(21-15-06)
Ross County v Club 12	-	-	-	-	-	-	(None)
St Johnstone v Hearts	-	-	-	2-2/1-0	0-2	2-0/2-1	(06-07-09)

SCOTTISH DIVISION ONE

Home team v Away team							Since 1988 HWDAW
Dumbarton v Livingston	-	-	-	-	1-2/0-3	-	(02-00-06)
Dunfermline v Hamilton	-	0-5/1-1	-	-	-	-	(07-01-02)
Falkirk v Cowdenbeath	-	-	-	-	5-1/2-0	-	(02-00-00)
Morton v Dundee	-	0-2/1-2	2-0/2-0	0-1/2-2	0-1/1-3	1-2/0-2	(04-06-09)
Partick v Raith	-	-	-	1-2/0-0	0-0/3-0	0-1/1-1	(08-07-09)

SCOTTISH DIVISION TWO

Home team v Away team							Since 1988 HWDAW
Airdrie v Alloa	-	2-0/1-1	-	-	0-1/0-2	-	(06-02-02)
Ayr v East Fife	-	-	4-2/2-0	-	0-4/1-1	-	(03-01-02)
Forfar v Arbroath	-	1-3/1-0	-	-	-	1-1/2-4	(06-07-06)
Queen of Sth v Brechin	-	-	-	-	-	-	(04-07-04)
Stenhsmuir v Albion	3-2/0-4	0-1/2-2	1-0/2-0	-	-	3-0/1-2	(12-04-06)

SCOTTISH DIVISION THREE

Clyde v E Stirling	-	-	-	-	1-2/2-0	7-1/3-0	(06-00-01)
Montrose v Stranraer	-	2-4/0-2	-	1-1/4-5	3-3/3-2	0-6/1-3	(06-03-11)
Peterhead v Annan	-	-	-	-	-	2-3/3-2	(01-00-01)
Queen's Park v Elgin	3-0/3-0	-	-	0-3/0-1	1-1/1-0	6-0/1-3	(10-03-05)
Stirling v Berwick	-	-	-	-	-	-	(09-02-01)

FRIDAY 21ST DECEMBER 2012

CHAMPIONSHIP

Derby v Hull	2-2	-	-	-	0-1	0-2	(00-02-02)

LEAGUE 2

Barnet v Burton	-	-	-	1-1	0-0	3-6	(01-03-02)
Rochdale v Cheltenham	-	-	-	0-1	-	-	(00-05-02)
Southend v Chesterfield	-	-	-	-	2-3	-	(02-01-03)

SATURDAY 22ND DECEMBER 2012

PREMIER LEAGUE

Chelsea v Aston Villa	1-1	4-4	2-0	7-1	3-3	1-3	(12-05-06)
Liverpool v Fulham	4-0	2-0	0-0	0-0	1-0	0-1	(06-04-01)
Man City v Reading	0-2	2-1	-	-	-	-	(02-01-02)
Newcastle v QPR	-	-	-	1-1	-	1-0	(03-01-02)
Southampton v Sunderland	1-2	-	-	-	-	-	(04-00-03)
Swansea v Man Utd	-	-	-	-	-	0-1	(00-00-01)
Tottenham v Stoke	-	-	3-1	0-1	3-2	1-1	(02-01-01)
West Brom v Norwich	0-1	2-0	-	-	-	1-2	(06-02-04)
West Ham v Everton	1-0	0-2	1-3	1-2	1-1	-	(04-05-09)
Wigan v Arsenal	0-1	0-0	1-4	3-2	2-2	0-4	(01-02-04)

CHAMPIONSHIP

Birmingham v Burnley	0-1	-	1-1	2-1	-	2-1	(03-01-02)
Blackburn v Brighton	-	-	-	-	-	-	(02-01-01)
Blackpool v Wolves	-	0-0	2-2	-	2-1	-	(01-02-01)
C Palace v Huddersfield	-	-	-	-	-	-	(00-05-00)
Ipswich v Bristol C	-	6-0	3-1	0-0	2-0	3-0	(06-02-00)
Leeds v Middlesboro	-	-	-	-	1-1	0-1	(05-03-04)
Leicester v Cardiff	0-0	0-0	-	1-0	2-1	2-1	(03-03-01)
Millwall v Barnsley	-	-	-	-	2-0	0-0	(04-02-03)
Peterborough v Bolton	-	-	-	-	-	-	(01-00-01)
Sheff Weds v Charlton	-	0-0	4-1	-	2-2	0-1	(04-03-01)
Watford v Nottm F	-	-	2-1	0-0	1-1	0-1	(02-04-04)

LEAGUE 1

Brentford v Stevenage	-	-	-	-	-	0-1	(00-00-01)
Bury v Shrewsbury	1-2	1-1	2-1	1-0	1-0	-	(07-05-02)
Coventry v Preston	0-4	2-1	0-0	1-1	1-2	-	(02-04-04)
Crawley v Sheff Utd	-	-	-	-	-	-	(None)
Crewe v Bournemouth	2-0	1-4	-	1-2	-	-	(04-00-03)
Doncaster v MK Dons	-	-	-	-	-	-	(01-01-00)
Hartlepool v Portsmouth	-	-	-	-	-	-	(None)
Notts Co v Leyton O	-	-	-	-	3-2	1-2	(03-01-02)
Scunthorpe v Carlisle	3-0	-	2-1	-	-	1-2	(09-03-04)
Swindon v Tranmere	-	1-0	3-1	3-0	0-0	-	(10-04-02)
Walsall v Colchester	-	-	2-0	1-0	0-1	3-1	(05-01-05)

Home team	Away team	Six-season fixture record, latest result at right					Since 1988 – HW D AW	
Yeovil v Oldham		1-0	0-0	2-2	3-0	1-1	3-1	(03-03-01)

LEAGUE 2

Accrington v Plymouth		-	-	-	-	-	0-4	(00-00-01)
Bristol R v Rotherham		-	-	-	-	-	5-2	(04-01-02)
Morecambe v Dagenham		1-1	1-0	1-2	1-0	-	1-2	(06-03-03)
Northampton v Aldershot		-	-	-	0-3	1-1	3-1	(01-01-01)
Oxford Utd v Fleetwood		-	-	-	-	-	-	(None)
Port Vale v Wimbledon		-	-	-	-	-	1-2	(00-00-01)
Torquay v Exeter		-	1-0	-	-	-	-	(07-01-05)
Wycombe v Bradford		-	2-1	1-0	-	1-0	-	(05-00-00)
York v Gillingham		-	-	-	-	-	-	(02-04-01)

SCOTTISH PREMIER LEAGUE

Aberdeen v St Johnstone		-	-	-	2-1/1-3	0-1/0-2	0-0/0-0	(07-10-07)
Celtic v Ross County		-	-	-	-	-	-	(None)
Hearts v Dundee Utd		4-0/0-4	1-3/1-0	0-0/3-0	0-0/0-0	1-1/2-1	0-1/0-2	(25-09-09)
Inverness v Club 12		-	-	-	-	-	-	(None)
Kilmarnock v Hibernian		2-1/0-2	2-1	1-0/1-1	1-1	2-1	4-1/1-3	(15-09-08)
St Mirren v Motherwell		2-0/0-0	0-1/3-1	0-0/1-3	3-3/0-0	1-1	0-1/0-0	(05-09-07)

CONFERENCE

Alfreton v Barrow		1-0	0-0	-	-	-	2-1	(03-03-02)
Cambridge U v Nuneaton		-	-	-	-	-	-	(None)
Ebbsfleet v Hereford		-	-	-	-	-	-	(01-00-03)
Gateshead v Stockport		-	-	-	-	-	2-0	(01-00-00)
Grimsby v Wrexham		2-1	1-0	-	-	2-1	1-3	(05-01-03)
Hyde v Mansfield		-	-	-	-	-	-	(None)
Kidderminstr v Dartford		-	-	-	-	-	-	(None)
Macclesfield v Lincoln		2-1	1-2	1-2	0-1	1-1	-	(04-05-05)
Newport Co v Braintree		0-1	2-0	2-1	1-0	-	3-4	(03-00-02)
Tamworth v Southport		1-1	1-3	1-1	-	0-1	2-2	(00-04-02)
Telford v Luton		-	-	-	-	-	0-2	(00-00-01)
Woking v Forest G		3-3	1-1	0-1	-	-	-	(04-04-03)

WEDNESDAY 26TH DECEMBER 2012

PREMIER LEAGUE

Arsenal v West Ham		0-1	2-0	0-0	2-0	1-0	-	(12-01-05)
Aston Villa v Tottenham		1-1	2-1	1-2	1-1	1-2	1-1	(12-09-03)
Everton v Wigan		2-2	2-1	4-0	2-1	0-0	3-1	(04-02-01)
Fulham v Southampton		-	-	-	-	-	-	(03-01-00)
Man Utd v Newcastle		2-0	6-0	1-1	-	3-0	1-1	(12-07-00)
Norwich v Chelsea		-	-	-	-	-	0-0	(03-02-03)
QPR v West Brom		1-2	0-2	-	3-1	-	1-1	(04-02-03)
Reading v Swansea		-	-	4-0	1-1	0-1	-	(06-03-01)
Stoke v Liverpool		-	-	0-0	1-1	2-0	1-0	(02-02-00)
Sunderland v Man City		-	1-2	0-3	1-1	1-0	1-0	(04-02-05)

CHAMPIONSHIP

Barnsley v Birmingham		1-0	-	1-1	-	-	1-3	(03-03-06)
Bolton v Sheff Weds		-	-	-	-	-	-	(03-00-00)
Brighton v Millwall		0-1	3-0	4-1	0-1	-	2-2	(04-02-04)
Bristol C v Watford		-	0-0	1-1	2-2	0-2	0-2	(03-07-03)
Burnley v Derby		0-0	-	3-0	-	2-1	0-0	(05-03-01)
Cardiff v C Palace		0-0	1-1	2-1	1-1	0-0	2-0	(03-04-01)
Charlton v Ipswich		-	3-1	2-1	-	-	-	(05-03-02)
Huddersfield v Blackpool		0-2	-	-	-	-	-	(04-04-02)
Hull v Leicester		1-2	2-0	-	-	0-1	2-1	(03-03-02)

Home team Away team	Six-season fixture record, latest result at right						Since 1988 – HW D AW
Middlesboro v Blackburn	0-1	1-2	0-0	-	-	-	(06-02-07)
Nottm F v Leeds	-	1-2	-	-	1-1	0-4	(03-06-02)
Wolves v Peterborough	-	-	-	-	-	-	(01-01-00)

LEAGUE 1

Bournemouth v Yeovil	0-2	2-0	-	-	2-0	0-0	(03-01-01)
Carlisle v Hartlepool	-	4-2	0-1	3-2	1-0	1-2	(08-00-07)
Colchester v Brentford	-	-	-	3-3	0-2	2-1	(02-04-04)
Leyton O v Swindon	-	2-1	1-2	0-0	3-0	-	(02-01-01)
MK Dons v Walsall	1-1	-	0-1	1-0	1-1	0-1	(03-04-03)
Oldham v Doncaster	4-0	1-1	-	-	-	-	(01-01-02)
Portsmouth v Crawley	-	-	-	-	-	-	(None)
Preston v Bury	-	-	-	-	-	1-1	(05-04-01)
Sheff Utd v Scunthorpe	-	0-0	-	0-1	0-4	2-1	(01-01-02)
Shrewsbury v Notts Co	2-0	0-0	3-2	0-1	-	-	(04-03-03)
Stevenage v Coventry	-	-	-	-	-	-	(None)
Tranmere v Crewe	1-0	1-1	2-0	-	-	-	(06-03-02)

LEAGUE 2

Wimbledon v Northampton	-	-	-	-	-	0-3	(00-00-01)
Aldershot v Bristol R	-	-	-	-	-	1-0	(01-00-00)
Bradford v Accrington	-	0-3	1-1	1-1	1-1	1-1	(00-04-01)
Burton v Rochdale	-	-	-	1-0	-	-	(01-00-00)
Cheltenham v Wycombe	-	-	-	-	1-2	-	(03-03-02)
Chesterfield v York	-	-	-	-	-	-	(04-04-01)
Dagenham v Southend	-	-	-	-	-	2-3	(00-00-01)
Exeter v Oxford Utd	2-1	2-0	-	-	-	-	(03-01-00)
Fleetwood v Morecambe	-	-	-	-	-	-	(01-02-03)
Gillingham v Barnet	-	-	0-2	-	2-4	3-1	(03-02-02)
Plymouth v Torquay	-	-	-	-	-	1-2	(02-03-01)
Rotherham v Port Vale	1-5	-	1-0	1-2	5-0	0-1	(04-01-04)

SCOTTISH PREMIER LEAGUE

Club 12 v Celtic	-	-	-	-	-	-	(None)
Dundee Utd v St Johnstone	-	-	-	3-3	1-0/2-0	0-0	(09-07-08)
Hibernian v Ross County	-	-	-	-	-	-	(None)
Inverness v St Mirren	1-2/2-1	1-0/0-0	1-2/2-1	-	1-2/1-0	2-1/0-0	(10-04-04)
Kilmarnock v Hearts	0-0/1-0	3-1/0-0	0-2	1-2	1-2/2-2	0-0/1-1	(12-12-11)
Motherwell v Aberdeen	0-2/0-2	3-0/2-1	0-1/1-1	1-1	1-1/2-1	1-0/1-0	(13-16-17)

SCOTTISH DIVISION ONE

Cowdenbeath v Livingston	-	-	-	-	-	-	(00-01-05)
Dumbarton v Raith	-	-	-	-	-	-	(01-00-05)
Dunfermline v Falkirk	0-3/0-3	-	-	-	1-1/3-0	-	(04-05-04)
Hamilton v Dundee	1-0/1-0	2-0/1-0	-	-	-	1-6/3-1	(08-03-09)
Partick v Morton	-	1-1/0-3	2-1/1-0	5-0/1-0	0-0/2-0	5-0/0-0	(09-07-06)

SCOTTISH DIVISION TWO

Albion v Ayr	-	-	-	-	-	-	(01-00-00)
Alloa v Forfar	2-0/2-0	-	-	-	3-2/0-3	-	(06-04-12)
Brechin v Arbroath	-	-	3-1/0-1	0-0/0-2	-	2-3/1-1	(06-05-05)
East Fife v Stenhsmuir	0-0/1-1	7-0/0-1	-	2-1/1-1	6-0/1-1	1-3/1-1	(14-09-08)
Queen of Sth v Airdrie	1-1/0-3	-	0-0/4-0	3-0/2-2	-	-	(05-04-02)

SCOTTISH DIVISION THREE

Berwick v Queen's Park	0-2	1-1/1-4	-	1-0/1-1	1-1/3-1	2-0/1-4	(10-08-10)
E Stirling v Annan	-	-	2-1/1-1	1-3/3-1	1-5/2-0	1-0/0-4	(04-01-03)
Elgin v Montrose	3-2/0-2	0-2/2-1	1-2/1-0	0-1/5-2	3-2/1-0	3-1/2-1	(11-04-09)
Stirling v Peterhead	2-0/2-1	-	0-0/2-1	2-1/2-0	-	-	(10-01-03)
Stranraer v Clyde	-	-	-	-	3-1/3-0	0-0/1-0	(07-08-02)

Home team	Away team	Six-season fixture record, latest result at right					Since 1988 – HW D AW	

CONFERENCE

Home v Away							
Barrow v Gateshead	-	-	-	3-3	1-3	1-2	(05-02-03)
Braintree v Cambridge U	-	-	-	-	-	3-2	(01-00-00)
Dartford v Ebbsfleet	-	-	-	-	1-1	-	(00-01-00)
Forest G v Newport Co	-	-	-	-	0-0	1-1	(00-02-00)
Hereford v Kidderminstr	-	-	-	-	-	-	(01-01-02)
Lincoln v Grimsby	2-0	1-2	1-1	0-0	-	1-2	(02-05-02)
Luton v Woking	-	-	-	-	-	-	(None)
Mansfield v Alfreton	-	-	-	-	-	3-2	(01-00-00)
Nuneaton v Tamworth	-	1-0	-	-	-	-	(02-00-01)
Southport v Macclesfield	-	-	-	-	-	-	(02-00-02)
Stockport v Hyde	-	-	-	-	-	-	(None)
Wrexham v Telford	-	-	-	-	-	4-0	(01-00-00)

SATURDAY 29TH DECEMBER 2012

PREMIER LEAGUE

Home v Away							
Arsenal v Newcastle	1-1	3-0	3-0	-	0-1	2-1	(13-02-04)
Aston Villa v Wigan	1-1	0-2	0-0	0-2	1-1	2-0	(01-03-03)
Everton v Chelsea	2-3	0-1	0-0	2-1	1-0	2-0	(07-08-08)
Fulham v Swansea	-	-	-	-	-	0-3	(05-02-01)
Man Utd v West Brom	-	-	4-0	-	2-2	2-0	(04-02-00)
Norwich v Man City	-	-	-	-	-	1-6	(03-05-04)
QPR v Liverpool	-	-	-	-	-	3-2	(03-02-04)
Reading v West Ham	6-0	0-3	-	-	-	3-0	(04-00-01)
Stoke v Southampton	2-1	3-2	-	-	-	-	(02-00-01)
Sunderland v Tottenham	-	1-0	1-1	3-1	1-2	0-0	(04-04-04)

CHAMPIONSHIP

Home v Away							
Barnsley v Blackburn	-	-	-	-	-	-	(02-02-03)
Bolton v Birmingham	-	3-0	-	2-1	2-2	-	(08-06-01)
Brighton v Watford	-	-	-	-	-	2-2	(05-01-02)
Bristol C v Peterborough	-	-	-	1-1	-	1-2	(06-02-03)
Burnley v Leicester	0-1	1-1	-	-	3-0	1-3	(02-02-03)
Cardiff v Millwall	-	-	-	-	2-1	0-0	(01-03-02)
Charlton v Derby	-	-	2-2	-	-	-	(04-03-04)
Huddersfield v Sheff Weds	-	-	-	-	1-0	0-2	(02-01-01)
Hull v Leeds	1-2	-	-	-	2-2	0-0	(01-02-03)
Middlesboro v Blackpool	-	-	-	0-3	-	2-2	(00-01-01)
Nottm F v C Palace	-	-	0-2	2-0	3-0	0-1	(09-02-04)
Wolves v Ipswich	1-0	1-1	0-0	-	-	-	(06-07-01)

LEAGUE 1

Home v Away							
Bournemouth v Crawley	-	-	-	-	-	-	(None)
Carlisle v Bury	-	-	-	-	-	4-1	(05-00-02)
Colchester v Swindon	-	-	3-2	3-0	2-1	-	(05-00-04)
Leyton O v Walsall	-	1-0	0-1	2-0	0-0	1-1	(02-03-01)
MK Dons v Coventry	-	-	-	-	-	-	(03-04-08)
Oldham v Crewe	1-0	3-2	1-1	-	-	-	(02-01-01)
Portsmouth v Yeovil	-	-	-	-	-	-	(None)
Preston v Doncaster	-	-	1-0	1-1	0-2	-	(03-02-01)
Sheff Utd v Hartlepool	-	-	-	-	-	3-1	(01-00-00)
Shrewsbury v Brentford	-	0-1	1-3	-	-	-	(05-01-03)
Stevenage v Notts Co	-	-	-	-	-	0-2	(00-00-01)
Tranmere v Scunthorpe	0-2	-	2-0	-	-	1-1	(02-01-02)

LEAGUE 2

Home team v Away team							Since 1988
Wimbledon v Oxford Utd	-	-	-	0-1	-	0-2	(00-00-02)
Aldershot v Torquay	-	0-3	-	0-2	1-0	0-1	(01-00-03)
Bradford v Rochdale	-	1-2	2-0	0-3	-	-	(01-00-02)
Burton v Southend	-	-	-	-	3-1	0-2	(01-00-01)
Cheltenham v Bristol R	-	1-0	2-1	-	-	0-2	(02-02-03)
Chesterfield v Morecambe	-	2-2	1-2	1-1	0-2	-	(00-02-02)
Dagenham v Port Vale	-	-	1-1	1-1	-	1-2	(00-02-01)
Exeter v Barnet	-	-	2-1	-	-	-	(04-05-02)
Fleetwood v York	-	-	-	-	2-1	0-0	(01-01-00)
Gillingham v Northampton	0-1	0-1	-	-	1-0	4-3	(07-02-04)
Plymouth v Wycombe	-	-	-	-	-	-	(03-02-00)
Rotherham v Accrington	-	0-1	0-0	1-0	2-0	1-0	(03-01-01)

SCOTTISH PREMIER LEAGUE

Home team v Away team							Since 1988
Club 12 v Aberdeen	-	-	-	-	-	-	(None)
Dundee Utd v St Mirren	1-0/0-2	2-0/1-1	2-0/3-2	3-2	1-2	1-1/0-0	(12-05-05)
Hibernian v Celtic	2-2/2-1	3-2/0-2	2-0/0-0	0-1/0-1	0-3	0-2/0-5	(08-10-26)
Motherwell v Kilmarnock	5-0/0-1	1-2/1-0	0-2/1-2	3-1/1-0	0-1/1-1	0-0	(14-08-12)
Ross County v Hearts	-	-	-	-	-	-	(None)
St Johnstone v Inverness	-	-	-	-	1-0/0-3	2-0/0-0	(05-01-02)

SCOTTISH DIVISION ONE

Home team v Away team							Since 1988
Dundee v Partick	0-1/3-1	3-0/1-0	0-0/4-0	2-0/1-0	2-1/3-2	0-1/0-3	(13-05-08)
Falkirk v Dumbarton	-	-	-	-	-	-	(01-01-00)
Morton v Dunfermline	-	0-1/3-0	1-1/2-1	0-2/1-2	2-1/0-2	-	(06-04-07)
Livingston v Hamilton	0-1/1-2	2-0/1-3	-	-	-	1-0/0-4	(04-03-08)
Raith v Cowdenbeath	1-3/1-2	2-0/3-2	-	-	2-1/2-2	-	(07-01-02)

SCOTTISH DIVISION TWO

Home team v Away team							Since 1988
Airdrie v Brechin	-	2-1/1-2	-	-	1-1/2-2	2-3/4-1	(06-03-04)
Arbroath v Albion	2-3/0-0	1-0/1-4	-	-	1-1/3-0	6-2/6-1	(12-05-07)
Ayr v Alloa	0-1/4-3	2-0/3-1	3-0/1-1	-	2-1/1-0	-	(11-03-03)
Forfar v East Fife	-	0-2/2-3	-	-	3-2/0-0	3-2/1-4	(06-02-11)
Stenhsmuir v Queen of Sth	-	-	-	-	-	-	(10-04-07)

SCOTTISH DIVISION THREE

Home team v Away team							Since 1988
Annan v Elgin	-	-	5-0/6-0	0-2/3-3	0-1/2-2	1-1/1-1	(02-04-02)
Clyde v Berwick	-	-	-	-	1-4/2-0	1-4/2-2	(06-02-05)
Montrose v Stirling	-	-	-	-	-	-	(03-04-08)
Peterhead v E Stirling	-	-	-	-	-	1-0/2-0	(10-00-02)
Queen's Park v Stranraer	-	-	2-2/1-1	1-2/2-5	1-3/3-3	2-0/3-2	(07-06-08)

CONFERENCE

Home team v Away team							Since 1988
Barrow v Macclesfield	-	-	-	-	-	-	(01-02-00)
Braintree v Woking	-	-	-	1-0	2-0	-	(02-00-00)
Dartford v Cambridge U	-	-	-	-	-	-	(None)
Forest G v Kidderminstr	2-1	2-2	2-2	1-1	1-1	1-1	(03-06-00)
Hereford v Newport Co	-	-	-	-	-	-	(None)
Lincoln v Gateshead	-	-	-	-	-	1-0	(01-00-00)
Luton v Ebbsfleet	-	-	-	2-3	-	3-0	(01-00-01)
Mansfield v Grimsby	1-2	1-2	-	-	0-2	2-1	(03-01-03)
Nuneaton v Alfreton	1-0	1-0	-	-	1-3	-	(03-01-01)
Southport v Hyde	-	2-1	2-0	4-1	-	-	(05-02-01)
Stockport v Telford	-	-	-	-	-	2-2	(00-01-00)
Wrexham v Tamworth	-	-	-	0-0	4-2	3-0	(02-01-00)

TUESDAY 1ST JANUARY 2013

PREMIER LEAGUE

Match							
Chelsea v QPR	-	-	-	-	-	6-1	(06-02-00)
Liverpool v Sunderland	-	3-0	2-0	3-0	2-2	1-1	(06-06-00)
Man City v Stoke	-	-	3-0	2-0	3-0	3-0	(07-00-01)
Newcastle v Everton	1-1	3-2	0-0	-	1-2	2-1	(12-04-03)
Southampton v Arsenal	-	-	-	-	-	-	(05-04-08)
Swansea v Aston Villa	-	-	-	-	-	0-0	(00-01-00)
Tottenham v Reading	1-0	6-4	-	-	-	-	(02-00-00)
West Brom v Fulham	-	-	1-0	-	2-1	0-0	(04-04-02)
West Ham v Norwich	-	-	-	-	-	-	(01-03-01)
Wigan v Man Utd	1-3	0-2	1-2	0-5	0-4	1-0	(01-00-06)

CHAMPIONSHIP

Match							
Birmingham v Cardiff	1-0	-	1-1	-	-	1-1	(02-03-00)
Blackburn v Nottm F	-	-	-	-	-	-	(05-01-01)
Blackpool v Hull	-	2-1	-	-	-	1-1	(04-02-02)
C Palace v Wolves	2-2	0-2	0-1	-	-	-	(03-04-05)
Derby v Middlesboro	-	0-1	-	2-2	3-1	0-1	(05-02-06)
Ipswich v Brighton	-	-	-	-	-	3-1	(04-01-03)
Leeds v Bolton	-	-	-	-	-	-	(01-01-03)
Leicester v Huddersfield	-	-	4-2	-	-	-	(02-00-00)
Millwall v Bristol C	1-0	-	-	-	0-0	1-2	(03-04-05)
Peterborough v Barnsley	-	-	-	1-2	-	3-4	(01-01-05)
Sheff Weds v Burnley	1-1	0-2	4-1	-	-	-	(02-02-03)
Watford v Charlton	2-2	1-1	1-0	-	-	-	(04-04-01)

LEAGUE 1

Match							
Brentford v Bournemouth	0-0	-	2-0	-	1-1	1-1	(08-06-03)
Bury v Tranmere	-	-	-	-	-	2-0	(03-01-02)
Coventry v Shrewsbury	-	-	-	-	-	-	(None)
Crawley v Colchester	-	-	-	-	-	-	(None)
Crewe v Carlisle	5-1	0-1	1-2	-	-	-	(05-00-03)
Doncaster v Sheff Utd	-	-	0-2	1-1	2-0	-	(01-01-01)
Hartlepool v Preston	-	-	-	-	-	0-1	(02-01-02)
Notts Co v MK Dons	2-2	1-2	-	-	2-0	1-1	(01-03-01)
Scunthorpe v Oldham	1-1	-	2-0	-	-	1-2	(02-01-02)
Swindon v Portsmouth	-	-	-	-	-	-	(02-04-04)
Walsall v Stevenage	-	-	-	-	-	1-1	(00-01-00)
Yeovil v Leyton O	2-1	0-1	0-0	3-3	2-1	2-2	(03-03-02)

LEAGUE 2

Match							
Accrington v Chesterfield	-	2-1	1-0	2-0	2-2	-	(03-01-00)
Barnet v Aldershot	-	-	0-3	3-0	1-2	2-1	(04-00-02)
Bristol R v Plymouth	-	-	-	-	2-3	2-3	(02-04-03)
Morecambe v Bradford	-	2-1	2-1	0-0	0-1	1-1	(02-02-01)
Northampton v Dagenham	-	-	-	1-0	-	2-1	(02-00-00)
Oxford Utd v Cheltenham	-	-	-	-	1-1	1-3	(03-02-01)
Port Vale v Fleetwood	-	-	-	-	-	-	(None)
Rochdale v Rotherham	-	4-1	1-2	4-0	-	-	(02-02-04)
Southend v Gillingham	-	3-0	-	1-0	2-2	1-0	(05-02-01)
Torquay v Wimbledon	-	-	-	-	-	4-0	(01-00-00)
Wycombe v Exeter	-	-	1-1	2-2	-	3-1	(01-02-00)
York v Burton	3-2	0-0	1-3	-	-	-	(01-01-03)

CONFERENCE

Alfreton v Mansfield	-	-	-	-	-	3-6 (00-00-01)
Cambridge U v Braintree	-	-	-	-	-	2-0 (01-00-00)
Ebbsfleet v Dartford	-	-	-	-	2-1	- (01-00-00)
Gateshead v Barrow	-	-	-	2-1	3-0	2-0 (04-04-02)
Grimsby v Lincoln	0-0	1-0	5-1	2-2	-	3-1 (06-02-01)
Hyde v Stockport	-	-	-	-	-	(None)
Kidderminstr v Hereford	-	-	-	-	-	(01-02-01)
Macclesfield v Southport	-	-	-	-	-	(03-00-01)
Newport Co v Forest G	-	-	-	-	3-1	0-0 (01-01-00)
Telford v Wrexham	-	-	-	-	-	0-2 (00-00-01)
Woking v Luton	-	-	-	-	-	(None)

WEDNESDAY 2ND JANUARY 2013

SCOTTISH PREMIER LEAGUE

Aberdeen v Dundee Utd	3-1/2-4	2-0/2-1	0-1/2-2	0-2/2-2	1-1	3-1/3-1 (21-09-13)
Celtic v Motherwell	2-1/1-0	3-0/0-1	2-0	0-0/2-1/4-0	1-0/4-0	4-0/1-0 (29-09-07)
Hearts v Hibernian	3-2/2-0	0-1/1-0	0-0/0-1	0-0/2-1	1-0	2-0/2-0 (24-13-06)
Ross County v Inverness	-	-	-	2-1/0-0	-	(06-03-07)
St Johnstone v Club 12	-	-	-	-	-	(None)
St Mirren v Kilmarnock	0-1/0-2	0-0/1-0	0-0/1-1	1-0/1-0	0-2	3-0/4-2 (06-03-06)

SCOTTISH DIVISION ONE

Dundee v Cowdenbeath	-	-	-	-	3-0/2-2	- (01-01-00)
Dunfermline v Raith	-	-	-	0-2/2-1	2-2/2-1	- (06-03-05)
Falkirk v Livingston	-	-	-	-	-	4-3/2-5 (06-04-03)
Morton v Dumbarton	-	-	-	-	-	(09-03-02)
Partick v Hamilton	3-1/0-2	0-3/3-0	-	-	-	1-1/2-0 (05-07-05)

SCOTTISH DIVISION TWO

Albion v Airdrie	-	-	-	-	-	7-2/0-1 (01-00-03)
Alloa v Stenhsmuir	-	-	-	1-4/2-1	1-0/1-2	- (09-02-07)
Arbroath v East Fife	1-1/1-3	2-3/0-1	0-1/0-2	0-1/2-2	-	3-0/2-2 (07-06-12)
Ayr v Queen of Sth	-	-	-	0-1/3-0	-	1-0/1-1 (05-04-04)
Forfar v Brechin	1-2/3-2	-	-	-	1-1/2-1	0-0/4-1 (08-04-05)

SCOTTISH DIVISION THREE

Annan v Stranraer	-	-	-	1-0/3-2	2-2/2-1	0-3/1-3 (03-01-02)
E Stirling v Stirling	-	-	-	-	-	(01-03-06)
Elgin v Peterhead	-	-	-	-	-	6-1/1-2 (04-01-07)
Montrose v Berwick	0-1/1-2	-	1-1/1-1	1-3/1-1	1-1/1-1	3-5/1-1 (03-09-15)
Queen's Park v Clyde	-	-	-	-	0-1/4-0	3-0/3-0 (04-00-03)

CONFERENCE

Tamworth v Nuneaton	-	1-2	-	-	-	- (01-01-01)

SATURDAY 5TH JANUARY 2013

LEAGUE 1

Brentford v Leyton O	2-2	-	-	1-0	2-1	5-0 (07-02-01)
Bury v Sheff Utd	-	-	-	-	-	0-3 (00-02-02)
Coventry v Tranmere	-	-	-	-	-	(None)
Crawley v Preston	-	-	-	-	-	(None)
Crewe v Stevenage	-	-	-	-	0-1	- (00-00-01)

Home team / Away team							Since 1988 – HW D AW
Doncaster v Colchester	-	-	-	-	-	-	(05-03-02)
Hartlepool v Bournemouth	-	1-1	-	-	2-2	0-0	(04-05-01)
Notts Co v Oldham	-	-	-	-	0-2	1-0	(04-01-06)
Scunthorpe v Shrewsbury	-	-	-	-	-	-	(04-03-01)
Swindon v Carlisle	-	2-2	1-1	2-0	0-1	-	(02-02-01)
Walsall v Portsmouth	-	-	-	-	-	-	(01-02-01)
Yeovil v MK Dons	-	-	0-0	1-0	1-0	0-1	(02-02-01)

LEAGUE 2

Home team / Away team							Since 1988 – HW D AW
Accrington v Dagenham	-	1-0	0-0	0-1	-	3-0	(03-01-03)
Barnet v Bradford	-	2-1	4-1	2-2	0-2	0-4	(02-01-03)
Bristol R v Gillingham	-	1-1	-	2-1	-	2-2	(03-03-02)
Morecambe v Aldershot	2-1	-	2-0	1-0	1-1	2-0	(06-02-00)
Northampton v Fleetwood	-	-	-	-	-	-	(None)
Oxford Utd v Burton	0-0	0-3	2-1	-	3-0	2-2	(02-02-01)
Port Vale v Plymouth	-	-	-	-	-	1-0	(06-00-02)
Rochdale v Wimbledon	-	-	-	-	-	-	(None)
Southend v Cheltenham	-	2-2	2-0	-	1-2	4-0	(04-01-04)
Torquay v Rotherham	-	-	-	0-2	1-1	3-3	(02-02-03)
Wycombe v Chesterfield	-	1-0	1-1	-	1-2	3-2	(07-04-02)
York v Exeter	0-0	3-2	-	-	-	-	(05-02-04)

SCOTTISH DIVISION ONE

Home team / Away team							Since 1988 – HW D AW
Cowdenbeath v Morton	1-2/1-1	-	-	-	2-2/0-2	-	(00-04-04)
Dumbarton v Dunfermline	-	-	-	-	-	-	(00-01-05)
Hamilton v Falkirk	-	-	1-1/0-1	0-0/2-2	-	0-1/0-1	(03-07-07)
Livingston v Partick	2-2/0-1	0-4/1-0	3-1/2-4	-	-	2-1/3-1	(08-07-05)
Raith v Dundee	-	-	-	2-2/1-0	1-2/2-1	0-1/0-1	(04-06-05)

SCOTTISH DIVISION TWO

Home team / Away team							Since 1988 – HW D AW
Airdrie v Ayr	-	0-0/0-2	-	3-1/1-1	2-2/0-5	-	(08-11-05)
Brechin v Alloa	2-0/2-3	0-0/0-0	3-1/1-0	2-1/1-1	3-1/3-2	-	(11-03-06)
East Fife v Albion	2-2/1-3	4-0/0-0	-	-	-	2-0/1-2	(10-09-06)
Queen of Sth v Arbroath	-	-	-	-	-	-	(07-04-04)
Stenhsmuir v Forfar	-	4-0/2-0	1-1/0-1	-	3-0/0-1	2-3/1-2	(09-04-10)

SCOTTISH DIVISION THREE

Home team / Away team							Since 1988 – HW D AW
Berwick v E Stirling	2-2/2-0	-	2-1/1-2	0-1/2-2	3-0/1-1	4-2/0-2	(13-06-08)
Clyde v Annan	-	-	-	-	0-2/0-2	0-0/1-1	(00-02-02)
Peterhead v Montrose	-	-	-	-	-	2-3/2-1	(08-02-02)
Stirling v Queen's Park	-	-	0-3/4-0	-	-	-	(08-03-04)
Stranraer v Elgin	-	3-3/0-0	-	0-2/2-1	2-1/1-2	1-0/5-2	(06-02-02)

CONFERENCE

Home team / Away team							Since 1988 – HW D AW
Alfreton v Dartford	-	-	-	-	-	-	(None)
Cambridge U v Stockport	-	-	-	-	-	2-2	(01-02-02)
Ebbsfleet v Lincoln	-	-	-	-	-	2-3	(00-00-01)
Gateshead v Nuneaton	-	-	-	-	-	-	(None)
Grimsby v Hereford	2-1	2-1	-	1-0	-	-	(03-01-01)
Hyde v Forest G	-	-	-	-	-	-	(None)
Kidderminstr v Barrow	-	-	0-1	1-2	2-0	1-2	(02-01-05)
Macclesfield v Luton	-	-	2-1	-	-	-	(02-01-00)
Newport Co v Wrexham	-	-	-	-	1-1	0-1	(00-01-01)
Tamworth v Braintree	-	-	-	-	-	1-0	(01-00-00)
Telford v Southport	-	1-5	1-0	0-2	-	0-1	(05-04-05)
Woking v Mansfield	-	-	2-2	-	-	-	(00-01-00)

SATURDAY 12TH JANUARY 2013

PREMIER LEAGUE

Home v Away							
Arsenal v Man City	3-1	1-0	2-0	0-0	0-0	1-0	(13-05-00)
Aston Villa v Southampton	-	-	-	-	-	-	(08-05-04)
Everton v Swansea	-	-	-	-	-	1-0	(01-00-00)
Fulham v Wigan	0-1	1-1	2-0	2-1	2-0	2-1	(11-04-02)
Man Utd v Liverpool	2-0	3-0	1-4	2-1	3-2	2-1	(13-06-05)
Norwich v Newcastle	-	-	-	-	-	4-2	(03-00-02)
QPR v Tottenham	-	-	-	-	-	1-0	(05-02-02)
Reading v West Brom	-	-	-	1-1	--	-	(03-03-02)
Stoke v Chelsea	-	-	0-2	1-2	1-1	0-0	(00-02-03)
Sunderland v West Ham	-	2-1	0-1	2-2	1-0	-	(06-05-03)

CHAMPIONSHIP

Barnsley v Leeds	3-2	-	-	-	5-2	4-1	(04-01-01)
Bolton v Millwall	-	-	-	-	-	-	(02-00-00)
Brighton v Derby	-	-	-	-	-	2-0	(02-01-02)
Bristol C v Leicester	-	0-2	-	1-1	2-0	3-2	(05-01-02)
Burnley v C Palace	1-1	1-1	4-2	-	1-0	1-1	(03-05-02)
Cardiff v Ipswich	2-2	1-0	0-3	1-2	0-2	2-2	(02-02-05)
Charlton v Blackpool	-	4-1	2-2	-	-	-	(01-01-00)
Huddersfield v Birmingham	-	-	-	-	-	-	(03-02-05)
Hull v Sheff Weds	2-1	1-0	-	-	-	-	(03-00-02)
Middlesboro v Watford	4-1	-	-	0-1	2-1	1-0	(04-02-04)
Nottm F v Peterborough	-	-	-	1-0	-	0-1	(02-00-01)
Wolves v Blackburn	-	-	-	1-1	2-3	0-2	(01-04-04)

LEAGUE 1

Bournemouth v Swindon	-	2-2	-	-	3-2	-	(04-04-02)
Carlisle v Coventry	-	-	-	-	-	-	(None)
Colchester v Scunthorpe	-	0-1	0-0	-	-	1-1	(06-04-03)
Leyton O v Crewe	1-1	0-1	1-0	-	-	-	(03-02-02)
MK Dons v Bury	2-1	1-2	-	-	-	2-1	(02-00-01)
Oldham v Brentford	3-0	-	-	2-3	2-1	0-2	(06-02-04)
Portsmouth v Notts Co	-	-	-	-	-	-	(02-02-00)
Preston v Walsall	-	-	-	-	-	0-0	(05-03-02)
Sheff Utd v Yeovil	-	-	-	-	-	4-0	(01-00-00)
Shrewsbury v Hartlepool	1-1	-	-	-	-	-	(01-03-04)
Stevenage v Doncaster	-	-	-	-	-	-	(02-02-01)
Tranmere v Crawley	-	-	-	-	-	-	(None)

LEAGUE 2

Wimbledon v Wycombe	-	-	-	-	-	-	(None)
Aldershot v Accrington	-	-	3-1	3-1	1-1	0-0	(03-03-01)
Bradford v Oxford Utd	-	-	-	-	5-0	2-1	(04-03-02)
Burton v Torquay	-	3-1	0-1	0-2	3-3	1-4	(01-01-03)
Cheltenham v York	-	-	-	-	-	-	(01-02-01)
Chesterfield v Northampton	0-0	-	-	1-0	2-1	-	(06-05-02)
Dagenham v Rochdale	-	1-1	3-2	1-2	0-1	-	(01-01-02)
Exeter v Southend	-	-	-	1-0	-	-	(05-01-02)
Fleetwood v Bristol R	-	-	-	-	-	-	(None)
Gillingham v Port Vale	3-2	1-2	1-0	-	3-0	1-1	(05-01-01)
Plymouth v Morecambe	-	-	-	-	-	1-1	(00-01-00)
Rotherham v Barnet	-	1-0	3-4	3-0	0-0	2-2	(04-04-02)

SCOTTISH DIVISION ONE

Dumbarton v Partick	-	-	-	-	-	-	(00-00-02)

Home team / Away team	Six-season fixture record, latest result at right						Since 1988 – HW D AW
Dunfermline v Dundee	-	0-1/0-1	0-1/1-1	1-1/2-1	3-1/0-0	-	(13-05-06)
Falkirk v Morton	-	-	-	-	2-1/1-0	1-0/0-2	(13-02-05)
Hamilton v Cowdenbeath	-	-	-	-	-	-	(05-02-01)
Livingston v Raith	-	-	-	-	-	1-1/4-0	(05-05-05)

SCOTTISH DIVISION TWO

Home team / Away team							
Albion v Queen of Sth	-	-	-	-	-	-	(02-03-01)
Arbroath v Alloa	-	-	4-1/1-0	2-2/0-0	-	-	(09-10-10)
East Fife v Brechin	-	-	0-0/2-1	2-0/2-0	1-3/0-0	1-1/2-2	(13-07-04)
Forfar v Ayr	0-1/1-1	-	-	-	4-1/3-2	-	(08-03-06)
Stenhsmuir v Airdrie	-	-	-	-	1-3/1-0	1-1/0-3	(02-02-04)

SCOTTISH DIVISION THREE

Home team / Away team							
Annan v Montrose	-	-	1-2/2-1	2-0/0-0	2-2/2-1	2-1/1-2	(04-02-02)
Clyde v Stirling	-	1-3/3-0	-	0-1/1-2	-	-	(07-01-06)
Elgin v E Stirling	5-0/2-1	6-0/3-0	0-4/0-2	1-2/0-1	0-2/2-0	2-0/3-1	(14-03-07)
Queen's Park v Peterhead	-	1-1/2-0	0-1/2-1	-	-	1-1/0-1	(05-03-06)
Stranraer v Berwick	-	-	-	2-4/3-1	1-1/3-1	2-1/1-3	(08-11-08)

CONFERENCE

Home team / Away team							
Barrow v Woking	-	-	0-1	-	-	-	(00-00-02)
Braintree v Telford	-	-	-	-	-	2-1	(01-00-00)
Dartford v Macclesfield	-	-	-	-	-	-	(None)
Forest G v Gateshead	-	-	-	1-0	1-1	2-1	(02-01-00)
Hereford v Alfreton	-	-	-	-	-	-	(None)
Lincoln v Newport Co	-	-	-	-	-	2-0	(01-00-00)
Luton v Hyde	-	-	-	-	-	-	(None)
Mansfield v Kidderminstr	-	-	4-2	3-3	1-2	0-3	(04-02-02)
Nuneaton v Grimsby	-	-	-	-	-	-	(None)
Southport v Cambridge U	1-2	-	-	-	1-1	1-0	(01-02-01)
Stockport v Tamworth	-	-	-	-	-	2-0	(01-00-00)
Wrexham v Ebbsfleet	-	-	3-2	1-1	-	1-0	(02-01-00)

FRIDAY 18TH JANUARY 2013

LEAGUE 2

Home team / Away team							
Morecambe v Cheltenham	-	-	-	1-0	1-1	3-1	(03-01-01)

SATURDAY 19TH JANUARY 2013

PREMIER LEAGUE

Home team / Away team							
Chelsea v Arsenal	1-1	2-1	1-2	2-0	2-0	3-5	(08-08-07)
Liverpool v Norwich	-	-	-	-	-	1-1	(05-02-02)
Man City v Fulham	3-1	2-3	1-3	2-2	1-1	3-0	(05-04-03)
Newcastle v Reading	3-2	3-0	-	3-0	-	-	(03-00-00)
Southampton v Everton	-	-	-	-	-	-	(06-07-04)
Swansea v Stoke	-	-	-	-	-	2-0	(04-00-01)
Tottenham v Man Utd	0-4	1-1	0-0	1-3	0-0	1-3	(04-06-14)
West Brom v Aston Villa	-	-	1-2	-	2-1	0-0	(01-03-02)
West Ham v QPR	-	-	-	-	-	-	(02-03-01)
Wigan v Sunderland	-	3-0	1-1	1-0	1-1	1-4	(03-03-02)

CHAMPIONSHIP

Home team / Away team							
Birmingham v Brighton	-	-	-	-	-	0-0	(00-02-01)
Blackburn v Charlton	4-1	-	-	-	-	-	(06-02-02)
Blackpool v Cardiff	-	0-1	1-1	1-1	-	1-1	(07-06-01)
C Palace v Bolton	-	-	-	-	-	-	(00-05-02)

Home team / Away team	Six-season fixture record, latest result at right						Since 1988 – HW D AW
Derby v Nottm F	-	-	1-1	1-0	0-1	1-0	(06-03-04)
Ipswich v Barnsley	5-1	0-0	3-0	1-0	1-3	1-0	(09-03-02)
Leeds v Bristol C	-	-	-	-	3-1	2-1	(02-00-00)
Leicester v Middlesboro	-	-	-	2-0	0-0	2-2	(06-03-04)
Millwall v Burnley	-	-	-	-	1-1	0-1	(04-04-04)
Peterborough v Hull	-	-	-	-	-	0-1	(05-01-02)
Sheff Weds v Wolves	2-2	1-3	0-1	-	-	-	(00-03-05)
Watford v Huddersfield	-	-	-	-	-	-	(00-01-02)

LEAGUE 1

Home team / Away team							
Brentford v Tranmere	1-1	-	-	2-1	2-1	0-2	(05-02-05)
Bury v Stevenage	-	-	-	-	3-0	1-2	(01-00-01)
Coventry v Oldham	-	-	-	-	-	-	(01-02-00)
Crawley v Carlisle	-	-	-	-	-	-	(01-00-00)
Crewe v MK Dons	-	-	2-2	-	-	-	(01-01-02)
Doncaster v Leyton O	0-0	4-2	-	-	-	-	(05-01-01)
Hartlepool v Colchester	-	-	4-2	3-1	1-0	0-1	(09-01-03)
Notts Co v Sheff Utd	-	-	-	-	-	2-5	(01-00-03)
Scunthorpe v Portsmouth	-	-	-	-	1-1	-	(00-01-00)
Swindon v Shrewsbury	2-1	-	-	-	-	2-1	(03-00-01)
Walsall v Bournemouth	-	1-3	-	-	0-1	2-2	(03-04-04)
Yeovil v Preston	-	-	-	-	-	2-1	(01-00-00)

LEAGUE 2

Home team / Away team							
Accrington v Wimbledon	-	-	-	-	-	2-1	(01-00-00)
Barnet v Fleetwood	-	-	-	-	-	-	(None)
Bristol R v Exeter	-	-	-	1-0	0-2	-	(01-03-01)
Northampton v Burton	-	-	-	1-1	2-3	2-3	(00-01-02)
Oxford Utd v Rotherham	-	-	-	-	2-1	2-1	(04-01-00)
Port Vale v Bradford	0-1	-	0-2	2-1	2-1	3-2	(04-04-05)
Rochdale v Gillingham	-	-	0-1	-	-	-	(05-01-02)
Southend v Plymouth	1-1	-	-	-	-	2-0	(05-02-01)
Torquay v Chesterfield	-	-	-	2-0	0-0	-	(04-05-00)
Wycombe v Dagenham	-	0-1	2-1	-	-	-	(02-00-01)
York v Aldershot	1-0	2-0	-	-	-	-	(03-00-01)

SCOTTISH PREMIER LEAGUE

Home team / Away team							
Celtic v Hearts	2-1/1-3	5-0/3-0	1-1/0-0	2-1/2-0	3-0/4-0	1-0/5-0	(30-13-05)
Hibernian v Club 12	-	-	-	-	-	-	(None)
Inverness v Aberdeen	1-1	1-2/3-4	0-3	-	2-0/0-2	2-1/0-2	(02-02-08)
Kilmarnock v Dundee Utd	0-0/1-0	2-1/1-2	2-0	0-2/4-4	1-2/1-1	1-1	(13-09-09)
Motherwell v St Johnstone	-	-	-	1-3	4-0	0-3/3-2/5-1	(12-05-07)
St Mirren v Ross County	-	-	-	-	-	-	(06-03-01)

SCOTTISH DIVISION ONE

Home team / Away team							
Cowdenbeath v Dunfermline	-	-	-	-	0-1	-	(00-00-03)
Dundee v Dumbarton	-	-	-	-	-	-	(01-01-00)
Morton v Livingston	-	2-2/1-1	1-2/2-2	-	-	2-1/1-3	(09-06-06)
Partick v Falkirk	-	-	-	-	1-0/1-2	2-2/1-1	(09-06-08)
Raith v Hamilton	-	-	-	-	-	3-2/2-1	(08-07-04)

SCOTTISH DIVISION TWO

Home team / Away team							
Airdrie v Arbroath	-	-	-	-	-	3-3/2-0	(04-01-01)
Alloa v East Fife	-	-	0-3/0-1	0-0/2-0	3-2/1-3	-	(06-05-06)
Ayr v Stenhsmuir	-	-	-	-	2-0/4-3	-	(03-01-02)
Brechin v Albion	-	-	-	-	-	1-4/2-1	(11-01-05)
Queen of Sth v Forfar	-	-	-	-	-	-	(06-03-06)

Home team	Away team	Six-season fixture record, latest result at right						Since 1988 – HW D AW

SCOTTISH DIVISION THREE

Home team	Away team							Since 1988
Berwick v Elgin		3-1/0-0	-	1-1/2-1	2-0/2-1	6-2/4-0	1-1/3-3	(07-05-00)
E Stirling v Queen's Park		2-1/0-2	-	-	1-0/0-3	0-1/3-2	1-3/1-2	(16-07-16)
Montrose v Clyde		-	-	-	-	8-1/3-1	4-0/5-0	(04-01-02)
Peterhead v Stranraer		5-2/5-0	-	4-0/1-0	-	-	1-3/1-1	(05-01-02)
Stirling v Annan		-	-	-	-	-	-	(None)

CONFERENCE

Home team	Away team							Since 1988
Braintree v Grimsby		-	-	-	-	-	5-0	(01-00-00)
Ebbsfleet v Tamworth		4-1	-	-	0-1	-	3-0	(05-00-01)
Gateshead v Woking		-	-	-	-	-	-	(02-02-02)
Hereford v Dartford		-	-	-	-	-	-	(None)
Hyde v Cambridge U		-	-	-	-	-	-	(None)
Lincoln v Wrexham		0-3	2-4	-	-	-	1-2	(04-04-03)
Macclesfield v Kidderminstr		-	-	-	-	-	-	(03-06-05)
Newport Co v Barrow		-	-	-	-	5-0	2-2	(01-01-00)
Nuneaton v Luton		-	-	-	-	-	-	(None)
Southport v Mansfield		-	-	-	-	1-2	3-1	(01-00-01)
Stockport v Forest G		-	-	-	-	-	0-1	(00-00-01)
Telford v Alfreton		-	3-0	0-0	2-0	2-1	1-0	(04-01-00)

TUESDAY 22ND JANUARY 2013

CONFERENCE

Home team	Away team							Since 1988
Barrow v Stockport		-	-	-	-	-	1-0	(01-00-00)
Cambridge U v Ebbsfleet		3-0	1-1	1-0	4-0	-	2-0	(04-02-00)
Dartford v Braintree		-	-	-	-	1-0	-	(01-00-00)
Forest G v Hereford		-	-	-	-	-	-	(01-03-04)
Grimsby v Hyde		-	-	-	-	-	-	(None)
Luton v Lincoln		-	-	3-2	-	-	1-0	(02-01-01)
Mansfield v Nuneaton		-	-	-	-	-	-	(None)
Tamworth v Macclesfield		-	-	-	-	-	-	(None)
Telford v Gateshead		4-0	-	1-0	-	-	1-2	(04-05-03)
Woking v Newport Co		-	-	-	0-1	-	-	(00-00-01)
Wrexham v Southport		-	-	-	-	2-1	2-0	(02-00-00)

FRIDAY 25TH JANUARY 2013

LEAGUE 2

Home team	Away team							Since 1988
Cheltenham v Rochdale		-	-	-	1-4	-	-	(01-02-04)

SATURDAY 26TH JANUARY 2013

CHAMPIONSHIP

Home team	Away team							Since 1988
Barnsley v Millwall		-	-	-	-	1-0	1-3	(03-02-04)
Bolton v Peterborough		-	-	-	-	-	-	(01-01-00)
Brighton v Blackburn		-	-	-	-	-	-	(02-00-02)
Bristol C v Ipswich		-	2-0	1-1	0-0	0-1	0-3	(03-02-03)
Burnley v Birmingham		1-2	-	1-1	2-1	-	1-3	(01-02-03)
Cardiff v Leicester		3-2	0-1	-	2-1	2-0	0-0	(04-02-01)
Charlton v Sheff Weds		-	3-2	1-2	-	1-0	1-1	(03-01-04)
Huddersfield v C Palace		-	-	-	-	-	-	(03-01-01)
Hull v Derby		1-2	-	-	-	2-0	0-1	(02-00-02)
Middlesboro v Leeds		-	-	-	-	1-2	0-2	(01-06-05)
Nottm F v Watford		-	-	3-2	2-4	1-0	1-1	(03-03-04)
Wolves v Blackpool		-	2-1	2-0	-	4-0	-	(04-00-00)

LEAGUE 1

Home v Away							
Bournemouth v Crewe	1-0	1-0	-	1-0	-	-	(03-02-02)
Carlisle v Scunthorpe	0-2	-	1-1	-	-	0-0	(04-03-09)
Colchester v Walsall	-	-	0-2	2-1	2-0	1-0	(07-01-03)
Leyton O v Notts Co	-	-	-	-	2-0	0-3	(03-01-02)
MK Dons v Doncaster	-	-	-	-	-	-	(00-00-02)
Oldham v Yeovil	1-0	3-0	0-2	0-0	0-0	1-2	(03-02-02)
Portsmouth v Hartlepool	-	-	-	-	-	-	(None)
Preston v Coventry	1-1	1-0	2-1	3-2	2-1	-	(08-02-00)
Sheff Utd v Crawley	-	-	-	-	-	-	(None)
Shrewsbury v Bury	1-3	0-1	1-0	1-1	0-3	-	(05-05-04)
Stevenage v Brentford	-	-	-	-	-	2-1	(01-00-00)
Tranmere v Swindon	-	2-1	1-0	1-4	0-2	-	(10-03-03)

LEAGUE 2

Home v Away							
Wimbledon v Port Vale	-	-	-	-	-	3-2	(01-00-00)
Aldershot v Northampton	-	-	-	2-1	1-1	0-1	(01-01-01)
Bradford v Wycombe	-	0-1	1-0	-	1-0	-	(03-00-02)
Burton v Barnet	-	-	-	2-0	1-4	1-2	(01-01-04)
Chesterfield v Southend	-	-	-	-	2-1	-	(03-02-01)
Dagenham v Morecambe	2-1	2-0	0-2	1-1	-	1-2	(06-03-03)
Exeter v Torquay	-	4-3	-	-	-	-	(05-06-02)
Fleetwood v Oxford Utd	-	-	-	-	-	-	(None)
Gillingham v York	-	-	-	-	-	-	(01-04-02)
Plymouth v Accrington	-	-	-	-	-	2-2	(00-01-00)
Rotherham v Bristol R	-	-	-	-	-	0-1	(03-02-02)

SCOTTISH PREMIER LEAGUE

Home v Away							
Aberdeen v Hibernian	2-1/2-2	3-1/2-1	1-2/2-1	0-2	4-2/0-1	1-0/1-2	(23-07-14)
Club 12 v St Mirren	-	-	-	-	-	-	(None)
Dundee Utd v Ross County	-	-	-	-	-	-	(None)
Hearts v Motherwell	4-1	1-2	3-2/2-1	1-0/0-2	0-2/0-0/3-3	2-0/0-1	(25-13-08)
Inverness v Kilmarnock	3-4	3-1/3-0	3-1/2-1	-	1-3	2-1/1-1	(05-03-04)
St Johnstone v Celtic	-	-	-	1-4	0-3/0-1	0-2	(06-03-12)

SCOTTISH DIVISION ONE

Home v Away							
Dumbarton v Hamilton	-	-	-	-	-	-	(04-03-07)
Dunfermline v Livingston	-	0-4/1-1	1-2/1-0	-	-	-	(09-04-05)
Falkirk v Dundee	-	-	-	-	3-3/2-2	2-1/1-1	(04-07-01)
Morton v Raith	2-0/1-0	-	-	5-0/1-1	0-1/0-0	1-1/1-3	(10-07-10)
Partick v Cowdenbeath	-	-	-	-	1-0/0-1	-	(01-00-01)

SCOTTISH DIVISION TWO

Home v Away							
Albion v Stenhsmuir	2-5/2-1	1-1/3-3	1-2/1-2	-	-	1-1/1-0	(04-07-10)
Alloa v Airdrie	-	0-6/1-2	-	-	2-3/1-0	-	(03-00-06)
Arbroath v Forfar	-	3-4/1-1	-	-	-	4-1/0-1	(02-09-08)
Brechin v Queen of Sth	-	-	-	-	-	-	(04-05-05)
East Fife v Ayr	-	-	3-0/0-1	-	2-3/3-2	-	(03-01-02)

SCOTTISH DIVISION THREE

Home v Away							
Annan v Peterhead	-	-	-	-	-	2-0/0-3	(01-00-01)
Berwick v Stirling	-	-	-	-	-	-	(03-08-02)
E Stirling v Clyde	-	-	-	-	0-0/2-0	1-1/0-1	(03-02-02)
Elgin v Queen's Park	1-2/0-3	-	-	0-1/0-1	4-2/0-1	2-0/1-1	(05-05-08)
Stranraer v Montrose	-	1-0/0-2	-	2-0	1-2/2-2	4-4/3-1	(11-02-05)

CONFERENCE

Home v Away							
Alfreton v Tamworth	-	1-2	1-1	-	-	5-2	(01-01-01)
Cambridge U v Grimsby	-	-	-	-	1-1	0-1	(04-01-03)

Home team & Away team							Since 1988 – HW D AW
Dartford v Barrow	-	-	-	-	-	-	(None)
Gateshead v Hereford	-	-	-	-	-	-	(00-01-00)
Hyde v Ebbsfleet	-	-	-	-	-	-	(None)
Kidderminstr v Woking	0-1	1-1	3-0	-	-	-	(07-02-03)
Lincoln v Forest G	-	-	-	-	-	1-1	(00-01-00)
Luton v Stockport	-	-	-	-	-	1-0	(02-03-00)
Macclesfield v Telford	-	-	-	-	-	-	(07-01-01)
Nuneaton v Braintree	-	-	-	-	-	-	(None)
Southport v Newport Co	-	-	-	-	2-1	1-1	(01-01-00)
Wrexham v Mansfield	0-0	1-1	2-0	2-1	1-1	1-3	(04-03-01)

TUESDAY 29TH JANUARY 2013

PREMIER LEAGUE

Arsenal v Liverpool	3-0	1-1	1-1	1-0	1-1	0-2	(09-09-06)
Aston Villa v Newcastle	2-0	4-1	1-0	-	1-0	1-1	(07-06-06)
Man Utd v Southampton	-	-	-	-	-	-	(15-02-00)
Norwich v Tottenham	-	-	-	-	-	0-2	(02-02-05)
QPR v Man City	-	-	-	-	-	2-3	(04-04-03)
Reading v Chelsea	0-1	1-2	-	-	-	-	(00-00-02)
Stoke v Wigan	-	-	2-0	2-2	0-1	2-2	(06-05-02)
Sunderland v Swansea	-	-	-	-	-	2-0	(01-00-00)

CONFERENCE

Kidderminstr v Telford	-	-	-	-	-	2-2	(06-04-03)

WEDNESDAY 30TH JANUARY 2013

PREMIER LEAGUE

Everton v West Brom	-	-	2-0	-	1-4	2-0	(04-01-01)
Fulham v West Ham	0-0	0-1	1-2	3-2	1-3	-	(01-01-06)

SCOTTISH PREMIER LEAGUE

Celtic v Kilmarnock	4-1/2-0	0-0/1-0	3-0	3-0/3-1	1-1	2-1	(26-07-00)
Hearts v Club 12	-	-	-	-	-	-	(None)
Motherwell v Dundee Utd	2-3	5-3/2-2	1-1/2-1	2-2/2-3	2-1/2-1	0-0/0-2	(19-11-15)
Ross County v Hibernian	-	-	-	-	-	-	(None)
St Johnstone v Aberdeen	-	-	-	1-0/1-1	0-1/0-0	1-2	(06-07-10)
St Mirren v Inverness	1-1/0-1	2-1/1-1	2-0/1-2	-	1-2/3-3	1-2/0-1	(04-06-08)

FRIDAY 1ST FEBRUARY 2013

LEAGUE 1

Sheff Utd v Coventry	-	2-1	1-1	1-0	0-1	-	(04-05-04)

LEAGUE 2

Bristol R v Barnet	2-0	-	-	-	-	0-2	(03-00-01)

SATURDAY 2ND FEBRUARY 2013

PREMIER LEAGUE

Arsenal v Stoke	-	-	4-1	2-0	1-0	3-1	(04-00-00)
Everton v Aston Villa	0-1	2-2	2-3	1-1	2-2	2-2	(07-10-07)
Fulham v Man Utd	1-2	0-3	2-0	3-0	2-2	0-5	(02-04-05)
Man City v Liverpool	0-0	0-0	2-3	0-0	3-0	3-0	(05-08-05)
Newcastle v Chelsea	0-0	0-2	0-2	-	1-1	0-3	(07-05-06)

Home team v Away team						Date
Home team / Away team — Six-season fixture record, latest result at right — Since 1988 – HW D AW						
QPR v Norwich	3-3	1-0	0-1	-	0-0	1-2 (07-06-05)
Reading v Sunderland	-	2-1	-	-	-	- (03-01-02)
West Brom v Tottenham	-	-	2-0	-	1-1	1-3 (02-02-02)
West Ham v Swansea	-	-	-	-	-	- (None)
Wigan v Southampton	-	-	-	-	-	- (None)

CHAMPIONSHIP

Birmingham v Nottm F	-	-	2-0	-	-	1-2 (01-01-05)
Blackburn v Bristol C	-	-	-	-	-	- (01-00-01)
Blackpool v Barnsley	-	1-1	1-0	1-2	-	1-1 (01-03-04)
C Palace v Charlton	-	0-1	1-0	-	-	- (04-01-03)
Derby v Huddersfield	-	-	-	-	-	- (01-00-00)
Ipswich v Middlesboro	-	-	-	1-1	3-3	1-1 (04-04-02)
Leeds v Cardiff	0-1	-	-	-	0-4	1-1 (00-02-03)
Leicester v Wolves	1-4	0-0	-	-	-	- (05-06-01)
Millwall v Hull	-	-	-	-	4-0	2-0 (02-02-00)
Peterborough v Burnley	-	-	-	-	-	2-1 (05-00-01)
Sheff Weds v Brighton	-	-	-	-	1-0	- (02-03-00)
Watford v Bolton	0-1	-	-	-	-	- (03-01-01)

LEAGUE 1

Bury v Doncaster	-	-	-	-	-	- (04-00-01)
Crawley v Swindon	-	-	-	-	-	0-3 (00-00-01)
Crewe v Scunthorpe	1-3	-	3-2	-	-	- (03-02-01)
Hartlepool v Notts Co	1-1	-	-	-	1-1	3-0 (02-03-00)
MK Dons v Bournemouth	-	-	-	-	2-0	2-2 (01-02-01)
Portsmouth v Colchester	-	-	-	-	-	- (None)
Preston v Shrewsbury	-	-	-	-	-	- (04-01-00)
Stevenage v Leyton O	-	-	-	-	-	0-1 (00-00-01)
Tranmere v Carlisle	0-2	2-0	4-1	0-0	2-1	1-2 (03-02-02)
Walsall v Oldham	-	0-3	1-2	3-0	1-1	0-1 (03-03-05)
Yeovil v Brentford	1-0	-	-	2-0	2-0	2-1 (04-00-01)

LEAGUE 2

Wimbledon v Burton	-	-	-	-	-	4-0 (01-00-00)
Bristol R v Barnet	2-0	-	-	-	-	0-2 (03-00-01)
Cheltenham v Torquay	-	-	-	1-1	2-2	0-1 (02-03-03)
Exeter v Aldershot	0-0	1-1	3-2	-	-	- (04-02-00)
Fleetwood v Bradford	-	-	-	-	-	- (None)
Gillingham v Wycombe	-	-	1-1	3-2	0-2	- (04-02-02)
Plymouth v Dagenham	-	-	-	-	2-1	0-0 (01-01-00)
Port Vale v Accrington	-	-	0-2	2-2	2-0	4-1 (02-01-01)
Rochdale v Chesterfield	-	0-1	2-1	2-3	-	1-1 (06-03-02)
Rotherham v Northampton	1-2	-	-	1-0	2-2	1-1 (05-02-01)
Southend v Oxford Utd	-	-	-	-	2-1	2-1 (05-02-03)
York v Morecambe	2-3	-	-	-	-	- (01-01-01)

SCOTTISH DIVISION TWO

Airdrie v East Fife	-	-	-	-	1-1/2-2	1-3/2-0 (02-05-01)
Ayr v Brechin	1-2/1-1	2-1/0-3	1-1/4-2	-	0-2/2-0	- (08-03-06)
Forfar v Albion	-	1-0/1-4	0-0/4-0	2-2/1-1	-	0-2/4-0 (11-05-02)
Queen of Sth v Alloa	-	-	-	-	-	- (03-04-07)
Stenhsmuir v Arbroath	1-2/1-2	1-0/0-3	-	3-0/1-1	-	2-0/1-3 (14-03-08)

SCOTTISH DIVISION THREE

Clyde v Elgin	-	-	-	-	1-1/3-3	1-2/0-2 (00-02-02)
Montrose v E Stirling	1-0/4-0	3-1/2-0	3-0/0-2	0-3/0-1	0-2/3-0	2-1/3-1 (26-07-09)
Peterhead v Berwick	-	4-3/9-2	-	-	-	1-0/1-2 (03-00-01)
Queen's Park v Annan	-	-	-	0-0/3-2	3-0/0-1	0-0/2-0 (03-02-01)
Stirling v Stranraer	3-3/0-2	-	3-2/1-2	-	-	- (07-06-05)

Home team	Away team	Six-season fixture record, latest result at right						Since 1988 – HW D AW

CONFERENCE

Fixture							Since 1988
Barrow v Luton	-	-	-	0-1	0-1	1-0	(01-00-02)
Braintree v Lincoln	-	-	-	-	-	1-0	(01-00-00)
Ebbsfleet v Macclesfield	-	-	-	-	-	-	(None)
Forest G v Wrexham	-	-	2-3	0-2	3-0	1-0	(02-00-02)
Grimsby v Alfreton	-	-	-	-	-	5-2	(01-00-00)
Hereford v Southport	-	-	-	-	-	-	(01-05-01)
Mansfield v Dartford	-	-	-	-	-	-	(None)
Newport Co v Kidderminstr	-	-	-	-	3-0	1-3	(01-00-01)
Stockport v Nuneaton	-	-	-	-	-	-	(None)
Tamworth v Gateshead	-	-	2-1	1-0	1-1	1-1	(02-02-00)
Telford v Cambridge U	-	-	-	-	-	1-2	(00-00-01)
Woking v Hyde	-	-	-	-	-	-	(None)

SATURDAY 9TH FEBRUARY 2013

PREMIER LEAGUE

Fixture							Since 1988
Aston Villa v West Ham	1-0	1-0	1-1	0-0	3-0	-	(08-07-03)
Chelsea v Wigan	4-0	1-1	2-1	8-0	1-0	2-1	(06-01-00)
Liverpool v West Brom	-	-	3-0	-	1-0	0-1	(05-00-01)
Man Utd v Everton	3-0	2-1	1-0	3-0	1-0	4-4	(16-05-03)
Norwich v Fulham	-	-	-	-	-	1-1	(00-01-03)
Southampton v Man City	-	-	-	-	-	-	(03-03-05)
Stoke v Reading	-	-	-	-	-	-	(06-03-06)
Sunderland v Arsenal	-	0-1	1-1	1-0	1-1	1-2	(03-05-04)
Swansea v QPR	-	-	0-0	2-0	0-0	1-1	(01-03-00)
Tottenham v Newcastle	2-3	1-4	1-0	-	2-0	5-0	(12-01-06)

CHAMPIONSHIP

Fixture							Since 1988
Blackburn v Ipswich	-	-	-	-	-	-	(04-03-02)
Blackpool v Millwall	0-1	-	-	-	-	1-0	(03-00-03)
Bolton v Burnley	-	-	-	1-0	-	-	(02-02-00)
Brighton v Hull	-	-	-	-	-	0-0	(10-04-00)
Bristol C v Nottm F	1-1	-	2-2	1-1	2-3	0-0	(00-05-02)
Charlton v Birmingham	-	-	0-0	-	-	-	(06-04-01)
Huddersfield v Cardiff	-	-	-	-	-	-	(04-01-01)
Middlesboro v Barnsley	-	-	-	2-1	1-1	2-0	(04-02-02)
Peterborough v Leicester	-	-	2-0	1-2	-	1-0	(03-01-01)
Sheff Weds v Derby	1-2	-	0-1	0-0	-	-	(02-03-06)
Watford v C Palace	-	0-2	2-0	1-3	1-1	0-2	(03-04-07)
Wolves v Leeds	1-0	-	-	-	-	-	(04-01-00)

LEAGUE 1

Fixture							Since 1988
Bournemouth v Portsmouth	-	-	-	-	-	-	(01-00-01)
Brentford v Bury	-	1-4	1-0	-	-	3-0	(05-02-04)
Carlisle v Stevenage	-	-	-	-	-	1-0	(01-00-01)
Colchester v Preston	1-0	2-1	-	-	-	3-0	(05-03-00)
Coventry v Yeovil	-	-	-	-	-	-	(None)
Doncaster v Walsall	-	2-3	-	-	-	-	(04-00-04)
Leyton O v Tranmere	3-1	3-0	0-1	2-1	0-3	0-1	(05-00-04)
Notts Co v Crewe	-	-	-	2-0	-	-	(02-01-02)
Oldham v MK Dons	-	-	2-0	2-1	1-2	2-1	(05-01-03)
Scunthorpe v Crawley	-	-	-	-	-	-	(None)
Shrewsbury v Sheff Utd	-	-	-	-	-	-	(None)
Swindon v Hartlepool	0-1	2-1	0-1	0-2	1-1	-	(02-03-03)

LEAGUE 2

Match							Since 1988
Accrington v Southend	-	-	-	-	3-1	1-2	(01-00-01)
Aldershot v Plymouth	-	-	-	-	-	0-0	(00-01-00)
Barnet v Port Vale	-	-	1-2	0-0	1-0	1-3	(01-01-03)
Bradford v Gillingham	4-2	-	2-2	-	1-0	2-2	(04-02-02)
Burton v Rotherham	-	-	-	0-1	2-4	1-1	(00-01-02)
Chesterfield v Wimbledon	-	-	-	-	-	-	(None)
Dagenham v Cheltenham	-	-	-	0-2	-	0-5	(00-00-02)
Morecambe v Exeter	2-2	-	1-1	-	-	-	(00-04-01)
Northampton v Rochdale	-	-	-	1-2	-	-	(05-03-04)
Oxford Utd v Bristol R	-	-	-	-	-	3-0	(05-04-04)
Torquay v Fleetwood	-	-	-	-	-	-	(None)
Wycombe v York	-	-	-	-	-	-	(03-01-01)

SCOTTISH PREMIER LEAGUE

Match							Since 1988
Aberdeen v St Mirren	2-0	4-0/1-1	2-0	1-0/2-1	2-0/0-1	2-2/0-0	(14-05-01)
Club 12 v Ross County	-	-	-	-	-	-	(None)
Dundee Utd v Hearts	0-1	4-1	3-0/0-1	2-0/1-0	2-0/2-1	1-0/2-2	(16-13-13)
Hibernian v St Johnstone	-	-	-	3-0/1-1	0-0/1-2	3-2/2-3	(08-07-06)
Inverness v Celtic	1-1/1-2	3-2	1-2/0-0	-	0-1/3-2	0-2	(02-03-06)
Kilmarnock v Motherwell	1-2	0-1	1-0/0-0	0-3	0-1/3-1	0-0/2-0	(14-05-14)

SCOTTISH DIVISION ONE

Match							Since 1988
Cowdenbeath v Falkirk	-	-	-	-	0-0/1-2	-	(00-01-01)
Dundee v Morton	-	2-1/2-0	1-0/0-0	1-0/3-1	2-1/1-1	0-1/0-1	(11-05-04)
Hamilton v Dunfermline	-	2-1/3-0	-	-	-	-	(04-02-04)
Livingston v Dumbarton	-	-	-	-	2-0/1-1	-	(04-03-01)
Raith v Partick	-	-	-	1-1/1-0	4-0/0-2	2-0/2-1	(11-08-06)

SCOTTISH DIVISION TWO

Match							Since 1988
Albion v Arbroath	1-3/0-3	5-2/0-2	-	-	0-2/3-0	1-0/1-1	(05-05-16)
Alloa v Ayr	0-1/1-1	2-1/1-2	0-2/3-2	-	4-1/0-1	-	(04-05-09)
Brechin v Airdrie	-	4-2/2-1	-	-	3-1/1-2	1-1/1-1	(03-05-06)
East Fife v Forfar	-	3-0/3-0	-	-	1-3/3-0	4-3/4-0	(12-03-04)
Queen of Sth v Stenhsmuir	-	-	-	-	-	-	(09-03-10)

SCOTTISH DIVISION THREE

Match							Since 1988
Berwick v Clyde	-	-	-	-	2-1/1-1	0-2/3-0	(04-03-06)
E Stirling v Peterhead	-	-	-	-	-	0-2/6-3	(03-01-08)
Elgin v Annan	-	-	1-2/0-1	1-1/1-0	2-0/2-3	3-0/1-2	(03-01-04)
Stirling v Montrose	-	-	-	-	-	-	(07-05-02)
Stranraer v Queen's Park	-	-	0-0/2-2	1-1/0-0	1-0/2-1	2-3/2-3	(10-06-05)

CONFERENCE

Match							Since 1988
Alfreton v Woking	-	-	-	-	-	-	(None)
Braintree v Hereford	-	-	-	-	-	-	(None)
Ebbsfleet v Gateshead	-	-	-	2-0	-	0-1	(01-00-01)
Grimsby v Telford	-	-	-	-	-	2-0	(01-00-00)
Hyde v Macclesfield	-	-	-	-	-	-	(None)
Kidderminstr v Cambridge U	1-0	1-0	1-3	1-0	0-0	0-0	(05-04-01)
Lincoln v Dartford	-	-	-	-	-	-	(None)
Luton v Forest G	-	-	-	2-1	6-1	1-1	(02-01-00)
Mansfield v Barrow	-	-	2-2	4-1	1-1	7-0	(02-02-00)
Newport Co v Tamworth	-	-	-	-	1-1	1-2	(02-01-03)
Nuneaton v Southport	-	0-2	-	-	-	-	(02-00-04)
Wrexham v Stockport	0-1	0-1	-	-	-	4-0	(05-01-07)

TUESDAY 12TH FEBRUARY 2013

CONFERENCE

Match							Since 1988
Cambridge U v Alfreton	-	-	-	-	-	3-0	(01-00-00)
Dartford v Luton	-	-	-	-	-	-	(None)
Forest G v Braintree	-	-	-	-	-	0-2	(00-00-01)
Gateshead v Kidderminstr	-	-	-	0-2	2-2	2-1	(07-01-03)
Hereford v Wrexham	2-0	2-0	-	-	-	-	(04-03-00)
Macclesfield v Nuneaton	-	-	-	-	-	-	(None)
Newport Co v Mansfield	-	-	-	-	1-0	1-0	(02-00-00)
Southport v Barrow	-	1-1	-	-	2-4	2-1	(02-04-02)
Stockport v Lincoln	2-0	1-3	-	-	3-4	4-0	(04-01-03)
Tamworth v Grimsby	-	-	-	-	2-1	1-1	(01-01-00)
Telford v Hyde	-	2-1	2-3	4-0	5-0	-	(03-00-01)
Woking v Ebbsfleet	2-2	1-0	1-0	-	3-0	-	(05-01-02)

FRIDAY 15TH FEBRUARY 2013

LEAGUE 2

Match							Since 1988
Exeter v Accrington	-	-	2-1	-	-	-	(02-00-02)

SATURDAY 16TH FEBRUARY 2013

CHAMPIONSHIP

Match							Since 1988
Barnsley v Brighton	-	-	-	-	-	0-0	(03-02-01)
Birmingham v Watford	-	-	3-2	-	-	3-0	(06-01-02)
Burnley v Huddersfield	-	-	-	-	-	-	(02-01-00)
Cardiff v Bristol C	-	2-1	0-0	3-0	3-2	3-1	(04-03-03)
C Palace v Middlesboro	-	-	-	1-0	1-0	0-1	(03-00-03)
Derby v Wolves	0-2	-	2-3	-	-	-	(01-03-06)
Hull v Charlton	-	1-2	-	-	-	-	(00-01-01)
Ipswich v Blackpool	-	2-1	1-1	3-1	-	2-2	(02-02-00)
Leeds v Peterborough	-	-	3-1	-	-	4-1	(02-00-00)
Leicester v Blackburn	-	-	-	-	-	-	(04-04-02)
Millwall v Sheff Weds	-	-	-	-	-	-	(04-00-02)
Nottm F v Bolton	-	-	-	-	-	-	(02-01-01)

LEAGUE 1

Match							Since 1988
Bury v Coventry	-	-	-	-	-	-	(None)
Crawley v Doncaster	-	-	-	-	-	-	(None)
Crewe v Brentford	3-1	-	-	-	-	-	(04-01-02)
Hartlepool v Leyton O	-	1-1	0-1	1-0	0-1	2-1	(10-03-04)
MK Dons v Swindon	0-1	-	1-2	2-1	2-1	-	(04-01-02)
Portsmouth v Carlisle	-	-	-	-	-	-	(None)
Preston v Bournemouth	-	-	-	-	-	1-3	(01-03-04)
Sheff Utd v Colchester	-	2-2	-	-	-	3-0	(01-01-00)
Stevenage v Oldham	-	-	-	-	-	1-0	(01-00-00)
Tranmere v Shrewsbury	-	-	-	-	-	-	(01-01-00)
Walsall v Notts Co	2-1	-	-	-	0-3	0-1	(04-02-02)
Yeovil v Scunthorpe	0-2	-	1-2	-	-	2-2	(02-01-03)

LEAGUE 2

Match							Since 1988
Wimbledon v Bradford	-	-	-	-	-	3-1	(01-00-00)
Bristol R v Wycombe	1-2	-	-	2-3	-	-	(05-00-06)
Cheltenham v Aldershot	-	-	-	1-2	1-2	2-0	(01-00-02)

Home team	Away team	Six-season fixture record, latest result at right						Since 1988 – HW D AW

Home team / Away team							Since 1988
Fleetwood v Burton	-	-	-	-	-	-	(None)
Gillingham v Dagenham	-	-	2-1	-	-	1-2	(01-00-01)
Plymouth v Oxford Utd	-	-	-	-	-	1-1	(04-03-00)
Port Vale v Morecambe	-	-	2-1	0-2	7-2	0-4	(02-00-02)
Rochdale v Torquay	2-0	-	-	2-1	-	-	(12-03-03)
Rotherham v Chesterfield	0-1	2-1	3-0	3-1	1-0	-	(04-01-04)
Southend v Northampton	-	1-1	1-0	-	1-1	2-2	(03-05-01)
York v Barnet	-	-	-	-	-	-	(04-01-00)

SCOTTISH PREMIER LEAGUE

Aberdeen v Club 12	-	-	-	-	-	-	(None)
Celtic v Dundee Utd	2-2	3-0/0-0	2-2/2-1	1-1/1-0	1-1/4-1	5-1/2-1	(31-11-02)
Hearts v Kilmarnock	0-2/1-0	1-1/0-2	1-2/3-1	1-0/1-0	0-3/0-2	0-1	(19-08-08)
Motherwell v Inverness	1-4/1-0	2-1/3-1	3-2/2-2	-	0-0	3-0/0-1	(05-02-05)
Ross County v St Johnstone	2-2/1-1	-	1-2/2-2	-	-	-	(03-05-04)
St Mirren v Hibernian	1-0/1-1	2-1	0-0/1-1	1-1	1-0/0-1	2-3/1-0	(08-06-07)

SCOTTISH DIVISION ONE

Dundee v Hamilton	1-1/1-0	1-0/1-1	-	-	-	0-1/2-2	(09-06-04)
Falkirk v Dunfermline	1-0/1-0	-	-	-	0-1/1-2	-	(07-02-05)
Morton v Partick	-	4-2/0-0	2-0/0-1	0-2/1-0	2-0/1-0	1-2/1-0	(14-04-05)
Livingston v Cowdenbeath	-	-	-	-	-	-	(03-01-01)
Raith v Dumbarton	-	-	-	-	-	-	(05-01-00)

SCOTTISH DIVISION TWO

Airdrie v Queen of Sth	2-2/0-3	-	2-0/2-0	1-1/0-1	-	-	(06-03-03)
Arbroath v Brechin	-	-	1-2/0-0	1-4/1-0	-	1-1/2-3	(03-05-08)
Ayr v Albion	-	-	-	-	-	-	(01-00-01)
Forfar v Alloa	0-2/0-2	-	-	-	1-1/3-1	-	(11-07-05)
Stenhsmuir v East Fife	0-1/3-5	2-1/0-1	-	1-1/1-1	1-1/0-2	2-1/1-0	(11-09-11)

SCOTTISH DIVISION THREE

Annan v E Stirling	-	-	2-1/4-0	0-1/1-0	3-1/2-1	3-0/2-2	(06-01-01)
Clyde v Stranraer	-	-	-	-	2-2/4-2	1-1/2-1	(06-09-02)
Montrose v Elgin	2-0/0-1	0-0/3-2	1-0/3-1	1-1/0-4	0-1/1-0	3-0/2-3	(14-04-06)
Peterhead v Stirling	2-3/2-1	-	1-1/1-1	3-2/1-1	-	-	(06-06-02)
Queen's Park v Berwick	1-0/1-0/0-2	1-0/3-1	-	2-0/2-3	0-2/1-0	1-1/2-2	(13-06-10)

CONFERENCE

Alfreton v Macclesfield	-	-	-	-	-	-	(None)
Barrow v Nuneaton	0-1	0-1	-	-	-	-	(00-00-04)
Braintree v Southport	-	-	-	-	-	0-0	(00-01-00)
Ebbsfleet v Stockport	-	-	-	-	-	2-1	(01-00-00)
Forest G v Dartford	-	-	-	-	-	-	(None)
Gateshead v Wrexham	-	-	-	1-0	0-1	1-4	(01-00-02)
Hereford v Lincoln	1-2	3-1	-	2-0	0-1	-	(05-02-06)
Hyde v Kidderminstr	-	-	-	-	-	-	(None)
Luton v Newport Co	-	-	-	-	1-1	2-0	(01-01-00)
Mansfield v Cambridge U	-	-	1-1	2-1	1-0	1-2	(05-04-02)
Telford v Tamworth	-	4-1	0-0	-	-	1-0	(03-01-00)
Woking v Grimsby	-	-	-	-	-	-	(None)

TUESDAY 19TH FEBRUARY 2013

CHAMPIONSHIP

Barnsley v Wolves	1-0	1-0	1-1	-	-	-	(06-03-06)
Birmingham v Sheff Weds	2-0	-	3-1	-	-	-	(03-00-01)
Burnley v Middlesboro	-	-	-	-	3-1	0-2	(01-00-02)

Home team	Away team	Six-season fixture record, latest result at right						Since 1988 – HW D AW
Cardiff v Brighton		-	-	-	-	-	1-3	(04-05-01)
C Palace v Bristol C		-	2-0	4-2	0-1	0-0	1-0	(05-01-01)
Derby v Bolton		-	1-1	-	-	-	-	(04-01-00)
Hull v Blackburn		-	-	1-2	0-0	-	-	(02-01-02)
Ipswich v Watford		-	1-2	0-0	1-1	0-3	1-2	(06-03-06)
Leeds v Blackpool		-	-	-	-	-	0-5	(00-00-01)
Leicester v Charlton		-	1-1	-	-	-	-	(03-05-02)
Millwall v Peterborough		-	-	2-0	-	-	2-2	(03-02-01)
Nottm F v Huddersfield		5-1	2-1	-	-	-	-	(04-00-02)

SATURDAY 23RD FEBRUARY 2013

PREMIER LEAGUE

Home team	Away team							
Arsenal v Aston Villa		1-1	1-1	0-2	3-0	1-2	3-0	(12-06-06)
Fulham v Stoke		-	-	1-0	0-1	2-0	2-1	(04-02-02)
Liverpool v Swansea		-	-	-	-	-	0-0	(00-01-00)
Man City v Chelsea		0-1	0-2	1-3	2-1	1-0	2-1	(05-03-11)
Newcastle v Southampton		-	-	-	-	-	-	(09-02-02)
Norwich v Everton		-	-	-	-	-	2-2	(04-04-01)
QPR v Man Utd		-	-	-	-	-	0-2	(01-03-05)
Reading v Wigan		3-2	2-1	-	-	-	-	(08-02-03)
West Brom v Sunderland		1-2	-	3-0	-	1-0	4-0	(04-05-05)
West Ham v Tottenham		3-4	1-1	0-2	1-2	1-0	-	(08-03-07)

CHAMPIONSHIP

Home team	Away team							
Blackburn v Leeds		-	-	-	-	-	-	(06-01-05)
Blackpool v Leicester		-	2-1	-	1-2	-	3-3	(01-01-01)
Bolton v Hull		-	-	1-1	2-2	-	-	(02-02-00)
Brighton v Burnley		-	-	-	-	-	0-1	(02-03-02)
Bristol C v Barnsley		-	3-2	2-0	5-3	3-3	2-0	(10-03-02)
Charlton v Nottm F		-	-	0-2	-	-	-	(02-02-03)
Huddersfield v Ipswich		-	-	-	-	-	-	(03-02-00)
Middlesboro v Millwall		-	-	-	-	0-1	1-1	(05-01-01)
Peterborough v Birmingham		-	-	-	-	-	1-1	(02-02-01)
Sheff Weds v C Palace		3-2	2-2	2-0	2-2	-	-	(06-05-02)
Watford v Derby		-	-	3-1	0-1	3-0	0-1	(05-05-04)

LEAGUE 1

Home team	Away team							
Bournemouth v Sheff Utd		-	-	-	-	-	0-2	(00-00-02)
Brentford v Walsall		-	-	-	1-1	1-2	0-0	(06-03-01)
Carlisle v MK Dons		-	-	3-2	5-0	4-1	1-3	(03-00-01)
Colchester v Tranmere		-	-	0-1	1-1	3-1	4-2	(04-03-03)
Coventry v Crewe		-	-	-	-	-	-	(02-01-01)
Doncaster v Yeovil		0-0	1-2	-	-	-	-	(01-01-07)
Leyton O v Crawley		-	-	-	-	-	-	(None)
Notts Co v Bury		0-1	1-3	0-1	5-0	-	2-4	(03-02-08)
Oldham v Portsmouth		-	-	-	-	-	-	(03-03-00)
Scunthorpe v Hartlepool		-	-	3-0	-	-	0-2	(09-03-02)
Shrewsbury v Stevenage		-	-	-	-	1-0	-	(02-00-00)
Swindon v Preston		-	-	-	-	-	-	(None)

LEAGUE 2

Home team	Away team							
Accrington v Cheltenham		-	-	-	4-0	2-4	0-1	(01-00-02)
Aldershot v Fleetwood		-	-	-	-	-	-	(None)
Barnet v Rochdale		3-2	0-0	2-1	1-0	-	-	(10-02-02)
Bradford v Rotherham		1-1	3-2	3-0	2-4	2-1	2-3	(08-01-06)
Burton v Exeter		1-0	4-4	-	-	-	-	(03-01-01)

Chesterfield v Gillingham	0-1	-	0-1	-	3-1	-	(06-07-02)
Dagenham v Wimbledon	-	-	-	-	-	0-2	(00-00-01)
Morecambe v Bristol R	-	-	-	-	-	2-3	(00-00-01)
Northampton v Plymouth	-	-	-	-	-	0-0	(02-03-00)
Oxford Utd v York	2-0	1-1	1-0	2-1	-	-	(05-03-01)
Torquay v Port Vale	-	-	-	1-2	0-0	2-1	(02-01-01)
Wycombe v Southend	-	-	-	1-1	3-1	-	(02-01-01)

SCOTTISH PREMIER LEAGUE

Celtic v Club 12	-	-	-	-	-	-	(None)
Dundee Utd v Hibernian	0-3/0-0	0-0/1-1/1-1	2-0/2-2	1-0/0-2	1-0/3-0	3-1	(16-16-10)
Hearts v Inverness	4-1/1-0	2-3/1-0	1-0/3-2	-	1-1	2-1	(07-02-02)
Kilmarnock v Aberdeen	1-0/1-2	0-1/3-1	1-2	1-1/2-0	2-0	2-0/1-1	(20-07-08)
Ross County v Motherwell	-	-	-	-	-	-	(None)
St Johnstone v St Mirren	-	-	-	1-0/2-2	2-1/0-0	0-1	(12-08-05)

SCOTTISH DIVISION ONE

Cowdenbeath v Raith	1-2/1-5	1-0/1-4	-	-	1-2/0-3	-	(02-01-07)
Dumbarton v Falkirk	-	-	-	-	-	-	(00-00-02)
Dunfermline v Morton	-	0-1/2-0	0-1/2-1	3-1/4-1	2-0/1-3	-	(11-02-05)
Hamilton v Livingston	1-1/3-0	1-1/3-1	-	-	-	1-1/0-1	(07-06-02)
Partick v Dundee	3-1/2-1	1-1/1-0	0-0/1-1	0-2/0-1	1-0/0-0	0-1/0-0	(10-08-10)

SCOTTISH DIVISION TWO

Airdrie v Stenhsmuir	-	-	-	-	1-0/2-2	5-2/0-3	(06-01-01)
Alloa v Arbroath	-	-	2-1/2-0	0-1/1-0	-	-	(13-08-09)
Ayr v Forfar	5-0/3-1	-	-	-	0-1/3-1	-	(08-05-03)
Brechin v East Fife	-	-	2-1/2-1	3-2/1-0	1-3/2-3	0-2/1-3	(14-04-06)
Queen of Sth v Albion	-	-	-	-	-	-	(01-01-04)

SCOTTISH DIVISION THREE

Berwick v Stranraer	-	-	-	1-0/1-0	2-2/3-3	2-2/1-0	(13-06-08)
E Stirling v Elgin	2-1/0-2	3-1/0-0	5-2/1-0	1-1/2-0	0-2/2-1	1-1/2-2	(10-05-09)
Montrose v Annan	-	-	1-1/0-3	0-0/1-2	1-1/0-1	2-3/1-1	(00-04-04)
Peterhead v Queen's Park	-	1-0/1-0	4-1/1-1	-	-	1-1/2-1	(08-05-01)
Stirling v Clyde	-	0-2/1-1	-	1-1/1-0	-	-	(03-04-07)

CONFERENCE

Cambridge U v Hereford	-	-	-	-	-	-	(02-01-02)
Dartford v Stockport	-	-	-	-	-	-	(None)
Grimsby v Ebbsfleet	-	-	-	-	-	4-3	(01-00-00)
Kidderminstr v Alfreton	-	-	-	-	-	3-1	(01-00-00)
Lincoln v Barrow	-	-	-	-	-	2-1	(01-00-00)
Luton v Mansfield	-	-	-	4-1	2-0	0-0	(03-01-01)
Macclesfield v Gateshead	-	-	-	-	-	-	(07-00-00)
Newport Co v Telford	-	-	-	-	-	0-0	(00-01-00)
Nuneaton v Forest G	-	-	-	-	-	-	(04-00-01)
Southport v Woking	0-0	-	-	-	-	-	(07-04-01)
Tamworth v Hyde	-	2-1	2-0	-	-	-	(02-00-00)
Wrexham v Braintree	-	-	-	-	-	5-1	(01-00-00)

SUNDAY 24TH FEBRUARY 2013

CHAMPIONSHIP

Wolves v Cardiff	1-2	3-0	2-2	-	-	-	(03-01-02)

TUESDAY 26TH FEBRUARY 2013

LEAGUE 1

Home v Away						Record
Bournemouth v Coventry	-	-	-	-	-	-	(None)
Carlisle v Walsall	-	2-1	1-1	1-1	1-3	1-1	(03-06-03)
Colchester v Yeovil	-	-	1-0	2-1	0-0	2-2	(04-02-01)
Crawley v Brentford	-	-	-	-	-	-	(None)
Hartlepool v Crewe	-	3-0	1-4	-	-	-	(01-00-02)
Portsmouth v MK Dons	-	-	-	-	-	-	(02-00-01)
Preston v Oldham	-	-	-	-	-	3-3	(02-02-00)
Scunthorpe v Stevenage	-	-	-	-	-	1-1	(00-01-00)
Sheff Utd v Leyton O	-	-	-	-	-	3-1	(01-00-00)
Shrewsbury v Doncaster	-	-	-	-	-	-	(02-00-01)
Swindon v Bury	2-1	-	-	-	-	-	(04-01-00)
Tranmere v Notts Co	-	-	-	-	0-1	1-1	(06-02-01)

LEAGUE 2

Home v Away						Record
Wimbledon v Plymouth	-	-	-	-	-	1-2	(00-00-01)
Barnet v Southend	-	-	-	-	0-2	0-3	(02-00-03)
Bradford v Dagenham	-	0-2	1-1	3-3	-	0-1	(00-02-02)
Burton v Morecambe	2-1	-	-	5-2	3-2	3-2	(04-00-04)
Chesterfield v Aldershot	-	-	5-1	0-1	2-2	-	(01-01-01)
Fleetwood v Cheltenham	-	-	-	-	-	-	(None)
Gillingham v Oxford Utd	-	-	-	-	0-0	1-0	(02-01-00)
Northampton v Bristol R	-	0-1	0-0	-	-	3-2	(06-02-03)
Port Vale v Exeter	-	-	1-3	-	-	-	(01-01-01)
Rochdale v Accrington	4-2	4-1	3-1	1-2	-	-	(03-00-01)
Rotherham v York	-	-	-	-	-	-	(04-01-02)
Torquay v Wycombe	3-0	-	-	-	0-0	-	(01-03-00)

CONFERENCE

Home v Away						Record
Alfreton v Hyde	2-2	0-3	3-2	4-0	0-0	-	(03-03-02)
Barrow v Wrexham	-	-	1-1	2-1	0-1	3-1	(02-01-01)
Braintree v Luton	-	-	-	-	-	3-1	(01-00-00)
Dartford v Grimsby	-	-	-	-	-	-	(None)
Lincoln v Mansfield	1-2	1-2	-	-	-	1-1	(06-03-06)
Newport Co v Gateshead	-	-	-	-	2-1	1-0	(02-00-00)
Nuneaton v Kidderminstr	-	-	-	-	-	-	(00-00-01)
Stockport v Hereford	0-2	2-3	4-1	-	0-5	-	(03-00-04)
Tamworth v Cambridge U	0-1	-	-	0-0	1-1	2-2	(00-04-01)

WEDNESDAY 27TH FEBRUARY 2013

SCOTTISH PREMIER LEAGUE

Home v Away						Record
Aberdeen v Ross County	-	-	-	-	-	-	(None)
Club 12 v St Johnstone	-	-	-	-	-	-	(None)
Hibernian v Kilmarnock	2-2/0-1	4-1/2-0	2-4	1-0/1-0	2-1/2-1	1-1/0-1	(16-10-08)
Inverness v Dundee Utd	0-0/1-0	0-3/1-1	1-3	-	0-2	2-3	(02-04-05)
Motherwell v Celtic	1-1	1-4/1-2	2-4/1-1	2-3	0-1/2-0	1-2/0-3	(09-15-21)
St Mirren v Hearts	2-2	1-3/1-1	0-1	2-1/1-1	0-2	0-0	(03-07-07)

FRIDAY 1ST MARCH 2013

CHAMPIONSHIP

Home v Away						Record
Derby v C Palace	1-0	-	1-2	1-1	5-0	3-2	(08-02-03)

SATURDAY 2ND MARCH 2013

PREMIER LEAGUE

Home v Away							
Aston Villa v Man City	1-3	1-1	4-2	1-1	1-0	0-1	(05-06-07)
Chelsea v West Brom	-	-	2-0	-	6-0	2-1	(06-01-00)
Everton v Reading	1-1	1-0	-	-	-	-	(01-01-00)
Man Utd v Norwich	-	-	-	-	-	2-0	(06-01-02)
Southampton v QPR	1-2	2-3	0-0	-	-	-	(04-02-06)
Stoke v West Ham	-	-	0-1	2-1	1-1	-	(01-02-03)
Sunderland v Fulham	-	1-1	1-0	0-0	0-3	0-0	(02-04-02)
Swansea v Newcastle	-	-	-	1-1	-	0-2	(00-01-01)
Tottenham v Arsenal	2-2	1-3	0-0	2-1	3-3	2-1	(07-12-05)
Wigan v Liverpool	0-4	0-1	1-1	1-0	1-1	0-0	(01-03-03)

CHAMPIONSHIP

Home v Away							
Barnsley v Bolton	-	-	-	-	-	-	(02-04-01)
Blackburn v Peterborough	-	-	-	-	-	-	(None)
Blackpool v Bristol C	0-1	1-1	0-1	1-1	-	5-0	(05-07-04)
Brighton v Huddersfield	0-0	1-1	0-1	0-0	2-3	-	(02-05-02)
Charlton v Burnley	-	1-3	1-1	-	-	-	(00-01-02)
Hull v Birmingham	2-0	-	-	0-1	-	2-1	(02-02-02)
Ipswich v Leicester	0-2	3-1	-	0-0	3-0	1-2	(11-03-02)
Leeds v Millwall	-	4-2	2-0	0-2	3-1	2-0	(05-01-01)
Middlesboro v Cardiff	-	-	-	0-1	1-0	0-2	(01-00-02)
Sheff Weds v Nottm F	-	-	1-0	1-1	-	-	(06-01-06)
Wolves v Watford	-	1-2	3-1	-	-	-	(05-09-01)

LEAGUE 1

Home v Away							
Brentford v Scunthorpe	0-2	-	-	-	-	0-0	(03-01-01)
Bury v Crawley	-	-	-	-	-	-	(None)
Coventry v Swindon	-	-	-	-	-	-	(00-01-00)
Crewe v Portsmouth	-	-	-	-	-	-	(03-01-01)
Doncaster v Hartlepool	-	2-0	-	-	-	-	(06-03-01)
Leyton O v Bournemouth	3-2	1-0	-	-	2-2	1-3	(05-04-01)
MK Dons v Preston	-	-	-	-	-	0-1	(03-01-01)
Notts Co v Carlisle	-	-	-	-	0-1	2-0	(02-01-01)
Oldham v Sheff Utd	-	-	-	-	-	0-2	(02-03-03)
Stevenage v Colchester	-	-	-	-	-	0-0	(00-01-00)
Walsall v Shrewsbury	1-0	-	-	-	-	-	(02-03-02)
Yeovil v Tranmere	0-2	1-1	1-0	2-0	3-1	2-1	(04-02-01)

LEAGUE 2

Home v Away							
Accrington v Torquay	1-0	-	-	4-2	1-0	3-1	(04-00-00)
Aldershot v Gillingham	-	-	2-1	-	1-1	1-2	(01-01-01)
Bristol R v Burton	-	-	-	-	-	7-1	(01-00-00)
Cheltenham v Wimbledon	-	-	-	-	-	0-0	(00-01-00)
Dagenham v Chesterfield	-	0-3	3-0	2-1	-	-	(02-00-01)
Exeter v Northampton	-	-	-	-	-	-	(00-01-03)
Morecambe v Rochdale	-	1-1	1-1	3-3	-	-	(00-03-00)
Oxford Utd v Port Vale	-	-	-	-	2-1	2-1	(05-03-01)
Plymouth v Barnet	-	-	-	-	-	0-0	(03-02-01)
Southend v Rotherham	-	-	-	-	1-0	0-2	(04-00-02)
Wycombe v Fleetwood	-	-	-	-	-	-	(None)
York v Bradford	-	-	-	-	-	-	(00-02-01)

SCOTTISH DIVISION ONE

Home v Away							
Dumbarton v Cowdenbeath	-	-	2-1/1-1	0-3/2-1	-	0-4/0-2	(10-06-08)
Dunfermline v Partick	-	1-0/1-1	1-0/0-1	3-1/1-2	0-0/0-0	-	(07-04-02)

Home team v Away team							Since 1988 – HW D AW
Falkirk v Raith	-	-	-	-	0-0/2-1	2-0/2-3	(17-02-06)
Hamilton v Morton	-	1-0/3-0	-	-	-	1-2/4-3	(11-06-06)
Livingston v Dundee	2-3/1-3	0-2/1-1	1-2/0-1	-	-	4-2/2-3	(03-05-08)

SCOTTISH DIVISION TWO

Albion v Alloa	-	-	-	-	-	-	(07-04-05)
Arbroath v Ayr	-	-	0-3/1-3	-	-	-	(02-02-04)
East Fife v Queen of Sth	-	-	-	-	-	-	(08-01-07)
Forfar v Airdrie	-	-	-	-	1-2/1-2	3-2/2-3	(02-04-06)
Stenhsmuir v Brechin	-	-	-	1-1/1-2	0-0/1-3	1-1/2-1	(09-07-06)

SCOTTISH DIVISION THREE

Annan v Berwick	-	-	1-2/1-1	1-1/0-1	1-1/2-3	2-2/1-1	(00-05-03)
Clyde v Peterhead	-	-	-	1-3/3-1	-	2-0/0-1	(02-00-02)
Elgin v Stirling	-	-	-	-	-	-	(01-01-04)
Queen's Park v Montrose	1-1/5-0	-	-	3-2/3-0	1-0/4-1	3-1/5-0	(16-11-09)
Stranraer v E Stirling	-	2-1/2-1	-	1-2/2-2	4-1/2-0	6-0/4-1	(11-04-04)

CONFERENCE

Barrow v Tamworth	-	2-0	-	1-0	0-2	1-1	(02-01-01)
Cambridge U v Forest G	1-1	2-0	0-1	7-0	1-1	1-1	(02-04-01)
Gateshead v Braintree	-	-	-	-	-	2-2	(00-01-00)
Hereford v Nuneaton	-	-	-	-	-	-	(01-03-00)
Hyde v Newport Co	-	-	-	-	-	-	(None)
Kidderminstr v Ebbsfleet	1-2	2-1	3-1	2-2	-	2-2	(02-02-02)
Macclesfield v Grimsby	2-1	1-2	1-0	0-0	-	-	(03-02-01)
Mansfield v Telford	-	-	-	-	-	1-1	(00-01-00)
Southport v Dartford	-	-	-	-	-	-	(None)
Stockport v Luton	-	-	-	-	-	1-1	(00-02-03)
Woking v Lincoln	-	-	-	-	-	-	(None)
Wrexham v Alfreton	-	-	-	-	-	0-1	(00-00-01)

TUESDAY 5TH MARCH 2013

CHAMPIONSHIP

Birmingham v Blackpool	-	-	0-1	-	2-0	3-0	(04-00-01)
Bolton v Blackburn	1-2	1-2	0-0	0-2	2-1	2-1	(05-05-05)
Bristol C v Brighton	1-0	-	-	-	-	0-1	(03-01-03)
Burnley v Barnsley	4-2	2-1	1-2	-	3-0	2-0	(05-01-02)
Cardiff v Derby	2-2	-	4-1	6-1	4-1	2-0	(05-02-01)
C Palace v Hull	1-1	1-1	-	-	0-0	0-0	(02-04-00)
Huddersfield v Middlesboro	-	-	-	-	-	-	(00-00-01)
Leicester v Leeds	1-1	-	1-0	-	2-2	0-1	(08-03-05)
Millwall v Wolves	-	-	-	-	-	-	(06-02-02)
Nottm F v Ipswich	-	-	1-1	3-0	2-0	3-2	(06-03-02)
Peterborough v Charlton	-	-	-	-	1-5	-	(00-01-02)
Watford v Sheff Weds	-	2-1	2-2	4-1	-	-	(06-02-01)

LEAGUE 2

Cheltenham v Chesterfield	0-0	-	-	0-1	0-3	-	(00-02-03)

SATURDAY 9TH MARCH 2013

PREMIER LEAGUE

Arsenal v Everton	1-1	1-0	3-1	2-2	2-1	1-0	(20-03-01)
Fulham v Chelsea	0-2	1-2	2-2	0-2	0-0	1-1	(01-05-05)
Liverpool v Tottenham	3-0	2-2	3-1	2-0	0-2	0-0	(15-07-02)
Man City v Wigan	0-1	0-0	1-0	3-0	1-0	3-0	(05-01-01)

Home team	Away team						Since 1988 – HW D AW
Newcastle v Stoke	-	-	2-2	-	1-2	3-0	(02-01-01)
Norwich v Southampton	0-1	2-1	2-2	0-2	-	-	(06-04-03)
QPR v Sunderland	1-2	-	-	-	-	2-3	(01-01-04)
Reading v Aston Villa	2-0	1-2	-	-	-	-	(01-00-01)
West Brom v Swansea	-	-	-	0-1	-	1-2	(01-00-03)
West Ham v Man Utd	1-0	2-1	0-1	0-4	2-4	-	(03-07-08)

CHAMPIONSHIP

Home team	Away team						Since 1988 – HW D AW
Birmingham v Derby	1-0	1-1	1-0	-	-	2-2	(03-03-01)
Bolton v Brighton	-	-	-	-	-	-	(00-00-01)
Bristol C v Middlesboro	-	-	-	2-1	0-4	0-1	(02-02-03)
Burnley v Hull	2-0	0-1	-	2-0	4-0	1-0	(08-00-01)
Cardiff v Barnsley	2-0	3-0	3-1	0-2	2-2	5-3	(04-02-01)
C Palace v Leeds	1-0	-	-	-	1-0	1-1	(04-03-03)
Huddersfield v Charlton	-	-	-	1-1	3-1	1-0	(03-02-02)
Leicester v Sheff Weds	1-4	1-3	-	3-0	-	-	(04-02-05)
Millwall v Blackburn	-	-	-	-	-	-	(01-00-01)
Nottm F v Wolves	-	-	0-1	-	-	-	(02-05-01)
Peterborough v Ipswich	-	-	-	3-1	-	7-1	(02-00-00)
Watford v Blackpool	-	1-1	3-4	2-2	-	0-2	(01-03-02)

LEAGUE 1

Home team	Away team						Since 1988 – HW D AW
Bournemouth v Doncaster	2-0	0-2	-	-	-	-	(03-00-01)
Carlisle v Brentford	2-0	-	-	1-3	2-0	2-2	(03-01-03)
Colchester v Crewe	-	-	0-1	-	-	-	(02-00-03)
Crawley v Notts Co	-	-	-	-	-	-	(None)
Hartlepool v Yeovil	-	2-0	0-0	1-1	3-1	0-1	(02-02-02)
Portsmouth v Bury	-	-	-	-	-	-	(01-01-00)
Preston v Stevenage	-	-	-	-	-	0-0	(00-01-00)
Scunthorpe v Coventry	-	2-1	-	1-0	0-2	-	(02-00-01)
Sheff Utd v MK Dons	-	-	-	-	-	2-1	(03-03-03)
Shrewsbury v Leyton O	-	-	-	-	-	-	(07-03-02)
Swindon v Walsall	1-1	0-3	3-2	1-1	0-0	-	(03-05-03)
Tranmere v Oldham	1-0	0-1	0-1	0-1	1-2	1-0	(07-02-05)

LEAGUE 2

Home team	Away team						Since 1988 – HW D AW
Wimbledon v York	-	-	-	0-1	1-0	-	(01-00-01)
Barnet v Morecambe	-	0-1	1-1	2-0	1-2	0-2	(04-02-03)
Bradford v Aldershot	-	-	5-0	2-1	2-1	1-2	(03-00-01)
Burton v Cheltenham	-	-	-	5-6	2-0	0-2	(03-02-03)
Chesterfield v Bristol R	-	-	-	-	-	-	(02-02-02)
Fleetwood v Exeter	-	-	-	-	-	-	(None)
Gillingham v Plymouth	-	-	-	-	-	3-0	(05-00-00)
Northampton v Accrington	-	-	-	4-0	0-0	0-0	(01-02-00)
Port Vale v Southend	-	1-2	-	-	1-1	2-3	(05-02-02)
Rochdale v Wycombe	0-2	0-1	0-1	-	-	2-1	(01-02-04)
Rotherham v Dagenham	-	2-1	1-1	2-0	-	3-1	(03-01-00)
Torquay v Oxford Utd	-	3-2	1-1	-	3-4	0-0	(02-04-02)

SCOTTISH PREMIER LEAGUE

Home team	Away team						Since 1988 – HW D AW
Aberdeen v Motherwell	2-1	1-2/1-1	2-0	0-0/0-3	1-2	1-2	(17-15-10)
Club 12 v Inverness	-	-	-	-	-	-	(None)
Hibernian v Hearts	2-2/0-1	1-1	1-1/1-0	1-1/1-2	0-2/2-2	1-3	(12-17-14)
Ross County v Celtic	-	-	-	-	-	-	(None)
St Johnstone v Kilmarnock	-	-	-	0-1	0-3/0-0	2-0	(05-06-07)
St Mirren v Dundee Utd	1-3/0-1	0-3	0-2	0-0/1-2	1-1/1-1	2-2	(02-09-10)

SCOTTISH DIVISION ONE

Home team	Away team						Since 1988 – HW D AW
Cowdenbeath v Hamilton	-	-	-	-	-	-	(03-01-04)

Home team v Away team						Since 1988 – HW D AW	
Home team v Away team	Six-season fixture record, latest result at right					Since 1988 – HW D AW	
Dundee v Dunfermline	-	1-1/0-0	0-0/1-0	1-0/3-2	2-2/1-1	-	(08-09-08)
Morton v Falkirk	-	-	-	-	0-0/2-2	3-2/0-0	(04-07-10)
Partick v Dumbarton	-	-	-	-	-	-	(02-00-00)
Raith v Livingston	-	-	-	-	-	0-1/0-3	(07-01-06)

<h3 align="center">SCOTTISH DIVISION TWO</h3>

Home team v Away team						Since 1988	
Airdrie v Albion	-	-	-	-	-	4-0/1-0	(03-00-00)
Brechin v Forfar	4-2/2-2	-	-	-	0-0/0-1	0-1/2-1	(07-03-07)
East Fife v Arbroath	2-1/1-2	0-2/2-1	3-2/0-0	1-1/3-1	-	2-2/1-3	(08-06-11)
Queen of Sth v Ayr	-	-	-	2-0/3-0	-	4-1/2-1	(05-04-05)
Stenhsmuir v Alloa	-	-	-	1-0/0-2	0-1/2-3	-	(07-03-07)

<h3 align="center">SCOTTISH DIVISION THREE</h3>

Home team v Away team						Since 1988	
Berwick v Montrose	1-2/1-0	-	3-2/0-1	2-0/0-2	1-0/0-1	1-2/2-2	(11-09-08)
Clyde v Queen's Park	-	-	-	-	2-3/0-2	0-2/1-2	(02-00-05)
Peterhead v Elgin	-	-	-	-	-	1-3/3-0	(08-03-01)
Stirling v E Stirling	-	-	-	-	-	-	(10-01-00)
Stranraer v Annan	-	-	-	2-0/3-2	2-2/1-1	4-2/4-2	(04-02-00)

<h3 align="center">CONFERENCE</h3>

Home team v Away team						Since 1988	
Braintree v Nuneaton	-	-	-	-	-	-	(None)
Cambridge U v Woking	3-0	1-0	4-1	-	-	-	(03-00-01)
Dartford v Wrexham	-	-	-	-	-	-	(None)
Ebbsfleet v Newport Co	-	-	-	-	-	1-1	(02-01-00)
Forest G v Barrow	-	-	2-1	1-0	2-3	3-0	(03-01-01)
Gateshead v Hyde	-	-	6-3	-	-	-	(06-00-03)
Grimsby v Kidderminstr	-	-	-	-	3-3	1-2	(01-01-01)
Lincoln v Southport	-	-	-	-	-	2-0	(01-00-00)
Luton v Hereford	-	-	-	-	-	-	(None)
Mansfield v Stockport	1-1	4-2	-	-	-	2-1	(05-01-00)
Tamworth v Alfreton	-	0-1	1-2	-	-	2-2	(00-01-02)
Telford v Macclesfield	-	-	-	-	-	-	(03-00-06)

<h2 align="center">TUESDAY 12TH MARCH 2013</h2>

<h3 align="center">LEAGUE 1</h3>

Home team v Away team						Since 1988	
Brentford v Swindon	-	-	-	2-3	0-1	-	(03-02-05)
Bury v Scunthorpe	-	-	-	-	-	0-0	(04-03-02)
Coventry v Colchester	2-1	1-0	-	-	-	-	(02-00-00)
Crewe v Sheff Utd	-	-	-	-	-	-	(03-01-04)
Doncaster v Carlisle	1-2	1-0	-	-	-	-	(03-03-05)
Leyton O v Portsmouth	-	-	-	-	-	-	(None)
MK Dons v Shrewsbury	2-0	3-0	-	-	-	-	(02-00-00)
Notts Co v Preston	-	-	-	-	-	0-0	(03-02-01)
Oldham v Hartlepool	-	0-1	2-1	0-3	4-0	0-1	(04-00-04)
Stevenage v Bournemouth	-	-	-	-	-	2-2	(00-01-00)
Walsall v Tranmere	-	2-1	0-1	2-1	1-4	0-1	(03-01-05)
Yeovil v Crawley	-	-	-	-	-	-	(None)

<h3 align="center">LEAGUE 2</h3>

Home team v Away team						Since 1988	
Accrington v Fleetwood	-	-	-	-	-	-	(03-00-00)
Aldershot v Burton	3-2	1-0	-	0-2	1-2	2-0	(05-01-02)
Bristol R v Port Vale	-	3-2	-	-	-	0-3	(03-02-02)
Dagenham v Torquay	-	-	-	5-3	-	1-1	(01-01-00)
Exeter v Gillingham	-	-	3-0	1-1	-	-	(03-02-00)
Morecambe v Northampton	-	-	-	2-4	1-2	1-2	(00-00-03)
Oxford Utd v Barnet	-	-	-	-	2-1	2-1	(03-00-00)
Plymouth v Bradford	-	-	-	-	-	1-0	(04-01-01)

CONFERENCE

SATURDAY 16TH MARCH 2013

PREMIER LEAGUE

CHAMPIONSHIP

LEAGUE 1

LEAGUE 2

Home v Away							HW-D-AW
Morecambe v Gillingham	-	-	0-1	-	1-1	2-1	(01-01-01)
Oxford Utd v Chesterfield	-	-	-	-	0-0	-	(02-01-00)
Plymouth v Fleetwood	-	-	-	-	-	-	(None)
Southend v Torquay	-	-	-	-	2-1	4-1	(04-03-02)
Wycombe v Northampton	-	-	-	-	2-2	-	(03-04-02)
York v Port Vale	-	-	-	-	-	-	(01-00-00)

SCOTTISH PREMIER LEAGUE

Home v Away							HW-D-AW
Celtic v Aberdeen	1-0/2-1	3-0/1-0	3-2/2-0	3-0	9-0/1-0	2-1	(35-04-06)
Dundee Utd v Club 12	-	-	-	-	-	-	(None)
Hearts v St Johnstone	-	-	-	1-2	1-1/1-0	1-2/2-0	(08-08-06)
Inverness v Ross County	-	-	-	1-3/3-0	-	-	(07-06-03)
Kilmarnock v St Mirren	1-1	0-0/1-0	0-1/2-1	1-2/1-1	2-1/2-0	2-1/0-2	(07-03-04)
Motherwell v Hibernian	1-6	2-1/1-0	1-4	1-3/1-0/6-6	2-3/2-0	4-3	(14-15-14)

SCOTTISH DIVISION ONE

Home v Away							HW-D-AW
Cowdenbeath v Dundee	-	-	-	-	2-1/1-3	-	(01-00-01)
Dumbarton v Morton	-	-	-	-	-	-	(08-01-05)
Hamilton v Partick	1-2/2-1	2-0/0-0	-	-	-	1-0/2-2	(04-06-07)
Livingston v Falkirk	-	-	-	-	-	1-1/1-2	(04-02-06)
Raith v Dunfermline	-	-	-	1-2/1-2	2-0/2-1	-	(05-02-06)

SCOTTISH DIVISION TWO

Home v Away							HW-D-AW
Albion v East Fife	0-1/0-3	1-4/2-2	-	-	-	0-3/1-1	(08-04-14)
Alloa v Brechin	2-2/2-3	2-2/0-4	2-1/3-2	2-1/2-3	2-2/2-2	-	(07-07-04)
Arbroath v Queen of Sth	-	-	-	-	-	-	(06-03-07)
Ayr v Airdrie	-	1-1/1-2	-	1-1/1-4	1-0/3-1	-	(08-04-13)
Forfar v Stenhsmuir	-	0-1/1-2	1-0/4-4	-	1-1/2-0	2-3/1-2	(10-07-06)

SCOTTISH DIVISION THREE

Home v Away							HW-D-AW
Annan v Clyde	-	-	-	-	1-0/0-2	1-0/1-0	(03-00-01)
E Stirling v Berwick	0-1/0-3	-	1-0/0-4	1-0/3-2	0-0/1-0	1-3/2-1	(12-04-11)
Elgin v Stranraer	-	0-5/2-3	-	1-2/2-3	1-2/2-1	1-1/1-2	(01-02-07)
Montrose v Peterhead	-	-	-	-	-	2-1/1-3	(03-01-08)

CONFERENCE

Home v Away							HW-D-AW
Alfreton v Gateshead	-	-	1-3	-	-	1-1	(00-01-01)
Ebbsfleet v Southport	0-4	-	-	-	-	1-2	(01-00-03)
Forest G v Mansfield	-	-	1-0	1-4	2-1	1-1	(02-01-01)
Grimsby v Cambridge U	-	-	-	-	1-1	2-1	(04-03-01)
Hereford v Barrow	-	-	-	-	-	-	(01-00-00)
Hyde v Dartford	-	-	-	-	-	-	(None)
Kidderminstr v Tamworth	0-2	-	-	0-0	2-2	2-0	(01-02-02)
Newport Co v Macclesfield	-	-	-	-	-	-	(None)
Nuneaton v Lincoln	-	-	-	-	-	-	(None)
Stockport v Braintree	-	-	-	-	-	1-1	(00-01-00)
Woking v Telford	-	-	-	-	-	-	(08-04-00)
Wrexham v Luton	-	-	-	3-0	1-0	2-0	(08-01-01)

SATURDAY 23RD MARCH 2013

LEAGUE 1

Home v Away							HW-D-AW
Bournemouth v Bury	-	-	2-0	1-2	-	1-2	(04-03-03)
Carlisle v Yeovil	1-4	2-1	4-1	1-0	0-2	3-2	(05-00-02)
Colchester v MK Dons	-	-	0-3	2-0	1-3	1-5	(02-00-04)
Crawley v Crewe	-	-	-	-	-	1-1	(00-01-00)
Hartlepool v Walsall	3-1	0-1	2-2	3-0	2-1	1-1	(04-04-02)
Portsmouth v Coventry	-	-	-	-	0-3	2-1	(02-01-01)
Preston v Leyton O	-	-	-	-	-	0-2	(03-00-03)

Home team v Away team	Six-season fixture record, latest result at right					Since 1988 – HW D AW	
Scunthorpe v Doncaster	2-0	-	-	2-2	1-3	-	(04-05-06)
Sheff Utd v Brentford	-	-	-	-	-	2-0	(01-01-00)
Shrewsbury v Oldham	-	-	-	-	-	-	(00-01-00)
Swindon v Notts Co	1-1	-	-	-	1-2	-	(06-01-03)
Tranmere v Stevenage	-	-	-	-	-	3-0	(01-00-00)

LEAGUE 2

Home team v Away team	Six-season fixture record, latest result at right					Since 1988 – HW D AW	
Wimbledon v Morecambe	-	-	-	-	-	1-1	(00-01-00)
Barnet v Cheltenham	-	-	-	1-1	3-1	2-2	(05-04-00)
Bradford v Bristol R	-	-	-	-	-	2-2	(01-01-02)
Burton v Wycombe	-	-	-	-	1-2	-	(00-00-01)
Chesterfield v Plymouth	-	-	-	-	-	-	(03-01-01)
Fleetwood v Dagenham	-	-	-	-	-	-	(None)
Gillingham v Accrington	-	-	1-0	-	3-1	1-1	(02-01-00)
Northampton v Oxford Utd	-	-	-	-	2-1	2-1	(05-00-01)
Port Vale v Aldershot	-	-	0-0	1-1	1-0	4-0	(02-02-00)
Rochdale v Southend	-	-	-	-	-	-	(03-01-04)
Rotherham v Exeter	-	-	0-1	-	-	-	(03-02-03)
Torquay v York	-	0-0	1-1	-	-	-	(04-06-01)

SCOTTISH DIVISION ONE

Home team v Away team	Six-season fixture record, latest result at right					Since 1988 – HW D AW	
Dundee v Raith	-	-	-	2-1/2-0	0-0/2-1	1-0/1-1	(08-06-02)
Dunfermline v Dumbarton	-	-	-	-	-	-	(05-01-00)
Falkirk v Hamilton	-	-	4-1/1-2	2-0/0-1	-	0-0/3-0	(08-05-04)
Morton v Cowdenbeath	1-0/3-0	-	-	-	1-2/3-0	-	(05-01-02)
Partick v Livingston	2-3/0-0	3-0/2-1	2-1/1-0	-	-	2-1/2-3	(08-06-07)

SCOTTISH DIVISION TWO

Home team v Away team	Six-season fixture record, latest result at right					Since 1988 – HW D AW	
Albion v Forfar	-	2-1/0-0	1-3/2-0	1-1/0-1	-	1-0/2-2	(05-04-10)
Alloa v Queen of Sth	-	-	-	-	-	-	(10-02-02)
Arbroath v Stenhsmuir	2-0/4-1	2-2/1-0	-	0-3/1-1	-	1-0/0-2	(14-06-05)
Brechin v Ayr	0-2/2-0	2-2/5-1	0-1/1-0	-	0-3/1-0	-	(07-04-07)
East Fife v Airdrie	-	-	-	-	3-3/0-1	2-0/2-0	(03-02-03)

SCOTTISH DIVISION THREE

Home team v Away team	Six-season fixture record, latest result at right					Since 1988 – HW D AW	
Annan v Queen's Park	-	-	-	3-1/0-2	2-1/1-2	5-2/2-3	(03-00-03)
Berwick v Peterhead	-	1-2/2-2	-	-	-	2-1/0-1	(01-01-02)
E Stirling v Montrose	0-3/0-2	0-3/3-1	5-0/2-1	1-0/2-3	2-1/1-2	1-0/3-1	(17-06-18)
Elgin v Clyde	-	-	-	-	0-1/0-1	0-3/1-1	(00-01-03)
Stranraer v Stirling	2-1/3-1	-	1-0/2-8	-	-	-	(05-07-07)

CONFERENCE

Home team v Away team	Six-season fixture record, latest result at right					Since 1988 – HW D AW	
Barrow v Ebbsfleet	-	-	0-3	2-0	-	1-1	(01-01-01)
Braintree v Alfreton	-	-	-	-	-	1-2	(00-00-01)
Dartford v Gateshead	-	-	-	-	-	-	(None)
Forest G v Grimsby	-	-	-	-	3-3	0-1	(00-01-01)
Hereford v Hyde	-	-	-	-	-	-	(None)
Lincoln v Telford	-	-	-	-	-	1-1	(00-01-00)
Luton v Tamworth	-	-	-	2-1	2-0	3-0	(03-00-00)
Mansfield v Macclesfield	1-2	5-0	-	-	-	-	(05-02-02)
Nuneaton v Woking	-	-	-	-	-	-	(01-02-01)
Southport v Kidderminstr	0-1	-	-	-	2-2	1-2	(02-03-06)
Stockport v Newport Co	-	-	-	-	-	2-2	(00-01-00)
Wrexham v Cambridge U	-	-	2-0	2-2	1-0	1-1	(05-05-02)

FRIDAY 29TH MARCH 2013

CHAMPIONSHIP

Home team v Away team	Six-season fixture record, latest result at right					Since 1988 – HW D AW	
Blackburn v Blackpool	-	-	-	-	2-2	-	(00-01-00)
Derby v Bristol C	-	-	2-1	1-0	0-2	2-1	(06-00-02)
Watford v Burnley	-	1-2	3-0	-	1-3	3-2	(06-02-05)

Home team	Away team	Six-season fixture record, latest result at right						Since 1988 – H W D AW
LEAGUE 1								
Brentford v Notts Co		-	0-0	1-1	-	1-1	0-0	(04-07-03)
Colchester v Bournemouth		-	-	-	-	2-1	1-1	(06-01-02)
Hartlepool v MK Dons		1-0	-	1-3	0-5	0-1	1-1	(03-01-03)
Preston v Portsmouth		-	-	-	-	1-0	-	(03-01-00)
Scunthorpe v Leyton O		3-1	-	2-1	-	-	2-3	(08-03-02)
Tranmere v Sheff Utd		-	-	-	-	-	1-1	(02-04-02)
LEAGUE 2								
Barnet v Dagenham		-	3-1	1-1	2-0	-	2-2	(05-02-01)
Bradford v Southend		-	-	-	-	0-2	2-0	(02-01-02)
Northampton v Torquay		-	-	-	0-0	2-2	0-0	(03-05-04)
Oxford Utd v Morecambe		0-0	-	-	-	4-0	1-2	(01-01-01)
Port Vale v Cheltenham		1-1	3-0	-	1-1	0-1	1-2	(01-02-03)
Rochdale v Aldershot		-	-	3-1	1-0	-	-	(02-00-00)
Rotherham v Wimbledon		-	-	-	-	-	1-0	(01-00-00)
Wycombe v Accrington		1-1	0-1	2-1	-	1-2	-	(01-01-02)

SATURDAY 30TH MARCH 2013

Home team	Away team							Since 1988
PREMIER LEAGUE								
Arsenal v Reading		2-1	2-0	-	-	-	-	(02-00-00)
Aston Villa v Liverpool		0-0	1-2	0-0	0-1	1-0	0-2	(07-08-09)
Everton v Stoke		-	-	3-1	1-1	1-0	0-1	(02-01-01)
Fulham v QPR		-	-	-	-	-	6-0	(03-00-00)
Man City v Newcastle		0-0	3-1	2-1	-	2-1	3-1	(08-04-01)
Southampton v Chelsea		-	-	-	-	-	-	(05-03-08)
Sunderland v Man Utd		-	0-4	1-2	0-1	0-0	0-1	(02-03-07)
Swansea v Tottenham		-	-	-	-	-	1-1	(00-01-00)
West Ham v West Brom		-	-	0-0	-	2-2	-	(02-02-03)
Wigan v Norwich		-	-	-	-	-	1-1	(00-02-00)
CHAMPIONSHIP								
Charlton v Bolton		2-0	-	-	-	-	-	(03-02-05)
C Palace v Birmingham		0-1	-	0-0	-	-	1-0	(05-03-04)
Huddersfield v Hull		-	-	-	-	-	-	(03-02-01)
Ipswich v Leeds		1-0	-	-	-	2-1	2-1	(06-03-03)
Leicester v Millwall		-	-	0-1	-	4-2	0-3	(06-02-03)
Nottm F v Brighton		2-1	0-0	-	-	-	1-1	(02-02-01)
Peterborough v Cardiff		-	-	-	4-4	-	4-3	(06-02-00)
Sheff Weds v Barnsley		2-1	1-0	0-1	2-2	-	-	(08-01-01)
Wolves v Middlesboro		-	-	-	-	-	-	(04-00-03)
LEAGUE 1								
Bury v Crewe		-	-	-	3-0	3-1	-	(05-01-03)
Carlisle v Shrewsbury		-	-	-	-	-	-	(04-03-02)
Coventry v Doncaster		-	-	1-0	1-0	2-1	0-2	(03-00-01)
Crawley v Stevenage		3-0	2-1	0-2	0-3	-	-	(02-00-04)
Swindon v Oldham		-	3-0	2-0	4-2	0-2	-	(08-02-06)
Yeovil v Walsall		-	0-2	1-1	1-3	1-1	2-1	(02-02-02)
LEAGUE 2								
Bristol R v York		-	-	-	-	-	-	(04-02-03)
Burton v Chesterfield		-	-	-	2-2	1-0	-	(01-01-00)
Fleetwood v Gillingham		-	-	-	-	-	-	(None)
Plymouth v Exeter		-	-	-	-	2-0	-	(06-01-01)

SCOTTISH PREMIER LEAGUE

Aberdeen v Hearts	1-3/1-0	1-1/0-1	1-0/0-0	1-1/0-1	0-1/0-0	0-0	(17-13-15)
Club 12 v Motherwell	-	-	-	-	-	-	(None)
Hibernian v Inverness	2-0	1-0/2-0	1-2	-	1-1/2-0	1-1	(05-02-03)
Ross County v Kilmarnock	-	-	-	-	-	-	(None)
St Johnstone v Dundee Utd	-	-	-	2-3/0-1	0-0	3-3/1-5/0-2	(05-09-12)
St Mirren v Celtic	1-3	1-5/0-1	1-3	0-2/4-0	0-1	0-2/0-2	(02-01-15)

SCOTTISH DIVISION ONE

Cowdenbeath v Partick	-	-	-	-	2-1/1-1	-	(01-01-00)
Dundee v Falkirk	-	-	-	-	2-0/1-0	4-2/3-1	(07-01-03)
Hamilton v Dumbarton	-	-	-	-	-	-	(12-02-00)
Livingston v Dunfermline	-	1-1/0-2	2-3/4-2	-	-	-	(06-07-06)
Raith v Morton	1-3/2-0	-	-	3-0/1-2	1-0/2-2	1-1/5-0	(13-07-06)

SCOTTISH DIVISION TWO

Airdrie v Alloa	-	2-0/1-1	-	-	0-1/0-2	-	(06-02-02)
Ayr v East Fife	-	-	4-2/2-0	-	0-4/1-1	-	(03-01-02)
Forfar v Arbroath	-	1-3/1-0	-	-	-	1-1/2-4	(06-07-06)
Queen of Sth v Brechin	-	-	-	-	-	-	(04-07-04)
Stenhsmuir v Albion	3-2/0-4	0-1/2-2	1-0/2-0	-	-	3-0/1-2	(12-04-06)

SCOTTISH DIVISION THREE

Clyde v E Stirling	-	-	-	-	1-2/2-0	7-1/3-0	(06-00-01)
Montrose v Stranraer	-	2-4/0-2	-	1-1/4-5	3-3/3-2	0-6/1-3	(06-03-11)
Peterhead v Annan	-	-	-	-	-	2-3/3-2	(01-00-01)
Queen's Park v Elgin	3-0/3-0	-	-	0-3/0-1	1-1/1-0	6-0/1-3	(10-03-05)
Stirling v Berwick	-	-	-	-	-	-	(09-02-01)

CONFERENCE

Alfreton v Lincoln	-	-	-	-	-	1-3	(00-00-01)
Cambridge U v Luton	-	-	-	3-4	0-0	1-1	(02-03-01)
Ebbsfleet v Forest G	1-1	0-2	0-1	4-3	-	1-1	(02-05-02)
Gateshead v Southport	-	-	1-1	-	1-0	2-3	(01-04-05)
Grimsby v Barrow	-	-	-	-	1-1	5-2	(01-01-00)
Hyde v Wrexham	-	-	-	-	-	-	(None)
Kidderminstr v Braintree	-	-	-	-	-	5-4	(01-00-00)
Macclesfield v Stockport	2-0	0-2	-	-	0-2	-	(02-00-02)
Newport Co v Dartford	-	-	-	-	-	-	(None)
Tamworth v Mansfield	-	-	-	2-4	0-2	0-1	(00-00-03)
Telford v Nuneaton	-	0-0	-	-	4-1	-	(03-01-02)
Woking v Hereford	-	-	-	-	-	-	(02-02-05)

MONDAY 1ST APRIL 2013

CHAMPIONSHIP

Barnsley v Leicester	0-1	0-1	-	1-0	0-2	1-1	(03-04-06)
Birmingham v Wolves	1-1	-	2-0	2-1	1-1	-	(05-05-04)
Blackpool v C Palace	-	1-1	2-2	2-2	-	2-1	(01-03-00)
Bolton v Huddersfield	-	-	-	-	-	-	(05-04-00)
Bristol C v Sheff Weds	-	2-1	1-1	1-1	-	-	(01-04-01)
Burnley v Nottm F	-	-	5-0	-	1-0	5-1	(06-01-01)
Cardiff v Blackburn	-	-	-	-	-	-	(None)
Hull v Watford	-	3-0	-	-	0-0	3-2	(02-03-02)
Leeds v Derby	0-1	-	-	-	1-2	0-2	(06-03-03)
Millwall v Ipswich	-	-	-	-	2-1	4-1	(04-03-02)

LEAGUE 1

Home v Away							
Bournemouth v Scunthorpe	1-1	-	-	-	-	2-0	(02-03-00)
Crewe v Preston	-	-	-	-	-	-	(05-01-03)
Doncaster v Swindon	-	2-0	-	-	-	-	(02-01-00)
Leyton O v Bury	-	-	-	-	-	1-0	(04-01-04)
MK Dons v Brentford	-	1-1	-	0-1	1-1	1-2	(00-03-03)
Notts Co v Yeovil	-	-	-	-	4-0	3-1	(02-00-01)
Oldham v Colchester	-	-	0-1	2-2	0-0	1-1	(04-06-02)
Portsmouth v Tranmere	-	-	-	-	-	-	(05-02-03)
Sheff Utd v Carlisle	-	-	-	-	-	1-0	(01-00-00)
Shrewsbury v Crawley	-	-	-	-	-	2-1	(01-00-00)
Stevenage v Hartlepool	-	-	-	-	-	2-2	(00-01-00)
Walsall v Coventry	-	-	-	-	-	-	(00-01-02)

LEAGUE 2

Home v Away							
Wimbledon v Barnet	-	-	-	-	-	1-1	(00-01-00)
Accrington v Burton	-	-	-	0-2	3-1	2-1	(05-01-01)
Aldershot v Oxford Utd	1-1	1-0	-	-	1-2	0-3	(01-01-02)
Cheltenham v Northampton	0-2	1-1	0-1	2-2	1-0	2-2	(05-04-02)
Chesterfield v Port Vale	3-0	-	2-1	0-5	2-0	-	(07-01-02)
Dagenham v Bristol R	-	-	-	-	0-3	4-0	(01-00-01)
Exeter v Rochdale	-	-	4-1	-	1-0	3-1	(09-04-01)
Gillingham v Rotherham	1-0	-	4-0	-	3-1	0-0	(08-03-00)
Morecambe v Wycombe	-	0-1	0-0	-	0-3	-	(00-01-02)
Southend v Fleetwood	-	-	-	-	-		(None)
Torquay v Bradford	-	-	-	1-2	2-0	1-2	(01-02-02)
York v Plymouth	-	-	-	-	-	-	(02-04-01)

CONFERENCE

Home v Away							
Barrow v Hyde	1-2	1-0	-	-	-	-	(05-06-03)
Braintree v Ebbsfleet	-	-	-	-	4-2	2-3	(01-00-02)
Dartford v Woking	-	-	-	-	3-2	2-3	(01-00-01)
Forest G v Telford	-	-	-	-	-	2-1	(02-05-00)
Hereford v Tamworth	-	-	-	-	-	-	(02-00-01)
Lincoln v Cambridge U	-	-	-	-	-	0-1	(03-04-02)
Luton v Kidderminstr	-	-	-	3-1	1-1	1-0	(03-01-00)
Mansfield v Gateshead	-	-	-	0-2	3-2	1-1	(01-01-01)
Nuneaton v Newport Co	-	-	-	-	-	-	(02-00-00)
Southport v Alfreton	-	1-0	0-1	1-3	-	2-1	(04-00-02)
Stockport v Grimsby	3-0	1-1	-	-	-	2-0	(07-03-01)
Wrexham v Macclesfield	0-0	1-1	-	-	-	-	(01-03-01)

TUESDAY 2ND APRIL 2013

CHAMPIONSHIP

Home v Away							
Brighton v Charlton	-	-	-	0-2	1-1	-	(01-01-02)
Middlesboro v Peterborough	-	-	-	1-0	-	1-1	(01-02-00)

SCOTTISH DIVISION THREE

Home v Away							
Queen's Park v Stirling	-	-	1-1/3-1	-	-	-	(05-06-03)

FRIDAY 5TH APRIL 2013

LEAGUE 2

Home v Away							
Port Vale v Burton	-	-	-	3-1	2-1	3-0	(03-00-00)

SATURDAY 6TH APRIL 2013

PREMIER LEAGUE

Chelsea v Sunderland	-	2-0	5-0	7-2	0-3	1-0	(10-01-02)
Liverpool v West Ham	2-1	4-0	0-0	3-0	3-0	-	(14-04-00)
Man Utd v Man City	3-1	1-2	2-0	4-3	2-1	1-6	(10-06-02)
Newcastle v Fulham	1-2	2-0	0-1	-	0-0	2-1	(04-03-03)
Norwich v Swansea	-	-	2-3	-	2-0	3-1	(02-00-01)
QPR v Wigan	-	-	-	-	-	3-1	(02-01-01)
Reading v Southampton	-	-	1-2	-	-	1-1	(01-01-01)
Stoke v Aston Villa	-	-	3-2	0-0	2-1	0-0	(02-02-00)
Tottenham v Everton	0-2	1-3	0-1	2-1	1-1	2-0	(14-07-03)
West Brom v Arsenal	-	-	1-3	-	2-2	2-3	(01-01-04)

CHAMPIONSHIP

Birmingham v Millwall	-	-	-	-	-	3-0	(03-02-00)
Bolton v Wolves	-	-	-	1-0	1-0	1-1	(06-03-02)
Brighton v Leicester	-	-	3-2	-	-	1-0	(04-02-03)
Burnley v Bristol C	-	0-1	4-0	-	0-0	1-1	(03-04-02)
Charlton v Leeds	-	-	-	1-0	-	-	(01-01-04)
C Palace v Barnsley	2-0	2-0	3-0	1-1	2-1	1-0	(10-03-02)
Derby v Ipswich	2-1	-	0-1	1-3	1-2	0-0	(03-05-05)
Huddersfield v Peterborough	-	-	1-0	-	1-1	-	(03-02-02)
Hull v Middlesboro	-	-	2-1	-	2-4	2-1	(02-02-01)
Nottm F v Blackpool	1-1	-	0-0	0-1	-	0-0	(00-04-01)
Sheff Weds v Blackburn	-	-	-	-	-	-	(03-04-02)
Watford v Cardiff	-	2-2	2-2	0-4	4-1	1-1	(03-04-01)

LEAGUE 1

Bournemouth v Notts Co	-	-	0-1	2-1	3-3	2-1	(05-02-04)
Colchester v Leyton O	-	-	1-0	1-0	3-2	1-1	(05-03-00)
Coventry v Brentford	-	-	-	-	-	-	(None)
Doncaster v Tranmere	0-0	0-0	-	-	-	-	(00-04-01)
Hartlepool v Bury	2-0	-	-	-	-	3-0	(03-02-01)
MK Dons v Crawley	-	-	-	-	-	-	(None)
Oldham v Carlisle	0-0	2-0	0-0	2-0	0-1	2-1	(04-02-01)
Portsmouth v Stevenage	-	-	-	-	-	-	(None)
Preston v Scunthorpe	-	0-1	-	3-2	2-3	0-0	(02-03-03)
Swindon v Crewe	-	1-1	0-0	-	-	3-0	(03-02-03)
Walsall v Sheff Utd	-	-	-	-	-	3-2	(02-00-03)
Yeovil v Shrewsbury	-	-	-	-	-	-	(01-00-00)

LEAGUE 2

Aldershot v Southend	-	-	-	-	1-0	2-0	(02-00-00)
Barnet v Chesterfield	-	0-2	1-3	3-1	2-2	-	(03-02-03)
Bradford v Northampton	1-2	-	-	2-0	1-1	2-1	(02-01-01)
Bristol R v Wimbledon	-	-	-	-	-	1-0	(01-00-00)
Exeter v Dagenham	3-2	-	2-1	-	2-1	-	(04-02-00)
Fleetwood v Rochdale	-	-	-	-	-	-	(None)
Gillingham v Torquay	-	-	-	-	1-1	2-0	(03-03-02)
Morecambe v Rotherham	-	5-1	1-3	2-0	0-0	3-3	(02-02-01)
Oxford Utd v Wycombe	-	-	-	-	2-2	-	(01-03-03)
Plymouth v Cheltenham	-	-	-	-	-	1-2	(03-01-01)
York v Accrington	-	-	-	-	-	-	(00-00-02)

SCOTTISH PREMIER LEAGUE

Celtic v Hibernian	2-1/1-0	1-1/2-0	4-2/3-1	1-2/3-2	2-1/3-1	0-0	(27-12-04)
Dundee Utd v Aberdeen	3-1	1-0/3-0	2-1/1-1	0-1	3-1/3-1	1-2	(16-17-09)

Home v Away							
Hearts v Ross County	-	-	-	-	-	-	(None)
Inverness v St Johnstone	-	-	-	-	1-1/2-0	0-1	(04-01-02)
Kilmarnock v Club 12	-	-	-	-	-	-	(None)
Motherwell v St Mirren	0-0/2-3	1-1	2-1/0-2	2-0	3-1/0-1	1-1	(10-05-04)

SCOTTISH DIVISION ONE

Dumbarton v Livingston	-	-	-	-	1-2/0-3	-	(02-00-06)
Dunfermline v Hamilton	-	0-5/1-1	-	-	-	-	(07-01-02)
Falkirk v Cowdenbeath	-	-	-	-	5-1/2-0	-	(02-00-00)
Morton v Dundee	-	0-2/1-2	2-0/2-0	0-1/2-2	0-1/1-3	1-2/0-2	(04-06-09)
Partick v Raith	-	-	-	1-2/0-0	0-0/3-0	0-1/1-1	(08-07-09)

SCOTTISH DIVISION TWO

Airdrie v Brechin	-	2-1/1-2	-	-	1-1/2-2	2-3/4-1	(06-03-04)
Arbroath v Albion	2-3/0-0	1-0/1-4	-	-	1-1/3-0	6-2/6-1	(12-05-07)
Ayr v Alloa	0-1/4-3	2-0/3-1	3-0/1-1	-	2-1/1-0	-	(11-03-03)
Forfar v East Fife	-	0-2/2-3	-	-	3-2/0-0	3-2/1-4	(06-02-11)
Stenhsmuir v Queen of Sth	-	-	-	-	-	-	(10-04-07)

SCOTTISH DIVISION THREE

Annan v Elgin	-	-	5-0/6-0	0-2/3-3	0-1/2-2	1-1/1-1	(02-04-02)
Clyde v Berwick	-	-	-	-	1-4/2-0	1-4/2-2	(06-02-05)
Montrose v Stirling	-	-	-	-	-	-	(03-04-08)
Peterhead v E Stirling	-	-	-	-	-	1-0/2-0	(10-00-02)
Queen's Park v Stranraer	-	-	2-2/1-1	1-2/2-5	1-3/3-3	2-0/3-2	(07-06-08)

CONFERENCE

Alfreton v Stockport	-	-	-	-	-	6-1	(01-00-00)
Barrow v Mansfield	-	-	2-1	3-1	2-2	2-3	(02-01-01)
Cambridge U v Newport Co	-	-	-	-	0-1	1-1	(00-01-01)
Ebbsfleet v Nuneaton	-	-	-	-	-	-	(01-01-00)
Gateshead v Luton	-	-	-	0-1	1-0	0-0	(01-01-01)
Grimsby v Southport	-	-	-	-	1-1	0-1	(00-01-01)
Hyde v Braintree	-	-	-	-	-	-	(None)
Kidderminstr v Lincoln	-	-	-	-	-	1-1	(01-03-02)
Macclesfield v Hereford	3-0	0-1	-	3-1	1-1	2-2	(02-02-01)
Tamworth v Forest G	1-1	-	-	0-0	2-1	0-1	(03-03-02)
Telford v Dartford	-	-	-	-	-	-	(None)
Woking v Wrexham	-	-	1-1	-	-	-	(00-01-00)

TUESDAY 9TH APRIL 2013

SCOTTISH DIVISION ONE

Cowdenbeath v Livingston	-	-	-	-	-	-	(00-01-05)
Dumbarton v Raith	-	-	-	-	-	-	(01-00-05)
Dunfermline v Falkirk	0-3/0-3	-	-	-	1-1/3-0	-	(04-05-04)
Hamilton v Dundee	1-0/1-0	2-0/1-0	-	-	-	1-6/3-1	(08-03-09)
Partick v Morton	-	1-1/0-3	2-1/1-0	5-0/1-0	0-0/2-0	5-0/0-0	(09-07-06)

FRIDAY 12TH APRIL 2013

LEAGUE 2

Southend v Bristol R	-	0-1	1-0	2-1	-	1-1	(06-04-02)

SATURDAY 13TH APRIL 2013

PREMIER LEAGUE

Home v Away							
Arsenal v Norwich	-	-	-	-	-	3-3	(05-03-01)
Aston Villa v Fulham	1-1	2-1	0-0	2-0	2-2	1-0	(07-04-00)
Chelsea v Tottenham	1-0	2-0	1-1	3-0	2-1	0-0	(15-07-01)
Everton v QPR	-	-	-	-	-	0-1	(04-02-03)
Man City v West Brom	-	-	4-2	-	3-0	4-0	(06-04-01)
Newcastle v Sunderland	-	2-0	1-1	-	5-1	1-1	(06-05-02)
Reading v Liverpool	1-2	3-1	-	-	-	-	(01-00-01)
Southampton v West Ham	-	-	-	-	-	1-0	(08-03-02)
Stoke v Man Utd	-	-	0-1	0-2	1-2	1-1	(00-01-03)
Wigan v Swansea	-	-	-	-	-	0-2	(04-00-04)

CHAMPIONSHIP

Home v Away							
Barnsley v Charlton	-	3-0	0-0	-	-	-	(05-03-02)
Blackburn v Derby	-	3-1	-	-	-	-	(03-01-02)
Blackpool v Burnley	-	3-0	0-1	-	-	4-0	(05-01-06)
Bristol C v Bolton	-	-	-	-	-	-	(02-02-01)
Cardiff v Nottm F	-	-	2-0	1-1	0-2	1-0	(03-02-01)
Ipswich v Hull	0-0	1-0	-	-	1-1	0-1	(02-04-02)
Leeds v Sheff Weds	2-3	-	-	-	-	-	(05-02-04)
Leicester v Birmingham	1-2	-	-	-	-	3-1	(04-01-02)
Middlesboro v Brighton	-	-	-	-	-	1-0	(03-01-00)
Millwall v C Palace	-	-	-	-	3-0	0-1	(04-02-03)
Peterborough v Watford	-	-	-	2-1	-	2-2	(02-02-01)
Wolves v Huddersfield	-	-	-	-	-	-	(01-04-02)

LEAGUE 1

Home v Away							
Brentford v Portsmouth	-	-	-	-	-	-	(01-00-00)
Bury v Oldham	-	-	-	-	-	0-0	(00-04-00)
Carlisle v Preston	-	-	-	-	-	0-0	(00-02-02)
Crawley v Coventry	-	-	-	-	-	-	(None)
Crewe v Doncaster	2-1	0-4	-	-	-	-	(04-00-02)
Leyton O v MK Dons	-	-	1-2	1-2	2-2	0-3	(00-01-03)
Notts Co v Colchester	-	-	-	-	2-0	4-1	(03-03-03)
Scunthorpe v Walsall	-	-	1-1	-	-	0-1	(03-02-03)
Sheff Utd v Swindon	-	-	-	-	-	-	(05-02-00)
Shrewsbury v Bournemouth	-	-	4-1	1-0	-	-	(05-02-02)
Stevenage v Yeovil	-	-	-	-	-	0-0	(02-05-01)
Tranmere v Hartlepool	-	3-1	1-0	0-0	0-1	1-1	(04-04-01)

LEAGUE 2

Home v Away							
Accrington v Morecambe	-	3-2	1-0	3-2	1-1	1-1	(08-03-01)
Burton v Plymouth	-	-	-	-	-	2-1	(01-00-00)
Cheltenham v Gillingham	1-1	1-0	-	-	1-2	0-3	(01-01-02)
Chesterfield v Bradford	3-0	1-1	0-2	1-1	2-2	-	(03-04-01)
Dagenham v Oxford Utd	0-1	-	-	-	-	0-1	(00-00-02)
Northampton v York	-	-	-	-	-	-	(04-03-00)
Rochdale v Port Vale	-	-	1-0	0-0	-	-	(01-01-00)
Rotherham v Fleetwood	-	-	-	-	-	-	(None)
Torquay v Barnet	1-1	-	-	0-1	1-1	1-0	(02-06-05)
Wimbledon v Exeter	-	-	-	-	-	-	(None)
Wycombe v Aldershot	-	-	3-0	-	2-2	-	(01-01-00)

SCOTTISH DIVISION ONE

Home v Away							
Dundee v Partick	0-1/3-1	3-0/1-0	0-0/4-0	2-0/1-0	2-1/3-2	0-1/0-3	(13-05-08)
Falkirk v Dumbarton	-	-	-	-	-	-	(01-01-00)

Home team / Away team	1	2	3	4	5	6	Since 1988
Morton v Dunfermline	-	0-1/3-0	1-1/2-1	0-2/1-2	2-1/0-2	-	(06-04-07)
Livingston v Hamilton	0-1/1-2	2-0/1-3	-	-	-	1-0/0-4	(04-03-08)
Raith v Cowdenbeath	1-3/1-2	2-0/3-2	-	-	2-1/2-2	-	(07-01-02)

SCOTTISH DIVISION TWO

Home team / Away team	1	2	3	4	5	6	Since 1988
Albion v Ayr	-	-	-	-	-	-	(01-00-00)
Alloa v Forfar	2-0/2-0	-	-	-	3-2/0-3	-	(06-04-12)
Brechin v Arbroath	-	-	3-1/0-1	0-0/0-2	-	2-3/1-1	(06-05-05)
East Fife v Stenhsmuir	0-0/1-1	7-0/0-1	-	2-1/1-1	6-0/1-1	1-3/1-1	(14-09-08)
Queen of Sth v Airdrie	1-1/0-3	-	0-0/4-0	3-0/2-2	-	-	(05-04-02)

SCOTTISH DIVISION THREE

Home team / Away team	1	2	3	4	5	6	Since 1988
Berwick v Queen's Park	0-2	1-1/1-4	-	1-0/1-1	1-1/3-1	2-0/1-4	(10-08-10)
E Stirling v Annan	-	-	2-1/1-1	1-3/3-1	1-5/2-0	1-0/0-4	(04-01-03)
Elgin v Montrose	3-2/0-2	0-2/2-1	1-2/1-0	0-1/5-2	3-2/1-0	3-1/2-1	(11-04-09)
Stirling v Peterhead	2-0/2-1	-	0-0/2-1	2-1/2-0	-	-	(10-01-03)
Stranraer v Clyde	-	-	-	-	3-1/3-0	0-0/1-0	(07-08-02)

CONFERENCE

Home team / Away team	1	2	3	4	5	6	Since 1988
Braintree v Mansfield	-	-	-	-	-	1-1	(00-01-00)
Cambridge U v Barrow	-	-	2-1	0-2	3-1	1-0	(03-00-01)
Ebbsfleet v Telford	-	-	-	-	-	3-2	(01-00-02)
Forest G v Southport	1-2	-	-	-	0-0	2-3	(04-01-04)
Hereford v Gateshead	-	-	-	-	-	-	(01-00-00)
Lincoln v Tamworth	-	-	-	-	-	4-0	(01-00-00)
Luton v Grimsby	-	-	2-1	-	1-0	1-1	(04-02-03)
Newport Co v Alfreton	-	-	-	-	-	1-0	(01-00-00)
Nuneaton v Hyde	0-0	1-0	-	-	1-2	2-0	(03-01-01)
Stockport v Dartford	-	-	-	-	-	-	(None)
Woking v Macclesfield	-	-	-	-	-	-	(04-00-01)
Wrexham v Kidderminstr	-	-	0-1	2-2	2-2	2-0	(01-02-02)

TUESDAY 16TH APRIL 2013

CHAMPIONSHIP

Home team / Away team	1	2	3	4	5	6	Since 1988
Barnsley v Derby	1-2	-	2-0	0-0	1-1	3-2	(05-03-03)
Blackpool v Sheff Weds	-	2-1	0-2	1-2	-	-	(02-00-03)
Bristol C v Birmingham	-	-	1-2	-	-	0-2	(03-00-03)
Cardiff v Charlton	-	0-2	2-0	-	-	-	(01-00-01)
Ipswich v C Palace	1-2	1-0	1-1	1-3	2-1	0-1	(06-02-08)
Leeds v Burnley	1-0	-	-	-	1-0	2-1	(04-00-01)
Leicester v Bolton	-	-	-	-	-	-	(00-03-01)
Middlesboro v Nottm F	-	-	-	1-1	1-1	2-1	(01-07-02)
Millwall v Watford	-	-	-	-	1-6	0-2	(05-02-08)
Peterborough v Brighton	-	-	0-0	-	0-3	1-2	(02-03-05)
Wolves v Hull	3-1	0-1	-	1-1	-	-	(02-02-02)

WEDNESDAY 17TH APRIL 2013

CHAMPIONSHIP

Home team / Away team	1	2	3	4	5	6	Since 1988
Blackburn v Huddersfield	-	-	-	-	-	-	(02-00-00)

SATURDAY 20TH APRIL 2013

PREMIER LEAGUE

Home team / Away team	1	2	3	4	5	6	Since 1988
Fulham v Arsenal	2-1	0-3	1-0	0-1	2-2	2-1	(03-01-07)
Liverpool v Chelsea	2-0	1-1	2-0	0-2	2-0	4-1	(15-03-05)

Home team · Away team							Since 1988 – HW D AW
Man Utd v Aston Villa	3-1	4-0	3-2	0-1	3-1	4-0	(17-06-01)
Norwich v Reading	-	-	0-2	-	2-1	-	(02-03-03)
QPR v Stoke	1-1	3-0	-	-	-	1-0	(04-03-01)
Sunderland v Everton	-	0-1	0-2	1-1	2-2	1-1	(04-04-04)
Swansea v Southampton	-	-	3-0	-	-	-	(01-00-00)
Tottenham v Man City	2-1	2-1	2-1	3-0	0-0	1-5	(11-04-03)
West Brom v Newcastle	-	-	2-3	1-1	3-1	1-3	(01-04-04)
West Ham v Wigan	0-2	1-1	2-1	3-2	3-1	-	(04-01-03)

CHAMPIONSHIP

Home team · Away team							Since 1988 – HW D AW
Birmingham v Leeds	1-0	-	-	-	-	1-0	(04-01-00)
Bolton v Middlesboro	0-0	0-0	4-1	-	-	-	(06-05-00)
Brighton v Blackpool	0-3	-	-	-	-	2-2	(04-03-02)
Burnley v Cardiff	2-0	3-3	2-2	-	1-1	1-1	(06-06-00)
Charlton v Wolves	-	2-3	1-3	-	-	-	(05-02-05)
C Palace v Leicester	2-0	2-2	-	0-1	3-2	1-2	(06-02-04)
Derby v Peterborough	-	-	-	2-1	-	1-1	(02-01-01)
Huddersfield v Millwall	4-2	1-0	1-2	1-0	-	-	(04-00-01)
Hull v Bristol C	-	0-0	-	-	2-0	3-0	(02-02-02)
Nottm F v Barnsley	-	-	1-0	1-0	2-2	0-0	(05-03-01)
Sheff Weds v Ipswich	2-0	1-2	0-0	0-1	-	-	(03-03-04)
Watford v Blackburn	2-1	-	-	-	-	-	(03-01-02)

LEAGUE 1

Home team · Away team							Since 1988 – HW D AW
Bournemouth v Carlisle	0-1	1-3	-	-	2-0	1-1	(04-01-02)
Colchester v Shrewsbury	-	-	-	-	-	-	(00-02-01)
Coventry v Leyton O	-	-	-	-	-	-	(None)
Doncaster v Notts Co	-	-	-	-	-	-	(00-00-01)
Hartlepool v Brentford	-	-	-	0-0	3-0	0-0	(03-02-04)
MK Dons v Scunthorpe	-	-	0-2	-	-	0-0	(01-01-01)
Oldham v Crawley	-	-	-	-	-	-	(None)
Portsmouth v Sheff Utd	3-1	-	-	-	1-0	-	(07-03-02)
Preston v Tranmere	-	-	-	-	-	2-1	(02-01-01)
Swindon v Stevenage	-	-	-	-	-	-	(None)
Walsall v Bury	0-1	-	-	-	-	2-4	(02-01-05)
Yeovil v Crewe	2-0	0-3	3-2	-	-	-	(02-00-01)

LEAGUE 2

Home team · Away team							Since 1988 – HW D AW
Aldershot v Dagenham	1-1	-	1-2	2-3	-	1-1	(05-02-02)
Barnet v Wycombe	2-1	2-1	1-1	-	0-1	-	(05-02-01)
Bradford v Burton	-	-	-	1-1	1-1	1-1	(00-03-00)
Bristol R v Accrington	4-0	-	-	-	-	5-1	(02-00-00)
Exeter v Cheltenham	-	-	-	-	-	-	(00-00-03)
Fleetwood v Chesterfield	-	-	-	-	-	-	(None)
Gillingham v Wimbledon	-	-	-	-	-	3-4	(00-00-01)
Morecambe v Torquay	-	-	-	2-0	2-1	1-2	(02-00-01)
Oxford Utd v Rochdale	-	-	-	-	-	-	(02-01-02)
Plymouth v Rotherham	-	-	-	-	-	1-4	(04-03-01)
Port Vale v Northampton	1-0	2-2	-	1-3	1-1	3-0	(03-03-03)
York v Southend	-	-	-	-	-	-	(05-02-00)

SCOTTISH DIVISION ONE

Home team · Away team							Since 1988 – HW D AW
Dumbarton v Dundee	-	-	-	-	-	-	(00-00-02)
Dunfermline v Cowdenbeath	-	-	-	-	2-1/5-0	-	(03-00-01)
Falkirk v Partick	-	-	-	-	2-3/2-0	2-1/1-1	(09-04-09)
Hamilton v Raith	-	-	-	-	-	2-2/2-1	(08-06-05)
Livingston v Morton	-	4-0/6-1	1-0/0-2	-	-	1-1/0-0	(10-05-05)

SCOTTISH DIVISION TWO

Home team · Away team							Since 1988 – HW D AW
Albion v Brechin	-	-	-	-	-	1-2/0-1	(02-04-10)

Home team	Away team	Six-season fixture record, latest result at right						Since 1988 – HW D AW
Arbroath v Airdrie		-	-	-	-	-	3-1/2-2	(02-02-02)
East Fife v Alloa		-	-	1-0/0-2	0-2/0-1	4-1/3-1	-	(07-04-07)
Forfar v Queen of Sth		-	-	-	-	-	-	(05-02-07)
Stenhsmuir v Ayr		-	-	-	-	3-1/2-1	-	(02-01-03)

SCOTTISH DIVISION THREE

Home team	Away team							Since 1988 – HW D AW
Annan v Stirling		-	-	-	-	-	-	(None)
Clyde v Montrose		-	-	-	-	2-0/1-1	1-0/1-2	(04-01-03)
Elgin v Berwick		1-2/2-1	-	0-2/2-0	3-3/1-5	1-2/3-2	4-1/4-0	(05-02-05)
Queen's Park v E Stirling		1-3/2-1	-	-	1-0/2-0	2-0/2-0	2-0/5-1	(24-06-09)
Stranraer v Peterhead		2-1/1-1	-	0-3/0-1	-	-	2-1/0-3	(02-02-04)

CONFERENCE

Home team	Away team							Since 1988 – HW D AW
Alfreton v Forest G		-	-	-	-	-	1-6	(00-00-01)
Barrow v Braintree		-	-	-	-	-	0-4	(00-00-01)
Dartford v Nuneaton		-	-	-	-	-	-	(None)
Gateshead v Ebbsfleet		-	-	-	1-3	-	2-3	(00-00-02)
Grimsby v Newport Co		-	-	-	-	2-0	2-2	(01-01-00)
Hyde v Lincoln		-	-	-	-	-	-	(None)
Kidderminstr v Stockport		-	-	-	-	-	1-1	(00-01-00)
Macclesfield v Cambridge U		-	-	-	-	-	-	(01-02-01)
Mansfield v Wrexham		3-0	2-1	1-2	0-1	2-3	2-0	(04-01-03)
Southport v Luton		-	-	-	-	2-1	3-3	(01-01-00)
Tamworth v Woking		3-1	-	-	-	-	-	(02-00-02)
Telford v Hereford		-	-	-	-	-	-	(01-02-04)

SATURDAY 27TH APRIL 2013

PREMIER LEAGUE

Home team	Away team							Since 1988 – HW D AW
Arsenal v Man Utd		2-1	2-2	2-1	1-3	1-0	1-2	(11-07-06)
Aston Villa v Sunderland		-	0-1	2-1	1-1	0-1	0-0	(05-05-02)
Chelsea v Swansea		-	-	-	-	-	4-1	(01-00-00)
Everton v Fulham		4-1	3-0	1-0	2-1	2-1	4-0	(11-00-00)
Man City v West Ham		2-0	1-1	3-0	3-1	2-1	-	(09-02-01)
Newcastle v Liverpool		2-1	0-3	1-5	-	3-1	2-0	(08-05-06)
Reading v QPR		-	-	0-0	1-0	0-1	-	(05-01-02)
Southampton v West Brom		0-0	3-2	-	-	-	-	(02-02-00)
Stoke v Norwich		5-0	2-1	-	-	-	1-0	(05-03-01)
Wigan v Tottenham		3-3	1-1	1-0	0-3	0-0	1-2	(01-03-03)

CHAMPIONSHIP

Home team	Away team							Since 1988 – HW D AW
Barnsley v Hull		3-0	1-3	-	-	1-1	2-1	(03-02-03)
Blackburn v C Palace		-	-	-	-	-	-	(04-02-01)
Blackpool v Derby		-	-	3-2	0-0	-	0-1	(01-01-01)
Bristol C v Huddersfield		1-1	-	-	-	-	-	(03-04-01)
Cardiff v Bolton		-	-	-	-	-	-	(01-00-01)
Ipswich v Birmingham		1-0	-	0-1	-	-	1-1	(04-02-03)
Leeds v Brighton		-	0-0	3-1	1-1	-	1-2	(03-04-01)
Leicester v Watford		-	4-1	-	4-1	4-2	2-0	(08-05-02)
Middlesboro v Charlton		2-0	-	-	-	-	-	(06-06-02)
Millwall v Nottm F		1-0	2-2	-	-	0-0	2-0	(05-05-01)
Peterborough v Sheff Weds		-	-	-	1-1	5-3	-	(01-02-01)
Wolves v Burnley		2-1	2-3	2-0	2-0	-	-	(08-00-02)

LEAGUE 1

Home team	Away team							Since 1988 – HW D AW
Brentford v Doncaster		0-4	-	-	-	-	-	(01-00-02)
Bury v Yeovil		-	-	-	-	-	3-2	(03-00-00)
Carlisle v Colchester		-	-	0-2	2-1	4-1	1-0	(06-01-03)
Crawley v Hartlepool		-	-	-	-	-	-	(None)

Home v Away							Since 1988
Crewe v Walsall	-	0-0	2-1	-	-	-	(06-01-04)
Leyton O v Oldham	2-2	1-0	2-1	1-2	1-0	1-3	(03-01-02)
Notts Co v Coventry	-	-	-	-	-	-	(01-00-00)
Scunthorpe v Swindon	-	-	3-3	-	-	-	(00-01-01)
Sheff Utd v Preston	-	1-1	1-0	1-0	1-0	2-1	(09-03-00)
Shrewsbury v Portsmouth	-	-	-	-	-	-	(00-00-01)
Stevenage v MK Dons	-	-	-	-	-	4-2	(01-00-00)
Tranmere v Bournemouth	1-0	3-1	-	-	0-3	0-0	(04-04-01)

LEAGUE 2

Wimbledon v Fleetwood	-	-	-	-	1-0	-	(01-00-00)
Accrington v Oxford Utd	-	-	-	-	0-0	0-2	(00-01-01)
Burton v Gillingham	-	-	-	-	1-1	1-0	(01-01-00)
Cheltenham v Bradford	1-2	-	-	4-5	4-0	3-1	(02-00-02)
Chesterfield v Exeter	-	-	2-1	-	-	0-2	(04-00-01)
Dagenham v York	2-1	-	-	-	-	-	(01-00-02)
Northampton v Barnet	-	-	-	1-3	0-0	1-2	(02-04-04)
Rochdale v Plymouth	-	-	-	-	1-1	-	(01-03-02)
Rotherham v Aldershot	-	-	1-2	0-0	1-0	2-0	(02-01-01)
Southend v Morecambe	-	-	-	-	2-3	1-1	(00-01-01)
Torquay v Bristol R	0-0	-	-	-	-	2-2	(03-02-01)
Wycombe v Port Vale	-	-	4-2	-	1-1	-	(04-01-01)

SCOTTISH DIVISION ONE

Cowdenbeath v Dumbarton	-	-	2-0/0-0	2-1/0-0	-	0-0/4-1	(10-06-08)
Dundee v Livingston	0-1/2-0	4-1/2-0	0-3/4-1	-	-	3-0/1-0	(15-02-04)
Morton v Hamilton	-	0-2/1-3	-	-	-	0-2/1-2	(06-07-10)
Partick v Dunfermline	-	1-1/0-1	1-0/2-3	2-0/1-4	0-2/2-0	-	(05-02-05)
Raith v Falkirk	-	-	-	-	2-1/1-2	1-0/2-2	(11-05-08)

SCOTTISH DIVISION TWO

Airdrie v Forfar	-	-	-	-	2-0/3-1	4-4/3-0	(07-05-01)
Alloa v Albion	-	-	-	-	-	-	(15-01-02)
Ayr v Arbroath	-	-	2-1/2-1	-	-	-	(04-03-01)
Brechin v Stenhsmuir	-	-	-	1-0/2-2	0-0/3-1	2-0/1-0	(10-09-03)
Queen of Sth v East Fife	-	-	-	-	-	-	(07-04-04)

SCOTTISH DIVISION THREE

Berwick v Annan	-	-	3-0/1-1	2-1/0-2	2-2/2-3	0-1/1-3	(02-02-04)
E Stirling v Stranraer	-	2-3/1-3	-	1-1/2-0	0-1/0-2	1-3/2-2	(02-04-13)
Montrose v Queen's Park	0-3/0-2	-	-	1-2/1-2	1-2/0-2	0-1/3-1	(13-08-14)
Peterhead v Clyde	-	-	-	2-0/0-0	-	0-0/1-1	(01-03-00)
Stirling v Elgin	-	-	-	-	-	-	(04-01-01)

SATURDAY 4TH MAY 2013

PREMIER LEAGUE

Fulham v Reading	0-1	3-1	-	-	-	-	(05-02-02)
Liverpool v Everton	0-0	1-0	1-1	1-0	2-2	3-0	(12-10-02)
Man Utd v Chelsea	1-1	2-0	3-0	1-2	2-1	3-1	(08-09-06)
Norwich v Aston Villa	-	-	-	-	-	2-0	(05-03-01)
QPR v Arsenal	-	-	-	-	-	2-1	(03-05-01)
Sunderland v Stoke	2-2	-	2-0	0-0	2-0	4-0	(07-05-01)
Swansea v Man City	-	-	-	-	-	1-0	(01-00-00)
Tottenham v Southampton	-	-	-	-	-	-	(11-02-04)
West Brom v Wigan	-	-	3-1	-	2-2	1-2	(03-02-02)
West Ham v Newcastle	0-2	2-2	3-1	-	1-2	-	(07-06-06)

CHAMPIONSHIP

Birmingham v Blackburn	-	4-1	-	2-1	2-1	-	(07-00-03)
Bolton v Blackpool	-	-	-	-	2-2	-	(02-02-00)
Brighton v Wolves	-	-	-	-	-	-	(01-04-01)

Home team v Away team							Since 1988 – HW D AW
Burnley v Ipswich	1-0	2-2	0-3	-	1-2	4-0	(04-02-03)
Charlton v Bristol C	-	1-1	0-2	-	-	-	(05-01-01)
C Palace v Peterborough	-	-	-	2-0	-	1-0	(03-00-00)
Derby v Millwall	-	-	-	-	0-0	3-0	(05-03-05)
Huddersfield v Barnsley	-	-	-	-	-	-	(04-02-02)
Hull v Cardiff	4-1	2-2	-	-	0-2	2-1	(06-02-03)
Nottm F v Leicester	-	-	-	5-1	3-2	2-2	(05-04-00)
Sheff Weds v Middlesboro	-	-	-	1-3	-	-	(05-00-03)
Watford v Leeds	-	-	-	-	0-1	1-1	(01-03-03)

SCOTTISH DIVISION ONE

Home team v Away team							Since 1988 – HW D AW
Dumbarton v Partick	-	-	-	-	-	-	(00-00-02)
Dunfermline v Dundee	-	0-1/0-1	0-1/1-1	1-1/2-1	3-1/0-0	-	(13-05-06)
Falkirk v Morton	-	-	-	-	2-1/1-0	1-0/0-2	(13-02-05)
Hamilton v Cowdenbeath	-	-	-	-	-	-	(05-02-01)
Livingston v Raith	-	-	-	-	-	1-1/4-0	(05-05-05)

SCOTTISH DIVISION TWO

Home team v Away team							Since 1988 – HW D AW
Albion v Queen of Sth	-	-	-	-	-	-	(02-03-01)
Arbroath v Alloa	-	-	4-1/1-0	2-2/0-0	-	-	(09-10-10)
East Fife v Brechin	-	-	0-0/2-1	2-0/2-0	1-3/0-0	1-1/2-2	(13-07-04)
Forfar v Ayr	0-1/1-1	-	-	-	4-1/3-2	-	(08-03-06)
Stenhsmuir v Airdrie	-	-	-	-	1-3/1-0	1-1/0-3	(02-02-04)

SCOTTISH DIVISION THREE

Home team v Away team							Since 1988 – HW D AW
Annan v Montrose	-	-	1-2/2-1	2-0/0-0	2-2/2-1	2-1/1-2	(04-02-02)
Clyde v Stirling	-	1-3/3-0	-	0-1/1-2	-	-	(07-01-06)
Elgin v E Stirling	5-0/2-1	6-0/3-0	0-4/0-2	1-2/0-1	0-2/2-0	2-0/3-1	(14-03-07)
Queen's Park v Peterhead	-	1-1/2-0	0-1/2-1	-	-	1-1/0-1	(05-03-06)
Stranraer v Berwick	-	-	-	2-4/3-1	1-1/3-1	2-1/1-3	(08-11-08)

SUNDAY 12TH MAY 2013

PREMIER LEAGUE

Home team v Away team							Since 1988 – HW D AW
Arsenal v Wigan	2-1	2-0	1-0	4-0	3-0	1-2	(06-00-01)
Aston Villa v Chelsea	0-0	2-0	0-1	2-1	0-0	2-4	(08-08-07)
Everton v West Ham	2-0	1-1	3-1	2-2	2-2	-	(11-05-02)
Fulham v Liverpool	1-0	0-2	0-1	3-1	2-5	1-0	(05-00-06)
Man Utd v Swansea	-	-	-	-	-	2-0	(01-00-00)
Norwich v West Brom	1-2	1-2	-	-	-	0-1	(03-04-05)
QPR v Newcastle	-	-	-	0-1	-	0-0	(02-01-03)
Reading v Man City	1-0	2-0	-	-	-	-	(04-00-01)
Stoke v Tottenham	-	-	2-1	1-2	1-2	2-1	(02-00-02)
Sunderland v Southampton	1-1	-	-	-	-	-	(02-03-02)

SUNDAY 19TH MAY 2013

PREMIER LEAGUE

Home team v Away team							Since 1988 – HW D AW
Chelsea v Everton	1-1	1-1	0-0	3-3	1-1	3-1	(11-10-02)
Liverpool v QPR	-	-	-	-	-	1-0	(07-01-01)
Man City v Norwich	-	-	-	-	-	5-1	(09-02-01)
Newcastle v Arsenal	0-0	1-1	1-3	-	4-4	0-0	(05-08-06)
Southampton v Stoke	1-0	3-2	-	-	-	-	(03-00-00)
Swansea v Fulham	-	-	-	-	-	2-0	(04-03-01)
Tottenham v Sunderland	-	2-0	1-2	2-0	1-1	1-0	(09-02-01)
West Brom v Man Utd	-	-	0-5	-	1-2	1-2	(00-00-06)
West Ham v Reading	0-1	1-1	-	-	-	2-4	(02-01-02)
Wigan v Aston Villa	0-0	1-2	0-4	1-2	1-2	0-0	(01-02-04)

Odds conversion

Frac	Dec	%	Frac	Dec	%
10-1	11	9.09	6-4	2.5	40.00
9-1	10	10.00	7-5	2.4	41.67
17-2	9.5	10.53	11-8	2.375	42.11
8-1	9	11.11	13-10	2.3	43.48
15-2	8.5	11.76	5-4	2.25	44.44
7-1	8	12.50	6-5	2.2	45.45
13-2	7.5	13.33	11-10	2.1	47.62
6-1	7	14.29	21-20	2.05	48.78
11-2	6.5	15.38	Evs	2	50.00
5-1	6	16.67	20-21	1.952	51.23
9-2	5.5	18.18	10-11	1.909	52.38
4-1	5	20.00	9-10	1.9	52.63
18-5	4.6	21.74	5-6	1.833	54.56
7-2	4.5	22.22	4-5	1.8	55.56
10-3	4.333	23.08	8-11	1.727	57.90
16-5	4.2	23.81	7-10	1.7	58.82
3-1	4	25.00	4-6	1.667	59.99
14-5	3.8	26.32	5-8	1.625	61.54
11-4	3.75	26.67	8-13	1.615	61.92
13-5	3.6	27.78	3-5	1.6	62.50
5-2	3.5	28.57	4-7	1.571	63.65
12-5	3.4	29.41	8-15	1.533	65.23
95-40	3.375	29.63	1-2	1.5	66.67
23-10	3.3	30.30	40-85	1.471	67.98
9-4	3.25	30.77	9-20	1.45	68.97
11-5	3.2	31.25	4-9	1.444	69.25
85-40	3.125	32.00	2-5	1.4	71.43
21-10	3.1	32.26	4-11	1.364	73.31
2-1	3	33.33	7-20	1.35	74.07
19-10	2.9	34.48	1-3	1.333	75.02
15-8	2.875	34.78	3-10	1.3	76.92
9-5	2.8	35.71	2-7	1.286	77.76
7-4	2.75	36.36	1-4	1.25	80.00
17-10	2.7	37.04	2-9	1.222	81.83
13-8	2.625	38.10	1-5	1.2	83.33
8-5	2.6	38.46	1-10	1.1	90.91

Asian handicaps

Conceding handicap			Receiving handicap	
Result of bet	Result of match	Handicap	Result of match	Result of bet
Win	Win	0	Win	Win
No bet	Draw		Draw	No bet
Lose	Lose		Lose	Lose
Win	Win	0,0.5	Win	Win
Lose half	Draw	0.25	Draw	Win half
Lose	Lose		Lose	Lose
Win	Win	0.5	Win	Win
Lose	Draw		Draw	Win
Lose	Lose		Lose	Lose
Win	Win by 2+	0.5,1	Lose by 2+	Lose
Win half	Win by 1	0.75	Lose by 1	Lose half
Lose	Draw		Draw	Win
Lose	Lose		Win	Win
Win	Win by 2+	1	Lose by 2+	Lose
No bet	Win by 1		Lose by 1	No bet
Lose	Draw		Draw	Win
Lose	Lose		Win	Win

Correct scores 2011-12

	Prem	Chmp	Lg1	Lg2	BSP	SPL	Sct 1	Sct 2	Sct 3
1-0	33	56	48	67	48	17	14	18	14
2-0	30	46	39	47	41	17	4	13	11
2-1	30	46	50	40	41	16	15	7	12
3-0	21	23	24	22	19	10	7	8	10
3-1	23	23	14	23	28	9	8	7	9
3-2	7	18	21	15	14	4	5	4	2
4-0	9	9	6	10	9	6	3	6	3
4-1	4	7	12	10	7	1	4	7	2
4-2	2	0	7	3	2	2	4	2	4
4-3	1	2	2	2	1	2	2	3	0
0-0	27	41	46	35	35	25	14	5	4
1-1	45	73	79	69	68	21	26	22	24
2-2	14	32	33	31	32	5	14	12	10
3-3	5	3	6	4	8	5	0	3	1
4-4	2	0	2	0	0	1	0	1	1
0-1	20	49	42	41	47	20	18	9	10
0-2	21	25	28	26	22	17	7	9	6
1-2	34	33	31	46	39	15	9	10	12
0-3	7	13	8	10	10	9	3	3	4
1-3	8	20	18	10	18	3	7	7	13
2-3	11	10	8	13	15	6	5	9	8
0-4	3	4	4	6	3	3	2	2	2
1-4	2	3	2	4	7	3	0	3	2
2-4	1	2	6	0	3	1	0	2	0
3-4	0	2	2	2	3	0	0	1	0
Other	20	12	15	16	32	10	9	7	16

Home win/draw/away win percentages 2011-12

	Prem	Chmp	Lg1	Lg2	BSP	SPL	Sct 1	Sct 2	Sct 3
Home	45	43	42	45	42	39	39	44	45
Draw	24	27	30	25	26	25	30	24	22
Away	31	30	28	30	32	36	31	32	33

under/over goals percentages 2011-12

	Prem	Chmp	Lg1	Lg2	BSP	SPL	Sct 1	Sct 2	Sct 3
<1.5	21	26	25	26	24	27	26	18	16
>1.5	79	74	75	74	76	73	74	82	84
<2.5	46	53	51	52	47	51	46	42	38
>2.5	54	47	49	48	53	49	54	58	62
<3.5	71	73	71	73	67	73	65	58	59
>3.5	29	27	29	27	33	27	35	42	41
<4.5	86	89	85	88	83	85	84	77	80
>4.5	14	11	15	13	17	15	16	23	20

Top goalscorers 2011-12 (strikers)

	P	Goals	First	Last
R van Persie (Arsenal)	38	30	9	9
W Rooney (Man Utd)	34	27	9	6
R Lambert (Southampton)	42	27	11	9

Top goalscorers 2011-12 (midfielders)

	P	Goals	First	Last
C Dempsey (Fulham)	37	17	7	6
C Burke (Birmingham)	46	13	4	4
D Shiels (Kilmarnock)	35	13	5	6

Top goalscorers 2011-12 (defenders)

	P	Goals	First	Last
C Mulgrew (Celtic)	30	8	3	3
G Halford (Portsmouth)	42	7	1	1
L Craig (St Johnstone)	36	7	1	2

Premier League, Championship and SPL matches only